1995

Microeconomics
Theory and Applications
FOURTH EDITION

Companion volumes prepared by Edwin Mansfield

Microeconomics: Selected Readings, *Fourth Edition*

Microeconomic Problems: Case Studies and Exercises
for Review, *Fourth Edition*

Microeconomics
Theory and Applications

Fourth Edition

Edwin Mansfield
University of Pennsylvania

W · W · Norton and Company · *New York and London*

Copyright © 1982, 1979, 1975, 1970 by W. W. Norton & Company, Inc.
Published simultaneously in Canada by George J. McLeod Limited,
Toronto.
Printed in the United States of America
All Rights Reserved

Library of Congress Cataloging in Publication Data
Mansfield, Edwin.
  Microeconomics: theory and applications.
  Includes bibliographies and index.
  1. Microeconomics. I. Title.
HB172.M36 1982   330   81–14219
ISBN 0–393–95218–5   AACR2

W. W. Norton & Company, Inc. 500 Fifth Avenue, New York, N.Y.
10110
W. W. Norton & Company Ltd., 37 Great Russell Street, London
WC1B 3NU

1 2 3 4 5 6 7 8 9 0

To Dixie

*who once again asked
that this dedication
be as short as possible*

Contents

3 The Tastes and Preferences of the Consumer   49

4 Consumer Behavior and Individual Demand   80

$\boxed{5}$ Market Demand   110

10 Price and Output under Pure Monopoly   277

11 Price and Output under Monopolistic Competition   311

12 Price and Output under Oligopoly   330

13 Price and Employment of Inputs under Perfect Competition   360

14 Price and Employment of Inputs under Imperfect Competition   387

17 Public Goods, Externalities, and the Role of Government   466

18 Intertemporal Choice and Technological Change   491

19 Decision-Making and Choice Involving Risk   526

Preface

Economic theory in recent years has catapulted into the public awareness—both because of its failures and its successes. The failures have been widely publicized. Far less heralded is the increased reliance on economic theory in government, business, and personal decision-making. The demand for new and refined applications of microeconomics, in particular, has pushed the discipline into areas well beyond its traditional boundaries. In previous editions of *Microeconomics: Theory and Applications* I have tried to keep pace with the state of the art. My aim in the fourth edition is no different.

How this edition differs from its predecessors can be summarized in a half-dozen categories. First, an entirely new Chapter 19 has been added on decision-making and choice involving risk. This is an increasingly important topic for the microeconomist, yet it is ignored or neglected in virtually all other intermediate texts. This chapter contains a discussion of probability, expected monetary value, the expected value of perfect information, decision trees, von Neumann and Morgenstern's concept of utility, and other relevant matters. In the past, much of this material has been considered beyond the realm of the intermediate course. To avoid that danger, I have worked hard to make it accessible, preparing a number of drafts for close review before incorporating the chapter in the text.

Second, there are improvements in the boxed examples, an innovation in the previous edition that appears to have stood the test of classroom use. Almost one-fifth of the examples are new. Some, like "The Economics of Gasohol" and "Automobile Prices and Japanese Imports," show how important microeconomic principles can be used to illuminate problems affecting both public and private policy. Others, like "The Supply of Shale Oil" and "Corn Production in Nebraska," show how major microeconomic relationships can be measured and how empirical results obtained by economists can be utilized. I have placed a premium in these new "Examples" on current issues. Each poses relevant questions which are followed by solutions. These are of necessity brief; references are provided to publications where more detailed discussions can be found.

Third, many topics have been clarified and updated. One learns through teaching that every class offers an opportunity to present theoretical material in a better and fresher way. What can be accomplished in the classroom ought to be replicated in a text. Thus the treatments of some traditional topics, such as the Edgeworth oligopoly model, have been completely rewritten.

Fourth, many new references are provided to relevant recent literature. These include discussions of economies of scope, optimum product diversity, and other topics treated recently in the literature. While this is not an appropriate place for voluminous bibliographies or extensive footnotes, an attempt has been made to extend and update references to both the theoretical and empirical literature.

Fifth, over half of the diagrams have been revised. Wherever possible, the labels have been simplified and clarified. An effort has been made to increase the precision of the diagrams, thereby making it easier for students to follow geometric arguments presented in the text.

Sixth, brief answers to the odd-numbered "Questions and Problems" at the ends of the chapters are included at the end of the book. This should enable students to test their understanding by working through these problems. More detailed answers to some of these questions are contained in *Microeconomic Problems: Case Studies and Exercises for Review,* fourth edition.

It remains my conviction in this edition that microeconomic theory is best presented in conjunction with real-world applications and cases. My experience has been that the most effective way to teach microeconomic theory is to demonstrate how economics can be, and has been, used by decision-makers. Once students recognize the relevance of microeconomic theory to policy issues in both the public and private sectors, they are usually motivated to learn it more thoroughly. Although many changes have been made in the fourth edition, it still retains its basic structure, proportions, and goals. As in earlier editions, the level of text discussion is designed for students who are taking the intermediate course in microeconomics. No mathematics beyond basic algebra is required, although mathematical explanations are often provided in the footnotes for students with a knowledge of calculus.

As with the previous editions, a workbook and reader accompany the text. *Microeconomic Problems: Case Studies and Exercises for Review,* fourth edition, has been revised and expanded, making it more effective in guiding students toward an understanding of the theories comprising and underlying microeconomics. In particular, many new problems and questions have been added in each chapter that test students' skills in applying microeconomic theory to real-world situations. *Microeconomic Problems* now contains about 1,000 questions and problems, together with their solutions.

Microeconomics: Selected Readings, fourth edition, includes new papers on decision-making and choice involving risk and on current problems facing the U.S. economy, among other topics. Articles that are dated or outmoded have been pruned. In my opinion, this reader continues to be broader and more varied than other books of readings at the intermediate level.

An *Instructor's Manual* is available for the text. In addition to some teaching suggestions for each chapter, it includes a test bank of multiple-choice questions and problem sets which not only reflects the decision-making emphasis of the text, but also develops theory as a set of principles that yields insights into everyday problems. Paul M. Sommers of Middlebury College, the author of the *Instructor's Manual,* has created a freshly varied diet of teaching materials for this new edition, and this is the place to record my thanks to him.

Since it would be impossible to list all of the many instructors and reviewers who have contributed in important ways to this and the previous editions, I must be content with thanking only a sample: Allan Braff, University of New Hampshire; Stephen R. Brenner, Grinnell College; James Cairns, Royal Military College of Canada; Joseph Cammarosano, Fordham University; Alvin Cohen, Lehigh University; Marshall Colberg, Florida State University; James Dolan, Regis College; Allan Feldman, Brown University; Alan Fisher, California State University at Fullerton; J. Fred Giertz, Miami University; Ellen Goldstein, California State University at Fullerton; Warren Gramm, Washington State University; William Gunther, University of Alabama; Kanji Haitani, State University of New York, Fredonia; Richard Harmstone, Pennsylvania State University; William Holohan, University of Wisconsin at Milwaukee; Jonathan Kesselman, University of British Columbia; Charles Knoeber, North Carolina State University; Steven Kohlhagen, University of California, Berkeley; Shou-Eng Koo, Indiana University and Purdue University; John Laitner, University of Michigan; Richard Levin, Yale University; J. Patrick Lewis, Otterbein College; Paul Malatesta, Colgate University; M. R. Metzger, George Washington University; Edwin Mills, Princeton University; Hajime Miyazaki, Stanford University; John Murphy, Canisius College; Richard Musgrave, Harvard University; K. R. Nair, West Virginia Wesleyan College; John Neufeld, University of North Carolina; Mancur Olson, University of Maryland; John Palmer, University of Western Ontario; R. D. Peterson, Colorado State University; Charles Plourde, York University; Robert Pollak, University of Pennsylvania; Richard Porter, University of Michigan; Charles Ratliff, Davidson College; Thomas Riddell, Bucknell University; Ray Roberts, Jr., Furman University; Anthony Romeo, University of Connecticut; Anthony Rufolo, Federal Reserve Bank of Philadelphia; Sol S. Shalit, University of Wisconsin at Milwaukee; Barry Siegel, University of Oregon; N. J. Simler, University of Minnesota; A. Michael Spence, Harvard University; James Stephenson, Iowa State University; Richard Sylla, North Carolina State University; W. James Truitt, Baylor University; Gordon Tullock, Virginia Polytechnic Institute; Hal

Varian, University of Michigan; David Vrooman, St. Lawrence University; Donald Walker, Indiana University of Pennsylvania; Joan Werner, University of Michigan; A. R. Whitaker, U.S. Naval Academy; Bronislaw Wojtun, Lemoyne-Owen College; Gary Yohe, Wesleyan University; and Richard Zeckhauser, Harvard University. Further, I would like to thank Donald S. Lamm, Mary Shuford, and Nancy Palmquist of Norton for doing a fine job with the publishing end of the work. And special thanks go to my wife, who again helped in countless ways.

E.M.

Philadelphia, 1982

1 Introduction to Microeconomics

1. Introduction

John Maynard Keynes, almost certainly the most influential economist of the twentieth century, said that "The ideas of economists ..., both when they are right and when they are wrong, are more powerful than is commonly understood. Indeed, the world is ruled by little else. Practical men, who believe themselves to be quite exempt from intellectual influences, are usually the slaves of some defunct economist."[1] Economics has such power because of its importance in nearly everyone's life. Economics helps us to understand the nature and organization of our society, the arguments underlying many of the great public issues of the day, and the operation and behavior of business firms and other economic decision-making units. To perform effectively and responsibly as a citizen, an administrator, a worker, or a consumer, one needs to know some economics.

Precisely what does economics deal with? According to one standard definition, economics is concerned with the way in which resources are allocated among alternative uses to satisfy human wants. It is customary to divide economics into two parts: microeconomics and macroeconomics. Microeconomics deals with the economic behavior of individual units such as consumers, firms, and resource owners; while macroeconomics deals with the behavior of economic aggregates such as gross national product and the level of employment.

This book is concerned with microeconomics. A general definition of microeconomics fraught with

---

1. J. M. Keynes, *The General Theory of Employment, Interest, and Money* (New York: Harcourt, Brace, reprinted in 1965), p. 383.

vague words like *resources* and *human wants* is unlikely to communicate to the reader the power of microeconomic theory or its usefulness in solving major problems in the real world. After wading through such an introductory discussion, the reader's interest in the subject is often banked, not kindled. To avoid this problem, we begin our discussion by giving five examples of the kinds of problems that microeconomics can help to solve. (Each of these examples is considered in detail in subsequent chapters.) Although these five examples cover only a small sample of the questions to which microeconomics is relevant, they give the student a reasonable first impression of the nature of microeconomics and its relevance to the real world.

2. Optimal Production Decisions

Business firms are constantly faced with the problem of choosing among alternative ways of manufacturing their products. For example, consider a textile mill that, among other things, finishes cotton cloth. Suppose that the output rate in the firm's finishing department is limited by the capacity of its finishing equipment and the amount of skilled labor it has available to carry out the work. The firm is considering the use of three finishing processes: processes 1, 2, and 3. Suppose that the firm knows that the profit per batch of cotton cloth finished with each of the processes is as shown in Table 1.1. For example, each batch of cotton cloth finished with process 1 yields a profit of $1. Suppose that the number of man-hours of skilled labor and the number of machine-hours of finishing equipment required to finish a batch of cotton cloth with each process is as shown in Table 1.1. For example, process 1 requires the use of 3 machine-hours of finishing equipment and 0.4 man-hours of skilled labor per batch of cotton cloth that is finished.

Under these circumstances, if 6,000 machine-hours per week is the maximum capacity of the finishing equipment and 600 man-hours per week is the maximum amount of skilled labor that the firm can hire, which processes should the firm use? And how many batches of cloth should be finished using each process? This is an example of one type of problem that microeconomics is designed to solve. It is a problem faced

Table 1.1   Characteristics of three processes for finishing cloth in a cotton mill

	Process 1	Process 2	Process 3
Profit per batch of cotton cloth finished *(dollars)*	1.00	0.90	1.10
Man-hours of skilled labor required per batch finished	0.40	0.50	0.35
Machine-hours of finishing equipment required per batch finished	3.00	2.50	5.25

by an individual firm that is trying to maximize its profit or attain some other set of objectives of its owners and managers. Microeconomics serves as the basis for, and is helpful in promoting an understanding of, the powerful modern tools of managerial decision-making that help to solve problems of this sort. These tools are applicable to government as well as business. Thus the techniques introduced in recent years in many government agencies to promote better decision-making are fundamentally applications of microeconomics.[2]

3. Pricing Policy

Most firms are also faced with the problem of pricing their products. For example, suppose that a firm is the sole producer of a product and that it can sell this product in New Jersey and Pennsylvania, but that the law prohibits the product from being carried from one state to the other. The amount of the product that the firm can sell at various prices in Pennsylvania is shown in Table 1.2. Similarly, the amount of the product that

Table 1.2   Relationship between price and quantity sold in New Jersey and Pennsylvania

NEW JERSEY		PENNSYLVANIA	
Price per ton in New Jersey (dollars)	Quantity sold in New Jersey (tons)	Price per ton in Pennsylvania (dollars)	Quantity sold in Pennsylvania (tons)
1.00	1,000	1.00	1,500
1.10	900	1.10	1,400
1.20	800	1.20	1,300
1.30	700	1.30	1,200
1.40	600	1.40	1,100
1.50	500	1.50	1,000
1.60	400	1.60	900
		1.70	800
		1.80	700

the firm can sell at various prices in New Jersey is also shown in Table 1.2. Since the product cannot be carried from one state to another, the firm is able to set different prices for the product in the two states. If it costs the firm $1.00 to produce each ton of product, what price should the firm charge in each state if it wants to maximize its profits?

This kind of problem faces many, many firms. Since many goods and services cannot be resold, it is often possible for the producer of such goods or services to sell them at different prices to different groups of consumers. For example, an operation to cure a particular type of cancer may be $500 for a rich person and $100 for a poor person. In these cases—as well as in the simpler and more straightforward case where a

2. For the answer to the problem posed in this section, see Chapter 8.

firm's product can be sold only at a single price—it is important that the firm know how to set price to achieve its objectives. Microeconomics provides a basis for analyzing and solving such problems. When a management consultant is hired to help solve a problem of this sort, his or her recommendations, if sound, will rely heavily on the application of well-established principles of microeconomics.[3]

As in the case of the previous example, this problem may seem quite simple to solve, at least to some readers, and they may wonder why special techniques are required to solve such easy problems. The reason is that the problems that occur in real life often involve more variables and are more complicated than those presented in these two sections. The examples given here were constructed to illustrate the type of problems with which microeconomics attempts to deal, and for this purpose, it is best to strip the problem to the simplest essentials. But it would be very misleading to conclude that because trial-and-error methods—and patience—can produce a solution to these examples, such methods—and perhaps a little more patience—can also produce a solution to most real problems. Microeconomics attempts to provide techniques to help solve problems of this sort when trial-and-error and other such methods are not adequate.

4. Rules for Optimal Resource Allocation

In the previous two sections we were concerned with problems facing business firms (or individual government agencies). Although such problems are important and interesting, they are by no means the only type dealt with by microeconomics. On the contrary, much of microeconomics is concerned with problems that face us all as citizens. Together we must somehow decide how we want to organize the production and marketing of goods and services in our country. We must also decide how these goods and services are to be distributed among the people. Some of the subtlest and most significant applications of microeconomics are in this area.

In recent years, there has been a great deal of talk concerning the restructuring of various aspects of the economy. Some people charge that many basic American industries like steel and automobiles are unable to compete with their foreign rivals, and that fundamental changes should be made. Suppose that we ask the following basic question: If we could restructure the entire economic system and if we agreed that the goal was to make anyone better off (in terms of his or her own tastes) as long as this did not make someone else worse off (in terms of the latter's tastes), what sort of changes would we be justified in making? More specifically, suppose that we could take resources away from some sectors of the economy and provide them to other sectors, or that we could prohibit consumers from consuming certain goods, or that we could pro-

---

3. For a description of the way in which a pricing problem like that described in this section can be solved, see Chapter 10.

Example 1.1   Automobile Prices and Japanese Imports

In the fall of 1980, the U.S. auto industry introduced new lines of smaller, fuel-efficient cars. The prices at which they and their Japanese competitors were offered were as follows:

Chevrolet Citation	$6,337	Subaru wagon	$5,612
GM "J" Cars	6,300	Datsun 310	5,439
Ford Escort	6,009	Subaru hatchback	5,212
Dodge Omni	5,713	Mazda GLC	4,755

(a) According to some observers, "Detroit has priced these cars relatively high to replenish its depleted coffers as soon as possible." Is it always true that this is the effect of charging relatively high prices? (b) Some auto executives have stated that the U.S. demand for smaller cars will be so great in the early 1980s that Detroit will be able to sell all such cars that it can produce. What implicit assumptions are they making? (c) In 1979, the International Trade Commission decided not to recommend curbing the imports of Japanese cars into the United States. In terms of promoting the vitality and efficiency of the U.S. automobile industry, what arguments can be made in favor of this decision? (d) Were imports of Japanese cars into the United States subsequently curbed?

Solution

(a) No. If a firm charges relatively high prices, it may sell relatively few units of its product, the result being that its profits are lower than if its price was somewhat lower. (b) They are assuming that U.S. consumers will not buy imported smaller cars (instead of U.S. smaller cars) in such numbers that Detroit will be unable to sell all it can produce. (c) American auto producers would have to reduce their costs and change the features of their cars to meet foreign competition, rather than rely on the government to protect them from such competition. (d) In 1981, the Japanese agreed to "voluntary" restraint on exports of cars to the United States.*

* For further discussion, see "Detroit's High-Price Strategy Could Backfire," *Business Week,* November 24, 1980.

hibit firms from charging certain prices. What actions of this sort would we be justified in taking?

Students sometimes complain that they are not confronted with significant or relevant questions. Surely such complaints cannot be lodged legitimately against this question! Having said this, it is important to add that microeconomics has progressed far enough to be able to provide at least partial answers to this kind of question, which is fortunate since the value of a field lies more in its power to answer questions than in the audacity with which it poses them. Nonetheless, the reader should not be encouraged to believe that microeconomics is the key that by itself will unlock the answers to the great social problems of the day.

Microeconomics provides a way of thinking about many of these problems that is valuable, as indicated perhaps by the formidable number of economists appointed by both Democratic and Republican administrations to positions of great responsibility. But microeconomics, although valuable, is only one of many disciplines that have important roles to play in this area.[4]

5. Public Policy Concerning Market Structure

Another problem that faces us all as citizens is the way that industries are structured. Suppose for simplicity that all industries sell to a large number of independent buyers, none of which is in a position to influence the price of the product. Suppose that we have three choices: to allow each industry to be taken over by a single firm, to allow each industry to become dominated by a few firms (but prevent a single firm from taking over), or to make sure that each industry is composed of a large number of independent firms. Which choice should we make?

This is a very important problem—and one that continues to be the center of considerable controversy. In the United States, the antitrust laws are designed to promote competition and to control monopoly. For example, the Sherman Act of 1890, the first major federal legislation directed against monopoly, outlaws conspiracies or combinations in restraint of trade and forbids the monopolizing of trade or commerce. This seems to indicate that we as a nation have decided not to allow industries to be taken over by a single firm. But is this policy justified? To what extent has it been outmoded by developments in the years that have elapsed since the passage of the Sherman Act?

According to some prominent observers, a policy designed to insure that each industry be composed of a large number of independent firms would be a mistake. They claim that very large firms are required in many industries to insure efficiency and promote progress. How can their arguments be evaluated? What criteria can be used to judge the relative advantages of alternative ways that industries can be structured? In various discussions, one often hears of the advantages of a competitive system in which industries are composed of many small firms. In what sense can such a system be shown to be optimal? Is it always optimal, or just under certain special conditions?

This problem is of the utmost importance, since it concerns the basic framework within which the nation's business activity is carried out. It is one of the most fundamental questions of public policy. Compared with the problems of the individual firms in Sections 2 and 3, it is—like the problem in Section 4—certainly more difficult to formulate and to solve, if for no other reason than that it is harder to decide what benefits the entire country than it is to decide what benefits a particular firm. By the same token, this problem is much broader than the problems discussed in

---

4. For a discussion of the problem described in this section, see Chapter 16.

Sections 2 and 3. Whereas our interest there was to find policies that would benefit a particular firm, our interest here is to find policies that will benefit the nation as a whole.

This is another example of a problem that microeconomics is aimed at helping to solve. Although it is not possible to solve this problem in as neat or as simple a fashion as one might solve a less complicated problem, it is possible to throw considerable light on the issues involved—and microeconomists have labored for generations to see to it that problems of this sort are analyzed as dispassionately and as scientifically as possible. Moreover, the results have been put to use in the world of action as well as in the world of speculation and study. The lawyer who argues an antitrust case, and the judge who decides one, must both rely on and use the principles of microeconomics.[5]

6. Public Policy Concerning Energy and Pollution

Finally, still another problem that faces us all is our limited energy supply. Given the great amount of attention paid to this issue in the press and in Congress, few people are likely to be unaware of the problem. But it is important for us to understand how the price of oil is established, and why some observers claim that there is a shortage of natural gas. We should also be aware of what measures might be taken to spur the development of new sources of energy or to reduce its consumption. All of these issues are at the heart of our recent energy crises.

Related to this problem is the question of how much environmental pollution we should tolerate. One way to expand our energy supplies might be to permit the use of more coal, but this would aggravate our pollution problems. In recent years, there has been a great deal of attention paid to these pollution problems, but nonetheless many people do not really understand why undesirably high levels of pollution occur in a free-enterprise economy, and what measures might be adopted to reduce pollution to proper levels. Why must the government intervene to curb pollution? Why won't private industry do the job by itself?

These are further examples of problems that microeconomics can help to solve. As in the previous examples, it is frequently not possible to come up with very precise or exact answers. But microeconomic analysis permits us to reach conclusions that are sufficiently precise to throw a great deal of light on the relevant questions of public policy. It is for this reason that government agencies like the Department of Energy and the Environmental Protection Agency hire economists and economic consultants. And it is for this reason that congressional committees dealing with these questions ask economists to testify and provide advice.[6]

5. For discussion of the problem described in this section, see Chapters 9 to 12, 16, and 18.
6. For discussions of the problems described in this section, see Chapters 2, 5, 12, 17, and 18.

7. Microeconomics: Problem-Solving and Science

Sections 2 through 6 have provided some examples of problems that microeconomics can help solve. These examples are useful in indicating the relevance of microeconomics but they may be misleading if they suggest that microeconomics is wholly a bag of techniques to solve practical problems. On the contrary, *microeconomics, like any branch of the natural or social sciences, is concerned with the explanation and prediction of observed phenomena regardless of whether these explanations or predictions have any immediate applications to practical problems.* As indicated in the previous sections, it has turned out that many parts of microeconomics have been relevant and useful in solving practical problems, but this does not mean that all of microeconomics *has* found an application of this sort or that all of microeconomics *should* find an application of this sort.

For example, one of the principal objectives of microeconomics is to answer questions like the following: What determines the price of various commodities? (Why is steak more expensive than chicken?) What determines the amount that a worker makes? (Why are physicians paid more than cab drivers?) What determines the way that a consumer allocates his or her income among various commodities? (How will an increase in the price of butter affect the amount of margarine purchased by Mrs. Brown?) What determines how much of a particular commodity will be produced? (What accounts for the woeful decrease in the number of cigar-store Indians produced?) What determines the number and size of firms in a particular industry? (Why are there so many producers of wheat and so few producers of automobiles?)

None of these questions is, as it stands, in the form of a practical problem. Yet to understand the world about us and to perform effectively as a citizen, administrator, or worker, it is obvious that one must have at least a minimal understanding of the answers to these questions. The situation is something like that of mathematics. Although pure mathematics is not concerned with the solution of particular problems, it has turned out that various branches of mathematics are of great value in solving practical problems. And a minimal knowledge of mathematics is extremely important as a basis for understanding the world around us and for further professional and technical training.

8. Human Wants and Resources

At the beginning of this chapter, we gave a very brief definition of economics which must now be expanded and explained. It will be recalled from Section 1 that we said that economics focuses on the way in which resources are allocated among alternative uses to satisfy human wants. This is a perfectly satisfactory definition, but it does not mean much unless we define what is meant by *human wants* and by *resources*. What do these terms mean?

Human wants are the things, services, goods, and circumstances that people desire. Wants vary greatly among individuals and over time for the same individual. Some people like sports, others like books; some want to travel, others want to putter in the yard. An individual's desire for a particular good during a particular period of time is not infinite, but in the aggregate human wants seem to be insatiable. Besides the basic desires for food, shelter, and clothing, which must be fulfilled to some extent if the human organism is to maintain its existence, wants arise from cultural factors. For example, society, often helped along by advertising and other devices to modify tastes, promotes certain images of the "full, rich life," which frequently entail the possession and consumption of certain types of automobiles, houses, appliances, and other goods and services.

Resources are the things or services used to produce goods which can be used to satisfy wants. Economic resources are scarce, while free resources, such as air, are so abundant that they can be obtained without charge. The test of whether a resource is an economic resource or a free resource is price: Economic resources command a nonzero price but free resources do not. In a world where all resources were free, there would be no economic problem since all wants could be satisfied.

An economic resource that is used in the production of a particular good is called an input. Thus, in the example in Section 2, the inputs in the finishing of cotton cloth were skilled labor and finishing equipment. Economic resources have alternative uses. A particular resource generally can be used in the production of many types of goods. For example, the skilled labor used by the cotton mill could be used by many other kinds of firms and in many other kinds of work. Of course, as resources become more specialized, there generally are fewer alternative jobs for them—but there are still some. Even the cotton mill's finishing equipment can probably be adapted for somewhat different uses.

Economic resources are of a variety of types. In the nineteenth century it was customary for economists to classify economic resources into three categories: land, labor, and capital. In recent years this sort of classification has tended to go out of style in part because each category contains such an enormous variety of resources. Nevertheless, it is worthwhile defining each of these general types of resources. Land is a shorthand expression for natural resources. Labor is human effort, both physical and mental. Capital includes equipment, buildings, inventories, raw materials, and other nonhuman producible resources that contribute to the production, marketing, and distribution of goods and services. Note that the economist's definition of capital is different from that of the man in the street who employs the word to mean money. For example, a man with a hot dog stand who has $100 in his pocket may say that he has $100 in capital; but his definition is different from that of the economist who would include in the man's capital the value of his stand, the value of his equipment, the value of his inventory of hot dogs and mustard, and the value of other nonlabor resources (other than land) that he uses.

9. Technology

Another term that must be defined at this point is *technology*. Technology is society's pool of knowledge regarding the industrial and agricultural arts. Technology consists of knowledge used in industry and agriculture concerning the principles of physical and social phenomena (such as the laws of motion and the properties of fluids), knowledge regarding the application of these principles to production (such as the application of various aspects of genetic theory to the breeding of new plants), and knowledge regarding the day-to-day operation of production (such as the rules of thumb of the skilled craftsman). Note that technology is different from the techniques in use, since not all that is known is likely to be in use. Also, technology is different from pure science, although the distinction is not very precise. Pure science is directed toward understanding, whereas technology is directed toward use.

The important thing about technology is that it sets limits on the amount and types of goods that can be derived from a given amount of resources. Put differently, it sets limits on the extent to which human wants can be satisfied by a given amount of resources. For instance, consider the cotton textile mill in Section 2. With the existing technology, the only three processes that are available require the input combinations shown in Table 1.1. Given the existing technology, Table 1.1 shows that there is no way to finish a batch of cotton cloth using only 0.10 man-hours of skilled labor and 1.0 machine-hours of finishing equipment. This is beyond the current state of the art. Engineers and craftsmen do not yet know how to accomplish this. It is obvious that this limitation of existing knowledge results in a corresponding limitation on how much the firm can produce with its 600 man-hours of skilled labor and its 6,000 machine-hours of finishing equipment. When, and if, technology advances to the point where it is possible to finish a batch of cotton cloth with 0.10 man-hours of skilled labor and 1.0 machine-hours of finishing equipment, the firm will be able to produce more with its existing amount of skilled labor and equipment. More will then be produced with the existing resources.

10. The Tasks Performed by an Economic System

Economics, of course, deals with the functioning of economic systems—just as, for example, biology deals with the functioning of biological systems. Perhaps the best way to define the economic system is to describe what it does. A society's economic system must allocate its resources among competing uses, combine and process these resources in such a way as to produce goods and services, determine the amount of various goods and services that will be produced, distribute these goods and services among the society's members, and determine what provision is to be made for the future growth of the society's per capita income. Put in a single sentence, these tasks do not seem quite as awesome as in fact they are. To do justice to each of these tasks, a fuller explanation is needed.

First, the economic system must allocate its resources among competing uses and combine and process these resources to produce the desired level and composition of output. Suppose that the desired level and composition of output is known. There usually are many ways of producing a commodity, and it is not easy to decide which way is best. For example, a plant can use different types and quantities of equipment, different amounts and qualities of raw materials, different amounts and qualities of labor, different locations, different means of transporting and distributing its product, and different ways of informing potential customers of the product's existence. Of the many combinations of resources that could be used, which should be used? Or looking at the problem from a somewhat different point of view, there is an enormous quantity and variety of resources in any society: How should each of these resources be used?

Even if some smart Philadelphia lawyer, or some other type of philosopher-king, could tell us which combination of resources is best for the production of each good, this would not be a complete solution to the problem. We would also have to find a way to insure that this combination would in fact be used. The difficulty of solving this aspect of the problem should not be underestimated. Even in highly disciplined organizations like armies, it is not unusual for a general's plan of action to be executed improperly or distorted considerably.

Second, an economic system must determine the level and composition of output. To what extent should society's resources be used to produce weapons systems? To what extent should they be used to rebuild the cities? To what extent should they be used to produce cotton and wool cloth? To what extent should they be used to produce artificial fibers like nylon? To what extent should they be used to produce dresses? To what extent should they be used to produce Levis? What is the proper combination of goods—weapons systems, rebuilt cities, natural fibers, artificial fibers, dresses, Levis, and so on—that should be produced? The enormous complexity of this question, as well as its importance, should be obvious. If the reader feels a bit overwhelmed by it, this is precisely the message we wish to convey.

Third, the economic system must also determine how the goods and services that are produced are distributed among the members of society. How much of each type of good and service is each person to receive? This is a subject that has generated, and continues to generate, heated controversy. Some people are in favor of a relatively egalitarian society where the amount received by one family varies little from that received by another family of the same size. Other people favor a less egalitarian society where the amount that a family or person receives varies a great deal. Few people favor a thoroughly egalitarian society, if for no other reason than that some differences in income are required to stimulate workers to do certain types of work.

Fourth, another task of an economic system is to provide for whatever rate of growth of per capita income the society desires and can achieve. The goal of economic growth is a relatively new one; most past societies have had economies that were unprogressive. Regardless of its newness, however, it has come to be regarded as an extremely important task, particularly in the less-developed countries of Africa, Asia, and South America. There is very strong pressure in these countries for changes in technology, the adoption of superior techniques, increases in the stock of capital resources, and better and more extensive education and training of the labor force. These are viewed as some of the major ways to promote the growth of per capita income. In the industrialized nations, the goal of rapid economic growth has become more controversial in recent years. This has been due in part to the fact that some observers have questioned the extent to which economic growth is worth its costs in social dislocation, pollution, and so forth. But there is no indication that most industrialized nations have lost interest in further economic growth.

11. Our Mixed Capitalist System

The previous section described the four basic functions that any economic system must perform. How does our economic system in the United States perform each of these functions? Let's begin with the determination of the level and composition of output in the society. How is this decided? In a substantially free-enterprise economy, such as ours, consumers choose the amount of each good that they want, and producers act in accord with these decisions. The importance that consumers attach to a good is indicated by the price they are willing to pay for it.

However, consumer sovereignty does not extend to all areas of our society. For example, with regard to the consumption of commodities like drugs, society imposes limits on the decisions of individuals. Moreover, some goods cannot be bought and sold in the marketplace, or even if they can be, it would be inefficient to do so. Such goods, called public goods, will not be provided in the right amounts by private industry, so the government tends to intervene. Examples of public goods are national defense and a healthful environment. Decisions regarding the provision of these goods tend to be made in the political arena.

Going back to the first function described in the previous section, how does our economic system allocate its resources among competing uses, and how does it process these resources to obtain the desired level and composition of output? Basically, the price system does the job by indicating the desires of workers and the relative value of various types of materials and equipment as well as the desires of consumers. For example, if bricklayers are scarce relative to the uses for them, their price in the labor market—their wage—will be bid up and they will tend to be used only in the places where they are most productive. The forces that push firms in the direction of actually carrying out the proper decisions take the form principally of profits or losses. Profits are the carrot and losses are the stick which are used to eliminate the less efficient and the less alert firms and to increase the more efficient and the more alert.

Although decentralized decision-making based on the price system is used to organize production in most areas of our economy, there are notable exceptions. For example, in the acquisition of new weapons by the Department of Defense, the price system, in anything like its customary form, has not been applied. Instead, the government has exercised control over sellers through the auditing of costs and through the intimate involvement of its agents in the managerial and operating structure of the sellers. Moreover, there is extensive government ownership of the seller's facilities; the government decides what weapons are to be created through its program decisions; and it often decides how they are to be created and produced.

Turning to the next function, how does our economic system determine how much in the way of goods and services each member of the society is to receive? In general, the income of individuals depends largely on the quantities of resources of various kinds that they own and the prices they get for them. For example, if a person both works and rents out houses he or she owns, the person's total income is the number of hours worked per year multiplied by his or her hourly wage rate plus the number of houses owned times the annual rental per house. Thus the distribution of income depends on the way that resource ownership is distributed. Some individuals own higher-priced labor resources than others, because of greater intelligence or superior training. Some individuals own a much greater amount of capital and land than others. However, this is only part of the story. The government modifies the resulting distribution of income by imposing progressive income taxes and by welfare programs such as aid to dependent children. In this way, an attempt is made to reduce income differentials somewhat.

Finally, how does our economic system determine our nation's rate of growth of per capita income? A nation's rate of growth of per capita income depends on the rate of growth of its resources and the rate of increase of the efficiency with which they are used. In our economy, the rate at which labor and capital resources are increased is motivated, at least in part, through the price system. Higher wages for more highly skilled work are an incentive for an individual to undergo further training and education. Capital accumulation occurs in response to expectations of profit. Increases in efficiency, due in considerable measure to the advance of technology, are also stimulated by the price system, but it must be recognized that the government plays an extremely significant role in supporting research and development. In areas like defense, space, atomic energy, and many aspects of agriculture and medicine, the government plays a dominant role in research and development.

12. The Price System and Microeconomics

From the discussion in the previous section it is clear that the price system plays a major role in the way our economy goes about performing the four principal functions that any economic system must perform. It is not the only means by which our economy goes about performing these tasks, but its role is very important. A person who wants to understand the way in which our economic system functions must therefore have at least a basic knowledge of how the price system works. Microeconomics—or at least a major part of it—is often called price theory because so much of it is concerned so directly with the workings of the price system.

At this point, we are in a position to bring together various strands of the preceding discussion in order to describe more fully the nature and purpose of microeconomics. Economics, it will be recalled from Sections 1 and 8, deals with the way in which scarce resources are allocated among alternative uses to satisfy human wants. Microeconomics, it will be recalled from Section 1, is the branch of economics that is concerned with the economic behavior of individual consumers, firms, and resource owners, not with the aggregate changes of the economy. According to the previous paragraph, one of the principal purposes of microeconomics is to provide an understanding of the workings and effects of the price system, which plays an important role in the way our economy functions.

In the course of providing such an understanding, microeconomics helps to answer questions of the kind discussed in Section 7: What determines the price of various commodities? What determines the amount that a worker makes? What determines the way that a consumer allocates his or her income among various commodities? What determines how much of a particular commodity will be produced? What determines the number and size of firms in a particular industry? Moreover, in the course of investigating these and related questions, microeconomics has shed considerable light on the kinds of problems discussed in Sections 2 to 6: How should a firm choose among alternative manufacturing processes if it wants to maximize its profits? What sort of pricing policy should it adopt? What kinds of social changes can be made if it is agreed that the goal is to make anyone better off if it does not make someone else worse off? What are the advantages and disadvantages of various ways in which industries might be organized?

13. Model-Building and the Role of Models

Before concluding this introductory chapter, it is important that we describe briefly the basic methodology used in microeconomics to answer the kinds of questions cited above. This methodology is much the same as that used in any other type of scientific analysis. The basic procedure is the formulation of models. A model is composed of a number of assumptions from which conclusions—or predictions—are deduced. For example, suppose that we want to formulate a model of the solar system. We might represent each of the planets by a point in space, and we might make the assumption that each would change position in accord with certain mathematical equations. Based on this model, we might predict when an eclipse would occur.[7]

To be useful, a model must in general simplify and abstract from the real situation. Although the assumptions that are made obviously must bear some relationship to the type of situation to which the model is

7. See Irwin Bross, *Design for Decision* (New York: Macmillan, 1953), pp. 161–82.

applicable (since randomly chosen asumptions are unlikely, for example, to predict eclipses very well), it is very important to understand that the assumptions need not be exact replicas of reality. Thus, in the example above, the fact that planets are in fact not points makes little or no difference. Moreover, even if the equations representing their movements are somewhat in error, this may make little difference since, despite these errors, the model may predict well enough to be useful. In both the natural and social sciences, models based on simplified and idealized circumstances have found many, many uses. Also, some assumptions may refer to things that are not directly measurable, like utility in economic theory. The fact that they are not directly measurable does not mean that they are useless: Their usefulness depends on whether or not they result in models that are more powerful and accurate.

There are a number of important reasons why economists, like other scientists, use models. One is that the real world is so complex that it is necessary to simplify and abstract if any progress is to be made. Another is that a simple model may be the cheapest way of obtaining needed information. Of course, although the use of models is well accepted throughout the various branches of the scientific community, this does not mean that all models are good or useful. A model may be so oversimplified and distorted that it is utterly useless. The trick is to construct a model in such a way that irrelevant and unimportant considerations and variables are neglected, but the important factors—those that have an important effect on the phenomena the model is designed to predict— are included.

14. The Evaluation of a Model

The purpose of a model is to make predictions concerning phenomena in the real world, and in many respects the most important test of a model is how well it predicts these phenomena. In this sense, a model that predicts the price of coffee within plus or minus 1 cent a pound is better than a model that predicts the price of coffee within plus or minus 2 cents a pound. Of course, this does not mean that a model is useless if it cannot predict very accurately. Under some circumstances, one does not need a very accurate prediction. For some purposes, it is sufficient that a model's predictions be accurate to within a mile; for other purposes, its predictions must be accurate to within a gnat's whisker. Also, for some purposes, a model's predictions must describe various aspects and dimensions of reality; for other purposes, only one aspect or dimension is important.

A model's predictions are derived by applying the rules of logic to the assumptions. For example, in the model of the solar system described above, we see at what point in time an eclipse will occur according to the model by making computations based on the model's assumptions and employing the rules of logic. One elementary test of a model's predictions is whether or not they really do flow logically from the model's assumptions. Sometimes errors of logic and computation creep in to mar a prediction. More fundamentally, another test of a model is whether its assumptions are logically consistent, one with another. Sometimes the natural or social scientist, in building a model, makes assumptions that are not really compatible.

Another important consideration in judging a model is the range of phenomena to which it applies. In any science, there is a great and understandable attempt to formulate models that are as general as possible. A model that can predict the behavior of any consumer in the economy is more valuable than one that can predict only the behavior of John Jones. Hence the economist is much more interested in a model that is relevant to many consumers in the economy than in one that is relevant to only one consumer. However, the more general a model is meant to be, the more difficult it is to attain a given degree of accuracy. It is relatively easy to construct empirically valid models with little or no generality. For example, if one wanted to go to the trouble of studying a particular person's eating habits, it is likely that one could formulate a model that would predict his or her choice of breakfast food cereals pretty well. But it would be much more difficult to find a model that would be equally accurate in predicting the choice of any type of food by any consumer in the economy. If a theory is to be general, it must ignore many details (and sometimes some variables that are considerably more important than details); the result is that its predictions are likely to fall short—perhaps considerably short—of a high degree of accuracy.

It is important to add another point that is frequently misunderstood: If one is interested in predicting the outcome of a particular event, one will be forced to use the model that predicts best, even if this model does not predict very well. The choice is not between a model and no model; it is between one type of model and another. After all, if one must make a forecast, one will use the most accurate device available to make such a forecast. And any such device is a model of some sort. Consequently, when economists make simplifying assumptions and derive conclusions that are only approximately true, it is somewhat beside the point to complain that the assumptions are simpler than reality or that the predictions are not always accurate. All of this may be true, but if the predictions are better than those obtained on the basis of other models, this model must be used until something better comes along. Thus, if a model can predict the price of coffee to within plus or minus 1 cent a pound and no other model can do better, this model will be used even if those interested in predicting the price of coffee bewail the model's limitations and wish it could be improved.

The basic point can perhaps be illustrated by the story of the man whose weakness was games of chance and whose wife told him one day that the local casino was dishonest and asked him to stop visiting it. He replied "It's a darned shame and I'd like to stop going . . . but it's the only game in town." Similarly, if a model is the best that is available, it will—and should—be used until a better model appears.

At this point, a final word should be added concerning the microeconomic models discussed in subsequent chapters. No claim is made

Example 1.2   The Bootlegging of Cigarettes

Cigarette bootleggers take cigarettes from states with low cigarette taxes and sell them in states with high cigarette taxes. Such smuggling results in a loss in tax revenue to the latter states. The Advisory Commission on Intergovernmental Relations estimated that this loss in 1979 and 1975 was as follows:

LOSS FROM CIGARETTE TAX EVASION

	1975	1979
	(MILLION OF DOLLARS)	
All states	337	280
Florida	36	43

(a) If you had to construct a model to predict the amount of cigarettes bootlegged, what factors would you include? (b) Based on the above figures, do you think that Florida's cigarette tax rate is lower than that of neighboring states? Why or why not? (c) Between 1975 and 1979, Florida changed its tax on a pack of cigarettes by 3 cents per pack. Do you think that it increased or decreased the tax? Why? (d) Could the change in the total loss from cigarette tax evasion have been due in part to the great increase in the price of gasoline in the late 1970s? Why or why not?

Solution

(a) The amount of cigarettes bootlegged into a particular state depends on this state's tax rate relative to that of its neighboring states. If a state's tax rate is much higher than that of its neighbors, bootleggers can make money by bringing cigarettes into this state. Also, the amount bootlegged into a particular state depends on the cost of transporting the cigarettes. The higher the cost per mile of transporting a truckload of cigarettes, the smaller the distance it is profitable to take them. (b) No. Florida's loss from tax evasion is over 15 percent of that in all states, which is disproportionately large. Thus, its tax rate would be expected to be higher than in neighboring states (which in fact is true). (c) Since its loss from tax evasion increased (while that in other states decreased) during 1975–79, one would expect that its tax increased relative to that in neighboring states. In fact, it increased its tax by 3 cents per pack. (d) Yes. The cost of transporting the cigarettes increased.*

* For further discussion, see "Inflation and Gas Prices Hinder the Cigarette Bootlegging Trade," *New York Times,* April 20, 1980.

that these models are sufficiently accurate or powerful to solve all—or most—of the problems that face firms, governments, or others. Some of these models have been used to predict reasonably well; others have not been nearly so successful. Still others have not really been tested, and no one knows how well they would predict. Moreover, no claim is made that the models discussed in subsequent chapters are the last word on the subject. Undoubtedly they will be improved. All that we do claim is that, according to a consensus of the economics profession, they are the best models we have. Like the local casino they may have their imperfections (although dishonesty is not among them), but they are the best in town.

15. Summary

Economics deals with the way in which resources are allocated among alternative uses to satisfy human wants. Economic activity is directed toward the satisfaction of human wants. Resources are the things and services used to produce goods that can satisfy wants. Economic resources are scarce and have a nonzero price; free resources are not scarce and can be obtained free of charge. Technology is society's pool of knowledge regarding the industrial and agricultural arts. It sets limits on the amount and types of goods and services that can be derived from a given set of resources.

Any economic system must accomplish four tasks: It must allocate resources, determine the composition of output, distribute the product, and provide for growth. In our society, individual consumers have great power in determining the composition of output; the prices they are willing to pay for a good indicate how much importance they attach to it. The price system also is an important determinant of how resources are allocated and how the product is distributed. However, since our economy is mixed, government also plays a very important role in these tasks. In some areas, the composition of output and the allocation of resources are determined by political decisions. Moreover, the government modifies the distribution of income, and it plays an important role in stimulating and maintaining growth.

The methodology used by economists is much the same as that used in any other type of scientific analysis; the basic procedure is the formulation of models. Economic theory is divided into two parts: microeconomics and macroeconomics. Microeconomics is concerned with the economic behavior of individual economic units like consumers, firms, and resource owners. One of the most important purposes of microeconomics is to provide an understanding of the working and effects of the price system. In the course of providing such an understanding, microeconomics helps to answer many practical problems of businesses and governments and throws important light on many fundamental issues that confront responsible citizens and elected representatives. Much of this chapter has been devoted to examples of the kinds of problems microeconomics can help to solve.

QUESTIONS AND PROBLEMS

1. On most questions of policy one can find disagreements among economists. Thus President Reagan's economic advisers have somewhat different views than President Carter's economic advisers. Does this prove that economics is not a science?

2. The median salary of teachers of economics has generally been higher than that of teachers of physics, chemistry, mathematics, or biology. Is this a powerful argument that economics is a science? Why or why not?

3. If a certain proposition holds true for a part of a system, must it hold true for the whole system? For example, suppose that a farmer will benefit from producing a larger crop. Does it follow that all farmers will benefit from producing a larger crop? Explain.

4. According to the principle of Occam's razor, if two models predict equally well, the one that is less complicated should be chosen. Do you agree? How can you tell how complicated a model is?

5. In evaluating the accuracy of their statements, should you distinguish between (1) economists' descriptive statements, propositions, and predictions about the world, and (2) their statements about what policies should be adopted? Explain.

6. Do you think that the industrialized nations of the world should forsake the goal of economic growth? Do you think that continued economic growth will result in our running out of raw materials, with the result that living standards will fall? Explain.

7. Describe the four basic tasks that must be performed by any economic system.

8. One purpose of microeconomics is to determine how we can achieve an optimal allocation of resources. Describe some of the problems involved in defining an "optimal" allocation. Do you think that there is an optimal allocation of resources in the United States at present? Why or why not?

9. What considerations must be taken into account in judging or evaluating a model?

10. Suppose that you were given the task of constructing a model to predict U. S. Steel's total sales next year. How would you go about it? What variables would you include?

SELECTED REFERENCES

FRIEDMAN, MILTON. "The Methodology of Positive Economics." *Essays in Positive Economics*. Chicago: University of Chicago Press, 1953.

HARROD, ROY. "Scope and Method of Economics." *Economic Journal*, 1938.

KOOPMANS, TJALLING. "Economics among the sciences." *American Economic Review*, March 1979. [Advanced]

LANGE, OSCAR. "The Scope and Method of Economics." *Readings in the Phi-*

losophy of Science, edited by Herbert Feigl and May Brodbeck. New York: Appleton-Century-Crofts, 1953.

MARSHALL, ALFRED. *Principles of Economics.* London: Macmillan, 1920.

ROBBINS, LIONEL. *An Essay on the Nature and Significance of Economic Science.* London: Macmillan, 1935.

2 Demand and Supply

1. Introduction

One of the most important purposes of microeconomics is to provide an understanding of the workings of the price system. In this chapter, we provide a brief glimpse of the mechanism at the center of that system: the market. We begin by discussing the basic concepts of demand and supply, as well as the price elasticity of demand and the price elasticity of supply. Then we describe briefly how price is determined. Finally, we show how our results can be used to throw important light on some major present-day policy issues. This chapter provides a brief, initial look at these central concepts, not an exhaustive treatment. In later chapters, each of these topics will be discussed in much more detail.[1]

2. Market

Since this chapter is concerned with the behavior of markets, it is necessary to describe at the outset what we mean by a market. This is not quite as straightforward as it may seem, since most markets are not well defined in a geographical or physical sense. (For example, the New York Stock Exchange is an atypical market in the sense that it is located principally in a particular building.) What is a market? A good working definition is that it is a group of firms and individuals in touch with each other in order to buy or sell some good. Of course, not every person in a market has to be in

1. Readers familiar with these concepts can use this chapter for review or go directly to Chapter 3 without loss of continuity.

contact with every other person in the market; a person or firm is part of a market even if in contact with only a subset of the other persons or firms in the market.

Markets vary enormously in their size, arrangements, and procedures. For some household goods, all of the consumers west of the Rocky Mountains may be members of the same market. For other goods, like Rembrandt paintings, only a few collectors, dealers, and museums scattered around the world are members of the market. Basically, however, all markets consist primarily of buyers and sellers, although third parties like brokers and agents may be present as well. In most markets, the sellers suggest the price, but this is not always the case. In this chapter, we assume that a market contains many small buyers and sellers so that none of them individually exerts a significant influence on the price.[2] We will relax that assumption in later chapters.

3. The Market Demand Curve

According to Thomas Carlyle, the famous nineteenth-century historian and essayist, "it is easy to train an economist; teach a parrot to say Demand and Supply." Although he may have exaggerated the susceptibility of parrots to an economics education, Carlyle certainly was right about the central role played by demand and supply in economics. The market for every good has a demand side and a supply side. The demand side can be represented by a *market demand schedule,* a table which shows the quantity of the good that would be purchased at each price. (The price of the good is, of course, the amount of money that must be paid for a unit of it.) For example, suppose that the market demand schedule for coal is as shown in Table 2.1. According to this table, 565 million tons of coal will be demanded per year if its price is $36 per ton, 570 million tons of coal will be demanded if its price is $35 per ton, and so on. Another way of presenting the data in Table 2.1 is by a *market demand curve,* which is a plot of the market demand schedule on a graph. The vertical axis of the graph measures the price per unit of the good, and the horizontal axis measures the quantity of the good demanded per unit of time. Figure 2.1 shows the market demand curve for coal, based on the figures in Table 2.1.

Two things should be noted concerning Figure 2.1. First, the market demand curve for coal *slopes downward to the right.* In other words, the quantity of coal demanded increases as the price falls. This is true of the demand curve for most goods: they almost always slope downward to the right. In subsequent chapters, we shall learn why this is not always the

2. More accurately, we assume that markets are perfectly competitive. A perfectly competitive market exists when no buyer or seller can influence price, output is homogeneous, resources are mobile, and knowledge is perfect. A fuller definition of a perfectly competitive market is given in Chapter 9.

Table 2.1   Market demand
schedule for coal, 1981

Price per ton (dollars)	Quantity demanded per year (millions of tons)
36	565
35	570
34	580
33	590
32	600
31	610
30	630

NOTE: These figures are hypothetical, but adequate for present purposes. In subsequent chapters, we shall provide data describing the actual relationship between the price and quantity demanded of various goods. At this point, the emphasis is on the concept of a market demand schedule, not on the detailed accuracy of these figures.

case, but these reasons need not concern us at present. Second, the market demand curve in Figure 2.1 pertains to a *particular period of time:* 1981. It is important to recognize that any demand curve pertains to some period of time, and that its shape and position depend on the length and other characteristics of this period. For example, if we were to estimate the market demand curve for coal for the first week in 1981, it

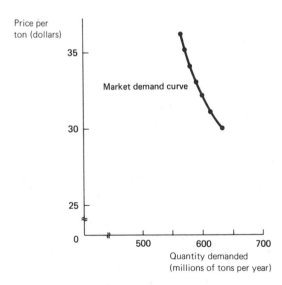

Figure 2.1   Market demand curve for coal, 1981

would be a different curve than the one in Figure 2.1, which pertains to the whole year. The difference arises partly because consumers can adapt their purchases more fully to changes in the price of coal in a year than in a week.

Besides the length of the time period, what other factors determine the position and shape of the market demand curve for a good? One important factor is the *tastes of consumers*. If consumers show an increasing preference for a product, the demand curve will shift to the right; that is, at each price, consumers will desire to buy more than previously. On the other hand, if consumers show a decreasing preference for a product, the demand curve will shift to the left, since, at each price, consumers will desire to buy less than previously. For example, let's turn from coal to the case of electricity. If consumers become more energy-conscious, and begin to take more pride in cutting back on the unnecessary use of electricity, the demand curve for electricity may shift to the left, as shown in Figure 2.2. The greater the shift in preferences, the larger the shift in the demand curve.

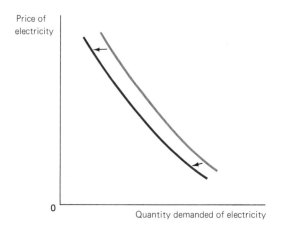

Figure 2.2   Effect of increased energy-consciousness on market demand curve for electricity

Another factor that influences the position and shape of a good's market demand curve is *the level of consumer incomes*. For some types of products, the demand curve shifts to the right if per capita income increases; whereas for other types of commodities, the demand curve shifts to the left if per capita income rises. In subsequent chapters, we shall analyze why some goods fall into one category and other goods fall into the other, but, at present, this need not concern us. All that is important here is that changes in per capita income affect the demand curve. In the case of electricity, all the available studies indicate that an increase in

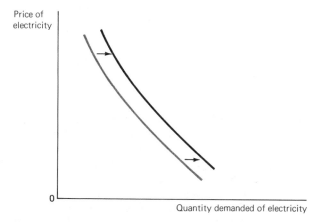

Figure 2.3 Effect of increase in per capita income on market
demand curve for electricity

per capita income would shift the demand curve to the right, as shown in
Figure 2.3.

Still another factor that influences the position and shape of a good's
market demand curve is the *level of other prices*. For example, since
natural gas can be substituted to some extent for electricity, the quantity of electricity demanded depends on the price of natural gas. If the
price of gas is high, more electricity will be demanded than if the price of
gas is low, because people and firms will be stimulated to substitute
electricity for the high-priced gas. Thus, as shown in Figure 2.4, increases

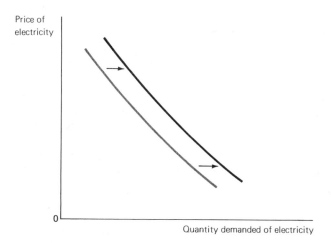

Figure 2.4 Effect of increase in the price of natural gas
on market demand curve for electricity

in the price of gas will shift the market demand curve for electricity to the right (and decreases in the price of gas will shift it to the left).[3]

4. The Price Elasticity of Demand

The shape of a good's market demand curve varies from one good to another and from one market to another. In particular, market demand curves vary in the sensitivity of quantity demanded to price. For some goods, a small change in price results in a large change in quantity demanded; for other goods, a large change in price results in a small change in quantity demanded. To gauge the sensitivity, or responsiveness, of the quantity demanded to changes in price, economists use a measure called the *price elasticity of demand*. The price elasticity of demand is defined to be *the percentage change in quantity demanded resulting from a 1 percent change in price.*[4]

For example, suppose that a 1 percent reduction in the price of electricity results in a 1.2 percent increase in the quantity demanded in the United States. If so, the price elasticity of demand for electricity is 1.2. Convention dictates that we give the elasticity a positive sign despite the fact that the change in price is negative and the change in quantity demanded is positive. Clearly, the price elasticity of demand will generally vary from one point to another on a demand curve. For example, the price elasticity of demand may be higher when the price of electricity is high than when it is low. Similarly, the price elasticity of demand will vary from market to market. For example, Japan may have a different price elasticity of demand for electricity than does the United States.[5]

Alfred Marshall, the great English economist who lived about sev-

---

3. Let the quantity demanded of a good per unit of time equal Q_D. In general,

$$Q_D = f(P, T, I, R, N),$$

where P is the price of the good, T stands for the tastes of consumers, I is the level of consumer income, R is the price of related goods, and N is the number of consumers in the market. The demand curve shows the relationship between Q_D and P when the other variables are held constant. In general, changes in the values at which these other variables are held constant will affect the relationship between Q_D and P, which is another way of saying that these other variables will generally influence the position and shape of the market demand curve.

4. For readers with a knowledge of calculus, it is worth noting that, if Q_D is the quantity demanded and P is the price, a more precise definition of the price elasticity of demand is

$$\eta = \frac{-dQ_D}{dP} \cdot \frac{P}{Q_D}.$$

More will be said about the measurement of the price elasticity of demand in Chapter 5.

5. A much more complete discussion of the demand curve for electricity is contained in Example 5.1 in Chapter 5.

enty years ago, was one of the first economists to give a clear formulation of the concept of the price elasticity of demand. It is a very important concept and one that will be used repeatedly throughout this book. One thing to note at the outset is that the price elasticity of demand is expressed in terms of *relative* changes in price and quantity demanded, not *absolute* changes in price and quantity demanded. This is because absolute changes are difficult to interpret. For example, suppose that a price goes up by a dime. This is a lot for a subway ride but little for a house. Similarly, it is a lot for a bottle of beer but little for a fifty-gallon keg. A frequent error is to confuse the price elasticity of demand with the slope of the demand curve. They are by no means the same thing.[6]

Suppose that we have a market demand schedule showing the quantity of a commodity demanded in the market at various prices. How can we estimate the price elasticity of market demand? Let ΔP be a change in the price of the good and ΔQ_D be the resulting change in its quantity demanded. If ΔP is very small, we can compute the *point elasticity of demand*:

$$\eta = -\frac{\Delta Q_D}{Q_D} \div \frac{\Delta P}{P} \qquad\qquad 2.1$$

For example, consider Table 2.2 where data are given for very small increments in the price of a commodity. If we want to estimate the price elasticity of demand when the price is between 99.95 cents and $1, we obtain the following result:

$$\eta = -\frac{40{,}002 - 40{,}000}{40{,}000} \div \frac{99.95 - 100}{100} = .1$$

Note that we used $1 as P and 40,000 as Q_D. We could have used 99.95 cents as P and 40,002 as Q_D, but it would have made no real difference to the answer. (Try it and see.)

Table 2.2   Quantity demanded at various prices (small increments in price)

Price (cents per unit of commodity)	Quantity demanded per unit of time (units of commodity)
99.95	40,002
100.00	40,000
100.05	39,998

6. The slope of the demand curve is dP/dQ_D. A glance at footnote 4 will show that this slope is not equal to the price elasticity of demand. Sometimes the price elasticity of demand is also confused with dQ_D/dP. This too is an error since they are by no means the same thing.

Table 2.3 Quantity demanded at various prices (large increments in price)

Price (dollars per unit of commodity)	Quantity demanded per unit of time (units of commodity)
3	40
4	20
5	3

However, if we have data concerning only large changes in price (that is, if ΔP and ΔQ_D are large), the answer may vary considerably depending on which value of P and Q_D is used in Equation 2.1. For example, take the case in Table 2.3. Suppose that we want to estimate the price elasticity of demand in the price range between \$4 and \$5. Then, depending on which value of P and Q_D is used, the answer will be

$$\eta = -\frac{20 - 3}{3} \div \frac{4 - 5}{5} = 28.33$$

$$\eta = -\frac{3 - 20}{20} \div \frac{5 - 4}{4} = 3.40$$

The difference between these two results is enormous. In a case of this sort, it is advisable to compute the *arc elasticity of demand*, which uses the average value of P and Q_D:

$$\eta = -\frac{\Delta Q_D}{(Q_{D1} + Q_{D2})/2} \div \frac{\Delta P}{(P_1 + P_2)/2}$$

$$= -\frac{\Delta Q_D(P_1 + P_2)}{\Delta P(Q_{D1} + Q_{D2})}$$
2.2

where P_1 and Q_{D1} are the first values of price and quantity demanded, and P_2 and Q_{D2} are the second set. Thus, in Table 2.3,

$$\eta = -\frac{20 - 3}{(20 + 3)/2} \div \frac{4 - 5}{(4 + 5)/2} = 6.65$$

This is the way economists get around this difficulty.

5. The Market Supply Curve

Each market has a supply side as well as a demand side. The supply side can be represented by a *market supply schedule,* a table which shows the quantity of the good that would be supplied at various prices. For example, suppose that the market supply schedule for coal is shown in Table 2.4. Then 500 million tons of coal will be supplied if its price is \$30 per

Table 2.4 Market supply
schedule for coal, 1981

Price per ton (dollars)	Quantity supplied per year (millions of tons)
30	500
31	550
32	600
33	650
34	675
35	700
36	725

NOTE: These figures are hypothetical, but adequate
for present purposes. In subsequent chapters, we shall
provide data describing the actual relationship
between the price and quantity supplied of various
goods. At this point, the emphasis is on the concept
of a market supply schedule, not on the detailed
accuracy of these figures.

ton, 550 million tons of coal will be supplied if its price is $31 per ton, and
so on. Another way of presenting the data in Table 2.4 is by a *market
supply curve,* which is a plot of the market supply schedule on a graph.
The vertical axis of the graph measures the price per unit of the good, and
the horizontal axis measures the quantity of the good supplied per unit
of time. Figure 2.5 shows the market supply curve for coal, based on the
figures in Table 2.4.[7]

Two things should be noted concerning Figure 2.5. First, the market

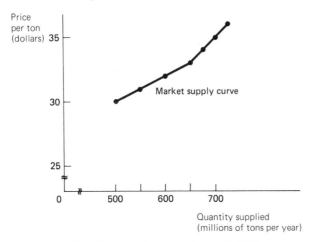

Figure 2.5 Market supply curve for coal, 1981

7. Note once more that we assume that the market for coal is perfectly competitive.
(See footnote 2.) This simplification is adopted throughout this chapter. In subsequent chapters we relax the assumption that markets are perfectly competitive.

supply curve for coal *slopes upward to the right.* In other words, the quantity of coal supplied increases as the price increases. This is because increases in its price give the makers of coal a greater incentive to produce it and offer it for sale. Empirical studies indicate that the market supply curves for a great many commodities share this characteristic of sloping upward to the right. In subsequent chapters, we will analyze in detail the factors responsible for the shape of a particular good's market supply curve. Second, the market supply curve in Figure 2.5 pertains to a *particular period of time:* 1981. Any supply curve pertains to some period of time, and its shape and position depend on the length and other characteristics of this period. For example, if we were to estimate the market supply curve for coal for the first week in 1981, it would be a different curve than the one in Figure 2.5, which pertains to the whole year. In part, the difference arises because coal producers can adapt their output rate more fully to changes in coal's price in a year than in a week.

Besides the length of the time period, what other factors determine the position and shape of the market supply curve for a good? One important factor is *technological change.* Recall that technology was defined in Chapter 1 as society's pool of knowledge concerning the industrial arts. As technology progresses, it becomes possible to produce commodities more cheaply, so that firms often are willing to supply a given amount at a lower price than formerly. Thus technological change often causes the supply curve to shift to the right. For example, this certainly has occurred in the case of coal, as indicated in Figure 2.6. There have been many important technological changes in coal production in the past fifty years, including the invention and improvement of continuous mining machinery, trackless mobile loaders, and shuttle cars.

Another factor that influences the position and shape of a good's market supply curve is the *level of input prices.* The supply curve for a commodity is affected by the prices of the resources (labor, capital, and land) used to produce it. Decreases in the prices of these inputs make it possible to produce commodities more cheaply, so that firms may be willing to supply a given amount at a lower price than they formerly

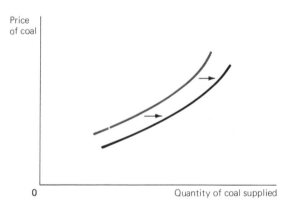

Figure 2.6   Effect of technological change on the market supply curve for coal

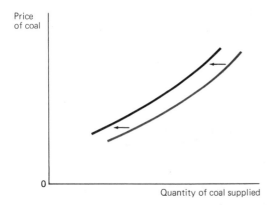

Price
of coal

0

Quantity of coal supplied

Figure 2.7   Effect of increase in wages of coal miners
on market supply curve for coal

would. Thus decreases in the price of inputs may cause the supply curve
to shift to the right. On the other hand, increases in the price of inputs
may cause it to shift to the left. For example, if the wage rates of coal
miners increase (as they did in 1981), the supply curve for coal may shift
to the left, as shown in Figure 2.7.[8]

6. The Price Elasticity of Supply

Like market demand curves, market supply curves vary in shape. In
particular, they vary with respect to the sensitivity of quantity supplied
to price. For some goods, a small change in price results in a large change
in quantity supplied; for other goods, a large change in price results in a
small change in quantity supplied. To gauge the sensitivity of the quantity supplied to changes in price, economists use a measure called the
price elasticity of supply, which is defined to be *the percentage change in
quantity supplied resulting from a 1 percent change in price.*[9] Thus, if a 1

8. Let the quantity supplied of a good per unit of time equal Q_S. In general,

$$Q_S = g(P, M, V),$$

where P is the price of the good, M is the level of input prices, and V stands for the
level of technology. The supply curve shows the relationship between Q_S and P
when the other variables are held constant. In general, changes in the values at
which these other variables are held constant will affect the relationship between
Q_s and P, which is another way of saying that these other variables will generally
influence the position and shape of the market supply curve.

9. More accurately, if Q_S is the quantity supplied and P is the price, the price elasticity of supply is

$$\eta_S = \frac{dQ_S}{dP} \cdot \frac{P}{Q_S}$$

More will be said about the measurement of the price elasticity of supply in
Chapter 9.

percent increase in the price of natural gas results in a 0.5 percent increase in the quantity supplied, the price elasticity of supply of natural gas is 0.5.

Clearly, the price elasticity of supply is analogous to the price elasticity of demand. Like the latter, it is expressed in terms of relative, not absolute, changes in price and quantity, and it should not be confused with the slope of the supply curve. Its value is likely to vary from one point to another on a supply curve. For example, the price elasticity of supply of natural gas may be higher when the price is low than when it is high. In general, the price elasticity of supply would be expected to increase with the length of the period to which the supply curve pertains. Why? Because, as noted in the previous section, manufacturers of the good will be able to adapt their output rates more fully to changes in its price if the period is long rather than short.

If we have a market supply schedule showing the quantity of a commodity supplied at various prices, we can readily estimate the price elasticity of supply. Let ΔP be the change in the price of the good and ΔQ_s be the resulting change in its quantity supplied. If ΔP is very small, we can compute the *point elasticity of supply:*

$$\eta_S = \frac{\Delta Q_S}{Q_S} \div \frac{\Delta P}{P} \qquad \text{2.3}$$

If ΔP is not so small, we can compute the *arc elasticity of supply* by using the average value of Q_S and P in Equation 2.3. These calculations are similar to (but not exactly the same[10]) as those required to compute the price elasticity of demand. To illustrate them, take the case in Table 2.4. Suppose that we want to compute the price elasticity of supply between $30 and $31. The arc elasticity of supply is

$$
\begin{aligned}
\eta_S &= \frac{\Delta Q_S}{(Q_{S1} + Q_{S2})/2} \div \frac{\Delta P}{(P_1 + P_2)/2} \\
&= \frac{550 - 500}{(550 + 500)/2} \div \frac{31 - 30}{(31 + 30)/2} \\
&= 2.90.
\end{aligned}
$$

7. The Equilibrium Price

Recall from the previous chapter that prices in a free-enterprise economy are important determinants of what is produced, how it is produced, who

10. In calculating the price elasticity of demand, we multiply the relative change in quantity demanded resulting from a 1 percent change in price by -1, so that the result will be a positive number. In calculating the price elasticity of supply, we do *not* have to multiply the relative change in quantity supplied resulting from a 1 percent change in price by -1, because it already is positive in the typical case. This is because, as we have already stressed, supply curves generally slope *upward* to the right, whereas demand curves generally slope *downward* to the right.

receives it, and how rapidly per capita income grows. It behooves us, therefore, to look carefully at how prices themselves are determined in a free-enterprise economy. As a first step toward describing this process, we must define the equilibrium price of a good. At various points in this book, you will encounter the concept of an equilibrium, which is very important in economics, as in many other scientific fields.

An equilibrium is a situation where there is no tendency for change; in other words, it is a situation that can persist. Thus *an equilibrium price is a price that can be maintained.* Any price that is not an equilibrium price cannot be maintained for long, since there are basic forces at work to stimulate a change in price. The best way to understand what we mean by an equilibrium price is to take a particular case, such as the market for coal. Let's put both the demand curve for coal (in Figure 2.1) and the supply curve for coal (in Figure 2.5) together in the same diagram. The result, shown in Figure 2.8, will help us determine the equilibrium price of coal.

We begin by seeing what would happen if various prices were established in the market. For example, if the price were $34 a ton, the demand curve indicates that 580 million tons of coal would be demanded, while the supply curve indicates that 675 million tons would be supplied. Thus, if the price were $34 a ton, there would be a mismatch between the quantity supplied and the quantity demanded per year, since the rate at which coal is supplied would be greater than the rate at which it is demanded. Specifically, as shown in Figure 2.8, there would be an *excess supply* of 95 million tons. Under these circumstances, some of the coal supplied by producers could not be sold, and as inventories of coal built up, suppliers would tend to cut their prices in order to get rid of unwanted inventories. Thus a price of $34 per ton would not be maintained for long—and for this reason, $34 per ton is not an equilibrium price.

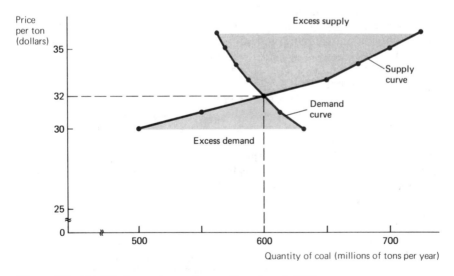

Figure 2.8 Equilibrium price and quantity of coal, 1981

If the price were $30 per ton, on the other hand, the demand curve indicates that 630 million tons of coal would be demanded, while the supply curve indicates that 500 million tons would be supplied. Again we find a mismatch between the quantity supplied and the quantity demanded per year, since the rate at which coal is supplied would be less than the rate at which it is demanded. Specifically, as shown in Figure 2.8, there would be an *excess demand* of 130 million tons. Under these circumstances, some of the consumers who want coal at this price would have to be turned away empty-handed. There would be a shortage. And given this shortage, suppliers would find it profitable to increase the price, and competition among buyers would bid the price up. Thus a price of $30 per ton could not be maintained for long—so $30 per ton is not an equilibrium price.

The equilibrium price must be the price where the quantity demanded equals the quantity supplied. Obviously this is the only price at which there is no mismatch between the quantity demanded and the quantity supplied; and consequently the only price that can be maintained for long. In Figure 2.8, the price at which the quantity supplied equals the quantity demanded is $32 per ton, the price where the demand curve intersects the supply curve. Thus $32 per ton is the equilibrium price of coal under the circumstances visualized in Figure 2.8, and 600 million tons is the equilibrium quantity.[11]

8. The Actual Price

What we set out to explain was the actual price, not the equilibrium price—since the actual price is all that is observed in the real world. In general, economists simply assume that the actual price will approximate the equilibrium price, which seems reasonable enough, since the basic forces at work tend to push the actual price toward the equilibrium price. Thus, if the demand and supply curves remain fairly stable for a time, the actual price should move toward the equilibrium price.

To see that this is the case, consider the market for coal, as described by Figure 2.8. What if the price somehow is set at $34 per ton? As we saw in the previous section, there is downward pressure on the price of coal under these conditions. Suppose the price, responding to this pressure, falls to $33. Comparing the quantity demanded with the quantity supplied at $33, we find that there is still downward pressure on price, since the quantity supplied exceeds the quantity demanded at $33. The price, responding to this pressure, may fall to $32.50, but comparing the quantity demanded with the quantity supplied at this price, we find that there is still a downward pressure on price, since the quantity supplied exceeds the quantity demanded at $32.50.

11. If $P = D(Q)$ is the demand curve and $P = S(Q)$ is the supply curve, we have two equations in two unknowns—price (P) and quantity (Q). To determine the equilibrium price, we can solve these equations simultaneously for P and Q.

So long as the actual price exceeds the equilibrium price, there will be a downward pressure on price. Similarly, so long as the actual price is less than the equilibrium price, there will be an upward pressure on price. Thus there is always a tendency for the actual price to move toward the equilibrium price. But it should not be assumed that this movement is always rapid. Sometimes it takes a long time for the actual price to get close to the equilibrium price. Sometimes the actual price never gets to the equilibrium price because by the time it gets close, the equilibrium price changes. All that safely can be said is that the actual price will move toward the equilibrium price. But of course this information is of great value, both theoretically and practically. For many purposes, all that is required is a prediction of whether the price will move up or down.

9. Effects on Price of Shifts in the Demand Curve

We have already seen that demand curves shift in response to changes in tastes, income, and prices of other products. Any supply-and-demand diagram like Figure 2.8 is essentially a snapshot of the situation during a particular period of time. The results in Figure 2.8 are limited to a particular period because the demand and supply curves in the figure pertain only to that period. What happens to the equilibrium price of a product (which we shall call good X) when its demand curve changes?

Suppose that consumer tastes shift in favor of good X, causing the demand curve for good X to shift to the right. This state of affairs is shown in Figure 2.9, where the demand curve shifts from DD' to D_1D_1'. It is not hard to see the effect on the equilibrium price of good X. When DD' is the demand curve, the equilibrium price is OP. But when the demand curve shifts to D_1D_1', a shortage of $(OQ_2 - OQ)$ develops at this price. That is, the quantity demanded exceeds the quantity supplied at this price by $(OQ_2 - OQ)$. Consequently, suppliers raise their prices. After

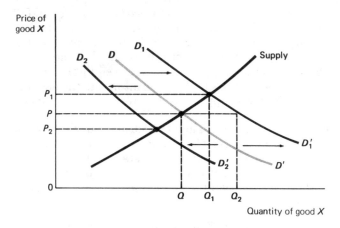

Figure 2.9   Effects of shifts in demand curve on equilibrium price

some testing of market reactions and trial-and-error adjustments, the price will tend to settle at OP_1, the new equilibrium price, and quantity will tend to settle at OQ_1.

On the other hand, suppose that consumer demand for good X falls off, perhaps because of a great drop in the price of a product that is an effective substitute for good X. The demand for good X now shifts to the left. Specifically, as shown in Figure 2.9, it shifts from DD' to D_2D_2'. What will be the effect on the equilibrium price of good X? Clearly, the new equilibrium price will be OP_2, where the new demand curve intersects the supply curve.

To illustrate the usefulness of this model, consider the market for fish. In 1966, the Roman Catholic Church abolished the requirement that no meat be consumed on Fridays, with the result that the demand curve for fish shifted markedly to the left. What happened to the price of fish? In accord with our model, it fell substantially in areas like New England where there is a large Catholic population. Specifically, the price of flounder, haddock, cod, and perch fell about 10 to 20 percent in New England.[12]

In general, a shift to the right in the demand curve results in an increase in the equilibrium price, and a shift to the left in the demand curve results in a decrease in the equilibrium price. This is the lesson of Figure 2.9. Of course, this conclusion depends on the assumption that the supply curve slopes upward to the right, but, as we noted in a previous section, this is generally the case.

10. Effects on Price of Shifts in the Supply Curve

Supply curves, like demand curves, shift over time. What happens to the equilibrium price of a good when its supply curve shifts? Suppose that, because of technological advances, producers of good X are willing and able to supply more of good X at a given price than they used to. Specifically, suppose that the supply curve shifts from SS' to S_1S_1' in Figure 2.10. What will be the effect on the equilibrium price? Clearly, it will fall from OP (where the SS' supply curve intersects the demand curve) to OP_3 (where the S_1S_1' supply curve intersects the demand curve). On the other hand, suppose that input prices rise, with the result that the supply curve shifts from SS' to S_2S_2' in Figure 2.10. Clearly, the equilibrium price will increase from OP (where the SS' supply curve intersects the demand curve) to OP_4 (where the S_2S_2' supply curve intersects the demand curve).

Lovers of peanut butter were shown in late 1980 and early 1981 what a shift to the left in the supply curve of a commodity will do. A severe drought in Georgia and other peanut-producing states wrecked havoc with the peanut crop, cutting output considerably. Because of the resulting increase in the price of peanuts, the supply curve for peanut

---

12. F. W. Bell, "The Pope and the Price of Fish," *American Economic Review*, December 1968.

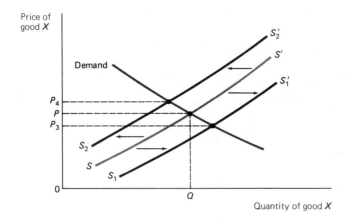

Figure 2.10   Effects of shifts in supply curve on equilibrium price

butter shifted to the left. The result of this big shift to the left in the
supply curve for peanut butter was just what our theory would predict: a
big jump in peanut butter prices. For example, peanut butter sold for
over $2 per pound in April 1981, compared to about $1 per pound before
the drought.

In general, a shift to the right in the supply curve results in a decrease in the equilibrium price, and a shift to the left in the supply curve
results in an increase in the equilibrium price. Of course, this conclusion
depends on the assumption that the demand curve slopes downward to
the right, but, as we noted in a previous section, this is generally the case.

11. Effects on Price of an Excise Tax

To illustrate how the models discussed in previous sections can be used
to throw light on the effects of various public-policy measures, we discuss
in this section the effects on price of an excise tax. Suppose that such a
tax is imposed on a particular good, say cigarettes.[13] In Figure 2.11, we
show the demand and supply curves, *DD'* and *SS'*, for cigarettes before
the imposition of the tax. Obviously, the equilibrium price of a pack of
cigarettes is 60 cents, and the equilibrium quantity is 50 million packs. If
a tax of 20 cents is imposed on each pack produced, what is the effect on
the price of each pack? Or to see it from the smoker's perspective, how
much of the tax is passed on to the consumer in the form of a higher
price?

Since the tax is collected from the sellers, the supply curve is shifted

---

13. For simplicity, we assume here that the market for cigarettes is perfectly competitive. In later chapters, we shall present models that pertain to cases where there
are relatively few producers.

Example 2.1   The Demand for Air Transportation

There is a considerable amount of air travel between Los Angeles and New York City; it is one of the most intensively traveled routes in the country. According to P. Verleger, the price elasticity of demand for air travel between Los Angeles and New York City is about 0.67. (a) Suppose that an economic consultant says that the demand curve for air travel between Los Angeles and New York City is as shown below:

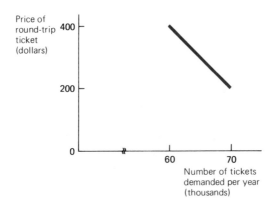

Is this graph in accord with Verleger's finding? Why or why not? (b) Suppose that the airlines double the price of a ticket between Los Angeles and New York City. Will this price increase affect the demand curve for air travel between these two cities? If so, in what way? (c) Suppose that a severe recession occurs. Will this affect the demand curve for air travel between these two cities? If so, in what way? (d) Because of the marked increase in the price of jet fuel (and other things), the cost of providing air transportation between Los Angeles and New York City has risen appreciably in recent years. Does such a cost increase affect the demand curve for air travel between these two cities? If so, in what way?

Solution

(a) According to the economic consultant's demand curve, about 60,000 tickets will be purchased if the price of a ticket is $400; about 70,000 will be purchased if the price is $200. Thus, the arc elasticity of demand is

$$\frac{-(70,000 - 60,000)}{(70,000 + 60,000)/2} \div \frac{(200 - 400)}{(200 + 400)/2} = 0.23.$$

This is quite different from Verleger's finding (that the price elasticity is 0.67). (b) Such an increase in price would reduce the *quantity of tickets demanded,* but it would *not* shift the demand curve. In other words, there would be a *movement along* the demand curve from a point corresponding to the old price to a point corresponding to the new price, but no *shift* in the demand curve. (c) Yes, it may

upward by the amount of the tax. In Figure 2.11, the posttax supply
curve is $S_T S'_T$. For example, if the pretax price had to be 40 cents a pack to
induce sellers to supply 40 million packs of cigarettes, the posttax price
would have to be 20 cents higher—or 60 cents a pack—to induce the same
supply. Similarly, if the pretax price had to be 60 cents a pack to induce
sellers to supply 50 million packs of cigarettes, the posttax price would
have to be 20 cents higher—or 80 cents a pack—to induce the same supply. The reason why the sellers require 20 cents more per pack to supply
the pretax amount is that they must pay the 20 cents per pack to the
government. Thus to wind up with the same amount as before (after
paying the tax), they require the extra 20 cents per pack.

Figure 2.11 shows that, after the tax is imposed, the equilibrium
price of cigarettes is 70 cents, an increase of 10 cents over its pretax level.
Consequently, in this case, half of the tax is passed on to consumers, who
pay 10 cents more for cigarettes. And half of the tax is swallowed by the
sellers, who receive (after they pay the tax) 10 cents per pack less for
cigarettes. But it is not always true that sellers pass half of the tax on to
consumers and absorb the rest themselves. On the contrary, in some

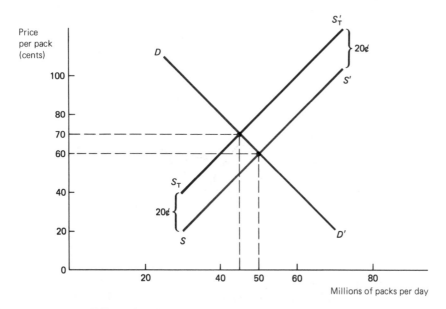

Figure 2.11 Effect of excise tax on price and output of cigarettes

cases, consumers may bear almost all of the tax (and sellers may bear practically none of it), while in other cases consumers may bear almost none of the tax (and sellers may bear practically all of it). The result will depend on how sensitive the quantity demanded and the quantity supplied are to the price of the good.

In particular, holding the supply curve constant, the less sensitive the quantity demanded is to the price of the good, the bigger the portion of the tax that is shifted to consumers. To illustrate this, consider panel A of Figure 2.12, which shows the effect of a 20 cents per pack tax on

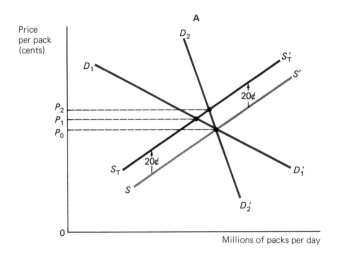

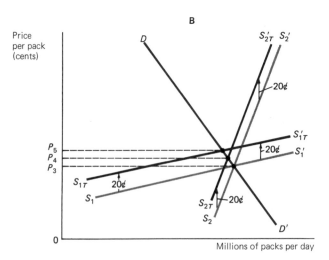

Figure 2.12   Effect of excise tax on price of cigarettes, under alternative assumptions concerning sensitivity of quantity demanded and quantity supplied to price

Example 2.2 The Market for Rental Housing

According to a recent study by F. deLeeuw and N. Ekanem, the price elasticity of demand for rental housing in American cities is 1.0, and the price elasticity of supply of rental housing is 0.5 in the long run. (a) Suppose that a particular city's government decides that the level of rent should be pushed up in order to encourage a greater supply of rental housing. If the government wants to increase the quantity of rental housing supplied by 2 percent, how big an increase in the rent is required? (b) Will such an increase in the rent result in the desired increase in the quantity of rental housing supplied in the short run? (c) What will be the effect on the total amount of rental housing that is demanded? (d) Suppose that the government's decision to increase the rent meets with widespread political opposition, and that it decides to lower it instead. If it pushes the rent down to a level that is 1 percent below its equilibrium value, the quantity of rental housing demanded will exceed the quantity supplied. How big will be the difference between the quantity demanded and quantity supplied, as a percent of the equilibrium quantity of rental housing?

Solution

(a) Since the price elasticity of supply is 0.5, a 4 percent increase in the rent will increase the quantity supplied by about 2 percent. (b) In the short run, there is likely to be a smaller effect, because there will be less time for construction of new housing and adaptation of old housing. (c) Since the price elasticity of demand is 1.0, a 4 percent increase in the rent will result in about a 4 percent decline in the quantity of rental housing demanded. (d) Suppose that the equilibrium rent and quantity are P and Q, respectively. If the rent is reduced by 1 percent, the quantity demanded will increase by 1 percent, which means it will increase by $.01Q$ (see the graph). At the

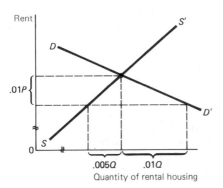

Quantity of rental housing

same time, the quantity supplied will fall by .5 percent, which means it will fall by $.005Q$. Thus the difference between the quantity supplied and the quantity demanded will equal $.01Q + .005Q$, or $.015Q$. In other words, it will equal 1.5 percent of the equilibrium quantity.*

* For further discussion, see F. deLeeuw and N. Ekanem, "The Supply of Rental Housing," *American Economic Review*, December 1971; and E. Hanushek and J. Quigley, "What Is the Price Elasticity of Housing Demand?" *Review of Economics and Statistics*, August 1980.

cigarettes in two markets, one where the quantity demanded $(D_1 D_1')$ is much more sensitive to price than in the other case $(D_2 D_2')$. Before the tax, the equilibrium price is OP_0, regardless of whether $D_1 D_1$ or $D_2 D_2$ is the demand curve. After the tax, the equilibrium price is OP_1 if the demand curve is $D_1 D_1$, or OP_2 if the demand curve is $D_2 D_2'$. Clearly, the increase in the price to the consumer is greater if the quantity demanded is less sensitive to price $(D_2 D_2')$ than if it is more sensitive $(D_1 D_1')$.

Also, holding the demand curve constant, the less sensitive the quantity supplied is to the price of the good, the bigger the portion of the tax that is absorbed by producers. To illustrate this, consider panel B of Figure 2.12, which shows the effect of a 20 cents per pack tax on cigarettes in two markets, one where the quantity supplied $(S_1 S_1')$ is much more sensitive to price than in the other case $(S_2 S_2')$. Before the tax, the equilibrium price is OP_3, regardless of whether $S_1 S_1'$ or $S_2 S_2'$ is the pretax supply curve. After the tax, the equilibrium price is OP_4, if the (pretax) supply curve is $S_2 S_2'$, or OP_5 if the (pretax) supply curve is $S_1 S_1'$. Clearly, the increase in price to the consumer is greater if the quantity supplied is more sensitive to price $(S_1 S_1')$ than if it is less sensitive $(S_2 S_2')$.[14]

12. Price Floors and Ceilings

As a further illustration of how the simple models taken up in this chapter can help to illuminate public-policy issues, consider the case of price floors or price ceilings. As is well known, governments often intervene in markets to prop up the price of a particular good or to see to it that its price does not exceed a certain level. At this point we will sketch only roughly the effects of such price floors or price ceilings. More details on this subject will be added in later chapters.

The effects of a price floor are shown in Figure 2.13. As is evident, the equilibrium price of the good is OP. Nonetheless, because the government feels that this price is not equitable, it sets a minimum price of OP_m. At this minimum price, the quantity supplied (OQ_S) exceeds the quantity demanded (OQ_D), and the government is faced with the problem of disposing of the surplus or of limiting production so that the quantity supplied is no more than OQ_D. One important area where price floors have been adopted in the United States has been agriculture. For major farm commodities like wheat and corn, there long have been minimum prices established by the government. As our model predicts, a major problem stemming from these price floors has been the disposal and limitation of farm surpluses.[15]

---

14. If government intervention is warranted to reduce cigarette smoking, one way of effecting such a reduction is by taxing cigarettes according to their tar and nicotine content. For an interesting discussion of such a tax, see J. Harris, "Taxing Tar and Nicotine," *American Economic Review,* June 1980.

15. In Chapters 9 and 16, we discuss these agricultural price floors and their effects in much more detail.

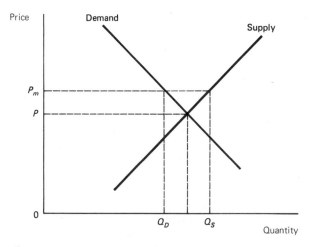

Figure 2.13 Effects of a price floor

The effects of a price ceiling are shown in Figure 2.14. Although the equilibrium price is OP, the government sets a maximum price of OP_n, because it does not want the price of the good to rise to its equilibrium level. At this maximum price, the quantity demanded (OQ_D) exceeds the quantity supplied (OQ_S); in other words, there is a shortage of the good. To allocate the limited supply among the many buyers who want to purchase the good, the government may resort to some form of rationing. For example, in World War II when price controls were in effect, families were issued ration coupons which determined how much they could buy of various commodities. Frequently, black markets develop under these circumstances, and the good is sold illegally at a price higher than the legal maximum. As our model predicts, a major problem stemming from price ceilings has been the resolution of the shortages that ensue.

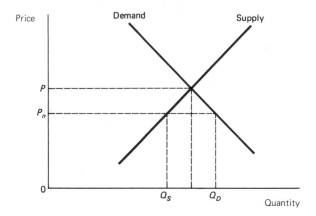

Figure 2.14 Effects of a price ceiling

13. In Vino Veritas: An Illustration of a Price Floor

In 1979, the weather conditions in many parts of Europe were ideal for cultivating grapes. In France, there was a record output of more than 2.2 billion gallons of wine. In Bordeaux, wine-makers took about 10 million gallons of wine off the market in an attempt to buttress the price of their wine. However, as indicated in the previous section, another way that industries can attempt to protect themselves against reductions in the price of their product is to prevail on the government to establish a price floor. Suppose that the French government had decreed that Bordeaux wine could not be sold in 1979 at less than its 1978 price. Would such a price floor have raised the price above the equilibrium price that otherwise would have prevailed?

If the market demand curve for Bordeaux wine was the same in 1979 as in 1978, and if the 1979 market supply curve for Bordeaux wine (S_{79}) is to the right of the 1978 supply curve (S_{78}), the situation is as shown in Figure 2.15. The equilibrium price in 1979 would be OP_0, and the price floor would be OP_1 (since this was the 1978 price). Thus the price floor would be above the equilibrium price.

Whether such a price increase would result in an increase in the total amount of money received by the Bordeaux wine makers depends on the price elasticity of demand for their wine. For example, if this price elasticity equals one, such a price increase would have no effect on the amount of money they receive. To see this, note that the total amount of money they receive is the quantity of wine sold multiplied by its price. If the price elasticity of demand equals 1, a 1 percent increase in price results in a 1 percent decrease in quantity sold. Thus the total amount they receive is not affected by the price increase. (More will be said on this score in Chapters 4 and 5.)[16]

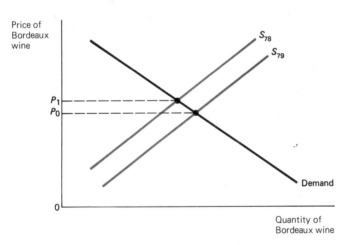

Figure 2.15   Effect of price floor on Bordeaux wine

16. For further information concerning economic aspects of the wine trade, see "Wine Talk: A Blow to the Law of Supply and Demand," *New York Times,* May 7, 1980.

14. Natural Gas and Oil: Illustrations of Price Ceilings

Price floors and ceilings can and do affect our everyday lives. In recent decades, the federal government has imposed a ceiling on the price of natural gas (in interstate commerce). In 1977 and 1978, there was a struggle between those who favored continuation of the price ceiling and those who opposed it. This struggle was waged with vigor, if not ferocity, since billions of dollars were at stake. Finally, in late 1978, legislation was passed which will deregulate the price of new gas, as of January 1, 1985.

To understand this controversy, some knowledge of microeconomics is essential. Basically, the opponents of the price ceiling argued that it was below the equilibrium price and that it was causing an undesirable shortage of natural gas. In their view, the situation was like that shown in Figure 2.14. To increase the quantity of gas supplied, they maintained that the price should be allowed to rise. In the words of President Gerald Ford's Council of Economic Advisers, "Deregulation of the price of new natural gas . . . would redirect supplies toward their most valuable uses, increase incentives to enlarge future supplies, and lead to reduced imports of oil and liquid natural gas."[17]

On the other hand, many who favored continuation of the price ceiling argued that the supply curve for natural gas has a very low price elasticity, with the result that increases in price would not elicit much additional supply. Thus, in their view, such price increases would mean a transfer of billions of dollars from consumers to gas producers—but little additional supply of gas. Further they argued that a fundamental assumption underlying Figure 2.14—namely, that the market was competitive—was not met in this case. It was their position that the major gas producers had appreciable control over the market.

Oil, like natural gas, has been subject to a price ceiling and it too has been the center of much controversy. At one time, the ceiling price on old oil was set at the 1972 price, while the price of new oil was uncontrolled. Subsequently, a variety of changes were made in the oil price ceilings. In early 1981, President Ronald Reagan announced that the remaining controls on the price of oil would be lifted. These controls were scheduled to expire in the fall of 1981 in any event.

Our purpose here is not to decide whether the opponents of price ceilings were right or wrong; instead, it is to indicate the central role played by the microeconomic concepts discussed in this chapter in understanding the issue. Even though this chapter deals only with the basic concepts of demand and supply, the results are of importance in illuminating this and many other major policy issues.

15. Summary

The market for every good has a demand side and a supply side. The demand side can be represented by a market demand curve which shows

17. *Economic Report of the President* (Washington, D.C.: U.S. Government Printing Office, 1976), p. 24.

the quantity of the good that would be purchased at each price. The market demand curve for a good almost always slopes downward to the right; that is, the quantity demanded increases as the price falls. The position and shape of the market demand curve for a good depends on the tastes of consumers, the level of consumer incomes, the prices of other goods, and the length of the time period to which the demand curve pertains. The price elasticity of demand, defined as the percentage change in the quantity demanded resulting from a 1 percent change in price, is a measure of the responsiveness of quantity demanded to changes in price. The price elasticity of demand will generally vary from one point to another on a demand curve. Estimated price elasticities are of two types: point elasticities and arc elasticities.

The supply side of a competitive market can be represented by a market supply curve which shows the quantity of the good that would be supplied at each price. The market supply curve for a good generally slopes upward to the right; that is, the quantity supplied increases as the price rises. The position and shape of the market supply curve for a good depends on the state of technology, input prices, and the length of the time interval to which the supply curve pertains. The price elasticity of supply, defined as the percentage change in the quantity supplied resulting from a 1 percent change in price, is a measure of the responsiveness of quantity supplied to changes in price. The price elasticity of supply will generally vary from one point to another on a supply curve.

An equilibrium price is a price that can be maintained. In a competitive market, it is the price where the quantity demanded equals the quantity supplied. In other words, it is the price where the demand curve intersects the supply curve. If the actual price exceeds the equilibrium price, there will be an excess supply of the good, and the actual price will tend to fall. If the actual price is less than the equilibrium price, there will be an excess demand for the good, and the actual price will tend to rise. Thus the actual price will tend to be pushed toward the equilibrium price. In general, a shift to the right in the demand curve results in an increase in the equilibrium price, and a shift to the left in the demand curve results in a decrease in the equilibrium price. In general, a shift to the right in the supply curve results in a decrease in the equilibrium price, and a shift to the left in the supply curve results in an increase in the equilibrium price.

To illustrate how this simple demand-and-supply analysis can be used to throw light on various policy issues, we showed how such an analysis can be used to predict the effect of an excise tax. Since the tax is collected from the sellers, the supply curve of the good on which the tax is imposed is shifted upward by the amount of the tax. How much the price of the good is increased by the tax depends on how sensitive the quantity demanded and quantity supplied are to changes in the price of the good. In addition, we used models of this type to analyze the effects of price floors and price ceilings imposed by the government. Price floors tend to result in surpluses, and price ceilings tend to result in shortages. Finally, we described how these simple microeconomic concepts are useful in understanding the recent controversies in Congress (and elsewhere) over the government's ceilings on the prices of natural gas and oil.

QUESTIONS AND PROBLEMS

1. Suppose that the number of bicycles demanded in the United States at various prices is as follows:

Price of a bicycle (dollars)	Quantity demanded per year (millions of bicycles)
80	20
100	18
120	16

Draw three points on the demand curve for bicycles. Calculate the arc price elasticity of demand when (a) the price is between $80 and $100, and (b) the price is between $100 and $120.

2. Suppose that the relationship between the quantity of bicycles supplied per year in the United States and the price per bicycle is as follows:

Price of a bicycle (dollars)	Quantity supplied per year (millions of bicycles)
60	14
80	16
100	18
120	19

Draw four points on the supply curve for bicycles, and estimate the price elasticity of supply when the price is between $80 and $100.

3. Based on the data presented in Questions 1 and 2, what is the equilibrium price of a bicycle in the United States? If the price is $80, will there be an excess demand? An excess supply? If the price is $120, will there be an excess demand? An excess supply?

4. Suppose that an excise tax of $40 is imposed on each bicycle. What will be the posttax equilibrium price of a bicycle? What will be the posttax equilibrium quantity? How does it compare with the pretax equilibrium quantity?

5. After the government imposes the tax in Question 4, it decides to set a price ceiling of $100 on the price of a bicycle. Will there be a surplus of bicycles? A shortage? If so, how big a surplus or shortage?

6. According to Richard Titmuss of the London School of Economics, no Englishman pays even a shilling for all the blood his physicians prescribe for him, and no blood donor is paid for his blood. Yet blood is more readily available for patients there than in the United States where we pay for the donation of blood. What hypotheses can be advanced to account for this?

7. Suppose that the demand curve for cantaloupes is:
$$P = 120 - 3\,Q_D,$$
where P is the price per pound (in cents) of a cantaloupe and Q_D is the quantity demanded per year (in millions of pounds). Suppose that the supply curve for cantaloupes is:
$$P = 5Q_S,$$
where Q_S is the quantity supplied per year (in millions of pounds). What is the equilibrium price per pound of a cantaloupe? What is the equilibrium quantity of cantaloupes produced?

8. Indicate whether each of the following will shift the demand curve for cantaloupes to the left, to the right, or have no effect on it: (a) a report by

the U.S. Surgeon-General that cantaloupes cause cancer; (b) a 10 percent increase in the price of honeydew melons; (c) a 20 percent increase in per capita income; (d) a 10 percent increase in the wages of workers producing cantaloupes.

9. Suppose that the government puts a price floor of 80 cents per pound on cantaloupes. How big will be the resulting surplus of cantaloupes, based on the data in Question 7? What measures can the government adopt to cut down on this surplus?

10. The market supply curve for good Y is a straight line through the origin. Does the price elasticity of supply vary with good Y's price? What is good Y's price elasticity of supply?

SELECTED REFERENCES

BOWEN, HOWARD. *Toward Social Economy.* New York: Rinehart, 1948.

FRIEDMAN, MILTON. *Capitalism and Freedom.* Chicago: University of Chicago Press, 1962.

MARSHALL, ALFRED. *Principles of Economics.* London: Macmillan, 1920.

SAMUELSON, PAUL. "The Economic Role of Private Activity." *A Dialogue on the Proper Economic Role of the State,* University of Chicago, Graduate School of Business, Selected Paper no. 7. Reprinted in E. Mansfield, *Economics: Readings, Issues, and Cases.* 3d ed. New York: Norton, 1980.

SCITOVSKY, TIBOR. *Welfare and Competition.* Rev. ed. Homewood, Ill.: Irwin, 1971.

3 The Tastes and Preferences of the Consumer

1. Introduction

Microeconomics is the branch of economics that deals with the behavior of individual decision-making units. One of the most important of these units is the consumer. For many purposes the consumer is not an individual but a household; the decisions regarding the purchase of a house or car, for example, often are household rather than individual decisions. In other cases, however, the individual person is the consumer, as, for example, when he or she buys a meal at a restaurant. Regardless of the precise way in which the consumer is defined, there are millions of consumers in the United States—and they spend a great deal of money. In recent years, the American consumer has spent over $1 trillion per year on final goods and services. About 70 percent of the final goods and services produced by the American economy go directly to consumers. Moreover, the importance of consumers is not a purely American phenomenon. For example, in our neighbor to the north, Canada, about two-thirds of the final goods and services produced by the Canadian economy go directly to consumers. Similar figures could be cited for many other countries.

In this chapter we present a simple model to represent the consumer's tastes and to help predict how much of various commodities he or she will buy. Besides being of interest for its own sake, this model is a first step toward analyzing the forces underlying the market demand curve, the importance of which was stressed in the previous chapter. Some of the major concepts that are introduced in this model are utility, indifference curves, the marginal rate of substitution, and the budget line. Finally, we show how this body of theory has been applied to help solve very important practical problems of budget allocation by government agencies.

2. The Nature of the Consumer's Preferences

Our purpose in this chapter is to present a simple model of consumer behavior that will enable us to predict how much of a particular commodity—hot dogs, paint, housing—a consumer buys during a particular period of time. Clearly, one of the most important determinants of a consumer's behavior is his or her tastes or preferences. After all, some consumers like Shakespeare while others like comic books; some like Verdi and others like the Rolling Stones. And it is obvious that these differences in tastes result in quite different decisions by consumers as to what commodities they buy. In this section we present three basic assumptions that the economist makes about the nature of the consumer's tastes.

To begin with, suppose that the consumer is confronted with any two market baskets, each containing various quantities of commodities. For example, one market basket might contain 1 ticket to a baseball game and 3 chocolate bars, while the other might contain 4 bottles of soda and a bus ticket. The first assumption that the economist makes is that consumers can decide whether they prefer the first market basket to the second, whether they prefer the second to the first, or whether they are indifferent between them.[1] This certainly seems to be a plausible assumption.

Second, we assume that the consumer's preferences are transitive. For example, if a man prefers Budweiser to Schlitz and Schlitz to Pabst, he must also prefer Budweiser to Pabst. Otherwise his preferences would not be transitive, which would mean that his preferences would be contradictory or inconsistent. Similarly, if he is indifferent between mince pie and pumpkin pie and between pumpkin pie and apple pie, he must also be indifferent between mince pie and apple pie. His tastes may be judged to be shallow or deep, lofty or mean, selfish or generous: this makes no difference to the theory. But his preferences must be transitive. Although not all consumers may exhibit preferences that are transitive, this assumption certainly seems to be a plausible basis for a model of consumer behavior.

Third, we assume that the consumer always prefers more of a commodity to less. For example, if one market basket (a very big one) contains 15 harmonicas and 2 gallons of gasoline, whereas another market basket (also big) contains 15 harmonicas and 1 gallon of gasoline, we assume that the first market basket, which unambiguously contains more commodities, is preferred. Also, we assume that, by adding a certain amount of harmonicas to the second market basket, we can make it

---

1. One way of telling whether the consumer prefers one market basket to another is to set equivalent prices for them and ask which one the consumer wants.

equally desirable in the eyes of the consumer to the first market basket; that is, we can make the consumer indifferent between them. These assumptions, like the previous two, seem quite plausible.

3. Utility

To understand the theory of consumer behavior, it is essential to understand the concept of utility. In Sections 3 to 7, we assume that utility is measurable, like a person's height or weight. Then, in Sections 8 to 16, we relax this simplifying assumption. To focus on the important factors at work here, let's assume that there are only two goods, food and medicine. This is an innocuous assumption, since the results we shall obtain can be generalized to include cases where any number of goods exists. For simplicity, food is measured in pounds, and medicine is measured in ounces.

Consider consumers making choices concerning how much of each good to buy. Undoubtedly, they regard certain market baskets—that is, certain combinations of food and medicine (the only commodities)—to be more desirable than others. For example, a consumer certainly would regard 2 pounds of food and 1 ounce of medicine to be more desirable than 1 pound of food and 1 ounce of medicine. For simplicity, suppose that it is possible to measure the amount of satisfaction that the consumer gets from each market basket by its utility. *A utility is a number that represents the level of satisfaction that the consumer derives from a particular market basket.* For example, the utility attached to the market basket containing 2 pounds of food and 1 ounce of medicine may be 13 utils, and the utility attached to the market basket containing 1 pound of food and 1 ounce of medicine may be 8 utils. (A util is the traditional unit in which utility is expressed.)

It is important to distinguish between total utility and marginal utility. The total utility of a market basket is the number described in the previous paragraph, whereas *the marginal utility measures the additional satisfaction derived from an additional unit of a commodity (when the levels of consumption of all other commodities are held constant).* To see how marginal utility is obtained, let's take a close look at Table 3.1. The total utility the consumer derives from the consumption of various amounts of food is given in the middle column of this table. (For simplicity, we assume for the moment that only food is consumed.) The marginal utility, shown in the right-hand column, is the extra utility derived from each amount of food over and above the utility derived from 1 less pound of food. Thus it equals the difference between the total utility of a certain amount of food and the total utility of 1 less pound of food.

For example, as shown in Table 3.1, the *total* utility of 3 pounds of food is 13 utils, which is a measure of the total amount of satisfaction that the consumer gets from this much food. In contrast, the *marginal* utility of 3 pounds of food is the extra utility obtained from the third pound of food—that is, the total utility of 3 pounds of food less the total utility of 2 pounds of food. Specifically, as shown in Table 3.1, it is 4 utils.

Table 3.1 Consumer's total and marginal utility
from consuming various amounts of
food per day

Pounds of food	Total utility	Marginal utility*
0	0	–
1	4	4 (= 4 – 0)
2	9	5 (= 9 – 4)
3	13	4 (= 13 – 9)
4	16	3 (= 16 – 13)
5	18	2 (= 18 – 16)

* These figures pertain to the interval between the indicated number of pounds of food and one pound less than the indicated number. This table assumes that no medicine is consumed.

Similarly, the *total* utility of 2 pounds of food is 9 utils, which is a measure of the total amount of satisfaction that the consumer gets from this much food. In contrast, the *marginal* utility of 2 pounds of food is the extra utility from the second pound of food—that is, the total utility of 2 pounds of food less the total utility of 1 pound of food. Specifically, as shown in Table 3.1, it is 5 utils.

4. The Law of Diminishing Marginal Utility

It seems reasonable to believe that, as a person consumes more and more of a particular commodity, there is, beyond some point, a decline in the extra satisfaction derived from the last unit of the commodity consumed. For example, if a person consumes 2 pounds of food in a particular period of time, it may be just what the doctor ordered. If he or she consumes 3 pounds of food in the same period of time, the third pound of food is likely to yield less satisfaction than the second. If he or she consumes 4 pounds of food in the same period of time, the fourth pound of food is likely to yield less satisfaction than the third. And so on.

This assumption or hypothesis is often called the law of diminishing marginal utility. This law states that, *as a person consumes more and more of a given commodity (the consumption of other commodities being held constant), the marginal utility of the commodity eventually will tend to decline.* In other words, it states that the relationship between the marginal utility of a commodity and the amount consumed will be as shown in Figure 3.1. Beyond some point (*OB* in Figure 3.1), the marginal utility declines as the amount consumed increases. Finally, note that the figures concerning the consumer in Table 3.1 are in accord with this law. Once the consumption of food exceeds 2 pounds, the marginal utility of food declines.

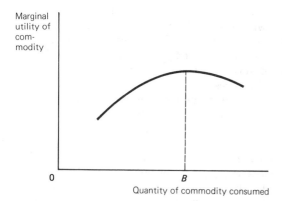

Figure 3.1   Diminishing marginal utility

5. The Rational Consumer

Assume for the moment that it is possible to measure the utility a consumer attaches to each market basket. If so, these measurements are a complete representation of his or her tastes and preferences. From them we can tell at a glance which market baskets the consumer would prefer over other market baskets. If the utility attached to the first market basket is higher than the second, he or she will prefer the first over the second market basket. If the utility attached to the first market basket is lower than the second, he or she will prefer the second over the first market basket. If the utility attached to the first market basket equals the second, he or she will be indifferent between the two market baskets.

Given the consumer's tastes, we assume that he or she is rational, in the sense that he or she tries to *maximize utility.* This assumption is so general and so reasonable that most people would accept it as a good approximation to reality. Of course, this is not to deny that some acts are irrational. However, by and large, people's actions seem to be such that they promote, not frustrate, the achievement of their goals. Even the ascetic, although his actions may seem irrational at first glance, can be regarded as attempting to maximize utility, if we recognize the very peculiar nature of his tastes.

Going a step further, we note that, although the consumer may attempt to maximize utility, he or she may not succeed in doing so because of miscalculation or for other reasons. The problem of maximizing utility may not be as simple as it looks. For·example, how many people know how much their cars really cost them? It is not that they do not know how to do the arithmetic; more important is the fact that what should or should not be regarded as a cost in a particular situation is not always straightforward. More will be said on this score in subsequent chapters. For the moment, all we want to point out is that consumers may not be able to achieve the maximization of utility, at least right away.

However, if the consumer is allowed some time to adapt and to learn, it seems likely that he or she will eventually find the market basket that maximizes his or her utility. Let us define the consumer's equilibrium behavior as a course of action that will not be changed by him or her in favor of some other course of action, if the consumer's money income, tastes, and the prices he or she faces remain the same. Then the consumer's equilibrium behavior will be to choose the market basket that maximizes his or her utility. And eventually one would expect the consumer to come very close to acting in accord with his or her equilibrium behavior.

To maximize utility, the consumer must take account of factors other than his or her own tastes. Account must be taken of the *prices* of various commodities and the level of the consumer's *money income,* since both of these factors limit, or constrain, the nature and size of the market basket that he or she can buy. The consumer's money income is the amount of money that he or she can spend per unit of time.[2] If a consumer had an infinite money income, there would be no need to worry that certain market baskets might be too expensive to purchase. The consumer could simply buy the market basket he or she liked best. But no one has an unlimited money income. Even the Rockefellers and Mellons cannot buy the market basket they like best, since this would mean the expenditure of more than even they have. For us poorer folk, the problem is much more difficult still, since our incomes are much smaller. What we can buy is much more severely constrained by our incomes.

Besides his or her money income, the consumer must also take account of the prices of all relevant commodities. The price of a commodity is the amount of money that the consumer must pay for a unit of the commodity. The higher prices are, the fewer units of a commodity can be bought with a given money income. For example, an income of $20,000 went a lot further when movies were 50 cents and sodas were 5 cents a bottle than it does now when movies are often $5 and sodas are 40 cents or so a bottle.

6. The Equilibrium Market Basket

What is the optimal market basket, the one that maximizes utility subject to these constraints? It is the one where *the consumer's income is allocated among commodities so that, for every commodity purchased, the marginal utility of the commodity is proportional to its price.* Thus, in the case of the consumer whose choices are limited to food and medicine, the optimal market basket is the one where

$$\frac{MU_F}{P_F} = \frac{MU_M}{P_M} \qquad \text{3.1}$$

2. To the extent that the consumer can borrow, the amount he or she can borrow can, for some purposes, also be included as income, since it increases the amount the consumer can spend during the period. More will be said about borrowing and lending in Chapter 18.

where MU_F is the marginal utility of food, MU_M is the marginal utility of medicine, P_F is the price of a pound of food, and P_M is the price of an ounce of medicine.

To understand why the rule in Equation 3.1 is correct, it is convenient to begin by pointing out that $MU_F \div P_F$ is the marginal utility of the *last dollar's worth* of food and that $MU_M \div P_M$ is the marginal utility of the *last dollar's worth* of medicine. To see why this is so, take the case of food. Since MU_F is the extra utility of the *last pound* of food bought, and since P_F is the price of this *last pound,* the extra utility of the *last dollar's worth* of food must be $MU_F \div P_F$. For example, if the last pound of food results in an extra utility of 4 utils and this pound costs \$2, then the extra utility from the last dollar's worth of food must be $4 \div 2$, or 2 utils. In other words, the marginal utility of the last dollar's worth of food is 2 utils.

Since $MU_F \div P_F$ is the marginal utility of the last dollar's worth of food and $MU_M \div P_M$ is the marginal utility of the last dollar's worth of medicine, what Equation 3.1 really says is that *the rational consumer will choose a market basket where the marginal utility of the last dollar spent on all commodities purchased is the same.* To see why this must be so, consider the numerical example in Table 3.2, which shows the marginal utility the consumer derives from various amounts of food and medicine. Rather than measuring food and medicine in physical units, we measure them in Table 3.2 in terms of the amount of money spent on them.

Given the information in Table 3.2, how much of each commodity should the consumer buy if his or her money income is only \$4 (a ridiculous assumption but one that will help to make our point)? Clearly, the first dollar the consumer spends should be on food since it will yield him or her a marginal utility of 9. The second dollar he or she spends should also be on food since a second dollar's worth of food has a marginal utility of 7. (Thus the total utility derived from the \$2 of expenditure is $9 + 7 = 16$.[3]) The marginal utility of the third dollar is 4 if it is spent on more food—and 4 too if it is spent on medicine. Suppose that he or she chooses

Table 3.2 Consumer's marginal utility from consuming various amounts of food and medicine per day

Dollars worth of each commodity	Food	Medicine
1	9	4
2	7	3
3	4	2
4	3	1
5	2	0

3. Since the marginal utility is the extra utility obtained from each dollar spent, the total utility from the total expenditure must be the sum of the marginal utilities of the individual dollars of expenditure.

more food. (The total utility derived from the $3 of expenditure is 9 + 7 + 4 = 20.) What about the final dollar? Its marginal utility is 3 if it is spent on more food and 4 if it is spent on medicine; thus he or she will spend it on medicine. (The total utility derived from all $4 of expenditure is then 9 + 7 + 4 + 4 = 24.)

Clearly, the consumer, if rational, will allocate $3 of his or her income to food and $1 to medicine. This is the equilibrium market basket, the market basket that maximizes consumer satisfaction. The important thing to note is that this market basket demonstrates the principle set forth at the beginning of this section. As shown in Table 3.2, the marginal utility derived from the last dollar spent on food is equal to the marginal utility derived from the last dollar spent on medicine. (Both are 4.) Thus this market basket has the characteristic described above: The marginal utility of the last dollar spent on all commodities purchased is the same. In the next section, we show that this will always be the case for market baskets that maximize the consumer's utility. If it were not true, the consumer could obtain a higher level of utility by changing the composition of his or her market basket.

7. The Budget Allocation Rule: Further Proof

In the previous section, we stated the proposition that the consumer, to maximize utility, will choose a market basket where the marginal utility of the last dollar spent on all commodities purchased is the same. In this section, we show that, if this budget allocation rule is not followed, the consumer cannot be maximizing utility. This is offered as further proof of the proposition in the previous section. For simplicity, we continue to assume that the consumer buys only two commodities, food and medicine.

Suppose that the marginal utility of the last dollar spent on food is 3 utils whereas the marginal utility of the last dollar spent on medicine is 2 utils. Clearly, the consumer is not maximizing utility, because spending $1 more on food will increase total utility by 3 utils,[4] and spending $1 less on medicine will reduce total utility by 2 utils. Thus the transfer of $1 of expenditure from medicine to food will increase total utility by 1 util— which means that the consumer currently isn't maximizing utility. More generally, a transfer of expenditure from medicine to food will always increase a consumer's utility so long as the marginal utility of the last dollar spent on food exceeds the marginal utility of the last dollar spent on medicine. Thus *the consumer will not be maximizing utility if the marginal utility of the last dollar spent on food exceeds the marginal utility of the last dollar spent on medicine.*

Suppose that the situation is reversed, with the marginal utility of the last dollar spent on food being 2 utils and the marginal utility of the

---

4. We assume here that the extra utility from an *extra* dollar spent on food equals the extra utility from the *last* dollar spent on food. This is an innocuous assumption.

last dollar spent on medicine being 3 utils. Clearly, the consumer is not maximizing utility, because spending $1 more on medicine will increase total utility by 3 utils,[5] and spending $1 less on food will reduce total utility by 2 utils. Thus the transfer of $1 of expenditure from food to medicine will result in a net increase of utility of 1 util—which means that the consumer currently isn't maximizing utility. More generally, a transfer of expenditure from food to medicine will always increase total utility so long as the marginal utility of the last dollar spent on medicine exceeds the marginal utility of the last dollar spent on food. Thus *the consumer will not be maximizing utility if the marginal utility of the last dollar spent on medicine exceeds the marginal utility of the last dollar spent on food.*

In the previous paragraph, we showed that the consumer will *not* be maximizing utility if the marginal utility of the last dollar spent on food is *less than* the marginal utility of the last dollar spent on medicine. In the paragraph before last, we showed that the consumer will *not* be maximizing utility if the marginal utility of the last dollar spent on food *exceeds* the marginal utility of the last dollar spent on medicine. Consequently, it follows that the consumer will be maximizing utility only when the marginal utility of the last dollar spent on food equals the marginal utility of the last dollar spent on medicine. This is what we set out to prove.[6]

8. Cardinal and Ordinal Utility

In previous sections, we assumed that utility is measurable, like weight or height. In this regard, we followed the example of such great nineteenth-century economists as William Stanley Jevons of England, Karl Menger of Austria, and Léon Walras of France. In their view, utility was measurable in a *cardinal* sense, which means that the difference between two measurements is itself numerically significant. For example, if I weigh 185 pounds and you weigh 170 pounds, the difference between these measurements has numerical significance: It says that I weigh 15 pounds more than you do. Moreover, if the difference between Ed McMahon's and Johnny Carson's weights is 60 pounds, it follows that the difference between my weight and yours is less than the difference between Ed McMahon's weight and Johnny Carson's. According to most nineteenth-century economists, utility was measurable in the same sense.

In contrast, most twentieth-century economists, following the lead of E. Slutsky, Vilfredo Pareto, Sir John Hicks, and other great figures of

5. We assume here that the extra utility from an *extra* dollar spent on medicine equals the extra utility from the *last* dollar spent on medicine. This, like the assumption in footnote 4, is innocuous.
6. For a mathematical proof of the budget allocation rule in Equation 3.1, see footnote 12.

the more recent past, assume that utility is measurable in an ordinal sense, which means that a consumer can only *rank* various market baskets with regard to the satisfaction they give him or her.[7] For example, you may be able to say with assurance that you prefer two tickets to the Super Bowl to two tickets to the San Francisco Opera, but you may not be able to say how many more utils of satisfaction you get from the former than the latter. For an ordinal measurement of utility, this is adequate, since all that is needed is a ranking. If the consumer prefers market basket 1 to market basket 2, and market basket 2 to market basket 3, the utility of market basket 1 must be higher than the utility of market basket 2, and the utility of market basket 2 must be higher than the utility of market basket 3. But any set of numbers conforming to these requirements is an adequate measure of utility in an ordinal sense. For example, the utility of market baskets 1, 2, and 3 may be 50, 40, and 30, or 10, 9, 8. Both are adequate utility measures, since all that counts is that the utility of market basket 1 be higher than that of market basket 2, which in turn should be higher than that of market basket 3.

The modern assumption that utility is ordinally measurable is less restrictive than the older assumption that utility is cardinally measurable. That is, we need not assume that a consumer can answer questions like: How many extra utils of satisfaction will you get from a second helping of mashed potatoes? Indeed, the concept of marginal utility loses much of its meaning if utility is ordinally measurable, since, as noted above, differences in ordinal utilities are arbitrary. For example, if the consumer prefers two helpings of mashed potatoes to one helping, ordinal utility is higher for two helpings than for one, but how much higher is arbitrary. Why? Because, to be a proper ordinal utility measure, all that is required is that market baskets giving equal satisfaction to the consumer must receive the same utility and that market baskets he or she prefers must receive higher utilities than those that are not preferred. No particular significance attaches to the scale that is used or to the size of the difference between the utilities attached to two market baskets.

The fact that modern economists generally assume that utility is ordinally, not cardinally, measurable does not mean that results based on the assumption of cardinal utility are wrong. If the consumer is able to characterize his or her preferences by attaching a cardinal utility to each market basket, these results are correct—and should be used. But what if the consumer cannot characterize his or her preferences in this way? In that case, a different kind of model of consumer behavior is required. The rest of this chapter provides such a model. This model, based on the assumption that utility is ordinally measurable, is the leading one at present. There is no contradiction between these two models. The model presented in previous sections (which assumes the existence of cardinal utilities) can be regarded as a special case of the one

7. For example, see J. Hicks, *Value and Capital* (New York: Oxford University Press, 1946); H. Hotelling, "Demand Functions with Limited Budgets," *Econometrica*, 1935; and P. Samuelson, *Foundations of Economic Analysis* (Cambridge, Mass.: Harvard University Press, 1947).

to be presented below (which assumes ordinal utilities). If utility is cardinally measurable, both models yield the same results.

9. Indifference Curves

Assuming utility is only ordinally measurable, we can represent the consumer's tastes or preferences by a set of indifference curves. *An indifference curve is the locus of points representing market baskets among which the consumer is indifferent.* For example, suppose we confine our attention to the ten market baskets in Table 3.3, in which the first market basket contains 1 pound of meat and 4 pounds of potatoes, the second market basket contains 1 pound of meat and 6 pounds of potatoes, and so on. Suppose that the consumer is asked to choose between various pairs of these market baskets and that he or she is indifferent between some of these market baskets. For example, the consumer may not care whether he or she consumes 4 pounds of meat plus 2 pounds of potatoes or 2 pounds of meat plus 3 pounds of potatoes. Suppose that we enlarge the number of market baskets (containing various quantities of meat and potatoes) under consideration, so that we include all market baskets in which from 1 to 8 pounds of meat are combined with from 1 to 8 pounds of potatoes. Then suppose we plot each of the market baskets on a diagram like Figure 3.2 and that *curve A is the set of points representing market baskets among which the consumer is indifferent.* For example, this curve includes all of the market baskets that the consumer regards as being equivalent (in terms of his or her satisfaction) to 4 pounds of meat plus 2 pounds of potatoes.

Curve *A* is an *indifference curve.* Of course there are many such indifference curves, each pertaining to a different level of satisfaction. For example, indifference curve *B* in Figure 3.2 represents a higher level of utility than indifference curve *A*, since it includes market baskets with more of both meat and potatoes than the market baskets represented by indifference curve *A*. One can visualize a series of indifference curves—

Table 3.3   Alternative market baskets

Market basket	Meat (pounds)	Potatoes (pounds)
	(per unit of time)	
1	1	4
2	1	6
3	2	3
4	2	4
5	3	2
6	3	3
7	4	1
8	4	2
9	5	0
10	5	1

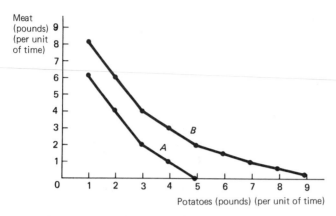

Figure 3.2 Indifference curves

one showing all market baskets that are equivalent (in the eyes—or belly—of the consumer) to 1 pound of potatoes and 2 pounds of meat, one showing all market baskets that are equivalent to 2 pounds of potatoes and 2 pounds of meat, and so on. The resulting series of indifference curves is called an indifference map.

A consumer's indifference map lies at the heart of the theory of consumer behavior, since such a map provides a representation of the consumer's tastes. To illustrate how a consumer's indifference map mirrors his or her tastes, consider the various indifference maps in Figure 3.3.

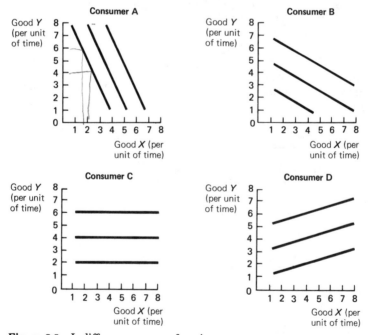

Figure 3.3 Indifference maps of various consumers

Consumer A's indifference curves are relatively steep, whereas consumer B's indifference curves are relatively flat. What does this mean? Apparently consumer A needs several extra units of good Y to compensate for the loss of a single unit of good X, whereas consumer B needs less than one extra unit of good Y to compensate for the loss of a single unit of good X. Thus, in this sense, good Y is less important (relative to good X) to consumer A than to consumer B.

What about consumers C and D in Figure 3.3? Apparently consumer C regards good X as useless, since he does not care whether he has more or less of it. Consumer D seems to regard good X as a nuisance, since she is willing to reduce the amount of good Y she consumes in order to get rid of some good X. But situations of this sort are ruled out by the third assumption in Section 2—namely, that the consumer prefers more of a commodity to less. This does not mean that some things are not a nuisance. It means only that in the case of consumer D we would define a commodity as the lack of good X, not the consumption of good X. Using this simple, legitimate trick, we no longer violate the third assumption in Section 2, since more of all commodities is now preferred to less.[8]

10. Characteristics of Indifference Curves

All indifference curves have certain characteristics that should be noted. First, given the fact (noted in the last section) that every commodity is defined so that more of it is preferred to less, it follows that indifference curves must have a negative slope. If more of both commodities is desirable, and if one market basket has more of good Y, it must have less of good X than another market basket if the two market baskets are to be equivalent in the eyes of the consumer. If the two market baskets are equivalent, and if one market basket contains more of both commodities—which would be the case if an indifference curve had a positive slope—it would mean that one or the other of the commodities is not defined so that more of it is preferred to less.

Second, given the fact that every commodity is defined so that more of it is preferred to less, it also follows that indifference curves that are higher in graphs like Figure 3.2 represent greater levels of consumer

---

8. Let U represent the consumer's utility, and let the consumer consume x_1 units of good 1, x_2 units of good 2, and so on. The *utility function* is the relationship between U and $x_1, x_2, \cdots, x_n$. It is

$$U = U(x_1, x_2, \cdots, x_n)$$

(In early formulations of utility theory, it was assumed that utility was an additive quality, that is,

$$U = U_1(x_1) + U_2(x_2) + \cdots + U_n(x_n)$$

but this assumption has been scrapped by modern economists.)

Using this utility function, one can define an indifference curve very simply. An indifference curve is given by the equation

$$U(x_1, x_2, \cdots, x_n) = a$$

where a is a constant.

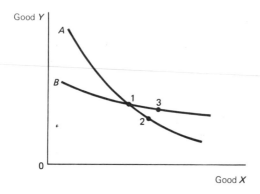

Figure 3.4   Intersecting indifference curves:
A contradiction of the assumptions

satisfaction than indifference curves that are lower. For example, curve
B in Figure 3.2 is preferred to curve A. Why? Because the higher curve,
Curve B, includes market baskets with as much of one good and more of
the other (or as much of the second good and more of the first) than the
lower curve, Curve A. This is what we mean when we say that a curve is
higher or lower. Put differently, the utility attached to all market baskets on a higher indifference curve is greater than the utility attached to
all market baskets on a lower indifference curve. However, the difference
between these utilities is arbitrary if utility is only ordinally measurable.

Third, indifference curves cannot intersect. To prove this statement,
let's show that a contradiction arises if two indifference curves were to
intersect. For example, take the case of two intersecting indifference
curves in Figure 3.4. On indifference curve A, market basket 1 is equivalent to market basket 2. On indifference curve B, market basket 1 is
equivalent to market basket 3. Hence, if the indifference curves intersect,
market basket 2 must be equivalent to market basket 3. But this cannot
be, since market basket 3 contains more of both commodities than market basket 2, and commodities are defined so that more of them is preferred to less. If the consumer's tastes are transitive, as we assumed in
Section 2, there cannot be an intersection of indifference curves.

11. The Marginal Rate of Substitution

We pointed out in Section 9 that consumers differ in the importance
that they attach to an extra unit of a particular good. Of course, this is
hardly news. For example, it is well known that an alcoholic will sometimes trade a valuable item like a watch for an extra drink of whiskey,
whereas the president of the Temperance Union will not give a cent for
an extra (presumably the first) dose of Demon Rum. However, news or
not, it is useful to have a measure of the relative importance attached by
the consumer to the acquisition of another unit of a particular good. The

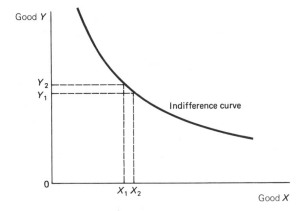

Figure 3.5 The marginal rate of substitution

measure that economists have devised is called the *marginal rate of substitution,* a term indicative of the economist's talent for elegant and graceful phrase-making.

The marginal rate of substitution is defined as the number of units of good Y that must be given up if the consumer, after receiving an extra unit of good X, is to maintain a constant level of satisfaction. For example, in Figure 3.5, the consumer can give up $(OY_2 - OY_1)$ units of good Y to receive $(OX_2 - OX_1)$ extra units of good X, and this trade will leave him or her no better or no worse off. Thus the marginal rate of substitution of good X for good Y is $(OY_2 - OY_1)/(OX_2 - OX_1)$. This is the number of units of good Y that must be given up—per unit of good X received—to maintain a constant level of satisfaction.

More precisely, the marginal rate of substitution is equal to minus one times the slope of the indifference curve.[9] Thus the marginal rate of substitution of good X for good Y is higher for consumer A (whose indifference curve on p. 60 is steeper) than for consumer B (whose indifference curve is flatter). In general, the marginal rate of substitution will vary from point to point on a given indifference curve, since the indifference curve's slope will vary from point to point. For example, on indifference

9. The definition in the previous paragraph is an approximation that is quite adequate when good X is measured in small units. Suppose that there are only two commodities and that an indifference curve is

$$U(x_1, x_2) = a$$

Taking the total differential, we obtain

$$\frac{\partial U}{\partial x_1} dx_1 + \frac{\partial U}{\partial x_2} dx_2 = 0$$

Thus the slope of the indifference curve is

$$\frac{dx_2}{dx_1} = -\frac{\partial U}{\partial x_1} \div \frac{\partial U}{\partial x_2}$$

which equals minus one times the marginal rate of substitution of the first good for the second good.

curve *A* (or curve *B*) in Figure 3.2, the marginal rate of substitution of potatoes for meat gets smaller as the consumer has more potatoes and less meat.

In the economist's model of consumer behavior it is generally assumed that indifference curves have the sort of shape exhibited by curves *A* and *B* in Figure 3.2. More specifically, it is assumed that they show that the more the consumer has of a particular good, the less will be the marginal rate of substitution of this good for any other good. Put somewhat crudely, this amounts to assuming that the more the consumer has of a particular good, the less important to him or her (relative to other goods) is an extra unit of this good. In mathematical terms, this assumption means that indifference curves are convex. In other words, an indifference curve lies above its tangent, as illustrated in panel A of Figure 3.6. This contrasts with the case presented in panel B of Figure 3.6 where the indifference curve is not convex.[10]

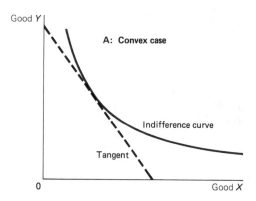

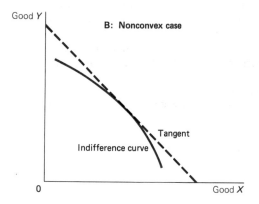

Figure 3.6 Indifference curves: Convexity

10. The assumption of convexity may not always hold, but a discussion of cases where it fails belongs in a more advanced book.

Example 3.1   The Experimental Determination
                   of Indifference Curves

In 1969 K. MacCrimmon and M. Toda published an experimental study in which they asked a group of college students to choose among market baskets containing various amounts of money and fountain pens. One of the students said she was indifferent among market baskets A to E below. MacCrimmon and Toda also asked the students to choose among market baskets containing various quantities of money and French pastries (to be eaten on the spot). The same student said she was indifferent among market baskets F to J below.

Market basket	Number of pens	Amount of money (dollars)	Market basket	Number of French pastries	Amount of money (dollars)
A	0	20.00	F	0	6.00
B	50	17.50	G	3	5.50
C	100	15.00	H	6	5.00
D	130	14.00	I	8	6.00
E	160	13.00	J	10	7.00

(a) Draw the student's indifference curve for money and fountain pens. (Assume that the points given in the table can be connected with straight lines.) (b) Draw her indifference curve for money and French pastries. (c) Do these indifference curves represent the same level of utility? (d) Are French pastries always a good? (e) If the French pastries could be taken home and eaten later, would the indifference curve for money and French pastries be the same as that given above?

Solution

(a) and (b) The indifference curves are shown below.

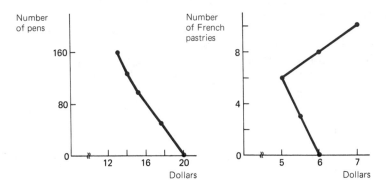

(c) No, since one indifference curve includes market basket A, which contains $20 alone, while the other indifference curve includes market basket F, which contains $6 alone. So long as more money is preferred to less, the former indifference curve must represent a higher level of utility than the latter. (d) No. For more than 6 French pastries, the indifference curve is upward sloped to the right because the student was willing to consume more French pastries only if she received more money. (e) No. The student would probably have not required more money to make her willing to consume more than 6 French pastries, if she did not have to eat them on the spot.*

* For further discussion, see K. MacCrimmon and M. Toda, "The Experimental Determination of Indifference Curves," *Review of Economic Studies,* October 1969.

12. The Budget Line

Earlier in this chapter, we presented a rule indicating which market basket the rational consumer would purchase, given that utility was cardinally measurable. Now we must do the same thing, under the assumption that utility is ordinally measurable. To begin with, we must show how the consumer's money income and the level of commodity prices influence the nature and size of the market baskets available to the consumer. It simplifies matters without distorting the essentials of the situation if we assume that there are only two commodities that the consumer can buy, good X and good Y. Since the consumer must spend all of his or her money income on one or the other of these two commodities,[11] it is evident that

$$Q_x P_x + Q_y P_y = I \qquad \text{3.2}$$

where Q_x is the amount the consumer buys of good X, Q_y is the amount the consumer buys of good Y, P_x is the price of good X, P_y is the price of good Y, and I is the consumer's money income. For example, if the price of good X is $1 a unit and the price of good Y is $2 a unit and the consumer's income is $100, it must be true that $Q_x + 2Q_y = 100$. Note that we assume that the consumer takes prices as given. This, of course, is generally quite realistic.

It is possible to plot the combinations of quantities of goods X and Y that the consumer can buy on the same sort of graph as the indifference map. Solving Equation 3.2 for Q_y, we have

$$Q_y = \frac{1}{P_y} I - \frac{P_x}{P_y} Q_x \qquad \text{3.3}$$

Equation 3.3, which is a straight line, is plotted in Figure 3.7. The first term on the right-hand side of Equation 3.3 is the intercept of the line on

11. Of course, the consumer can also save some of his or her income, but, from the point of view of this model, savings can be viewed as a commodity like any other. Thus, with this amendment, Equation 3.2 can easily encompass saving.

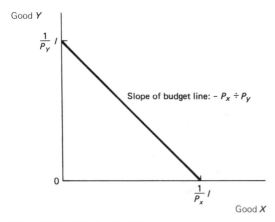

Figure 3.7 The budget line

the vertical axis: It is the amount of good Y that could be bought by the consumer if he or she spent all of his or her income on good Y. The slope of the line is equal to the negative of the price ratio, P_x/P_y.

The straight line in Equation 3.3 is called the *budget line*. It shows all of the combinations of quantities of good X and good Y that the consumer can buy. In subsequent sections, we shall be interested in the effects of changes in product prices and money income on consumer behavior. These changes are reflected by changes in the budget line. Equation 3.3 shows that increases in money income increase the intercept of the budget line, but leave unaffected the slope of the budget line. For example, Figure 3.8 shows the effect of an increase in income, with C the original budget line and D the budget line after the increase in income. Conversely, decreases in income lower the intercept of the budget line. In Figure 3.8, E is the budget line after a decrease in income, with C once again the original budget line.

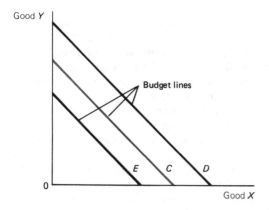

Figure 3.8 Effect of change in income on the budget line

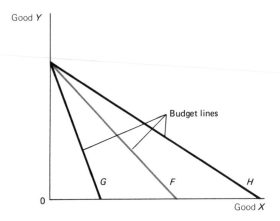

Figure 3.9   Effect of change in price of good X
on budget line

Equation 3.3 also shows what happens to the budget line if the price of good X changes. Increases in P_x increase the absolute value of the slope of the budget line; decreases in P_x decrease the absolute value of the slope. The vertical intercept of the line is unaffected. Figure 3.9 shows the effect of changes in P_x on the budget line. Suppose that the original budget line is F. If P_x increases, the budget line becomes G. If P_x decreases, the budget line becomes H. Intuitively, it is easy to see why an increase (decrease) in the price of good X results in the budget line's cutting the X axis at a point closer to (farther from) the origin. The point where the budget line cuts the X axis equals the maximum number of units of good X that the consumer can buy with his or her fixed money income, and this number obviously is inversely related to the price of good X.

13. The Equilibrium of the Consumer

At the beginning of the previous section, we said that we would show which market basket the rational consumer will purchase, if utility is ordinal. To do this, we must answer the question, What market basket will maximize the consumer's utility? Figure 3.10 brings together the consumer's indifference map and his or her budget line. All of the relevant information needed to answer this question is contained in Figure 3.10. *The indifference map shows what the consumer's preferences are.* For example, any market basket on indifference curve 3 is preferred to any on indifference curve 2; and any market basket on indifference curve 2 is preferred to any on indifference curve 1. The consumer would like to choose a market basket on the highest possible indifference curve. This is the way to maximize his or her utility.

But not all market baskets are within reach. *The budget line shows what the consumer can do.* He or she can choose any market basket such as U, V, or W on the budget line, but he or she cannot obtain a market

Example 3.2   The Food-Stamp Program

In 1980 the food-stamp program in the United States included about
20 million individuals, and cost about $10 billion. Suppose that if a
family is eligible for food stamps, it pays $80 per month to obtain
$150 worth of food. (a) If the family's cash income is $250 and it is
not eligible for food stamps, draw its budget line on a graph where
the quantity of food consumed per month is measured along the
horizontal axis and the quantity of nonfood items consumed per
month is measured along the vertical axis. (b) Draw the family's
budget line on this graph if it is eligible for food stamps. (c) Show
that if the family were given $70 in cash (rather than in food), it
might achieve a higher level of satisfaction.

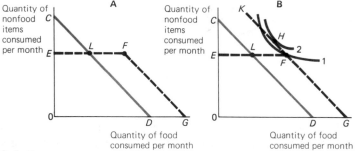

Solution

(a) Without food stamps, the family's budget line is *CD* in panel A.
In this panel, *OC* is the quantity of nonfood items the family can
obtain with its entire income ($250) and *OD* is the quantity of food it
can obtain with it. (b) With food stamps, the family's budget line is
CLFG in panel A. *EC* is the quantity of nonfood items the family
can buy with $80. If the family buys food stamps, *OE* is the max-
imum quantity of nonfood items it can obtain once it pays for the
food stamps. *EF* is the $150 worth of food it receives with the food
stamps, and *DG* (= *LF*) is the $70 worth of food that it can obtain
with food stamps that it couldn't otherwise obtain, when the quantity of nonfood items is held constant. If the quantity of nonfood
items consumed by the family exceeds *OE,* it does not have enough
money left for food to buy food stamps, so the budget line is the
same as without food stamps. (That is, it is *CL.*) If the quantity of
nonfood items consumed by the family does not exceed *OE,* it can
buy food stamps, and consume an extra amount of food equal to
DG, so the budget line is *FG.* (c) If the family were given $70 in cash
(rather than in food), its budget line would be *GK* in panel B. Because its money income increases by $70, the budget line is higher,
but parallel to, the old budget line, *CD.* With this budget line, the
family can reach point *H* on indifference curve 2, whereas with
budget line *CLFG,* the best it can do is reach point *F* on indifference
curve 1. Since indifference curve 2 is higher than indifference curve
1, the family achieves a higher level of satisfaction if it receives the
cash rather than the food. Of course, not all families have indifference curves of this sort; some have indifference curves such that
they achieve as high a level of satisfaction with the food as with the
cash. This is the case for families with indifference curves that are
tangent to the budget line between *F* and *G.**

* For further discussion, see K. Clarkson, "Welfare Benefits of the Food
Stamp Program," *Southern Economic Journal,* July 1976; and M. MacDon-
ald, *Food, Stamps, and Income Maintenance* (New York: Academic, 1977).

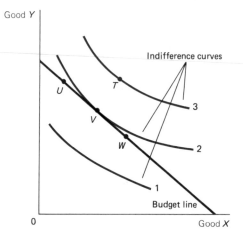

Figure 3.10   Equilibrium of the consumer

basket like T which is above the budget line. (Of course, the consumer can also buy any market basket below the budget line, but any such market basket lies on a lower indifference curve than a market basket on the budget line.) Since this is the case, *the market basket that will maximize the consumer's utility is the one on the budget line that is on his or her highest indifference curve*—which is V in Figure 3.10. It can readily be seen that this market basket is at a point where the budget line is tangent to an indifference curve. This market basket, V, is the one that the rational consumer would, according to our model, be predicted to buy in equilibrium.[12]

12. Mathematically, one can state the conditions for equilibrium as follows: Suppose that the consumer's utility function is

$$U = U(x_1, x_2, \cdots, x_n)$$

Then he or she maximizes U subject to the constraint that

$$x_1 p_1 + x_2 p_2 + \cdots + x_n p_n = I$$

where p_i is the price of the ith good. To maximize U subject to the constraint, we construct the function

$$L = U(x_1, x_2, \cdots, x_n) - \lambda(x_1 p_1 + \cdots + x_n p_n - I)$$

where λ is a Lagrangian multiplier. The first-order conditions for a maximum are

$$\frac{\partial L}{\partial x_1} = \frac{\partial U}{\partial x_1} - \lambda p_1 = 0$$

$$\frac{\partial L}{\partial x_2} = \frac{\partial U}{\partial x_2} - \lambda p_2 = 0$$

$$\cdots\cdots\cdots\cdots\cdots\cdots\cdots\cdots$$

$$\frac{\partial L}{\partial x_n} = \frac{\partial U}{\partial x_n} - \lambda p_n = 0$$

$$\frac{\partial L}{\partial \lambda} = x_1 p_1 + x_2 p_2 + \cdots + x_n p_n - I = 0$$

14. Revealed Preference and the Measurement of Indifference Curves

Thus far we have assumed that the consumer's indifference curves were measured by asking him or her to choose between various market baskets in the way described in Section 9. However, after thinking about this procedure for a short while, one might object that people cannot, or will not, provide trustworthy answers to direct questions concerning their preferences. The man who surreptitiously visits an erotic stage show (and repeatedly buys the best seats in the house) may claim that such shows are sinful and repugnant to him. Is there any way to measure a person's indifference curves other than by asking direct questions concerning the person's tastes? Is there any way to deduce a consumer's indifference curves from his or her actual behavior rather than from his or her professed preferences?

The theory of revealed preference, a relatively new part of microeconomics, is an attempt to do just that. We assume that we can vary the consumer's money income and the prices he or she faces, changing these factors in accord with the experiment. Then assuming that the consumer's tastes remain fixed during the course of the experiment, we see how he or she reacts to the various levels of money income and prices. The basic idea behind the formulation and interpretation of the experiments is as follows: The consumer may choose one market basket over a second market basket either because he or she prefers the first to the second or because the first is cheaper than the second. Thus, if we vary prices so that the first market basket is not cheaper than the second and if the first is still chosen over the second, we can be sure that the first market basket is preferred over the second.

Consider the case of two commodities, good X and good Y. Let A in Figure 3.11 represent the market basket (Oa of good X and Oa' of good Y) that the consumer purchases when his or her budget line is QQ'. From this it follows that every point (each representing a market basket) on or below QQ' is revealed to be inferior to A in the eyes of this consumer, since all of these points were available to the consumer and he or she chose A. Moreover, every point in the shaded area above and to the right of A is preferred to A because each such point represents a market basket with at least as much of both commodities as A. Thus, since a commodity is defined so that more of it is preferred to less, each such point must be

---

From these equations it follows that

$$\frac{\partial U}{\partial x_1} \div p_1 = \frac{\partial U}{\partial x_2} \div p_2 = \cdot \quad \cdot \quad \cdot = \frac{\partial U}{\partial x_n} \div p_n$$

$$x_1 p_1 + x_2 p_2 + \ldots + x_n p_n - I = 0$$

Note that if utility is assumed to be cardinally measurable, this result is equivalent to the budget allocation rule in Equation 3.1. We ignore the possibility of corner solutions where the optimal value of some of the Xs is zero. This remains true until Chapter 8 when linear programming is described.

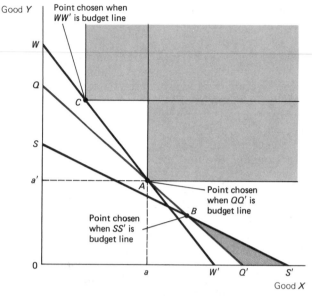

Figure 3.11   Revealed preference

preferred to A. Therefore the indifference curve running through point A must lie in between the budget line and the shaded area.

To get a better idea of the location and shape of this indifference curve, consider any other point on QQ'—for example, B. This point is inferior to A but there is some budget line that will make the consumer purchase it. Suppose that this budget line is SS'. Then we can deduce that the blackened area is inferior to A in the eyes of the consumer, since it is inferior to B, and B is inferior to A. This procedure can be used to narrow the zone of ignorance—the zone where we are unsure whether the included points are inferior or superior to A—that is below and to the right of A. To narrow the zone of ignorance above and to the left of A, we adopt the following procedure. We establish a new budget line, WW', which includes point A. Let C be the market basket the consumer chooses when he or she has the new money income and prices represented by this new budget line. Since C is no more expensive than A under these conditions, C is shown to be preferred to A. Moreover, all points above and to the right of C are also preferred to A, since they are preferred to C, and C is preferred to A.

If these procedures were repeated over and over again, one would eventually derive an indifference curve. Obviously, however, this would be a long and laborious process. The theory of revealed preference is more important as a means of demonstrating that indifference curves can, in principle, be derived in this way, than as a means of actually deriving indifference curves.[13]

13. The theory of revealed preferences assumes the following: First, if a market basket is purchased when this market basket is more expensive than another

15. Determinants of Consumer Tastes and Preferences

In previous sections of this chapter, we have discussed how the consumer's tastes can be represented and the way his or her tastes influence the market basket that is chosen. But we have said nothing about the factors that determine his tastes. Clearly, the consumer's tastes can be changed by various forms of experience. The child whose widest grins of satisfaction are reserved for candy and other sweets grows into the man who politely declines a sweet drink in favor of a dry martini. The boy who regards the ballet as sissy stuff grows to be the man who pays $40 for a ticket to the Royal Ballet and gives away complimentary ringside tickets to the fights. Age has a great effect on a person's tastes; so does education. Indeed, one of the benefits of education is that it allows people to appreciate and enjoy various forms of experience more keenly than they otherwise would.

Another factor influencing a consumer's tastes is his or her observation of what other consumers have. These effects are sometimes called demonstration effects. For example, if the Joneses have a Cadillac, their neighbors, the Smiths, may feel that they should have one, too. Or if the Jones's daughter can buy expensive clothes, Mrs. Smith may feel that her daughter should have them, too. (Whether Mr. Smith feels this way is another matter—which indicates the importance of asking in a particular case what individuals are regarded as the "consumer," and how decisions are made.) Sometimes an opposite kind of effect is at work: If many consumers have a certain commodity, others may not want it. For example, the snobbish Crandalls may take pride in having tastes that are different from the common herd of mankind.

Another important determinant of a consumer's tastes is the advertising and selling expenses incurred by manufacturers and sellers of various goods and services. There can be no doubt that advertising influences consumers, although the extent of its influence varies greatly from one product to another, and from one consumer to another. For goods where quality is hard for the consumer to measure, and where the relative advantages of a particular good or brand are not very great, advertising may play a very important role. Of course, advertising also plays a significant role merely by informing the consumer of the existence and characteristics of new products. Much more will be said about the effects of advertising in subsequent chapters.[14]

Finally, we have assumed in previous sections that a consumer's tastes (that is, his or her indifference map) are independent of the struc-

---

market basket, it must also be purchased when it is no more expensive. This rules out snob effects, where preferences are affected by prices. Second, if one market basket is chosen over a second and the second is chosen over a third, the first must be chosen over the third. This is the assumption of transitivity. Third, given any market basket, it is assumed that there exists some budget line that will lead the consumer to buy it.

14. See J. K. Galbraith, "Consumer Behavior and the Dependence Effect," and F. Hayek, "The *Non-Sequitur* of the Dependence Effect," reprinted in E. Mansfield, *Microeconomics: Selected Readings,* 4th ed. (New York: Norton, 1982.)

ture of prices. For example, changes in the prices of meat and potatoes are not supposed to affect the indifference map in Figure 3.2. This rules out cases in which goods are consumed because they are expensive—conspicuous consumption—and cases in which quality is judged by price. This assumption is a reasonable first approximation but it obviously does not hold for all cases. It is possible to extend our model to allow for violations of this assumption, but a discussion of such extensions properly belongs in a more advanced text.

16. Budget Allocation by a Government Agency: An Application

In Chapter 1 we said that microeconomics has turned out to be useful in helping to solve many important practical problems; yet in this chapter we have provided no evidence so far to support that statement. The material provided in previous sections of the present chapter must be understood if the reader is to understand the theory of consumer behavior. But it is by no means obvious how it would enable anyone to solve any kind of a practical problem. Appearances, however, can be deceiving. The kind of analysis discussed in this chapter can be useful in many contexts. The purpose of this section is to show how the model described in previous sections has been used to solve problems of budget allocation by government agencies.

For concreteness's sake, let's consider a particular agency, the Department of Transportation. And let's consider the decision that it (and Congress) must make with regard to the allocation of funds between urban highways and urban mass transit (buses and rail lines), both of which can be used to meet the transportation needs of our urban population. Suppose that the Department of Transportation has $2 billion to spend on urban highways and/or mass transit. How should it allocate this sum between them? In other words, how much should it spend on highways, and how much should it spend on mass transit? This is an important decision, one that involves huge sums of money and the time, comfort, and convenience of many of our people.

The reader may be forgiven if he or she asks in a somewhat bewildered tone, "What in the world has this problem got to do with the theory of consumer preferences we discussed in previous sections of this chapter?" The answer is that, strange as it may seem, economists have used the theory discussed above to help solve this kind of problem. The way in which they have solved the problem is instructive in many respects, one being that it illustrates how simple models can be adapted to throw light on very complicated problems.

In effect, the economists have said, "Let's view the Department of Transportation as a consumer. Let's regard highways and mass transit as two goods that the department can buy, with each good having a price and the total amount that can be spent on them both being fixed. Assuming that the department is interested in maximizing the effectiveness of the nation's transportation system, let's use as indifference curves for

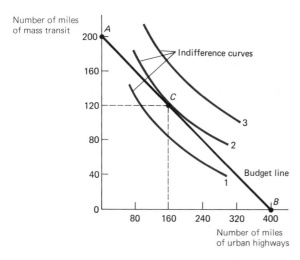

Figure 3.12 Allocation of transportation budget between urban highways and mass transit

the department the combinations of extra miles of highway and of extra miles of mass transit that will result in a certain expected addition to the nation's total transportation capability. Clearly, the bigger the expected addition to this capability, the higher the indifference curve. Then let's find the point on the budget line (which can be derived from the price of a mile of highway, the price of a mile of mass transit, and the total budget to be allocated) that lies on the highest indifference curve. This point will indicate the optimal allocation of the budget."

To actually attack the problem in this way, the first step, of course, is to determine various "indifference curves" of the "consumer," the Department of Transportation. Figure 3.12 shows what they might look like. As in Figure 3.5, each indifference curve slopes downward, since highways can be substituted for mass transit, and vice versa. Moreover, they are likely to be convex. What exactly does each of these indifference curves mean? Consider indifference curve 1. Each point on this indifference curve represents a combination of highways and mass transit that results in the same addition to transportation capability, that is, the same expected addition to our ability to transport people quickly and safely. The Department of Transportation is viewed as being interested in maximizing the nation's transportation capability. In other words, transportation capability (measured in this way) is a measure of this consumer's "utility." Thus the consumer is indifferent among all of the points on curve 1. And the consumer clearly prefers indifference curve 2 to indifference curve 1, because points on indifference curve 2 result in more transportation capability than those on indifference curve 1.

Having constructed the indifference curves, the next step is to construct the appropriate budget line. If the Department of Transportation has $2 billion to spend, if each mile of mass transit costs $10 million, and if each mile of highway costs $5 million, the budget line is AB in Figure 3.12. Based on our discussion in Section 12, this should be clear enough. Given this budget line and the indifference map, the problem boils down to finding the point on the budget line that lies on the highest indifference curve. A careful inspection of Figure 3.12 shows that this optimal point is point C, where the Department of Transportation funds the construction of 120 miles of mass transit and 160 miles of urban highways.

In recent years, economic analysis of this kind has played an important role in policy-making in many government agencies.[15] In practice, of course, the measurement of "transportation capability" or "social worth" often presents extremely difficult problems, with the result that it is not possible to draw curves like 1, 2, and 3 with great accuracy. Nevertheless, this does not mean that this type of analysis is not useful. On the contrary, it has proved very useful, since it provides a correct way of thinking about the problem. It focuses attention on the relevant factors, and it puts them in their proper place.[16]

This example also illustrates the fact that most aspects of microeconomics are concerned with means to achieve specified ends, not with the choice of ends. Thus economists in this case were interested in increasing the transportation capability to be obtained from a given budget. But they took as given the hypothesis that it was a good thing to increase transportation capability. In other words, they took as given the fact that the "utility" of the "consumer" should be increased. In certain circumstances, this hypothesis could perhaps be wrong. For example, suppose that the department wants to maximize its power and influence in the federal government, or to maximize the political fortunes of its top officials, rather than the nation's transportation capability. The same techniques could be used; all that would be required is a reinterpretation of the indifference curves.[17] Of course, this does not mean that it is not valuable to have techniques like those discussed here. They are obviously of great value. What it does mean is that one cannot expect them to do more than they are designed to do. They cannot tell us what our goals or ends should be.

15. Some of the pioneering studies of this kind occurred in the Department of Defense. See C. Hitch and R. McKean, *The Economics of Defense in the Nuclear Age,* Cambridge, Mass.: Harvard University Press, 1960.

16. It should be emphasized, however, that the particular example presented in this section is highly simplified. For one thing, costs incurred by parties other than the federal government are ignored. Also, the indifference curves may not always have the shape shown in Figure 3.12. Further, miles of highway or mass transit are rather crude units of measurement. Nonetheless, despite these and other limitations, this example communicates the spirit of this sort of analysis.

17. Under these circumstances, each indifference curve would show the combinations of highways and mass transit that result in the same level of power for the department or the same level of political fortunes for the department's top officials.

17. Summary

The consumer is, of course, one of the most important types of decision-making units in the economy. Clearly, among the most important determinants of a consumer's behavior are his or her tastes or preferences. We assume that, when confronted with two market baskets, a consumer can say which one is preferred, or whether he or she is indifferent between them. Also, we assume that the consumer's tastes are transitive and that a commodity is defined in such a way that more is preferred to less. Utility is a number that indexes the level of satisfaction derived from a particular market basket. Market baskets with higher utilities are preferred over market baskets with lower utilities. The consumer is assumed to be rational in the sense that he or she tries to maximize utility. If this is accomplished, the consumer's income is allocated among commodities so that, for every commodity he or she buys, the marginal utility of the commodity is proportional to its price. In other words, the marginal utility of the last dollar spent on each commodity is made equal for all commodities.

An indifference curve is the locus of points representing market baskets among which the consumer is indifferent. A consumer's tastes can be represented by a set of indifference curves. An indifference curve must have a negative slope, and two indifference curves cannot intersect. The slope of an indifference curve (multiplied by minus one) is called the marginal rate of substitution. The marginal rate of substitution shows approximately how many units of one good must be given up if the consumer, after receiving an extra unit of another good, is to maintain a constant level of satisfaction. Market baskets on higher indifference curves have higher utilities than those on lower indifference curves.

The budget line indicates all of the combinations of quantities of goods—all of the market baskets—that the consumers can buy, given his or her money income and the level of each price. In equilibrium, we would expect the consumer to attain the highest level of satisfaction that is compatible with the budget line. This means that in equilibrium the consumer will choose the market basket on the budget line that is on the highest indifference curve. This market basket is at a point where the budget line is tangent to an indifference curve.

The theory of revealed preference shows how one could measure an indifference curve by watching the consumer's behavior rather than recording his or her professed preferences. A consumer's tastes are affected by age and education, the behavior and purchases of others, and by advertising and other selling expenses. Finally, we showed how the model of consumer behavior presented in this chapter has been used to solve problems of budget allocation by government agencies. In particular, we took up a case study involving expenditures on urban transportation.

QUESTIONS AND PROBLEMS

1. Suppose that James Gray spends his entire income on goods X and Y. The marginal utility of each good (shown below) is independent of the amount

consumed of the other good. The price of X is $100 and the price of Y is $500.

Number of units of good consumed	MR. GRAY'S MARGINAL UTILITY (UTILS)	
	Good X	Good Y
1	20	50
2	18	45
3	16	40
4	13	35
5	10	30
6	6	25
7	4	20
8	2	15

If Mr. Gray has an income of $1,000 per month, how many units of each good should he purchase?

2. Draw Mr. Gray's budget line from the data in the previous question. At what point does it cut the axis along which the quantity of good Y is measured?

3. In the diagram below, we show one of Ellen White's indifference curves and her budget line. If the price of good A is $50, what is Ms. White's income? What is the equation for her budget line? What is the slope of the budget line? What is the price of good B? What is her marginal rate of substitution in equilibrium?

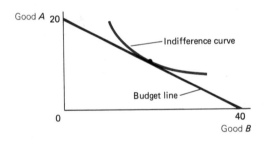

4. "A survey shows that most people prefer Cadillacs to Chevrolets." What exactly does this mean? If this is true, why do more people drive Chevrolets than Cadillacs?

5. One of Ms. Jones's indifference curves includes the following market baskets. Each of these market baskets gives her equal satisfaction.

Market basket	Meat (pounds)	Potatoes (pounds)
1	2	8
2	3	7
3	4	6
4	5	5
5	6	4
6	7	3
7	8	2
8	9	1

In her case, what is the marginal rate of substitution of potatoes for meat? How does the marginal rate of substitution vary as she consumes more meat and less potatoes? Is this realistic?

6. According to John Kenneth Galbraith, "as a society becomes increasingly affluent, wants are increasingly created by the process by which they are satisfied." Do you agree? Why or why not? Assuming that this is true, what would be the implications of this proposition for the theory of consumer behavior?

7. Define utility. How does cardinal utility differ from ordinal utility? Which concept is generally used by economists today?

8. According to Armen Alchian, "whether or not utility is some kind of glow or warmth, or happiness, is here irrelevant; all that counts is that we can assign numbers to entities or conditions which a person can strive to realize." Comment on this statement. Do you agree with it? Why or why not?

9. Suppose that consumers in San Francisco pay twice as much for apples as for pears, whereas consumers in Los Angeles pay 50 percent more for apples than for pears. If consumers in both cities maximize utility, will the marginal rate of substitution of pears for apples be the same in San Francisco as in Los Angeles? If not, in which city will it be higher?

10. A consumer is willing to trade one pound of steak for three pounds of hamburger. He currently is purchasing as much steak as hamburger per month. The price of steak is twice that of hamburger. Should he increase his consumption of hamburger and reduce his consumption of steak? Or should he reduce his consumption of hamburger and increase his consumption of steak?

SELECTED REFERENCES

HICKS, JOHN. *Value and Capital.* New York: Oxford University Press, 1946.

HENDERSON, JAMES, AND RICHARD QUANDT. *Microeconomic Theory.* 3d ed. New York: McGraw-Hill, 1980.

MARSHALL, ALFRED. *Principles of Economics.* London: Macmillan, 1920.

STIGLER, GEORGE. "The Development of Utility Theory." *Journal of Political Economy,* August 1950.

————. *The Theory of Price.* New York: Macmillan, 1966.

SAMUELSON, PAUL. *Foundations of Economic Analysis.* Cambridge, Mass.: Harvard University Press, 1947. (Advanced)

LEIBENSTEIN, HARVEY. "Bandwagon, Snob, and Veblen Effects in the Theory of Consumers' Demand." Reprinted in E. Mansfield, *Microeconomics: Selected Readings,* 4th ed. New York: Norton, 1982.

4 Consumer Behavior and Individual Demand

1. The Equilibrium of the Consumer: Review and Another Viewpoint

In this chapter, we proceed further with the development of a model of consumer behavior. Building on the results of the previous chapter, we show how the consumer responds to changes in his or her money income and to changes in the prices of commodities. In addition, we present some illustrations of how this theory has been applied to help solve important problems of public policy. Specifically, we describe how it has been applied to an important water problem of New York City and to the interpretation and construction of price indexes.

To begin with, it is useful to review briefly the conditions under which the consumer is in equilibrium. However, rather than merely parrot what has already been said in the previous chapter, we look at these conditions from a somewhat different point of view. We said in Section 13 of the previous chapter that the consumer's equilibrium market basket is at a point where the budget line is tangent to an indifference curve: This is the market basket that maximizes the consumer's utility. Since the slope of the indifference curve equals minus one times the marginal rate of substitution of good X for good Y (see Section 11, Chapter 3) and since the slope of the budget line is $-P_x/P_y$ (see Section 12, Chapter 3), it follows that the rational consumer will choose in equilibrium to allocate his or her income between good X and good Y so that the marginal rate of substitution of good X for good Y equals P_x/P_y.

This is a famous result—and a very useful one that should be understood fully. It is easier to agree that it is true than it is to see what it really means and why it is true. Perhaps the best way to understand this result is to define once again the marginal rate of substitution: The marginal rate of substitution is the rate at which the consumer is *willing* to substitute good X for good Y, holding his or her total level of satisfaction constant. Thus, if the marginal rate of substitution is three, the consumer is willing to give up three units of good Y in order to get one more unit of good X.

On the other hand, the price ratio, P_x/P_y, is the rate at which the consumer is *able* to substitute good X for good Y. Thus, if P_x/P_y is two, he or she *must* give up two units of good Y to get one more unit of good X. What the result described in this section is really saying is: The rate at which the consumer is willing to substitute good X for good Y (holding satisfaction constant) must equal the rate at which he or she is able to substitute good X for good Y. Otherwise it is always possible to find another market basket that will increase the consumer's satisfaction. And this means, of course, that the present market basket is not the equilibrium one that maximizes consumer satisfaction.

To see that this must be the case, suppose that the consumer has chosen a market basket in which the marginal rate of substitution of good X for good Y is three. Suppose that the ratio, P_x/P_y, is two. If this is the case, the consumer can trade two units of good Y for an extra unit of good X in the market, since the price ratio is two. But this extra unit of good X is worth three units of good Y to the consumer, since the marginal rate of substitution is three. Consequently, he or she can increase satisfaction by trading good Y for good X—and this will continue to be the case as long as the marginal rate of substitution exceeds the price ratio. Conversely, if the marginal rate of substitution is less than the price ratio, the consumer can increase satisfaction by trading good X for good Y. Only when the marginal rate of substitution equals the price ratio does the consumer's market basket maximize his or her utility.

2. Effects of Changes in Consumer Money Income

With this review in mind, let us turn to new territory and consider the effect of changes in money income on the amounts of good X and good Y purchased by the consumer. For example, suppose that the consumer is a student and that the amount of money he earns and receives from home increases from $5,000 to $7,000 a year. What effect will this have on his purchases? How much of the extra money will he spend on books? On entertainment? On clothes? On food?

In the previous chapter, we saw that an increase in money income results in an increase in the intercept of the budget line, but leaves unaffected the slope of the budget line (as long as the prices of commodities remain constant). Similarly, a decrease in money income results in a decrease in the intercept of the budget line, but leaves unaffected the slope of the budget line (as long as the prices of commodities remain

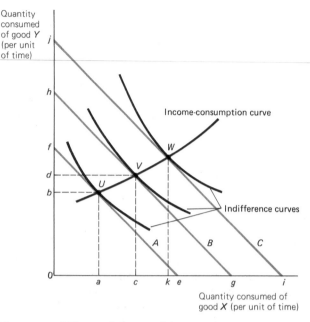

Figure 4.1   Effects of changes in money income on consumer
equilibrium

constant). To determine the effect of a change in money income on the
market basket chosen by the consumer, one can compare the equilibrium
position based on the budget line corresponding to the old level of money
income with the equilibrium position based on the budget line corresponding to the new level of money income.

For example, suppose that the budget line corresponding to the old
level of income—$5,000 in the case of the student—is A in Figure 4.1.
Given the consumer's indifference map, the market basket that maximizes his utility is comprised of Oa units of good X and Ob units of good
Y, if his income is at the old level. Now suppose that his income rises—to
$7,000 in the case of the student—and that the new budget line is B in
Figure 4.1. With these new conditions, the market basket that maximizes
his utility is comprised of Oc units of good X and Od units of good Y.

Clearly, the way in which an increase in money income influences a
consumer's purchases depends on his tastes. In other words, the nature
of the market basket chosen at the old income, the nature of the market
basket chosen at the new income, and consequently the nature of the
difference between these two market baskets is influenced by the shape
of the consumer's indifference curves. Also, the way in which an increase
in money income influences a consumer's purchases depends on the price
ratio, P_x/P_y. Of course, this price ratio is held constant when we analyze
the effects of changes in money income on consumer behavior, but the
level at which the price ratio is held constant will influence the results.

3. Income-Consumption and Engel Curves

Holding commodity prices constant, we find that each level of money income results in an equilibrium market basket for the consumer. That is, corresponding to each level of money income is an equilibrium market basket for a particular consumer. For example, the equilibrium market baskets corresponding to three income levels are represented by points U, V, and W in Figure 4.1. If we connect all of the points representing equilibrium market baskets corresponding to all possible levels of money income, the resulting curve is called the income-consumption curve. Figure 4.1 shows such a curve.

The income-consumption curve can be used to derive Engel curves, which are important for studies of family expenditure patterns. An Engel curve is the relationship between the equilibrium quantity purchased of a good and the level of income.[1] Ernst Engel was a nineteenth-century German statistician who did pioneering work related to such curves; economists have named them after him.

It is easy to see how an Engel curve can be derived from the income-consumption curve. Take the case in Figure 4.1 as an example. When money income equals P_x times Oe (or P_y times Of, since they are equal), the income-consumption curve shows that the consumer buys Oa units of good X. When money income equals P_x times Og (or P_y times Oh), the income-consumption curve shows that the consumer buys Oc units of good X. When money income is P_x times Oi (or P_y times Oj), the income-consumption curve shows that the consumer buys Ok units of good X. These are three points on the Engel curve for good X for this consumer. Each of these points shows the equilibrium amount of good X that he or she purchases at a certain level of money income. As more and more points are included, all of the points on the Engel curve for good X for this consumer are traced out. The result is shown in Figure 4.2.

Of course, the shape of a consumer's Engel curve for a particular good will depend on the nature of the good, the nature of the consumer's tastes, and the level at which commodity prices are held constant. For example, Engel curves with quite different shapes are shown in panels A and B of Figure 4.3. According to the Engel curve in panel A, the quantity consumed of the good increases with income, but at a *decreasing* rate. According to the Engel curve in panel B the quantity consumed of the good increases with income, but at an *increasing* rate. A comparison of panel A with panel B shows that a change in income from Ou to Ov does not have as great an effect on consumption of the good in panel B as on consumption of the good in panel A.

1. Often an Engel curve is defined to be the relationship between the consumer's *expenditure* on a commodity and his or her money income. But since the commodity prices are held constant, the consumer's expenditure on the product is proportional to the number of units of the commodity that he or she consumes. So it makes no real difference for present purposes whether we use expenditure or quanity demanded of the commodity as the relevant variable.

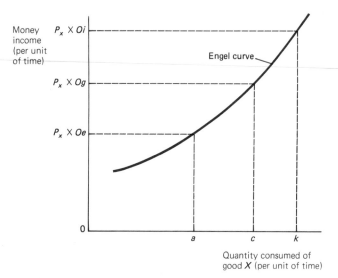

Figure 4.2   The Engel curve for good X

In general, one would expect that Engel curves for goods like salt and shoelaces would show that the consumption of these commodities does not change very much in response to changes in income. For example, only a rather unusual type of person would respond to a large increase in income by gorging himself or herself with salt and shoelaces—singly or in combination. On the other hand, goods like caviar and filet mignon might be expected to have Engel curves showing that their consumption increases considerably with increases in income. In general, this is probably so. But one should be careful about such generalizations. For example, if the consumer were a vegetarian, this would not hold true for filet mignon.

4. Effects of Changes in Commodity Price

In the previous two sections we have been concerned with the effect of changes in money income on the market basket that, in equilibrium, will be chosen by the consumer. Another important question is: Holding the consumer's money income constant, what will be the effect of a change in the price of a certain commodity on the amount of this commodity that the consumer will purchase? For example, take the case of the college student mentioned in Section 2. Suppose that his income remains constant at $5,000 and that the prices of all commodities other than food are held constant. Suppose that the price of food is allowed to vary and that we watch how the quantity of food that he consumes (per unit of time) varies in response to changes in the price of food. What sort of relationship exists between the price of food and the quantity of food that he consumes (per unit of time)?

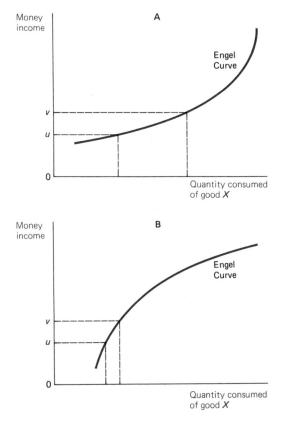

Figure 4.3 Engel curves: Various shapes

This case is unnecessarily specific. Let's pose the question more generally. Let's assume that there are only two commodities, good X and good Y. Suppose that the price of good Y and the money income of the consumer are held constant, but the price of good X is allowed to vary from one level to another. Suppose that the budget line corresponding to the original price of good X is B in Figure 4.4. If the price of good X is increased and the new budget line is C, the new equilibrium market basket for the consumer will be T, rather than the original equilibrium market basket of S. (In the previous chapter, we saw that an increase in the price of good X increases the absolute value of the slope of the budget line but does not affect the vertical intercept of the line.) Thus the increase in the price of good X will result in the consumer's buying Ou units of good X and Ov units of good Y, rather than the original market basket composed of Or units of good X and Os units of good Y.

Corresponding to each price of good X is an equilibrium market basket that can be determined in this way. The curve that connects the various equilibrium points is called the *price-consumption curve*. Figure 4.4 shows the price-consumption curve for this consumer, given the level

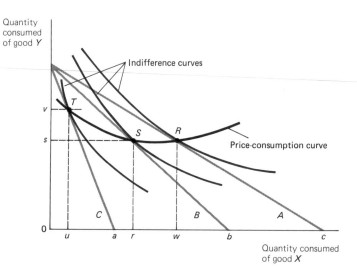

Figure 4.4   Effects of changes in price of good X on consumer equilibrium

of his or her money income and the price of good Y. One reason why the price-consumption curve is of interest is that it can be used to derive the consumer's individual demand curve for the commodity in question. The individual demand curve shows how much of a given commodity the consumer would purchase (per unit of time) at various prices of the commodity, holding constant the consumer's money income, his or her tastes, and the prices of other commodities. The individual demand curve is one of the central concepts in the theory of consumer behavior.

How can the individual demand curve be derived from the price-consumption curve? To illustrate the procedure, consider the case in Figure 4.4. When the price of good X is I/Oa (where I is the money income of the consumer), the price-consumption curve shows that the consumer buys Ou units of good X.[2] When the price of good X is I/Ob, the price-consumption curve shows that the consumer buys Or units of good X. When the price of good X is I/Oc, the price-consumption curve shows that the consumer buys Ow units of good X. These are three points on the individual demand curve. By deriving more and more points in this way, one can obtain the entire individual demand curve for good X. The result, DD', is shown in Figure 4.5.

5. The Individual Demand Curve: Location and Shape

The location and shape of an individual demand curve will depend on the level of money income and the level at which the prices of other goods are

2. From Figure 4.4, we know that the price of good X must be I/Oa when the budget line is C because, if the consumer devotes all of his or her money income, I, to good X, he or she can get Oa units of good X.

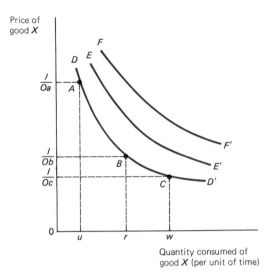

Figure 4.5   Individual demand curve for good X

held constant, as well as on the nature of the commodity and the tastes of the consumer. For example, suppose that we consider the demand curve for good X of the consumer represented in Figure 4.5. If his or her income were to be held constant at a level higher than I, a different demand curve would result. Rather than DD' it might be EE' in Figure 4.5. Also, if the price of good Y were higher than that assumed in Figure 4.4, a different demand curve would result. Rather than DD', it might be FF' in Figure 4.5. An important point to remember about a demand curve is that it is always drawn with certain assumptions about the level of the consumer's money income and the level of other prices in mind. In general it is only valid if these assumptions are correct.

It is important to differentiate between shifts in a consumer's demand curve for a particular commodity and changes in the amount of the commodity that he or she consumes. As we have seen, a consumer's demand curve may shift because of changes in his or her income or tastes, as well as because of changes in the prices of other goods. Such shifts in the consumer's demand curve are likely to result in changes in the amount of the commodity that he or she consumes, but they are not the only reason for such changes. In addition, changes in the price of the good will result in changes in the amount of the commodity that he or she consumes. We must be careful to distinguish between cases where the demand curve remains the same and changes in the consumption of the commodity occur because of changes in the commodity's price, and those cases where the demand curve shifts. The movement from point A to point B in Figure 4.5 is an example of the former; the shift of the demand curve from DD' to EE' is an example of the latter.

6. Price Elasticity of Demand: Individual Demand Curves

Individual demand curves differ greatly in shape. In the case of some commodities a consumer's consumption of the commodity is quite sensitive to its price; small changes in price result in considerable changes in the amount he or she consumes. On the other hand, in the case of other commodities, the consumer's consumption of the commodity is not at all sensitive to its price; large changes in price result in only small changes in the amount that he or she consumes. To gauge the sensitivity or responsiveness of the quantity demanded to changes in price, economists use the price elasticity of demand, as we know from Chapter 2. Recall that the price elasticity of demand is defined to be the percentage change in quantity resulting from a 1 percent change in price.[3]

For example, suppose that a 1 percent reduction in the price of thumbtacks results in a 2 percent increase in the quantity demanded by young Billy Jones, who delights in putting them on dimly lit park benches. For this budding juvenile delinquent, the price elasticity of demand for thumbtacks is two. As has been noted, convention dictates that we give the elasticity a positive sign despite the fact that the change in price is negative and the change in quantity demanded is positive. Clearly, the price elasticity of demand will generally vary from one point to another on an individual demand curve. For example, in the case of Master Jones, the price elasticity of demand may be higher when thumbtacks are a penny apiece than when they are two for a penny. Similarly, the price elasticity of demand will vary from consumer to consumer. For example, Mary Jones, Billy's sister, may have a much lower price elasticity of demand for thumbtacks than he does.

7. Price Elasticity, Total Expenditure, and the Price-Consumption Curve

The demand for a commodity is said to be *price elastic* if the elasticity of demand exceeds one. The demand for a commodity is said to be *price inelastic* if the elasticity of demand is less than one. And the demand for a commodity is said to be of *unitary elasticity* if the price elasticity of demand is equal to one.

Suppose that a consumer's demand for a commodity is elastic, that is, the price elasticity of demand exceeds one. In this situation, if the price is reduced, the percentage increase in the quantity consumed is greater than the percentage reduction in price. (That this is the case follows from the definition of the price elasticity of demand.) Conse-

---

3. More accurately, if q is the quantity demanded and p is the price, the price elasticity of demand is

$$\eta = \frac{-dq}{dp} \frac{p}{q}$$

quently, a price reduction must lead to an increase in the consumer's expenditure on the product, and a price increase must lead to a decrease in the consumer's expenditure on the product. On the other hand, suppose that the consumer's demand for a commodity is inelastic, that is, the price elasticity of demand is less than one. In this situation, if the price is reduced, the percentage increase in the quantity consumed is less than the percentage reduction in price. Thus a price reduction must lead to a decrease in the consumer's expenditure on the product, and a price increase must lead to an increase in the consumer's expenditure on the product. Finally, if the demand for a product is of unitary elasticity, price increases or decreases do not affect the consumer's expenditure on the product.

Whether the demand for a commodity is price elastic, price inelastic, or of unitary elasticity can be determined from the slope of the price-consumption curve if we construct the price-consumption curve in the following way: Suppose that the commodity in question is good X. Suppose that we define as good Y the money spent by the consumer on goods other than good X. Admittedly, good Y is a peculiar sort of commodity but there is nothing to prevent us from defining a commodity in this way. In weighing every purchase, the consumer must decide whether to give up money he or she can spend on other goods—that is, good Y—for good X. Since good Y is money, its price is always one. For example, it takes a quarter to buy a quarter. The introduction of this kind of good Y is a useful trick that we will adopt elsewhere in this chapter.

Figure 4.6 shows the price-consumption curve, which is constructed in the way described in Section 4, for three different consumers. In panel A, the consumer's indifference curves are such that the price-consumption curve has zero slope. Thus the amount of the consumer's income *not spent* on good X (the amount of good Y) remains constant at OU, when the price is decreased from P_1 to P_2. Consequently, the amount spent on good X must also have remained constant, which means that the demand for good X is of unitary elasticity. In panel B, the upward sloping price-consumption curve indicates that this consumer's demand for good X is price inelastic. Why? Because a decrease in price from P_1 to P_2 results in an increase (from OA to OB) in the amount not spent on good X, which means that the consumer's expenditure on good X must have declined with a decrease in price.

In panel C, the downward sloping price-consumption curve indicates that the third consumer's demand for good X is price elastic. Why? Because a decrease in price from P_1 to P_2 results in a decrease (from OU to OW) in the amount not spent on good X, which means that the consumer's expenditure on good X must have increased with a decrease in its price. Thus, to summarize, a horizontal price-consumption curve implies that demand is of unitary elasticity; an upward sloping price-consumption curve implies that demand is price inelastic; and a downward sloping price-consumption curve implies that demand is price elastic.

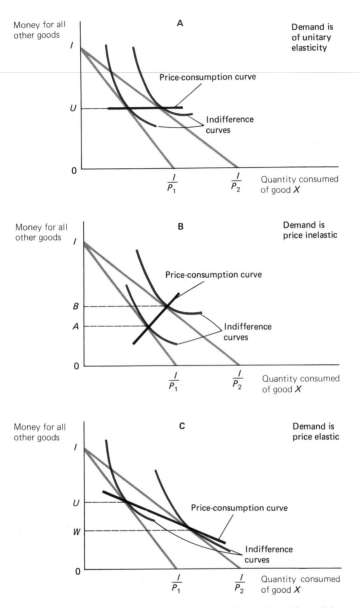

Figure 4.6 Price-consumption curves and the elasticity of demand

8. Substitution and Income Effects

When the price of a good changes, the consumer is affected in two ways:
First, he or she attains a different level of satisfaction, and second, he or
she is likely to substitute now cheaper goods for more expensive goods.
The total effect of a price change is illustrated in Figure 4.7. The original

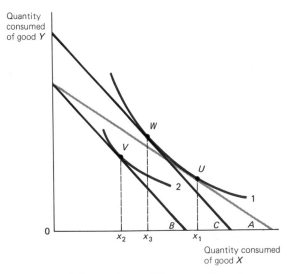

Figure 4.7   Substitution and income effects for a normal good

price ratio is given by the slope of the budget line A. Given this price
ratio, the consumer chooses point U on indifference curve 1, and consumes Ox_1 units of good X. Now suppose that the price of good X is
increased and B is the new budget line. Given the new price ratio, the
consumer chooses point V on indifference curve 2, and consumes Ox_2
units of good X. The total effect of the price change on the quantity
demanded of good X is a reduction of $Ox_1 - Ox_2$ units.

The total effect of this—or any—price change can be divided concep-
tually into two parts: the substitution effect and the income effect. First,
consider the substitution effect. In Figure 4.7, when the price of good X
increases, it is clear that a decrease occurs in the consumer's level of
satisfaction: He or she winds up on indifference curve 2 rather than
indifference curve 1. Suppose that, when the price goes up, we could
increase the consumer's money income by an amount sufficient to keep
him or her on the old indifference curve. If this could be done, it would
mean that the budget line would be parallel to the budget line B, but
that it would be tangent to indifference curve 1. This hypothetical budget line is labeled C in Figure 4.7. The substitution effect is defined to be
the movement from the original equilibrium point U to the imaginary
equilibrium point W, which corresponds to the hypothetical budget line
C. The substitution effect is the reduction of the quantity consumed
from Ox_1 to Ox_3 units of good X. Put differently, it is the change in
quantity demanded of good X resulting from a price change when the
level of satisfaction is held constant.

Next, consider the income effect. The movement from the imaginary
equilibrium point W to the actual new equilibrium point V is the income
effect. This movement does not involve any change in prices; the price
ratio is the same in budget line C as in budget line B. It is due to a change
in total satisfaction; such a change is a movement from one indifference

curve to another. If we define the consumer's real income as his or her level of satisfaction (or utility), the income effect is the change in quantity demanded of good X due entirely to a change in real income, *all prices being held constant.* In Figure 4.7, it is the reduction from Ox_3 to Ox_2 units. The total effect of a change in price is obviously the sum of the income effect and the substitution effect. [4]

9. Normal and Inferior Goods

The substitution effect is always negative. That is, if the price of good X increases and real income is held constant, there will always be a decrease in the consumption of good X; and if the price of good X decreases and real income is held constant, there will always be an increase in the consumption of good X. This result follows from the fact that indifference curves have a negative slope (see Chapter 3). However, the income effect is not predictable from the theory alone. In most cases, one would expect that increases in real income will result in increases in consumption of a good and that decreases in real income will result in decreases in consumption of a good. This is the case for so-called *normal goods.* But not all goods are normal. Some goods are called *inferior goods* because the income effect is the opposite (of that of a normal good) for them. An illustration of an inferior good is given in Figure 4.8, where real income is assumed to increase from indifference curve 1 to indifference

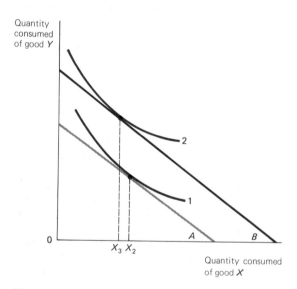

Figure 4.8   An inferior good

4. For an explanation of substitution and income effects in elementary mathematical terms, see J. Henderson and R. Quandt, *Microeconomic Theory,* 3d ed. (New York: McGraw-Hill, 1980).

curve 2. Prices are assumed to be the same before and after the increase in real income; the original budget line is A and the subsequent budget line is B. Figure 4.8 shows that, because of the shapes of the indifference curves, the consumer purchases $(OX_2 - OX_3)$ fewer units of good X after the increase in real income than he originally did.

Ordinarily, the substitution effect of a price change is strong enough to offset an inferior good's income effect, with the consequence that the quantity demanded of a good is inversely related to its price. However, it is possible for an inferior good to have an income effect that is so strong that it offsets the substitution effect, with the result that the quantity demanded is directly related to the price, at least over some range of variation of price. A case of this sort is known as *Giffen's paradox.* For Giffen's paradox to occur, a good must be an inferior good, but not all inferior goods exhibit Giffen's paradox.

Oleomargarine is likely to be an inferior good for many consumers. Increases in real income are likely to lead to a substitution of butter for oleomargarine. Many other examples of inferior goods could be put forth, although, as stated above, inferior goods are in the minority. Giffen's paradox is a much, much rarer phenomenon. In the rest of this book, we shall assume that goods do not exhibit Giffen's paradox. That is, all demand curves are assumed to have a negative slope.

10. The New York Water Crisis: An Application

Previous sections have presented a model of how consumers respond to changes in price and money income. But no attempt has been made to indicate how this model can be used to help solve practical problems. In the balance of this chapter, we discuss some applications of this model. To begin with, we describe a major problem that confronted New York City in 1949 and 1950.[5] At that time New York City experienced a water crisis, because the average rate of use of water exceeded the yield of the water system. Various solutions to the problem were proposed. For example, the Board of Water Supply requested approval of the construction of a new dam and reservoir. In response to the crisis, the mayor asked his Committee on Management Survey to examine the question and make recommendations. After looking into the problem, the committee recommended that no new dam be built. Instead they recommended the use of universal metering, together with the elimination of leakage and waste from street mains.

The idea behind metering was quite simple. Many consumers paid only a flat fee for water and were not metered. With metering, consumers would be charged about 15 cents per hundred cubic feet of water. Obviously, since metering would increase the price of using an extra hun-

5. The theory presented in this chapter has been used in many recent studies of transportation projects, water projects, and other projects. But we have chosen an older example because it is a classic illustration of the use of this theory. Throughout this book, we try to incorporate the best illustrations, not necessarily the most recent ones.

dred cubic feet of water from zero to 15 cents, it would result in the consumer's decreasing his or her use of water. According to the mayor's Committee on Management Survey, universal metering would save about two hundred million gallons of water per day.

The problem facing the city of New York, however, was whether or not metering was the best way of meeting the crisis. Another possible way to meet the crisis was to build the new dam proposed by the Board of Water Supply. Which solution was the best? After some deliberation it was decided to build the new dam. Was this the right decision?

11. The RAND Study and Consumer's Surplus

A few years after it was decided to build the dam, a group of economists at the RAND Corporation studied this decision. Their purpose was to show how microeconomic techniques could help to solve such problems.[6] Although the RAND study could not affect the decision of New York, it was hoped that it would affect such decisions at other times and places. In this section, we describe the way that the RAND economists attacked the problem. To begin with, one of the most important considerations in deciding whether New York should have adopted more extensive metering or built the new dam was the cost of meeting the crisis in each way. Which would be less costly?

According to various estimates the cost of providing water with the new dam would be about $1,000 per million gallons per day. According to the Committee on Management Survey, the cost of metering would be about $50 per million gallons per day. But this was only part of the cost of metering, since it did not include the loss to consumers arising from the fact that they would be led to consume less water. To make a fair comparison of the cost of metering with the cost of a new dam, one should include such losses. But how can one make estimates of the monetary value of these losses? This is a very difficult question, more difficult than one may recognize at first glance.

The RAND economists attempted to answer this question by using some results based on the sort of model we have discussed in this and the previous chapter. Suppose that a consumer is obliged to consume Q gallons of water per day rather than $Q + \Delta$ gallons of water per day. To measure the monetary value of the loss of Δ gallons of water per day, the RAND economists, following earlier economists like Jules Dupuit and Alfred Marshall,[7] used the maximum amount that the consumer would be willing to pay for the Δ gallons of water per day. Thus, if John Jones

---

6. See J. Hirshleifer, J. Milliman, and J. De Haven, *Water Supply* (Chicago: University of Chicago Press, 1960), Chapter 10. This application is also cited, but in somewhat less detail, in G. Stigler, *The Theory of Price* (New York: Macmillan, 1966), pp. 78–81.

7. J. Dupuit, *Annales des Ponts et Chaussées* (1844); and A. Marshall, *Principles of Economics* (London: Macmillan, 8th ed., 1920) p. 842.

were willing to pay up to 10 cents a day to avoid losing 100 gallons of water per day, this would be the monetary value to him of the loss of this much water.

It is important to note that the monetary value to the consumer of the Δ gallons of water—that is, the maximum amount that he or she would pay for the Δ gallons of water—may be considerably more than the consumer actually pays for the Δ gallons of water. This is true for other commodities as well. For example, a man may be willing to pay up to $200 to avoid spending a weekend with his in-laws, but a merciful Providence may enable him to pay only $10 to avoid such a weekend. The difference between the maximum amount that the consumer would pay and the amount he or she actually pays is called _consumer's surplus_. For example, the consumer's surplus of the man who avoids his in-laws at a cost of $10 is $190.

Is there any way to tell from a consumer's demand curve for water how much—at the most—he or she is willing to pay to avoid the loss of Δ gallons of water per day? Under certain very special assumptions, there is a way. Suppose that we plot the consumer's indifference curves in Figure 4.9, in which the amount of water consumed per day is one good and the amount of money that the consumer can spend on all goods other than water is the other good. Suppose that the indifference curves (1, 2, and 3, as well as others not shown) are parallel; that is, the vertical distance between any two indifference curves is the same regardless of where along the horizontal axis one measures this distance. This is a very restrictive assumption, but according to some economists it may be a

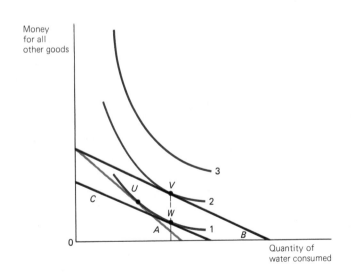

Figure 4.9 Special assumption underlying calculations of the RAND study

reasonable approximation for commodities, like water, on which the consumer spends only a small amount of his or her income.[8]

What does it mean when we assume that the indifference curves in Figure 4.9 are parallel? If they are parallel, their slopes must be equal at a given point along the horizontal axis. This means that, if a change occurs in the price of water, the income effect (on the consumption of water) of the price change is zero. To see this, suppose that the price of water decreases so that the consumer's equilibrium point shifts from U to V. The income effect of this price decrease can be measured by inserting a budget line, C, which has the slope of the new budget line, B, but which is tangent to the old indifference curve, 1. If this fictitious budget line were the real one, the equilibrium point would be W. The income effect is the movement along the horizontal axis from W to V, which is clearly equal to zero.

12. The RAND Solution

The RAND economists' analysis rested on the assumption that the indifference curves in Figure 4.9 are parallel. Given this assumption, one can calculate from a consumer's demand curve for water how much—at the most—he or she is willing to pay to avoid having to consume Q gallons of water per day rather than $Q + \Delta$ gallons of water per day. The calculation is simple: *One simply computes the area under his or her demand curve for water between Q and $Q + \Delta$.* The first object of this section is to show why this procedure is sensible. Then we will show how the RAND economists used this result to help solve the problem.

To see why the maximum amount that the consumer will pay for the extra Δ gallons of water per day is the area under the demand curve between Q and $Q + \Delta$, consider Figure 4.10, which shows his or her demand curve for water. For simplicity, we assume that the consumer's water consumption can be varied only in units of one gallon of water per day. Thus the consumer can increase his or her consumption from Q gallons to $Q + 1$ gallons, $Q + 2$ gallons, and so on. What is the maximum amount that the consumer will pay for the $(Q + 1)$st gallon of water? The demand curve, DD', shows that OP_1 is the maximum price that the consumer will pay for the extra gallon of water. (If the price exceeds OP_1 the consumer will demand only Q gallons.) What is the maximum amount that the consumer will pay for the $(Q + 2)$nd gallon of water? The demand curve shows that OP_2 is the maximum price that the consumer will pay for the extra gallon of water. (If the price exceeds OP_2, the consumer will demand only $Q + 1$ gallons.) And by repeated use of the same reasoning, we find that OP_3 is the maximum amount that the

---

8. Basically, the assumption underlying the analysis is that the marginal utility of income is constant. If this is the case, the indifference curves in Figure 4.9 will be parallel. This assumption is stringent, indeed. See P. Samuelson, *Foundations of Economic Analysis* (Cambridge, Mass.: Harvard University Press, 1947), pp. 189–202; and J. Hicks, *Value and Capital* (New York: Oxford University Press, 1946), pp. 38–41.

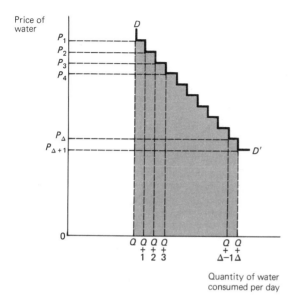

Figure 4.10   The maximum amount the consumer will pay
to consume $Q + \Delta$ rather than Q gallons
of water per day

consumer will pay for the $(Q + 3)$rd gallon, that OP_4 is the maximum
amount that the consumer will pay for the $(Q + 4)$th gallon, and so on.

Thus the maximum amount that the consumer will pay for one
extra gallon is OP_1 (which equals the area under the demand curve from
Q gallons to $Q + 1$ gallons). Similarly, the maximum amount that the
consumer will pay for two extra gallons is OP_1 (which equals the area
under the demand curve from Q gallons to $Q + 1$ gallons) plus OP_2
(which equals the area under the demand curve from $Q + 1$ to $Q + 2$
gallons). And the maximum amount that the consumer will pay for three
extra gallons is OP_1 (which equals the area under the demand curve from
Q gallons to $Q + 1$ gallons) plus OP_2 (which equals the area under the
demand curve from $Q + 1$ to $Q + 2$ gallons) plus OP_3 (which equals the
area under the demand curve from $Q + 2$ to $Q + 3$ gallons). And, in
general, the maximum amount that the consumer will pay for Δ extra
gallons is OP_1 (which equals the area under the demand curve from Q to
$Q + 1$ gallons) plus OP_2 (which equals the area under the demand curve
from $Q + 1$ to $Q + 2$ gallons) ... plus OP_Δ (which equals the area under
the demand curve from $Q + \Delta - 1$ to $Q + \Delta$ gallons). Since $OP_1 + OP_2$
$+ \cdots + OP_\Delta$ equals the area under the demand curve from Q to $Q + \Delta$
gallons, it follows that this area measures the maximum amount that the
consumer will pay for the extra Δ gallons of water per day.

Returning to New York's problem, the RAND study also assumed,
in effect, that the demand curve was approximately linear. Under this
assumption, the relevant area under the demand curve for each consumer would be about 7.5 cents per hundred cubic feet times the number
of cubic feet that was saved. This fact is shown in Figure 4.11. This

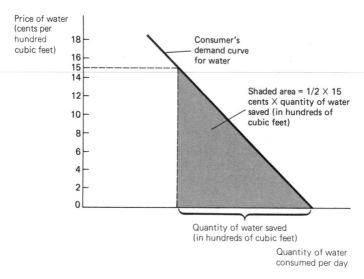

Figure 4.11   Area under the consumer's demand curve for water

amounts to about $100 per million gallons. Thus the total cost of saving water through metering—including the costs of metering, which were $50 per million gallons saved—was estimated by the RAND study to be about $150 per million gallons. This seemed to be lower than the cost of providing water with the new dam. Thus the RAND study seemed to suggest that metering might have been cheaper than building the dam.

This is an interesting example of the use of the theory of consumer demand. However, it should be recognized that this kind of analysis is fraught with many difficulties. For one thing, the assumption of parallel indifference curves may not be a good approximation. For another, there are problems, described in Chapter 16, involved in comparing and combining the results for different consumers.[9] Still further, the proper decision depends on forecasts of rainfall as well as on growth in water usage. Subsequent studies have shown that the RAND study seriously overestimated the level of rainfall in the mid-sixties.[10]

13. Indexes of the Cost of Living

Another area where the theory described in previous sections has proved useful is in the construction of index numbers of the cost of living. The phrase *cost of living* means the cost of living at a constant level of satisfaction. Cost-of-living indexes have always been closely associated

9. For example, who will receive the benefits? Who will pay the costs? How can we tell whether one set of citizens should reap benefits at the expense of some other set of citizens?

10. See J. Hirshleifer and J. Milliman, "Urban Water Supply: A Second Look," *American Economic Review,* May, 1967. I am indebted to E. Burmeister and R. Pollak for helpful discussions of these topics.

Example 4.1 Economic Aspects of Outdoor Recreation

Lewis and Clark Lake is a large reservoir in South Dakota created on the Missouri River by the Gavins Point Dam. It is located in an area where there are few natural bodies of water, and it has become very popular as a recreational area. Suppose that 10,000 families are potential users of the lake for recreational purposes and that each family's demand curve for recreational trips to the lake is as follows:

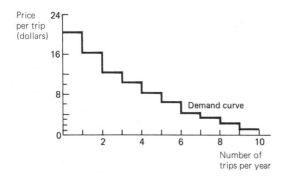

(a) If an ordinance were passed which limited each family to no more than 5 trips per year to the lake, what is the loss (in money terms) to each family? (b) If an ordinance were passed which allowed a family to use the lake for recreational purposes only if it purchased a permit for $75 a year, would it be worthwhile for each family to buy the permit, if it could not use the lake without the permit (and it could use the lake as much as it liked with one)? (c) Suppose that we consider two goods: trips to the lake and money that can be spent on things other than trips to the lake. In answering questions (a) and (b), what assumption are you making regarding each family's indifference curves concerning these two goods?

Solution

(a) The loss is the area under the demand curve from 5 to 10 trips, which equals $6 + $4 + $3 + $2 + $1, or $16. (b) Once a family buys the permit, a trip to the lake is free. Thus, if it buys the permit, it will make 10 trips per year, as shown by the demand curve. The maximum amount that each family would pay for these 10 trips is the area under the demand curve from 0 to 10 trips, which is $20 + $16 + $12 + $10 + $8 + $6 + $4 + $3 + $2 + $1, or $82. Since this maximum amount exceeds $75, each family would find it worthwhile to buy the permit. (c) The calculations assume that these indifference curves are parallel. That is, if we measure the number of trips along the horizontal axis and the amount of money for all other goods along the vertical axis, the vertical distance between any two indifference curves is assumed to be the same regardless of where along the horizontal axis one measures this distance.*

---

* For further discussion, see M. Clawson and J. Knetsch, *Economics of Outdoor Recreation* (Baltimore, Md.: Johns Hopkins University Press, 1966).

with the measurement and problems of inflation. For example, labor unions want to know whether wages are keeping pace with the cost of living. Automatic adjustments in wages based on changes in cost-of-living indexes are incorporated in many wage contracts. And cost-of-living indexes are used to measure changes in the purchasing power of the dollar for a variety of purposes, including the adjustment of pensions and welfare payments (and even alimony payments).

The most famous index of the cost of living is the Consumer Price Index, which the Bureau of Labor Statistics has been calculating for over fifty years. This index includes the prices of practically everything people buy for living—food, clothing, homes, automobiles, household supplies, house furnishings, fuel, drugs, doctors' fees, rent, transportation, and so forth. It pertains to urban consumers, and is based on data concerning the spending habits and prices paid by such consumers. Prices are obtained by personal visits to a sample of about twenty-five thousand retail stores and service establishments in the United States. Prices are collected at intervals ranging from once every month to once every three months. Based on these data, the Bureau of Labor Statistics publishes each month the Consumer Price Index for the urban population as a whole and for each of twenty-eight metropolitan areas.

14. The Laspeyres Index and the Paasche Index

How can indexes of the cost of living be constructed? To what extent can we infer from these indexes that increases or decreases have occurred in consumer welfare? For example, if a family earned $20,000 in 1975 and $30,000 in 1980, was it really better off in 1980, or were prices so much higher in 1980 that it really was worse off then? Ideally, a cost-of-living index is constructed so that the consumer's real income can be determined by dividing his or her money income by the index. Thus, if the ideal index went up by less than 50 percent between 1975 and 1980, the family in question was better off in 1980; otherwise it was not.

In practice, cost-of-living indexes, like most things in life, are not ideal. The two basic types of indexes that can be used are the Laspeyres index and the Paasche index. To illustrate how these indexes are constructed, suppose that the family in the previous paragraph buys only two commodities. (We can easily show that the results are true for any number.) Suppose that it buys x_1 units of good X and y_1 units of good Y in 1980 and x_0 units of good X and y_0 units of good Y in 1975. Suppose that the price of good X is P_{x1} in 1980 and P_{x0} in 1975 and that the price of good Y is P_{y1} in 1980 and P_{y0} in 1975.

The Laspeyres index measures the change in the cost of the market basket purchased by the consumer in the original year, in this case 1975. Thus it equals

$$L = \frac{x_0 P_{x1} + y_0 P_{y1}}{x_0 P_{x0} + y_0 P_{y0}}$$

On the other hand, the Paasche index measures the change in the cost of the market basket purchased in the later year, in this case 1980. Thus it equals

$$P = \frac{x_1 P_{x1} + y_1 P_{y1}}{x_1 P_{x0} + y_1 P_{y0}}$$

15. The Laspeyres Index, Paasche Index, and Changes in Consumer Welfare

Given the prices paid by the family $(P_{x0}, P_{x1}, P_{y0}, P_{y1})$ and the quantities consumed (x_0, x_1, y_0, y_1), suppose that we computed these two indexes. What could we conclude from them? Recall that the family's money income went up by 50 percent between 1975 and 1980. If the Laspeyres index, L, is greater than 1.50, can we be sure that the consumer, that is, the family, was worse off in 1980 than in 1975? If the Laspeyres index is less than 1.50, can we be sure that the consumer was better off in 1980 than in 1975? What about the Paasche index? If P is greater than 1.50, can we be sure that the consumer was worse off in 1980 than in 1975? If P is less than 1.50, can we be sure that the consumer was better off in 1980 than in 1975?

The first thing to note is that the cost of the market basket actually chosen in 1975 equaled

$$x_0 P_{x1} + y_0 P_{y1}$$

in 1980. Thus, if the family's income in 1980 exceeded this amount, it must have been better off in 1980 than in 1975, since it could buy the 1975 market basket—and more—in 1980. But the family's income in 1980 exceeded this amount if

$$x_0 P_{x1} + y_0 P_{y1} < x_1 P_{x1} + y_1 P_{y1}$$

since the quantity on the right-hand side must equal the family's income in 1980. If we divide both sides of the inequality by $(x_0 P_{x0} + y_0 P_{y0})$, it follows that the family must have been better off in 1980 than in 1975 if the Laspeyres index, L, was less than the ratio of 1980 to 1975 income— 1.50 in this case.

The next thing to note is that the family must have been better off in the earlier year if it could have bought the 1980 market basket in 1975 but did not do so. Thus it must have been better off in 1975 if

$$x_0 P_{x0} + y_0 P_{y0} > x_1 P_{x0} + y_1 P_{y0}$$

since the quantity on the left-hand side must equal the family's income in 1975. Dividing both sides of this inequality by $(x_1 P_{x1} + y_1 P_{y1})$, we find that the family must have been better off in 1975 than in 1980 if the ratio of the family's 1975 to 1980 money income exceeded $1/P$, or if the ratio of 1980 to 1975 money income was less than the Paasche index.

In summary, we can be sure that a family's welfare has increased if the ratio of its later money income to its earlier money income is greater than the Laspeyres index. And we can be sure that its welfare has decreased if the ratio of its later money income to its earlier money income is less than the Paasche index. If neither of these conditions holds, we cannot tell whether an increase or a decrease has occurred in the consumer's welfare. Of course, these results are based on the assumption that the consumer's tastes and the quality of the goods remain constant during the relevant time interval. Otherwise the problem is completely intractable if not meaningless.

16. A Graphical Interpretation

The results of the previous section throw considerable light on an important and difficult problem. Basically, these results are nothing more than simple applications of the theory of consumer behavior. To see this, consider panel A of Figure 4.12, which shows the family's indifference

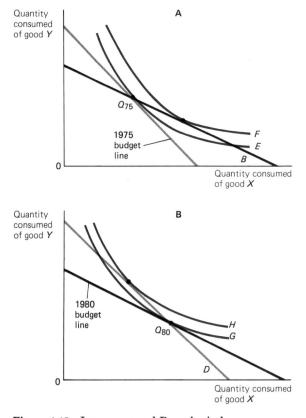

Figure 4.12 Laspeyres and Paasche indexes

curves, E and F, the budget line in 1975, and the family's 1975 market basket, Q_{75}. Suppose that we calculate how much the family's 1975 market basket would have cost in 1980 and that we see how well off the family would have been in 1980 with this much money income. Under these circumstances, the 1980 budget line would have been

$$x_1 P_{x1} + y_1 P_{y1} = I'$$

where $I' = x_0 P_{x1} + y_0 P_{y1}$. This budget line is shown as B in panel A of Figure 4.12.

It is obvious from Figure 4.12, panel A, that, if its 1980 income was I', the family was at least as well off in 1980 as it was in 1975. It could certainly attain the indifference curve, E, that it attained in 1975. Moreover, in general, it could attain a higher indifference curve, F. Thus the ratio of the 1980 cost of attaining the 1975 indifference curve to the 1975 cost of attaining it was at most

$$\frac{I'}{x_0 P_{x0} + y_0 P_{y0}} = \frac{x_0 P_{x1} + y_0 P_{y1}}{x_0 P_{x0} + y_0 P_{y0}} = L$$

since the family's 1975 income was $x_0 P_{x0} + y_0 P_{y0}$. This, of course, is precisely the result we obtained in the previous section: If the ratio of the family's money income in 1980 to its money income in 1975 was greater than the Laspeyres index, we can be sure that its welfare increased.

Turning to the Paasche index, consider panel B of Figure 4.12, which shows the family's indifference curves, G and H, the budget line in 1980 and the family's 1980 market basket, Q_{80}. Suppose that we calculate how much the 1980 market basket would have cost in 1975 and that we see how well off the family would have been in 1975 with this much money income. Under these circumstances, the 1975 budget line would have been

$$x_0 P_{x0} + y_0 P_{y0} = I''$$

where $I'' = x_1 P_{x0} + y_1 P_{y0}$. This budget line is shown as D in Figure 4.12, panel B.

It is obvious from Figure 4.12, panel B, that, if its 1975 income was I'', the family was at least as well off as in 1980. It could certainly attain the indifference curve, G, that it attained in 1980. Moreover, in general, it could attain a higher indifference curve, H. Thus the ratio of the 1980 cost of attaining the 1980 indifference curve to the 1975 cost of attaining it was at least

$$\frac{x_1 P_{x1} + y_1 P_{y1}}{I''} = \frac{x_1 P_{x1} + y_1 P_{y1}}{x_1 P_{x0} + y_1 P_{y0}} = P$$

since the family's 1980 income was $x_1 P_{x1} + y_1 P_{y1}$. This, too, is precisely the result we obtained in the previous section: If the ratio of the family's

Example 4.2   Index Numbers and Changes in Economic
                  Welfare

According to the Bureau of Labor Statistics, the price of food was 8
percent higher in the United States in 1980 than in 1979, and the
price of housing was 16 percent higher in 1980 than in 1979*. Suppose that a family spent half of its 1979 money income on food and
half on housing. (a) For this family, what was the Laspeyres price
index in 1980 (if the original or base year is 1979)? (b) If this family's
income was 13 percent higher in 1980 than in 1979, can we be sure its
welfare increased from 1979 to 1980? (c) If prices increased more
rapidly in the city where this family lives than in the nation as a
whole, can we be sure its welfare increased from 1979 to 1980?

Solution
(a) From p. 100, we know that the equation for the Laspeyres price
index is

$$L = \frac{x_0 P_{x1} + y_0 P_{y1}}{x_0 P_{x0} + y_0 P_{y0}}$$

Let good X be food and good Y be housing, let x_0 be the number of
units of food bought in 1979 and x_1 be the amount bought in 1980,
and let y_0 be the number of units of housing bought in 1979 and y_1 be
the amount bought in 1980. The price of a unit of food is P_{x0} in 1979
and P_{x1} in 1980, and the price of a unit of housing is P_{y0} in 1979 and
P_{y1} in 1980. Another way of writing this equation is

$$L = \frac{x_0 P_{x0} \left(\dfrac{P_{x1}}{P_{x0}}\right) + y_0 P_{y0} \left(\dfrac{P_{y1}}{P_{y0}}\right)}{x_0 P_{x0} + y_0 P_{y0}}$$

$$= \left(\frac{x_0 P_{x0}}{x_0 P_{x0} + y_0 P_{y0}}\right)\left(\frac{P_{x1}}{P_{x0}}\right) + \left(\frac{y_0 P_{y0}}{x_0 P_{x0} + y_0 P_{y0}}\right)\left(\frac{P_{y1}}{P_{y0}}\right).$$

Since $x_0 P_{x0} + y_0 P_{y0}$ equals the family's money income in 1979, $x_0 P_{x0}$
$\div (x_0 P_{x0} + y_0 P_{y0})$ equals the proportion of its 1979 money income
spent on food, which equals $\frac{1}{2}$. Similarly, $y_0 P_{y0} \div (x_0 P_{x0} + y_0 P_{y0})$
equals the proportion of its 1979 money income spent on housing,
which equals $\frac{1}{2}$. Thus, since $P_{x1}/P_{x0} = 1.08$ and $P_{y1}/P_{y0} = 1.16$,

$$L = \frac{1}{2}(1.08) + \frac{1}{2}(1.16) = 1.12,$$

which means that the Laspeyres index equaled 1.12. (Frequently,
index numbers are expressed as percentages; if this is done here, the
index equaled 112.) (b) Since the ratio of the family's 1980 money
income to its 1979 money income is 1.13, it barely exceeds the Laspeyres index, which has been shown to equal 1.12. Thus its welfare
seems to have increased. (c) No. The calculations above assume that
the prices paid by the family increased at the same rate as in the
nation as a whole. If they increased more rapidly, the Laspeyres
price index for the family exceeded 1.12. We cannot tell (from the
information given) whether it exceeded 1.13; if it did, the family's
welfare may have decreased.

---

* The figures for both 1980 and 1979 pertain to July. See *Monthly Labor
Review,* October 1980, p. 85.

money income in 1980 to its money income in 1975 was less than the Paasche index, we can be sure that its welfare decreased.[11]

17. Information and Search Activity by Consumers

Finally, we must recognize that our model of consumer behavior assumes that the consumer knows the minimum price that he or she must pay for each commodity. The consumer, however, frequently does not have such information. For example, if a person is shopping for a new car, he or she does not know which auto dealer will sell a particular model at the lowest price. In fact, studies show that a particular model of Chevrolet may sell for several hundred dollars more at one dealer than at another. But unless the consumer shops around, there is no way to determine which dealer will quote the lowest price, or what the lowest price is.

The reasons for such price dispersion are not difficult to find. Because of changes in market conditions (described in subsequent chapters), some firms find it profitable to change their prices. Since it takes time for other firms to find out about the price changes and to react to them, temporary price disparities occur. Also, some buyers (and sellers) are inexperienced and/or uninformed, with the result that they are willing to pay (or charge) prices that are out of line with current market conditions. Clearly, the greater the amount of instability in market conditions and the greater the amount of ignorance among buyers and sellers, the greater the amount of price dispersion.

How much search activity will the rational consumer carry out? In other words, how much shopping around will the consumer do? The answer depends on the cost of search, among other things. For example, if it is very costly to determine the price charged by a seller, the consumer will contact fewer sellers than if it is cheap to do so. The cost of search will be influenced by the geographical size of the market and whether the consumer must contact a seller in person to obtain a price quotation. Obviously, the cost of obtaining each quotation tends to be higher if the sellers are far apart and if the consumer must contact them personally.

The optimal amount of search activity also depends on the expected gains to the consumer from search. In general, one would expect that, the larger the fraction of the consumer's income that is spent on a particular commodity, the greater the prospective gains to the consumer from search, and thus the greater the amount of search carried out. Conse-

11. This discussion of index numbers has benefited from the lucid presentation in G. Stigler, *The Theory of Price,* pp. 74–78. Also, note that index numbers are often expressed as 100 times L or 100 times P, rather than L or P. Which is used should be clear from the context in which they appear.

For further discussion, see R. A. Pollak, "Welfare Evaluation and the Cost-of-Living Index in the Household Production Model," *American Economic Review,* June 1978; and W. E. Diewert, "The Economic Theory of Index Numbers: A Survey," Discussion paper 79–09, Department of Economics, University of British Columbia, March 1979.

quently, one might expect consumers to shop around more for major items like cars and houses than for minor items like candy and shoelaces.[12]

18. Summary

Another way of expressing the conditions for consumer equilibrium is as follows: The rational consumer will choose in equilibrium to allocate his or her income between good X and good Y in such a way that the marginal rate of substitution of good X for good Y equals the ratio of the price of good X to the price of good Y. If we hold commodity prices constant, each level of money income results in an equilibrium market basket for the consumer, and the curve that connects the points representing all of these equilibrium market baskets is called the income-consumption curve. The income-consumption curve can be used to derive the Engel curve, which is the relationship between the equilibrium amount of a good purchased by a consumer and the level of the consumer's money income. Engel curves play an important role in family expenditure studies.

Holding constant the consumer's money income as well as the prices of other goods, we can determine the relationship between the price of a good and the amount of this good that a consumer will consume. This relationship is called the consumer's individual demand curve for the good in question. The individual demand curve, one of the central concepts in the theory of consumer behavior, can be derived from the price-consumption curve, which includes all of the equilibrium market baskets corresponding to various prices of the good.

The location and shape of an individual demand curve will depend on the level of money income and the level at which the prices of other goods are held constant, as well as on the nature of the good and the tastes of the consumer. It is important to differentiate between shifts in a consumer's demand curve for a particular commodity and changes in the amount of the commodity that he or she consumes. Individual demand curves differ greatly in shape. In some cases, small changes in a good's price result in large changes in the amount of it that is consumed by the consumer; in other cases, large changes in a good's price result in small changes in the amount of it that is consumed by the consumer. To gauge the sensitivity or responsiveness of the quantity demanded to changes in price, economists use the price elasticity of demand, a measure we encountered in Chapter 2.

12. For a pioneering analysis of this topic, see G. Stigler, "The Economics of Information," *Journal of Political Economy,* June 1961. In recent years, a considerable amount of interesting and important work has been carried out in this area by G. Stigler, J. Marschak, J. Hirshleifer, L. Telser, and others. See A. M. Spence, *Market Signaling* (Cambridge, Mass.: Harvard University Press, 1974), for an analysis of the role of information in labor markets. Also, see the papers by J. Stiglitz, S. Salop, S. Grossman, J. Green, G. Butters, R. Wilson, and others in the "Symposium on Information," *Review of Economic Studies,* October 1977.

The demand for a commodity is price elastic if the elasticity is greater than one, price inelastic if the elasticity is less than one, and of unitary elasticity if the elasticity equals one. A price reduction increases the consumer's total expenditure on the commodity if the demand is price elastic, decreases the consumer's total expnditure on the commodity if the demand is price inelastic, and does not affect the consumer's total expenditure on the commodity if the demand is of unitary elasticity. Using this fact, the price-consumption curve can be used to indicate whether the demand for a commodity is price elastic, price inelastic, or of unitary elasticity. Of course, the price elasticity of demand varies in general from point to point on the individual demand curve.

The total effect of a price change on the quantity demanded can be divided into two parts: the substitution effect and the income effect. The substitution effect is the change in quantity demanded of a good resulting from a price change when the level of satisfaction, or real income, is held constant. The income effect shows the effect of the change in real income that is due to the price change. The substitution effect is always negative. The income effect is not predictable from the theory alone: Its sign is different for normal goods than for inferior goods.

An illustration of how this model of consumer behavior has been used to help solve practical problems is provided by the RAND Corporation's study of solutions to New York City's water crisis in the early fifties. An important question in this case was: How can one make estimates of the monetary value of the loss to consumers arising from the fact that, if metering were adopted, they would be led to consume less water? If certain restrictive assumptions are made, this question can be answered, at least approximately. Another type of problem where this sort of model has proved useful is in the construction of index numbers of the cost of living. The two basic types of indexes that can be used are the Laspeyres index and the Paasche index. Using these indexes, it is often possible to determine whether a consumer's welfare has increased or decreased during a particular period. Finally, we recognized that the consumer does not always have complete information concerning prices, and we discussed the determinants of the amount of search activity carried out by a consumer.

QUESTIONS AND PROBLEMS

1. Suppose that all consumers pay 15 cents for a telephone call and 25 cents for a newspaper (and that all consumers purchase some of both goods).
(a) If all consumers are maximizing utility, is it possible to determine each consumer's marginal rate of substitution of telephone calls for newspapers?
(b) Suppose that a local economist applies for a grant to estimate this marginal rate of substitution; his proposed procedure is to ask a sample of consumers. Can you suggest a simpler procedure? (c) Based on these facts alone, can you estimate this marginal rate of substitution? If so, what is it?

2. A representative of the dairy industry asserts that, as income increases, the proportion of income spent on food tends to rise. (a) Do you think this

proposition is true? Why or why not? (b) Indicate the general shape of the Engel curve for food, based on this proposition.

3. According to some observers, the typical Irish peasant in the nineteenth century was so poor he spent almost all his income for potatoes. When the price of potatoes fell, he could get the same amount of nutrition for a smaller expenditure on potatoes, so some of his income was diverted to vegetables and meat. Since the latter also provided calories, he could even reduce his consumption of potatoes under these circumstances. If this is true, were potatoes (a) a normal good? (b) an inferior good? (c) a good exhibiting Giffen's paradox?

4. Suppose that a family consumes a quite different set of commodities in a later period than in an earlier one, and that many of the goods it consumes in the later period were not available in the earlier one. What difficulties does this cause the economist who would like to construct a cost-of-living index?

5. Suppose that a 1 percent increase in the price of pork chops results in Ms. Smith's buying 3 percent fewer pork chops per week. What is the price elasticity of demand for pork chops on the part of Ms. Smith? Is her demand for pork chops price elastic or price inelastic? Will an increase in the price of pork chops result in an increase, or a decrease, in the total amount of money that she spends on pork chops?

6. Suppose that you were asked by the mayor of New York to write a report evaluating and criticizing the methods used in the RAND study of New York's water crisis. What points would you emphasize? On balance, would you recommend that he accept the RAND results? Why or why not?

7. Suppose Ms. Smith's utility function can be described by $U = Q_c Q_p$, where U is her utility, Q_c is the number of pounds of corn she consumes, and Q_p is the number of pounds of potatoes she consumes. Suppose that the total amount of money she can spend on these two commodities is $100 and the price of corn is $1 per pound. How many potatoes will she buy if potatoes are 50 cents per pound?

8. Explain in detail how price indexes have been, and are being, used to measure inflation and in collective bargaining. Give specific instances where they were employed, and indicate whether Laspeyres or Paasche indexes (or some other type) were used.

9. Calculate the Laspeyres and Paasche indexes for a family that consumes the following amounts of bread and clothing (and no other goods) in 1980 and 1985.

	1980	1985
Amount consumed of bread	100	140
Amount consumed of clothing	120	130
Price of bread (dollars)	0.30	0.50
Price of clothing (dollars)	30.00	40.00

10. In Example 4.1, how much is the consumer's surplus from each family's utilization of the lake if there is a charge of $8 for each trip to the lake?

SELECTED REFERENCES

HICKS, JOHN. *A Revision of Demand Theory.* Oxford: Oxford University Press, 1956.

HENDERSON, JAMES, AND RICHARD QUANDT. *Microeconomic Theory.* 3d ed. New York: McGraw-Hill, 1980.

MARSHALL, ALFRED. *Principles of Economics.* London: Macmillan, 1920.

STIGLER, GEORGE. *The Theory of Price,* New York: Macmillan, 1966.

SAMUELSON, PAUL. *Foundations of Economic Analysis.* Cambridge, Mass.: Harvard University Press, 1947. (Advanced)

5 Market Demand

1. Introduction

The previous chapter was concerned with the determinants of the quantity of a good demanded by an individual consumer. For many purposes, it is not so much the quantity demanded by a particular consumer that counts; instead it is the quantity demanded by all the consumers in a market. For example, the auto industry is much more concerned with the quantity of cars that will be demanded by the entire national market than with the quantity of cars that you or I will purchase next year. Economists, too, when confronted with many problems, are much more interested in the quantity of a good demanded in a market than in the quantity of a good demanded by a particular individual. For example, as we saw in Chapter 2, it is the market demand curve, not the individual demand curve, that (together with the market supply curve) determines the equilibrium price of a good.

In this chapter we are concerned with market demand. After showing how the market demand curve is related to the demand curves of the individual consumers in the market, we discuss some major determinants of the price elasticity of market demand. Then we take up the effects of two other factors, besides the good's price, on the quantity of the good that is demanded in the market—aggregate money income and the prices of other commodities. Next, we look at market demand from the seller's side of the market, placing emphasis on the concept of marginal revenue and the differences between the demand curve for the industry and the demand curve for the firm. Finally, we discuss the measurement of market demand curves, and we describe two cases where such measurements were used to help guide public and private decision-makers.

2. Derivation of the Market Demand Curve

In Section 4 of Chapter 4, we showed how an individual demand curve can be derived from a consumer's indifference map. This demand curve is of course the relationship between the quantity of the good demanded by the consumer (per unit of time) and the good's price, when the money income of the consumer and the prices of other goods are held constant. The shape and level of the individual demand curve obviously depend on the consumer's tastes, as reflected in his or her indifference map. They also depend on the level of the consumer's money income and the level of the prices of other goods.

The market demand curve for a commodity is simply the *horizontal* summation of the individual demand curves of all the consumers in the market. Put differently, to find the market quantity demanded at each price, we add up the individual quantities demanded at that price. For example, Table 5.1 shows the individual demand schedules[1] for four consumers. If these four consumers comprise the entire market, the market demand schedule is given in the last column of Table 5.1. Figure 5.1 shows the individual demand curves based on these same data, as well as the resulting market demand curve.

Table 5.1   Individual and market demand schedules

PRICE (CENTS PER UNIT OF THE COMMODITY)	QUANTITY DEMANDED (PER UNIT OF TIME)				QUANTITY DEMANDED IN MARKET (PER UNIT OF TIME)
	Individual A	Individual B	Individual C	Individual D	
	(units of the commodity)				
1	50	40	30	20	140
2	40	30	25	19	114
3	30	20	18	18	86
4	25	15	13	17	70
5	20	14	13	16	63
6	15	13	11	15	54
7	10	12	9	14	45
8	8	11	7	13	39
9	6	10	5	12	33
10	5	9	3	11	28

1. Recall from Chapter 2 that a demand schedule is a table showing the quantity demanded at various prices.

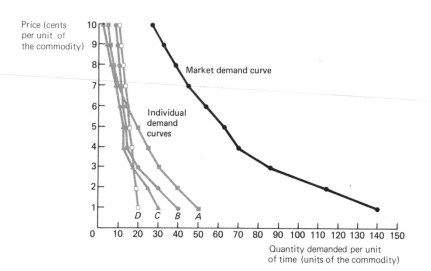

Figure 5.1   Individual and market demand curves

The market demand curve for a commodity is one of the most important concepts in microeconomics. The market demand curve shows how much of the commodity will be purchased (per unit of time) by the consumers in the market at each possible price (given that the level of money income of the consumers and the prices of other commodities are held constant). Information regarding the market demand curve is of the utmost importance to producers of the commodity. Obviously, they need to know how much can be sold at various prices. The market demand curve is also of great importance to economists because, as pointed out in Chapter 2, it plays an important role in determining the price of the commodity.

3. Graphical Measurement of the Price Elasticity of Demand

At each point on the market demand curve, the price elasticity of demand, defined as the percentage change in the quantity demanded resulting from a 1 percent change in price, gauges the sensitivity of the quantity demanded to changes in price. Chapter 2 pointed out the significance of the price elasticity of demand. In the next three sections of this chapter, we go further in discussing its measurement, effects, and determinants. To begin with, let's consider how it can be measured. In Chapter 2, we described how one can compute the price elasticity of demand from a table showing the quantity demanded at each of a number of prices. But suppose that we are given a demand curve, such as that shown in Figure 5.1. Is there any way to make a rough estimate of the price elasticity at a given point on this demand curve by means of visual inspection of the demand curve? The answer is yes; the following method is applicable to problems of this sort.

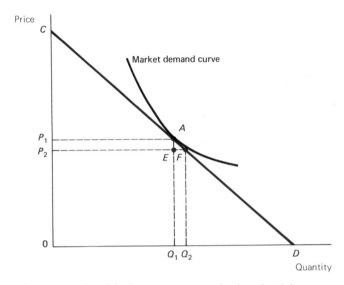

Figure 5.2   Graphical measurement of price elasticity

Suppose that the problem is to estimate the price elasticity of demand at point A on the demand curve in Figure 5.2. The first step is to construct the tangent to the demand curve at point A; this tangent is labeled CAD. If the price falls from OP_1 to OP_2, the resulting change in the quantity demanded can be approximated by Q_1Q_2. This approximation should be reasonably good if the change in price is small or if the demand curve is close to linear. Thus the elasticity at point A can be approximated by

$$\frac{Q_1Q_2}{OQ_1} \div \frac{P_2P_1}{OP_1} = \frac{Q_1Q_2}{P_2P_1} \cdot \frac{OP_1}{OQ_1}$$

It is obvious that $Q_1Q_2 \div P_2P_1 = EF \div EA$. Also, since AEF and AQ_1D are similar right triangles, $EF \div EA = Q_1D \div Q_1A = Q_1D \div OP_1$. Thus, the price elasticity of demand (denoted by η) equals:

$$\eta = \frac{Q_1D}{OP_1} \cdot \frac{OP_1}{OQ_1} = \frac{Q_1D}{OQ_1}$$

and since $Q_1D \div OQ_1 = AD \div CA$,

$$\eta = AD \div CA \tag{5.1}$$

This result, which is easy to interpret and apply, is exact if the demand curve is linear. If the price change is small, it is a good approximation even if the demand curve is not linear.

Let us apply this result to the case of a linear demand curve, such as BA in Figure 5.3. It is obvious from inspection of this figure that the price elasticity of demand exceeds one at prices exceeding OP, that the price elasticity of demand is less than one at prices under OP, and that there is

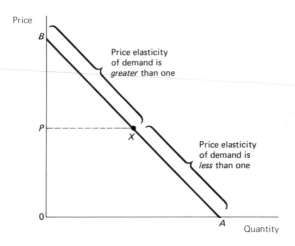

Figure 5.3   Graphical measurement of price elasticity:
Linear demand curve

unitary price elasticity of demand at a price of *OP*. To prove that there is
unitary elasticity of demand at a price of *OP*, we need only note that *XA*
= *BX*. To prove that the elasticity of demand is greater than one at
prices above *OP*, choose any price above *OP* and find the point corresponding to this price on the demand curve; it is clear that the distance
from this point to *A* is greater than the distance from this point to *B*. To
prove that the elasticity of demand is less than one at prices under *OP*,
choose any price below *OP* and find the point corresponding to this price
on the demand curve; it is clear that the distance from this point to *A* is
less than the distance from this point to *B*.

4. Price Elasticity and Total Money Expenditure

The price elasticity of demand is of interest to economists because it is a
useful way to describe an important aspect of the market for a commodity. Whether they know it or not, the producers of a commodity should
also be interested in the price elasticity of demand. Why? Because they
are interested in questions like: Will an increase in price result in an
increase in the total amount spent by consumers on the product? Or will
an increase in price result in a decrease in the total amount spent by
consumers on the product? The answers to these questions depend on
the price elasticity of demand, as we shall show in this section.

Suppose that the demand for the product is price elastic, that is, the
price elasticity of demand exceeds one. The total amount of money spent
by consumers on the product equals the quantity demanded times the
price per unit. In this situation, if the price is reduced, the percentage
increase in quantity demanded is greater than the percentage reduction
in price (since this follows from the definition of the price elasticity of

demand). It then follows that a price reduction must lead to an increase in the total amount spent by consumers on the commodity.

The reasoning used here is, of course, just the same as that used in Section 7 of Chapter 4 where we showed that the same kind of result holds at the level of the individual consumer. If we apply this reasoning to other possible cases as well, we find that, if the demand is price elastic, a price increase leads to a reduction in the amount of money spent on the commodity. If the demand is price inelastic, a price decrease leads to a reduction in the total amount spent on the commodity, and a price increase leads to an increase in the amount spent on the commodity. If the demand is of unitary elasticity, an increase or decrease in price has no effect on the amount spent on the commodity.

These results can be illustrated with the linear demand curve in Figure 5.3. As we move down the demand curve from B to X, the elasticity of demand gets smaller, but it always exceeds one. Thus the total amount spent on the good increases continually as we move from B to X. At point X, since there is unitary elasticity, there is no change in the total amount spent on the good. Moving from X to A, the elasticity of demand is always less than one. Thus the total amount spent on the good decreases continually as we move from X to A.

Another interesting case is shown in Figure 5.4. The demand curve shown there is a rectangular hyperbola, which means that

$$q = \frac{a}{p} \qquad\qquad 5.2$$

where q is the quantity demanded of the good, p is its price, and a is some constant. It can be shown that this kind of demand curve is of unitary elasticity at all points. Thus changes in price have no effect on the total

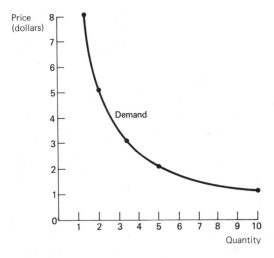

Figure 5.4 Demand curve with unitary elasticity at all points

amount spent on the product. It is evident from Equation 5.2 that, regardless of the price, the total amount spent on the product will be a ($10 in Figure 5.4).

5. Determinants of the Price Elasticity of Demand

In previous sections we have stressed the importance of the price elasticity of demand, but nothing has been said about the determinants of the price elasticity of demand. What determines whether the demand for a commodity is price elastic or price inelastic in a certain price range? Why does the price elasticity of demand for one commodity equal 3.0 and the price elasticity of demand for another commodity equal 1.5? This is a very important question, and the one to which we turn our attention in this section.

First, and foremost, the price elasticity of demand for a commodity depends on the number and closeness of the substitutes that are available. If a commodity has many close substitutes, its demand is likely to be price elastic. If increases occur in the price of the product, a large proportion of its buyers will turn to the close substitutes that are available; if decreases occur in its price, a great many buyers of substitutes will switch to this product.

Of course, the extent to which a commodity has close substitutes depends on how narrowly it is defined. In general, one would expect that, as the definition of the product becomes narrower and more specific, the product has more close substitutes and its demand becomes more price elastic. Thus the demand for a particular brand of cigarettes is likely to be more price elastic than the overall demand for cigarettes and the demand for cigarettes is likely to be more price elastic than the demand for tobacco products as a whole. If a commodity is defined so that it has perfect substitutes, its price elasticity of demand is infinite. Thus, if the cotton produced by Farmer Jones is exactly the same as the cotton produced by other farmers and if he increases his price slightly (to a point above the market level), his sales would be reduced to nothing.

Second, it is sometimes asserted that the price elasticity of demand for a commodity is likely to depend on the importance of the commodity in consumers' budgets. For example, the demand for commodities like thumbtacks, pepper, and salt may be quite inelastic. The typical consumer spends only a very small fraction of his income on such goods. On the other hand, for commodities that bulk larger in the typical consumer's budget, like major appliances, the elasticity of demand may tend to be higher. Consumers may be more conscious of, and influenced by, price changes in the case of goods that require larger outlays. However, although a tendency of this sort is sometimes hypothesized, there is no guarantee that it exists. As some economists have pointed out, the link between a commodity's price elasticity of demand and its importance in consumer's budgets may in fact be much weaker than is implied by this hypothesis.

Third, the price elasticity of demand for a commodity is likely to depend on the length of the period to which the demand curve pertains. (Every market demand curve—like every individual demand curve—pertains, of course, to a certain time interval.) In general, demand is likely to be more elastic, or less inelastic, over a long period of time than over a short period of time. The longer the period of time, the easier it is for consumers and business firms to substitute one good for another. If, for example, the price of natural gas should decline relative to other fuels, the consumption of natural gas in the week after the price decline would probably increase very little. But over a period of several years, people would have an opportunity to take account of the price decline in choosing the type of fuel to be used in new houses and renovated old houses. In the longer period of several years, the price decline would have a greater effect on the consumption of natural gas than in the shorter period of one week.

6. The Income Elasticity of Demand

Up to this point, we have been concerned solely with the effect of price on the quantity of the commodity demanded in the market. Yet price is not the only factor that influences the quantity demanded in the market. Another important factor is the level of money income among the consumers in the market. For example, if housewives have plenty of money to spend, the quantity demanded of beef is likely to be greater than if they are poverty-stricken. Or if incomes in a particular community are high, the quantity demanded of caviar is likely to be greater than if incomes are low.

For an individual consumer, we saw in Chapter 4 that the relationship between money income (per period of time) and the amount consumed of a particular commodity (per period of time) can be represented by an Engel curve. Recall that this curve is based on the condition that the prices of all commodities remain constant. At any point on the Engel curve, one can characterize the sensitivity of the amount consumed to changes in the consumer's money income by the *income elasticity of demand,* which is defined as

$$\eta_I = \frac{\Delta Q}{Q} \div \frac{\Delta I}{I} \qquad\qquad 5.3$$

where ΔQ is the change in quantity consumed that results from a small change in the consumer's money income ΔI, Q is the original quantity consumed, and I is the original money income of the consumer.[2]

2. More precisely, the income elasticity of demand is

$$\frac{dQ}{dI} \div \frac{Q}{I}$$

The definition in the text is the same except that finite differences are substituted for derivatives.

Some goods have positive income elasticities, indicating that increases in the consumer's money income result in increases in the amount of the good consumed. For example, one would generally expect steak and caviar to have positive income elasticities. Other goods have negative income elasticities, indicating that increases in the consumer's money income result in decreases in the amount of the good consumed. For example, margarine and poor grades of vegetables and other types of food might have negative income elasticities.[3] However, one must be careful to point out that the income elasticity of demand for a good is likely to vary considerably, depending on the level of the consumer's money income. Thus, in some ranges of income, the income elasticity may be positive; in other ranges of income, it may be negative.

The concept of income elasticity of demand can be applied to an entire market as well as to a single consumer, the only change in Equation 5.3 being that we must interpret Q as the total quantity demanded in the market, I as the aggregate money income of all consumers in the market, and ΔQ and ΔI as the changes in total quantity demanded and in aggregate money income. As in the case of the individual consumer, it is assumed that the prices of all commodities are held constant. Figure 5.5 shows a variety of possible relationships between the total quantity demanded in the market and the aggregate money income of the consumers. Curve A shows a case in which the income elasticity is greater than one, which means that a 1 percent increase in money income results in more than a 1 percent increase in the total quantity demanded. Curve B shows a case in which the income elasticity is less than one, which means that a 1 percent increase in money income results in less than a 1 percent increase in the total quantity demanded. Case C shows a case in which the income elasticity is negative, indicating that increases in aggregate money income result in decreases in the total quantity demanded.[4]

There are, of course, enormous differences among goods with respect to their income elasticity of demand. No refined statistical surveys are needed to tell us that the income elasticity of demand for high-quality food and clothes is generally higher than the income elasticity of demand for salt and Kleenex. Luxury items are generally assumed to have high income elasticities of demand. Indeed, one way to define luxuries and necessities is to say that luxuries are goods with high income elasticities of demand, and necessities are goods with low income elasticities of demand.

An empirical law of consumption, *Engel's law*, was developed in the nineteenth century by Ernst Engel (whose work was noted in Chapter 4). Based on data concerning the budgets and expenditures of a large

---

3. The similarity between goods with a negative income elasticity and inferior goods should be obvious.

4. Of course, the quantity demanded may be influenced by the distribution of money income among consumers as well as the aggregate money income. We assume that the income distribution is held constant.

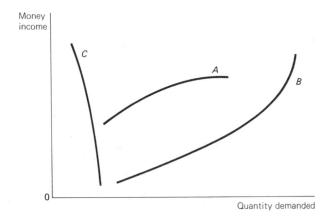

Figure 5.5   Various types of relationships between quantity
demanded and aggregate income

number of families, Engel found that the income elasticity of demand for
food was quite low. He concluded from this result that the proportion of
its income spent on food by a nation (or a family) was a good index of its
welfare, with the better-off nations spending a smaller proportion on
food than the poorer ones. This generalization is crude, but still service-
able within limits.[5]

7. Cross Elasticities of Demand

In previous sections we have discussed the effects of two factors—the
price of the commodity and the level of aggregate money income—on the
quantity of the commodity demanded in the market. These two factors
are not the only important ones; another important factor is the price of
other commodities. Holding constant the commodity's own price (as well
as the level of money incomes) and allowing the price of another commodity to vary, there may be important effects on the quantity demanded in the market for the commodity in question. By observing these
effects, we can classify pairs of commodities as *substitutes* or *complements,* and we can measure how close the relationship (either substitute
or complementary) is.

Consider two commodities, good X and good Y. Suppose that good
Y's price goes up. What is the effect on the quantity of good X that is
bought (per unit of time)? The *cross elasticity of demand* is defined as

$$\eta_{xy} = \frac{\Delta Q_x}{Q_x} \div \frac{\Delta P_y}{P_y}$$
    5.4

5. For an excellent study of Engel's law, see H. Houthakker, "An International Comparison of Household Expenditures Patterns," *Econometrica,* October 1957.

Example 5.1 Electricity Demand in the United States

D. Chapman, T. Tyrell, and T. Mount estimated that the long-run price elasticity of demand for electricity by all U.S. residential consumers is 1.2, that the income elasticity of demand for electricity by such consumers is 0.2, and that the cross elasticity of demand for electricity with respect to the price of natural gas is 0.2. (a) If the price of electricity is expected to rise by 1 percent in the long run, by how much would the price of natural gas have to change to offset the effect of this increase in electricity's price on the quantity of electricity consumed? (b) Among residential consumers in a Chicago suburb, holding other factors constant, there was the following relationship between their aggregate money income and the amount of electricity they consumed:

Aggregate income (millions of dollars)	Quantity of electricity consumed
100	300
110	303
121	306

Is this evidence consistent with the results presented by Chapman, Tyrell, and Mount? If not, what factors might account for the discrepancy? (c) Does your answer to question (b) depend on the units in which the quantity of electricity consumed is measured in the table above? (d) Would you expect the income elasticity of demand and the cross elasticity of demand to be higher or lower in the short run than in the long run? Why?

Solution

(a) A 1 percent increase in the price of electricity would cut electricity consumption by 1.2 percent, because the price elasticity of demand is 1.2. A 6 percent increase in the price of natural gas would raise electricity consumption by about 1.2 percent, because the cross elasticity of demand is 0.2. Thus, if the price of natural gas were to increase by about 6 percent, this would offset the effect of the increase in electricity's price. (b) Based on the data in the table given above, a 10 percent increase in income seems to result in about a 1 percent increase in electricity consumption. Thus the income elasticity seems to be about 0.1, not 0.2, as reported by Chapman, Tyrell, and Mount. This discrepancy could be due to the fact that the inhabitants of this suburb regard electricity to be more of a necessity than do all Americans. (c) No. Regardless of what the units may be, the income elasticity is the same—namely, about 0.1, as pointed out in the answer to question (b). (d) Both would be expected to be lower in the short run because consumers have less time to adapt to changes in income or price. In fact, Chapman, Tyrell, and Mount found both to be about 0.02 in the short run.[*]

[*] For further discussion, see L. Taylor, "The Demand for Electricity: A Survey," *Bell Journal of Economics,* Spring 1975; R. Pindyck, "Interfuel Competition and the Industrial Demand for Energy," *Review of Economics and Statistics,* May 1979; and M. Murray, R. Spann, L. Pulley, and E. Beauvais, "The Demand for Electricity in Virginia," *Review of Economics and Statistics,* November 1978.

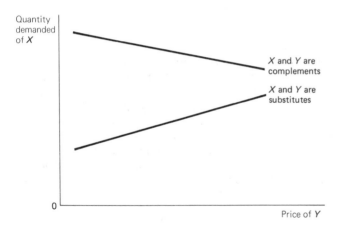

Figure 5.6   Relationship between consumption of good X and price
of good Y, given that they are substitutes or complements

where ΔP_y is the change in the price of good Y, P_y is the original price of
good Y, ΔQ_x is the resulting change in the quantity demanded of good X,
and Q_x is the original quantity demanded of good X. Thus the cross
elasticity of demand is the relative change in the quantity of good X
resulting from a 1 percent change in the price of good Y.[6]

Whether goods X and Y are classified as substitutes or complements
depends on whether the cross elasticity of demand is positive or negative.
For example, an increase in the price of lamb, when the price of pork
remains constant, will tend to increase the quantity of pork demanded;
thus η_{xy} is positive, and lamb and pork are classified as substitutes. On
the other hand, an increase in the price of fishing licenses may tend to
decrease the purchase of fishing poles, when the price of fishing poles
remains constant; thus η_{xy} is negative, and fishing licenses and fishing
poles are classified as complements. Figure 5.6 shows the relationship
between the consumption of good X and the price of good Y, given that
they are substitutes or complements.

The cross elasticity of demand looks at the change in quantity demanded that results from a change in price *without* compensating for the
change in the level of real income. This is the only feasible procedure
because we seldom have data concerning the indifference maps of individual consumers. Moreover, we are generally interested in the relation-

6. More precisely the cross elasticity of demand is

$$\frac{dQ_x}{dP_y} \div \frac{Q_x}{P_y}$$

The definition in the text is the same except that finite differences are substituted
for derivatives.

In subsequent discussions of marginal revenue, marginal product, marginal
cost, and other such terms, we shall use finite differences and not bother to repeat
each time the alternate definition based on the use of derivatives (since the alternative definition is obvious in each case).

ship between commodities in the whole market rather than the relationship for a particular consumer.[7]

Finally, one other point should be noted. Whether goods X and Y are substitutes or complements can be determined by looking at the relative change in the quantity demanded of good X divided by the relative change in the price of good Y, that is, η_{xy}. It can also be determined by looking at the relative change in the quantity demanded of good Y divided by the relative change in the price of good X, η_{yx}. However, it should not be expected that the two elasticities will have the same numerical value. For example, goods X and Y may be substitutes, but the consumption of good X may be more sensitive to changes in the price of good Y than the consumption of good Y is to changes in the price of good X.

8. The Sellers' Side of the Market and Marginal Revenue

Up to this point, we have looked at the subject of demand chiefly from the point of view of consumers. But, as we have already noted, the expenditures of the consumers are the receipts of the sellers. In the next three sections, we look at demand from the other side of the market—the seller's side. We begin by defining marginal revenue. Then, in the following section, we show how marginal revenue can be estimated from the demand curve. Next, in Section 10, we discuss the differences between the demand curve for the industry and the demand curve for the firm. Finally, in Section 11, we discuss the relationship between marginal revenue and the price elasticity of demand. These results are of great importance and they form a bridge to the theory of the firm, which is presented in succeeding chapters.

The sellers of a commodity are interested, of course, in the total amount of money spent by consumers on the commodity. This amount is called *total revenue* by economists. From the market demand curve, one can easily determine the total revenue of the sellers at each price, since total revenue is, by definition, price times quantity. Thus, in Table 5.2, total revenue is $36 at a price of $9. The value of total revenue at various prices is shown in the third column of Table 5.2.

Economists and firms are also concerned with *marginal revenue,* which is defined as the addition to total revenue attributable to the addition of one unit to sales. Thus, if $R(q)$ is total revenue when q units are sold and $R(q - 1)$ is total revenue when $(q - 1)$ units are sold, the marginal revenue between q units and $(q - 1)$ units is $R(q) - R(q - 1)$. This is illustrated in Table 5.2. For example, when only one unit is sold, it is possible to charge a price of $12 and the total revenue is $12. The

---

7. For a single individual, goods can be classified as substitutes or complements more accurately on the basis of his or her utility function. Good Y is a substitute (complement) for good X if the marginal rate of substitution of good Y for money is reduced (increased) when good X is substituted for money in such a way as to leave the consumer no better or worse off than before. See J. Hicks, *Value and Capital* (New York: Oxford University Press, 1946), p. 44.

Table 5.2 Quantity demanded, total revenue, and marginal revenue

Price (dollars per unit of the commodity)	Quantity demanded (units of the commodity)	Total revenue (dollars)	Marginal revenue (dollars per unit of the commodity)
13	0	0	
			12
12	1	12	
			10
11	2	22	
			8
10	3	30	
			6
9	4	36	
			4
8	5	40	
			2
7	6	42	
			0
6	7	42	
			-2
5	8	40	
			-4
4	9	36	
			-6
3	10	30	

marginal revenue between one unit of output and zero units of output is total revenue at one unit of output minus total revenue at zero units of output. Since the latter is zero, the marginal revenue between one unit of output and zero units of output is $12.

It is evident from Table 5.2 that total revenue from a given number of units of output—say n units—is equal to the sum of marginal revenue between 0 and 1 units of output, marginal revenue between 1 and 2 units of output, marginal revenue between 2 and 3 units of output, and so on up to marginal revenue between $(n - 1)$ and n units of output. For example, total revenue for 2 units of output is $22, which equals the sum of marginal revenue between 0 and 1 units of output ($12) and marginal revenue between 1 and 2 units of output ($10). It is easy to prove that this will always be true. By the definition of marginal revenue, the sum of the marginal revenue between 0 and 1 units of output, 1 and 2 units of output, and so on up to $(n - 1)$ and n units of output is

$$[R(1) - R(0)] + [R(2) - R(1)]$$
$$+ [R(3) - R(2)] + \cdots + [R(n) - R(n - 1)].$$

Since $R(1)$, $R(2)$, $\cdots$, $R(n - 1)$ appear with both positive and negative signs, they cancel out; and since $R(0) = 0$, this sum must equal $R(n)$.

The *marginal revenue curve* shows marginal revenue at various levels of output of a commodity. For example, panel A of Figure 5.7 shows the marginal revenue curve for the situation in Table 5.2. Note that the marginal revenue curve lies above zero when total revenue is increasing, that it lies below zero when total revenue is decreasing, and that it equals zero when total revenue is at a maximum. For example, in panel A of Figure 5.7, the marginal revenue curve is zero between 6 and 7 units of output, and inspection of Table 5.2 confirms that they are the output levels where total revenue is maximized. Also, marginal revenue is shown

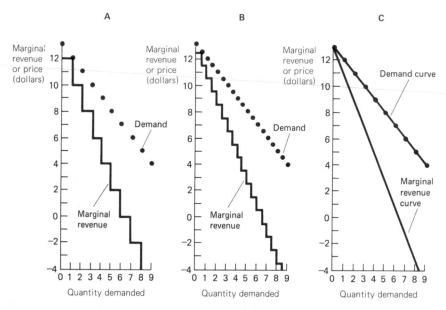

Figure 5.7   Demand curve and marginal revenue curve

to be positive for output levels of less than 6 units and negative for output levels of greater than 7 units; inspection of Table 5.2 confirms that total revenue is increasing up to 6 units of output and is decreasing beyond 7 units of output.

The marginal revenue curve consists of a number of "steps" when the demand curve is defined for only a relatively few points. For example, this is the case in panel A of Figure 5.7. However, as the demand curve is defined for more and more points, the "teeth" of the saw-toothed marginal revenue curve become finer and finer. For example, they are finer in panel B than in panel A. Finally, when the demand curve is continuous, as in panel C, the marginal revenue curve becomes continuous, too.

9. Determination of the Marginal Revenue Curve

Presented with a table like Table 5.2, it is no problem to calculate marginal revenue. But often one is given a demand curve, like DD' in Figure 5.8. How does one go about determining the marginal revenue curve in this case? To begin with, we assume that the demand curve is linear. The results in panel C of Figure 5.7 suggest quite correctly that, if the demand curve is a straight line, the marginal revenue curve will be a straight line, too. Also, they suggest that the marginal revenue curve and the demand curve start out at the same point on the vertical axis.[8] Since the marginal

8. Of course, this does not prove that the marginal revenue curve will have these characteristics. To prove that this is the case, let the demand curve be
$$P = a - bQ$$

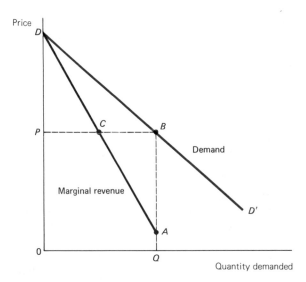

Figure 5.8   Graphical estimation of the marginal revenue curve:
The case in which the demand curve is linear

revenue curve is a straight line that intersects the vertical axis at D, we
need to determine only one additional point on this curve to identify the
entire curve, since two points determine a straight line.

Consider any output level, OQ, in Figure 5.8. What is the marginal
revenue at this point? The total revenue at this point is OP times OQ,
which is the area of the quadrangle $OPBQ$. The total revenue at this
point must also equal the sum of all the marginal revenues up to this
point, which is the area $ODAQ$. Thus the unknown A (which is what we
are trying to determine) must be such that the area of $OPBQ$ equals the
area of $ODAQ$. These two areas have in common the area $OPCAQ$.
Deducting this common area, it follows that A must be such that the
triangle CBA equals the area of the triangle DPC. But these two triangles are similar, since angle PCD equals angle BCA, and angle DPC
equals angle CBA (both being $90°$). Thus, if they have the same area,
these triangles must be congruent, and PD must equal AB. Consequently, one can find the unknown point A on the marginal revenue
curve by dropping a perpendicular from B to the x axis and a perpendic-

---

Then the total revenue curve is
$$R = PQ = aQ - bQ^2$$
and the marginal revenue curve is
$$\frac{dR}{dQ} = \frac{d(PQ)}{dQ} = a - 2bQ$$

Thus the marginal revenue curve is a straight line and it has the same intercept on
the y axis (that is, a) as the demand curve. (P is price, and Q is quantity demanded.)

ular from B to the y axis, and by marking off a distance of PD from B on the perpendicular QB. Given the determination of A, the entire marginal revenue curve can be constructed by drawing a straight line through D and A.

Another method that is sometimes used is as follows: First, drop a perpendicular from B to the x axis and from B to the y axis. Second, find the midpoint of the perpendicular to the y axis. Call this midpoint C. (In fact, in Figure 5.8, it will accord with C.) Finally, draw a line through D and C. This line is also the marginal revenue curve. Naturally, this method amounts to the same thing as the method described in the previous paragraph, and the results are precisely the same.[9]

Thus far, we have assumed that the demand curve is linear. Fortunately, our procedure needs to be changed only slightly even if the demand curve is not linear. To illustrate, consider the demand curve shown in Figure 5.9. To derive the marginal revenue curve, we begin by finding the marginal revenue of quantity OQ_1. First, drop perpendiculars from B_1 to both axes. Second, form the tangent to the demand curve at B_1 and extend it to intersect the price axis at G_1. Third, to find marginal revenue at OQ_1, deduct an amount equal to P_1G_1 from Q_1B_1, the result being Q_1A_1 which indicates that point A_1 is on the marginal revenue curve. Having found the point on the marginal revenue curve at quantity OQ_1.

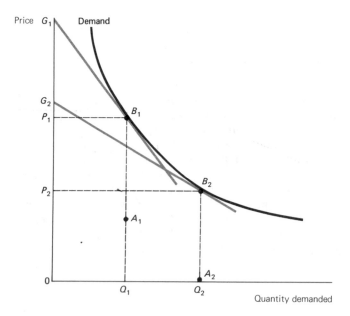

Figure 5.9   Graphical estimation of the marginal revenue curve: The case in which the demand curve is nonlinear

9. The results of footnote 8 show that this is the case.

we can do the same for OQ_2 (the resulting point on the marginal revenue curve is A_2), and so forth. Connecting the resulting points, we can approximate the true marginal revenue curve.

10. Industry and Firm Demand Curves

Throughout this chapter we have been concerned with the market demand curve for a commodity. It is important to distinguish between the market demand curve for a commodity and the market demand curve for the output of a single firm producing the commodity. Of course, if only one firm produces the commodity (in which case the industry in question is a *monopoly*) there is no difference between these demand curves. But if there is more than one firm producing the commodity, as is usually the case, the demand curve for the output of each firm will generally be quite different from the demand curve for the commodity. In particular, the firm's demand curve will generally be more price elastic than that facing the industry as a whole, since the products of other firms are close substitutes for the products of any one firm.

Suppose that there are a great many sellers of the product in question, say 50,000 sellers of the same size, and that the conditions in the industry are close to *perfectly competitive*. (In perfect competition, the number of firms is large and their products are homogeneous, and for simplicity it is assumed that the firms have full knowledge of the market. Much more will be said about perfect competition in subsequent chapters.) In a case of this sort, if any one firm were to triple its output and sales, the total industry output would increase by only .004 percent. Since this change in total output is too small to have any noticeable effect on the price of the commodity, each seller can act as if variations in its own output will have no real effect on market price. Put differently, it appears to each firm that it can sell all it wants—within the range that is within its capabilities—without influencing the price. Thus the demand curve facing the individual firm in perfect competition is *horizontal*.

The firm in a perfectly competitive market can increase its sales rate without shading its price to get the extra business. Its demand curve, shown in Figure 5.10, is infinitely elastic: A very small decrease in price would result in an indefinitely large increase in the quantity it could sell, and a very small increase in price would result in its selling nothing. Moreover, since price remains constant, each additional unit sold increases total revenue by the amount of the price, the consequence being that price and marginal revenue are always equal. Thus, in the case of perfect competition, the demand curve facing a particular firm and the marginal revenue curve facing that firm are one and the same.

In a situation where the industry is not perfectly competitive, the demand curve for the output of a particular firm will not be horizontal, but it is likely to be more elastic than the demand curve for the commodity. If competition is not perfect, marginal revenue will not equal price, as it does in perfect competition. Instead, it will be less than price

Figure 5.10   Demand curve for the output of a firm in a perfectly
competitive industry

because demand is less than infinitely elastic.[10] (As we shall see in the
next section, there is a simple relationship between marginal revenue and
the price elasticity of demand.)

11. Marginal Revenue and the Elasticity of Demand

Before turning to the measurement of market demand curves, one additional theoretical result should be presented, since it is of widespread use.
This result states that there is the following relationship between the
elasticity of demand at a certain output level and marginal revenue at
that output level

$$MR = P\left[1 - \frac{1}{\eta}\right]$$

5.5

where MR is marginal revenue, P is price, and η is the price elasticity of
demand. To prove that this is true, consider Figure 5.11. For simplicity,
we assume that the demand curve, DD', is linear, but the result holds for
any shape of demand curve. Consider point B on DD'. Using the method
described in Section 9, we find that QA is the marginal revenue at B.
Using the method described in Section 3, the elasticity of demand at B is
$BD' \div DB$. Since $PD \div PB = QB \div QD'$ and $AB = PD$, we know that

$$AB = PB\left[\frac{QB}{QD'}\right] = QB\left[\frac{PB}{QD'}\right]$$

10. Let p be price and q be quantity demanded. If the demand curve is $p = f(q)$,
marginal revenue is

$$\frac{d(pq)}{dq} = f(q) + q\frac{df(q)}{dq} = p + q\frac{dp}{dq}$$

Thus marginal revenue must be less than price as long as $dp/dq < 0$.

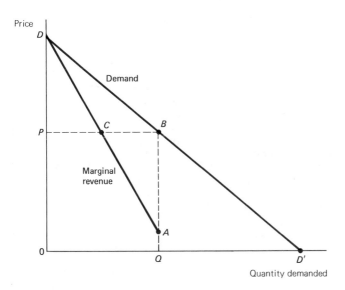

Figure 5.11   Relationship between marginal revenue and price elasticity of demand

Since $QA = QB - AB,$

$$QA = QB - QB\left[\frac{PB}{QD'}\right]$$

$$= QB\left[1 - \frac{PB}{QD'}\right]$$

Since QA is marginal revenue, QB is price, and $PB \div QD' = OQ \div QD' = DB \div BD' = 1/\eta$, Equation 5.5 follows.[11]

12. Measurement of Demand Curves

The market demand curve plays a very important role in microeconomics, and there have been literally hundreds of published studies—and many more unpublished ones—that attempt to measure the market de-

11. Of course, it is easy to derive the result of this section from the result of footnote 10, which is

$$MR = p + q\frac{dp}{dq}$$

It follows from this equation that

$$MR = p\left(1 + \frac{q}{p}\frac{dp}{dq}\right)$$

$$= p\left(1 - \frac{1}{\eta}\right)$$

Example 5.2   The Demand for Steel

The steel industry has long maintained that the demand for steel is price inelastic. According to a well-known study by T. Yntema, the price elasticity of demand for steel is no more than 0.4. (a) Are there any major substitutes for steel? If so, what are some of them? (b) Some years ago the chief executive officer of Bethelehem Steel testified before a Senate committee that the price elasticity of demand for steel was much less than 1. If so, can we deduce that the demand for Bethlehem's steel is price inelastic? (c) If the demand for Bethlehem's steel is inelastic at the price it is charging, is it maximizing its profits? (d) Is the cross elasticity of demand between Bethlehem's steel and imported Japanese steel positive or negative? Why?

Solution

(a) There are a considerable number of important substitutes, notably plastics, aluminum, and concrete. For example, buildings and bridges formerly requiring structural steel can now use prestressed concrete. (b) No, because the demand curve for the output of a single firm (Bethlehem) is not the same as the demand curve for the output of the steel industry as a whole. In general, we would expect the demand curve for the output of a single firm to be more price elastic than the industry's demand curve, because the output of other firms in the industry can be substituted for the output of the firm in question. (c) If the demand for a firm's product is inelastic, this means that its price elasticity of demand, η, is less than one. Based on Equation 5.5, it follows that, if η is less than one, the firm's marginal revenue must be *negative*. Since marginal revenue is the change in total revenue attributable to the increase of one unit to sales, it follows that a *reduction* in the amount produced and sold by the firm would *increase* total revenue (because price would be raised enough to more than offset the smaller number of units sold). In a case of this sort, the firm could increase its profit by reducing its output (and raising its price). Why? Because profit equals total revenue minus total cost, and a reduction in output would increase total revenue and reduce total cost (since it would cost less to produce fewer units). Consequently, a reduction in output would increase profit, which means that the firm is not currently maximizing its profit. (d) The cross elasticity of demand is positive because Bethlehem's steel and imported Japanese steel are substitutes.*

* For further discussion, see *Administered Prices: Steel*, Committee on the Judiciary, U.S. Senate, 85th Congress, 2d Session (Washington, D.C.: U.S Government Printing Office).

mand curves for particular commodities. This section describes briefly various ways in which such empirical studies have been carried out. The following two sections provide examples of the ways in which the results of such studies have been used to help solve important practical problems.

One technique that is frequently used to estimate the demand curve for a particular commodity is the direct market experiment. The idea is to vary the price of the product while attempting to keep other market conditions fairly stable (or to take changes in other market conditions into account). For example, the Parker Pen Company conducted an experiment some years ago to determine the price elasticity of demand for Quink. They raised the price from 15 cents to 25 cents in four cities and found that demand was quite inelastic. Also, in some stores, the old package selling at 15 cents was put next to a package marked "New Quink, 25 cents"; the results also indicated that demand was quite inelastic. Attempts were also made to estimate the cross elasticity of demand with other brands.

Another technique that is sometimes employed is to interview consumers and administer questionnaires concerning their buying habits, motives, and intentions. Unfortunately, the direct approach of simply asking people how much they would buy of a particular commodity at particular prices does not seem to work very well in most cases. The snap judgments of consumers in response to such a hypothetical question do not seem to be very accurate. However, more subtle approaches can be of value. For example, interviews indicated that most buyers of a certain baby food selected it on their doctor's recommendation, and that most of them knew very little about prices or substitutes. This information, together with other data, led the manufacturer to the conclusion that the price elasticity of demand was quite low.[12]

Still another very popular technique is the use of statistical methods to extract information from data regarding sales, prices, incomes, and other variables in the past. Basically, what is involved is a comparison of various points in time or various sectors of the market; the point of this comparison is to see what effect the observed variation in price, income, and other relevant variables, had on the quantity demanded. For example, to estimate the price elasticity of demand, one might plot the quantity demanded in 1982 versus the 1982 price, the quantity demanded in 1981 versus the 1981 price, and so on. If the results were as shown by the points in Figure 5.12, one might construct a curve like DD' as an estimate of the demand curve.

Although this example provides some understanding of the type of analysis that is involved, it makes the naïve assumption that the demand curve has remained constant over the period. Suppose that the 1982 demand curve was $D_1D'_1$, that the 1981 demand curve was $D_2D'_2$, and so on. Then the estimated demand curve DD' is a hybrid that resembles none of the true demand curves. Sophisticated econometric techniques have been developed for dealing with this so-called *identification problem*. Econometric techniques have also been devised to measure at the same time the effect of money income and the prices of other commodities on the quantity demanded; thus estimates can be made of the relationship between a commodity's price and the quantity demanded, when

12. J. Dean "Estimating the Price Elasticity of Demand," in E. Mansfield, *Managerial Economics and Operations Research,* 4th ed. (New York: Norton, 1980).

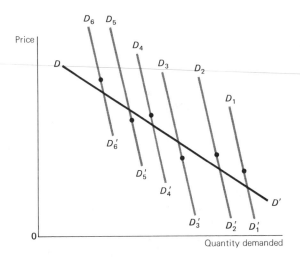

Figure 5.12 Illustration of identification problem

these other factors are held constant. However, even an elementary description of these econometric techniques lies outside the scope of this book.[13]

Each of the approaches to the measurement of demand curves has its disadvantages. Direct experimentation can be expensive or risky because customers may be lost and profits cut by the experiment. Also, since they are seldom really controlled experiments and since they are often of relatively brief duration and the number of observations is small, experiments often cannot produce all of the information that is needed. Interviews and questionnaires suffer from a great many disadvantages, some of which are noted above. So do consumer clinics where consumers are placed in simulated market conditions and changes in their behavior are observed as the conditions of the experiment are changed; consumer clinics are expensive and they cannot avoid the distortion due to the consumers' realizing that they are in an experimental situation.[14]

The difficulties involved in the application of statistical and econometric techniques are also very considerable. Unreliable and biased results can be obtained if important variables are unwittingly (or wittingly) omitted from the analysis. If some of the variables influencing the quantity demanded are highly correlated among themselves, it may not be possible to obtain reliable estimates of the separate effects of each of them. Also, the demand function is likely to be only one of a number of equations that connect the relevant variables, and it may be difficult to unscramble these equations adequately from the available statistics.

There are no easy remedies for these problems. Nevertheless, these

13. For a good description of these techniques, see L. Klein, *An Introduction to Econometrics* (Englewood Cliffs, N.J.: Prentice-Hall, 1962).

14. W. Baumol, "The Empirical Determination of Demand Relationships," reprinted in E Mansfield, *Microeconomics: Selected Readings,* 4th ed. (New York: Norton, 1982).

Table 5.3 Estimated price elasticity of demand for selected commodities, United States

Commodity	Price elasticity
Electricity	1.20
Beef	0.92
Women's hats	3.00
Sugar	0.31
Corn	0.49
Cotton	0.12
Wheat	0.08
Potatoes	0.31
Oats	0.56
Barley	0.39
Buckwheat	0.99
Haddock	2.20
Tires	1.20
Movies	3.70

SOURCE H. Schultz, *Theory and Measurement of Demand*, (Chicago: University of Chicago Press, 1938); M. Spencer and L. Siegelman, *Managerial Economics* (Homewood, Ill.: Irwin, 1959); F. Bell, "The Pope and the Price of Fish," *American Economic Review*, December 1968; L. Taylor, "The Demand for Electricity: A Survey," *Bell Journal of Economics*, Spring 1975; and H. Houthakker and L. Taylor, *Consumer Demand in the United States* (Cambridge, Mass.: Harvard, 1970).

problems, although sometimes formidable, are not insolvable. Many interesting and important studies have been made of the demand curves for particular commodities. And many interesting estimates have been made of the price elasticity, the income elasticity, and the cross elasticity of demand of various commodities. For example, Table 5.3 shows the results of Henry Schultz's pioneering study of the price elasticity of various farm products, as well as selected results from other studies. Table 5.4 shows various cross elasticities of demand estimated by Her-

Table 5.4 Estimated cross elasticities of demand for selected commodities

Commodity	Cross elasticity with respect to price of:	Cross elasticity
Beef	Pork	+0.28
Butter	Margarine	+0.67
Margarine	Butter	+0.81
Pork	Beef	+0.14
Electricity	Natural gas	+0.20
Natural gas	Fuel oil	+0.44

SOURCE H. Wold, *Demand Analysis* (New York: Wiley, 1953); L. Taylor and R. Halvorsen, "Energy Substitution in U.S. Manufacturing," *Review of Economics and Statistics*, November 1977.

Table 5.5 Estimated income elasticity of
demand for selected commodities

Commodity	Income elasticity
Butter	0.42
Cheese	0.34
Cream	0.56
Eggs	0.37
Fruits and berries	0.70
Flour	−0.36
Electricity	0.20
Liquor	1.00
Margarine	−0.20
Meat	0.35
Milk and cream	0.07
Restaurant consumption	1.48
Tobacco	1.02
Haddock	0.46
Dentists' services	1.41
Furniture	1.48
Books	1.44

SOURCE H. Wold, p. 265; F. Bell; H. Houthakker
and L. Taylor; and L. Taylor.

man Wold, in his well-known study, and others. Table 5.5 shows the
income elasticity of demand for selected commodities, as estimated by
Wold and others. The reader should study these tables carefully.[15]

13. Government Policy-Making in the 1973 Fuel Crisis: An Illustration

The concepts presented in this chapter are of great importance in helping
to solve problems of public and private policy. To illustrate how they can
be used, consider the famous energy crisis that confronted top government policy-makers at the end of 1973. When the Arab oil-producing
countries announced a cutback of exports of oil to the United States, the
first official estimates were that American consumers would have to
reduce their consumption of gasoline by 20 or 30 percent. William E.
Simon, the newly appointed federal "energy czar," stated repeatedly that
he wanted to avoid rationing gasoline, if possible. So did other government officials, on the grounds that rationing would lead to black markets
and create a large bureaucracy.

How could gasoline consumption be cut by 20 or 30 percent without
rationing? By increasing the price of gasoline. But how much of a price
hike would be required? Clearly, the answer depends on the price elasticity of demand for gasoline. For example, if the arc elasticity of demand
is about 1, the price of gasoline would have to increase by about 33

15. For a description of a study of the price and income elasticity of demand for
cigarettes, see S. Sackrin, "The Demand for Cigarettes," reprinted in E. Mansfield,
ibid.

percent to achieve a 25 percent reduction in the quantity demanded. On the other hand, if the arc elasticity of demand is about .3, the price of gasoline would have to increase by about 182 percent to achieve a 25 percent reduction in the quantity demanded.[16]

Many economists pointed out to Simon and other government policy-makers that the short-term demand for gasoline is quite inelastic. According to a preliminary estimate from the Transportation Department's research center, the price elasticity of demand is about 0.2. According to Hendrik Houthakker of Harvard University and Phillip Verleger of Data Resources, Inc., the short-run elasticity is about 0.3. And according to Alan Greenspan of Townsend-Greenspan and Company, it is about 0.4. Although these estimates differ somewhat, they are close enough to indicate that the short-term price elasticity of demand is quite low.[17]

Given that this is the case, huge increases in price would be required to cut gasoline consumption by 20 or 30 percent. For example, Houthakker and Verleger suggested that gasoline prices might have to be doubled to produce significant reductions in demand, and the late Arthur Okun of the Brookings Institution indicated that a 50 cent per gallon price increase might be required. These results were taken seriously in the deliberations within the Congress and the executive branch. Faced with the fact that such large increases in price would be needed to produce the desired reduction in gasoline consumption, many people began to feel that rationing might be the lesser of the two evils. Fortunately, however, subsequent analysis indicated that gasoline consumption did not have to be cut so severely, and it was possible to avoid both rationing and so enormous an increase in price.

Nonetheless, in the discussions that took place at the end of 1973, the concept of the price elasticity of demand played an important role in illuminating a central public issue. Relatively simple measurements based on this concept showed that, if price increases were used to reduce gasoline consumption by the amount then thought necessary, the increases would have to be far larger than many officials realized, or felt comfortable with.[18]

16. To obtain these figures, note that it follows from Equation 2.2 that $-\Delta Q \, (P_1 + P_2) \div \Delta P (Q_1 + Q_2) = \eta$. If Q_2 is 25 percent below Q_1, it follows that $Q_2 = .75 \, Q_1$ and that $\Delta Q = -.25 Q_1$. Thus $.25 Q_1 \, (P_1 + P_2) \div 1.75 \, Q_1 \Delta P = \eta$, or $\Delta P \div (P_1 + P_2) = .25 \div 1.75 \eta = 1/7\eta$. Consequently, if $\eta = 1$, $7(P_2 - P_1) = P_1 + P_2$, which implies that $6P_2 = 8P_1$, or $P_2 = 1.33 \, P_1$. That is, if the price elasticity of demand is 1, the price must increase by 33 percent. And if $\eta = .3$, $2.1(P_2 - P_1) = P_1 + P_2$, which implies that $1.1 \, P_2 = 3.1 \, P_1$, or $P_2 = 2.82 \, P_1$. That is, if the price elasticity of demand is 0.3, the price must increase by 182 percent. (In this footnote, we have dropped the $_D$ subscript used in Equation 2.2, since it is unnecessary here. That is, we use ΔQ, Q_1, and Q_2 rather than ΔQ_D, Q_{D1}, and Q_{D2}.)

17. *Business Week,* December 15, 1973, p. 23.

18. Of course, one can still argue that the officials should not have been deterred by the size of the required price increase. Our purpose here is not to determine whether this is true. (Material bearing on this question is taken up in Chapter 16.) The sole point we want to make at present is that the price elasticity of demand played a major role in the decision-making process regarding this important issue.

14. A Business Pricing Problem

The concepts discussed in this chapter are obviously of fundamental importance in the formulation of business policy, as well as public policy. To illustrate the use of the concept of price elasticity by business, let's go back several decades and consider a famous case involving Columbia Records. In 1938, the Columbia Broadcasting Company purchased the American Record Company and changed its name to Columbia Records. When the new company began operations, classical records were sold by the industry at about $1.50, semiclassical and well-established popular records were sold at $0.75, and popular records were sold at $0.35. Among classical records, a sale of 5,000 was considered good; although extremely popular releases might reach a sales volume of 50,000, some records might not sell more than 200.

In November 1938, a New York newspaper began a promotion scheme whereby it offered classical albums to its readers at prices averaging about $0.50 a record. The results were very impressive; more than 50,000 records of a single symphony were sold in a few weeks. Observing this fact, and the enthusiastic reception of the radio broadcasts of symphonic and operatic performances, the executives of the Columbia Broadcasting System concluded that there was a very good opportunity to increase the market for classical records by price reductions. However, during the first couple of years, the new company maintained the high level of prices on classical records while it improved the mechanical quality of its records and the skill and reputation of the artists it recorded.

Before instituting a price reduction, Columbia obviously had to estimate more precisely what the effect of a price reduction would be on its revenues and costs. The answers to these questions clearly depended upon the price elasticity of demand for classical records, as well as on the way in which the firm's costs varied with the quantity of records it produced (a subject that is discussed at length in Chapter 7). Edward Wallerstein, president of Columbia Records, began by trying to estimate the public's reaction to lower prices. He asked a number of dealers to keep detailed records of their customary sales and then for one month to offer all people who entered their stores regular classical and semiclassical records at two-thirds of list price. These dealers found that the unannounced price reduction of $33\frac{1}{3}$ percent more than doubled the number of records sold. Thus the apparent price elasticity of demand, based on this crude experiment, was well above one. This evidence, in addition to the other indications, convinced Wallerstein that Columbia should go further in analyzing the pros and cons of a price reduction of substantial magnitude.

Based on the estimated price elasticity of demand, it was possible to estimate the effect of a price cut on the firm's total revenue. In addition, a close examination was made of the firm's cost structure to determine the effect of a price cut on the firm's total costs. Since many costs were fixed, total costs would not increase in proportion to the increased volume resulting from the price cut. After considerable study, it was decided to reduce the price of 10-inch classical records from about $1.25 to $0.75 and to reduce the price of 12-inch classical records from about $1.75 to $1.00. Presumably a price reduction of this extent was chosen because it was felt to be the most profitable one. The response was overwhelming. Other firms followed Columbia's lead. To the surprise of much of the industry, total expenditure on classical records rose greatly.[19]

This is a good illustration of how the price elasticity of demand must be taken into account in pricing strategy. It also illustrates the claim, frequently made by critics, that firms tend to underestimate the price elasticity of demand. There have been many congressional investigations of pricing in key industries like steel and automobiles, and it is frequently alleged in these hearings that the firms in question should, in their own interest as well as the public's, lower their prices. It is difficult to generalize concerning the accuracy of this allegation. In some instances, like the record industry, there seems to have been an underestimation of the elasticity of demand. Whether there are many other cases of this sort is difficult to say.[20]

15. Summary

The market demand curve for a commodity is simply the horizontal summation of the individual demand curves of all the consumers in the market. Since individual demand curves almost always slope downward to the right, it follows that market demand curves will do so, too. As pointed out in previous chapters, the price elasticity of demand measures the responsiveness of quantity demanded to changes in price. Graphical techniques are available to estimate the elasticity at a given point. The price elasticity of demand for a commodity depends on the number and closeness of substitutes that are available. If a commodity has many close substitutes, its demand is likely to be elastic. Of course, the extent to which a commodity has close substitutes depends on how narrowly it is defined. The sellers of a product are particularly interested in the relationship between price changes and changes in the amount of money spent on the product. If the price elasticity of demand is greater (less) than one, reductions in price lead to an increase (decrease) in the total expenditure on the commodity.

The income elasticity of demand is the percentage change in quantity demanded resulting from a 1 percent change in money income. Commodities differ greatly in their income elasticities. Goods that people regard as luxuries are generally assumed to have high income elasticities

19. For further details concerning this case, see M. McNair and H. Hansen, *Problems in Marketing* (New York: McGraw-Hill, 1949), pp. 596–603.

20. For some discussion of whether or not this is true in the automobile industry, see *Administered Prices: Automobiles,* Senate Subcommittee on Antitrust and Monopoly.

of demand. Indeed, one way to define luxuries and necessities is to say that luxuries are goods with high income elasticities of demand, and necessities are goods with low income elasticities of demand. The cross elasticity of demand is the relative change in the quantity demanded of good X divided by the relative change in the price of good Y. Whether commodities are classified as substitutes or complements depends on whether the cross elasticity is positive or negative.

Marginal revenue is the addition to total revenue attributable to the addition of the last unit to sales. Obviously, total revenue from n units of output is equal to the sum of marginal revenue in the intervals between 0 and 1 unit of output, 1 and 2 units of output, and so on up to $(n - 1)$ to n units of output. The marginal revenue curve shows marginal revenue at various levels of output of the commodity. Graphical techniques are available to estimate the marginal revenue curve from the demand curve. There is a very simple relation between the price elasticity of demand at a certain output level and marginal revenue at the output level. It is important to distinguish between the market demand curve for a commodity and the market demand curve for the output of a single firm producing the commodity. In a perfectly competitive industry, the firm's demand curve will be horizontal. If the industry contains more than one firm but is not perfectly competitive, the firm's demand curve will not be horizontal, but it is likely to be more price elastic than the demand curve for the commodity.

The market demand curve plays a very important role in microeconomics, and there have been many studies that have attempted to measure the demand curve for particular commodities. One technique used to estimate the demand curve is direct market experimentation. Another technique is to interview consumers and administer questionnaires concerning their habits, motives, and intentions. Still another technique is the use of statistical and econometric techniques to extract information from data regarding sales, prices, incomes, and other variables in the past. Each of these approaches has its disadvantages, and there is no easy remedy to the estimation problem. Nevertheless, the difficulties generally are not insurmountable. Many interesting and important estimates have been made of the demand curves for various goods.

One case that illustrates the use of these concepts in important practical problems is the energy crisis at the end of 1973. According to the first official estimates, American consumers had to reduce their consumption of gasoline by 20 or 30 percent. The extent of the price increase required to reduce gasoline consumption by this amount depends on the price elasticity of demand. Because the short-run market demand for gasoline is quite inelastic, huge increases in price would have been required. Another illustration is the case of Columbia Records. After conducting small-scale experiments, Columbia became convinced that the demand for classical records was quite elastic and that profits would be increased by a drastic cut in price. Columbia cut the price in 1940 and the response was in keeping with Columbia's expectations.

QUESTIONS AND PROBLEMS

1. Suppose that a consumer considers Geritol of supreme importance and that he spends all of his income on Geritol. To this consumer, what is the price elasticity of demand for Geritol? What is the income elasticity of demand for Geritol? What is the cross elasticity of demand between Geritol and any other good?

2. In the automobile industry, is the demand curve for the output of each firm horizontal? (Why or why not?) Is it less elastic than the demand curve for automobiles as a whole? (Why or why not?) If the price of an automobile is $7,000, is marginal revenue less than, equal to, or greater than $7,000?

3. Which of the following are likely to have a positive cross elasticity of demand? (a) automobiles and oil, (b) wood tennis rackets and metal tennis rackets, (c) gin and tonic, (d) fishing poles and fishing licenses, (e) a Harvard education and a Stanford education.

4. The demand for buggy whips has declined precipitously in the past century. Given that this shift to the left of the demand curve for buggy whips has resulted in a reduction in the total revenue of buggy-whip producers, can we be sure that the price elasticity of demand for buggy whips is (a) less than one, (b) greater than one, (c) greater than zero?

5. Suppose the mayor of New York asked you to advise him concerning the proper fare that should be charged by the New York City subway. In what way might information concerning the price elasticity of demand be useful?

6. According to the Senate Subcommittee on Antitrust and Monopoly, the income elasticity of demand for automobiles in the United States is between 2.5 and 3.9. What does this mean? If incomes rise by 5 percent, what effect will this have on the quantity of autos demanded? How might this fact be used by General Motors?

7. Suppose you are a trustee of a major university. At a meeting of the board of trustees, one university official argues that the demand for places at this university is completely inelastic. As evidence, he cites the fact that, although the university has doubled its tuition in the last decade, there has been no appreciable decrease in the number of students enrolled. Do you agree? Comment on his argument.

8. According to William Baumol, "Some mail-order houses have employed systematic programs in which a few experimental pages were bound inconspicuously into the catalogues distributed to customers within restricted geographical regions, thus permitting observation of the effects of price, product, or even catalogue display variations." Comment on the accuracy of this technique. What might be some of the problems in estimating a product's price elasticity of demand in this way? What techniques might be better than this one?

9. Show that, if the Engel curve for a good is a straight line through the origin, the income elasticity of demand for the good is one.

10. The cross elasticity of demand can be used to determine which products belong to the same market. For example, in the famous cellophane case, the U.S. Department of Justice brought suit against the duPont Company for having monopolized the sale of cellophane. In its defense, duPont claimed that cellophane had many close substitutes, such as aluminum foil, waxed

paper, and polyethylene. Can you guess how duPont used cross elasticities of demand in this case? (Incidentally, the Supreme Court accepted duPont's argument in its landmark decision handed down in 1953.)

SELECTED REFERENCES

HICKS, JOHN. *Value and Capital.* New York: Oxford University Press, 1946.

SCHULTZ, HENRY. *The Theory and Measurement of Demand.* Chicago: University of Chicago Press, 1938.

DEAN, JOEL. *Managerial Economics.* Englewood Cliffs, N.J.: Prentice-Hall, 1951.

MARSHALL, ALFRED. *Principles of Economics.* London: Macmillan, 1920.

STIGLER, GEORGE. 'The Limitations of Statistical Demand Curves." *Journal of the American Statistical Association,* 1939.

BAUMOL, WILLIAM. "The Empirical Determination of Demand Relationships." Reprinted in E. Mansfield *Microeconomics: Selected Readings.* 4th ed., New York: Norton, 1982.

6 The Firm and Its Technology

1. The Assumption of Profit Maximization

Both General Electric and the Ford Foundation have assets that run into the billions of dollars. Both are large, powerful organizations, but only one of them is a firm. What is a firm? Put briefly, it is a unit that produces a good or service for sale. In contrast to not-for-profit institutions like the Ford Foundation, firms attempt to make a profit. There are literally millions of firms in the United States: Some are proprietorships (owned by a single person), some partnerships (owned by two or more people), and some corporations (which are fictitious legal persons). About six-sevenths of the goods and services produced in the United States are produced by firms; the rest are provided by government and not-for-profit institutions. It is obvious that an economy like ours is centered around the activities of firms.

As a first approximation, economists generally assume that firms attempt to maximize profits. However, the economist's definition of profits does not coincide with the accountant's. The economist does not assume that the firm attempts to maximize the current, short-run profits measured by the accountant. Instead he or she assumes that the firm will attempt to maximize the sum of profits over a long period of time, these profits being properly discounted to the present. Also, when the economist speaks of profits, he or she means profit after taking account of the capital and labor provided by the owners. More will be said on this score in the next chapter.

Although the assumption of profit maximization serves as a reasonable first approximation, it has obvious limitations. For one thing, the making of profits generally requires time and energy, and if the owners of the firm are the managers as well, they may decide that it is preferable to sacrifice profits for leisure. (Profit-maximizers in Miami Beach and the Virgin Islands encourage this type of thinking.) In a case of this sort, it is more accurate to assume that the owner-manager, like the consumer, is maximizing utility, since utility is a function of his or her profits and the amount of leisure he or she enjoys. Using the kind of analysis described in Chapter 3, we can determine how much money the owner-manager will give up for leisure (see Example 6.1).

It should also be noted that, in an uncertain world, the concept of maximum profit is not clearly defined. Since any particular course of action will not result in a unique, certain level of profit, but in a variety of possible levels of profit, each with a certain probability of occurrence, it makes no sense to speak about the maximization of profits. However, if the firm is able, explicitly or implicitly, to attach a probability to each level of profit that could result from each course of action, it is meaningful to assume that the firm attempts to maximize expected profits.[1] For simplicity, we shall assume in the following pages that the firm has full knowledge of the relevant variables, and that there is no uncertainty.

Observers of the modern corporation often state that profits are not the sole objective of these firms. Industry spokesmen often claim that the following objectives are also of importance: achieving better social conditions in the firm's community, increasing (or at least maintaining) its market share, creating an image as a good employer and a useful part of the community, and so forth. For example, oil firms often stress their concern over the environment and over the reduction of wasteful uses of fuel. Besides the question of how seriously one should take such self-proclaimed goals, the important question is how distinct these goals are from the goal of profit maximization. To the extent that many of these goals are simply means to achieve profits *in the long run,* there may be less inaccuracy in the profit maximization assumption than might appear at first glance.

In recent years economists have begun to experiment with models of the firm that do not assume profit maximization. A brief introduction to such models is contained in the Appendix to this chapter. Although these models are useful for certain purposes, profit maximization remains the standard assumption in microeconomics. In large part, this is because it is a close enough approximation for many of the most important purposes of microeconomics. For example, even some of the proponents of alternative models admit that profit maximization may be a suitable assumption in models designed to show how the price system functions.

In addition economists are interested in the theory of the profit-maximizing firm because it provides rules of behavior for firms that do

1. Expected profit is defined as the long-term average value of profit—the sum of the various possible levels of profit, after each level is weighted by the probability of its occurrence. The firm may be interested in the variance, as well as the expected value of profits, in which case it will maximize some function of both the expected value and the variance. For further discussion of this and related topics, see Chapter 19, which deals with decision-making under conditions of risk.

Example 6.1   Utility Maximization by the Entrepreneur

In a famous article, Tibor Scitovsky suggested that the entrepreneur (that is, the owner-manager of the firm) maximizes utility, which is a function of the firm's profits and the amount of leisure the entrepreneur enjoys. Suppose that a particular entrepreneur's indifference curves between profit and leisure are as shown in the graph below. Also, suppose that the amount of work that the entrepreneur must do is proportional to his or her firm's output. If this is the case, the relationship between leisure and profit is given by the curved line $ABCD$. (a) Why does the relationship between leisure and profit have the shape indicated by $ABCD$? (b) Will the entrepreneur maximize profit? (c) If the entrepreneur's indifference curves were horizontal lines, would he or she maximize profit?

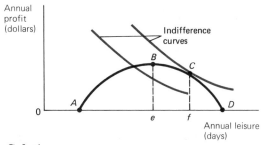

Solution

(a) Up to some point, increases in the firm's output result in increases in profit; beyond this point, they result in decreases in profit. Thus, since the entrepreneur's days of work are assumed to be proportional to the firm's output, up to some point, increases in the number of days he or she works result in increases in profit; beyond this point, they result in decreases in profit. Finally, since the entrepreneur's number of days of leisure equals the total time during the year minus his or her number of days of work, it follows that, up to some point, increases in his or her number of days of leisure are associated with increases in profit; beyond that point (indicated by e in the graph), they are associated with decreases in profit. (b) No. He or she maximizes utility by choosing point C, where there are Of days of leisure, and profit is below the maximum that could be achieved. (c) Yes. He or she would choose point B, where profits are a maximum.*

* For further discussion, see T. Scitovsky, "A Note on Profit Maximization and Its Implications," *Review of Economic Studies,* Winter 1943.

want to maximize profits. The theory of the profit-maximizing firm suggests how a firm should operate if it wants to make as such money as possible. Even if a firm does not want to maximize profit, the theory can be useful. For example, it can show how much the firm is losing by taking certain courses of action. In recent years the theory of the profit-maximizing firm has been studied more and more for the sake of determining rules of business behavior.[2]

2. Technology and Inputs

One of the fundamental determinants of a firm's behavior is the state of technology. Whether a firm produces textiles or locomotives, whether a firm is big or small, whether a firm is run by a genius or a moron (or even your brother-in-law), the firm cannot do more than is permitted by existing technology. Technology, as we defined it in Chapter 1, is the sum total of society's pool of knowledge concerning the industrial and agricultural arts. Although this definition is accurate, it is not very useful in indicating how we can represent the state of technology in a model of the firm. The purpose of the rest of this chapter is to show how economists represent the state of technology.

To begin with, an *input* is defined as anything that a firm uses in its production process. Most firms require a wide variety of inputs. For example, some of the inputs in the iron and steel industry are iron ore, coal, oxygen, skilled labor of various types, the services of blast furnaces, open hearths, electric furnaces, and rolling mills, as well as the services of the people managing the companies. To give a more humble example, the inputs in the production and sale of hot dogs by a street vendor are the hot dogs, the rolls, the stove, the truck, and the services of the vendor.

In representing and analyzing production processes, we assume that all inputs can be divided into two categories: fixed inputs and variable inputs. A *fixed input* is an input whose quantity cannot be changed during the period of time under consideration. This period will vary from problem to problem. Of course, the amount of most inputs can be varied to some extent, no matter how brief the time interval. But for some inputs, the cost of quick variation in their amount is so large as to make such variation impractical. For simplicity, we regard these inputs as being fixed. The firm's plant and equipment are examples of inputs that often are included in this category.

On the other hand, a *variable input* is an input whose quantity can be changed during the relevant period. For example, the number of workers hired to perform a job like construction can often be increased or decreased on short notice. The amount of raw material used in the production of a commodity like ladies' dresses can often be increased or decreased by using up or building up the firm's inventories. The amount of water used in the production of a service like a car wash can sometimes be varied within limits simply by turning the relevant knobs.

2. For example, see W. Baumol, *Economic Theory and Operations Analysis,* 4th ed. (Englewood Cliffs, N.J.: Prentice-Hall, 1977).

3. The Short Run and the Long Run

Whether or not an input is regarded as variable or fixed depends on the length of the period under consideration. The longer the period, the more inputs are variable, not fixed. Although the length of the relevant period varies from problem to problem, economists have found it useful to focus special attention on two time periods: the short run and the long run. The *short run* is defined to be that period of time in which some of the firm's inputs are fixed. More specifically, since the firm's plant and equipment are among the most difficult inputs to change quickly, the short run is generally understood to mean the length of time during which the firm's plant and equipment are fixed. On the other hand, the *long run* is that period of time in which all inputs are variable. In the long run, the firm can make a complete adjustment to any change in its environment.

In both the short run and the long run, a firm's productive processes ordinarily permit substantial variation in the proportions in which inputs are used. In the long run, there can be no question but that input proportions can be varied considerably. For example, an automobile die can be made on conventional machine tools with more labor and less expensive equipment, or it can be made on numerically controlled machine tools with less labor and more expensive equipment. Similarly, an airplane can be almost handmade or it can be made using much equipment and relatively little labor. In the short run, there are also considerable opportunities for changes in input proportions. For one thing, the ratio between fixed and variable inputs can vary greatly.

Production processes with fixed, not variable, proportions are ones where there is one, and only one, ratio of inputs that can be used. For example, to produce a certain product, 2 hours of labor must be combined with a certain amount of capital. Consequently, if output is increased or decreased, the quantity of all inputs must be varied in proportion to output. There seem to be very few cases where all inputs must be combined in fixed proportions. However, there are cases where the amount of a *certain* input can be varied only within narrow limits. For example, a particular drug may have to contain a certain amount of aspirin per ounce of the drug. Thus it is not unusual for some inputs to be required in relatively fixed proportions but it is very unusual for this to be the case for all, or most, inputs.

4. The Production Function

For any commodity, the *production function* is the relationship between the quantities of various inputs used per period of time and the maximum quantity of the commodity that can be produced per period of time. More specifically, the production function is a table, a graph, or an equation showing the maximum output rate that can be achieved from any specified set of usage rates of inputs. The production function summarizes the characteristics of existing technology at a given point in

Table 6.1   Output of corn when
various amounts of
labor are applied to an
acre of land

Amount of labor (annual number of man-years)	Output of corn (bushels per year)
1	6
2	13.5
3	21
4	28
5	34
6	38
7	38
8	37

time; it shows the technological constraints that the firm must reckon with. In most of this book, we assume that the firm takes the production function as given; in Chapter 18, when we analyze the process of technological change, we study the firm's attempts to change the production function.

To illustrate the production function, consider the simplest case—when there is one fixed input and one variable input. Suppose that the fixed input is the service of an acre of land, the variable input is labor (in man-years), and the output is corn (in bushels). Suppose that a scientifically inclined farmer decides to find out what the effect on annual output will be if he or she applies various numbers of man-years of labor during the year to the acre of land. (The farmer can vary the number of man-years of labor by hiring fewer or more laborers.) If he or she obtains the results in Table 6.1, then these results might be regarded as the production function in this situation. Alternatively, the curve in Figure 6.1, which presents exactly the same results, might be regarded as the production function.

The production function is an important starting point for the analysis of the firm's technology: It gives us the maximum *total output* that can be realized by using each combination of quantities of inputs. But there is more that we need to know about the production process. In particular, two other important concepts are the average product and the marginal product of an input. The *average product* of an input is total product (that is, total output) divided by the amount of the input used to produce this amount of output. The *marginal product* of an input is the addition to total output due to the addition of the last unit of the input, when the amounts of other inputs used are held constant.

To illustrate these concepts, let us go back to the farmer in Table 6.1. On the basis of the production function shown in this table, we can compute the average product and marginal product of labor. Both the average product and the marginal product of labor will vary, of course, depending on how much labor is used. If $Q(L)$ is the total output rate when L man-years of labor are used per year, the average product of

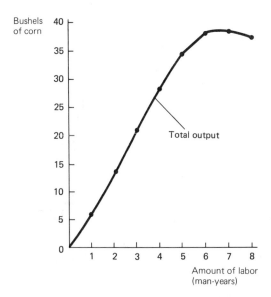

Bushels of corn

Total output

Amount of labor
(man-years)

Figure 6.1 Relationship between total output and amount
of labor used on one acre of land

labor when L man-years of labor are used per year is $Q(L)/L$. And the
marginal product of labor when between L and $(L - 1)$ man-years of
labor are used per year is

$$[Q(L) - Q(L - 1)].$$

Thus the average product of labor is 6 bushels of corn per man-year of
labor when 1 man-year of labor is used, and the marginal product of
labor is 7.5 bushels of corn per man-year of labor when between 1 and 2
man-years of labor are used. The results for other levels of utilization of
labor are shown in Table 6.2.

Panel A of Figure 6.2 shows the average product curve for labor. The

Table 6.2 Average and marginal products of labor

Amount of labor	Total output	Average product of labor	Marginal product of labor*
0	0	—	—
1	6.0	6.00	6.0
2	13.5	6.75	7.5
3	21.0	7.00	7.5
4	28.0	7.00	7.0
5	34.0	6.80	6.0
6	38.0	6.30	4.0
7	38.0	5.40	0.0
8	37.0	4.60	−1.0

* These figures pertain to the interval between the indicated amount
of labor and one unit less than the indicated amount of labor.

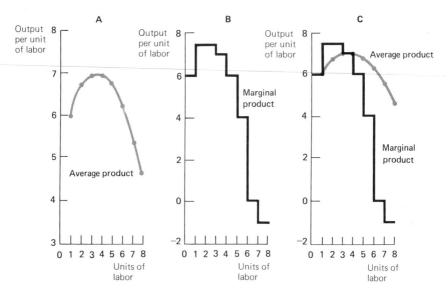

Figure 6.2   Average and marginal product curves for labor

numbers are taken from Table 6.2. As is typically the case for production processes, the average product of labor (which is the only variable input in this case) rises, reaches a maximum, and then falls. Panel B of Figure 6.2 shows the marginal product curve for labor. (These numbers also are taken from Table 6.2) The marginal product of labor also rises, reaches a maximum, and then falls. This, too, is typical of many production processes.[3] Finally, panel c of Figure 6.2 shows both the average product curve and the marginal product curve for labor. As is always the case, marginal product exceeds average product when the latter is increasing, equals average product when the latter reaches a maximum, and is less than average product when the latter is decreasing. This is simply a matter of arithmetic: If the addition to a total is greater (less) than the average, the average is bound to increase (decrease).[4]

Tables 6.1 and 6.2 are constructed on the assumption that land, the fixed input, is equal to one acre. Suppose that we could increase the amount of land to two acres. What effect would this have on the total, average, and marginal products of labor? Generally, over the relevant range of production, an increase in the fixed input will result in an increase in all of them. For example, the result might be like that shown in Figure 6.3.

3. Sometimes, however, an input's marginal product decreases throughout the entire range of its utilization.

4. If x is the amount of the variable input that is used and
$$Q = f(x)$$
where Q is the output rate, then the average product of the variable input is $Q \div x = f(x) \div x$, and the marginal product of the variable input is $dQ/dx = df(x)/dx$.

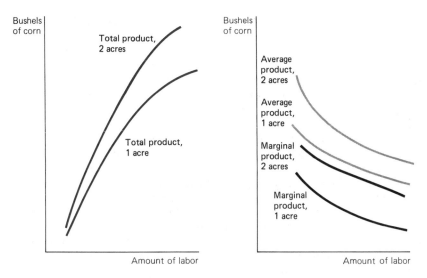

Figure 6.3   Total, average, and marginal product curves for labor, with one and two acres of land*

* Note that only part of each of these curves is shown; the region where average or marginal product is increasing is omitted.

5. The Law of Diminishing Marginal Returns and the Geometry of Average and Marginal Product Curves

Previous sections have defined the production function and the average and marginal products of an input. We are now in a position to discuss one of the most famous laws of microeconomics—the law of diminishing marginal returns. The law of diminishing marginal returns, like the Scriptures, is often quoted and frequently misinterpreted. Put very briefly, this law states that *if equal increments of an input are added, the quantities of other inputs held constant, the resulting increments of product will decrease beyond some point; that is, the marginal product of the input will diminish.* This law is illustrated by Table 6.2; beyond 3 man-years of labor, the marginal product of labor decreases.

Several things should be noted concerning this law. First, the law of diminishing marginal returns is an empirical generalization, not a deduction from physical or biological laws. In fact, it seems to hold for most

---

Thus average product is a maximum when

$$\frac{d(Q/x)}{dx} = \left(\frac{dQ}{dx} - \frac{Q}{x} \right) \frac{1}{x} = 0$$

which means that dQ/dx must equal Q/x when the average product is a maximum. But since dQ/dx is the marginal product and Q/x is the average product, this proves the proposition in the text: When the average product is a maximum, the average product equals the marginal product.

production functions in the real world. Second, it is assumed that technology remains fixed. The law of diminishing marginal returns cannot predict the effect of an additional unit of input when technology is allowed to change. Third, it is assumed that there is at least one input whose quantity is being held constant. The law of diminishing marginal returns does not apply to cases where there is a proportional increase in all inputs. Fourth, it must be possible, of course, to vary the proportions in which the various inputs are used.

If there is a fixed input and only one variable input, the typical form of the relationship between the amount of the variable input and the total output is given by OT in Figure 6.4.[5] Given such a graph, how can we determine the average product and the marginal product of the variable input? To make the analysis more concrete, suppose that Figure 6.4 refers to another farm like the one in Table 6.1, that the output is corn, and that the variable input is labor. First, consider the average product of the variable input, labor. Since average product equals total product divided by the amount of variable input, the average product of any amount of variable input, OA equals $AB(=OC)$ divided by OA. And AB/OA is obviously the slope of the line, OB, which joins the origin and the point on the total product curve corresponding to this amount of variable input. Thus the slope of the line joining the origin and the relevant point on the total product curve is equal to the average product of the variable input, labor.

Second, consider the marginal product of the variable input, labor. Given the total product curve in Figure 6.5 (which is the same as that in Figure 6.4), how can we determine the marginal product? If the amount

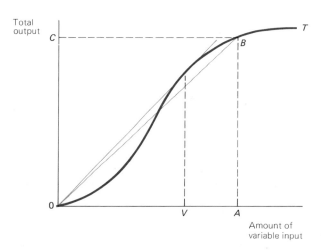

Figure 6.4   Measurement of the average product

5. In Figure 6.4, we assume that the amount of the variable output is varied continuously, with the result that the total product, the average product, and the marginal product curves are continuous.

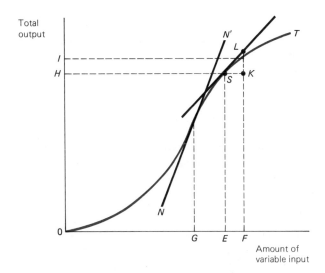

Figure 6.5 Measurement of marginal product

of variable input increases from *OE* to *OF,* total output increases from *OH* to *OI.* Clearly, as the increment in the amount of variable input becomes smaller and smaller, the extra product divided by the extra variable input, *HI/EF,* approaches the slope of the total product curve at *S.* (Even if the increment is *EF,* the approximation is not too bad: The slope of the total product curve is *KL/SK = KL/EF,* which is fairly close to *HI/EF.*) Thus, since the slope of a curve at any point equals the slope of its tangent at that point, we can determine the marginal product of any amount of variable input by drawing the tangent to the total product curve at that amount of variable input and measuring its slope. For example, the slope of *NN'* is the marginal product of variable input when *OG* units of variable input are used.

Using these results, it is possible to prove a number of interesting results concerning the average product curve (the curve showing the relationship between average product and the amount of variable input used) and the marginal product curve (the curve showing the relationship between marginal product and the amount of variable input used). To begin with, in Figure 6.4, since a line joining the origin and a point on the total product curve is bound to be steepest (that is, has the maximum slope) when the line is tangent to the total product curve, it follows that the average product must be a maximum if *OV* units of variable input are used. Moreover, since the tangent to the total product curve is exactly the same as the line joining the origin and the total product curve when *OV* units of the variable input are used, the slope of the tangent must equal the slope of this line, and marginal product must equal average product. Thus *marginal product must equal average product when the latter is a maximum.*[6] Also, since the marginal product is a maximum at

6. Of course this is precisely the same result as that stated at the end of Section 4.

OG (Figure 6.5), where the slope of the tangent to the total product curve is greatest, and since *OG* is less than *OV*, it follows that *the maximum marginal product occurs at a lower level of variable input than the maximum average product.*

6. The Production Function: Two Variable Inputs

In the previous sections, we were concerned with the case in which there is only one variable input. In the next four sections, we take up the more general case in which there are two variable inputs. These variable inputs can be thought of as working with one or more fixed inputs, or they may be thought of as the only two inputs (in which case the situation is the long run). In either case, it is easy to extend the results to as many inputs as one likes. This section takes up the production function, Sections 7 and 8 are concerned with its representation through a system of geometric constructs called isoquants, and Section 9 deals with substitution among inputs.

If we increase the number of variable inputs from one to two, the production function becomes slightly more complicated, but it is still the relationship between various combinations of inputs and the maximum amount of output that can be obtained from them. Really, the only change is that the output is a function of two variables rather than one. For example, suppose in our agricultural example that we allow both land and labor to vary; the results might be given by Table 6.3. This is the production function in tabular form. Note that we can obtain the marginal product of each input by holding the other input constant. For example, the marginal product of land when 4 man-years are used and when between 1 and 2 acres of land are used is 51 bushels per acre; the marginal product of labor when 2 acres are used and when between 3 and 4 man-years of labor are used is 20 bushels per man-year. Similarly, the average product of either land or labor can be computed simply by dividing the total output by the amount of either land or labor that is used.[7]

Another way to present the production function is by a surface, like that in Figure 6.6. The production surface is *OAQB*[8]. The height of a point on this surface denotes the quantity of output. Dropping a perpendicular down from a point on the production surface to the "floor" and seeing how far the resulting point is from the labor and land axes indicates how much of each input is required to produce this much

---

7. If x_1 is the amount of the first input and x_2 is the amount of the second input, the production function is

   $$Q = f(x_1, x_2)$$

   where Q is the output rate. The marginal product of the first input is $\partial Q/\partial x_1$; the marginal product of the second input is $\partial Q/\partial x_2$.

8. Note that this surface is not meant to represent the numerical values in Table 6.3 but is a general representation of how a production surface of this sort is likely to appear.

Table 6.3 Hypothetical production
function for corn, two
variable inputs

AMOUNT OF LABOR (MAN-YEARS)	NUMBER OF ACRES			
	1	*2*	*3*	*4*
	(Bushels of corn produced per year)			
1	5	11	18	24
2	14	30	50	72
3	22	60	80	99
4	29	80	115	125
5	34	84	140	145

output. For example, to produce $U'U$ units of output requires OB_1 (= A_1U') man-years of labor and OA_1 (= B_1U') acres of land. Conversely, one can take any amounts of land and labor, say OA_2 acres of land and OB_2 man-years of labor, and find out how much output they will produce by measuring the height of the production surface at D', the point where labor input is OB_2 and land input is OA_2. According to Figure 6.6, the answer equals $D'D$.

Note that this hypothetical production function illustrates the fact that a given amount of output can be produced in quite different ways. For example, in Table 6.3, 80 bushels of corn can be produced with either 4 man-years of labor and 2 acres of land or with 3 man-years of labor and 3 acres of land. (Moreover, the production function does not include many of the different ways in which a given output can be produced

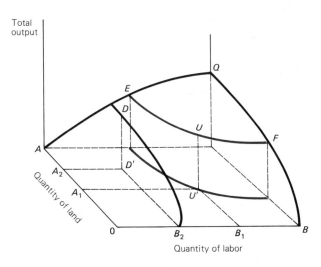

Figure 6.6 Production function, two variable inputs

because it includes only efficient combinations of inputs.[9]) Generally there is a variety of ways to produce a given output and a variety of efficient input combinations; thus it is possible for the firm to substitute one input for another in producing a specified amount of output.

7. Isoquants

An isoquant is a curve showing all possible (efficient) combinations of inputs that are capable of producing a certain quantity of output. Given the production function, one can readily derive the isoquant pertaining to any level of output. For example, in Figure 6.6, suppose that we want to find the isoquant corresponding to an output of $U'U$. All that we need to do is to cut the production surface at the height of $U'U$ parallel to the base plane, the result being EUF, and to drop perpendiculars from EUF to the base. Clearly, this results in a curve that includes all efficient combinations of land and labor that can produce $U'U$ bushels of corn.[10]

A number of isoquants, each pertaining to a different output rate, is shown in Figure 6.7. The two axes measure the quantities of inputs that are used. In contrast to the previous diagrams, we assume that labor and capital—not labor and land—are the relevant inputs in this case. The curves show the various combinations of inputs that can produce 50, 100,

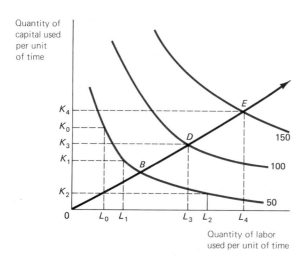

Figure 6.7 Isoquants

9. For example, if 2 units of labor and 3 units of capital can produce 1 unit of output, this combination of inputs and output will not be included in the production function if it is also possible to produce 1 unit of output with 2 units of labor and 2 units of capital. The former input combination is clearly inefficient, since it is possible to obtain the result with the same amount of labor and less capital.
10. Using the notation in footnote 7, an isoquant shows all combinations of x_1 and x_2 such that $f(x_1, x_2)$ equals a certain output rate.

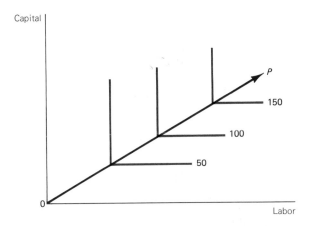

Figure 6.8 Isoquants in the case of fixed proportions

and 150 units of output. For example, consider the isoquant pertaining to 50 units of output per period of time. According to this isoquant, it is possible to attain this output rate if OL_0 units of labor and OK_0 units of capital are used per period of time. Alternatively, this output rate can be attained if OL_1 units of labor and OK_1 units of capital—or OL_2 units of labor and OK_2 units of capital—are used per period of time.

A ray is a line that starts from some point and goes off into space. A ray from the origin, such as $OBDE$, describes all input combinations where the capital-labor ratio is constant, with the slope of the ray being equal to the constant capital-labor ratio. For example, at points D and E, 100 and 150 units of output are produced with a capital-labor ratio of $OK_3/OL_3 = OK_4/OL_4$. Moving out from the origin along any ray, such as $OBDE$, we see that various output levels can be produced with the same ratio of one input to another. Of course, the absolute amount of each input increases as we move out to higher and higher output levels, but the ratio of one input to the other remains constant. It is important to understand the difference between such a ray and an isoquant; an isoquant pertains to a fixed, not a changing, output rate and a changing, not a fixed, ratio of inputs.

An isoquant plays much the same kind of role in production theory that an indifference curve plays in demand theory. An indifference curve shows the various combinations of two commodities that provide equal satisfaction to the consumer; an isoquant shows the various combinations of two inputs that result in an equal output for the firm. It is obvious that, like indifference curves, two isoquants cannot intersect. If an intersection were to occur, it would mean that two different output rates are the maximum obtainable from a given combination of resources; this is obviously absurd.

Isoquants can be used to illustrate the case in which inputs must be used in fixed proportions. Figure 6.8 shows a case of this sort; the necessary ratio of capital to labor is the slope of the ray OP. The isoquants are right angles, indicating that, if one input is changed while the other input is held constant, there is no increase in the output rate. In other words, the marginal product of either input is zero if the other input is held constant. Sometimes there are a number of processes that can be used to produce a given commodity, each utilizing the inputs in fixed proportions (but with the proportions fixed at different levels). This case is discussed at length in Chapter 8, where we take up linear programming.

8. The Economic Region of Production

In some cases, isoquants may have positively sloped segments, or bend back upon themselves, as shown in Figure 6.9. Above OA and below OB, the slope of the isoquants is positive, which implies that increases in both capital and labor are required to maintain a certain output rate. If this is the case, the marginal product of one or the other input must be negative. Above OA, the marginal product of capital is negative; thus output will increase if less capital is used, while the amount of labor is held constant. Below OB, the marginal product of labor is negative; thus output will increase if less labor is used, while the amount of capital is held constant. The lines OA and OB are called *ridge lines*.

Clearly, no profit-maximizing firm will operate at a point outside the ridge lines, since it can produce the same output with less of both inputs, which must be cheaper. To illustrate this, consider point C in Figure 6.9. Because this is a point where the isoquant is positively sloped—and thus outside the ridge lines—it requires a greater amount of both labor and capital than some other point (for example, point D) on the same isoquant. Since both capital and labor have positive prices, it must be cheaper to operate at point D than at point C. In general, it is always possible to find a cheaper way to produce a given quantity of output than to operate at a point outside the ridge lines. Thus the zone between the ridge lines is often called the *economic region of production*. For exam-

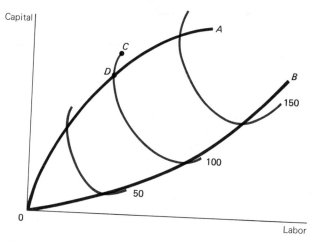

Figure 6.9   The economic region of production

ple, in Figure 6.9, the economic region of production is the zone between OA and OB. No rational firm will venture outside this region.

9. Substitution among Inputs

From both a practical and a theoretical point of view, it is important to study the rate at which one input must be substituted for another to maintain a constant output rate. Consider the isoquant, ZZ', in Figure 6.10. The relevant output rate can be produced with OL_0 units of labor and OK_0 units of capital. However, if the amount of labor is increased to OL_1, the same output rate can be attained with less capital: OK_1 units rather than OK_0. Thus, in the relevant range, the rate at which labor can be substituted for capital is $-(OK_0 - OK_1)/(OL_0 - OL_1) = BA/BC$; the minus sign is added to make the result a positive number. If we consider a very small increase in labor (OL_1 being very close to OL_0), BA/BC equals minus one times the slope of the tangent, GG', to the isoquant at A, which is called the *marginal rate of technical substitution*. It measures, for small changes in labor, the change in capital required per unit change in labor. The reader will note that, as its name indicates, it is analogous to the marginal rate of substitution in demand theory. (Economists, having found an elegant and felicitous phrase like the marginal rate of substitution, did not want to abandon it for anything cumbersome.)

Using the diagram in Figure 6.10, it is easy to demonstrate that the marginal rate of technical substitution of labor for capital is equal to the ratio of the marginal product of labor to the marginal product of capital. Suppose that labor input is held at the OL_0 level, while capital is increased from OK_1 to OK_0. Output would increase from the level (say Q_1) corresponding to isoquant WW' to the level (say Q_0) corresponding to isoquant ZZ'. The marginal product of capital is $(Q_0 - Q_1) \div (OK_0 -$

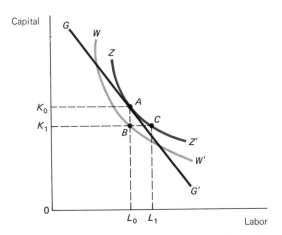

Figure 6.10   The marginal rate of technical substitution

$OK_1) = (Q_0 - Q_1) \div BA$. On the other hand, suppose that capital is held at OK_1, while labor is increased from OL_0 to OL_1. The marginal product of labor is $(Q_0 - Q_1) \div (OL_1 - OL_0) = (Q_0 - Q_1) \div BC$. Thus the ratio of the marginal product of labor to the marginal product of capital equals $BA \div BC$, which (in the limit for small changes in the amount of labor) equals the marginal rate of technical substitution.[11]

It is also easy to show that the marginal rate of technical substitution of labor for capital tends to decrease as an increasing amount of labor is substituted for capital. As labor is substituted for capital, the marginal product of labor tends to fall. Increases in labor, holding capital constant, result in a decrease in the marginal product of labor in the economic region of production. When capital is decreased, even more of a decrease occurs in the marginal product of labor, since a decrease in capital results in a downward shift in the marginal product curve for labor. At the same time, the marginal product of capital rises (for the same kinds of reasons) as more labor is substituted for capital. Thus, since the marginal rate of technical substitution equals the marginal product of labor (which is falling) divided by the marginal product of capital (which is rising), it must be falling as labor is substituted for capital.

Since the marginal rate of technical substitution falls as labor is substituted for capital, it follows that isoquants must be convex. (See Chapter 3, Section 11.) Because the marginal rate of technical substitution equals minus one times the slope of the isoquant and because the marginal rate of technical substitution falls as we move to the right along an isoquant, the absolute value of the slope of the isoquant must be getting smaller as we move to the right along an isoquant. But if the absolute value of the slope is getting smaller as we move to the right, the isoquant must be convex.

10. The Long Run and Returns to Scale

Previous sections have shown how a firm's technology can be represented by a production function and have described the characteristics of pro-

---

11. Using the notation in footnote 7, the total differential of the production function is

$$dQ = \frac{\partial f}{\partial x_1} dx_1 + \frac{\partial f}{\partial x_2} dx_2$$

Since output remains constant along an isoquant, $dQ = 0$ along an isoquant. Thus

$$\frac{\partial f}{\partial x_1} dx_1 + \frac{\partial f}{\partial x_2} dx_2 = 0$$

and the marginal rate of technical substitution, defined as $-dx_2/dx_1$, is

$$\frac{\partial f}{\partial x_1} \div \frac{\partial f}{\partial x_2}$$

which is the ratio of the marginal product of the first input to the marginal product of the second input. This is another proof of the proposition in the text.

Example 6.2 Milk Production

Based on data obtained by the U.S. Department of Agriculture, 8,500 pounds of milk can be produced during a specified time period by a cow fed the following combinations of quantities of hay and grain:

Quantity of hay (pounds)	Quantity of grain (pounds)
5,000	6,154
5,500	5,454
6,000	4,892
6,500	4,423
7,000	4,029
7,500	3,694

(a) Plot these data as an isoquant. (b) Calculate the marginal rate of technical substitution at all points along this isoquant. (c) Is this isoquant convex? (d) If the price of a pound of hay equals the price of a pound of grain, should a cow be fed 5,000 pounds of hay and 6,154 pounds of grain?

Solution

(a) The isoquant is as follows:

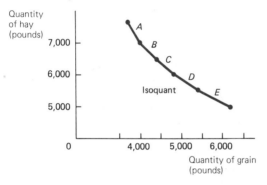

(b) For each segment (A, B, ... , E) of the isoquant, the marginal rate of technical substitution is as follows:

Segment	Marginal rate of technical substitution
A	$-(7,500 - 7,000) \div (3,694 - 4,029) = 1.49$
B	$-(7,000 - 6,500) \div (4,029 - 4,423) = 1.27$
C	$-(6,500 - 6,000) \div (4,423 - 4,892) = 1.07$
D	$-(6,000 - 5,500) \div (4,892 - 5,454) = 0.89$
E	$-(5,500 - 5,000) \div (5,454 - 6,154) = 0.71$

(c) Yes, since the marginal rate of technical substitution falls as more grain is substituted for hay. (d) No, because other combinations of quantities of hay and grain are cheaper. If P equals the price of a pound of either hay or grain, the cost of 5,000 pounds of hay and 6,154 pounds of grain is 11,154P. In contrast, the cost of 6,000 pounds of hay and 4,892 pounds of grain is 10,892P, which is lower.*

---

* For further discussion, see E. Heady, *Economics of Agricultural Production and Resource Use* (New York: Prentice Hall, 1952).

duction functions (and of related concepts like the marginal and average product) that seem to hold in general for production processes. However, one important characteristic of production functions has not been described: how output responds in the long run to changes in the *scale* of the firm. In other words, suppose that we consider a long-run situation in which all inputs are variable, and suppose that the firm increases the amount of all inputs by the same proportion. What will happen to output? This is an important question, the answer to which (as we shall see in subsequent chapters) helps to determine whether firms of certain sizes can survive in the industry.

To repeat, what will happen to output under the assumed conditions? Clearly, there are three possibilities: First, output may increase by a larger proportion than each of the inputs. For example, a doubling of all inputs may lead to more than a doubling of output. This is the case of *increasing returns to scale*. Second, output may increase by a smaller proportion than each of the inputs. For example, a doubling of all inputs may lead to less than a doubling of output. This is the case of *decreasing returns to scale*. Third, output may increase by exactly the same proportion as the inputs. For example, a doubling of all inputs may lead to a doubling of output. This is the case of *constant returns to scale*.

At first glance it may seem that production functions must necessarily exhibit constant returns to scale. After all, if two factories are built with the same plant and the same types of workers, it would seem obvious that twice as much output will result. Unfortunately (or fortunately, depending on your point of view), it is not as simple as that. For instance, if a firm doubles its scale, it may be able to use techniques that could not be used at the smaller scale. Some inputs are not available in small units; for example, we cannot install half an open-hearth furnace. Because of indivisibilities of this sort, increasing returns to scale may occur. Thus, although one could double a firm's size by simply building two small factories, this may be inefficient. One large factory may be more efficient than two smaller factories of the same total capacity because it is large enough to use certain techniques and inputs that the smaller factories cannot use.

Another reason for increasing returns to scale stems from certain geometrical relations. For example, since the volume of a box that is 4 × 4 × 4 feet is 64 times as great as the volume of a box that is 1 × 1 × 1 foot, the former box can carry 64 times as much as the latter box. But since the area of the six sides of the 4 × 4 × 4-foot box is 96 square feet and the area of the six sides of the 1 × 1 × 1-foot box is 6 square feet, the former box only requires 16 times as much wood as the latter. Greater specialization also can result in increasing returns to scale: As more men and machines are used, it is possible to subdivide tasks and allow various inputs to specialize. Also, economies of scale may arise because of probabilistic considerations: For example, because the aggregate behavior of a bigger number of customers tends to be more stable, a firm's inventory may not have to increase in proportion to its sales.

Decreasing returns to scale can also occur; the most frequently cited reason is the difficulty of coordinating a large enterprise. It can be diffi-

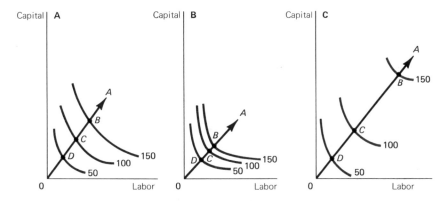

Figure 6.11 Constant, increasing, and decreasing returns to scale

cult even in a small firm to obtain the information required to make important decisions; in a large firm, the difficulties tend to be greater. It can be difficult even in a small firm to be certain that management's wishes are being carried out; in a larger firm these difficulties too tend to be greater. Although the advantages of a large organization seem to have captured the public fancy, there are often very great disadvantages. For example, in certain kinds of research and development, there is evidence that large engineering teams tend to be less effective than smaller ones and that large firms tend to be less effective than small ones.

Diagrams like those in Figure 6.11 can be used to analyze and describe the situation in a particular firm. Panel A describes a case in which there are constant returns to scale. Examination of the isoquants for outputs of 50, 100, and 150 units shows that they intersect any ray from the origin, like OA, at equal distances. (That is, $OD = DC = CB$.) In other words, twice as much of both inputs are needed to produce 100 units of output than to produce 50 units of output, and three times as much of both inputs are needed to produce 150 units of output than to produce 50 units of output. Panel B describes a case in which there are increasing returns to scale. In this case, successive isoquants, as one moves out from the origin, become closer and closer together. For example, $OD > DC > CB$. Panel C describes a case in which there are decreasing returns to scale. In this case, successive isoquants become farther and farther apart as we move out from the origin. For example, $OD < DC < CB$.

Whether or not there are constant, increasing, or decreasing returns to scale in a particular situation is an empirical question that must be settled case by case. There is no simple, all-encompassing answer.[12] In some industries the available evidence may indicate that increasing returns are present over a certain range of output. In other industries,

12. Also, it is important to note that the answer is likely to depend on the level of output that is considered. There may be increasing returns to scale at small output levels and constant or decreasing returns to scale at larger output levels.

decreasing or constant returns may be present. In the next section, we turn to a discussion of empirical studies.

11. Measurement of Production Functions

Economists and statisticians have devoted a great deal of time and effort, particularly in the past forty years, to the measurement of production functions. Three methods have been used in most of these studies. The first method is based on the statistical analysis of time-series data concerning the amount of various inputs used in various periods in the past and the amount of output produced in each period. For example, one might obtain data concerning the amount of labor, the amount of capital, and the amount of various raw materials used in the steel industry during each year from 1948 to 1982. On the basis of such data and information concerning the annual output of steel during 1948 to 1982, one might estimate the relationship between the amounts of the inputs and the resulting output.

The second method is based on the statistical analysis of cross-section data concerning the amount of various inputs used and output produced in various firms or sectors of the industry at a given point in time. For example, one might obtain data concerning the amount of labor, the amount of capital, and the amount of various raw materials used in various firms in the steel industry in 1982. On the basis of such data and information concerning the 1982 output of each firm, one might estimate the relationship between the amounts of the inputs and the resulting output.

The third method is based on technical information supplied by the engineer or the agricultural scientist. This information is collected by experiment or from experience with the day-to-day workings of the technical process. There are considerable advantages to be gained from approaching the measurement of the production function from this angle because the range of applicability of the data is known, and, unlike time-series and cross-section studies, we are not restricted to the narrow range of actual observations. However, there are also some difficult problems in this approach, which are discussed in the following paragraphs.

All three approaches are handicapped by the fact that the data may not always represent technically efficient combinations of inputs and output. For example, because of errors or constraints, the amount of inputs used by the steel industry in 1982 may not have been the minimum required to produce the 1982 output of the steel industry. Since the production function theoretically includes only efficient input combinations, a case of this sort should be excluded, if our measurements are to be pristine pure. In practice, however, such cases are not always excluded (or recognized) and the resulting estimate of the production function is in error for this reason.

Another important problem is the measurement of capital input. The principal difficulty stems from the fact that the stock of capital is composed of various types and ages of machines, buildings, and inventories. Combining them into a single measure—or a few measures—is a formidable problem. In addition, errors can arise in the first two techniques because various data points, which are assumed to be on the same production function, are in fact on different ones. Moreover, biases can occur because of identification problems somewhat similar to those discussed in Chapter 5, Section 12.[13]

With regard to the third method, it is difficult to combine the results for the processes for which engineers have data into an overall plant or firm production function. Since engineering data generally pertain to only a part of the firm's activities, this is often a very hard job. For example, engineering data tell us little or nothing about the firm's marketing or financial activities. Moreover, engineering data are generally available for only parts of the firm's fabricating activities.

Despite these difficulties, estimates of production functions have proved of considerable interest and value. Many of these estimates have been based on the assumption that the production function is a so-called Cobb-Douglas function, which is

$$Q = AL^{\alpha_1}K^{\alpha_2}M^{\alpha_3} \qquad\qquad 6.1$$

where Q is the output rate; L is the quantity of labor; K is the quantity of capital; and M is the quantity of raw materials; and A, α_1, α_2, and α_3 are parameters that vary from case to case. Ordinarily it is assumed that the value of each α is less than one, which assures that the marginal product of each input (which equals its α times its average product) decreases with increases in its utilization. Increasing returns to scale occur if $\alpha_1 + \alpha_2 + \alpha_3 > 1$; decreasing returns to scale occur if $\alpha_1 + \alpha_2 + \alpha_3 < 1$.

Table 6.4 shows the estimates of α_1, α_2, and α_3 for a number of industries in the United States and abroad. They provide interesting information concerning production relations in these industries. To see more clearly the implications of these results, note that α_1 is the percentage increase in output resulting from a 1 percent increase in labor, holding the quantities of the other inputs constant. For example, in the Canadian telephone industry in about 1972, a 1 percent increase in labor would have resulted in a 0.70 percent increase in output. Similarly, α_2 is the percentage increase in output resulting from a 1 percent increase in capital, holding the quantities of other inputs constant.

The results also cast light on returns to scale. In 6 of the 18 cases, there seem to be decreasing returns; in 12 of the 18 cases there seem to be increasing returns to scale. Finally, it is possible to construct isoquants from the results in Table 6.4. For example, Figure 6.12 shows some isoquants for the French gas industry. Note that these isoquants (A, B, and C) are similar in shape to the hypothetical isoquants introduced earlier in this chapter.[14]

13. For an excellent review of empirical studies of the production function, see A. A. Walters, "Production and Cost Functions," *Econometrica,* January 1963.

14. For further discussion, see M. Brown, *The Theory and Empirical Analysis of Production* (New York: National Bureau of Economic Research, 1967). There has

Table 6.4   Estimates of α_1, α_2, and α_3 for selected industries

Industry	Country	α_1	α_2	α_3	$\alpha_1 + \alpha_2 + \alpha_3$
Gas	France	.83	.10	—	0.93
Railroads	United States	.89	.12	.28	1.29
Coal	United Kingdom	.79	.29	—	1.08
Food	United States	.72	.35	—	1.07
Metals and machinery	United States	.71	.26	—	0.97
Communications	Soviet Union	.80	.38	—	1.18
Cotton	India	.92	.12	—	1.04
Jute	India	.84	.14	—	0.98
Sugar	India	.59	.33	—	0.92
Coal	India	.71	.44	—	1.15
Paper	India	.64	.45	—	1.09
Chemicals	India	.80	.37	—	1.17
Electricity	India	.20	.67	—	0.87
Food*	United States	.63	.44	—	1.07
Paper*	United States	.62	.37	—	0.98
Telephone	Canada	.70	.41	—	1.11
Chemicals†	United States	.54	.38	.11	1.03
Aircraft†	United States	.79	.18	.04	1.01

SOURCE A. A. Walters, "Production and Cost Functions," *Econometrica,* January 1963; J. Moroney, "Cobb-Douglas Production Functions and Returns to Scale in U.S. Manufacturing," *Western Economic Journal,* 1967; A. Dobell, L. Taylor, L. Waverman, T. Liu, and M. Copeland, "Communications in Canada," *Bell Journal of Economics and Management Science,* 1972; J. P. Lewis, "Postwar Economic Growth and Productivity in the Soviet Communications Industry," *Bell Journal of Economics and Management Sciences,* Autumn 1975; and Z. Griliches, "Returns to Research and Development Expenditures in the Private Sector," in J. Kendrick and B. Vaccara, *New Developments in Productivity Measurement and Analysis* (Chicago: National Bureau of Economic Research, 1980).

* The figure for α_1 is the sum of the figures given for production workers and nonproduction workers.

† In these cases, M is cumulated past expenditure on research and development, not the quantity of raw materials, and K is the quantity of capital services.

12. Summary

As a first approximation, economists generally assume that firms attempt to maximize profits. In recent years, there have been a number of attempts to experiment with alternative assumptions concerning the goals of the firm; most of these alternative assumptions stem from a more detailed view of the firm's organization. Although these theories are useful for some purposes, profit maximization remains the standard assumption in economics, because it is a close enough approximation for many important purposes and because it provides rules of behavior for firms that do want to make as much money as possible.

also been much use made of the transcendental logarithmic production function described in L. Christenson, D. Jorgenson, and L. Lau, "Conjugate Duality and the Transcendental Logarithmic Production Function," *Econometrica,* July 1971.

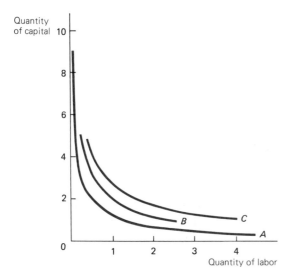

Figure 6.12   Isoquants for French gas industry

SOURCE M. Verhulst, "Pure Theory of Production Applied to
the French Gas Industry," *Econometrica*, 1948. Of course,
these isoquants are merely illustrative. The mathematical expression for an isoquant in this case is $L = H \div K^{\frac{10}{83}}$, where L
is the quantity of labor, K is the quantity of capital, and H is
a constant that differs from one isoquant to another.

The production function is used by economists to represent the
technology available to the firm. For any commodity, the production
function is the relationship between the quantities of various inputs used
per period of time and the maximum quantity of the commodity produced per period of time. In analyzing production processes, we generally
assume that all inputs can be divided into two categories: fixed and
variable. Corresponding to the idea of fixed and variable inputs is the idea
of the short and the long run. Both in the short run and in the long run, a
firm's production processes ordinarily permit substantial variation in
input proportions.

The law of diminishing marginal returns states that as equal increments of one input are added, the quantities of other inputs held
constant, the resulting increments of product will decrease beyond some
point; that is, the marginal product of the input will diminish. An input's
marginal product must equal its average product when the latter is a
maximum. The maximum marginal product occurs at a lower level of
variable input than the maximum average product. An isoquant is a
curve that shows all possible combinations of inputs that are capable of
producing a certain quantity of output. We can construct ridge lines so
that all points where the isoquants are positively sloped lie outside the
ridge lines. No rational firm will operate outside the ridge lines because
the marginal product of one or the other input is negative in this region.

If the firm increases all inputs by the same proportion and output increases by more (less) than this proportion, there are increasing (decreasing) returns to scale. Increasing returns to scale may occur because of indivisibility of inputs, various geometrical relations, or specialization. Decreasing returns to scale can also occur; the most frequently cited reason is the difficulty of managing a huge enterprise. Whether or not there are constant, increasing, or decreasing returns to scale is an empirical question that must be settled case by case.

Economists and statisticians have devoted a great deal of time and effort in the past forty years to the measurement of production functions. Three methods have been used in most of these studies: statistical analysis based on time series of inputs and output, statistical analysis based on cross-section data, and analysis based on engineering data. Although there are a great many difficulties in existing measurement techniques, estimates of production functions have proved of considerable interest and value.

APPENDIX   Organization of the Firm and Alternative Models of Firm Behavior

In recent years, there have been a number of attempts to experiment with models of the firm based on assumptions other than profit maximization. Most of these alternative models are tied to a more detailed look at the organization of the firm and its divisions. Until recently, economists have proceeded on the basis of extremely simple assumptions regarding the organization of the firm. Traditionally, they have posited the existence in each firm of an entrepreneur who exercises control over the firm's activities. The entrepreneur decides whether the firm should continue its existence (or be founded in the first place); he or she sets the price or decides what price to accept; and he or she decides whether output and capacity should be increased or decreased. The entrepreneur is the locus of decision-making in the firm. This concept of the organization of the firm is not unrealistic in many cases. In the United States, millions of small businessmen satisfy, more or less, the definition of the entrepreneur. For example, in a small tool-and-die shop, there is typically a single owner-manager who makes practically all of the major decisions.

However, in large corporations, the concept of the entrepreneur seems strained, since in most cases there is no single entrepreneur and it is difficult to know exactly where, how, and by whom decisions are made. Rather than a single entrepreneur, there are large numbers of people in middle management, as well as the top brass occupying key management positions, all of whom participate in varying degrees in the formulation of company policy. Various groups within the firm develop their own party lines, and intrafirm politics is an important part of the process determining company policy. For example, if a firm is composed of two divisions (each making a different product), each division may fight to maintain and expand its share of the firm's budget, and each may try to put the other in a subordinate position. Whereas in a small firm it may be fairly accurate to regard the goals of the firm as being the goals of the entrepreneur, in the large corporation the decision on the goals of the firm is in a real sense a matter of politics.

It has been suggested by Herbert Simon[15] (1978 Nobel laureate in economics) and others that the firm "satisfices" rather than maximizes profit. That is, business firms aim at a satisfactory rate of profit rather than the maximum figure. A firm's aspiration level is the boundary between unsatisfactory and satisfactory outcomes. The firm abandons the attempt to maximize profits because the calculations required are too complicated and the available data are too poor. Instead the firm tries to attain certain minimal standards of performance.

This theory would, of course, be incomplete if it did not specify how the firm's aspiration level will change, the aspiration level being a certain goal like "our profit for this year should be $2,000,000." According to some economists, if the environment facing the firm is relatively constant, the aspiration level will tend to be slightly higher than the firm's performance. If performance is improving, the aspiration level will tend to lag behind actual performance; and if performance is decreasing, the aspiration level will tend to be above actual performance. Of course, if the aspiration level is close to the maximum profit, there is little difference between the results obtained by assuming profit maximization and those obtained using satisficing.

An interesting feature of this theory is that it focuses attention on internal slack in the firm, a concept that has no place in traditional theory. One implication of the traditional assumption that firms maximize profits is that they produce whatever volumes of output they choose at minimum cost. Although this may be a reasonable first approximation, it seems likely that there is a certain amount of slack in most firms, in the sense that costs are not pushed down to the minimum. This slack acts as a cushion when the firm is submitted to pressures from the outside and from within. For example, if profits are reduced by a fall in demand, the firm is sometimes able to recoup part of the losses by eliminating slack, that is, by lowering its costs. However, this slack is usually not created to provide stability; instead it arises in part from the bargaining process within the firm.[16]

Simon's satisficing model is not the only alternative to the assumption of profit maximization. It has also been suggested that, when differences arise between profit maximization and the interests of the management group, executives are likely to follow policies favoring their own

15. For example, see H. Simon, "Theories of Decision-Making in Economic and Behavioral Science," reprinted in E. Mansfield, *Microeconomics: Selected Readings,* 4th ed. (New York: Norton, 1982).

16. See R. Cyert and J. March, *A Behavioral Theory of the Firm* (Englewood Cliffs, N.J.: Prentice-Hall, 1963), and other works of these authors for a discussion of the topics included in the last few paragraphs. Also, see H. Leibenstein, "Allocative Efficiency vs. X-Efficiency," reprinted in E. Mansfield, *Microeconomics: Selected Readings.*

interests.[17] Important in this regard is the separation of ownership from control in the large corporation in the United States. The owners of the firm—the stockholders—usually have little detailed knowledge of the firm's operations. Even if the board of directors is made up largely of people other than top management, top management usually has a great deal of freedom as long as it seems to be performing reasonably well. Under these circumstances, one might suppose that the behavior of the firm often will be dictated in part by the interests of the management group, the result being larger salaries, more perquisites, and a bigger staff than otherwise would be the case.

Still another alternative to the assumption of profit maximization has been proposed by William Baumol,[18] who suggests that firms attempt to maximize total sales, rather than profits. However, profits are not ignored; it is assumed that there is a certain minimum level of profits that the firm attempts to attain. Thus the firm can wind up in one of two types of equilibrium: one where the profit constraint bars the firm from maximizing sales, and one where it does not. According to Baumol, sales represent a measure of management's success, especially since many observers focus attention on a firm's share of the market as an indicator of its performance. Also, according to Baumol, there is a closer correlation between the salaries of the executives and the company's sales than between their salaries and profits.

In his *New Industrial State,*[19] John Kenneth Galbraith argues that the large corporation is run by the "technostructure"—the professional managers, engineers, and technicians that are the corporate bureaucracy—and that the large corporation's overriding goal is its own survival and autonomy. Consequently, the large corporation tries to avoid risk and emphasizes planning and stability. It is interested in corporate growth, even if this means some sacrifice of profits. Moreover, it is often interested in technological leadership.

Although each of these theories is useful for certain purposes and under certain conditions, profit maximization remains the standard assumption in microeconomics. In part, this is because it is a close enough approximation for many important purposes; in part, it is because some of these alternative theories require more in the way of data than does the simpler theory of profit maximization. Even some of the proponents of these alternative theories admit that profit maximization is an adequate assumption for a wide range of important purposes. Also as we have noted before, the theory of the profit-maximizing firm is of great interest because it provides rules of rational behavior for firms that do want to maximize profits.

17. See R. Marris, *The Economic Theory of "Managerial" Capitalism* (New York: Free Press, 1964). For a recent study of intrafirm organization see O. Williamson, *Markets and Hierarchies: Analysis and Antitrust Implications* (New York: The Free Press, 1975).

18. See W. Baumol, *Business Behavior, Value and Growth,* 2d ed. (New York: Macmillan, 1959).

19. Galbraith, *The New Industrial State* (Boston: Houghton Mifflin, 1967).

QUESTIONS AND PROBLEMS

1. Fill in the blanks in the following table:

Number of units of variable input	Total output (number of units)	Marginal product* of variable input	Average product of variable input
3	—	Unknown	30
4	—	20	—
5	130	—	—
6	—	5	—
7	—	—	$19\frac{1}{2}$

* These figures pertain to the interval between the indicated amount of the variable input and one unit less than the indicated amount of the variable input.

2. In Question 1, does the production function exhibit diminishing marginal returns? If so, at what number of units of variable input do diminishing marginal returns begin to set in? Can you tell on the basis of the table in Question 1?

3. As the quantity of a variable input increases, explain why the point where *marginal* product begins to decline is encountered before the point where *average* product begins to decline. Explain, too, why the point where *average* product begins to decline is encountered before the point where *total* product begins to decline.

4. Suppose that a good is produced with two inputs, labor and capital, and that the production function is

$$Q = 10\sqrt{L}\sqrt{K},$$

where Q is the quantity of output, L is the quantity of labor, and K is the quantity of capital. Does this production function exhibit increasing returns to scale? Decreasing returns to scale? Constant returns to scale? Explain.

5. Econometric studies of the cotton industry in India indicate that the Cobb-Douglas production function can be applied, and that the exponent of labor is .92 and the exponent of capital is .12. Suppose that both capital and labor were increased by 1 percent. By what percent would output increase?

6. According to Herbert Simon, "Models of satisficing behavior are richer than models of maximizing behavior, because they treat not only of equilibrium but of the method of reaching it as well." Comment on this statement. Do you agree? Why or why not?

7. (Advanced) Suppose you are assured by the owner of an aluminum plant that his plant is subject to constant returns to scale, with labor and capital the only inputs. He claims that output per worker in his plant is a function of capital per worker only. Is he right?

8. According to Fritz Machlup, the model of the firm is not "designed to serve to explain and predict the behavior of real firms; instead, it is designed to explain and predict changes in observed prices.... [The] firm is only a theoretical link, a mental construct helping to explain how one gets from the cause to the effect." Comment on this statement. Do you agree? Why or why not?

9. The following graph shows the combinations of quantities of grain and

protein that must be used to produce 150 pounds of pork. Curve A assumes that no aureomycin is added, while curve B assumes that some of it is added.

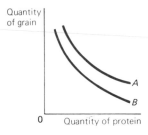

(a) If aureomycin can be obtained free, should pork producers add it? (b) Does the addition of aureomycin affect the marginal rate of technical substitution? If so, how?

10. Suppose that an entrepreneur's utility depends on the size of his or her firm (as measured by its output) and its profits. In particular, the indifference curves are as follows:

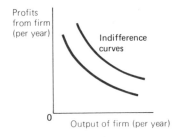

(a) Will the entrepreneur maximize profit? (b) If not, will he or she produce more or less than the profit-maximizing output? (c) Draw a graph to indicate the point he or she will choose. (Hint: Reread Example 6.1.)

SELECTED REFERENCES

CARLSON, SUNE. *A Study on the Pure Theory of Production.* London: P. S. King, 1939.

CASSELS, JOHN. "On the Law of Variable Proportions." *Explorations in Economics.* New York: McGraw-Hill, 1936.

MACHLUP, FRITZ. "On the Meaning of the Marginal Product." *Explorations in Economics.* New York: McGraw-Hill, 1936.

SHEPHARD, R. *Theory of Cost and Production Functions.* Princeton: Princeton University Press, 1970.

WALTERS, A. A. "Production and Cost Functions." *Econometrica,* January 1963.

MACHLUP, FRITZ. "Theories of the Firm: Marginalist, Behavioral, Managerial." Reprinted in E. Mansfield, *Microeconomics: Selected Readings.* 4th ed. New York: Norton, 1982.

SIMON, HERBERT. "Theories of Decision-Making in Economic and Behavioral Science." Reprinted in E. Mansfield *Microeconomics: Selected Readings.*

_____. "Rational Decision Making in Business Organizations," *American Economic Review,* September 1979.

7 Optimal Input Combinations and Cost Functions

1. Decisions Regarding Input Combinations

In the previous chapter we were concerned with the motivation of the firm and the way in which the technology available to the firm can be represented. We decided to assume, as a first approximation, that firms attempt to maximize profit. We also decided that the technology available to the firm can be represented by a production function, which conforms to certain rules like the law of diminishing marginal returns. These decisions take us part way—but only part way—toward a model of the firm. The next step is to determine how a profit-maximizing firm will combine inputs to produce a given quantity of output. That is the purpose of this chapter.

To be specific, suppose that a producer of steel decides for some reason to produce 1 million tons of steel next year. Suppose that, in accord with the conclusions of the previous chapter, we assume that the firm is an out-and-out profit-maximizer, and that we are given its production function, derived largely through engineering studies and statistical analysis. On the basis of this information, can we predict what combination of inputs the firm will use to produce 1 million tons of steel next year and how much it will cost to produce this amount? Or putting the problem somewhat differently, suppose that we are hired by the firm to help with this decision. Can we tell the firm what combination of inputs it *should* use and how much it *should* cost to produce this amount?

In this chapter, we begin by determining which combination of inputs a firm will choose if it minimizes the cost of producing a given amount of output. Then we discuss the nature of costs—what is meant by a cost and how various concepts of cost differ from one another. Finally, we show how the short-run and long-run cost functions of the firm can be derived theoretically, and we provide a brief discussion of the measurement of cost functions.

2. The Optimal Combination of Inputs

For the sake of generality, let's consider a firm of any sort, not just the steel firm noted previously. If the firm maximizes profit, it will minimize the cost of producing a given output or maximize the output derived from a given level of cost.[1] This seems obvious. Suppose that the firm is a perfect competitor in the input markets, which means that it takes input prices as given. (The case in which the firm can influence input prices is taken up in Chapter 14.) Suppose that there are two inputs, capital and labor, that are variable in the relevant time period. What combination of capital and labor should the firm choose if it wants to maximize the quantity of output derived from the given level of cost?

As a first step toward answering this question, let's determine the various combinations of inputs that the firm can obtain for a given expenditure. For example, if capital and labor are the inputs and the price of labor is P_L per unit and the price of capital is P_K per unit, the input combinations that can be obtained for a total outlay of R are such that

$$P_L L + P_K K = R \qquad \text{7.1}$$

where L is the amount of the labor input and K is the amount of the capital input. Given P_L, P_K, and R, it follows that

$$K = \frac{R}{P_K} - \frac{P_L}{P_K} L \qquad \text{7.2}$$

Thus the various combinations of capital and labor that can be purchased, given P_L, P_K, and R, can be represented by a straight line like that shown in Figure 7.1. (Capital is plotted on the vertical axis, labor is plotted on the horizontal.) This line, which has an intercept on the vertical axis equal to R/P_K and a slope of $-P_L/P_K$, is called an *isocost curve*.

If we superimpose the relevant isocost curve on the firm's isoquant map, we can readily determine graphically which combination of inputs will maximize the output for the given expenditure. Obviously, the firm should pick that point on the isocost curve that is on the highest isoquant, for example, P in Figure 7.2. This clearly is a point where the isocost curve is tangent to the isoquant. Thus, since the slope of the

1. The conditions for minimizing the cost of producing a given output are the same as those for maximizing the output from a given cost. This is shown in the present section. Thus we can view the firm's problem in either way.

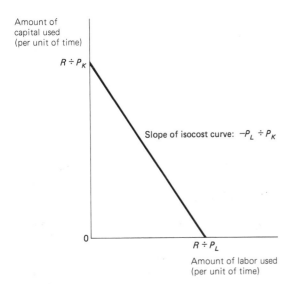

Figure 7.1 Isocost curve

isocost curve is the negative of P_L/P_K and the slope of the isoquant is the negative of the marginal rate of technical substitution, it follows that the optimal combination of inputs must be such that the ratio of input prices, P_L/P_K, equals the marginal rate of technical substitution. And since it will be recalled that the marginal rate of technical substitution of labor for capital is MP_L/MP_K, it follows that the optimal combination of inputs is one where $MP_L/MP_K = P_L/P_K$. Or put differently, the firm should choose an input combination where $MP_L/P_L = MP_K/P_K$.

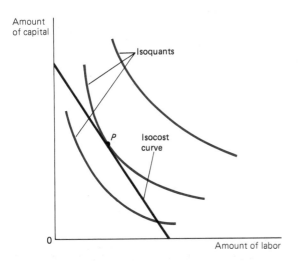

Figure 7.2 Maximization of output for given cost

In general, the firm will maximize output by distributing its expenditures among various inputs in such a way that the marginal product of a dollar's worth of any one input is equal to the marginal product of a dollar's worth of any other input used. Thus the firm will choose an input combination such that

$$\frac{MP_a}{P_a} = \frac{MP_b}{P_b} = \cdots = \frac{MP_m}{P_m} \qquad\qquad 7.3$$

where MP_a, MP_b, ... MP_m are the marginal product of inputs $a, b, \ldots m$, and P_a, P_b, ... P_m are the prices of inputs $a, b, \ldots m$.

Returning to the case where labor and capital are the only two inputs, suppose that a firm decides to spend $200 on these inputs and that the price of labor is $10 per unit and the price of capital is $20 per unit. Table 7.1 shows the marginal product of each input when various combinations of inputs (the total cost of each combination being $200) are used. What combination is best? According to Equation 7.3, the marginal product of capital should be set at twice the marginal product of labor, since the price of a unit of capital is twice the price of a unit of labor. This occurs at 14 units of labor and 3 units of capital; thus this is the optimal combination.

To prove that this allocation of cost ($140 to labor and $60 to capital) is optimal, suppose that we shift $20 from labor to capital (with the result that $120 is devoted to labor and $80 to capital). Since the marginal product of the extra unit of capital that is gained is 14 units of output and the marginal product of the two units of labor given up is 2 times 8 units of product,[2] this change will reduce output by 2 units. Similarly, the transfer of $20 from capital to labor will reduce output.

Table 7.1 Marginal products of capital and labor

| AMOUNT OF INPUT USED | | MARGINAL PRODUCT* | |
Labor	Capital	Labor	Capital
2	9	20	4
4	8	18	6
6	7	16	8
8	6	14	10
10	5	12	12
12	4	10	14
14	3	8	16
16	2	6	18
18	1	4	20

* The marginal products are defined for the interval between the indicated amount of labor or capital and one unit (capital) or two units (labor) less than this amount.

2. The marginal product of labor between 12 and 14 units of labor is 8 units of output per unit of labor. The marginal product of capital between 3 and 4 units of capital is 14 units of output per unit of capital.

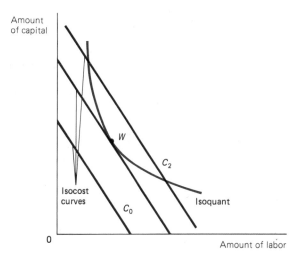

Amount
of capital

W

C_2

Isocost
curves

C_0

Isoquant

0

Amount of labor

Figure 7.3   Minimization of cost for given output

A graph similar to Figure 7.2 can be used to determine the input combination that will minimize the cost of producing a given output. Moving along the isoquant corresponding to the stipulated output level, we must find that point on the isoquant that lies on the lowest isocost curve, for example, W in Figure 7.3. Input combinations on isocost curves like C_0 that lie below W are cheaper than W, but they cannot produce the desired output. Input combinations on isocost curves like C_2 that lie above W will produce the desired output but at a higher cost than W. It is obvious that the optimal point, W, is a point where the isocost curve is tangent to the isoquant. Thus, to minimize the cost of producing a given output or to maximize the output from a given cost outlay, the firm must equate the marginal rate of technical substitution and the input-price ratio.[3]

3. Suppose that Q is the output rate and that the production function is $Q = f(x_1, x_2)$, where x_1 and x_2 are the amounts of the two inputs used. If we want to find the values of x_1 and x_2 that maximize Q for the given cost, C_0, we set up the Lagrangian function:

$$L = f(x_1, x_2) - \lambda(P_1 x_1 + P_2 x_2 - C_0)$$

where P_1 is the price of the first input, P_2 is the price of the second input, and λ is the Lagrange multiplier. Some first-order conditions are

$$\frac{\partial L}{\partial x_1} = \frac{\partial f}{\partial x_1} - \lambda P_1 = 0 \; ; \; \frac{\partial L}{\partial x_2} = \frac{\partial f}{\partial x_2} - \lambda P_2 = 0$$

which imply that $\partial f / \partial x_1 \div P_1 = \partial f / \partial x_2 \div P_2 = \lambda$, the condition in Equation 7.3.
  If we want to minimize the cost for the given input, Q_0, we set up the Lagrangian function:

$$P_1 x_1 + P_2 x_2 - M[f(x_1, x_2) - Q_0]$$

where M is the Lagrange multiplier. Some first-order conditions are

$$P_1 - \frac{M \partial f}{\partial x_1} = 0 \; ; \; P_2 - \frac{M \partial f}{\partial x_2} = 0$$

Note that this tells us how to solve the problem posed at the beginning of the chapter—the problem of the steel firm that decides for some reason to produce 1 million tons of steel next year and wants to know what combination of inputs to use. All that we need to do is to estimate the isoquant that pertains to an output by the firm of 1 million tons of steel per year. (If we are given the firm's production function, this is simple enough.) Then using data concerning the prices of the inputs, we can draw isocost curves, as in Figure 7.3, and determine the point, like W, where the isoquant is tangent to an isocost curve. This point represents the optimal combination of inputs.

3. The Production of Corn: An Application

To show how the theory presented in previous sections can be applied to help improve decision-making, this section describes how Earl Heady, a prominent agricultural economist, helped to determine the optimal combination of fertilizers in the production of Iowa corn.[4] He carried out experiments to determine the effect of various quantities of nitrogen (N) and phosphate (P) on corn yield per acre (Y), and found that

$$Y = -5.682 - .316N - .417P$$
$$+ 6.3512 \sqrt{N} + 8.5155 \sqrt{P} + .3410 \sqrt{PN}$$

7.4

where P and N are measured in pounds per acre and Y is measured in bushels per acre. This equation is, of course, a production function: It shows the amount of output (Y) that can be derived from various amounts of the inputs (N and P). Various isoquants are shown in Figure 7.4.

What is the least-cost combination of nitrogen and phosphate fertilizers? This is an important question, both to farm managers and to the general public. Corn is a very large and valuable crop, and it is important that it be produced as economically as possible. To solve this problem, Heady used the result we derived in Section 2; he said that the optimal N and P must be such that the ratio of the marginal product of nitrogen to its price must equal the ratio of the marginal product of phosphate to its price. At the time of the experiment, the price of nitrogen was 18 cents per pound and the price of phosphate was 12 cents per pound. From Equation 7.4 it follows that

$$MP_N = -.316 + 3.1756 \sqrt{\frac{1}{N}} + .1705 \sqrt{\frac{P}{N}}$$

7.5

which imply that $\partial f/\partial x_1 \div P_1 = \partial f/\partial x_2 \div P_2 = 1/M$, the condition in Equation 7.3. If the output level is the same, the values of x_1 and x_2 that are chosen must be the same, regardless of whether the output is maximized for the given cost or the cost is minimized for the given output.

4. See E. Heady, "An Econometric Investigation of the Technology of Agricultural Production Functions," *Econometrica,* April 1957.

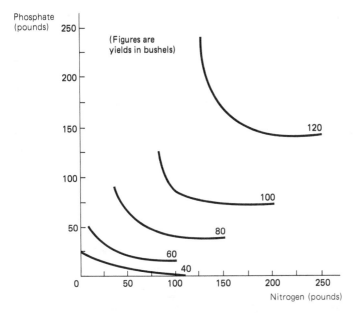

Figure 7.4   Corn isoquants from Equation 7.4

$$MP_P = -.417 + 4.2578 \sqrt{\frac{1}{P}} + .1705 \sqrt{\frac{N}{P}} \qquad\qquad 7.6$$

where MP_N is the marginal product of nitrogen and MP_P is the marginal product of phosphate.

Suppose that a farm manager is thinking of spending $30 per acre on fertilizers and that he wants to know how this expenditure should be allocated between nitrogen and phosphate. Following Equation 7.3, the optimal N and P must be such that

$$\frac{1}{18}\left\{-.316 + 3.1756 \sqrt{\frac{1}{N}} + .1705 \sqrt{\frac{P}{N}}\right\}$$

$$= \frac{1}{12}\left\{-.417 + 4.2578 \sqrt{\frac{1}{P}} + .1705 \sqrt{\frac{N}{P}}\right\},$$

and since he is going to spend $30

$$18N + 12P = 3,000.$$

Solving these two equations simultaneously, Heady's results indicate that the optimal input combination is about 91 pounds of nitrogen per acre and about 113.5 pounds of phosphate per acre. Of course, the figure of $30 was chosen arbitrarily but regardless of the total expenditure that is chosen, this method will provide the optimal allocation.

4. The Nature of Costs

The costs incurred by a firm are often thought to include only the money outlays the firm must make to obtain the use of resources. However, the firm's money outlays are only part of the cost picture. In many cases, economists are interested in the social costs of production, the costs to society when its resources are employed to make a given commodity. Since economic resources are, by definition, limited, when resources are used to produce a certain product, less can be produced of some other product that can be made with those resources. For example, aluminum can be used to produce airplanes, cooking utensils, outdoor furniture, and cans, among other things. Thus, when aluminum is used in the making of airplanes, some value of alternative products is given up.

According to the economist's definition, the cost of producing a certain product is the value of the other products that the resources used in its production could have produced instead. For example, the cost of producing airplanes is the value of the goods and services that could be obtained from the manpower, equipment, and materials used currently in aircraft production. The costs of inputs to a firm are their values in their most valuable alternative uses. These costs, together with the firm's production function (which indicates how much of each input is required to produce various amounts of the product), determine the cost of producing the product. This is called the *alternative cost doctrine* or the *opportunity cost doctrine*.

It is important to note that the alternative cost of an input may not equal its historical cost, which is defined to be the amount the firm actually paid for it. For example, if some gullible Dubuque contractor buys the Brooklyn Bridge for $1,000, this does not mean that its value, either to the contractor or to society, is $1,000. Similarly, if a firm invests $1 million in a piece of equipment that is quickly outmoded and is too inefficient relative to new equipment to be worth operating, its value is clearly not $1 million. Although conventional accounting rules place great emphasis on historical costs, the economist—and the sophisticated accountant and businessman—stress that historical costs should not be accepted uncritically.

Of course, the alternative cost of an input depends on the use for which the cost is being determined. For example, the cost of a pound of aluminum to transportation uses is the amount the aluminum is worth in nontransportation uses; the cost of a pound of aluminum to the aircraft industry is the amount the aluminum is worth to other transportation industries as well as in nontransportation uses; and the cost of a pound of aluminum to Boeing is the amount the aluminum is worth to other aircraft manufacturers as well as in all nonaircraft uses. If all aluminum were homogeneous in all relevant respects, all three of these alternative costs would tend to be the same, because aluminum would be transfered from low-value uses to high-value uses until the yields in all uses were the same. However, if aluminum is not homogeneous, it is not necessary that these alternative costs be equal.[5]

5. See G. Stigler, *The Theory of Price* (New York: Macmillan, 1966), Chapter 6.

The alternative uses of a resource will often be different in the long run than in the short run. For example, in the short run, a plumber generally cannot enter fields requiring specialized skills unrelated to plumbing. But given time he or she can acquire other skills and become a programmer or a machinist. In the long run, alternatives tend to be greater and more varied than in the short run. Frequently, the alternative cost of an input is underestimated because people look only at its alternative uses in the short run.

5. The Enforcement of the Laws: An Application

Many of the concepts of microeconomics are useful for the formulation of public policy, as well as for business decision-making. To illustrate this point, let's consider how the concept of alternative costs can be used to shed light on the optimal enforcement of the laws. The question here is: What proportion of the people who commit crimes of a certain kind should society try to apprehend and convict? Your first reaction may be that they all should be caught and convicted; but, if so, it is easy to show that you ought to reconsider.

To answer this question properly, let's begin by looking at how the costs to society from crime depend on the level of law enforcement. Clearly, the damage to the victims will tend to increase as the laws are enforced more leniently because people will be encouraged to engage in criminal activities. In other words, as the chance of getting caught decreases, more people will be willing to take the chance, with the result that criminal activity will increase, and the damage to crime victims will increase. Thus, as shown in Figure 7.5, the costs to society from crime will increase if society permits a decrease in the probability that a criminal will be apprehended and convicted. For example, in Figure 7.5, these costs will be OC_1 if the probability is 0.4, but OC_2 if the probability is 0.6.

Looking only at the costs to society from crime, it appears that the optimal level of this probability is 1.00; that is, that the optimal policy is to catch and convict all criminals. But this ignores another important type of cost—the cost to society of apprehending and convicting criminals. After all, the services of policemen, detectives, prosecutors, judges, and wardens, as well as other resources used to apprehend and convict criminals, are not free. On the contrary, these resources all have alternative costs—since they can be used in other activities. For example, the policeman who tries to nail a purse snatcher could be working in industry or in some other part of government.[6]

How do the social costs of apprehending and convicting criminals depend on the level of law enforcement? Clearly, they go up as the laws are enforced more stringently because more people and nonhuman resources are required to ferret out and convict criminals. Thus, as shown

---

6. Even the conscription of juries results in social costs, since the jurors could be performing other services. According to one estimate, this cost was over $200 million in 1962. See D. Martin, "The Economics of Jury Conscription," *Journal of Political Economy,* July 1972.

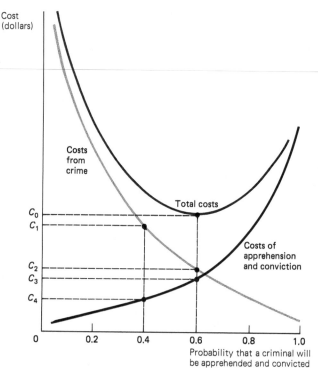

Figure 7.5   The optimal level of law enforcement

in Figure 7.5, the costs to society of apprehending and convicting criminals will increase with increases in the probability that a criminal will be
apprehended and convicted. For example, these costs will be OC_4 if the
probability is 0.4, but OC_3 if it is 0.6.

Recognizing that both of these costs must be taken into account, it
is clear that the optimal level of law enforcement is at the point where
the sum of both costs is a minimum. Thus, under the circumstances
shown in Figure 7.5, the optimal value of the probability of apprehension
and conviction is 0.6. To increase it beyond 0.6 would not be socially
desirable because the extra cost of apprehension and conviction would
exceed the resulting reduction in the cost to society from crime. Among
others, Gary Becker, George Stigler, and Simon Rottenberg have carried
out a number of illuminating studies of the economics of crime and
punishment. Of course, economics is only one of many disciplines that
have a role to play here. But as illustrated by Figure 7.5, relatively simple
microeconomic concepts can throw a great deal of light on many fundamental questions in this area.[7]

7. See G. Becker, "Crime and Punishment: An Economic Approach," *Journal of
   Political Economy*, March 1968; S. Rottenberg, "The Clandestine Distribution of
   Heroin, Its Discovery and Suppression," *Journal of Political Economy*, January
   1968; and G. Stigler, "The Optimum Enforcement of Laws," *Journal of Political
   Economy*, May 1970.

6. Social vs. Private Costs and Explicit vs. Implicit Costs

The social costs of producing a given commodity do not always equal the private costs, which are defined to be the costs to the individual producer. For example, a steel plant may discharge waste products into a river located near the plant. To the plant, the cost of disposing of the wastes is simply the amount paid to pump the wastes to the river. However, if the river becomes polluted and if its recreational uses are destroyed and the water becomes unfit for drinking, additional costs are incurred by other people. Differences of this sort between private and social costs occur frequently; in Chapters 16 and 17 we shall see that such differences may call for remedial public-policy measures.

Turning to the private costs of production, it is important to recognize that there are two types of costs, both of which are generally important. The first type is explicit costs, which are the ordinary expenses that accountants include as the firm's expenses. They are the firm's payroll, payments for raw materials, and so on. The second type is implicit costs, which include the costs of resources owned and used by the firm's owner. The second type of costs is often omitted in calculating the costs of the firm.

Implicit costs arise because the alternative cost doctrine must be applied to the firm as well as to society as a whole. Consider Martin Moran, the proprietor of a firm who invests his own labor and capital in the business. These inputs should be valued at the amount he would have received if he had used these inputs in another way. For example, if he could have received a salary of $50,000 if he worked for someone else, and if he could have received dividends of $10,000 if he invested his money in someone else's firm, he should value his labor and his capital at these rates. It is important that these implicit costs be included in a firm's total costs. Their exclusion can result in serious error.

7. The Proper Comparison of Alternatives

It is also important to note that, in making decisions, costs incurred in the past often are irrelevant. Suppose that you are going to make a trip and that you want to determine whether it will be cheaper to drive your car or to go by bus. What costs should be included if you drive your car? Since the only *extra* costs that will be incurred will be the gas and oil (and a certain amount of wear and tear on tires, engine, etc.), they are the only costs that should be included. Costs incurred in the past, such as the original price of the car, and costs that will be the same regardless of whether you make the trip by car or bus, such as your auto insurance, should not be included. On the other hand, if you are thinking about buying a car to make this and many other trips, these costs should be included.[8]

Note that the kind of model utilized in this section will be discussed further and in more detail when we discuss enviromental pollution in Chapter 17.

8. This example is worked out in more detail in the paper by E. Grant and W. Ireson in E. Mansfield, *Managerial Economics and Operations Research* 4th ed. (New York: Norton, 1980).

As an illustration, consider the case of Continental Air Lines, which deliberately runs extra flights that do no more than return a little more than their out-of-pocket costs. Suppose that Continental is faced with the decision of whether or not to run an extra flight between City X and City Y. Suppose that the fully allocated costs—the out-of-pocket costs plus a certain percent of overhead, depreciation, insurance, and other such costs—is $4,500 for the flight. Suppose that the out-of-pocket costs—the actual sum that Continental has to disburse to run the flight—are $2,000 and the expected revenue from the flight is $3,100. In a case of this sort, Continental will run the flight. This is the correct decision, since the flight will add $1,100 to profit. It will increase revenue by $3,100 and costs by $2,000. Overhead, depreciation, and insurance would be the same whether the flight is run or not. In this decision, the correct concept of cost is out-of-pocket, not fully allocated costs. Fully allocated costs are irrelevant and misleading here. The importance of this way of looking at costs cannot be overemphasized.[9]

8. Cost Functions in the Short Run

In Sections 2 and 3, we showed how the profit-maximizing firm will choose the combination of inputs to produce any given level of output. (Recall that this input combination is the one that minimizes the firm's cost of producing this level of output.) Given this optimal input combination, it is a simple matter to determine the profit-maximizing firm's cost of producing any level of output, since this cost is the sum of the amount of each input used by the firm multiplied by the price of the input. Given the firm's cost of producing each level of output, we can define the firm's *cost functions*, which play a very important role in the theory of the firm. A firm's cost functions show various relationships between its costs and its output rate. The firm's production function and the prices it pays for inputs determine the firm's cost functions. Since the production function can pertain to the short run or the long run, it follows that the cost functions can also pertain to the short run or the long run. In Sections 8 to 11, we discuss the short-run cost functions; in Sections 12 to 14, the long-run cost functions.

The short run is a time period so brief that the firm cannot change the quantity of some of its inputs. As the length of the time period increases, the quantities of more and more inputs become variable. Any time interval between one where the quantity of no input is variable and one where the quantity of all inputs is variable could reasonably be called the short run. However, as we pointed out in Chapter 6, we use a more restrictive definition: We say that the short run is the time period

9. See "Airline Takes the Marginal Route," *Business Week*, April 20, 1963. This article is reprinted in ibid.

It is very important in applied work to recognize what are the relevant alternatives and their effects. In this connection, it may be worthwhile to cite the case of Maurice Chevalier, who, when asked how it felt to have reached his advanced age, is said to have replied, "Fine, relative to the alternative."

so brief that the firm cannot vary the quantities of plant and equipment. These are the firm's *fixed inputs,* and they determine the firm's *scale of plant.* Inputs like labor, which the firm can vary in quantity in the short run, are the firm's *variable inputs.*

The amount of calendar time corresponding to the short run will be longer in some industries than in others. In industries where the amount of fixed inputs are small and relatively easily modified, the short run may be very short. For example, this may be the case in cotton textiles. On the other hand, in other industries the short run may be measured in years. For example, in the steel industry, it takes a long time to expand a firm's basic productive capacity.

Three concepts of total cost in the short run are important: total fixed cost, total variable cost, and total cost. *Total fixed costs* are the total obligations per period of time incurred by the firm for fixed inputs. Since the quantity of the fixed inputs is fixed (by definition), the total fixed cost will be the same regardless of the firm's output rate. Examples of fixed costs are depreciation of buildings and equipment and property taxes. In Table 7.2, the firm's total fixed costs are assumed to be $1,000; the firm's total fixed cost function is shown graphically in Figure 7.6A.

Total variable costs are the total costs incurred by the firm for variable inputs. They increase as the firm's output rate increases, since larger output rates require larger variable input rates, which mean higher variable costs. For example, the larger the product of a cotton mill, the larger the quantity of cotton that must be used, and the higher the total cost of the cotton. A hypothetical total variable cost schedule is shown in Table 7.2; Figure 7.6B shows the corresponding total variable cost function. Up to a certain output rate (2 units of output), total variable costs are shown to increase at a decreasing rate; beyond that output level, total variable costs increase at an increasing rate. *This latter characteristic of the total variable cost function follows from the law of diminishing marginal returns.* At small levels of output, increases

Table 7.2   Fixed, variable, and total costs

Units of output	Total fixed cost (dollars)	Total variable cost (dollars)	Total cost (dollars)
0	1,000	0	1,000
1	1,000	50	1,050
2	1,000	90	1,090
3	1,000	140	1,140
4	1,000	196	1,196
5	1,000	255	1,255
6	1,000	325	1,325
7	1,000	400	1,400
8	1,000	480	1,480
9	1,000	570	1,570
10	1,000	670	1,670
11	1,000	780	1,780
12	1,000	1,080	2,080

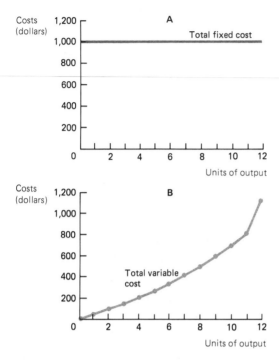

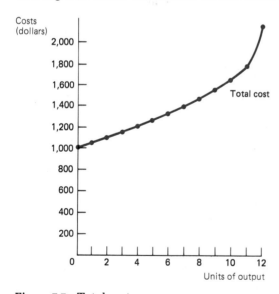

Figure 7.6   Total fixed and total variable costs

in the variable inputs may result in increases in their productivity, with the result that total variable costs increase with output, but at a decreasing rate. More will be said on this score in the next section.

Figure 7.7   Total costs

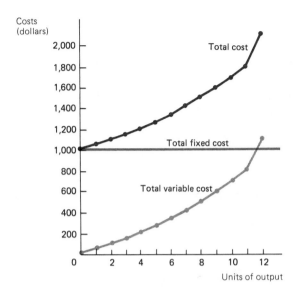

Figure 7.8   Fixed, variable, and total costs

Finally, *total costs* are the sum of total fixed costs and total variable costs. To derive the total cost column in Table 7.2, add total fixed cost and total variable cost at each output. The corresponding total cost function is shown in Figure 7.7. The total cost function and the total variable cost function have the same shape, since they differ by only a constant amount. All of the total cost functions are shown together in Figure 7.8.

9. Average and Marginal Costs

The total cost functions are of great importance, but it is possible to get a better understanding of the behavior of cost by looking at the average cost functions and the marginal cost function as well. There are three average cost functions, corresponding to the three total cost functions. The *average fixed cost* is total fixed cost divided by output. Table 7.3 and Figure 7.9 show the average fixed cost function in the example given in Section 8. The average fixed cost declines with increases in output; mathematically, the average fixed cost function is a rectangular hyperbola.

The *average variable cost* is total variable cost divided by output. For the example in the previous section, the average variable cost function is shown in Table 7.3 and Figure 7.10. At first, increases in output result in decreases in average variable cost, but beyond a point, they result in higher average variable cost. The results of the theory of production in Chapter 6 lead us to expect this curvature of the average variable cost function. If AVC is the average variable cost, TVC is the total variable cost, Q is the quantity of output, V is the quantity of the

Table 7.3 Average and marginal costs

Units of output	Average fixed cost (dollars)	Average variable cost (dollars)	Average total cost (dollars)	Marginal cost* (dollars)
1	1,000.00 (= 1,000 ÷ 1)	50.00 (= 50 ÷ 1)	1,050.00 (= 1,050 ÷ 1)	50 (= 1,050 − 1,000)
2	500.00 (= 1,000 ÷ 2)	45.00 (= 90 ÷ 2)	545.00 (= 1,090 ÷ 2)	40 (= 1,090 − 1,050)
3	333.33 (= 1,000 ÷ 3)	46.67 (= 140 ÷ 3)	380.00 (= 1,140 ÷ 3)	50 (= 1,140 − 1,090)
4	250.00 (= 1,000 ÷ 4)	49.00 (= 196 ÷ 4)	299.00 (= 1,196 ÷ 4)	56 (= 1,196 − 1,140)
5	200.00 (= 1,000 ÷ 5)	51.00 (= 255 ÷ 5)	251.00 (= 1,255 ÷ 5)	59 (= 1,255 − 1,196)
6	166.67 (= 1,000 ÷ 6)	54.17 (= 325 ÷ 6)	220.83 (= 1,325 ÷ 6)	70 (= 1,325 − 1,255)
7	142.86 (= 1,000 ÷ 7)	57.14 (= 400 ÷ 7)	200.00 (= 1,400 ÷ 7)	75 (= 1,400 − 1,325)
8	125.00 (= 1,000 ÷ 8)	60.00 (= 480 ÷ 8)	185.00 (= 1,480 ÷ 8)	80 (= 1,480 − 1,400)
9	111.11 (= 1,000 ÷ 9)	63.33 (= 570 ÷ 9)	174.44 (= 1,570 ÷ 9)	90 (= 1,570 − 1,480)
10	100.00 (= 1,000 ÷ 10)	67.00 (= 670 ÷ 10)	167.00 (= 1,670 ÷ 10)	100 (= 1,670 − 1,570)
11	90.91 (= 1,000 ÷ 11)	70.91 (= 780 ÷ 11)	161.82 (= 1,780 ÷ 11)	110 (= 1,780 − 1,670)
12	83.33 (= 1,000 ÷ 12)	90.00 (= 1,080 ÷ 12)	173.33 (= 2,080 ÷ 12)	300 (= 2,080 − 1,780)

* Note that marginal cost pertains to the interval between the indicated output level and one unit less than this output level.

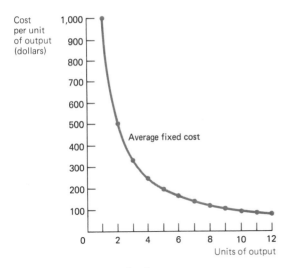

Figure 7.9   Average fixed cost

variable input and P is the price of the variable input, it is obvious that

$$AVC = \frac{TVC}{Q} = P\,\frac{V}{Q}$$

Thus, since Q/V is the average product of the variable input (AVP),

$$AVC = P\frac{1}{AVP} \qquad \text{7.7}$$

Consequently, since AVP generally rises and then falls with increases in output (see Figure 6.2, p. 148) and since P is constant, AVC must decrease and then rise with increases in output. The fact that the shape of the average variable cost curve follows in this way from the characteris-

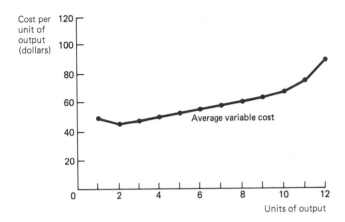

Figure 7.10   Average variable cost

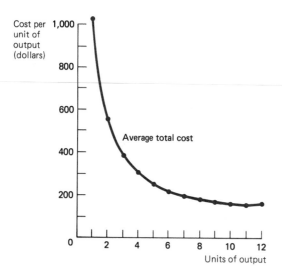

Figure 7.11   Average total cost

tics of the production function is important and should be fully understood.

The *average total cost* is total cost divided by output. For the example in the previous section, the average total cost function is shown in Table 7.3 and Figure 7.11. The average total cost equals the sum of average fixed cost and average variable cost, which helps to explain the shape of the average total cost function. For those levels of output where both average fixed cost and average variable cost decrease, average total cost must decrease too. However, average total cost achieves its minimum after average variable cost, because the increases in average variable cost are for a time more than offset by decreases in average fixed cost. (All of the average cost curves are shown in Figure 7.13.)

The *marginal cost* is the addition to total cost resulting from the addition of the last unit of output. That is, if $C(Q)$ is the total cost of producing Q units of output, the marginal cost between Q and $(Q - 1)$ units of output is $C(Q) - C(Q - 1)$. For the example in the previous section, the marginal cost function is shown in Table 7.3 and Figure 7.12.

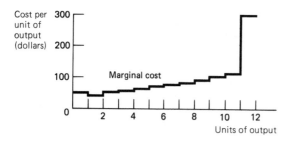

Figure 7.12   Marginal cost

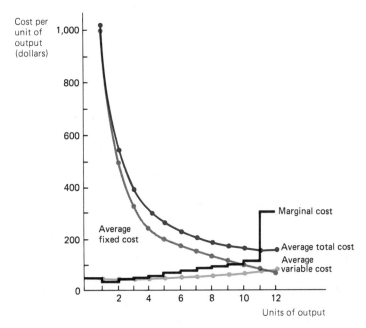

Figure 7.13   Average and marginal cost curves

At low output levels, marginal cost may decrease (as it does in Figure 7.12) with increases in output, but after reaching a minimum, it increases with further increases in output. The reason for this behavior is found in the law of diminishing marginal returns. If ΔTVC is the change in total variable costs resulting from a change in output of ΔQ and if ΔTFC is the change in total fixed costs resulting from a change in output of ΔQ, marginal cost equals

$$\frac{\Delta TVC + \Delta TFC}{\Delta Q}.$$

But since ΔTFC is zero (fixed costs being fixed), marginal cost equals

$$\frac{\Delta TVC}{\Delta Q}.$$

Moreover, if the price of the variable input is taken as given by the firm, $\Delta TVC = P(\Delta V)$, where ΔV is the change in the quantity of the variable input resulting from the increase of ΔQ in output. Thus the marginal cost equals

$$MC = P\frac{\Delta V}{\Delta Q} = P\frac{1}{MP} \qquad 7.8$$

where MP is the marginal product of the variable input. Since MP generally increases, attains a maximum, and declines with increases in output (see Figure 6.2, p. 148), marginal cost normally decreases, attains a minimum, and then increases.[10] The fact that the shape of the marginal cost function depends in this way on the law of diminishing marginal returns is important and should be fully understood.

10. Geometry of Average and Marginal Cost Functions

Given the total cost function, we frequently want to derive the average and marginal cost functions. The purpose of this section is to show how this can be done graphically. The procedures are quite similar to those used in Chapter 6, Section 5, to derive average and marginal product curves. Figure 7.14 shows how the average cost function can be derived from the total cost function, OTT', which is shown in panel A. (Note that, when we refer to average cost, we mean average *total* cost.) The average cost at any output level is given by the slope of the ray from the origin to the relevant point on the total cost function. For example, the average cost at an output OQ_0 is the slope of OR. We plot this slope, which equals OU, against OQ_0 in panel B. For each output, we plot in panel B the slope of the ray (from the origin to the relevant point on the total cost function) against the output, which results in AA', the average cost function. Beginning with a very small output, it is clear from Figure 7.14 that increases in output result in decreases in average cost, since the slope of such rays decreases with increases in output. However, it is also clear that average cost reaches a minimum at OQ_1, since beyond OQ_1 the slope of these rays increases with increases in output.

Figure 7.15 illustrates the derivation of the marginal cost function. As output increases from OQ_2 to OQ_3, total cost (OTT' in panel A)

---

10. If C is total cost, $C = F + V(Q)$, where F is the total fixed costs and $V(Q)$ is total variable costs. Thus average fixed cost is F/Q, average variable cost is $V(Q)/Q$, and average total cost is $F/Q + V(Q)/Q$. The marginal cost equals $dC/dQ = dV(Q)/dQ$.

It is easy to show that marginal cost equals average variable cost when average variable cost is a minimum. If average variable cost is a minimum,

$$\frac{d[V(Q)/Q]}{dQ} = \left[\frac{dV(Q)}{dQ} - \frac{V(Q)}{Q}\right]\frac{1}{Q} = 0$$

which means that $dV(Q)/dQ = V(Q)/Q$, which means that marginal costs equals average variable cost. It is also easy to show that marginal cost equals average total cost when average total cost is a minimum. When average total cost is a minimum,

$$\frac{d[F/Q + V(Q)/Q]}{dQ} = \left\{\frac{dV(Q)}{dQ} - \left[\frac{F}{Q} + \frac{V(Q)}{Q}\right]\right\}\frac{1}{Q} = 0$$

which means that $dV(Q)/dQ = F/Q + V(Q)/Q$, which means that marginal cost equals average total cost.

Total cost is related to both Q and input prices. If one knows this relationship, one can determine a great deal about the firm's technology. According to a fundamental principle of duality in production, this relationship summarizes all of the economically relevant aspects of the technology. See H. Varian, *Microeconomic Analysis,* New York: Norton, 1978.

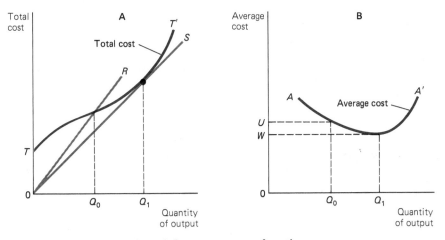

Figure 7.14 Construction of the average cost function

increases from OC_2 to OC_3. Thus the extra cost per unit of output is

$$\frac{OC_3 - OC_2}{OQ_3 - OQ_2} = \frac{BA}{CB}.$$

If we increase OQ_2 until the distance between OQ_2 and OQ_3 is extremely small, the slope of the tangent (UU') at A becomes a very good estimate of BA/CB. In the limit, for changes in output in a very small neighborhood around OQ_3, the slope of the tangent to the total cost function at OQ_3 is marginal cost. In panel B, MM' shows the slope of the tangent to the total cost curve at each output; this is the marginal cost function. It is evident from Figure 7.15 that, at small output rates, marginal cost

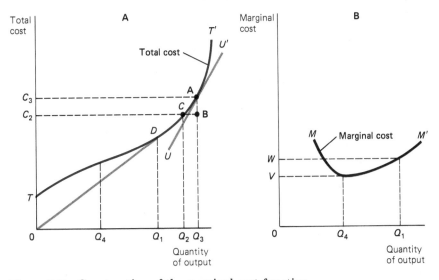

Figure 7.15 Construction of the marginal cost function

decreases with increases in output, since the slope of the tangent to the total cost function decreases with increases in output. However, it is also evident that marginal cost reaches a minimum, OV, at OQ_4 and increases thereafter, since the slope of the tangent to the total cost function is a minimum at OQ_4 and increases thereafter.

It should also be noted that when average cost is a minimum (at output OQ_1), the slope of the ray OD equals the slope of the tangent to the total cost function, since OD is the tangent to the total cost function. Thus, since average cost equals the slope of the ray OD and marginal cost equals the slope of the tangent to the total cost function, it follows that *average cost must equal marginal cost at the output level where average cost is a minimum.* In Figures 7.14 and 7.15, both equal OW.

11. The Break-Even Chart: An Application

A standard tool used by economists to help solve certain kinds of managerial problems is the break-even chart, which is an important practical application of cost functions. Typically, a break-even chart assumes that the firm's average variable costs are constant in the relevant output range. Thus the firm's total cost function is assumed to be a straight line, as shown in Figure 7.16. In Figure 7.16, we assume that the firm's fixed costs are $300 per month and that its variable costs are $1 per unit of

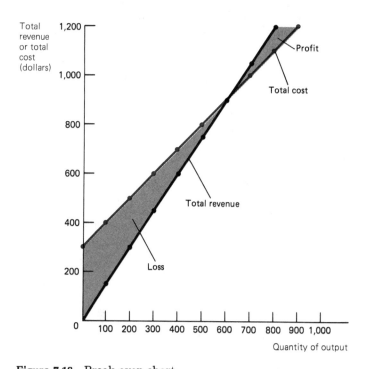

Figure 7.16   Break-even chart

Example 7.1   U.S. Steel's Cost Function

Economist T. Yntema estimated the short-run total cost function of the United States Steel Corporation in the 1930s to be as follows:

$$C = 182.1 + 55.73Q,$$

where C is total annual cost (in millions of dollars) and Q is millions of tons of steel produced. (a) What was U.S. Steel's fixed cost? (b) If U.S. Steel produced 10 million tons of steel, what was its average variable cost? (c) What was U.S. Steel's marginal cost? (d) Do you think that this equation provided a faithful representation of U.S. Steel's short-run total cost function, regardless of the value of Q? (e) If you needed to estimate U.S. Steel's current marginal cost, would you use this equation? (f) In recent years, there have been charges that Japanese steel makers have been "dumping" steel in the United States—that is, selling here below cost. Can this equation be used to tell whether this is so?

Solution

(a) Its fixed cost equaled $182.1 million, because, when $Q = 0$, $C = 182.1$, according to the equation. (b) If U.S. Steel produced 10 million tons of steel, $Q = 10$. Thus $C = 182.1 + 55.73 (10) = 739.4$. This is total cost, not total variable cost. To obtain total variable cost, we subtract the fixed cost, 182.1, from 739.4, the result being $557.3 million. Since 10 million tons were produced, average variable cost was $557.3 million divided by 10 million, or $55.73 per ton. (c) If output increased by 1 ton, the equation indicates that total cost increased by $55.73. Thus, marginal cost was $55.73 per ton. (d) No. Beyond some point, as output increased, marginal cost was bound to increase, because of the law of diminishing marginal returns. (See Section 15 for further discussion of this point.) (e) This equation is not appropriate for present conditions, because it is based on the input prices and technology of the 1930s, not those of today. (f) No, because it is based on input prices and technology in the United States in the 1930s, not on those in Japan now.

output per month. Since average variable cost is constant, the extra cost of an extra unit—marginal cost—must be constant, too, and equal to average variable cost.

To construct a break-even chart, the firm's total revenue curve must be plotted on the same chart with its total cost function. It is generally assumed that the price the firm receives for its product will not be affected by the amount it sells, with the result that total revenue is proportional to output and the total revenue curve is a straight line through the origin. Figure 7.16 shows the total revenue curve, assuming that the price of the product will be $1.50 per unit. The break-even chart, which combines the total cost function and the total revenue curve, shows the monthly profit or loss resulting from each sales level. For example, Figure 7.16 shows that, if the firm sells 300 units per month, it will make a loss of $150 per month. The chart also shows the break-even point, the output level that must be reached if the firm is to avoid losses; in Figure 7.16, the break-even point is 600 units of output per month.

In recent years, break-even charts have been used extensively by company executives, government agencies, and other groups. Under the proper circumstances, break-even charts can produce useful projections of the effect of the output rate on costs, receipts, and profits. For example, a firm may use a break-even chart to determine the effect of a projected decline in sales on profits. Or it may use it to determine how many units of a particular product it must sell in order to break even. However, break-even charts must be used with caution, since the assumptions underlying them may be inappropriate. If the product price is highly variable or costs are difficult to predict, the estimated total cost function and the estimated total revenue curve may be subject to considerable error.

Although the total cost function generally is assumed to be a straight line in break-even charts, this assumption can easily be dropped and a curvilinear total cost function can be used instead. However, for fairly small changes in output, a linear approximation is probably good enough in many cases. As we shall see in Section 15, empirical studies suggest that the total cost function is often close to linear, as long as the firm is not operating at capacity.[11]

12. Cost Functions in the Long Run

In the long run, the firm can build any scale or type of plant that it wants. All inputs are variable; the firm can alter the amounts of land, buildings, equipment, and other inputs per period of time. There are no fixed cost functions (total or average) in the long run, since no inputs are fixed. A useful way to look at the long run is to consider it a *planning horizon*. While operating in the short run, the firm must continually be planning ahead and deciding its strategy in the long run. Its decisions concerning the long run determine the sort of short-run position the firm will occupy in the future. For example, before a firm makes the decision to add a new type of product to its line, the firm is in a long-run situation, since it can choose among a wide variety of types and sizes of equipment to produce the new product. But once the investment is made, the firm is confronted with a short-run situation, since the type and size of equipment is, to a considerable extent, frozen.

Suppose that it is possible for a firm to construct only three alternative scales of plant; the short-run average cost function for each scale of plant is represented by S_1S_1', S_2S_2', and S_3S_3', in Figure 7.17. In the long run, the firm can build (or convert to) any one of these possible scales of plant. Which scale is most profitable? Obviously, the answer depends on the long-run output rate to be produced, since the firm will want to

11. Note, however, that the results of some of these studies have been subjected to criticism of various sorts. See Section 15.

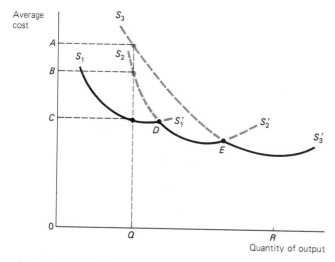

Figure 7.17 Short-run average cost functions for various scales of plant

produce this output at a minimum average cost. For example, if the anticipated output rate is OQ, the firm should choose the smallest plant, since it will produce OQ units of output per period of time at a cost per unit, OC, which is smaller than what the medium-sized plant (its cost per unit being OB) or the large plant (its cost per unit being OA) can do. However, if the anticipated output rate is OR, the firm should choose the largest plant.

The *long-run average cost function* shows the minimum cost per unit of producing each output level when any desired scale of plant can be built. In Figure 7.17, the long-run average cost function is the solid portion of the short-run average cost functions, S_1DES_3'. The broken-line segments of the short-run functions are not included because they are not the lowest average costs, as is evident from the figure.

At this point, we must abandon the simplifying assumption that there are only three alternative scales of plant. In fact, there are a great many alternative scales, with the result that the firm is confronted with a host of short-run average cost functions, as shown in Figure 7.18. The minimum cost per unit of producing each output level is given by the long-run average cost function, LL'. The long-run average cost function is tangent to each of the short-run average cost functions at the output where the plant corresponding to the short-run average cost function is optimal. Mathematically, the long-run average cost function is the envelope of the short-run functions.

Note, however, that the long-run average cost function (LL') is not tangent to the short-run functions at their minimum points, unless the LL' curve is horizontal. When the LL' curve is decreasing, it is tangent to the short-run functions to the left of their minimum points. When the LL' curve is increasing, it is tangent to the short-run functions to the right of their minimum points. A famous mistake was made by the well-

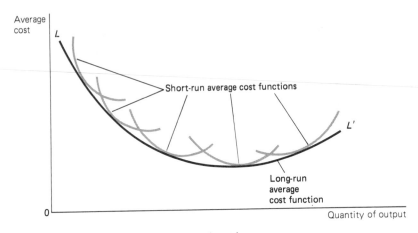

Figure 7.18   Long-run average cost function

known Princeton economist, Jacob Viner, in his pathbreaking 1931 article regarding cost functions. He tried to get the LL' curve to be tangent to the short-run functions at their minimum points. As noted above, this in general cannot be done.

In terms of least-cost input combinations, the long-run average cost function can be interpreted in the following way: For any specified output, the total cost—and the average cost—is the smallest in the long run when all inputs (not just those that were variable in the short run) are combined in such a way that the marginal product of a dollar's worth of one input equals the marginal product of a dollar's worth of any other input used. Only if the firm uses the least-cost combination of all inputs to produce each level of output can the levels of cost shown by the long-run average cost function be reached.

Given the long-run average cost of producing a given output, it is easy to derive the long-run total cost of the output, since the latter is simply the product of long-run average cost and output. Figure 7.19 shows the relationship between long-run total cost and output; this relationship is called the *long-run total cost function*. Given the long-run

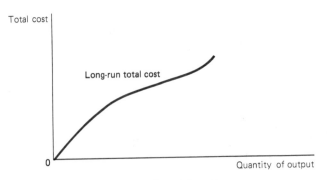

Figure 7.19   Long-run total cost function

total cost function, it is easy to derive the *long-run marginal cost function,* which shows the relationship between output and the cost resulting from the production of the last unit of output, if the firm has plenty of time to make the optimal changes in the quantities of all inputs used. Of course, long-run marginal cost must be less than long-run average cost when the latter is decreasing, equal to long-run average cost when the latter is a minimum, and greater than long-run average cost when the latter is increasing. It can also be shown that, when the firm has built the optimal scale of plant for producing a given level of output, long-run marginal cost and short-run marginal cost will be equal at that output.[12]

13. The Expansion Path and Long-Run Total Costs

At this point, it is also worthwhile to show how a firm's long-run total cost function can be derived from its isoquants. Figure 7.20 shows a firm's isoquants corresponding to output levels of 50, 100, and 150. As we know from Section 2, the least-cost combination of inputs to produce 50 units of output is represented by point E_0, where the isoquant is tangent to the relevant isocost curve. Similarly, the least-cost combination of inputs to produce 100 units of output is represented by point E_1, and the least-cost combination of inputs to produce 150 units of output is represented by point E_2. These tangency points (E_0, E_1, E_2), as well as those representing the least-cost combinations of inputs to produce other quantities of output, lie along a curve known as the *expansion path,* shown in Figure 7.20. The expansion path indicates how, as the output rate changes (but input prices remain fixed), the quantity of each input changes.

If capital and labor are the only inputs, it is a simple matter to derive the long-run total cost function from the expansion path. Each point on the expansion path represents the least-cost combination of inputs to produce a certain output in the long run (since neither input is fixed).

12. Suppose that the long-run average cost of producing an output rate of Q is $L(Q)$ and that the short-run average cost of producing this output with the ith scale of plant is $A_i(Q)$. Let $M(Q)$ be the long-run marginal cost and $R_i(Q)$ be the short-run marginal cost with the ith scale of plant. If the firm is maximizing profit, it is operating where short-run and long-run average costs are equal; in other words, $L(Q) = A_i(Q)$. Also, the long-run average cost function is tangent to the short-run average cost function, which means that

$$\frac{dL(Q)}{dQ} = \frac{dA_i(Q)}{dQ} \quad \text{and} \quad Q\frac{dL(Q)}{dQ} = Q\frac{dA_i(Q)}{dQ}$$

From these conditions, it is easy to prove that the long-run marginal cost, $M(Q)$, equals the short-run marginal cost, $R_i(Q)$.

$$M(Q) = \frac{d[QL(Q)]}{dQ} = L(Q) + \frac{QdL(Q)}{dQ}$$

$$R_i(Q) = \frac{d[QA_i(Q)]}{dQ} = A_i(Q) + \frac{QdA_i(Q)}{dQ}$$

Since we know from the previous paragraph that $L(Q) = A_i(Q)$ and $Q\, dL(Q)/dQ = Q\, dA_i(Q)/dQ$, it follows that $R_i(Q)$ must equal $M(Q)$.

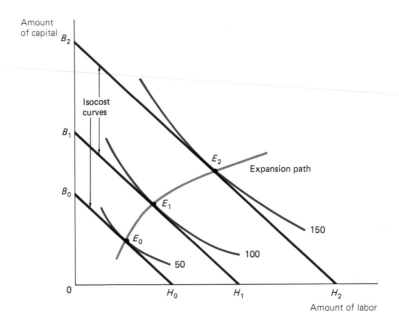

Figure 7.20   The expansion path

Consider point E_0, which corresponds to an output of 50 units. The total cost of the combination of inputs represented by E_0 is OH_0 times P_L, the price of a unit of labor. Why? Because point E_0 is on isocost curve B_0H_0, which means that the input combination at point E_0 costs the same as that at point H_0. And the cost of the input combination at point H_0 equals OH_0 times P_L.

Consequently, to obtain one point on the long-run total cost function, we plot OH_0 times P_L against 50 units of output, as shown in Figure 7.21. To obtain a second such point, consider point E_1 on the expansion path, which corresponds to an output of 100 units. Using the same reasoning as in the previous paragraph, the total cost of the combination of inputs represented by E_1 is OH_1 times P_L. Thus the minimum cost of producing 100 units of output in the long run is OH_1 times P_L, which means that the point on the long-run total cost function corresponding to an output of 100 units is OH_1 times P_L. Consequently, OH_1 times P_L is plotted against 100 units of output in Figure 7.21. Repeating this procedure for each of a number of different output levels, we obtain the long-run total cost function shown in Figure 7.21.

14. The Shape of the Long-Run Average Cost Function

The long-run average cost function in Figure 7.18 is drawn with much the same sort of shape as the short-run average cost function. Both decrease with increases in output up to a certain point, reach a minimum, and increase with further increases in output. However, the factors

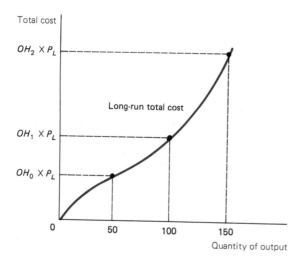

Figure 7.21 Derivation of long-run total cost function

responsible for this shape are not the same in the two cases. In the case of the short-run average cost function, the theory of diminishing marginal returns is operating behind the scenes. The short-run average cost function turns upward because decreases in average fixed costs are eventually counterbalanced by increases in average variable costs due to decreases in the average product of the variable input. However, the law of diminishing marginal returns is not responsible for the shape of the long-run average cost function, since there are no fixed inputs in the long run.

The determinants of the shape of the long-run average cost function are economies and diseconomies of scale. As pointed out in Chapter 6, increases in scale often result in important economies, at least up to some point. Because larger scale permits the introduction of different kinds of techniques, because larger productive units are more efficient, and because larger plants permit greater specialization and division of labor, the long-run average cost function declines, up to some point, with increases in output. Of course, the range of output over which the average cost function declines varies from industry to industry. (Moreover, in a given industry, this range varies over a period of time, particularly in response to changes in technology.)

Why does the long-run average cost function turn upward? The answer that is generally given is that, beyond a point, increases in scale result in inefficiencies in management. More and more responsibility and power must be given by top management to lower level employees. Coordination becomes more difficult, red tape increases, and flexibility is reduced. It is not easy to determine just when these diseconomies of scale begin to offset the economies of scale already cited. In many industries, the available empirical studies seem to indicate that after an initial decline, long-run average cost is constant over a considerable range of output. The situation is like that shown in Figure 7.22. Eventually, however, one would expect the long-run average cost function to rise.

Example 7.2   Ammonia's Production Costs

The following graph shows the average total cost of producing a ton of ammonia using the partial oxidation process and the steam reforming process, with plants of various sizes (as measured by daily capacities). In particular, curve C pertains to the partial oxidation process when naptha is used as a raw material, curve D pertains to the steam reforming process when naptha is used as a raw material, and curve E pertains to the steam reforming process when natural gas is used as a raw material.

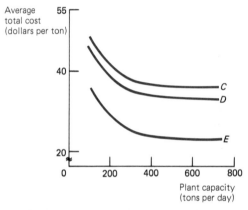

(a) Can the short-run cost function for ammonia be derived from this graph? (b) This graph assumes that naptha costs $0.008 per pound and natural gas costs $0.20 per mcf; if this assumption is true, which process should be used? (c) Does this graph suggest that there are economies of scale in ammonia production? (d) The graph above pertains to conditions in the early 1960s. In the late 1960s, a new process for producing ammonia was introduced. Using this new process, a plant with a capacity of 1,400 tons per day had an average cost of about $16 per ton. Did the long-run cost function for the production of ammonia shift between the early and late 1960s?

Solution

(a) No, since no information is given concerning the way in which cost varies with output when capacity is held constant. (b) The steam reforming process using natural gas, since its cost is lowest. (c) Yes, because costs tend to fall as the scale of a plant increases. (d) Yes, the function shifted downward. In the early 1960s, it was not possible to produce ammonia for $16 a ton, as is evident from the graph.*

*For further discussion, see D. Bixby, D. Rucker, and S. Tisdale, *Phosphatic Fertilizers: Properties and Processes,* Technical Bulletin no. 8 (Washington, D.C.: The Sulphur Institute, February 1964); and E. Mansfield. "The Diffusion of Eight Major Industrial Innovations in the United States," in N. Terleckyj, ed., *The State of Science and Research* (Washington, D.C.: National Planning Association, 1977).

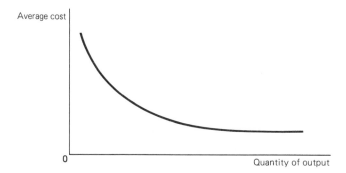

Figure 7.22   Apparent shape of many long-run average cost
                functions

It is important to note that the shape of the long-run average cost function is of great significance from the viewpoint of public policy. If the long-run average cost function decreases markedly up to a level of output that corresponds to all, or practically all, that the market demands of the commodity, it makes little sense to force competition in this industry, since costs would be higher if the output were divided among a number of firms than if it were produced by only one firm. In this case, the industry is a natural monopoly, and government agencies like the Federal Energy Regulatory Commission and the Federal Communications Commission, rather than competition, are relied on to regulate the industry's performance. (This will be discussed further in Chapter 10.)

15. Measurement of Cost Functions

Economists have made a great many studies to estimate cost functions—or *cost curves,* as they are often called—in particular firms and industries. Typically, these studies have been based on the statistical analysis of historical data regarding cost and output. Some studies have relied primarily on time-series data, in which the output level of a firm is related to its costs. For example, Figure 7.23 plots the output level of a hypothetical firm against its costs in various years in the past. Other studies have relied primarily on cross-section data, in which the output levels of various firms at a given point in time are related to their costs. For example, Figure 7.24 plots the 1982 output of eight firms in a given industry against their 1982 costs. Using data of this sort, as well as engineering data, economists have attempted to estimate the relationship between cost and output.

There are a number of important difficulties in estimating cost functions in this way. First, accounting data, which are generally the only cost data available, suffer from a number of deficiencies, when used for this purpose. The time period used for accounting purposes generally is longer than the economist's short run. The depreciation of an asset over a period of time is determined largely by the tax laws rather than economic criteria. Many inputs are valued at historical, rather than

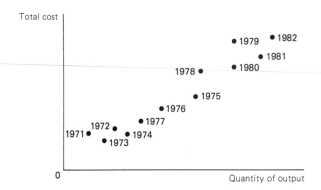

Figure 7.23   Relationship between total cost and output:
Time series for a given firm

alternative, cost. Moreover, accountants often use arbitrary allocations of overhead and joint costs.

Second, engineering data also suffer from important limitations. Engineering data, like cost accounting data, relate to processes within the firm. One difficulty in using them to estimate cost functions for an entire firm is that the costs of various processes may affect one another and may not be additive. Also, there is the inevitable arbitrariness involved in allocating costs that are jointly attached to the production of more than one commodity in multiproduct firms.

Third, an important criticism of cross-section studies is that they are subject to the so-called regression fallacy. It is often argued that the output produced and sold by the firm is only partly under the control of the firm and that actual and expected output will differ. When firms are classified by actual output, firms with very high output levels are likely

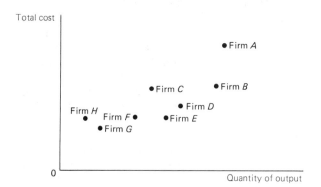

Figure 7.24   Relationship between total cost and output:
Cross-section

to be producing at an unusually high level, and firms with very low output levels are likely to be producing at an unusually low level. Since firms producing at an unusually high level of output are likely to be producing at lower unit costs than firms producing at an unusually low level of output, cross-section studies are likely to be biased, the observed cost of producing various output levels being different from the minimum cost of producing these output levels.

Despite these and other problems, estimates of cost functions have proved of considerable use, both to economists interested in promoting better managerial decisions and to economists interested in testing and extending economic theory. From the latter point of view, one of the most interesting conclusions of the empirical studies is that the long-run average cost function in most industries seems to be L-shaped (as in Figure 7.22), not U-shaped. That is, there is no evidence that it turns upward, rather than remaining horizontal, at high output levels (in the range of observed data). A summary of the results of some of the major studies carried out in recent years is presented in Tables 7.4 and 7.5. The reader should study these tables carefully, since they summarize a great many interesting results.

Another interesting conclusion of the empirical studies is that marginal cost in the short run tends to be constant in the relevant output range. As shown in Tables 7.4 and 7.5, this is a frequent result of these studies. This result seems to be at variance with the theory presented in Section 9 which says that marginal cost curves should be U-shaped. To explain this variance, critics have asserted that the empirical studies are biased toward constant marginal cost by the nature of accounting data and the statistical methods used. Another reason why marginal costs appear constant is that the data used in these studies often do not cover periods when the firm was operating at the peak of its capacity. Although marginal costs may well be relatively constant over a wide range, it is inconceivable that they do not eventually increase with increases in output.

An illustration of the sort of empirical work that has been done in this area is Joel Dean's pioneering study of the short-run cost functions in a hosiery mill. This study, published in 1941, was one of the first attempts by an economist to measure a firm's cost function. Dean found that the total cost function was linear within the range of observation, marginal cost being constant. His estimate of the total cost function is shown in Figure 7.25; his estimates of the average and marginal cost functions are shown in Figure 7.26.[13]

Another illustration of studies of this kind is Martin Feldstein's study of cost functions in British hospitals, Among other things, he found that the long-run average cost function "is a shallow U-shaped curve with a minimum at the current average size (310 beds), [which

13. See J. Dean, "Statistical Cost Functions of a Hosiery Mill," *Studies in Business Administration* 14 (no. 3), University of Chicago Press, 1941. See also A. A. Walters, "Production and Cost Functions," *Econometrica,* January 1963.

Table 7.4   Results of studies of cost functions: General industry studies*

Author	Industry	Type	Period	Result
Bain	Manufacturing	Q	L	Small economies of scale of multiplant firms.
Eiteman and Guthrie	Manufacturing	Q	S	MC below AC at all outputs below "capacity."
Hall and Hitch	Manufacturing	Q	S	Majority have MC decreasing.
Lester	Manufacturing	Q	S	Decreasing average variable cost to capacity.
Moore	Manufacturing	E	L	Economies of scale generally.
T.N.E.C. Monograph 13	Various industries	CS	L	Small- or medium-size plants usually have lowest costs. Blair draws different conclusions.
Alpert	Metal	E	L	Economies of scale to 80,000 pounds/month; then constant returns.
Johnston	Multiple product	TS	S	"Direct" cost is linearly related to output. MC is constant.
Dean	Leather belts	TS	S	Significantly increasing MC rejected by Dean.
Dean	Hosiery	TS	S	MC constant. SRAC "failed to rise."
Dean and James	Shoe stores	CS	L	LRAC is U-shaped (interpreted as not due to diseconomies of scale).
Holton	Retailing (Puerto Rico)	E	L	LRAC is L-shaped. But Holton argues that inputs of management may be under-valued at high outputs.
Ezekiel and Wylie	Steel	TS	S	MC declining, but large sampling errors.
Yntema	Steel	TS	S	MC constant.
Ehrke	Cement	TS	S	Ehrke interprets as constant MC. Apel argues that MC is increasing.
Nordin	Light plant	TS	S	MC is increasing.
Gupta	29 manufacturing industries (India)	CS	L	LRAC is L-shaped in 18 industries, U-shaped in 5, and linear in the rest.
Jansson and Schneerson	Shipping	CS	L	Economies of scale in hauling, but not in handling.
Norman	Cement	CS,E	L	Substantial economies of scale.

* The following abbreviations are used: MC = marginal cost, AC = average cost, SRAC = short-run average cost, LRAC = long-run average cost, S = short run, and L = long run, Q = questionnaire, E = engineering data, CS = cross-section, and TS = time series.

source A. A. Walters, "Production and Cost Functions," *Econometrica*, January 1963; V. Gupta, "Cost Functions, Concentration, and Barriers to Entry in 29 Manufacturing Industries in India," *Journal of Industrial Economics*, 1968; J. Jansson and D. Schneerson, "Economies of Scale of General Cargo Ships," *Review of Economics and Statistics*, May 1978; and G. Norman, "Economies of Scale in the Cement Industry," *Journal of Industrial Economics*, June 1979.

Table 7.5 Results of studies of cost functions: Public utilities

Author	Industry	Type*	Result†
Lomax	Gas (U.K.)	CS	LRAC of production declines (no analysis of distribution)
Gribbin	Gas (U.K.)	CS	LRAC of production declines (no analysis of distribution)
Lomax	Electricity (U.K.)	CS	LRAC of production declines (no analysis of distribution)
Johnston	Electricity (U.K.)	CS	LRAC of production declines (no analysis of distribution)
Johnston	Electricity (U.K.)	TS	SRAC falls, then flattens tending toward constant MC up to capacity.
McNulty	Electricity (U.S.A.)	CS	Average costs of administration are constant.
Nerlove	Electricity (U.S.A.)	CS	LRAC excluding transmission costs declines, then shows signs of increasing.
Johnston	Coal (U.K.)	CS	Wide dispersion of costs per ton.
Johnston	Road passenger transport (U.K.)	CS	LRAC either falling or constant.
Johnston	Life assurance	CS	LRAC declines.
Dhrymes and Kurz	Electricity (U.S.A.)	CS, TS	Substantial economies of scale.
Eads, Nerlove, and Raduchel	Airlines (U.S.A.)	CS, TS	No evidence of substantial economies of scale.
Knapp	Sewage Purification (U.K.)	CS	Significant economies of scale up to 10 million gallons daily.
Stevens	Refuse collection (U.S.A.)	CS	Considerable economies of scale in cities up to 20,000 population.

RAILWAYS

Author	Industry	Type*	Result†
Borts	U.S.A.	CS	LRAC increasing in East, decreasing in South and West.
Broster	U.K.	TS	Operating cost per unit of output falls.
Mansfield and Wein	U.S.A.	TS	MC is contant.
Griliches	U.S.A.	CS	No significant economies of scale to an indiscriminate expansion of traffic.

* CS means cross-section; TS means time-series.
† LRAC means long-run average cost; SRAC means short-run average cost; MC means marginal cost.

SOURCE A. A. Walters, "Production and Cost Functions," *Econometrica*, January 1963; P. Dhrymes and M. Kurz, "Technology and Scale in Electricity Generation," *Econometrica*, July 1964; G. Eads, M. Nerlove, and W. Raduchel, "A Long-Run Cost Function for the Local Service Airline Industry, " *Review of Economics and Statistics*, August 1969; Z. Griliches, "Railroad Cost Analysis," *Bell Journal of Economics and Management Science*, 1972; M. Knapp, "Economies of Scale in Sewage Purification and Disposal," *Journal of Industrial Economics,* December 1978; and B. Stevens, "Scale, Market Structure, and the Cost of Refuse Collection," *Review of Economics and Statistics,* August 1978.

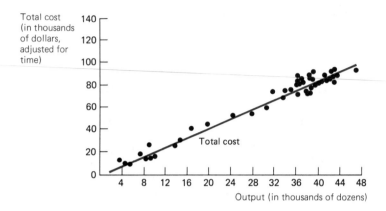

Figure 7.25   Total cost curve: Hosiery mill (monthly costs)

SOURCE J. Dean, op. cit.

indicates] ... that the medium size hospital of 300 to 500 beds is at least as efficient at providing general ward care as are larger hospitals."[14] Figure 7.27 shows the average cost function he estimated. His study illustrates the fact that microeconomic concepts are useful for nonprofit (and government) organizations as well as for firms. In recent years, a considerable amount of research has been carried out concerning the economics of health. More will be said about this topic in Chapters 10 and 13, where we shall analyze price discrimination in medicine and important aspects of the labor market for nurses.

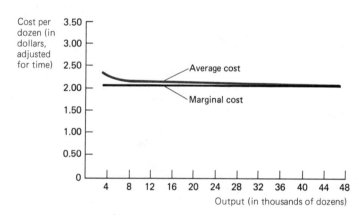

Figure 7.26   Average and marginal cost curves: Hosiery mill

SOURCE Ibid.

14. M. Feldstein, *Economic Analysis for Health Service Efficiency* (Chicago: Markham, 1968), p. 86.

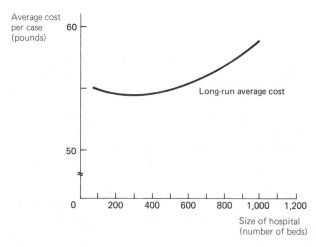

Figure 7.27   Long-run average cost function: British hospitals

16. Summary

To minimize the cost of producing a given output, a firm must combine inputs so that the marginal product of a dollar's worth of any one input is equal to the marginal product of a dollar's worth of any other input used. The optimal combination of inputs can be determined graphically by superimposing the relevant isocost curves on the firm's isoquant map, and by determining the point at which the relevant isoquant touches the lowest isocost curve. To illustrate the use of this theory, we described how it was used to derive the optimal combination of fertilizers in the production of Iowa corn.

The cost of producing a certain product is the value of the other products that the resources used in its production could have produced instead. This is the alternative cost doctrine. The alternative cost of an input may not be equal to its historical cost, and it is likely to be smaller in the short run than in the long run. The social costs of producing a given commodity do not always equal the private costs, as in the case of a steel mill that discharges wastes into a river. In making decisions, costs incurred in the past and costs that are the same for all alternative courses of action are irrelevant.

A cost function is a relation between a firm's costs and its output rate. The firm's production function and the prices it pays for inputs determine a firm's cost function. Three concepts of total cost are important in the short run: total fixed costs, total variable costs, and total costs. The average fixed costs, average variable costs, average costs, and marginal costs are also important. The short-run average cost function decreases at first, but eventually it turns up because of the law of diminishing marginal returns. Similarly, the marginal cost curve eventually turns up for the same reason.

A useful way to look at the long run is to view it as a planning horizon. The determinants of the shape of the long-run average cost function are economies and diseconomies of scale. Because of economies of scale, the long-run average cost curve is likely to decrease, up to some point, with increases in output. As output becomes greater and greater, it is often stated that diseconomies of scale will result, with the consequence that the long-run average cost curve will turn upward. The shape of the long-run average cost curve in a particular industry is of great importance from the viewpoint of public policy.

Economists have made a great many studies to estimate the cost functions of particular firms and industries. Typically, these studies have been based on historical data regarding cost and output, although accounting data, which are generally the only cost data available, suffer from a number of deficiencies when used for this purpose. One of the most interesting conclusions of these studies is that the long-run average cost curve seems to be L-shaped. However, the evidence is limited. Another interesting conclusion is that the short-run marginal cost function often seems to be horizontal, not U-shaped. But this may be due in considerable part to the limited range of the observations.

QUESTIONS AND PROBLEMS

1. Fill in the blanks in the table below:

Output	Total cost (dollars)	Total fixed cost (dollars)	Total variable cost (dollars)	Average fixed cost (dollars)	Average variable cost (dollars)
0	50	—	—	—	—
1	70	—	—	—	—
2	100	—	—	—	—
3	120	—	—	—	—
4	135	—	—	—	—
5	150	—	—	—	—
6	160	—	—	—	—
7	165	—	—	—	—

2. In Question 1, suppose that the price of an important input increased greatly, with the result that each of the figures concerning total cost rose by 50 percent. What effect would this have on the value of marginal cost?

3. As we saw in Example 6.2, 8,500 pounds of milk can be produced by a cow fed the following combinations of quantities of hay and grain:

Quantity of hay (pounds)	Quantity of grain (pounds)
5,000	6,154
5,500	5,454
6,000	4,892
6,500	4,423
7,000	4,029
7,500	3,694

If the price of a pound of hay equals one-half the price of a pound of grain (which equals P), what is the cost of each combination? What is the minimum-cost combination (of those shown above)?

4. In Question 3, plot the isocost curves and the isoquant. Use this graph to determine the minimum-cost combination. Compare your results with those obtained in Question 3.

5. Suppose that a steel plant's production function is $Q = 5LK$, where Q is its output rate, L is the amount of labor it uses per period of time, and K is the amount of capital it uses per period of time. Suppose that the price of labor is $1 a unit and the price of capital is $2 a unit. The firm's vice-president for manufacturing hires you to figure out what combination of inputs the plant should use to produce 20 units of output per period. What advice would you give?

6. According to Frederick Moore, "The '.6 rule' derived by engineers is a rough method of measuring increases in capital cost as capacity is expanded. Briefly stated the rule says that the increase in cost is given by the increase in capacity raised to the .6 power." Give some reasons why this rule holds for tanks, columns, compressors and similar types of equipment. (Hint: Capacity of a container is related to volume, whereas cost is related to surface area.)

7. Suppose that you are a consultant to a firm that publishes books. Suppose that the firm is about to publish a book that will sell for $10 a copy. The fixed costs of publishing the book are $5,000; the variable cost is $5 a copy. What is the break-even point for this book?

8. Suppose that you are given the job of estimating the short-run cost function for the United States Steel Corporation. How would you go about making such estimates? What data would you need, and where would you get such data? How accurate do you think your results would be?

9. In recent years, there has been considerable pressure from consumer advocates and other groups for more and better safety devices in automobiles. What effect do you think the adoption of these devices would have on the total cost function of an automobile manufacturer? Would it affect total fixed costs? Marginal costs? If so, how?

10. A plant producing widgets can produce any number of widgets (up to 100 per week) at a total cost of $100, but it cannot produce more than 100 widgets per week, regardless of how much its costs are. Graph its marginal cost curve. Indicate why few (if any) plants in the real world have a marginal cost curve of this sort.

SELECTED REFERENCES

CLARK, J. M. *The Economics of Overhead Costs.* Chicago: University of Chicago Press, 1923.

VINER, JACOB. "Cost Curves and Supply Curves." *Zeitschrift Fur Nationaloekonomie,* 1931. Reprinted in American Economic Association, *Readings in Price Theory.* Homewood, Ill.: Irwin, 1952.

STIGLER, G. *The Theory of Price.* New York: Macmillan, 1966.

SHEPHERD, R. *Theory of Cost and Production Functions.* Princeton: Princeton University Press, 1970.

JOHNSTON, JACK. *Statistical Cost Analysis.* New York: McGraw-Hill, 1960.

MOORE, F. "Economies of Scale, Some Statistical Evidence." Reprinted in E. Mansfield, *Microeconomics: Selected Readings.* 4th ed. New York: Norton, 1982.

MANSFIELD, E. "Statistical Cost Functions," in E. Mansfield, *Microeconomics: Selected Readings.*

8 Optimal Production Decisions and Linear Programming

1. Decisions Regarding Output Levels

The previous chapter showed how a profit-maximizing firm will combine inputs to produce a given amount of output, and indicated how one can determine the relationship between a firm's costs and its output from a knowledge of input prices and the firm's production function. These results are extremely useful but they fall short of providing us with a complete model of the firm. All that they tell us is how the profit-maximizing firm will—or should—produce a given amount of output. They do not tell us how much output the firm will choose to produce. The purpose of this chapter is to answer that question for the short run, assuming that the firm takes the price of its product (as well as the price of each input) as given.

In addition, we consider a situation where the firm produces more than one product. This, of course, is frequently the case. For example, General Electric produces goods ranging from toasters to jet engines and from generators to light bulbs. In a case of this sort, how does the firm decide how much of each good to produce? This is a very important question. Again, we assume that the firm takes as given the price of each of the commodities it produces.

These results, together with those in Chapters 6 and 7, provide a reasonably complete model of the firm in the short run, assuming that it takes all prices as given. Having gotten this far, we could go on to the theory of price and output in perfectly competitive markets, which is presented in Chapter 9. However, there are advantages at that point in describing linear programming, a very important tool of microeconomics, and reexamining the theory of the firm from the point of view of linear programming. The advantage of this is that, when looked at from the point of view of linear programming, the theory of the firm gains in realism and becomes much more powerful in handling actual production problems.

2. The Output of the Firm in the Short Run

The first question we take up in this chapter is: How much output will the firm produce in the short run? In the short run, the firm can expand or contract its output rate by increasing or decreasing the rate at which it employs variable inputs. For simplicity, assume that the firm cannot affect the price of its product and that it can sell any amount of its product that it wants at this price (that is, it is a perfectly competitive firm). Also, assume, as in previous chapters, that the firm maximizes its profits. To illustrate the firm's situation, consider the example in Table 8.1. The market price is $10 a unit, and the firm can produce as much as it chooses. Thus the firm's total revenue at various output rates is given in column 3 of Table 8.1. The firm's total fixed cost, total variable cost, and total cost are given in columns 4, 5, and 6 of Table 8.1. Finally, the last column shows the firm's total profit, the difference between total revenue and total cost, at various output rates.

Figure 8.1 provides a graphical description of the relationship between total revenue and total cost, on the one hand, and output, on the other. Of course, the vertical distance between the total revenue curve and the total cost curve is the profit at the corresponding output rate. (Note once again that cost curves are another name for cost functions. Both terms are in common use.) Below 2 units of output and above 7 units of output, this distance is negative. Since the firm can sell either large or small volumes of output at the same price per unit, the total revenue curve will be a straight line through the origin. This is always the case when the firm takes the price as given. The total cost curve has

Table 8.1 Cost and revenue of a firm: Prices taken as given by the firm

Output per period	Price (dollars)	Total revenue (dollars)	Total fixed cost (dollars)	Total variable cost (dollars)	Total cost (dollars)	Total profit (dollars)
0	10	0	12	0	12	−12
1	10	10	12	2	14	−4
2	10	20	12	3	15	5
3	10	30	12	5	17	13
4	10	40	12	8	20	20
5	10	50	12	13	25	25
6	10	60	12	23	35	25
7	10	70	12	38	50	20
8	10	80	12	69	81	−1

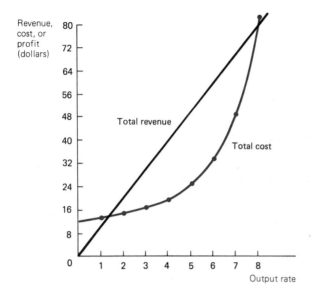

Figure 8.1   Relationship between total cost and total revenue:
Prices taken as given by the firm

the kind of shape we would expect, on the basis of Chapter 7, of a short-run total cost curve.

Based on an examination of either Table 8.1 or Figure 8.1, the output rate that will maximize the firm's profits is either 5 or 6 units per time period. These are the output rates where the profit figure in the last column of Table 8.1 is the largest and where the vertical distance between the total revenue and total cost curves in Figure 8.1 is the greatest.

For many purposes it is convenient to present the marginal revenue and marginal cost curves, as well as the total revenue and total cost curves. Table 8.2 shows marginal revenue and marginal cost at each

Table 8.2   Marginal revenue and marginal cost: Prices taken as given by the firm

Output per period	Marginal revenue (dollars)	Marginal cost* (dollars)
1	10	2
2	10	1
3	10	2
4	10	3
5	10	5
6	10	10
7	10	15
8	10	31

* This is the marginal cost between the indicated output level and one unit less than this output level.

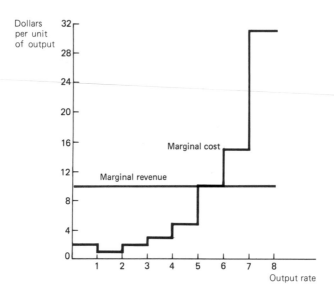

Figure 8.2   Marginal revenue and marginal cost: Prices taken
as given by the firm

output rate. These figures were derived in the way shown in Chapters 5
and 7. Figure 8.2 shows the resulting marginal revenue and marginal cost
curves. Since the firm takes the price as given, marginal revenue equals
price, since the change in total revenue resulting from a one-unit change
in sales necessarily equals the price.

The important thing to note is that the maximum profit is achieved
at the output rate where price ($=$ marginal revenue) equals marginal
cost. Both the figures in Table 8.2 and the curves in Figure 8.2 indicate
that price equals marginal cost at an output rate between 5 and 6 units,
which we know from Table 8.1 or Figure 8.1 to be the profit-maximizing
output. Is this merely a chance occurrence, or will it usually be true that
price will equal marginal cost at the profit-maximizing output rate?

3. Price Equals Marginal Cost

The fact that price equals marginal cost at the optimal output rate is not
merely a chance occurrence; it will usually be true if the firm takes as
given the price of the product. To prove that this is the case, consider
Figure 8.3, which shows a typical short-run marginal cost curve. Suppose
that the price is OP_0. At any output rate (after perhaps an irrelevant
range in which marginal cost is falling) less than OX, price exceeds
marginal cost; thus increases in output will increase profit since they will
add more to total revenues than to total costs. At any output rate above
OX, price is less than marginal cost; thus decreases in output will increase profits, since they will reduce total cost more than total revenue.

Since increases in output up to OX result in increases in profit and further increases in output result in decreases in profit, OX must be the profit-maximizing output.

Even if the firm is doing the best it can, it may not be able to earn a profit. For example, if the price is OP_2 in Figure 8.3, short-run average costs exceed the price at all possible outputs. Since the short run is too short to allow the firm to alter the scale of its plant, it cannot liquidate its plant in the short run. All that the firm can do is to produce at a loss or discontinue production. The firm's decision will depend on whether the price of the product will cover average variable costs. If there exists an output rate where price exceeds average variable costs, it will pay the firm to produce, even though price does not cover average total costs. If there does not exist an output rate where price exceeds average variable costs, the firm is better off to produce nothing at all. Thus, if the average variable cost curve is as shown in Figure 8.3, the firm will produce if the price is OP_2, but not if it is OP_1.

The reasoning behind this conclusion is as follows: If the firm produces nothing, it must still pay its fixed costs. Consequently, if the loss resulting from production is less than the firm's fixed costs, it is more profitable (in the sense that losses are smaller) to produce than not to produce. On a per unit basis, this means that it is better to produce than to discontinue production if the loss per unit of production is less than average fixed costs, that is, if $ATC - P < AFC$, where ATC is average total costs, P is price, and AFC is average fixed cost. But this will be so if $ATC < AFC + P$, since P has merely been added to both sides of the inequality. Subtracting AFC from both sides, this will be so if $ATC - AFC < P$. But $ATC - AFC$ is average variable costs, which means that we have proved what we set out to prove: that it is better to produce than to discontinue production if price exceeds average variable costs.

Thus if the firm maximizes profit or minimizes losses, it sets its

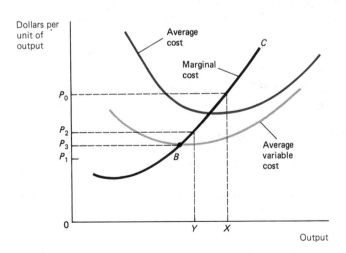

Figure 8.3 Short-run average and marginal cost curves

output rate so that short-run marginal cost equals price.[1] But this rule, like most others, has an exception: If the market price is too low to cover the firm's average variable costs at any conceivable output rate, the firm will minimize losses by discontinuing production.

4. The Multiproduct Firm: The Choice of Output Combinations

In previous sections, we assumed that the firm produced only one product. Clearly this is not the case for all firms. Some companies like General Motors or General Electric are engaged in the production of many, many types of products. To keep things simple, suppose that we are concerned with a firm that produces only two products, windshield wipers and hearing aids. (From the point of view of sheer glamor, the firm's product line is, of course, an advertising man's dream.) Suppose that this firm cannot affect the price of either product, that it takes each price as given, and that it can sell as much as it wants of each product at these prices. If it maximizes profits, how much of each product will the firm choose to produce?

For simplicity, we shall assume that the firm has some given quantity of resources: plant, equipment, and so forth. Using this fixed total quantity of resources, the firm can produce various combinations of windshield wipers and hearing aids. For example, the possible combinations of quantities of these two products, given this amount of resources, might be given by T_1 in Figure 8.4. This curve depends, of course, on the amount of resources used by the firm. For example, T_2 is a curve that pertains to a higher level of resources.

Curves like T_1 and T_2 are called *product transformation curves*. A product transformation curve must have a negative slope, since an increase in the output of one product must result in a decrease in the output of the other product.[2] The negative of the slope of the product transformation curve is called the *marginal rate of product transforma-*

---

1. Let the total cost be $C(Q)$, where Q is the output rate. The total profit per period is
$$\Pi = PQ - C(Q)$$
where P is the price of the product. If Π is a maximum,
$$P - \frac{dC(Q)}{dQ} = 0$$
or price must equal marginal cost. The second-order condition for a maximum is
$$\frac{d^2C(Q)}{dQ^2} > 0$$

2. Suppose that $g(Z_1, Z_2) = k$ is the product transformation curve, where Z_1 is the output of one good and Z_2 is the output of the other good. The total differential is
$$dk = \frac{\partial g}{\partial Z_1} dZ_1 + \frac{\partial g}{\partial Z_2} dZ_2$$
Since k is a constant, $dk = 0$, and the slope of the product transformation curve, dZ_2/dZ_1, is $-\partial g/\partial Z_1 \div \partial g/\partial Z_2$.

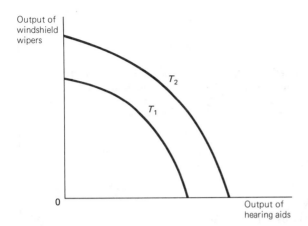

Figure 8.4   Product transformation curves

tion between the two products. It is generally assumed that the marginal rate of product transformation increases as we move to the right along a product transformation curve and decreases as we move to the left. In other words, product transformation curves are generally expected to be concave. For each additional unit of the one product that is given up, the increase in the output of the other product becomes smaller and smaller.

However, two special cases exist where this is not the case. Panel A of Figure 8.5 shows the case in which there is no substitutability at all between the two outputs. This might occur if the products in question (product 1 and product 2) are joint products that occur in fixed proportions. Panel B of Figure 8.5 shows the case in which there is complete substitutability between the two products. This might occur if the two products (again called product 1 and product 2 in Figure 8.5) are two versions of the same commodity. In the rest of this section we assume that some substitutability is possible but that it is less than complete.

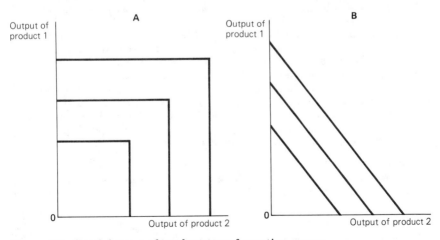

Figure 8.5   Special types of product transformation curves

Example 8.1   Corn Production in Nebraska

Richard Webster is a Nebraska farmer who produces corn on 1,000 acres of land, 500 of which are rented and 500 of which are owned. In an interview reported in the *New York Times,* he estimated that his costs per acre for corn produced in 1980 on his rented land were as follows:

Fertilizer	$ 41.84
Herbicides	2.76
Insecticides	5.50
Fuel	18.00
Seed	16.50
Electricity	15.00
Cost of services of plant and equipment	85.46
Labor	15.00
Insurance	10.00
Land rent	110.00
Total	$320.06

(a) Does this mean that the average cost of producing corn is $320.06? Why or why not? (b) On each acre of land that he owns, Mr. Webster does not have to pay a rent of $110, included above. Does this mean that the cost of using his own land is less than that of using rented land? (c) If each acre of land yields 120 bushels of corn, and if the price of a bushel of corn were expected to be 80 cents, should Mr. Webster produce any corn? (d) If the price were expected to be $1.50, should he produce any corn?

Solution

(a) No. This is the cost per acre, not the cost per bushel of corn produced. (b) If Mr. Webster could rent the land that he owns for $110 per acre, the alternative cost of using an acre of land he owns is $110. Thus, based on the concept of alternative cost, the cost of using his own land is the same as that of using rented land. (c) If each acre of land yields 120 bushels of corn, the cost per bushel of corn of fertilizers, herbicides, insecticides, fuel, seed, electricity, and labor equals ($41.84 + 2.76 + 5.50 + 18.00 + 16.50 + 15.00 + 15.00) ÷ 120, or 95.5 cents. Assuming that these inputs (and no others) are variable, average variable cost is 95.5 cents per bushel. Since the price of 80 cents is less than average variable cost, he should not produce any corn (unless, of course, he can somehow reduce his average variable cost by altering his output or by taking some other measures). (d) Since the price of $1.50 per bushel exceeds the average variable cost of 95.5 cents per bushel, he should produce corn, even though the price is less than average total cost.*

* For the interview with Mr. Webster see "Planting Season Arrives in the American Corn Belt ... With an Export Cutoff Adding to a Bad Price Picture," *New York Times,* April 20, 1980.

Since the firm's costs are fixed (because it is using a fixed set of resources), it will maximize profit by maximizing the total revenue from the two products. If π_1 is the price of windshield wipers and π_2 is the price of hearing aids, the total revenue is

$$V = X_1\pi_1 + X_2\pi_2$$

where X_1 is the amount of windshield wipers produced and X_2 is the amount of hearing aids produced. Thus, if the firm takes the prices as given, we can draw an *isorevenue line,*

$$X_1 = \frac{V}{\pi_1} - \frac{\pi_2}{\pi_1} X_2$$

which shows all combinations of outputs of the two commodities that result in a total revenue of V. There is a different isorevenue line for each value of V, but the slope of all such lines is the same and equal to the negative of π_2/π_1. The higher the value of V, the higher the isorevenue line.

By superimposing isorevenue lines on the graph showing the product transformation curve, we can obtain a graphical solution to the firm's problem. Figure 8.6 shows that the optimal combination of outputs is OQ_1 of windshield wipers and OQ_2 of hearing aids. This is the point on the product transformation curve that lies on the highest isorevenue line. If the firm were to produce elsewhere on the product transformation curve, it would be on a lower isorevenue line. Clearly, the isorevenue line is tangent to the product transformation curve at the optimum point. Therefore, π_2/π_1 (the negative of the slope of the isorevenue line) must equal the marginal rate of product transformation (the negative of the slope of the product transformation curve) at the optimum point.

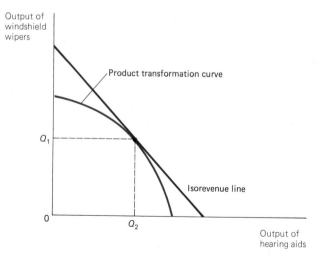

Figure 8.6   Optimal combination of outputs

5. Decision-Making in Municipal Government: An Application

The sort of analysis described in the previous section has a wide range of applications and is useful for many problems confronting public agencies as well as private firms. For example, a major snowstorm produced a snow emergency in New York City in 1969. As many parts of the city continued to be paralyzed for many days after the storm, politicians, labor leaders, businessmen, and even a high United Nations official complained of the slowness with which the snow was cleared. There was an atmosphere of intense dissatisfaction. Eight days after the storm, Mayor John Lindsay directed that a study be made to determine how the city's snow-fighting operations could be improved.

The analysts who carried out the study began by determining how much snow-fighting capability the city had and how this capability was distributed among various parts of the city. To simplify matters, let's divide New York City into two parts: (1) Manhattan and (2) boroughs other than Manhattan. Then let's view New York's snow-fighting capability as a productive unit that can produce two goods: (1) snow removal in Manhattan and (2) snow removal in boroughs other than Manhattan. Clearly, the more of one good that the city's snow-fighting capability produces, the less of the other good it can produce. Given the city's total capability, the various combinations of these two outputs that can be produced are shown in Figure 8.7. This, of course, is a product transformation curve, pure and simple. The points on this curve, like any product transformation curve, are efficient points in the sense that, holding constant the quantity of one output, they show the maximum amount that can be produced of the other output.

Which of the infinity of points on the product transformation curve should the City of New York choose? At one extreme, point U provides

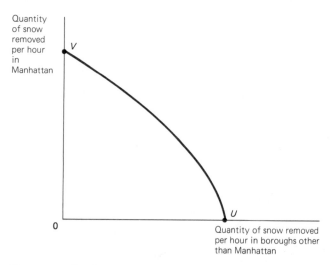

Figure 8.7   Product transformation curve: New York City snow removal

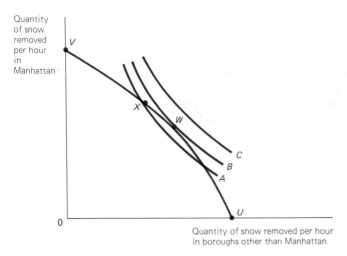

Figure 8.8   Solution of New York snow removal problem

no snow removal at all for Manhattan; at the other extreme, point V provides no snow removal at all for the boroughs other than Manhattan. Clearly, the answer lies somewhere in between, but where? In principle, the solution is simple: Choose that point which maximizes the welfare of the city as a whole. Suppose that each curve, like A, B, and C, in Figure 8.8 represents a set of combinations of the two outputs with equal "municipal worth." These curves are analogous to the isorevenue lines of the previous sections. (They are curved, not straight, because the relative worth of the two outputs is assumed constant in the previous section, but not here.) Thus the optimal combination is W, the point at which the product transformation curve touches the highest isorevenue line.

In fact, the analysts' investigations of the extent and distribution of the city's snow-fighting capability showed that the city was allocating its snow plows in such a way that snow was removed much more quickly in Manhattan than in other boroughs of the city. In other words, the municipal government was operating at point X on the product transformation curve. This was not due to a conscious decision, but because most of the plows were fitted on refuse-collection trucks. Since densely populated Manhattan generated more refuse per mile of street than the other boroughs, it had more refuse-collection trucks per mile of street—and also more plows! Once this was recognized, Mayor Lindsay reallocated the city's snow-fighting capability so as to move from point X toward point W. In other words, he moved plows and other equipment from Manhattan to the other boroughs. Once this was done, the available evidence indicated that it was very unlikely that the city would be paralyzed in this way again.

This was an interesting and apparently effective application of microeconomic (and engineering) analysis. Before leaving it, note that because the measurement of municipal worth presents difficult problems, it is often hard to draw curves like A, B, and C with confidence. Nonetheless, based on the available evidence (and the intuition of the decision-maker), it may be possible to approximate these curves accurately enough to support a useful analysis. For example, in the case of New York's snow disposal problem, this did not seem to pose an insurmountable problem. Of course, in the case of business firms, the measurement of the isorevenue lines is much more straightforward. Finally, note too that this same kind of analysis can be used if the decision-maker is viewed as maximizing his or her political fortunes, not the welfare of the city. Under these circumstances, curves like A, B, or C represent combinations of outputs with equal political worth to the decision-maker, not equal municipal worth.[3]

6. Linear Programming[4]

Previous sections of this chapter have shown how the profit-maximizing firm chooses its output level—or its combination of output levels, if it produces more than one commodity—in the short run, given that it takes the price of each of its inputs and outputs as given. At this point, we could go on to the theory of price and output in perfectly competitive markets. However, we choose to take a somewhat different path. In the rest of this chapter, we describe linear programming and reexamine the theory of the firm from the point of view of linear programming. Then, in Chapter 9, we discuss the theory of price and output in perfectly competitive markets.

Linear programming is the most famous of the mathematical programming methods that have come into existence since World War II. It is a technique that allows decision-makers to solve maximization and minimization problems where there are certain constraints that limit what can be done. One of the principal figures in the development of linear programming was George Dantzig, an American mathematician now at Stanford. First used shortly after World War II to help schedule the procurement activities of the United States Air Force, linear programming has become an extremely important part of microeconomic theory and a very powerful tool for the solution of managerial problems.

---

3. Needless to say, this brief discussion can only provide part of the results of the New York study. For a fuller account, see E. S. Savas, "The Political Properties of Crystalline H_2O: Planning for Snow Emergencies in New York," *Management Science*, October 1973, reprinted in E. Mansfield, *Managerial Economics and Operations Research*, 4th ed. (New York: Norton, 1980). The New York analysts did not couch their procedure or their results in the terms used here, but these terms and concepts seem to capture the spirit of their analysis in a sufficiently accurate way to be useful for present purposes. In reality, all that we have done here is to indicate one way in which the New York study can be interpreted in terms of the model discussed in the previous section. There may, of course, be other interpretations.

4. This chapter and Chapter 9 have been written so that the reader who is not interested in linear programming can go directly to Chapter 9 at this point. An understanding of the material in Chapter 9 does not depend on a reading of the material on linear programming.

Example 8.2 File Cabinets and Desks

The Universal Metal Products Company produces file cabinets and desks. If its usage of resources, and hence its cost, remains constant at the current level, the firm's product transformation curve is as shown below:

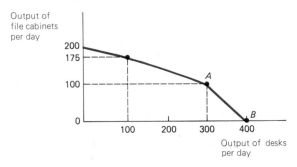

(a) What is the marginal rate of product transformation when the number of desks produced per day is less than 100? (b) If the firm produces an additional desk per day, how many fewer file cabinets must it produce per day if it is currently producing 330 desks per day? (c) If the price of a desk is the same as the price of a file cabinet, what output combination should the firm choose? (d) Why does the marginal rate of product transformation tend to increase as more and more desks are produced by the firm?

Solution

(a) The marginal rate of product transformation equals minus one times the slope of the product transformation curve. When the number of desks produced per day is between zero and 100, the slope of the product transformation curve is $-\frac{1}{4}$, so the answer is $\frac{1}{4}$. That is, a one-unit increase in the daily output of desks results in a $\frac{1}{4}$-unit decrease in the daily output of file cabinets. (b) When the number of desks produced per day is between 300 and 400, the slope of the product transformation curve is minus one, which means that the production of an additional desk per day requires the production of one less file cabinet per day. (c) Since the ratio of the price of a desk to the price of a file cabinet is one, the firm should choose a point where the marginal rate of product transformation equals one. This is true for all points on the product transformation curve between A and B. Thus the firm should choose any point between A and B. That is, it can produce 300 desks and 100 file cabinets per day, or 400 desks and no file cabinets, or any point in between. (d) When the firm produces relatively few desks, it can use those resources that are best suited for this purpose. But as it produces more and more desks, it must use resources that are much better suited for the production of file cabinets rather than desks. Consequently, the marginal rate of product transformation tends to increase as more and more desks are produced.

Its remarkable growth has been helped along by the development of computers which can handle the many computations that are required to solve large linear programming problems.

Although linear programming is an important tool of microeconomists, it is purely a mathematical technique. By itself it can only tell us the implications of the data that the decision-maker or the analyst has gathered (or assumed). If these data (or assumptions) are wrong, the solution will in general be wrong, too. The great advantage of linear programming is that it provides computational advantages, not that it performs magic.

Why is it important to reexamine the theory of production from the point of view of linear programming? There are at least two reasons. First, the programming analysis is more fundamental in one respect than the conventional analysis presented in Chapters 6 and 7. The conventional theory is built on the foundation of the production function, which assumes that the technically efficient production processes have been determined and given to the economist before he or she attacks the problem. But in the real world, the economist is usually confronted with a number of feasible production processes, and it is very difficult to tell which ones—or which combinations—are efficient. The choice of the optimal combination of production processes is an extremely important decision, and it can be analyzed by linear programming.

Second, the programming analysis seems to conform more closely to the way that businessmen tend to view production. The language and concepts of linear programming, though abstract and by no means the same as those of management, seem to be closer to those of management people than the ones used by the conventional theory. Although this is less important than the first reason, it is of some importance, since it makes it easier to apply linear programming than conventional theory. The development of linear programming has enabled the economist to solve many types of production problems for industry and government.

7. The Firm's Production Decisions as a Linear Programming Problem

Linear programming views the technology available to the firm as being composed of a finite number of processes. A *process* uses inputs and produces one or more outputs. For example, a man using a wheelbarrow to carry bricks is a process. An important assumption in linear programming is that each process uses inputs in fixed proportions. Consequently, each process can be described by a set of technical coefficients, $(a_1, \cdots, a_m)$, that shows the amount of the first input, $\cdots$, mth input that is needed to produce one unit of output. For example, if the first input were man-hours, the second input were wheelbarrow-hours, and a unit of output were the transportation of 1 ton-mile of bricks, the technical coefficients for the "man-wheelbarrow" process might be (5, 5), which would indicate that it takes 5 man-hours of labor and 5 hours of use of the wheelbarrow to "produce" 1 ton-mile of transportation of bricks.

Each process can be operated at various *activity levels*. The activity level of a process is the number of units of output that is produced with the process. For example, if 2 ton-miles of bricks are "produced" with the "man-wheelbarrow" process described above, its activity level is 2; on the other hand, if 0.5 ton-miles of bricks are transported with this process, its activity level is 0.5. It is assumed that, if the output of any process is varied, the quantity of inputs used by the process varies proportionately with the output of the process. Thus the quantity of any input used by a process is equal to the activity level of the process multiplied by the input's technical coefficient for this process. For example, the amount of labor used by the "man-wheelbarrow" process is $5 \times 5 = 25$ man-hours, if this process is operated at an activity level of 5. When two or more processes are used simultaneously, it is assumed that they do not interfere with one another or make each other more productive. (In other words, it is assumed that the processes are additive in the inputs.)

Viewed in the context of linear programming, the firm's production problem is as follows: The firm has certain fixed amounts of a number of inputs at its disposal. For example, if the firm is a steel mill, it has a limited amount of land, raw materials, managerial labor, and equipment of various types. (These limitations on the amounts of inputs that the firm can use are called *constraints*.) Each unit of output resulting from a particular process yields the firm a certain amount of profit. This amount of profit varies in general from process to process; indeed, the product itself may vary from process to process. Knowing the profit to be made from a unit of output from each process and recognizing the limited amount of inputs at its disposal, the firm must determine the activity level at which each process should be operated to maximize profit.

8. The Finishing of Cotton Cloth: An Illustration

The previous section provided a general description of the firm's production decision, as it is pictured from the viewpoint of linear programming. But such a description is of limited use unless it is supplemented by illustrations. Recognizing this fact, the next few sections of this chapter are devoted to a fairly detailed description of several cases that illustrate how linear programming can be used to solve the production problems of the firm.

To begin with, consider the following situation. Suppose that one of the operations of a textile mill is the finishing of cotton cloth. The output rate of the finishing department is limited by the capacity of its finishing equipment and the amount of skilled labor available to carry out the work. The firm is considering three finishing processes: processes 1, 2, and 3. Suppose that the firm knows that the profit per batch of cotton cloth finished with process 1 is $1.00; similarly, it is $0.90 for process 2, and $1.10 for process 3. Suppose too that process 1 uses 3 machine-hours of finishing capacity per batch of cotton cloth processed, that process 2 uses 2.50 machine-hours, and that process 3 uses 5.25 machine-hours. Also, suppose that process 1 uses 0.4 man-hours of skilled labor per batch of cotton cloth processed, that process 2 uses 0.50 man-hours, and that process 3 uses 0.35 man-hours. These are the technical coefficients.[5] Finally, suppose that 6,000 machine-hours per week is the maximum finishing capacity, and 600 man-hours per week is the maximum amount of skilled labor that the firm can use.

If Q_1 is the number of batches of cotton cloth processed per week on process 1, Q_2 is the number processed on process 2, and Q_3 is the number processed on process 3, the firm's production problem can be regarded as the following linear programming problem: Maximize

$$\pi = 1.00Q_1 + 0.90Q_2 + 1.10Q_3 \qquad \text{8.1}$$

subject to the constraints

$$3Q_1 + 2.50Q_2 + 5.25Q_3 \leq 6{,}000 \qquad \text{8.2}$$

$$0.40Q_1 + 0.50Q_2 + 0.35Q_3 \leq 600 \qquad \text{8.3}$$

$$Q_1 \geq 0;\ Q_2 \geq 0;\ Q_3 \geq 0 \qquad \text{8.4}$$

The *objective function*, sometimes called the criterion function, is the function to be maximized in a linear programming problem. In this case, it is the expression for the firm's profits given in Equation 8.1. The *constraints* are given in Inequalities 8.2 to 8.4. Inequality 8.2 states that the total machine-hours per week of finishing capacity must be less than or equal to 6,000. Inequality 8.3 states that the total man-hours of skilled labor per week must be less than or equal to 600. Inequality 8.4 contains nonnegativity constraints, which may seem so obvious as to be unnecessary to state. But they are not obvious to a dumb electronic computer, which might otherwise come up with a solution with a negative output. Finally, note that the objective function and the constraints are all linear in Q_1, Q_2, and Q_3, the levels at which the processes are operated.

To see how this problem can be solved, we begin by providing a graphical representation of the feasible input combinations and of a process.[6] Figure 8.9, which has the total man-hours per week of skilled labor-time used by all three processes along the horizontal axis and the total machine-hours per week of finishing capacity used by all three processes along the vertical axis, shows the combinations of total man-hours and total machine-hours that are feasible. The feasible region is the rectangle $OXYZ$, since a maximum of 600 man-hours and 6,000 machine-hours are available.

5. If machine-time is the first input and skilled labor is the second input, the a's, in the terminology of Section 7, are (3, 0.4) for process 1, (2.50, 0.5) for process 2, and (5.25, 0.35) for process 3. A unit of output is a batch of cotton cloth finished.

6. The ensuing discussion of this problem is similar in many respects (although the problem itself is quite different) to W. Baumol, *Economic Theory and Operations Analysis* 3d ed. (Englewood Cliffs, N.J.: Prentice-Hall, 1972), pp. 296–310. Baumol's discussions in Chapters 5, 6, and 12 of his book are highly recommended for those readers who are interested in a more detailed treatment of linear programming.

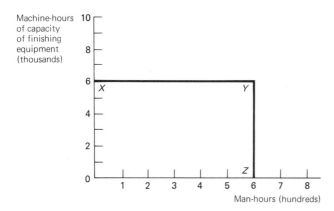

Figure 8.9   Feasible input combinations

Recall that a process is defined to have fixed input proportions. Since all points where input proportions are unchanged lie along a straight line through the origin, we can represent each process by such a line, or *ray*. In Figure 8.10, the ray OR_1 represents process 1. Process 1 uses 3 machine-hours of finishing capacity and 0.4 hours of skilled labor per batch processed. That is, it uses 7.5 machine-hours of finishing capacity for every hour of skilled labor. Thus the ray OR_1 includes all points at which finishing capacity is combined with skilled labor in the ratio of 7.5 : 1. Each point on this ray implies a certain output level. For example, point A, where 100 hours of labor and 750 machine-hours of finishing capacity are used, implies an output of 250 batches per week, since process 1 uses 0.4 hours of skilled labor and 3 machine-hours of finishing capacity per batch. Moreover, since all points at which labor and finishing capacity are combined in the ratio of 7.5 : 1 are included in the ray OR_1, every possible output corresponds to some point on OR_1.

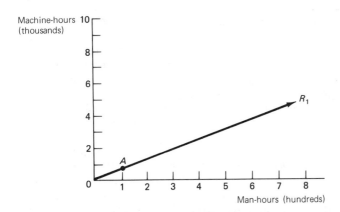

Figure 8.10   Representation of process 1 by a ray

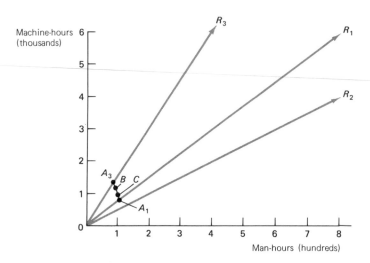

Figure 8.11 Rays for processes 1, 2, and 3

It is possible to construct rays representing each of the three processes. Figure 8.11 shows all of them, with OR_2 representing process 2, and OR_3 representing process 3. Each ray is constructed in the same way as OR_1 was constructed for process 1. Using these rays, we can draw isoquants—curves that include all input combinations that can produce a particular amount of output. An isoquant means the same thing here as in Chapter 6; the only difference is that an isoquant here does not exhibit the smoothness of the isoquants in Chapter 6.

To begin with, we focus on processes 1 and 3. In Figure 8.11, point A_1 on OR_1 is the point corresponding to an output of 250 batches per week, and point A_3 on OR_3 is the point corresponding to an output of 250 batches per week. Thus A_1 and A_3 are points on the isoquant corresponding to an output of 250 batches per week. Moreover, any point on the line segment that joins A_1 to A_3 is also on this isoquant, because the firm can simultaneously use both process 1 and process 3 to produce 250 batches per week. For example, point B corresponds to the case in which process 1 is used to produce 25 batches and process 3 is used to produce 225 batches, and point C corresponds to the case in which process 1 is used to produce 150 batches and process 3 is used to produce 100 batches. By varying the proportion of total output produced by each process, one can obtain all points on the line segment that joins A_1 to A_3.

In Figure 8.12, to complete the isoquant corresponding to an output of 250 batches per week, we join A_1 to A_2, the point on OR_2 that represents an output of 250 batches per week. Thus the entire isoquant is $A_3A_1A_2$. (At first glance, one might wonder why the line segment joining A_3 to A_2 is not part of the isoquant. After all, it does represent various combinations of skilled labor and finishing capacity that can produce 250

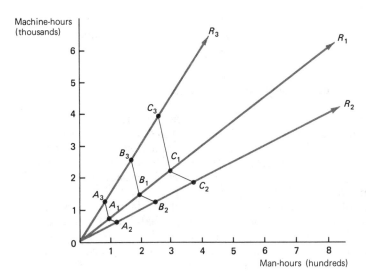

Figure 8.12 Isoquants for selected output levels

batches a week. The reason for its exclusion is that all points on the line segment joining A_3 to A_2 are inefficient. They use as much of one input and more of the other input than some point on $A_3A_1A_2$. Thus the points on A_3A_2 are clearly not on the isoquant—and they are not part of the solution to the firm's problem.) Other isoquants are also shown in Figure 8.12; $B_3B_1B_2$ is the isoquant corresponding to an output of 500 batches per week and $C_3C_1C_2$ is the isoquant corresponding to an output of 750 batches per week.

Several things should be noted about the characteristic shape of isoquants in linear programming problems. First, they consist of a series of connected line segments, not the smooth curves of conventional theory. If the number of possible processes is very large, however, the isoquants may approximate the smooth conventional curves.[7] Second, their slope is negative, or at least nonpositive. Third, they are convex, which means that the marginal rate of technical substitution of one input for another decreases as more of the first input is substituted for the other. Disregarding the fact that they do not exhibit the smoothness assumed in conventional theory, the isoquants of linear programming have the same basic shape as the isoquants of conventional theory.

Since the isoquants show a decreasing marginal rate of technical substitution of one input for another, linear programming is quite compatible with the law of diminishing returns, which plays an important role in conventional theory. However, the linearity assumptions in linear programming problems imply that there are neither diminishing nor

---

7. The basic reason why they are not smooth is that only a finite number of processes is assumed to be available to the firm. As the number of processes grows larger and larger, the isoquants become closer and closer to the smooth isoquants of conventional theory.

increasing returns to scale. In other words, the production function is always assumed to be linear and homogeneous, which means that there are constant returns to scale.

10. Isoprofit Curves and a Graphical Solution

Returning to the firm's problem, our next step toward a solution of this linear programming problem is the construction of isoprofit curves. Once this is done, we can obtain a solution by graphical means. Just as each isoquant in Figure 8.12 represents the locus of input combinations that can produce a given output, each *isoprofit curve* is constructed to include all input combinations that can produce a given level of profit.

For example, suppose that we construct the isoprofit curve corresponding to a profit of $200. Since the profit per batch is $1.00 for process 1, the point on OR_1 corresponding to an output of 200 batches per week is on this isoprofit curve. Since each batch produced with process 1 requires 3 machine-hours of finishing capacity and 0.4 man-hours of labor, the point on OR_1 corresponding to an output of 200 batches per week is A in Figure 8.13. Similarly, since the profit per batch is $0.90 for process 2, the point on OR_2 corresponding to an output of 222.2 batches per week is on this isoprofit curve. This is point B. Moreover, since the profit per batch is $1.10 for process 3, the point on OR_3 corresponding to an output of 181.8 batches per week is also on this isoprofit curve. This is point C. Finally, for the same reason as in the case of the isoquants, we can also include all points on the lines that join these points. Thus the isoprofit curve corresponding to a profit of $200 per week is CAB in Figure 8.13.

Isoprofit curves corresponding to other levels of profit can be constructed in a similar manner. As in the case of the isoquants in Figure

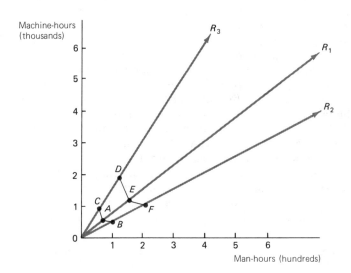

Figure 8.13 Isoprofit curves for selected profit levels

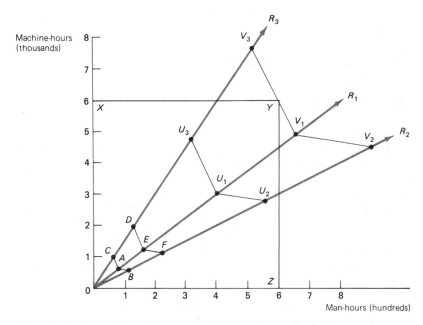

Figure 8.14 Isoprofit curves and feasible input combinations

8.12, the isoprofit curves in Figure 8.13 are parallel to one another. For example, if we compare DEF, the isoprofit curve corresponding to $400, with CAB, the isoprofit curve corresponding to $200, we find that they are parallel. That is, the slope of CA equals the slope of DE, and the slope of AB equals the slope of EF.

Given the isoprofit curves, we can easily solve the firm's problem. All that we need to do is add the isoprofit curves to the diagram (Figure 8.9) showing the feasible input combinations. This is done in Figure 8.14. Clearly, the problem is to find the point in the rectangle $OXYZ$ of feasible input combinations that lies on the highest profit curve. It is evident from Figure 8.14 that this optimal point is Y. If we construct various isoprofit curves, like $U_3U_1U_2$, $V_3V_1V_2$, and so forth, the highest isoprofit curve we can construct that includes any points in $OXYZ$ is $V_3V_1V_2$. And the only point in $OXYZ$ that lies on $V_3V_1V_2$ is Y.

Granting that Y is the optimum point, how can we tell what the original values of Q_1, Q_2, and Q_3 are? First, since Y lies on the line segment V_3V_1, it means that it is optimal only to use processes 3 and 1. This illustrates the fact that the optimal solution of a linear programming problem of this sort will generally entail the use of no more processes than there are constraints: two, in this case (excluding the nonnegativity constraints). Second, since Y is the point where a total of 6,000 machine-hours of finishing capacity and 600 hours of skilled labor are used,

$$3Q_1 + 5.25Q_3 = 6,000 \qquad\qquad \textbf{8.5}$$

$$0.40Q_1 + 0.35Q_3 = 600 \qquad\qquad \textbf{8.6}$$

Solving Equations 8.5 and 8.6 simultaneously, we find that the optimal values are $Q_3 = 571.4$ and $Q_1 = 1,000$. In other words, the firm will maximize its profit if it produces about 571 batches per week on process 3 and 1,000 batches per week on process 1.

11. Minimization of Costs

As another simple illustration of the use of linear programming in solving production problems, consider a variant of the above example. Suppose that the textile firm is no longer constrained by limits on the amount of skilled labor and finishing capacity it can use. Instead, it can hire all of the skilled labor it wants at $6.00 an hour, and it can rent all of the finishing capacity it wants at $0.80 per machine-hour. Suppose that it can use any of the three processes just described, and that its problem is to choose that combination of processes that will produce 400 batches per week of finished cotton cloth at minimum cost. The price received per batch is the same for all processes. (Note that the figures given in Section 8 concerning the profit per batch made by each process are no longer valid, since the price received per batch is now the same for all processes.)

In this case the firm's production problem can be regarded as the following linear programming problem: Minimize

$$C = 4.80Q_1 + 5.00Q_2 + 6.30Q_3 \tag{8.7}$$

subject to the constraints

$$Q_1 + Q_2 + Q_3 = 400 \tag{8.8}$$

$$Q_1 \geq 0; \; Q_2 \geq 0; \; Q_3 \geq 0 \tag{8.9}$$

The objective function in this case is cost, C, which is given in Equation 8.7. To derive this equation, note that the cost of each batch produced by process 1 is $4.80, since process 1 requires 3 machine-hours of finishing capacity (at $0.80 a machine-hour) and 0.4 man-hours of skilled labor (at $6.00 an hour). Thus the total cost of the batches produced by process 1 is $4.80Q_1$. Similarly, the total cost of the batches produced by process 2 is $5.00Q_2$, and the total cost of the batches produced by process 3 is $6.30Q_3$. The only constraint, other than the nonnegativity constraints in Inequality 8.9, is Equation 8.8, which states that the total production from all processes must equal 400.

It is easy to solve this problem. Using the methods described in Section 9, we can construct the isoquant corresponding to an output of 400 batches per week. This isoquant, labeled ABC, is shown in Figure 8.15. Next we can construct isocost curves, each of which shows the various combinations of quantities of skilled labor and finishing capacity that can be obtained at a given level of cost. The isocost curves corresponding to costs of $2,000 and $1,800 are labeled KK' and MM' in Figure 8.15. Clearly, the problem is to find the point on the isoquant, ABC, that lies on the lowest isocost curve. It is evident that the optimal point is B, which means that all of the output should be produced with process 1.

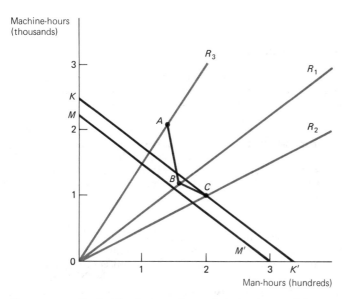

Figure 8.15 Optimal solution: Cost minimization problem

Two things should be noted at this point. First, a comparison of this problem with the one at the end of Section 2 of Chapter 7 shows that they are one and the same. In both cases, we are determining the input combination and production technique that minimize the cost of producing a given output. Moreover, Figure 7.3 (p. 175), which shows the solution according to conventional theory, is very similar to Figure 8.15, which shows the solution in this case. What is the difference between the two cases? It boils down to the fact that in Chapter 7 we assumed that we were somehow given a smooth production function, whereas here we assume that there are three processes that can be used and that their characteristics are as described here and in Section 8.

Second, was it really necessary to use linear programming—even the simplified version relying only on graphical techniques that we use here—to solve this problem? The answer clearly is no. All that the problem entails is a choice among three methods of production in a case in which the unit costs of production are constant for each process and there is no constraint on the amount that can be produced using a particular process. In such a case the answer is obvious: Produce the required volume of output with the process with the lowest unit cost. The moral is clear. Although relatively high-powered analytical devices like linear programming are often required to help solve large and complicated problems, nothing is gained by using them to handle problems that can just as readily be solved by simpler means. Students—and economists long out of school—sometimes become so infatuated with new tools that they use them even when much simpler methods would do just as well.

Example 8.3   The Choice of Production Processes

A firm can use three processes, A, B, or C, to produce a particular good. To make one unit of the good, process A requires 2 man-hours of labor and 1 hour of machine-time, process B requires 1.5 man-hours of labor and 1.5 hours of machine-time, and process C requires 1.1 man-hours of labor and 2.2 hours of machine-time. The firm must pay $3 per man-hour for labor and $2 per hour for machine-time, but it cannot use more than 120 hours of machine-time, since this is all that is available in the short run. If it has committed itself to produce 100 units of the product, how many units should it produce with process A?

Solution

The following graph contains the isoquant corresponding to an output of 100 units of the product. U_A is the input combination if all 100 units are produced with process A; U_B is the input combination if all 100 units are produced with process B; and U_C is the input combination if all 100 units are produced with process C. The graph also contains isocost curves, which show the combinations of labor-time and machine-time that can be purchased for a certain amount. (Specifically, the isocost curves corresponding to expenditures of $600 and $780 are given.)

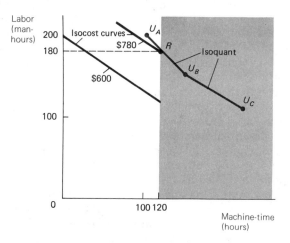

To minimize the cost of producing the 100 units of product, this firm should choose the point on the isoquant that is on the lowest isocost curve. However, the shaded area in the graph is not feasible since it requires more than 120 hours of machine-time. Thus the firm should choose the feasible point on the isoquant that is on the lowest isocost curve. Clearly, this is point R, where 120 hours of machine-time and 180 man-hours of labor are used. Since this point lies on the line segment between U_A and U_B, the firm should use process A to make some units of the product and process B to make the rest. Let Q_1 be the number of units that should be made with process A and Q_2 be the number that should be made with process B. Because process A uses 2 man-hours of labor per unit of product, process B uses 1.5 man-hours per unit of product, and a total of 180 man-hours should be used, it follows that

$$2\,Q_1 + 1.5\,Q_2 = 180.$$

And since $Q_1 + Q_2 = 100$ (since 100 units in all are produced),

$$2\,Q_1 + 1.5\,(100 - Q_1) = 180$$
$$.5Q_1 = 30$$
$$Q_1 = 60.$$

Thus the number of units of product produced with process A should be 60, and the number of units produced with process B should be 40 (since $Q_2 = 100 - Q_1$).

12. The Production of Automobiles and Trucks: Another Illustration

Turning now to a more complex case, suppose that a firm produces two kinds of output, automobiles and trucks.[8] It has four kinds of facilities, each of which is fixed in capacity: automobile assembly, truck assembly, engine assembly, and sheet metal stamping. The problem is: How many automobiles and how many trucks should the firm produce? The profit per automobile or the profit per truck depends on the price of an automobile or a truck, the variable costs of producing an automobile or a truck, and the firm's fixed costs. Assume that the price and average variable cost of each product are constant; that is, they do not vary with output in the relevant range. Specifically, assume that the price of an automobile is $7,000, the price of a truck is $9,000, the average variable costs of an automobile are $6,700, and the average variable costs of a truck are $8,750.

The firm wants to maximize profits. Neglecting fixed costs (which will be the same regardless of what the firm does), the firm's profits (per hour) equal

$$\pi = 300Q_a + 250Q_t \qquad\qquad 8.10$$

where Q_a is the number of automobiles produced by the firm per hour and Q_t is the number of trucks produced by the firm per hour. Since the firm receives $300 ($7,000 $-$ $6,700) above variable cost for each automobile that it produces, and since the firm receives $250 ($9,000 $-$ $8,750) above the variable cost for each truck it produces, the firm's profits (before deducting fixed costs) must equal $300 times the output of automobiles plus $250 times the output of trucks.

8. This is an adaptation of the well-known example found in R. Dorfman, "Mathematical or Linear Programming: A Nonmathematical Exposition," reprinted in E. Mansfield, *Microeconomics: Selected Readings,* 4th ed. (New York: Norton, 1982). Different numbers have been used to simplify the results.

Table 8.3   Percent of capacity of each
division of plant required to
make a car or a truck (per hour)

Capacity	Car	Truck
Auto assembly	5	0
Engine assembly	2	$3\frac{1}{3}$
Sheet metal	$3\frac{1}{3}$	$2\frac{1}{2}$
Truck assembly	0	4

The constraints on the firm's decisions are the fixed capacities for
automobile assembly, truck assembly, engine assembly, and sheet metal
stamping. Table 8.3 shows the proportion of each facility's total capacity
required to produce one automobile or one truck. From this table, we can
represent the constraints on the production of automobiles and trucks
by the following inequalities:

$$.05 Q_a \leq 1 \tag{8.11}$$

$$.04 Q_t \leq 1 \tag{8.12}$$

$$.02 Q_a + .033 Q_t \leq 1 \tag{8.13}$$

$$.033 Q_a + .025 Q_t \leq 1 \tag{8.14}$$

$$Q_a \geq 0; \; Q_t \geq 0 \tag{8.15}$$

To begin with, Inequalities 8.11 and 8.12 represent the constraints
imposed by existing automobile and truck assembly capacity. Since each
automobile that is produced per hour takes up 5 percent of the automobile assembly capacity, it follows that .05 times the output per hour of
automobiles must be less than or equal to one. Figure 8.16 plots the
firm's automobile production against its truck production. The vertical
line at 20 automobiles per hour shows the effects of this constraint, since

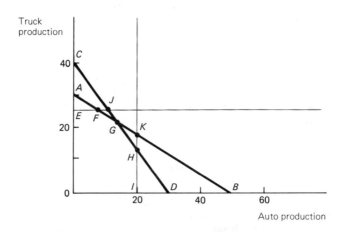

Figure 8.16   Feasible output combinations

20 is the maximum automobile output compatible with this constraint. Similarly, since each truck that is produced per hour takes up 4 percent of the truck assembly capacity, it follows that .04 times the output per hour of trucks must be less than or equal to one. The horizontal line in Figure 8.16 at 25 trucks per hour shows the effects of this constraint, since 25 is the maximum truck output compatible with this constraint.

Inequality 8.13 states that no more than the existing capacity for engine assembly can be used. Since each automobile produced per hour takes up 2 percent of the existing engine assembly capacity and since each truck produced per hour takes up $3\frac{1}{3}$ percent of the existing engine assembly capacity, it follows that .02 times the output per hour of automobiles plus .033 times the output per hour of trucks, must be less than or equal to one. Thus the line AB in Figure 8.16 separates feasible combinations of automobile and truck outputs from those that are beyond the existing engine assembly capacity. To be feasible, the combination of outputs must be on, or within, the triangle OAB.

Inequality 8.14 states that no more than the existing sheet metal stamping capacity can be used. Since each automobile produced per hour takes up $3\frac{1}{3}$ percent of the available metal stamping capacity and since each truck produced per hour takes up $2\frac{1}{2}$ percent of the available metal stamping capacity, it follows that .033 times the output per hour of automobiles plus .025 times the output per hour of trucks, must be less than or equal to one. Thus the line CD in Figure 8.16 separates feasible combinations of automobile and truck outputs from those that are beyond the existing sheet metal stamping capacity. To be feasible, the combination of outputs must be on, or within, the triangle OCD.

Combining these constraints, the combination of output of automobiles and trucks must lie within the area $OEFGHI$ in Figure 8.16. Any point outside this area violates at least one of the constraints. For example, point C uses more engine assembly capacity and truck assembly capacity than is available, and point K uses more sheet metal stamping capacity than is available.

This is a linear programming problem. The objective function is given by Equation 8.10, and the constraints are given in Inequalities 8.11 to 8.15. There are two processes, automobile production and truck production, each of which uses the four types of capacities in fixed (but different) proportions. The optimal solution to this problem can be found graphically by adding a family of isoprofit lines to Figure 8.16. This is done in Figure 8.17. Each black line shows the various combinations of automobile production and truck production that will result in the same total profit (gross of fixed costs). If π is this profit, the equation for an isoprofit line is

$$Q_t = \frac{\pi}{250} - \frac{300}{250} Q_a \qquad\qquad 8.16$$

Obviously, one should find that point in the feasible area, $OEFGHI$, that lies on the highest isoprofit line, that is, the highest black line.

Figure 8.17 shows that the optimal solution is at point G, where the firm produces 13.6 automobiles and 21.8 trucks per hour. With these

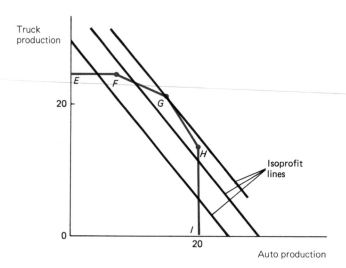

Figure 8.17 Optimal output combination

output rates, the firm's profit (gross of fixed costs) is $9,547 per hour.[9]

Before leaving this example, it is important to note that this problem is almost exactly the same as the problem we solved with conventional theory in Section 4 of this chapter. In both cases, the firm, taking the price of each product as given, is faced with the task of deciding how much of each product to produce. A comparison of Figure 8.17 with Figure 8.6 (p. 219) shows the similarities quite clearly. In both cases, there are isoprofit lines plotted against a product transformation curve; the isorevenue line in Figure 8.6 is the same as an isoprofit line under the circumstances posited there. However, an important dissimilarity is that in Section 4 we had to assume that someone handed us a production function; here we assume only that we are given the technological data in Table 8.3.

13. Computational Efficiency and the Comparison of Solutions at Extreme Points

Thus far we have emphasized the similarities between the conventional theory of production and production theory based on linear programming. Given that there are so many similarities, one might ask why there is any advantage in the linear programming approach. As we pointed out in Section 6, one important reason why the linear programming approach is used is that powerful computational techniques have been

9. How can a firm produce 13.6 autos per hour? By producing 68 autos every 5 hours. In cases in which the solution must be composed of integers, an extension of linear programming called integer programming must be used. See W. Baumol, *Economic Theory*, Chapter 8. Note that it is easy to find the coordinates of G by making Inequalities 8.13 and 8.14 into equations and solving them simultaneously for Q_a and Q_t.

developed to find the numerical solutions to linear programming problems. These computational techniques make use of the following fact: The optimal solution will lie at one of the *extreme points*—or corners—of the feasible area.[10] This rule is consistent with the cases discussed in the previous paragraphs. For example, in Figure 8.17, the optimal point, G, was an extreme point of the feasible area $OEFGHI$; and in Figure 8.14, the optimal point Y, was an extreme point of the feasible area $OXYZ$. This fact reduces very greatly the number of points that must be examined to find the optimal solution, since it shows that all one needs to bother with are the extreme points of the feasible area.

To illustrate, consider Figure 8.17. There are 6 extreme points of the feasible area $OEFGHI$. To find the optimal solution, we need only compute the profit (gross of fixed costs) at each of these points. At the origin O, profit obviously is zero. At E ($Q_a = 0$ and $Q_t = 25$), profit is \$6,250. At I($Q_a = 20$ and $Q_t = 0$), profit is \$6,000. We must find the coordinates of the other three extreme points before we can compute the level of profit at them. To find the coordinates of F, we must make Inequalities 8.12 and 8.13 into equations and solve them simultaneously; to find the coordinates of G, we must make Inequalities 8.13 and 8.14 into equations and solve them simultaneously; and to find the coordinates of H, we must make Inequalities 8.11 and 8.14 into equations and solve them simultaneously. We find that point F is $Q_a = 8\frac{1}{3}$ and $Q_t = 25$, the result being that profit is \$8,750. Point G is $Q_a = 13.6$ and $Q_t = 21.8$, the result being that profit is \$9,547. Point H is $Q_a = 20$ and $Q_t = 13\frac{1}{3}$, the result being that profit is \$9,333$\frac{1}{3}$. Thus, on the basis of these few computations, we know that point G must be the optimal solution.

In problems where the number of processes and constraints are too large for the graphical analysis used in previous sections, this kind of comparison of extreme point or corner solutions is employed to find the optimal solution. The *simplex method,* which is generally used for this purpose, is a systematic procedure for comparing extreme point or corner solutions. Combined with the speed and capacity of modern computers, it can solve extremely large problems in a very short period of time. There is a large literature on the simplex method, much of it involving a good deal of mathematics.[11] For present purposes, it is only necessary to know of the existence and general nature of this method.

14. The Dual Problem and Shadow Prices

Linear programming can do more than just find an optimal production program, the objective discussed in previous sections of this chapter. It can also find values to be placed on particular resources or inputs. For example, one could carry out the programming problem considered in

---

10. Of course, it sometimes happens that other points are as good as (but not better than) any extreme point. See Harvey Wagner, *Principles of Operations Research,* 2d ed. (Englewood cliffs, N.J.: Prentice-Hall, 1975).

11. For example, see G. Dantzig, *Linear Programming and Extensions* (Princeton, N.J.: Princeton University Press, 1963).

Section 12 under the assumption that the firm had a small amount of additional engine assembly capacity. Then one could compare the maximum profit obtainable with the extra amount of engine assembly capacity with the maximum profit obtainable without it. The increase, if there is an increase, in maximum profit is, of course, a measure of the value of the extra amount of engine assembly capacity.

Although this method of finding the value of an extra unit of a particular input is perfectly correct, it is cumbersome. A very interesting characteristic of linear programming problems is that one can obtain such values without going through this cumbersome procedure. Every linear programming problem has a corresponding problem called its *dual*. (The original problem is called the *primal* problem). If the primal is a maximization problem, the dual is a minimization problem; if the primal is a minimization problem, the dual is a maximization problem. The solutions to the dual are *shadow prices*, the values we seek.

For example, the shadow price of each type of capacity (in the problem in Section 12) tells us what would happen to the firm's profits if the company were somehow able to increase this type of capacity. Obviously, these shadow prices are of great practical importance. They show which types of capacity are bottlenecks, or effective constraints on output, since capacity that is underutilized receives a zero shadow price. More important, they indicate how much it would be worth to management to expand each type of capacity. A comparison can then be made between the extra profit due to expansion and the extra costs that must be incurred. If the costs are lower than the extra profits, as indicated by the shadow price, the expansion seems desirable. For example, if the firm producing automobiles and trucks can rent an additional 1 percent of engine assembly capacity at $100 an hour and if an extra 1 percent of such capacity would increase profits by $200, it would be well worth it to rent the extra capacity.[12]

15. Application of Linear Programming in the Petroleum Industry

Linear programming has been used in countless ways by many segments of industry and government. To illustrate the sorts of problems it has helped to solve, we present in this section one of its applications in the petroleum industry. The petroleum industry became aware of linear programming through the pioneering studies in the early fifties by Charnes, Cooper, and Mellon; and Manne.[13] As is true of most new

---

12. See R. Dorfman, P. Samuelson, and R. Solow, *Linear Programming and Economic Analysis* (New York: McGraw-Hill, 1958).

13. See A. Charnes, W. Cooper, and B. Mellon, "Blending Aviation Gasolines," *Econometrica*, April 1952; "A Model for Programming and Sensitivity Analysis in an Integrated Oil Company," *Econometrica*, April 1954. Also A. Manne, *Scheduling of Petroleum Refinery Operations* (Cambridge, Mass.: Harvard University Press, 1956).

techniques, it took some time before the industry recognized linear programming's full potentialities, but once the initial educational process was over, its use spread very rapidly.

The petroleum industry is composed of various phases: exploration, production, refining, and distribution and marketing. An integrated oil firm must explore in order to locate places where oil is most likely to be found. It must drill for oil, and refine it to produce gasoline and other products. It must transport the oil, both to and from the refinery. Finally, the oil and oil products enter the distribution system and are marketed by the firm. The petroleum industry is as large as it is complex. The international oil companies like Exxon, Texaco, and Mobil are among the giants of American industry.

Each phase of the petroleum business is full of unanswered problems and questions. The oil potentialities of a region can be explored in various ways. How should these ways be combined for maximum effectiveness? There are a number of different ways of planning and organizing production in an oil field. Which is best? A modern oil refinery is an extremely complex type of plant. What is the best way of operating it? And what do we mean by *best*? Of course, linear programming has not been able to solve all of these problems, but it has helped to solve some of them. For example, it has been useful in solving the following problem, which obviously is an important one to oil producers.

Consider the production phase of the petroleum industry. Suppose that a firm has a number of oil fields, or reservoirs, which are producing at various rates. The total production of the reservoirs must be adjusted to meet a commitment, such as keeping a pipeline full or a refinery supplied. An outside source of crude oil also exists. Technological factors require that the production rates do not exceed certain levels. The profit per barrel of crude oil produced is given, as is the number of years the operation is to be run on this basis. The problem is to determine a schedule of production rates so that the profit over the entire period is a maximum.

This can be viewed as a linear programming problem. For simplicity, assume that the firm has only two reservoirs and that the firm is planning for only two years. The results can easily be extended to larger numbers of reservoirs and longer periods of time. Let Q_{11} be the number of gallons of crude oil produced from the first reservoir in the first year, Q_{12} be the number of gallons of crude oil produced from the first reservoir in the second year, Q_{21} be the number of gallons of crude oil produced from the second reservoir in the first year and Q_{22} be the number of gallons of crude oil produced from the second reservoir in the second year. Let Q_1 be the number of barrels of crude oil purchased from the outside source in the first year, and Q_2 be the corresponding number in the second year.

The objective function is the total profit over the two years, which is

$$\text{II} = G_{11}Q_{11} + G_{12}Q_{12} + G_{21}Q_{21} + G_{22}Q_{22} \\ + G_1Q_1 + G_2Q_2 \qquad \text{8.17}$$

where G_{11} is the profit per barrel of crude oil produced from the first reservoir in the first year, G_{12} is the profit per barrel of crude oil produced from the first reservoir in the second year, G_{21} is the profit per barrel of crude oil produced from the second reservoir in the first year, G_{22} is the profit per barrel of crude oil produced from the second reservoir in the second year, G_1 is the profit per barrel of crude oil obtained from the outside source in the first year, and G_2 is the profit per barrel of crude oil obtained from the outside source in the second year.

The constraints are as follows. First, there are certain maximum levels of production. Thus,

$$Q_{11} \leq Q_{11}^* \tag{8.18}$$
$$Q_{12} \leq Q_{12}^* \tag{8.19}$$
$$Q_{21} \leq Q_{21}^* \tag{8.20}$$
$$Q_{22} \leq Q_{22}^* \tag{8.21}$$

where Q_{11}^* is the maximum production level of the first reservoir in the first year, Q_{12}^* is the maximum production level of the first reservoir in the second year, Q_{21}^* is the maximum production level of the second reservoir in the first year, and Q_{22}^* is the maximum production level of the second reservoir in the second year.[14]

Second, the total production from the two reservoirs in each year plus the amount purchased from the outside source must equal the commitment for that year. That is,

$$Q_{11} + Q_{21} + Q_1 = M_1 \tag{8.22}$$
$$Q_{12} + Q_{22} + Q_2 = M_2 \tag{8.23}$$

where M_1 is the commitment for the first year and M_2 the commitment for the second year. Also, Q_{11}, Q_{12}, Q_{21}, Q_{22}, Q_1 and Q_2 must be non-negative.

Using linear programming, this problem can be solved to determine the values of Q_{11}, Q_{12}, Q_{21}, Q_{22}, Q_1 and Q_2 that maximize the firm's profits. The Magnolia Petroleum Company and the Arabian American Oil Company have done a considerable amount of work on this problem, using a simple model like that described above and more complicated variants of this model. The results have been useful to these companies and others in the industry.[15]

---

14. See W. Garvin, H. Crandall, J. John, and R. Spellman, "Applications of Linear Programming in the Oil Industry," *Management Science,* July 1957, reprinted in part in E. Mansfield, *Managerial Economics and Operations Research,* 4th ed. This section is based largely on their paper. The model in the text is simplified in various respects to make it more easily comprehensible to students. In particular, the constraints in Inequalities 8.18 to 8.21 are not the only ones that were actually used. But this should make little difference in this context.

15. Ibid. As presented above, the problem is, of course, much simpler than the one dealt with by these companies. (As it stands, it can be solved in an elementary way.) For present purposes, it seemed wise to strip it down to its simplest form.

16. Summary

If the firm takes the price of its product as given, it maximizes profit—or minimizes losses—in the short run by producing the quantity of output at which marginal cost equals the price of the product. However, if the price of the product is less than the firm's average variable cost for every quantity of output, the firm will minimize losses by discontinuing production. If a firm produces two products and takes the price of each product as given, it will maximize profit by choosing the output levels of the two products so that the marginal rate of product transformation is equal to the ratio of the prices of the two products. The marginal rate of product transformation is minus one times the slope of the product transformation curve.

Linear programming is the most famous of the mathematical programming methods that have come into existence since World War II. It is a technique that allows decision-makers to solve maximization and minimization problems where there are certain constraints that limit what can be done. It is useful to look at production decisions from the programming point of view because, unlike conventional theory, it does not take the production function as being given to the economist before he or she attacks the problem. Also the programming analysis is easier to apply in many respects, and powerful computational techniques are available to obtain solutions.

Linear programming views the technology available to the firm as being a finite number of processes, each of which uses inputs in fixed proportions. The firm has a certain amount of each of the inputs at its disposal. Each unit of output resulting from a particular process yields the firm a certain amount of profit; this amount of profit varies from process to process. Knowing the profit to be made from a unit of output from each process and bearing in mind the limited amount of the various inputs at its command, the firm is visualized as attempting to determine the output from each process that will maximize profit.

To illustrate the use of linear programming, we discussed a case in which a hypothetical textile firm had to choose which combination of a number of alternative processes to use, given that it has only a limited amount of certain inputs. We solved the problem by graphical techniques. Isoprofit curves were constructed and superimposed on a diagram showing the feasible input combinations, and the point was chosen that, among those that were feasible, was on the highest isoprofit curve. In addition, we considered a variant of this problem in which the firm is no longer constrained by limitations on inputs.

Turning to a more complex case, we discussed the problem of a firm that produces more than one product and has various fixed facilities which set limits on the amount of each product that can be produced. The problem is to determine the optimal combination of outputs of the two products. This problem was also solved by graphical means, with isoprofit lines superimposed on a diagram showing feasible output combinations. In addition, in the context of this example, we discussed the fact that the optimal solution of a linear programming problem will lie at one of the extreme points or corners of the feasible area.

Every linear programming problem has a corresponding problem called its dual; the original problem is called the primal problem. If the primal is a maximization problem, the dual is a minimization problem; if the primal is a minimization problem, the dual is a maximization problem. In the example concerning the optimal combination of outputs of two products, whereas the primal looked for optimal output rates for the two products, the dual seeks to impute values to the fixed facilities. These imputed values, or shadow prices, are very useful, since they show what would happen to the firm's profits if the company somehow were able to increase each type of capacity. Finally, we presented an application of linear programming to an important practical problem of the petroleum industry. The problem is to determine the optimal schedule of production rates for a number of oil fields, or reservoirs.

QUESTIONS AND PROBLEMS

1. Suppose that a perfectly competitive firm's total costs are as follows:

Output rate	Total cost (dollars)
0	10
1	12
2	15
3	19
4	24
5	30

If the price of the product is $5, how many units of output should the firm produce?

2. According to some firms in the paper industry, price controls during the early 1970s resulted in price being below average variable cost. What do you think that these firms did? If you had been a consultant to these firms, what advice would you have given them?

3. A family is composed of a husband and wife. The husband needs 3,000 calories per day and the wife requires 2,000 calories per day. The doctor says that these calories must be obtained by eating not less than a certain amount of fats and a certain amount of proteins. The family wants to minimize its food bill, but it does not want to violate the doctor's orders. Is this a linear programming problem? If so, what are the objective function and the constraints?

4. Describe various ways in which linear programming might be used in your own university. What are some of the most important problems in applying it to university problems?

5. Suppose that a firm's marginal cost curve is a horizontal line at $3 per unit of output, if output is less than or equal to 100 units per month. If the price of the product is $4 per unit, should the firm produce at least 100 units per month? Why or why not?

6. Suppose that a firm's product transformation curve is as shown below:

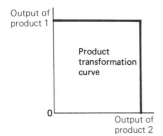

To what extent will changes in the price of product 1 and product 2 alter the slope of the isorevenue lines? To what extent will they alter the optimal amount of each product that the firm should produce?

7. Suppose that a firm's product transformation curve is as follows:

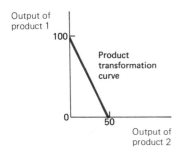

If the price of a unit of product 1 equals the price of a unit of product 2, draw several isorevenue lines in this graph. What is the optimal amount of each product that the firm should produce? Is this a point where an isorevenue line is tangent to the product transformation curve?

8. In the previous question, is the optimal point at an extreme point of the feasible area?

9. In Example 8.3, suppose that the firm was not constrained to use no more than 120 hours of machine-time. Under these circumstances, how many units should it produce with process *A*? process *B*? process *C*?

10. In analyzing New York's snow removal problem, should each curve (like *A*, *B*, and *C*) in Figure 8.8 be regarded as containing a set of combinations of outputs with the same municipal worth? Or should it be regarded as containing a set of combinations of outputs resulting in the same number of votes for the incumbents? What arguments can be presented on each side?

SELECTED REFERENCES

BAUMOL, WILLIAM. *Economic Theory and Operations Analysis.* 4th ed. Englewood Cliffs, N.J.: Prentice-Hall, 1977.

DORFMAN, ROBERT; PAUL SAMUELSON; AND ROBERT SOLOW. *Linear Programming and Economic Analysis.* New York: McGraw-Hill, 1958.

DANTZIG, GEORGE. *Linear Programming and Extensions*. Princeton, N.J.: Princeton University Press, 1963.

HENDERSON, A., AND R. SCHLAIFER. "Mathematical Programming." In Edwin Mansfield. *Managerial Economics and Operations Research*. 4th ed. New York: Norton, 1980.

HITCH, CHARLES, AND ROLAND MCKEAN. *The Economics of Defense in the Nuclear Age*. Cambridge, Mass.: Harvard University Press, 1960.

DORFMAN, ROBERT. "Mathematical or Linear Programming: A Nonmathematical Exposition." In Edwin Mansfield *Microeconomics: Selected Readings*. 4th ed. New York: Norton, 1982.

KOOPMANS, TJALLING, "Concepts of Optimality and Their Uses." *American Economic Review*. June 1977.

9 Price and Output under Perfect Competition

1. Market Structure: An Introduction

Previous chapters have provided models of the behavior of consumers and firms. In Chapters 9 to 12 we turn to the analysis of markets; our principal purpose is to explain the behavior of price and output. We will be concerned with questions of the following sort: What determines the price of a product? What determines how much of a product is produced? How are resources allocated among alternative uses? These are some of the most basic—and most important—questions in economics. In Chapter 2, we provided some preliminary answers to these questions. In Chapters 9 to 12, we discuss them in much more detail.

To begin with, we must distinguish between various types of markets. Economists have found it useful to classify markets into four general types: perfect competition, monopoly, monopolistic competition, and oligopoly. This classification is based largely on the number of firms in the industry that supplies the product. In perfect competition and monopolistic competition, there are many sellers, each of which produces only a small part of the industry's output. In monopoly, on the other hand, the industry consists of only a single firm. Oligopoly is an intermediate case where there are few sellers.

In this chapter we investigate how price and output are determined in perfectly competitive markets. Monopoly, monopolistic competition, and oligopoly are taken up in subsequent chapters. The analysis in this chapter brings together, and builds on, the topics discussed in previous chapters. In Chapter 2, we emphasized the important role played by the market demand and market supply curves. In Chapter 5, we used the tools devised in Chapters 3 and 4 to show how a product's market demand curve can be derived. In the present chapter, we use the tools devised in Chapters 6 to 8 to show how a product's market supply curve can be derived. Then we discuss in detail the way in which the demand and supply sides of the market interact to determine the equilibrium price and output of the firm and the industry in the market period, the short run, and the long run.

2. Perfect Competition

What do economists mean by perfect competition? When first exposed to this concept, students sometimes find it difficult to grasp because it is quite different from the concept of competition used by their relatives and friends in the business world. When businessmen speak of a highly competitive market, they generally mean a market where each firm is keenly aware of its rivalry with a few others and where advertising, packaging, styling, and other competitive weapons are used to attract business away from them. In contrast, the basic feature of the economist's definition of perfect competition is its impersonality. Because there are so many firms in the industry, no firm views another as a competitor, any more than one small wheat farmer views another small wheat farmer as a competitor.

More specifically, perfect competition is defined by four conditions. First, perfect competition requires that the product of any one seller be the same as the product of any other seller. This is an important condition because it makes sure that buyers do not care whether they purchase the product from one seller or another, as long as the price is the same. Note that the *product* may be defined by a great deal more than the physical characteristics of the good. Although various English pubs may serve the same beer, their products may not be identical because the atmosphere may be friendlier in one place than another, the location may be better, and so forth.

Second, perfect competition requires each participant in the market, whether buyer or seller, to be so small, in relation to the entire market, that he or she cannot affect the product's price. No buyer can be large enough to wangle a better price from the sellers than some other buyer. No seller can be large enough to influence the price by altering his or her output rate. Of course, if all producers act together, changes in output will certainly affect price, but any producer acting alone cannot do so. It will be recalled from Chapter 5 that this means that the firm's demand curve is horizontal.

Third, perfect competition requires that all resources be completely mobile. In other words, each resource must be able to enter or leave the market, and switch from one use to another, very readily.[1] More specifi-

---

1. Of course, this does not mean that such movements of resources do not take time. In the short run, many resources cannot be transferred from one use to another.

cally, it means that labor must be able to move from region to region and from job to job; it means that raw materials must not be monopolized; and it means that new firms can enter and leave an industry. Needless to say, this condition is often not fulfilled in a world where considerable retraining is required to allow a worker to move from one job to another and where patents, large investment requirements, and economies of scale make difficult the entry of new firms.

Fourth, perfect competition requires that consumers, firms, and resource owners have perfect knowledge of the relevant economic and technological data. Consumers must be aware of all prices. Laborers and owners of capital must be aware of how much their resources will bring in all possible uses. Firms must know the prices of all inputs and the characteristics of all relevant technologies. Moreover, in its purest sense, perfect competition requires that all of these economic decision-making units have an accurate knowledge of the future together with the past and present.

Having described these four requirements, it is obvious that no industry is perfectly competitive. Some agricultural markets may be reasonably close, since the first three requirements are frequently met; but even they do not meet all of the requirements.[2] Nevertheless, this does not mean that the study of the behavior of perfectly competitive markets is useless. Recall from Chapter 1 that a model may be quite useful even though some of its assumptions are unrealistic. The conclusions derived from the model of perfect competition have proved very useful in explaining and predicting behavior in the real world. They have permitted a reasonably accurate view of resource allocation in important segments of our economy.

3. Price Determination in the Market Period

Besides the short run and the long run, discussed in previous chapters, there is also the market period during which the supply of a good is fixed. For example, retailers may have only a certain number of Rolling Stones records in stock, and it may take a certain period of time before they can obtain more from the producers. Or the quantity of an agricultural commodity may be fixed for some time after a harvest. Also, in some cases, the quantity of a certain commodity may be fixed for a long period of time. For example, the quantity of Renoir paintings cannot be augmented—although forgers sometimes try.

Whereas the quantity of output is variable in the short and long runs, it is fixed in the *market period,* the consequence being that the *supply curve,* the curve that shows the quantity of output supplied at each price, is a vertical straight line. For example, in Figure 9.1, the quantity available for sale is *OA,* and the market supply curve is *AA'.* Since each seller has a fixed supply that it sells for the market-estab-

2. Some agricultural markets in which the conditions would otherwise be reasonably close to perfect competition are heavily affected by government programs. See Sections 15 and 16 at the end of this chapter.

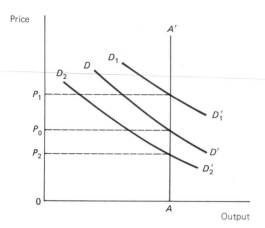

Figure 9.1   Price determination in the market period

lished price, the behavior of the sellers is perfectly straightforward: They simply sell what they have for as much as they can get.[3]

Equilibrium is achieved, of course, at that price which clears the market by equating the amount demanded with the amount supplied. At a lower price, buyers will want more of the commodity than exists in the market; at a higher price they will want less of the commodity than exists in the market. In Figure 9.1, if the market demand curve is DD', the equilibrium price is OP_0. If the demand curve were higher (like D_1D_1') the equilibrium price would be higher (like OP_1). If the demand curve were lower (like D_2D_2'), the equilibrium price would be lower (like OP_2). But the quantity would be the same, since it is fixed. Consequently, in the market period, quantity is set by supply alone and (given supply) price is set by demand alone.

The role played by prices as rationing devices is particularly obvious in the market period, where this is the major function of price. When the market equilibrium price is reached, the available supply has been rationed, without resort to fights among consumers or government intervention. Those consumers who can and will pay the price have the commodity—and there are just enough such consumers to exhaust the available supply.

4. The Supply Curve of the Firm in the Short Run

Having dealt with the determination of price and output in the market period, we proceed to the case of price and output determination in the short run. The first step is to construct each firm's short-run supply curve: the curve that shows how much the firm will produce at each price. Based on the results in Chapter 8, it is a simple matter to derive the

3. Of course, the sellers themselves may be among those who can use and want the good, the result being that their demand is included in the market demand curve. If this is the case, it may turn out they sell some of the good to themselves; that is, they keep it.

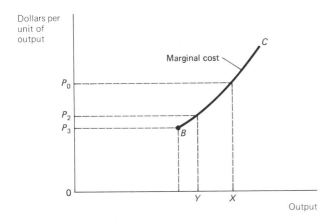

Figure 9.2   The supply curve of the perfectly competitive firm

firm's short-run supply curve. Recall from Chapter 8 that a firm that takes the price of its product as given (and can sell all it wants at that price) will choose the output level at which price equals marginal cost. Or if the price is less than the firm's average variable cost at every output, the firm will discontinue production. Thus, suppose that the firm's short-run cost curves are those in Figure 8.3 (p. 215). The marginal cost curve intersects the average variable cost curve at the latter's minimum point, B. If the price of the product is below OP_3, the firm will produce nothing, because there is no output level where price exceeds average variable cost.

If the price of the product exceeds OP_3, the firm will set its output rate at the point at which price equals marginal cost. This is the output rate that maximizes profit, as we saw in Chapter 8. Thus, if the price is OP_0, the firm will produce OX; if the price is OP_2, the firm will produce OY, and so forth. The resulting supply curve is that shown in Figure 9.2 as OP_3BC. *Given the way it was constructed, this curve is exactly the same as the firm's short-run marginal cost curve for prices above OP_3; at or below OP_3, the supply curve coincides with the price axis.*

5. Short-Run Supply Curve of the Industry

The price of the industry's product in the short run was given to us in the previous section. What we want to do is to see how it is determined. This price is influenced by both the consumers that demand the good and the firms that supply it. The determinants of the industry demand curve (that is, the market demand curve) have been discussed in previous chapters, particularly in Chapter 5. In this section, we discuss the determinants of the short-run industry supply curve (that is, the short-run market supply curve), and in the next section, we combine the demand and supply curves to determine the industry's price and output in the short run.

As a rough approximation, the industry's short-run supply curve

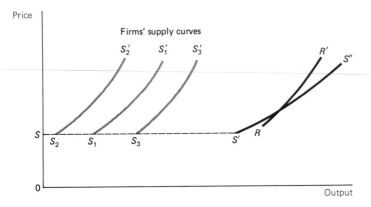

Figure 9.3 Horizontal summation of short-run supply curves of firms

can be regarded as the horizontal summation of the short-run supply curves of all of the firms in the industry. For example, if there were three firms in the industry and if their supply curves were OSS_1S_1', OSS_2S_2', and OSS_3S_3' in Figure 9.3, the industry's supply curve would be $OSS'S''$, since $OSS'S''$ shows the amounts of the product that all of the firms together would supply at various prices. Of course, if there were only three firms, the industry would not be perfectly competitive, but we can ignore this inconsistency. The point of Figure 9.3 is to illustrate the fact that the industry supply curve is the horizontal summation of the firm supply curves, at least under one important assumption.

The assumption underlying this construction of the short-run industry supply curve is that supplies of inputs to the industry as a whole are perfectly elastic. In other words, it is assumed that increases or decreases in output by all firms simultaneously do not affect input prices. This is a strong assumption. Although changes in the output of one firm alone often cannot affect input prices, the simultaneous expansion or contraction of output by all firms may well alter input prices, with the result that the individual firm's cost curves—and supply curve—will shift. For example, an expansion of the whole industry may bid up the price of certain inputs, with the result that the cost curves of the individual firms will be pushed upward.[4]

If contrary to the assumption underlying Figure 9.3, input prices are influenced in this way by expansion of the industry, what will be the effect on the short-run industry supply curve? It will make the short-run industry supply curve less elastic than $OSS'S''$. In the relevant price range, the curve might be more like RR'. To see this, note that expansion of the industry causes the short-run average cost curve and the short-run marginal cost curve to move upward, because of the resulting increase in input prices. But if the marginal cost curve moves upward, price will

---

4. More will be said about the effect of industry output on individual cost curves in subsequent sections of this chapter. Note, too, that in this chapter (and the rest of this book) we go back to the conventional, rather than the linear programming, view of production.

Example 9.1   The Supply of Shale Oil

According to a 1978 study by Neil Ericsson and Peter Morgan, the supply curve for shale oil was as shown below:

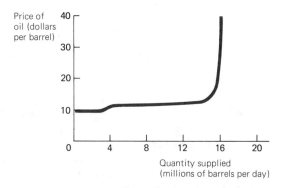

Two problems in producing shale oil is that the producer must dispose of the spent shale and that air pollution may occur. This supply curve assumes that the disposal of spent shale costs $5 per ton, and that federal air pollution standards are applied. (a) If the disposal of spent shale costs $10 per ton, would you expect the quantity supplied to be more or less than 16 million barrels per day if the price of oil is $40 per barrel? (b) Colorado air pollution standards are stricter than federal standards. If the Colorado standards are applied, would you expect the quantity supplied to be more or less than 16 million barrels per day if the price of oil is $40 per barrel? (c) Since no commercial-scale shale oil plants have been built, the above supply curve is based on engineering estimates. Do you think that this supply curve is very accurate? Why or why not? (d) A shale oil plant is estimated to cost over $1 billion. Would an investment in such a plant be risky? Why or why not? Would this influence the position and shape of the supply curve?

Solution

(a) Less. The supply curve will be to the left of the one shown above.
(b) Less. The supply curve will be to the left of the one shown above.
(c) There commonly are substantial errors in estimates of this sort, if they are based on no actual operating experience. Many unanticipated problems can arise in operating new types of plants. (d) Because of the uncertainties cited in part (c), such an investment would clearly be risky. Thus, less shale oil is likely to be produced than under riskless conditions.*

* For further discussion, see Neil Ericsson and Peter Morgan, "The Economic Feasibility of Shale Oil," *The Bell Journal of Economics,* August 1978.

equal marginal cost at a lower output than would have been the case if the marginal cost curve had not moved.

In summary, the shape of the short-run supply curve is determined by the number of firms in the industry, the size of the plant and other factors determining the shape of the marginal cost curve of each firm, and the effect of changes in industry output on input prices.

6. Short-Run Equilibrium Price and Output for the Industry

As we know from Chapter 2, the short-run equilibrium price level is the price at which the quantity demanded and the quantity supplied of the product in the short run are equal. For example, if the demand curve is DD' and the supply curve is as shown in Figure 9.4, the equilibrium price is OP and the equilibrium industry output is OQ, this point being the intersection of the demand and supply curves. Once enough time has elapsed for firms to adjust their utilization of the variable inputs, the price will tend to equal this equilibrium level, aside from the effects of certain factors that will be discussed in Section 12. If the price is above this equilibrium level, the quantity supplied will tend to exceed the quantity demanded, with the result that the price will tend to fall. If the price is below this equilibrium level, the quantity demanded will tend to exceed the quantity supplied, with the result that the price will tend to rise. There is no tendency for the price to move in one direction or the other if and only if it is at the equilibrium level.

At the equilibrium price, price will equal marginal cost for all firms that choose to produce, rather than shut down their plants. Price may be above or below average total cost, since there is no necessity that profits be zero or that fixed costs be covered in the short run. An increase in demand will increase equilibrium price and output in the short run. For example, suppose that demand shifts from DD' to EE' in Figure 9.4. The

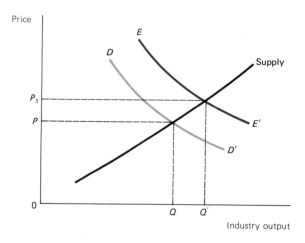

Figure 9.4   Determination of price and output in the short run

shift in the demand curve will cause a shortage at the old price, $OP,$ with the result that the price will eventually be pushed up to OP_1. At the same time, each firm will adjust its output rate upward so that its marginal cost will equal the higher price, with the result that industry output will grow to OQ'.

7. The Long-Run Adjustment Process

In the long run, the firm can change its plant size. This means that established firms may leave an industry if the industry has below-average profits, or that new firms may enter an industry if the industry has above-average profits. The next two sections are concerned with the long-run equilibrium of a perfectly competitive industry. We begin in this section by describing the adjustment process for an established firm.

Suppose that the firm has a plant with short-run average and marginal cost curves of A_0A_0' and M_0M_0', shown in Figure 9.5. Suppose that the price of the product is OP. With its existing plant the firm makes a small profit on each unit of output. However, in the long run, the firm is not limited to this plant. The firm could build a plant corresponding to any of the short-run cost curves in Figure 9.5. For example, it could build a medium-sized plant corresponding to short-run cost curves of A_1A_1' and M_1M_1', or it could build a large plant corresponding to short-run cost curves of A_2A_2' and M_2M_2'. What will the firm do in the long run? If it attempts to maximize profit it will choose to build the plant corresponding to short-run cost curves of A_2A_2' and M_2M_2'. The maximum attainable profit under the postulated circumstances will be earned by using this plant and producing OQ_2 units of output per period of time.

In general, maximum profit will be obtained by producing at an output rate and with a plant such that the *long-run marginal cost is equal to price at the point where the short-run marginal cost of the plant*

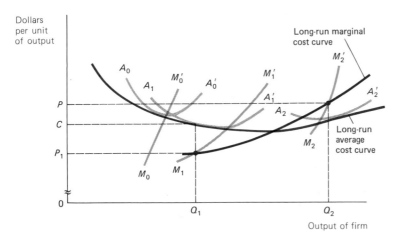

Figure 9.5   Change of plant size in the long run

is equal to price. This, of course, is true at the output of OQ_2 units and with the plant corresponding to short-run cost curves A_2A_2' and M_2M_2' in Figure 9.5. The plant will be chosen so that long-run marginal cost equals price, since this clearly is a condition for profit maximization in the long run. To maximize profit, the firm will operate this plant at the point where short-run marginal cost equals price. Thus the equality of long-run marginal cost, short-run marginal cost, and price follows from the assumption of profit maximization. (See footnote 12, Chapter 7.)

If all firms in the industry except this one had plants of optimal size, the expansion of this one firm would have no significant influence on price. Consequently, since OP is greater than the average cost of producing OQ_2 units, all firms would be earning a profit. Recall from Chapter 7 that costs, as reckoned by economists (but not accountants), include the returns that could be gotten from the most lucrative alternative use of the firm's resources. Consequently, an *economic profit* means that the firm is making more than it could make with its resources in other industries. Of course, the existence of above-average profits in this industry attracts new entrants; when these new firms enter the industry, the adjustment process must go on.

The arrival of new entrants shifts the industry supply curve to the right. That is, more will be supplied at a given price than before. For example, suppose that the industry supply curve shifts from SS' to S_1S_1' in Figure 9.6, with the result that the price drops from OP to OP_1 and industry output increases from OQ to OQ_1. Although total industry output increases (because of the new entrants), the output of each of the firms is smaller. Given that the price is now OP_1 the optimal output of each firm is OQ_1, rather than OQ_2 (see Figure 9.5). And the optimal plant is the one corresponding to the short-run cost curves, A_1A_1' and M_1M_1'. Firms that have built plants corresponding to the short-run cost curves A_2A_2' and M_2M_2' will lose a great deal of money. But even those firms that have plants of optimal size (corresponding to the short-run curves A_1A_1' and M_1M_1') will lose P_1C dollars per unit.

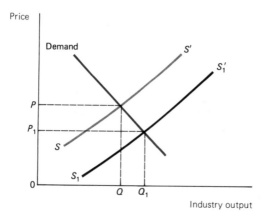

Figure 9.6   Effects of entry of new firms

This does not mean that firms with plants of optimal size are not maximizing profits. On the contrary, it is evident from Figure 9.5 that, with the price at OP_1, long-run marginal cost equals short-run marginal cost equals price when the firm produces OQ_1 units of output with the plant corresponding to the short-run cost curves, A_1A_1' and M_1M_1'. Thus this is the profit-maximizing solution for the firm. The trouble is that, even if the firm does the best it can, it cannot make an economic profit. The result will be an out-migration of firms from the industry. Since the returns that could be obtained from the firm's resources are greater in other industries, entrepreneurs will transfer these resources to other industries. In this way, the adjustment process will go on, since the exit of the firms will shift the industry's supply curve to the left.

8. Long-Run Equilibrium of the Firm

When and where will this adjustment process end? Eventually, enough firms will leave the industry so that economic losses are eliminated, but profits are avoided, too. At this point the remaining firms will be in equilibrium. In other words, the long-run equilibrium position of the firm is at the point at which its long-run average total costs equal price. If price is in excess of average total costs for any firm, economic profits are being earned and new firms will enter the industry. If price is less than average total costs for any firm, that firm will eventually leave the industry.

Going a step further, we can show that price must be equal to the *lowest value* of long-run average total costs. In other words, firms must be producing at the minimum point on their long-run average cost curves. The reason for this is as follows: To maximize their profits, firms must operate where price equals long-run marginal cost. Also, we have just seen that they must operate where price equals long-run average cost. But if both of these conditions are satisfied, it follows that long-run marginal cost must equal long-run average cost. And we know from Chapter 7 that long-run marginal cost is equal to long-run average cost only at the point at which long-run average cost is a minimum. Thus this must be the equilibrium position of the firm.

This equilibrium position is illustrated in Figure 9.7. When all adjustments are made, price equals OB. Since the demand curve is horizontal, the marginal revenue curve is the same as the demand curve, both being BB'. The equilibrium output of the firm is OV, and its plant corresponds to short-run average and marginal cost curves, AA' and MM'. At this output and with this plant, long-run marginal cost equals short-run marginal cost equals price: This insures that the firm is maximizing profit. Also, long-run average cost equals short-run average cost equals price. This insures that economic profits are zero. Since the long-run marginal cost and long-run average cost must be equal, the equilibrium point is at the bottom of the long-run average cost curve.

Since price must be the same for all firms in the industry, this implies that the minimum of the long-run average cost curve must be the same for all firms. However, this is not as unrealistic as it appears at first

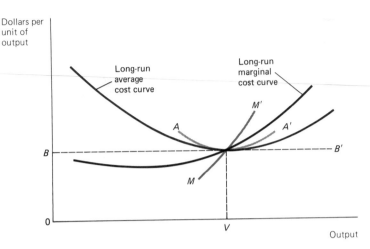

Figure 9.7   Long-run equilibrium of a perfectly competitive firm

glance. Firms that appear to have lower costs than others in the industry often have unusually good resources or particularly able managements. The owners of superior resources (including management ability) can obtain a higher price for them if they are put to alternative uses than more ordinary resources. Consequently, the alternative costs, or implicit costs, of one's using superior resources are higher than those of using ordinary resources. If this is taken into account, and if these superior resources are costed properly, the firms with apparently lower costs have no lower costs at all.

9. Constant-Cost Industries

In the previous two sections, it was assumed implicitly that the industry exhibited constant costs, which means that expansion of the industry does not result in an increase in input prices. Figure 9.8 shows long-run equilibrium under conditions of constant cost. The left-hand panel shows the short- and long-run cost curves of a typical firm in the industry. The right-hand panel shows the demand and supply curves in the market as a whole, DD' being the original demand curve and SS' being the original short-run supply curve. It is assumed that the industry is in long-run equilibrium, with the result that the price line is tangent to the long-run (and short-run) average cost curve at its minimum point. (OP is the price).

Assume now that the demand curve shifts to D_1D_1'. In the short run, with the number of firms fixed, the price of the product will rise from OP to OP_1; each firm will expand output from OQ to OQ_1; and each firm will be making economic profits since OP_1 exceeds the short-run average costs of the firm at OQ_1. The consequence is that firms will enter the industry and shift the supply curve to the right. In the case of a constant-cost industry, the entrance of the new firms does not affect the costs of the existing firms. The inputs used by this industry are used by

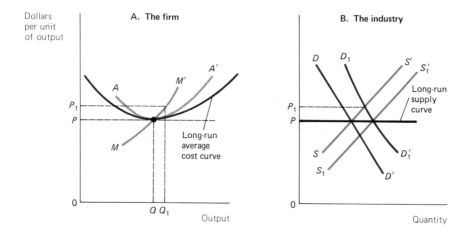

Figure 9.8   Long-run equilibrium: Constant-cost industry

many other industries as well, and the appearance of the new firms in this industry does not bid up the price of inputs and consequently raise the costs of existing firms. Neither does the appearance of the new firms lower the costs of existing firms.

Consequently, *a constant-cost industry has a horizontal long-run supply curve.* Since output can be increased by increasing the number of firms producing OQ units at an average cost of OP, the long-run supply curve is horizontal at OP. So long as the industry remains in a state of constant costs, its output can be increased indefinitely. If price exceeds OP, firms would enter the industry; if price were less than OP, firms would leave the industry. Thus long-run equilibrium can only occur in this industry when price is OP. And industry output can be expanded or contracted, in accord with demand conditions, without altering this long-run equilibrium price.

10. Increasing- and Decreasing-Cost Industries

An increasing-cost industry is shown in Figure 9.9. The original conditions are the same as in Figure 9.8, DD' being the original demand curve, SS' being the original supply curve, OP being the equilibrium price, and the long-run and short-run average cost curves of each firm being LL' and AA' in the left panel. As in Figure 9.8, the original position is one of long-run equilibrium, since the price line is tangent to the average cost curves at their minima.

Now suppose that the demand curve shifts to D_1D_1', with the result that the price of the product increases and firms earn economic profits, thus attracting new entrants. More and more inputs are required by the industry, and in an increasing-cost industry, the price of inputs increases with the amount used by the industry. Consequently, the cost of inputs increases for the established firms as well as the new entrants and the average cost curves are pushed up to L_1L_1' and A_1A_1'.

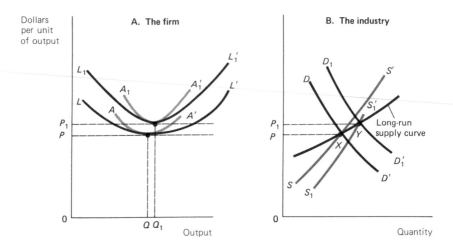

Figure 9.9   Long-run equilibrium: Increasing-cost industry

If the marginal cost curve of each firm is shifted to the left by the increase in input prices, the industry supply curve will also tend to shift to the left. However, this tendency is more than counterbalanced by the effects of the increase in the number of firms, which shifts the industry supply curve to the right. The latter effect must more than offset the former effect because otherwise there would be no expansion in total industry output. (No new resources would have been attracted to the industry.) The process of adjustment must go on until a new point of long-run equilibrium is reached. In Figure 9.9, this point is where the price of the product is OP_1 and each firm produces OQ_1 units;[5] the new short-run supply curve is $S_1 S_1'$.

An increasing-cost industry has a positively sloped long-run supply curve. That is, after long-run equilibrium is achieved, increases in output require increases in the price of the product. For example, points X and Y in Figure 9.9 are both on the long-run supply curve for this industry. The difference between constant-cost and increasing-cost industries is as follows: In constant-cost industries, new firms enter in response to an increase in demand until price returns to its original level; whereas in increasing-cost industries, new firms enter until the minimum point on the long-run cost curve has increased to the point where it equals the new price.[6]

A decreasing-cost industry is shown in Figure 9.10. Once again, we begin with an industry in long-run equilibrium, the demand curve being

5. We cannot be sure that OQ_1 exceeds OQ, as shown in Figure 9.9. It is possible for OQ_1 to be less than or equal to OQ.

6. This is only one way in which equilibrium can be achieved in increasing-cost industries. It is also possible that the increase in input prices (due to the expansion of industry output) raises average cost more than the increase in demand raises average revenue. Thus, firms may experience losses, some may leave the industry, and the remaining firms may produce at a larger scale.

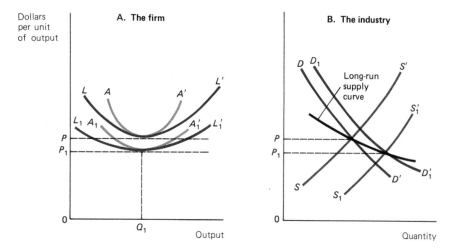

Figure 9.10   Long-run equilibrium: Decreasing-cost industry

DD', the short-run supply curve being SS', price being OP, and the long-run and short-run average cost curves of each firm being LL' and AA'. As before, we postulate an increase in demand to D_1D_1', the result being economic profit for established firms and the entry of new firms. However, in the case of a decreasing-cost industry, the expansion of the industry results in a decrease in the costs of the established firms. Thus the new long-run equilibrium is at a price of OP_1, the equilibrium output of each firm being OQ_1, and the new long-run and short-run average cost curves being L_1L_1' and A_1A_1'.

A *decreasing-cost industry has a negatively sloped long-run supply curve.* That is, after long-run equilibrium is reached, increases in output are accompanied by decreases in price. *External economies,* which are cost reductions that occur when the industry expands, may be responsible for the existence of decreasing-cost industries. An example of an external economy is an improvement in transportation that is due to the expansion of an industry and that reduces the costs of each firm in the industry. If there are important external economies, an industry may be subject to decreasing costs. Note that external economies are quite different from economies of scale: The individual firm has no control over external economies.

Most economists seem to regard increasing-cost industries as being the most frequently encountered of the three types. Decreasing-cost industries are the most unusual situation, although quite young industries may fall into this category. In Section 13, we present estimates of the shape of the long-run supply curve in various industries.

11. The Allocation Process: Short and Long Run

At this point, it is instructive to describe the process by which a perfectly competitive economy—an economy composed of perfectly competitive industries—would allocate resources. In Chapter 1, we noted that the allocation of resources among alternative uses is one of the major functions of an economic system. Equipped with the concepts of this and previous chapters, we can now go much farther than we could in Chapter 1 in describing how a perfectly competitive economy goes about shifting resources in accord with changes in consumer demand.

To be specific, suppose that a change occurs in tastes, with the result that consumers are more favorably disposed toward corn and less favorably disposed toward potatoes than in the past. What will happen in the short run? The increase in the demand for corn increases the price of corn, and results in some increase in the output of corn. However, the output of corn cannot be increased very substantially because the capacity of the industry cannot be expanded in the short run. Similarly, the fall in the demand for potatoes reduces the price of potatoes, and results in some reduction in the output of potatoes. But the output of potatoes will not be curtailed greatly because firms will continue to produce as long as they can cover variable costs.

The change in the relative prices of corn and potatoes tells producers that a reallocation of resources is called for. Because of the increase in the price of corn and the decrease in the price of potatoes, corn producers are earning economic profits and potato producers are showing economic losses. This will trigger a redeployment of resources. If some variable inputs in the production of potatoes can be used as effectively in the production of corn, these variable inputs may be withdrawn from potato production and switched to corn production. Even if there are no variable inputs that are used in both corn and potato production, adjustment can occur in various interrelated markets, with the result that corn production gains resources and potato production loses resources.

When short-run equilibrium is attained in both the corn and potato industries, the reallocation of resources is not yet complete since there has not been enough time for producers to build new capacity or liquidate old capacity. In particular, neither industry is operating at minimum average cost. The corn producers are operating at greater than the output level where average cost is a minimum; and the potato producers are operating at less than the output level where average cost is a minimum.

What will happen in the long run? The shift in consumer demand from potatoes to corn will result in greater adjustments in production and smaller adjustments in price than in the short run. In the long run, existing firms can leave potato production and new firms can enter corn production. Because of short-run economic losses in potato production, some potato land and related equipment will be allowed to run down, and some firms engaged in potato production will be liquidated. As firms leave potato production, the supply curve shifts to the left, causing the price to rise above its short-run level. The transfer of resources out of potato production will stop when the price has increased, and costs have decreased, to the point where losses are avoided.

While potato production is losing resources, corn production is gaining them. The short-run economic profits in corn production will result in the entry of new firms. The increased demand for inputs will raise input prices and cost curves in corn production, and the price of corn will be depressed by the movement to the right of the supply curve because of the entry of new firms. Entry ceases when economic profits are no longer being earned. At that point, when long-run equilibrium is achieved, there will be more firms and more resources used in the corn industry than in the short run.

Finally, long-run equilibrium is established in both industries, and the reallocation of resources is complete. It is important to note that this reallocation can affect industries other than corn and potatoes. If potato land and equipment can be easily adapted to the production of corn, which seems unlikely, potato producers can simply change to the production of corn. If not, the resources used in potato production are converted to some use other than corn, and the resources that enter corn production come from some use other than potato production. The full repercussions can be analyzed by general equilibrium analysis, which is discussed in Chapter 15.

12. The Path to Equilibrium and the Cobweb Theorem

A great deal of attention has been devoted in this chapter to the equilibrium levels of price and output. However, disequilibrium, rather than equilibrium, has to be the usual state of most real-life markets. Demand curves are constantly shifting in response to changes in tastes and incomes, among other things. Supply curves are constantly shifting in response to changes in technology and resource limitations, among other things. Thus the equilibrium levels of prices are constantly changing, and actual prices differ from them. We must recognize the importance of disequilibrium but it would be a mistake to conclude from this that theories based on equilibrium prices are of no use. On the contrary, equilibrium theories help us to predict the direction of change of price and output. With careful study one can sometimes say a good deal about the way in which price and output are likely to move.

To illustrate how actual price may converge on the equilibrium price, consider one of the simplest dynamic models[7] in economics, the cobweb model or theorem.[8] Suppose that the amount supplied of a commodity, say hogs, is a function of price in the *previous* period. This might be the case because it takes one period to raise a hog. On the other hand, suppose that the amount demanded of the commodity is a function of price in the *present* period. Finally, suppose that the demand and supply curves are as shown in Figure 9.11 and OP_0 was the price in the previous period.

Under these assumptions, the amount supplied in the first period will be OQ_1. But given that OQ_1 is supplied, the demand curve shows that the price will be OP_1 in the first period (since this is the price at

7. Dynamic models indicate the movement over a period of time of economic variables and the way in which such variables move from one equilibrium to another (or one disequilibrium to another).

8. The name *cobweb* is derived from the appearance of diagrams like Figure 9.11.

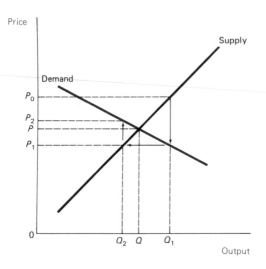

Figure 9.11 The cobweb theorem

which OQ_1 units of output will be demanded). With this price in the first period, the supply curve shows that the amount supplied in the second period will be OQ_2. And with OQ_2 as the amount supplied in the second period, the demand curve shows that the price in the second period will be OP_2. This process will go on and on, with price and output each moving in a cycle. In one period, price is above the equilibrium level, with the result that the quantity supplied in the next period is above the equilibrium level. Because quantity is then above the equilibrium level, price will be below the equilibrium level. And so on.

In the case described in Figure 9.11, the process converges. The actual price and output move closer and closer to the equilibrium levels, OP and OQ. This is because the supply curve is steeper than the demand curve. If the slopes of the demand and supply curves are equal (in absolute value), the cycles of price and output continue undiminished. If the demand curve is steeper than the supply curve, the amplitude of the cycles increases over time.

Although the cobweb model is extremely simple and mechanical, it may be of use in explaining why the prices and outputs of some commodities have shown pronounced cyclical movements. Jan Tinbergen of the Netherlands, a Nobel laureate, has suggested that this model may be relevant in explaining the patterns of hog prices. Clearly, however, the cobweb theorem is a very simple model that captures only a limited amount of the richness of the real world.

13. Estimates of Price Elasticity of Supply

Previous sections of this chapter have dealt at length with the role of demand curves and supply curves, both short-run and long-run, in the determination of price. Chapter 5 presented the results of various empirical studies of the demand curve for selected commodities. In this section we present the results of various empirical studies of the supply curve for selected commodities. The econometric techniques used to estimate the supply curve are much like those used to estimate the demand curve, which were discussed in Chapter 5.

To illustrate the kind of studies that have been carried out, consider the investigation sponsored by the Environmental Protection Agency of the elasticity of supply of construction services in the United States.[9] Based on data for 1958–72, studies made for EPA estimated that a 1 percent increase in the price of construction leads to an increase of 6.5 percent in the supply of construction services. EPA is extremely interested in the price elasticity of supply of construction services because it wants to know how much construction prices must rise in order to bring forth the extra construction services required to build the treatment plants and other equipment needed to meet new environmental protection standards.

Of course, there is a considerable difference between short-run and long-run elasticities of supply. Turning to agriculture, Marc Nerlove and William Addison have estimated short-run and long-run elasticities of supply for a number of vegetables produced for fresh market in the United States during 1919–55. The short-run elasticity is defined to be the elasticity over one production period. The results are shown in Table 9.1.[10] Note that the short-run elasticities are considerably lower than the long-run elasticities, as would be expected. For example, the short-run elasticity of supply for cabbage is estimated to be 0.36, whereas the long-run elasticity is estimated to be 1.2. According to these estimates the long-run elasticity of supply is greater for cucumbers, green peas, and spinach than for the other commodities. Although these estimates are based on quite sophisticated techniques, Nerlove and Addison caution that they are tentative and presented mainly for purposes of illustration.

14. The Cotton Textile Industry: A Case Study[10]

The cotton textile industry has been described as being closer to perfect competition than any other manufacturing industry in the United States. The industry's major product, gray cotton print cloth, can be viewed as homogeneous. Many buyers and sellers exist, no one of which is

---

9. See *The Economics of Clean Water—1973,* Environmental Protection Agency (Washington, D.C.: U.S. Government Printing Office, 1973).

10. M. Nerlove and W. Addison, "Statistical Estimation of Long-Run Elasticities of Supply and Demand," *Journal of Farm Economics,* November 1958.

11. This section is based largely on L. Reynolds, "Competition in the Textile Industry," in W. Adams and L. Traywick, ed., *Readings in Economics* (New York: Macmillan, 1948). K. Cohen and R. Cyert, *Theory of the Firm* (Englewood Cliffs, N.J.: Prentice-Hall, 1965), pp. 157–59, also draw on Reynolds's paper and use it in a similar way.

Table 9.1   Estimated price elasticities of supply

PRICE ELASTICITY

Commodity	Short run	Long run
Green lima beans	0.10	1.70
Green snap beans	0.15	∞*
Cabbage	0.36	1.20
Carrots	0.14	1.00
Cucumbers	0.29	2.20
Lettuce	0.03	0.16
Onions	0.34	1.00
Green peas	0.31	4.40
Green peppers	0.07	0.26
Tomatoes	0.16	0.90
Watermelons	0.23	0.48
Beets	0.13	1.00
Cantalopes	0.02	0.04
Cauliflower	0.14	1.10
Celery	0.14	0.95
Eggplant	0.16	0.34
Kale (Va. only)	0.20	0.23
Spinach	0.20	4.70
Shallots (La. only)	0.12	0.31

* According to Nerlove and Addison, this estimate holds only
  for a limited range of output.

SOURCE M. Nerlove and W. Addison, *op. cit.*

big enough to influence the price. Entry into the industry is not difficult.
Looking at the cotton textile industry during the interwar period, how
closely did its behavior accord with the theory presented in this chapter?

Considerable excess capacity existed in the cotton textile industry
from about 1924 to 1936. Evidence of this overcapacity is presented in
Table 9.2, which shows that the profit rate in cotton textiles was considerably below that in other manufacturing. For example, during 1924–28
and 1933–36, textile profits averaged less than 4 percent of the firms'
capitalization, whereas profits as a percent of capitalization in all manufacturing averaged 8 percent. It is also important to note that profit

Table 9.2   Profits as a percent of capitalization:
Cotton textile industry and
all manufacturing, 1919–36

Period	Cotton textiles	All manufacturing
1919–23	15.3	11.0
1924–28	4.7	11.0
1933–36	2.4	4.3

SOURCE Lloyd Reynolds, "Competition in the Cotton
Textile Industry," in W. Adams and D. Traywick,
op. cit.

rates in cotton textiles were higher in the South than in the North. Profits in the South averaged 6 percent, whereas profits in the North averaged 1 percent. This was due to the fact that the prices of many inputs—like labor and raw cotton—were lower in the South.

If we are given a situation of this sort, what would the perfectly competitive model predict? Clearly, the industry was not in long-run equilibrium, since the industry was not earning as great a return as other manufacturing industries and the returns obtained by mills in the South were greater than those obtained by mills in the North. What sort of changes would be required to make the industry approach long-run equilibrium? First, many firms would have to leave the industry, until eventually the profit rate in cotton textiles would increase to the point at which it approximated the profit rate in other industries. Second, the industry would tend to become concentrated more heavily in the South, the exit rate being higher in the North than in the South. It should be obvious from previous sections that the model would predict these two occurrences.

In fact, did the industry perform as expected on the basis of the model? According to careful studies of the industry's history during this period, the answer is yes. Under the pressure of economic losses, elimination of weaker firms proceeded steadily, the total number of spindles falling from a peak of 38 million in 1925 to 27 million in 1938. Moreover, the chief loser of capacity was the North, not the South. As one observer put it, "Competition has thus performed, though tardily and haphazardly, its traditional function of adjusting productive capacity to effective demand."[12]

15. Agricultural Prices and Output: An Application

Perhaps the most important sector of the American economy that contains industries that are reasonably close to perfect competition is agriculture. Farming is still our most important single industry, although it includes a much smaller percentage of our people than it once did. One of the most important points to note about American agriculture is that agricultural prices generally fell, relative to other prices, from World War I to the early 1970s. That is, if we correct for changes in the general price level resulting from overall inflation, there was a declining trend in farm prices. Another important fact is that farm incomes vary between good times and bad to a much greater extent than nonfarm incomes, whereas farm output is much more stable than industrial output.

The theory presented in this and previous chapters is useful in explaining the reasons for these characteristics of American agriculture. Figure 9.12 shows the demand and supply curves for farm products at various points in time. Since we know from Chapter 5 that the demand for food does not grow very rapidly in this country, we would expect the demand curve to shift relatively slowly to the right, from DD' in the first

12. Reynolds, ibid., p. 151

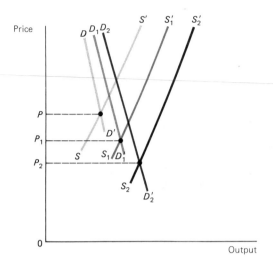

Figure 9.12   Shifts in demand and supply: Agriculture

period to D_1D_1' in the second period to D_2D_2' in the third period. On the other hand, because of very great technological improvements in agriculture, the supply curve has been shifting relatively rapidly to the right, from SS' in the first period to S_1S_1' in the second period to S_2S_2' in the third period. The consequence is that agriculture prices fell (relative to other prices) from OP to OP_1 to OP_2.

It is also easy to see why farm incomes are so unstable. We know from Chapter 5 that the demand curve for basic farm products is relatively inelastic. Also, the supply curve for basic farm products is relatively inelastic in the short run. Since both the demand curve and the supply curve are inelastic, a small shift (to the right or left) in either

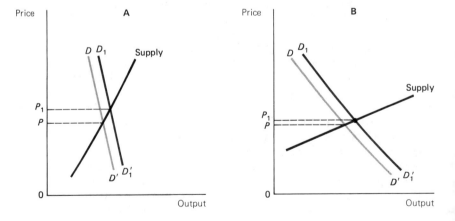

Figure 9.13   Relationship between elasticity of supply and demand and instability of price

curve, or both, results in a large change in price. To illustrate, consider Figure 9.13. In panel A, the demand and supply curves are much less elastic than in panel B, with the result that a small shift in the demand curve results in a much bigger change in price in panel A than in panel B. [13]

Although agricultural prices have generally fallen (relative to industrial prices) over the past sixty years, this trend was reversed sharply in 1973 and 1974, when farm prices rose at an astonishing rate. Due to poor harvests in other countries and the devaluation of the dollar, as well as trade with the Communist world, there was a marked upward shift to the right of the demand curve for American farm products. As would be predicted by our theory, farm prices rose rapidly in response to this shift in the demand curve. For example, the price of wheat rose from under $2 to over $5 per bushel. Anyone who witnessed the proceedings would have been quick to agree that farm prices behaved in accord with our model.

16. Government Subsidy Programs

Another important fact about American agriculture that must be added to this picture is government intervention and aid. Both Figures 9.12 and 9.13 are based on the supposition that agricultural markets are free. For about half of all farm products, the government has established price support programs of one sort or another. These programs vary in many respects, but the general idea behind them is that the federal government has tried to increase farm prices in various ways. For products where such programs exist, the perfectly competitive model is clearly an inap-

13. For simplicity, suppose that the demand and supply curves exhibit the same elasticity at each point, in which case

$$Q_D = \alpha_0 P^{-\beta_0} \qquad\qquad 9.1$$
$$Q_S = \alpha_1 P^{\beta_1} \qquad\qquad 9.2$$

where P is price, Q_D the quantity demanded, and Q_S the quantity supplied. Equation 9.1 is the demand function in which β_0 is the price elasticity of demand. Equation 9.2 is the supply function in which β_1 is the price elasticity of supply. Suppose that the demand curve shifted slightly, with α_0 increasing or decreasing by a small amount. What would be the effect on the equilibrium price? Suppose that the supply curve shifted slightly, with α_1 increasing or decreasing by a small amount. What would be the effect on the equilibrium price?

Since $Q_D = Q_S (= Q)$ in equilibrium, it follows from Equations 9.1 and 9.2 that

$$\log P = \frac{\log \alpha_0 - \log \alpha_1}{\beta_0 + \beta_1}$$

Thus,

$$\frac{dP}{P} \div \frac{d\alpha_0}{\alpha_0} = \frac{1}{\beta_0 + \beta_1}$$

$$\frac{dP}{P} \div \frac{d\alpha_1}{\alpha_1} = \frac{-1}{\beta_0 + \beta_1}$$

Consequently, as stated in the text, the relative change in price resulting from a small relative change in α_0 or α_1 is bigger if β_0 and β_1 are small than if β_0 or β_1 is large.

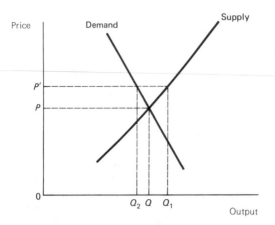

Figure 9.14   Effect of price support

propriate device to predict price and output. But, as we shall see in this section, the basic elements of the theory remain useful in analyzing the effects of these programs.

More specifically, the programs in operation until 1973 can be described in terms of Figure 9.14. A support price, OP', was set which was above the equilibrium price, OP, with the consequence that output equaled OQ_1, consumers bought OQ_2, and the rest (which equaled $OQ_1 - OQ_2$) had to be purchased by the government. The imposition of the support price meant, of course, that farmers received more for their crop than they otherwise would have, and the difference in their receipts was $OP' \times OQ_1 - OP \times OQ$.

To cut down on the amount that the government had to purchase (and store or dispose of), production controls were imposed as well. These controls often took the form of quotas on the acreage used to grow the product. With such controls, the situation is shown in Figure 9.15, where OQ_3 is the total quota—in terms of output—for all farms. Because of the imposition of the production control, the government's expenditures were reduced from $OP' \times (OQ_1 - OQ_2)$ in Figure 9.14 to $OP' (OQ_3 - OQ_2)$ in Figure 9.15.

In 1973, an alternative plan, proposed earlier by President Harry Truman's Secretary of Agriculture, Charles Brannan, and President Dwight Eisenhower's Secretary, Ezra Taft Benson, was adopted. According to this plan, which is illustrated in Figure 9.16, farmers are still guaranteed a "target" price of OP', but rather than allow the amount the government buys (which equals $OQ_3 - OQ_2$) to waste in storage, they sell this amount at whatever consumers will pay for it. Or, what amounts to the same thing, the government lets the competitive market alone, with the result that an output of OQ_3 is produced and sold at a price of OP_2; then the government issues subsidy checks to farmers to cover the difference between the price they received and the target price, OP'.

Clearly, the cost to the government under the Brannan plan is $(OP' - OP_2) \times OQ_3$. An important question is: Will the cost to the Treasury

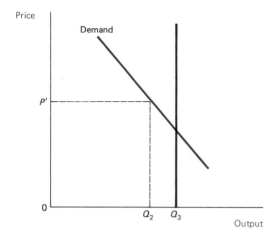

Figure 9.15   Effect of price support and production control

be greater than under the support plan shown in Figure 9.15? The answer depends on the elasticity of demand. If demand is inelastic, it will be greater; if demand is elastic, it will be smaller. To prove this, recall that the cost under the Brannan plan would be $(OP' - OP_2)OQ_3$, and the cost in Figure 9.15 would be $OP'(OQ_3 - OQ_2)$. Thus the former cost would be less than the latter if $OP_2 \times OQ_3 > OP' \times OQ_2$. But since $OP_2 \times OQ_3$ is the revenue at price OP_2 and $OP' \times OQ_2$ is the revenue at price OP', the former will be more than the latter only if the price elasticity of demand exceeds one. (Recall the discussion on p. 115.)

Since the demand for agricultural products is generally inelastic, this means that the Brannan plan will cost the Treasury more than the support plan in Figure 9.15, if the market price is less than the target price. But this is not a necessarily overwhelming argument against the Brannan plan. For one thing, the market price may be above the target

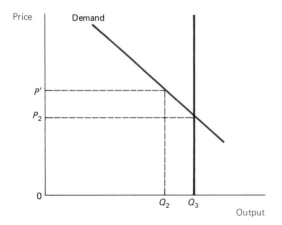

Figure 9.16   Effect of the Brannan plan

Example 9.2   Rent Control in New York City

Since the 1940s, New York City has had a system of rent control which imposes ceilings on rent. According to estimates made by the RAND Corporation, rent increases have fallen far short of cost increases. For housing units built before 1943, the average increase in rents was about 2 percent per year during 1943–70, whereas the average increase in landlords' costs was about 6 percent per year. (a) Under these circumstances, would you expect the vacancy rate for rent-controlled housing units to be relatively high or low? (b) What predictions would you make concerning the response of landlords to rent controls? (c) According to some observers, New York City has a shortage of about $3 billion worth of new rental housing. If this is interpreted as the size of the gap between the quantity supplied and the quantity demanded, how long will it take the price system to close this gap under existing conditions? (d) What segment of the populations are rent controls aimed at helping?

Solution

(a) The vacancy rate would be expected to be very low. The rent is the price of using an apartment for a month. This price, denoted by OR, is below the equilibrium price, as shown below, with the result that the quantity of rental housing demanded (OQ_D) is greater than the quantity supplied (OQ_S). Thus prospective tenants would be expected to snap up apartments as soon as they become available. In fact, in 1971, the rental vacancy rate was reported to be under 1 percent, which was a relatively low rate.

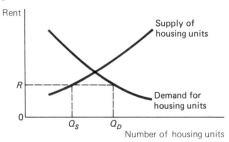

(b) Landlords will have an incentive to accept side payments or bribes from those looking for housing. They will curtail maintenance of their properties in many cases; because there is a shortage, renters are willing to accept poorer service and do more things for themselves. To the extent possible, landlords may try to subdivide apartments, since the ceiling on the rents from the subdivisions may exceed that of the original apartment. (c) Under existing conditions, the gap never will be closed by the price system. So long as rents are kept below their equilibrium level, the quantity of rental housing supplied will be less than the quantity demanded. (d) One important purpose is to help the poor.*

* For further discussion, see RAND Corporation, *Rental Housing in New York City,* RM-6190-NYC, February 1970; and J. Moorhouse, "Optimal Housing under Rent Control," *Southern Economic Journal,* July 1972.

price, in which case the Brannan plan will cost the Treasury nothing. For another, the Brannan plan has the advantage that the market price is closer to the true social cost of producing agricultural products. More will be said about the economic advantages and disadvantages of various types of agricultural price support programs in Chapter 16, when we continue this discussion of agricultural subsidies.

17. Effects of Transaction Costs on Price and Quantity

In previous sections, we have assumed that no middlemen existed who facilitated the workings of the market by helping to match up buyers and sellers. In many real-life markets, such middlemen play an important role. Among other things, they often help to provide relevant information to buyers and/or sellers, to execute whatever sales contracts are involved, and to help guarantee that the good is of the proper quality and that the buyer will pay the seller promptly and fully. For services of this sort, the middlemen receive a share of the price paid for the good. For example, in the New York Stock Exchange, a purchaser or seller of a stock must pay a commission to the broker handling the transaction. Also, there is a spread between the bid price (the price to a seller) and the ask price (the price to a buyer); that is, the former price is less than the latter price. This spread goes principally to the Exchange's specialist who continually stands ready to buy or sell this particular stock. To stay in business, the specialist must pay less, on the average, for a share of the stock than what he or she receives for it.

The costs of these middlemen's services are often called *transaction costs*. What are the effects of these transaction costs on the equilibrium price and the equilibrium output of a good? For simplicity, assume that the transaction cost is proportional to the amount spent on the good. In particular, suppose that the transaction cost per unit of the good sold equals AB in Figure 9.17. That is, for every unit of the good that is sold,

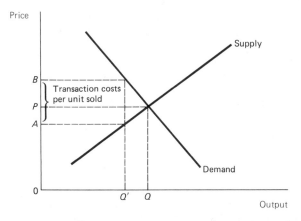

Figure 9.17   Effect of transaction costs on price and quantity

middlemen must be paid an amount equal to AB. Under these circumstances, there will be a gap between the price to the buyer and the price to the seller. In Figure 9.17, the equilibrium price will not be OP, as it would be if transaction costs were zero. Instead, the price to the buyer must exceed the price to the seller by AB, because this spread is required to pay the middlemen. Consequently, the price to the buyer must be OB and the price to the seller must be OA, because this is the only pair of prices differing by AB where the quantity supplied equals the quantity demanded.

Clearly, the effect of a transaction cost of this type is to drive a wedge between the price to the seller and the price to the buyer—and the larger the transaction cost per unit of the good sold, the bigger the wedge driven between these prices. Further, the effect of the transaction cost is to reduce the quantity of the good that is bought or sold. Whereas the equilibrium quantity is OQ when the transaction cost is zero, it is OQ' when the transaction cost is AB per unit of the good sold. This demonstrates an important point: As the transaction cost per unit of good sold increases, the amount of the good sold will tend to decrease. Eventually, if the transaction cost becomes big enough, the market for the good will cease to function at all; that is, the good will no longer be traded. This has happened to some commodities. For example, the market for used clothes has largely disappeared in the United States in recent years. Because the cost of selling used clothes is now so high relative to what people are willing to pay for them, there is no longer any profit to be made by trying to sell most types of used clothes; instead, they are thrown out or given away.

18. Summary

Perfect competition is defined by four conditions: No participant in the market can influence price; output must be homogeneous; resources must be mobile; and there must be perfect knowledge. In the market period, where the quantity supplied is fixed, the price of a product is demand-determined. In the short run, the firm maximizes profit or minimizes losses by producing the output at which marginal cost equals price. However, if market price is less than the firm's average variable costs at all levels of output, the firm will minimize losses by discontinuing production. The firm's short-run supply curve is the same as its marginal cost curve, as long as price exceeds average variable cost.

The short-run price of a product is determined by the interaction between the demand and supply sides of the market. As a rough approximation, the industry's short-run supply curve can be regarded as the horizontal summation of the short-run supply curves of the individual firms. However, this is not the case if the supply of inputs to the industry is not perfectly elastic. The short-run equilibrium price level is the price at which the quantity demanded and the quantity supplied in the short run are equal. At the equilibrium price, price will equal marginal cost for all firms that choose to produce, rather than shut down their plants.

In the long run, firms can change their plant size and leave or enter the industry. The long-run equilibrium position of the firm is at the point at which its long-run average costs equal price. Moreover, firms must be operating at the minimum point on their long-run average cost curves. Industries can be divided into three types: constant cost, increasing cost, and decreasing cost. Constant-cost industries have horizontal long-run supply curves; increasing-cost industries have positively sloped long-run supply curves; and decreasing-cost industries have negatively sloped long-run supply curves. Increasing-cost industries are generally regarded as being the most numerous of the three types.

Having presented this basic theory, we described the way in which resources are allocated in a perfectly competitive economy. Then we discussed the process by which actual price may converge on the equilibrium price, using as an illustration the cobweb model. Next we presented estimates of the elasticity of supply for a number of commodities. Then, after a brief case study of the cotton textile industry, we used the theory to explain some of the characteristics of American agriculture and to analyze government subsidy programs. Finally, we showed that transaction costs can drive a wedge between the price to the buyer and the price to the seller, and that they tend to reduce the quantity of a good that is traded.

QUESTIONS AND PROBLEMS

1. A perfectly competitive firm has the following total cost function:

Total output (dollars)	Total cost (dollars)
0	20
1	30
2	42
3	55
4	69
5	84
6	100
7	117

   How much will the firm produce if the price is (a) $13, (b) $14, (c) $15, (d) $16, or (e) $17?

2. Explain how it is possible for an industry to be a constant-cost industry even though each firm in the industry has increasing marginal costs.

3. Suppose that there are 100 firms producing the good in Question 1, and that each firm has the total cost function shown there. If input prices remain constant (regardless of industry output), draw the industry supply curve.

4. If the textile industry is a constant-cost industry, and the demand curve for textiles shifts upward, what are the steps by which a competitive market insures an increased amount of textiles. What happens if the government will not allow textile prices to rise?

5. An economist estimates that, in the short run, the quantity of widgets supplied at each price is as follows:

Price (dollars)	Quantity supplied per year (millions)
1	5
2	6
3	7
4	8

Calculate the arc elasticity of supply when the price is between $3 and $4 per widget. (Review Chapter 2 if you do not recall the definition of the arc elasticity of supply.)

6. "In long-run equilibrium, every firm in a competitive industry earns zero profit. Thus, if the price falls, all of these firms will be unable to stay in business." Evaluate this statement.

7. According to the U.S. Census Bureau, the largest four producers of flat glass account for about 92 percent of the industry's value-added. Do you think that the perfectly competitive model will work as well in flat glass as in cotton textiles? Why or why not?

8. According to George Stigler, the criticism that the concept of perfect competition is unrealistic can be dealt with by replying that "all concepts sufficiently general and sufficiently precise to be useful in scientific analysis must be abstract." Comment on this proposition. Do you agree? Why or why not?

9. According to D. Suits and S. Koizumi, the supply function for onions in the United States is $\log q = 0.134 + .0123\,t + 0.324 \log P - 0.512 \log C$, where q is the quantity supplied in a particular year, t is the year (less 1924), P is the price last season, and C is the cost index last season. Suppose that price is estimated by one forecaster to be 10 cents this season, whereas another says that it will be 11 cents. Holding other factors constant, how much difference will this make in forecasting the quantity supplied next season?

10. According to Kenneth Boulding, "The most jaundiced antiagrarian cannot deny that, of all people, farmers have the least opportunity for monopoly." Have farmers rejoiced over this fact? Why or why not? If you were a member of Congress, what sort of a farm program would you favor?

SELECTED REFERENCES

AMERICAN ECONOMIC ASSOCIATION. *Readings in Price Theory*, edited by George Stigler and Kenneth Boulding. Homewood, Ill.: Irwin, 1952.

BOULDING, KENNETH. "Agriculture: Problems of a Competitive Industry." In Mansfield, *Microeconomics: Selected Readings.*

KNIGHT, FRANK. *Risk, Uncertainty, and Profit.* London School Reprints of Scarce Works, no. 16, 1933.

MARSHALL, ALFRED. *Principles of Economics.* London: Macmillan, 1920.

SMITH, VERNON. "An Experimental Study of Competitive Market Behavior." *Journal of Political Economy,* April 1962.

SAMUELSON, PAUL. *Foundations of Economic Analysis.* Cambridge, Mass.: Harvard University Press, 1947. (Advanced)

STIGLER, GEORGE. "Perfect Competition, Historically Contemplated." in E. Mansfield, *Microeconomics: Selected Readings.* 4th ed. New York: Norton, 1982.

10 Price and Output under Pure Monopoly

1. Pure Monopoly

Most Americans are familiar with the word *monopoly*. On rainy afternoons, children in the United States often play a game called Monopoly in which they try hard to become the sole owners of related pieces of property. (According to the rules of the game, the amount that a player can get from the other players is greater if he is the sole owner of related pieces of property.) Whether or not you have ever played this game, the concept of a monopoly is probably familiar: A monopoly is a situation where there is a single source of supply. And whether you live in the United States or Canada or Australia or the United Kingdom, you have probably encountered some firms that are monopolies, or close to it. Electric companies, telephone companies, and water companies often are examples.

In microeconomics, pure monopoly, like perfect competition, is a useful model. The conditions defining pure monopoly are easy to state: There must exist one, and only one, seller in a market. Pure monopoly, like perfect competition, does not correspond more than approximately to conditions in real industries. But, as we have noted several times before, a model must be judged by its predictive ability, not the "realism" of its assumptions. The theory of pure monopoly has proved to be a very useful analytical device. Pure monopoly and perfect competition are opposites in the following sense: The firm in a perfectly competitive market has so many rivals that competition becomes impersonal in the extreme; the firm under pure monopoly has no rivals at all. Under pure monopoly, one firm is the sole supplier. There is no competition.

Having said this, it is important to add that the policies adopted by a pure monopolist are affected by certain indirect and potential forms of competition. Clearly, the monopolist is not completely insulated from the effects of actions taken in the rest of the economy. All commodities are rivals for the consumer's favor, as we saw in Chapter 3. Clearly this rivalry occurs among different products, as well as among the producers of a given commodity. For example, meat competes in this sense with butter, eggs, and even men's suits. Of course, the extent of the competition from other products depends on the extent to which other products are substitutes for the monopolist's product. For example, even if a firm somehow could obtain a monopoly on the supply of steel in a particular market, it would still face considerable competition from producers of aluminum, plastics, and other materials that are reasonably good substitutes for steel.

In addition, the threat of potential competition also acts as a brake on the policies of the monopolist. The monopolist often can maintain its monopoly position only if it does not extract as much short-run profit as possible. If it sets prices above a certain point, other firms may enter its market and try to break its monopoly. If entry can occur, the monopolist must take this possibility into account. Failure to do so may make it an ex-monopolist.

2. Reasons for Monopoly

Why do monopolies arise? There are many reasons, but four seem particularly important. First, a single firm may control the entire supply of a basic input that is required to manufacture a given product. The example that is cited repeatedly to illustrate this situation is the prewar aluminum industry. Bauxite is an input used to produce aluminum; and for some time, practically every source of bauxite in the United States was controlled by the Aluminum Company of America (Alcoa). For this reason (and others), Alcoa was, for a long time, the sole producer of aluminum in the United States. More will be said about the case of Alcoa in Section 17.

Second, a firm may become a monopolist because the average cost of producing the product reaches a minimum at an output rate that is big enough to satisfy the entire market at a price that is profitable. In a situation of this sort, if there is more than one firm producing the product, each must be producing at a higher-than-minimum level of average cost. Each may be inclined to cut the price to increase its output rate and reduce its average costs. The result is likely to be economic warfare—and the survival of a single victor, the monopolist. Cases in which costs behave in this fashion are called *natural monopolies*. When an industry is a natural monopoly, the public often insists that its behavior be regulated by the government.[1]

Third, a firm may acquire a monopoly over the production of a good by having patents on the product or on certain basic processes that are used in its production. The patent laws of the United States permit an inventor to get the exclusive right to make a certain product or to use a particular process. (The patent is in force for seventeen years.) Patents can be very important in keeping competitors out. For example, Alcoa held important patents on basic production processes used to make aluminum. However, it is often possible to "invent around" another company's patents. That is, although a firm cannot use a product or process on which another firm has a patent (without the latter's permission), it may be able to develop a closely related product or process and obtain a patent on it. Further discussion of the patent system is contained in Chapter 18.

Fourth, a firm may become a monopolist because it is awarded a market franchise by a government agency. The firm is granted the exclusive privilege to produce a given good or service in a particular area. In exchange for this right, the firm agrees to allow the government to regulate certain aspects of its behavior and operations. For example, as we shall see in Section 16, the government may set limits on the firm's price. Regardless of the form of regulation, the important point is that the monopoly has been created by the government.

3. The Monopolist's Demand Curve

Since the monopolist is the only firm producing a product, it is obvious that the monopolist's demand curve is precisely the same as the market demand curve for the product. Consequently, the factors determining the shape of the monopolist's demand curve are the same factors that determine the shape of the demand curve for the product. As we saw in Chapter 5 these factors are the prices of other related products (substitutes and complements), incomes, and tastes. However, it should be noted that the monopolist sometimes can affect the prices of related products, as well as consumer tastes. To influence consumer tastes, monopolists often make considerable expenditures on advertising, the purpose being, of course, to shift the demand curve to the right.

Since the monopolist's demand curve is negatively sloped (because

1. For relevant discussions of industries producing more than one product, see W. Baumol, "On the Proper Cost Tests for Natural Monopoly in a Multiproduct Industry," *American Economic Review*, December 1977; J. Panzar and R. Willig, "Economies of Scale in Multi-Output Production," *Quarterly Journal of Economics*, August, 1977; and Panzar and Willig, "Economies of Scope," *American Economic Review*, May, 1981. *Economies of scope* result from the scope rather than the scale of the enterprise. There are economies of scope where it is less costly to combine two or more product lines in one firm than to produce them separately.

the demand curve for a product is negatively sloped, save for a few cases of little significance), average and marginal revenue are not the same. This is quite different from the case of perfect competition where average and marginal revenue were equal. To illustrate the situation faced by a monopolist, consider the hypothetical case in Table 10.1. The price at which each quantity (shown in column 1) can be sold is shown in column 2. The total revenue, the product of the first two columns, is shown in column 3. Obviously, the average revenue corresponding to each output is the price corresponding to that output.

Marginal revenue is of great importance to the profit-maximizing firm. How can we estimate marginal revenue from the figures in Table 10.1? Marginal revenue between q and $(q - 1)$ units of output is defined as $R(q) - R(q - 1)$, where $R(q)$ is the total revenue when the output equals q. The problem in Table 10.1 is that the data are not provided for each level of output; we only have data for $q = 3, 8, 15$, and so on. To cope with this problem, we assume that $R(q)$ is approximately a linear function of q between 3 and 8, 8 and 15, 15 and 21, and so on. If this is the case, the marginal revenue is ($640 - $300) ÷ 5 at an output of between 7 and 8, ($1,110 - $640) ÷ 7 at an output of between 14 and 15, and so forth. The results are shown in the last column of Table 10.1.

Table 10.1   Demand and revenue of monopolist

Quantity sold	Price (dollars)	Total revenue (dollars)	Marginal revenue* (dollars)
3	100.00	300.00	—
8	80.00	640.00	68.00 ($= \frac{340}{5}$)
15	74.00	1,110.00	67.14 ($= \frac{470}{7}$)
21	70.00	1,470.00	60.00 ($= \frac{360}{6}$)
26	67.50	1,755.00	57.00 ($= \frac{285}{5}$)
30	65.50	1,965.00	52.50 ($= \frac{210}{4}$)
33	62.00	2,046.00	27.00 ($= \frac{81}{3}$)
35	60.00	2,100.00	27.00 ($= \frac{54}{2}$)

* These figures pertain to the interval between the indicated quantity of output and one unit less than the indicated quantity of output.

4. The Monopolist's Costs

Although a firm is a monopolist in the product market, it may be a perfect competitor in the market for inputs, in which case it buys so small a proportion of the total supply of each input that it cannot affect input prices. If this is the case, there is no need to dwell further on the monopolist's costs, since the theory in Chapter 7 will apply without modification.

In many cases, however, the monopolist is not a perfect competitor in the input markets, because it buys a large proportion of certain spe-

Table 10.2 Costs of monopolist

Output	Total variable cost (dollars)	Fixed cost (dollars)	Total cost (dollars)	Marginal cost* (dollars)
0	0	500	500	—
3	110	500	610	36.67 $(= \frac{110}{3})$
8	240	500	740	26.00 $(= \frac{130}{5})$
15	390	500	890	21.43 $(= \frac{150}{7})$
21	560	500	1,060	28.33 $(= \frac{170}{6})$
26	750	500	1,250	38.00 $(= \frac{190}{5})$
30	960	500	1,460	52.50 $(= \frac{210}{4})$
33	1,190	500	1,690	76.67 $(= \frac{230}{3})$
35	1,440	500	1,940	125.00 $(= \frac{250}{2})$

* These figures pertain to the interval between the indicated quantity of output and one unit less than the indicated quantity of output.

cialized resources that have little use other than to produce the commodity in question. In a case of this sort, the price that the firm has to pay for this input depends on how much it buys. The more the firm wants of this resource, the more it will generally have to pay. Cases of this sort are discussed at some length in Chapter 14. In the present chapter we assume that the firm is a perfect competitor in the market for inputs.

Table 10.2 shows the costs of our hypothetical monopolist. Column 1 shows various output rates, column 2 shows the total variable cost at each output rate, and column 3 shows the firm's fixed costs. Finally, column 4 shows the firm's total cost at each output rate, and column 5 shows the firm's marginal costs.

5. Short-Run Equilibrium Price and Output

The monopolist, if unregulated and free to maximize profits, will, of course, choose the price and output at which the difference between total revenue and total cost is largest. For example, combining the data from Tables 10.1 and 10.2 into Table 10.3, we find that our hypothetical mon-

Table 10.3 Cost, revenue, and profit of monopolist

Output	Total revenue (dollars)	Total cost (dollars)	Total profit (dollars)
3	300	610	−310
8	640	740	−100
15	1,110	890	220
21	1,470	1,060	310
26	1,755	1,250	505
30	1,965	1,460	505
33	2,046	1,690	356
35	2,100	1,940	160

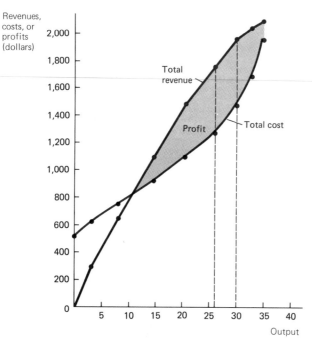

Figure 10.1   Total revenue, total cost, and total profit
of monopolist

opolist will choose an output rate of either 26 or 30 units per time period
and a price of $65.50 or $67.50. Figure 10.1 shows the situation graphically.

Note that either of these optimal output rates is less than the output rate where price equals marginal cost. Under perfect competition,
the profit-maximizing output was the one at which price equals marginal
cost; indeed, this fact was used to derive the firm's supply curve. It is
obvious from Tables 10.1 and 10.2 that this result is not true for pure
monopoly.

Table 10.4   Marginal cost and marginal revenue of monopolist

Output	Marginal cost* (dollars)	Marginal revenue* (dollars)	Total profit (dollars)
3	36.7	—	−310
8	26.0	68.0	−100
15	21.4	67.1	220
21	28.3	60.0	310
26	38.0	57.0	505
30	52.5	52.5	505
33	76.7	27.0	356
35	125.0	27.0	160

* These figures pertain to the interval between the indicated quantity of
output and one unit less than the indicated quantity of output.

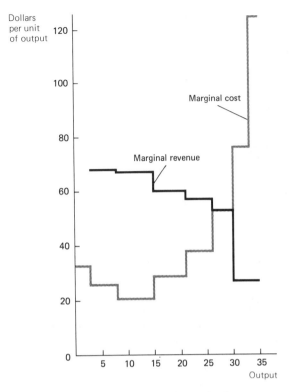

Figure 10.2   Marginal cost and marginal revenue of monopolist

Under monopoly, the firm will maximize profit if it sets its output rate at the point at which marginal cost equals marginal revenue. Table 10.4 and Figure 10.2 show that this is true in this example. It is easy to prove that this is generally a necessary condition for profit maximization. At any output rate at which marginal revenue exceeds marginal cost, profit can be increased by increasing output, since the extra revenue will exceed the extra cost. Thus profit will not be a maximum when marginal revenue exceeds marginal cost. At any output rate at which marginal cost exceeds marginal revenue, profit can be increased by reducing output, since the decrease in cost will exceed the decrease in revenue. Thus profit will not be a maximum when marginal cost exceeds marginal revenue. Since profit is not a maximum when marginal revenue exceeds marginal cost or when marginal cost exceeds marginal revenue, it must be a maximum only when marginal revenue equals marginal cost.[2]

2. Suppose that the monopolist's demand function is $P = D(q)$, where P is price and q is output. Let $C(q)$ be the monopolist's total cost function. Then the monopolist's profit is

$$\Pi = qD(q) - C(q)$$

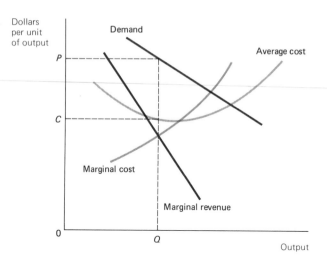

Figure 10.3   Equilibrium position of monopolist

Using this result, it is also simple to represent graphically the short-run equilibrium of the monopolist. Figure 10.3 shows the demand curve, the marginal revenue curve, the marginal cost curve, and the average total cost curve faced by the firm. Short-run equilibrium will occur at the output, OQ, where the marginal cost curve intersects the marginal revenue curve. If the monopolist produces OQ units, the demand curve shows that it must set a price of OP. Moreover, since the average cost curve shows that average costs are OC at an output of OQ units, the profit per unit of output is $(OP - OC)$, and the firm's total profit is $OQ[OP - OC]$.

In this case, the monopolist earns a profit, but this need not always be the case. It does not follow that a firm that holds a monopoly over the production of a particular product must make a profit. The demand curve for the product may be such that, even when the firm produces at the point at which marginal revenue equals marginal cost, average cost exceeds price. For example, even if one could somehow obtain a monopoly on the sale of cigar-store Indians, it might not be a profitable business to enter. Indeed, in the short run, a monopolist may not be able to cover its variable costs, in which case it will discontinue production.

---

and

$$\frac{d\Pi}{dq} = D(q) + qD'(q) - C'(q)$$

Setting $d\Pi/dq = 0$ to obtain the conditions under which profit is a maximum, we find that

$$D(q) + qD'(q) = C'(q)$$

Thus marginal revenue must equal marginal cost when profits are maximized, since the expression on the left-hand side is marginal revenue and the expression on the right-hand side is marginal cost. Of course, this is only the first-order condition for a local maximum. The second-order conditions must also be met, and the maximum may be only a local maximum.

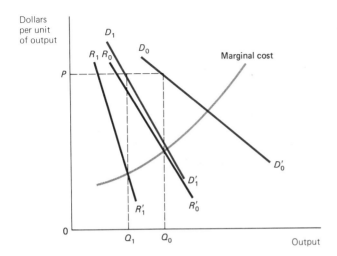

Figure 10.4   More than one output level corresponding
to a given price

6. Relationship between Price and Output

In perfect competition, one can define a unique relationship between the price of the product and the amount supplied. This is the industry's supply curve, which we discussed in Section 5 of Chapter 9. In monopoly, there is no such unique relationship between the product's price and the amount supplied. At first, this is likely to strike the reader as being extremely strange; indeed, one can be pardoned for questioning whether it really is so. The rest of this section is aimed at convincing the reader that it is true.

Figure 10.4 shows the marginal cost curve of the monopolist. It is assumed that the demand curve shifts from D_0D_0' to D_1D_1'. When the demand curve is D_0D_0', the firm produces OQ_0 units (since the marginal cost curve intersects the marginal revenue curve, R_0R_0', at OQ_0) and the price must be OP. When the demand curve is D_1D_1', the firm produces OQ_1 units (since the marginal cost curve intersects the new marginal revenue curve, R_1R_1', at OQ_1) and the price must be OP. This result shows that there is no unique relationship between price and quantity. A price of OP can result in an output of OQ_0 or OQ_1. Thus a particular price can result in a wide variety of output levels, depending on the shape and level of the demand curve.

7. Long-Run Equilibrium Price and Output

In contrast to perfect competition, the long-run equilibrium of a monopolistic industry is not marked by the absence of economic profits or losses. If a monopolist earns a short-run economic profit, it will not be confronted in the long run with competitors, unless the industry is no longer a monopoly. (The entrance of additional firms into the industry is, of course, not compatible with the existence of monopoly.) Thus the long-run equilibrium of an industry under monopoly may be characterized by economic profits.

On the other hand, if the monopolist incurs a short-run economic loss, it will be forced to look for other, more profitable uses for its resources. One possibility is that its existing plant is not optimal and that it can earn economic profits if it alters the scale and characteristics of its plant appropriately. If this is the case, it will make these alterations in the long run and remain in the industry. However, if there is no scale of plant that will enable the monopolist to avoid economic losses, it will leave the industry in the long run.

Returning to the case in which the monopolist earns short-run profits, it must decide in the long run whether it can make even larger profits by altering its plant. For example, assume that the monopolist's demand curve, marginal revenue curve, long-run average cost curve, and long-run marginal cost curve are as shown in Figure 10.5. Suppose that the firm currently has a plant corresponding to short-run average cost curve, A_0A_0', and short-run marginal cost curve, M_0M_0'. In the short run, it will produce OQ_0 units and set a price of OP_0. Since short-run average cost is OB, the firm's short-run profits will be $OQ_0[OP_0 - OB]$.

However, the firm can adjust its plant in the long run so as to make bigger profits than $OQ_0[OP_0 - OB]$. It is easy to show that the monopolist will maximize profit in the long run when it produces the output at which long-run marginal cost equals long-run marginal revenue. The reasoning behind this rule is precisely the same as that given in Section 5.

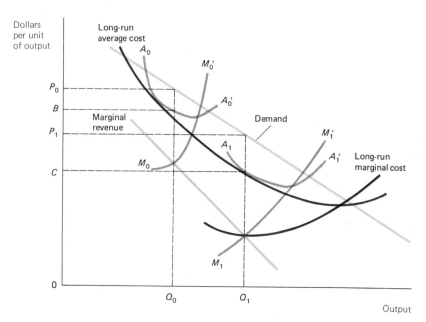

Figure 10.5 Long-run equilibrium for monopolist

Thus the firm will produce OQ_1 units in the long run, since this is the point at which the long-run marginal cost curve intersects the marginal revenue curve. The long-run average cost will be OC, the price will be OP_1, and total profit will be $OQ_1[OP_1 - OC]$. The resulting plant will have short-run average and marginal cost curves of A_1A_1' and M_1M_1', respectively.

8. Multiplant Monopoly

In previous sections we have assumed that the monopolist operated only one plant. This, of course, is an unrealistic assumption in many industries. Even readers with the most superficial knowledge of the structure of various industries will recognize that many firms operate more than one plant and that cost conditions may vary among these plants. This section extends the analysis in previous sections to cover the case where the monopolist operates more than one plant.

An illustrative case is shown in Table 10.5, which assumes that the monopolist operates two plants with marginal cost curves shown in columns 2 and 3, output being shown in column 1. Judging from the figures in these columns, if the firm decides to produce only one unit of output, it should use plant A, since the marginal cost between zero and one unit is lower in plant A than plant B. Thus, for the firm as a whole, the marginal cost between zero and one unit of output is $5 (the marginal cost between zero and one unit for plant A). Similarly, if the firm decides to produce two units of output, both should be produced in plant A, and the marginal cost between the first and second unit of output for the firm as a whole is $6 (the marginal cost between the first and second unit in plant A). If the firm decides to produce three units of output, two should be produced in plant A and one in plant B, and the marginal cost between the second and third unit of output for the firm as a whole is $7 (the marginal cost between zero and one unit of output for plant B). Alternatively, all three could be produced at plant A.

Continuing in this fashion, we can derive the marginal cost curve for the firm as a whole, shown in column 4 of Table 10.5. To maximize profits, the firm should find that output at which marginal revenue

Table 10.5   Costs of multiplant monopoly

Output	Marginal cost* Plant A (dollars)	Plant B (dollars)	Marginal cost for firm* (dollars)	Price (dollars)	Marginal revenue* (dollars)
1	5	7	5	20.00	—
2	6	9	6	15.00	10
3	7	11	7	13.00	9
4	10	13	7	11.50	7
5	12	15	9	8.00	−6

* These figures pertain to the interval between the indicated output and one unit less than the indicated output.

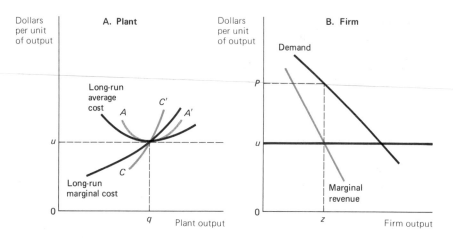

Figure 10.6 Equilibrium in the long run of a multiplant monopoly

equals the marginal cost of the firm as a whole. This is the optimum output. In this case, it is 3 or 4 units: Suppose that the firm picks 4 units.[3] To find out what price to charge, the firm must see what price corresponds to this output on the demand curve. In this case, the answer is $11.50.

This solves most of the monopolist's problems, but not quite all. Given that it will produce 4 units of output per year, how should it divide this production between the two plants? The answer is that it should set the marginal cost in plant A equal to the marginal cost in plant B. Table 10.5 shows that this means that plant A will produce 3 units per year and plant B will produce 1 unit per year. It should also be noted that the common value of the marginal costs of the two plants is also the marginal cost of the firm as a whole. Consequently, this common value must also be set equal to marginal revenue if the firm is maximizing profits.

In the long run the firm can vary the number and size of its plants. The monopolist can construct each plant of optimal size. In other words, in Figure 10.6, the short-run average cost, AA', will equal the long-run average cost, and it will be at the minimum point on the long-run average cost curve. The firm will build plants, each of which produces Oq units of output at an average cost of Ou dollars per unit. Thus, once it has reached Oq units of output, further expansion of output will be accommodated by building more plants of optimal size. Consequently the long-run marginal cost curve is a horizontal line at Ou. Since long-run marginal cost must equal marginal revenue, the firm's total output in the long run will be Oz; it will operate $Oz \div Oq$ plants; and it will charge a price of OP.[4]

3. If the firm maximizes profit, it is a matter of indifference to the firm whether it produces 3 or 4 units since the profit is the same. Suppose that the firm flips a coin to determine which output it will choose and that 4 units is the winner.

4. Of course, we ignore here the problem that Oz/Oq may not be an integer. For simplicity we assume that it is an integer. Also, Oz will generally be bigger than Oq, the scale in panel A of Figure 10.6 being different from that in panel B.

9. Effects of Changes in Demand and Cost

When the demand curve for a product shifts to the right, one ordinarily thinks that the product's price will rise. This expectation is correct under perfect competition, as long as the supply curve does not change (and is upward sloping). But under monopoly it may not be the case. For example, suppose that the monopolist's marginal cost curve is horizontal in the relevant range. Moreover, suppose that, at the price that prevailed before the shift in the demand curve, the elasticity of demand was 3; but that, at the price that prevailed after the shift in the demand curve, the elasticity of demand was 4. That is, the demand curve, when it shifted to the right, also became more elastic. Will such a shift in the demand curve increase price?

The answer is no. To prove this, note that, if the firm maximized profits before the shift in demand, it set marginal cost equal to marginal revenue. Thus,

$$M_1 = P_1\left(1 - \frac{1}{n_1}\right)$$

10.1

where M_1 is marginal cost before the shift in demand, P_1 is price before the shift in demand, and n_1 is the elasticity of demand before the shift in demand. As shown in Chapter 5, the right-hand side of Equation 10.1 equals marginal revenue. Similarly, if the firm maximized profits after the shift in demand, it set

$$M_2 = P_2\left(1 - \frac{1}{n_2}\right)$$

10.2

where M_2 is marginal cost after the shift in demand, P_2 is price after the shift in demand, and n_2 is the elasticity of demand after the shift in demand. Since the marginal cost curve is assumed horizontal, $M_1 = M_2$. And since $n_1 = 3$ and $n_2 = 4$, it follows that $P_2 = \frac{8}{9}P_1$. Thus price will be reduced by about 11 percent, despite the shift of the demand curve to the right.

If a monopolist's costs increase, one might think that the monopolist would pass all of the additional costs along to the consumer. For example, suppose that an excise tax were imposed on the monopolist's product, with the result that its marginal cost curve shifts upward as shown in Figure 10.7. For simplicity we assume again that the marginal cost curve is horizontal in the relevant range. Under these conditions, will the monopolist increase its price by an amount equal to the vertical distance between OM and ON? Or will it pass along only part of the additional costs to the consumer, in which case its price will increase by an amount less than the vertical distance between OM and ON?

The answer is: It will pass along only part of the additional costs to the consumer. If the monopolist maximized profits, it set marginal revenue equal to OM before the tax, with the result that it produced OQ_0 units of output and the price was OP_0 (Figure 10.7). After the imposition of the tax, it sets marginal revenue equal to ON, with the result that it produces OQ_1 units of output and the price is OP_1. It is obvious from

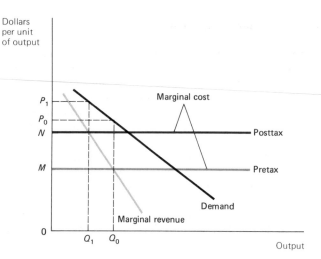

Figure 10.7   Effect of tax on price charged by monopolist

Figure 10.7 that the difference between OP_1 and OP_0 is less than the difference between ON and OM, which means that it passes along only part of the additional costs.

10. Comparison of Monopoly with Perfect Competition

It is important to note the differences between the long-run equilibrium of a monopoly and a perfectly competitive industry. Suppose that we could perform an experiment in which an industry was first operated under conditions of perfect competition and then under conditions of monopoly. Assuming that the demand curve for the industry's product and the industry's cost curves would be the same in either case,[5] what would be the difference in the long-run equilibrium?

First, under perfect competition, each firm operates at the point at which both long-run and short-run average costs are a minimum. However, under monopoly, although the plant that is used will produce the monopolist's long-run equilibrium output at minimum average cost, it is not the plant that will produce the product at the lowest possible average cost. In general, if the monopolist expanded its long-run equilibrium output, it could utilize a plant with lower average costs. This is clearly shown by Figure 10.8, which compares the long-run equilibrium of a firm under perfect competition and monopoly. The monopolist produces OQ_M units of output, which is less than the output corresponding to the minimum point on the long-run average cost curve. Consequently, society's resources tend to be used more effectively in perfectly competitive in-

5. However, the cost and demand curves need not be the same, as we noted above. For further discussion of this point, see George Stigler, *Theory of Price* (New York: Macmillan, 1966), Chapter 11.

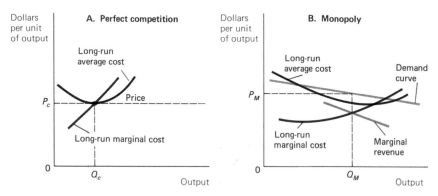

Figure 10.8   Comparison of long-run equilibria

dustries than in monopolized industries.[6] More will be said about this in Chapter 16.

Second, the output of a perfectly competitive industry tends to be greater and price tends to be lower than under monopoly. The perfectly competitive firm operates at the point at which price equals marginal cost, whereas the monopolist operates at a point at which price exceeds marginal cost. Under various circumstances, as we shall see in Chapter 16, price is a good indicator of the marginal social value of the good. Consequently, under these conditions, a monopoly produces at a point at which the marginal social value of the good exceeds the good's marginal social cost. In a static sense, society would be better off if more resources were devoted to the production of the good, and if the marginal social value of the product were set equal to the marginal social cost of the product—as it is in perfect competition. Again, more will be said on this score in Chapter 16.

Assuming that the demand curve for the product is linear and that the marginal cost is constant, we compare the equilibrium price and output in monopoly and perfect competition in Figure 10.9. The monopoly price is OP_1 and the competitive price is OM; the monopoly output is OQ_1 and the competitive output is OQ_0. It is assumed, of course, that the marginal cost curve is the long-run supply curve in perfect competition. Under these very special assumptions, the monopoly output will be exactly one-half the competitive output, the reason being that the marginal revenue curve cuts in half any horizontal line from the vertical axis to the demand curve.[7] In general, of course, the ratio of the monopoly to the competitive output could be more or less than one-half, depending on the shape of the demand and cost curves.

Using the concept of consumer's surplus described in Chapter 4, some economists believe that the welfare loss to society due to monopoly, rather than perfect competition, can be measured by the so-called wel-

6. In multiplant monopoly the monopolist operates fewer plants than would a competitive industry.

7. For a proof of this point, see Chapter 5, Section 9.

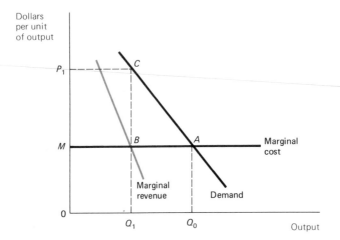

Figure 10.9   Comparison of price and output: Perfect competition
versus monopoly

fare triangle, ABC, in Figure 10.9. Basically, the idea is that the value to
society of the extra output resulting from perfect competition is equal to
Q_1CAQ_0, whereas the cost to society of the extra output is equal to
Q_1BAQ_0. Thus the net loss due to the smaller output under monopoly is
equal to ABC. One important limitation of this kind of measure is that it
assumes that one can simply add up the utilities gained and lost by
various members of society. No attention is paid to the effects of monopoly on the distribution of income.

About twenty years ago, Arnold Harberger of the University of Chicago estimated the area of the welfare triangle in each manufacturing
industry, based on the assumption that marginal cost is constant (as in
Figure 10.9) and that the price elasticity of demand is about one. The
results suggested that the misallocation of resources due to monopoly
was quite small. Specifically, he found that the elimination of this resource misallocation would result in an increase in consumer welfare of
about .1 percent. These conclusions have been challenged on several
counts. For example, as Harvey Leibenstein and others have pointed out,
Harberger's results do not recognize that monopolies may be less inclined to minimize costs than competitive firms. Further, as Gordon
Tullock has pointed out, Harberger's results ignore the social waste
which arises because firms use scarce resources in their attempts to obtain monopoly power.[8]

---

8. See A. Harberger, "Monopoly and Resource Allocation," and H. Leibenstein, "Allocative Efficiency vs. X-Efficiency," both reprinted in E. Mansfield, *Microeconomics: Selected Readings,* 4th ed. (New York: Norton, 1982); and G. Tullock,
   "The Welfare Costs of Monopoly and Theft," *Western Economic Journal,* June
   1967. Also, see A. Bergson, "On Monopoly Welfare Losses," *American Economic
   Review,* December 1973.

11. Bilateral Monopoly

Bilateral monopoly occurs when a monopolistic seller is confronted with only a single buyer. In other words, it is a case where the market is composed of a single buyer and a single seller. For example, if all tin plate were produced by a single firm and if only a single firm used tin plate, this would be a case of bilateral monopoly. Clearly, there are few cases of this sort, except perhaps in the labor markets. The market for labor may be dominated, particularly in small areas, by a single firm and a single union. For example, in a small coal town in Appalachia, a single union may include all, or practically all, coal miners, and a single firm may be the only employer of coal miners.[9]

Suppose that the seller's marginal cost curve is as shown in Figure 10.10. The buyer's demand curve is also shown in Figure 10.10; this curve shows the number of units of output demanded by the buyer at each price, given that the price is determined outside the control of the buyer. Under these conditions, the seller would like to set a price that will maximize its profits. Taking the buyer's demand curve as given, the seller's marginal revenue curve is as shown in Figure 10.10; and it would like to operate at the point at which its marginal revenue curve intersects its marginal cost curve. Thus it would like to charge a price of OP_0 and supply OQ_0 units of the good.

Turning to the buyer, what price would it like to pay and how many units of output would it like to buy? The buyer views the seller's marginal cost curve as a supply curve. Given a certain price, determined outside the control of the seller, we know that this curve shows how much the seller will supply.[9] Like the seller, the buyer would like to maximize its profits. The buyer's profits will be maximized when the curve showing the buyer's marginal expenditure on the good intersects the buyer's demand curve. The marginal expenditure on the good when between x and $(x - 1)$ units are bought is $R(x) - R(x - 1)$, where $R(x)$ is the total amount spent by the buyer on x units. The marginal expenditure on the good is shown by the CC' curve in Figure 10.10. Thus the buyer would like to operate at the point at which the CC' curve intersects the buyer's demand curve, which means that it would like to pay a price of OP_1 and buy OQ_1 units of output.

The price and output that will result in a situation of this sort is indeterminate. It seems likely that the price will lie somewhere between

---

9. However, even here there are problems in applying the theory. As pointed out in Chapter 14, the assumption that labor unions can be represented in this way implies a very special kind of motivation on the part of unions.

10. In Section 6, we showed that a monopoly has no supply curve. The seller's marginal cost curve is a supply curve only under the condition that the monopolist is constrained to sell at fixed prices outside its control. In other words, the monopolist is assumed to be stripped of its monopoly power. Similarly, in the preceding paragraph, the monopsonist (that is, the sole buyer) is assumed to be stripped of its monopsony power. These assumptions are made to obtain a range within which the outcome is likely to be.

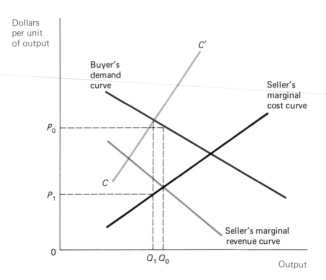

Figure 10.10   Bilateral monopoly

OP_0 and OP_1 and that output will lie somewhere between OQ_0 and OQ_1, but we cannot make any more specific predictions. A theory based on profit maximization is unable to yield a more specific prediction. Other factors, like bargaining power and negotiating skill and public opinion, are likely to play an important role in determining the nature of the final outcome.

12. Price Discrimination

Price discrimination occurs when the same commodity is sold at more than one price. For example, an operation to cure a particular form of cancer may be "sold" to a rich person for $500 and to a poor person for $100. Even if the commodities are not precisely the same, price discrimination is said to occur if very similar products are sold at prices that are in different ratios to marginal costs. For example, if a firm sells ballpoint pens with a label (cost of label: 1 cent) saying "Super Deluxe" in rich neighborhoods for $2 and sells the same ballpoint pens without this label in poor neighborhoods for $1, this is discrimination. Note that the mere fact that differences in price exist among similar goods is not evidence of discrimination. Only if these differences do not reflect cost differences is there evidence of this sort.

Under what conditions will a monopolist be able and willing to engage in price discrimination? The necessary conditions are that buyers fall into classes with considerable differences in the price elasticity of demand for the product, and that these classes can be identified and segregated at moderate cost. Also, it is important that buyers be unable to transfer the commodity easily from one class to another, since otherwise it would be possible for persons to make money by buying the commodity from the low-price classes and selling it to the high-price classes, thus making it difficult to maintain the price differentials between classes. The differences between classes of buyers in the price elasticity of demand may be due to differences between classes in income level, differences between classes in tastes, or differences between classes in the availability of substitutes. For example, the price elasticity of demand for a certain good may be lower for the rich than for the poor.

If a monopolist practices discrimination of this sort, it must decide two questions: How much output should it allocate to each class of buyer, and what price should it charge each class of buyer? To avoid unnecessary complications, let us assume that there are only two classes of buyers. Also, for the moment, assume that the monopolist has already decided on its total output, and consequently that the only real question is how it should be allocated between the two classes. In each class, there is a demand curve showing how many units of output would be bought by buyers in this class at various prices. In each class, there is also a marginal revenue curve that can be derived from the demand curve.

Given these marginal revenue curves, the monopolist will maximize its profits by allocating the total output between the two classes in such a way that marginal revenue in one class is equal to marginal revenue in the other class. The reason for this is clear. For example, if marginal revenue in the first class is \$5 and marginal revenue in the second class is \$3, the allocation is not optimal, since profits can be increased by allocating one less unit of output to the second class and one more unit of output to the first class. Only if the two marginal revenues are equal is the allocation optimal. And if the marginal revenues in the two classes are equal, the ratio of the price in the first class to the price in the second class will equal

$$\left(1 - \frac{1}{n_2}\right) \div \left(1 - \frac{1}{n_1}\right)$$

where n_1 is the elasticity of demand in the first class and n_2 is the elasticity of demand in the second class. Thus it will not pay to discriminate if the two elasticities are equal. Moreover, if discrimination does pay, the price will be lower in the class in which demand is more elastic.

Next consider the more realistic case where the monopolist must also decide on its total output. In this case, the monopolist must look at its costs, as well as demand in the two classes. It can be shown that it will choose the output where the marginal cost of the monopolist's entire output is equal to the common value of the marginal revenue in the two classes. To see this, consider Figure 10.11, which shows D_1D_1', the demand curve in class 1; D_2D_2', the demand curve in class 2; R_1R_1', the marginal revenue curve in class 1; R_2R_2', the marginal revenue curve in class 2; and the firm's marginal cost curve. The monopolist begins to determine its total output by summing horizontally over the two marginal revenue curves, R_1R_1' and R_2R_2'. The curve representing the horizontal summation of the two marginal revenue curves is ZZ'. This curve shows, for each level of marginal revenue, the total output that is needed if marginal revenue in each class is to be maintained at this level.

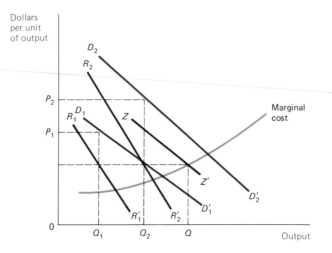

Figure 10.11   Price discrimination: Third degree

The optimal output is shown by the point where the ZZ' curve intersects the marginal cost curve, since marginal cost must be equal to the common value of marginal revenue in each class. If this were not the case, profits could be increased by expanding output (if marginal cost were less than marginal revenue) or by contracting output (if marginal cost were greater than marginal revenue). Thus the firm will produce an output of OQ units and sell OQ_1 units in the class 1 market and OQ_2 units in the class 2 market. Price will be OP_1 in the class 1 market and OP_2 in the class 2 market.[11]

11. Let p_1 be the price in the first class, p_2 the price in the second class, q_1 the quantity sold in the first class, and q_2 the quantity sold in the second class. If $C(q)$ is the monopolist's total cost, with q being equal to the sum of q_1 and q_2,

$$\Pi = p_1 q_1 + p_2 q_2 - C(q)$$

where Π is the monopolist's profits. Then

$$\frac{\partial \Pi}{\partial q_1} = \frac{\partial(p_1 q_1)}{\partial q_1} - \frac{\partial C(q)}{\partial q_1} = \frac{d(p_1 q_1)}{dq_1} - \frac{dC(q)}{dq}\frac{\partial q}{\partial q_1}$$

$$= \frac{d(p_1 q_1)}{dq_1} - \frac{dC(q)}{dq} = 0$$

$$\frac{\partial \Pi}{\partial q_2} = \frac{\partial(p_2 q_2)}{\partial q_2} - \frac{\partial C(q)}{\partial q_2} = \frac{d(p_2 q_2)}{dq_2} - \frac{dC(q)}{dq}\frac{\partial q}{\partial q_2}$$

$$= \frac{d(p_2 q_2)}{dq_2} - \frac{dC(q)}{dq} = 0$$

Thus, if Π is to be a maximum,

$$\frac{d(p_1 q_1)}{dq_1} = \frac{d(p_2 q_2)}{dq_2} = \frac{dC(q)}{dq}$$

13. Other Types of Price Discrimination

Price discrimination can take a number of forms. The type discussed in the previous section is often called *third-degree price discrimination.* (This expression was coined by A. C. Pigou, the English economist.[12]) Besides third-degree price discrimination, there are also first-degree and second-degree price discrimination. In *discrimination of the first degree,* the monopolist is aware of the maximum amount that each and every consumer will pay for each amount of the commodity. Since it is assumed that the product cannot be resold, the monopolist can charge each consumer a different price. And since the monopolist is assumed to be a profit-maximizer, it will establish prices so as to extract from each consumer the full value of his or her consumer's surplus.

To illustrate this case, suppose that each consumer buys only one unit of the commodity. In this very simple case, the monopolist will establish a price for each consumer that is so high that the consumer is on the verge of refusing to buy the commodity. In the more realistic case, where each consumer can buy more than one unit of the commodity, it is assumed that the monopolist knows each consumer's demand curve for the commodity and that it adjusts its offer accordingly. For example, suppose that the maximum amount that a particular consumer would pay for 20 units of the commodity is $50 and that 20 units is the profit-maximizing amount for the monopolist to sell to this consumer. Then the monopolist will make an all-or-nothing offer of 20 units of the commodity for $50.

First-degree price discrimination is a limiting case that could occur only in the few cases when a monopolist has a small number of buyers and when it is able to guess the maximum prices they are willing to accept. *Second-degree price discrimination* is an intermediate case. In second-degree price discrimination, the monopolist takes part, but not all, of the buyers' consumers' surpluses. For example, consider the case of a gas company. Suppose that each of its consumers has the demand curve shown in Figure 10.12. The company charges a high price, OP_0, if the consumer purchases less than OX units of gas per month. For any amount beyond OX units per month, the company charges a me-

---

In other words, $MR_1 = MR_2 = MC$, where MR_1 is marginal revenue in the first class, MR_2 is marginal revenue in the second class, and MC is marginal cost.
Since

$$MR_1 = P_1\left(1 - \frac{1}{n_1}\right) \text{ and } MR_2 = P_2\left(1 - \frac{1}{n_2}\right),$$

as proved in Chapter 5, it follows that, if $MR_1 = MR_2$,

$$P_1\left(1 - \frac{1}{n_1}\right) = P_2\left(1 - \frac{1}{n_2}\right)$$

$$\frac{P_1}{P_2} = \frac{[1 - (1/n_2)]}{[1 - (1/n_1)]}$$

12. A. C. Pigou, *The Economics of Welfare,* 4th ed. (London: Macmillan, 1950).

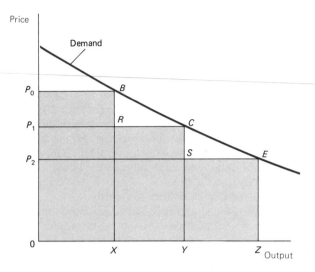

Figure 10.12   Price discrimination: Second degree

dium price, OP_1. For purchases beyond OY, the company charges an even lower price, OP_2. Consequently, the company's total revenues from each consumer are equal to the shaded area in Figure 10.12, since the consumer will purchase OX units at a price of OP_0, $(OY - OX)$ units at a price of OP_1, and $(OZ - OY)$ units at a price of OP_2.[13]

It is obvious that the gas company, by charging different prices for various amounts of the commodity, is able to increase its revenue and profits considerably. After all, if it were permitted to charge only one price and if it wanted to sell OZ units, it would have to charge a price of OP_2. Thus the firm's total revenue would equal only the rectangle, OP_2EZ, which is considerably less than the shaded area in Figure 10.12. By charging different prices, the monopolist is able to take part of the consumers' surplus. According to some authorities, the schedules of rates charged by many public utilities—gas, water, electricity, and others—can be viewed as a type of second-degree price discrimination.[14]

14. Price Discrimination: A Case Study

In Section 12, we began our discussion of price discrimination by citing the case of a physician who charges different prices to different patients for the same operation. It is widely recognized that price discrimination

13. Of course, this assumes for simplicity that each consumer purchases OZ units. Also, other simplifying assumptions (which need not concern us here) are made as well in this and the next paragraph.

14. Ralph Davidson, *Price Determination in Selling Gas and Electricity* (Baltimore: Johns Hopkins University Press, 1955); and C. Cicchetti and J. Jurewitz, *Studies in Electric Utility Regulation* (Cambridge, Mass.: Ballinger, 1975).

Example 10.1 Allocating Sales between Two Markets

The Erratic Book Company is a (hypothetical) monopolist that sells in two markets. The marginal revenue curve in the first market is

$$MR_1 = 20 - 2Q_1,$$

where MR_1 is the marginal revenue in the first market and Q_1 is the number of books sold per day in the first market. The marginal revenue curve in the second market is

$$MR_2 = 15 - 3Q_2,$$

where MR_2 is the marginal revenue in the second market and Q_2 is the number of books sold per day in the second market. If the marginal cost of a book is $6, how many books should the Erratic Book Company sell in each market?

Solution

If we follow the procedure in Section 12, the first step is to sum the two marginal revenue curves horizontally. To do so, we first express Q_1 and Q_2 as functions of MR_1 and MR_2. From the above equations, it follows that

$$Q_1 = 10 - \tfrac{1}{2} MR_1 \qquad\qquad\qquad 10.3$$
$$Q_2 = 5 - \tfrac{1}{3} MR_2. \qquad\qquad\qquad 10.4$$

Then setting $MR_1 = MR_2 = MR$, we find the value of $(Q_1 + Q_2)$ for each value of MR, with the result,

$$Q_1 + Q_2 = (10 - \tfrac{1}{2} MR) + (5 - \tfrac{1}{3} MR) = 15 - \tfrac{5}{6} MR.$$

Turning this equation around,

$$MR = 18 - \tfrac{6}{5}(Q_1 + Q_2),$$

which corresponds to the ZZ' curve in Figure 10.11. Since the marginal cost curve is a horizontal line at $6, the ZZ' curve intersects the marginal cost curve when

$$18 - \tfrac{6}{5}(Q_1 + Q_2) = 6,$$

or when $(Q_1 + Q_2) = 10$. When $MR_1 = MR_2 = \$6$, it follows from Equations 10.3 and 10.4 that $Q_1 = 7$ and $Q_2 = 3$. Thus the Erratic Book Company should sell 7 books per day in the first market and 3 books per day in the second market. (Of course, in this elementary case, the answer can be obtained simply by setting MR_1 and MR_2 in Equations 10.3 and 10.4 equal to $6.)

of this sort is practiced in medicine. Rich patients tend to be charged more than poor patients for the same medical services. Since the rich are willing and able to pay more than the poor, such a pricing policy is understandable because it allows doctors to raise their incomes. The doctors themselves often argue that it enables them to treat needy patients at very low fees—which may be the case in some instances, although economists tend to doubt that charitable inclinations are the sole reason for this form of price discrimination.

One of the most interesting questions concerning price discrimination in medicine is why some doctors do not reduce the fees they charge the affluent in order to get business away from other doctors. Such price cutting would be likely to be profitable for many of them, and if carried out, would tend to undermine the pattern of price discrimination. According to Reuben Kessel of the University of Chicago, [15] the explanation lies in the fact that the American Medical Association can (and will) punish severely any doctor who engages in such price cutting. Since the AMA can withhold internships from hospitals, it is in a position to bring pressure to bear on hospitals to use only doctors who are members of local medical societies. And doctors who engage in price cutting can be expelled from local medical societies. Thus any doctor who is tempted to cut prices is faced with the possibility that he may incur very great losses. In Kessel's view, this accounts for the fact that so little price cutting takes place.

15. Discrimination and the Existence of the Industry

Economists generally regard price discrimination as a socially inefficient way of pricing a commodity, for reasons discussed in Chapter 16. It should be recognized, however, that a good or service sometimes cannot be produced without discrimination. For example, consider the case in Figure 10.13, where there are two types of consumers, their demand curves being $D_0 D_0'$ and $D_1 D_1'$. Adding the two demand curves, we find that the total demand for the commodity is $D_0 UV$. As shown in Figure 10.13, no output exists at which price is greater than or equal to average total cost if price discrimination is not practiced. However, with price discrimination, an output of OQ_0 can be sold at a price of OP_0 to one type

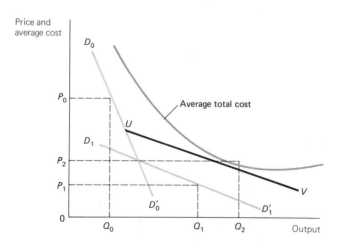

Figure 10.13 Discrimination necessary for existence of industry

15. R. Kessel, "Price Discrimination in Medicine," reprinted in E. Mansfield, *Microeconomics: Selected Readings*.

of consumer; an output of OQ_1 can be sold at a price of OP_1 to the second type of consumer; and the total output (which equals OQ_2) brings an average price of OP_2, which is greater than average total costs.

16. Public Regulation of Monopoly

State regulatory commissions often have substantial power over the prices charged by public utilities like gas and electric companies. As pointed out in Section 2, these public utilities often are natural monopolies. Consider the firm whose demand curve, marginal revenue curve, average cost curve, and marginal cost curve are shown in Figure 10.14. Without regulation, the firm would charge a price of OP_0 and it would produce OQ_0 units of the commodity. By setting a maximum price of OP_1, the commission can make the monopolist increase output, thus making price and output correspond more closely to what they would be if the industry were organized competitively. For instance, if the commission imposes a maximum price of OP_1, the firm's demand curve becomes P_1BD', its marginal revenue curve becomes P_1BCR', its optimum output becomes OQ_1, and it will charge the maximum price of OP_1. By establishing the maximum price, the commission helps consumers who pay a lower price for more of the good. By the same token, the commission deprives the monopolist of some of its monopoly power.

Commissions often set the price—or the maximum price—at the level at which it equals average total cost, including a "fair" rate of return on the company's investment. For example, in Figure 10.15, the price would be established by the commission at OP_2, where the demand curve intersects the average total cost curve. The latter curve includes what the

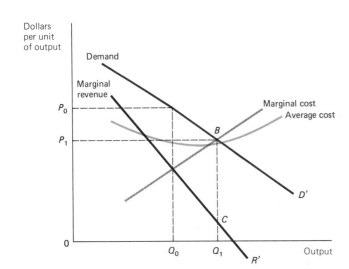

Figure 10.14   Regulation of monopoly: Maximum price

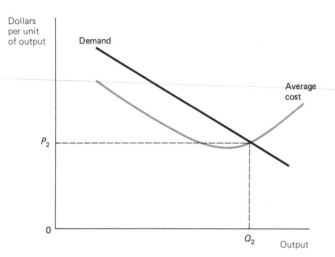

Figure 10.15   Regulation of monopoly: Fair rate of return

commission regards as a fair profit per unit of output. Needless to say, there has been considerable controversy over what constitutes a fair rate of return. There has also been a good deal of controversy over what should be included in the company's investment on which the fair rate of return is to be earned. For example, these questions have been discussed, argued, and examined in great detail—and sometimes with heat—in connection with the telephone industry in the famous investigation conducted by the Federal Communications Commission in the late sixties of American Telephone and Telegraph's pricing policies and rate of return. One suggestion is that public utilities should set price equal to marginal cost, not average cost. This suggestion will be discussed in Chapter 16.

The regulatory commissions also govern the extent to which price discrimination is used by the public utilities. Intricate systems of price discrimination exist in the rate structures of the electric and gas companies, the telephone companies, and so forth. Although some types of discrimination are prohibited, other types can be practiced if they are "reasonable." For example, a company may be permitted to charge a lower rate for a service where it must meet stiff competition. It should be noted that rate discrimination raises important questions of equity and of redistribution of income, as well as questions regarding economic efficiency. Particularly in transportation, some of the most nettlesome problems of rate regulation are concerned with questions of discrimination.

17. Alcoa: A Case Study of Unregulated Monopoly

The Aluminum Company of America was the sole manufacturer of virgin aluminum ingot in the United States from its inception in the late

Example 10.2   Economics of the Post Office

Postal service which, since 1845, has been established as a government monopoly in the United States, has been the object of continual controversy. Suppose that the short-run demand and cost curves of the Philadelphia post office are as follows:

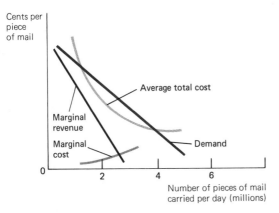

(a) Does the post office appear to be a natural monopoly, as some claim? (b) If the post office is a natural monopoly, must it be operated under government ownership? (c) If the Philadelphia post office wants to carry as many pieces of mail as it can without incurring a short-run deficit, how many should it carry per day? (d) The available evidence indicates that average revenue (per piece of mail) has exceeded average total cost and marginal cost for first-class mail, but not for third-class mail. Which type of mail is likely to attract private competitors? (e) What advantages might accrue if the post office were to face increased private competition?

Solution

(a) One cannot tell, because the answer depends on the long-run (not the short-run) average cost curve. A firm is a natural monopolist if its long-run average cost reaches a minimum at an output rate that is big enough to satisfy the market at a price that is profitable. (b) Many natural monopolies—for example, telephone companies and electric-power producers—are privately owned, so it is by no means clear that government ownership is implied. (c) 4 million pieces, since this is the point where the average total cost curve intersects the demand curve. (d) First-class mail, because it earns a profit. With respect to parcels, there is already considerable competition (from United Parcel Service, in particular). (e) More competition might prod the post office to increase its own efficiency.*

* For further discussion, see M. Baratz, "Cost Behavior and Pricing Policy in the Post Office," *Land Economics*, November 1962.

nineteenth century until World War II. Its monopoly position was based originally on patents regarding the production process. These patents terminated in 1909, and Alcoa attempted to maintain its monopoly position by (1) agreements with foreign aluminum producers not to export into their markets in exchange for their not intruding into its market, and (2) long-term contracts with companies controlling sources of raw materials to bar these companies from selling their raw materials to companies other than Alcoa. However, these agreements and contracts were nullified by the courts in 1912.

Alcoa maintained its monopoly position after 1912 largely by the constant expansion of its productive capacity to meet the increased demand for aluminum at the established price. According to Judge Learned Hand, Alcoa "insists that it never excluded competitors; but we can think of no more effective exclusion than progressively to embrace each new opportunity as it opened, and to face every newcomer with new capacity already geared into a great organization, having the advantage of experience, trade connections, and the elite of personnel."[16]

With regard to pricing, Alcoa did not attempt to maximize short-run profits. Instead, it recognized that foreign imports would be stimulated if it set its prices above a certain point. Moreover, according to some observers, it recognized "the advantages accruing to the company from an orderly reduction of aluminum prices over the years as necessary to penetrate new markets, coupled with a policy of stabilized prices between price reductions.... This policy also served to discourage potential competitors."[17] Thus Alcoa seemed to gear its pricing policy to the pursuit of long-run profits, recognizing the importance from its point of view of discouraging entry.

An antitrust suit was carried out against Alcoa in the forties. The company denied that it was a monopoly, arguing that it had many competitors: sellers of secondary aluminum ingot, foreign producers, and producers of other materials that to some extent are substitutes for aluminum. However, Judge Hand ruled that Alcoa had a monopoly position since it controlled over 90 percent of the domestic market for virgin aluminum ingots (with foreign producers supplying the rest). Alcoa was not allowed to buy government-financed aluminum plants built during World War II. These plants went to Kaiser and Reynolds, thus transforming the industry into a triopoly.[18]

---

16. See *United States* v. *Aluminum Company of America (1945),* in E. Mansfield, *Monopoly Power and Economic Performance,* 4th ed. (New York: Norton, 1978), p. 299. Also see *United States v. United States Shoe Machinery Corporation,* in E. Mansfield, *Microeconomics: Selected Readings.*

17. R. Lanzilotti, "The Aluminum Industry," in W. Adams, ed., *The Structure of American Industry* (New York: Macmillan, 1961), pp. 209–11.

18. This case is frequently used to illustrate pure monopoly. For a somewhat similar account, see K. Cohen and R. Cyert, *Theory of the Firm* (Englewood Cliffs, N.J.: Prentice-Hall, 1965), pp. 200–203.

18. The Michigan Telephone Industry: A Case Study of Regulation

The previous section described a case of unregulated monopoly. To illustrate the case of regulated monopoly, we turn to the telephone industry in Michigan. The two groups that have played a key role in the regulation of the telephone industry in Michigan are one firm, Michigan Bell Telephone System (a subsidiary of A. T. & T.), and one commission, the Public Service Commission in Michigan.[19] Although Michigan Bell is not the only telephone company in the state, it is the dominant firm, and there is no direct competition in the industry between firms. The commission, which is composed of three members appointed by the governor, has had authority over the telephone industry for about fifty years.

A general-rate case has been the common sort of regulatory "contest" in the Michigan telephone industry. Such cases have been initiated by the firms and have been based on company claims that earnings are deficient and a higher price level is required. It is generally assumed, though not proved, that demand is inelastic and that higher prices will mean greater revenues. The industry usually has received less than it asked for. Moreover, commission decisions have lagged behind the industry's revenue requests. However, it should be recognized that the fact that the commission has not approved all Bell requests does not mean that the company has been constrained much by the commission. The company may ask for more than it thinks it will get.

Nothing in public utility controls is more conventional, more securely established in regulatory methods, than the idea of a "reasonable return on the value of a firm's existing plant."[20] This is what the commission has been interested in establishing. Yet there are a host of questions, some obvious to the most naïve schoolchild, others difficult for a trained engineer or accountant to understand, concerning what is a "reasonable return" and what is "the value of a firm's existing plant." The original cost or historical cost of the plant is the measure on which most commissions base their estimates of the value of the plant; but some allow firms to use replacement-cost valuations instead. In the early 1980s, regulated firms often sought a rate of return of about 10 to 15 percent; commissions in recent years have approved rates of return of about 6 to 10 percent.[21] There are lots of detailed and difficult questions in each case of this sort that provide employment for a great many lawyers, accountants, engineers, and economists.

19. See C. E. Troxel, "Telephone Regulation in Michigan," in W. G. Shepherd and T. Gies, *Utility Regulation* (New York: Random House, 1966). Also, see M. Irwin, "The Telephone Industry," in W. Adams, *The Structure of American Industry,* 5th ed. (New York: Macmillan, 1977).

20. Ibid., p. 162.

21. See W. Shepherd and C. Wilcox, *Public Policies Toward Business,* 6th ed (Homewood, Ill.: Irwin, 1979); and W. Shepherd, *Public Policies Toward Business: Readings and Cases* (Homewood, Ill.: Irwin, 1979).

19. Transportation: Another Case Study of Regulation

Considerable controversy has centered on the regulatory process, with many observers feeling that the commissions are lax and that they tend to be captured by the industries they are supposed to regulate. Also, in some cases, regulation, although effective, seems to have had unfortunate consequences. For example, according to many experts, the Interstate Commerce Commission has set prices of various modes of transportation so as to prevent low-cost firms or industries from taking business away from high-cost firms or industries. The result has been an inefficient use of the nation's resources.

The Interstate Commerce Commission arose in response to the monopolies held by the railroads in the nineteenth century. After the Civil War, the Granger movement and the clamor by farmers and merchants for protection against arbitrary pricing by railroads resulted in the creation in 1887 of the ICC to regulate railroad rates. Almost a century old, the ICC currently faces a transportation scene quite different from that which existed at its birth. The railroads now must compete with trucks and airplanes, as well as with water carriers. Each of these modes of transportation has its own advantages and disadvantages. And each should be permitted to carry those kinds of freight and passengers that it can carry most cheaply.

However, the ICC often has prevented low-cost firms from cutting their prices, and thus taking business away from high-cost firms. For example, railroads have often been prevented from lowering prices and taking long-distance trucking business away from the trucks. The ICC has defended this practice by claiming that the nation needs a balanced transportation system where shippers have a wide choice of modes of transportation. However, this practice has prevented the lowest-cost firms from supplanting the higher-cost firms, and thus has resulted in more resources being used in the transportation sector than are required.

According to John Meyer, Merton Peck, John Stenason, and Charles Zwick, "trucks have a clear cost advantage for traffic of less than 100 miles, the rails a narrow cost advantage at 100 miles, and a clear and increasing cost advantage for traffic moving over 200 miles.[22] But since over 90 percent of all trucking shipments are sent for distances exceeding 200 miles, it is clear that much traffic goes by truck that could be moved more cheaply by rail. An important reason for this is that the ICC has refused to let rates reflect relative costs. Ann Friedlander of the Massachusetts Institute of Technology has estimated that the social cost of this misallocation of resources may have been as large as $500 million a year.[23] Faced with evidence of this sort, many policy-makers have advocated less emphasis on regulation, and more emphasis on competition, in transportation. For example, the President's Council of Economic Ad-

---

22. J. Meyer, M. Peck, J. Stenason, and C. Zwick, *Competition in the Transportation Industries* (Cambridge, Mass.: Harvard University Press, 1959), pp. 194–95.

23. Ann Friedlander, *The Dilemma of Freight Transport Regulation* (Washington, D.C.: Brookings Institution, 1969), p. 65.

visers concluded in 1970 that "a policy of permitting and encouraging competition of all kinds would, if general economic experience is any guide, make the industry more efficient as well as benefit the public."[24]

In 1980, President Carter signed bills to deregulate the railroads and the trucking industry. Railroads and trucking firms were given much more power over the prices they charge. The railroads hoped that greater freedom to change rates would enable them to earn a profit. The trucking industry hoped that deregulation would enable it to attract more business and to enjoy other benefits of competition. It will take a number of years to determine how well deregulation works out, both from the point of view of these industries and of the general public.

20. Summary

Pure monopoly exists when there is one, and only one, seller in a market. From some points of view, pure monopoly and perfect competition are polar opposites. Monopolies arise because a single firm controls the entire supply of a basic input, because a firm has a patent on the product or on certain basic processes, because the average cost of producing the product reaches a minimum at an output rate that is big enough to satisfy the entire market at a price that is profitable, because the firm is awarded a franchise, or for other reasons. The demand curve facing the monopolist is the demand for the product. The cost conditions facing a monopolist may be no different from those facing a perfectly competitive firm, if the monopolist is a perfect competitor in the input markets.

Under monopoly, the firm will maximize profit if it sets its output rate at the point where marginal cost equals marginal revenue. It does not follow that a firm that holds a monopoly over the production of a particular product must make a profit. If the monopolist cannot cover its variable costs, it will shut down, even in the short run. Under monopoly, there is no unique relationship between the product's price and the amount supplied. The long-run equilibrium of the industry is not necessarily marked by the absence of economic profits. If the monopolist has more than one plant, it should allocate production among its plants so that marginal costs are the same in each plant, and it should set its overall output rate so that this common marginal cost equals marginal revenue.

There are a number of important differences between the long-run equilibrium of a monopoly and of a perfectly competitive industry. Under perfect competition, each firm operates at the point where both long-run and short-run average costs are at a minimum; under monopoly, if the monopolist expanded its long-run equilibrium output, it could utilize a plant with lower average costs. The output of a perfectly competitive industry tends to be greater and price tends to be lower than under monopoly. The perfectly competitive firm operates at the point where price equals marginal cost, whereas the monopolist operates at a

24. *Economic Report of the President* (Washington, D.C.: U.S. Government Printing Office, 1970), p. 108

point where price exceeds marginal cost. Some economists measure the loss in economic welfare due to monopoly by the welfare triangle.

Bilateral monopoly occurs when a monopolistic seller confronts a monopsonistic buyer. The price and output that will result in this situation is indeterminate. Price discrimination occurs when the same commodity is sold at more than one price, or when similar products are sold at prices that are in different ratios to marginal costs. A monopolist will be able and willing to practice price discrimination if various classes of buyers with different elasticities of demand can be identified and segregated, and if the commodity cannot be transferred easily from one class to another. There are three types of price discrimination, and we have discussed the monopolist's behavior in each case. Economists generally regard price discrimination as a socially inefficient way of pricing a commodity, but it is sometimes true that, without discrimination, a commodity cannot be produced at all.

Regulatory commissions frequently have the power to set the prices charged by public utilities like gas or electric companies. They often set the price—or the maximum price—at the level at which it equals average total cost, including a "fair" rate of return on the company's investment. There has been considerable controversy over what constitutes a fair rate of return, and over what should be included in the company's investment. Finally, we presented three very brief case studies, the history of the Aluminum Company of America illustrating the case of an unregulated monopoly, the telephone industry in Michigan illustrating the case of a regulated monopoly, and certain pricing policies of the Interstate Commerce Commission illustrating some of the problems in regulation.

QUESTIONS AND PROBLEMS

1. A monopolist has the following total cost function and demand curve:

Price (dollars)	Output (units)	Total cost (dollars)
8	5	20
7	6	21
6	7	22
5	8	23
4	9	24
3	10	30

   What price should it charge?

2. Monopolists sometimes are said to be less interested in maximizing profit than perfectly competitive firms. Why might this be the case, and what nonprofit goals might a monopolist be interested in achieving?

3. A monopolist has two plants, with the following marginal cost functions:
$$MC_1 = 20 + 2Q_1$$
$$MC_2 = 10 + 5Q_2,$$

where MC_1 is marginal cost in the first plant, MC_2 is marginal cost in the second plant, Q_1 is output in the first plant, and Q_2 is output in the second plant. If the monopolist is minimizing its costs, and if it is producing 5 units of output at the first plant, how many units is it producing at the second plant?

4. A. C. Harberger, in his study cited in footnote 8, assumed that the price elasticity of demand was unity everywhere. Will a rational monopolist operate at a point where the price elasticity of demand is unity? Can one be sure that monopoly gains are not included in the cost items reported by accountants?

5. Authors customarily receive a royalty that is a fixed percentage of the price of the book. For this reason, economists have pointed out that an author has an interest in a book's price being lower than the price which maximizes the publisher's profits. Prove that this is true.

6. "Regulatory commissions tend to be captured by the industries they are supposed to regulate. They have little or no effect on price." Do you agree? Why or why not? What sorts of analyses can you devise to test these propositions?

7. Suppose that you are the owner of a metals-producing firm that is an unregulated monopoly. After considerable experimentation and research, you find that your marginal cost curve can be approximated by a straight line, $MC = 60 + 2Q$, where MC is marginal cost (in dollars) and Q is your output. Moreover, suppose that the demand curve for your product is $P = 100 - Q$, where P is the product price and Q is your output. If you want to maximize profit, what output should you choose?

8. According to Arnold Harberger, "Elimination of resource misallocations in American manufacturing in the late twenties would bring with it an improvement in consumer welfare of just a little more than a tenth of a percent. In present values, this welfare gain would amount to about $2.00 per capita." What sorts of techniques could one use to test this proposition? How accurate do you think this result is?

9. Suppose that you are hired as a consultant to a firm producing ball bearings. This firm is a monopolist which sells in two distinct markets, one of which is completely sealed off from the other. The demand curve for the firm's output in the one market is $P_1 = 160 - 8Q_1$, where P_1 is the price of the product and Q_1 is the amount sold in the first market. The demand curve for the firm's output in the second market is $P_2 = 80 - 2Q_2$, where P_2 is the price of the product and Q_2 is the amount sold in the second market. The firm's marginal cost curve is $5 + Q$, where Q is the firm's entire output (destined for either market). The firm asks you to suggest what its pricing policy should be. How many units of output should it sell in the second market? How many units of output should it sell in the first market? What prices should it charge?

10. According to John McGee, "Standard Oil did not use predatory price discrimination to drive out competing refiners.... Standard discriminated in price, but it did so to maximize profits given the elasticities of demand of markets in which it sold." Describe how you would test this conclusion against historical evidence. Also, indicate how you would go about determining whether such discrimination was good or bad.

SELECTED REFERENCES

HARBERGER, ARNOLD. "Monopoly and Resource Allocation." Reprinted in *Microeconomics: Selected Readings*.

HARROD, ROY. "Doctrines of Imperfect Competition." *Quarterly Journal of Economics,* 1934.

HICKS, JOHN. "Annual Survey of Economic Theory: The Theory of Monopoly." *Econometrica,* 1935. Reprinted in E. Mansfield, *Microeconomics: Selected Readings*. 4th ed. New York: Norton, 1982.

KAHN, ALFRED. *The Economics of Regulation: Principles and Institutions*. New York: Wiley, 1970.

MANSFIELD, EDWIN. *Monopoly Power and Economic Performance*. 4th ed. New York: Norton, 1978.

MCGEE, JOHN. "Predatory Price Cutting: The Standard Oil (N.J.) Case." Reprinted in *Microeconomics: Selected Readings*.

ROBINSON, JOAN. *The Economics of Imperfect Competition*. London: Macmillan, 1933.

KESSEL, REUBEN. "Price Discrimination in Medicine." reprinted in *Microeconomics: Selected Readings*.

JUDGE WYZANSKI. "United States v. United States Shoe Machinery Corporation." Reprinted in *Microeconomics: Selected Readings*.

Price and Output under Monopolistic Competition

1. Historical Background

Perfect competition and pure monopoly are two polar extremes. There is an extremely large number of firms in a perfectly competitive industry, but only one firm in a pure monopoly. For many years economists felt that these two models enabled them to analyze any market. They knew that some markets were quite different from either perfect competition or pure monopoly, but it was felt that the two models could be combined somehow to treat such cases. With the exception of a few oversimplified duopoly models, discussed in the following chapter, the whole of price theory consisted of the theory of perfect competition and the theory of pure monopoly. This situation lasted until the late twenties and early thirties.

During the twenties and thirties there was a marked change in attitude. Economists began to stress the importance of more and better research to develop models to handle the important middle ground between perfect competition and pure monopoly. An English economist, Piero Sraffa,[1] was one of the first to emphasize this point, and he was soon joined by many others who shared his feeling that the theories of perfect competition and pure monopoly dealt with polar extremes, between which fell practically all of the empirically relevant cases.

In response to this challenge, there was a flurry of activity in this area among the members of the eco-

---

1. P. Sraffa, "The Laws of Returns under Competitive Conditions," *Economic Journal,* 1926.

nomics profession in the period around 1930. One of the most noteworthy achievements that was produced was the theory of monopolistic competition, put forth by Harvard's Edward Chamberlin.[2] In this chapter, we present a detailed description of Chamberlin's theory, which unquestionably has had an important impact on the development of microeconomic theory in the past forty years. In addition, we discuss some of the criticisms that have been made of this theory.

2. Product Differentiation, the Group, and Other Assumptions

The basic idea behind Chamberlin's theory is that most firms face relatively close substitutes and that most commodities are not completely homogeneous from one seller to another. For example, Brooks Brothers has a monopoly on the sale of its men's suits. However, other firms like Macy's and Gimbel's sell roughly similar suits. Each firm has a monopoly over the sale of its own product, but the various brands are close substitutes.

This is a case of *product differentiation*. In other words, there is no single, homogeneous commodity called a man's suit; instead, each seller differentiates its product from that of the next seller. This, of course, is a prevalent case in the modern economy. Each seller tries to make its product a little different, by altering the physical makeup of the product, the services it offers, and other such variables. Other differences—which may be spurious—are based on brand name, image-making, advertising claims, and so forth. In this way, each seller has some amount of monopoly power, but it usually is small, because the products of other firms are very similar.

In perfect competition, the firms included in an industry are easy to determine, because they all produce the same product. But if there is product differentiation, it is no longer easy to define an industry, since each firm produces a somewhat different product. Nevertheless, Chamberlin believes that it is useful to group together firms producing similar products and call them a *product group*. For example, we can formulate a product group called men's suits. Of course, the process by which we combine firms into product groups is bound to be somewhat arbitrary, since there is no way to decide how close a pair of substitutes must be in order to be included in the same product group. However, Chamberlin asserts that meaningful product groups can be formulated.

The assumptions underlying Chamberlin's theory are as follows: First, he assumes that the product, which is differentiated, is produced by a large number of firms, with each firm's product being a fairly close substitute for the products of the other firms in the product group. Second, he assumes that the number of firms in the product group is sufficiently large so that each firm expects its actions to go unheeded by

2. E. Chamberlin, *The Theory of Monopolistic Competition* (Cambridge, Mass.: Harvard University Press, 1933). Another very important work of the same period was J. Robinson, *The Economics of Imperfect Competition* (New York: Macmillan, 1933).

its rivals and to be unimpeded by any retaliatory measures on their part. Third, he assumes that both demand and cost curves are the same for all of the firms in the group. This, of course, is a very restrictive assumption since, if the products are dissimilar, one would ordinarily expect their demand and cost curves to be dissimilar, too.

Retail trade is often cited as an industry that has many of the characteristics of monopolistic competition. For example, gasoline stations, clothing stores, and drugstores are regarded by some economists as fairly close approximations to Chamberlin's model. A firm under monopolistic competition can do three things to affect its rate of sales. It can change its price, change the characteristics of its product, or change its advertising and promotional expenditures. We take up each of these three types of decisions in the following sections. Sections 3 to 5 are concerned with price variation, Section 6 with product variation, and Section 7 with selling costs.

3. Demand Curves under Monopolistic Competition

Two kinds of demand curves play an important role in the theory of monopolistic competition. On the one hand, there is a demand curve that shows how much the firm will sell if it varies its price from the going level and if other firms maintain their existing prices. As an example of this demand curve, consider the situation in Figure 11.1. The firm is currently in equilibrium at the point A, with price OP and output OQ. If the firm reduces its price and if other firms maintain their prices, the firm can expect a considerable increase in sales, since it will be able to attract buyers away from other firms in the group (and increase sales to existing customers). If the firm increases its price and if other firms maintain

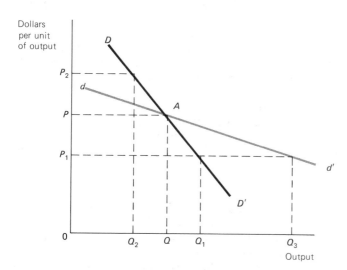

Figure 11.1   The two demand curves under monopolistic competition

their prices, the firm can expect a considerable decrease in sales, since it will lose business to other firms in the group (because buyers will switch allegiance). Thus, assuming that each firm expects its actions to go unheeded by its rivals, each firm believes its demand curve to be quite elastic. This demand curve is shown as dd' in Figure 11.1.

In addition, there is another important type of demand curve, based on the supposition that *all* firms raise or lower their prices by the same amount as this firm. This demand curve is shown as DD' in Figure 11.1. Thus, if this firm reduces its price to OP_1 and all other firms reduce their prices to OP_1 as well, this firm will sell OQ_1 units of output. Similarly, if this firm increases its price to OP_2 and all other firms increase their price to OP_2 as well, this firm will sell OQ_2 units of output. Of course, this second type of demand curve, DD', is less elastic than the first type, dd', since price reductions by this firm will expand its sales by a greater amount if other firms do not meet the price reduction, and price increases by this firm will decrease its sales by a greater amount if other firms do not meet the price increase. For example, if other firms do not meet the price reduction, this firm's sales will increase to OQ_3, rather than OQ_1, if it reduces its price to OP_1.

4. Equilibrium Price and Output in the Short Run

In discussing the pricing behavior of firms under monopolistic competition, it simplifies matters to assume that the firms have already decided on the characteristics of product and extent of selling expense that are most profitable. (In Sections 6 and 7, we shall deal with the way in which firms determine these variables.) It is also convenient to analyze the behavior of a product group in terms of a "representative firm." Since the demand and cost curves of each firm are assumed to be identical, it is legitimate to think in terms of a representative firm.

To see how the equilibrium price and output of each firm in the group is determined in the short run, consider the situation in Figure 11.2. The market price is OP_0 and the firm is producing and selling OQ_0 units. Suppose that the firm believes that any alteration in its price will not be matched by its rivals in the group, and that it tries to act as a monopolist. Then dd' is the relevant demand curve, RR' is the relevant marginal revenue curve, and the firm will decide to produce and sell an output of OQ_1, since this is the output at which its marginal cost curve intersects its marginal revenue curve, RR'. The price charged by the firm will change to OP_1.

This new price would boost the firm's profits, if the firm were correct in believing that the price charged by other firms in the group would remain constant. However, since all of the firms in the group are confronted with the same situation and since they all make the assumption that the other firms will not change price, they all do the same thing. Thus every firm changes its price to OP_1 and DD', not dd', becomes the relevant demand curve. This means that OQ_2 not OQ_1, units of output are sold by each firm at the new price, OP_1.

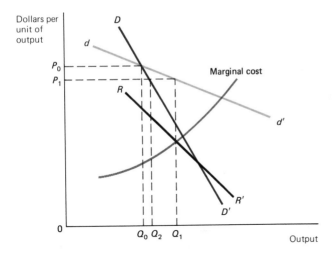

Figure 11.2   Initial change of price and output

The results are shown in Figure 11.3. Because all firms are now charging a price of OP_1, the dd' demand curve has now moved down until it intersects the DD' demand curve at OP_1. Clearly, the new dd' demand curve must intersect the DD' demand curve at OP_1, since the new dd' demand curve shows how much the firm will sell at various prices if other firms' prices remain constant at OP_1, not OP_0. Thus, at the point on the dd' demand curve corresponding to a price of OP_1, all firms are charging a price of OP_1, and the firm's sales must correspond to the point on the DD' demand curve corresponding to OP_1.

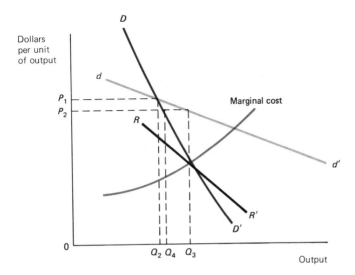

Figure 11.3   Situation after initial change of price and output

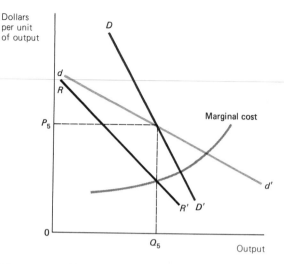

Figure 11.4 Short-run equilibrium

Again, the firm acts as a monopolist and attempts to maximize profits on the basis of the new dd' demand curve. It sets a price of OP_2 and expects to produce and sell OQ_3 units of output. But since this change in price seems profitable for all firms, they all take the same action, with the result that the DD' demand curve, not the new dd' demand curve, is the relevant one. Consequently, each firm produces OQ_4, not OQ_3, units of output. Again the dd' demand curve shifts to intersect the DD' demand curve at the new price, OP_2. And the process goes on.

This process continues until a point is reached where the firm has no reason to change its price. In the short run, an equilibrium will be reached when the situation is like that in Figure 11.4. That is, the short-run equilibrium price and output of each firm are OP_5 and OQ_5, respectively. It can easily be verified that the firm has no incentive to change its price from OP_5. Since marginal revenue based on the dd' demand curve and a going price of OP_5 equals marginal cost at an output of OQ_5, the firm believes that it is maximizing profits by maintaining its price at OP_5. Of course, the representative firm may not earn profits in short-run equilibrium. But as long as OP_5 exceeds the firm's average variable costs, the firm will continue to produce in the short run.

5. Equilibrium Price and Output in the Long Run

As in perfect competition, firms in the long run are able to change the scale of their plant and to leave or enter the industry. The long-run equilibrium price and output of the representative firm are shown in Figure 11.5; the equilibrium price is OP and the equilibrium output is OQ. Since there is free entry and exit in a monopolistic competitive industry, the long-run equilibrium is a situation in which all firms in the

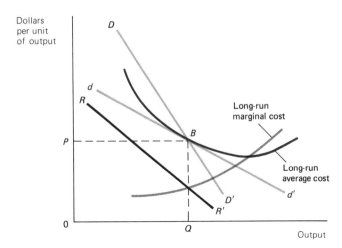

Figure 11.5   Long-run equilibrium

industry, although they are maximizing profits, have zero economic profits. This, of course, is similar to the long-run equilibrium in a perfectly competitive industry. Note that the cost curves in Figure 11.5 are long-run cost curves, not the short-run cost curves shown in Figure 11.4. The long-run equilibrium position is the point where (1) the long-run average cost curve, is tangent to the dd' demand curve, and where (2) the DD' demand curve intersects the dd' demand curve and the long-run average cost curve at the tangency point. (The marginal revenue curve is RR').

How is this long-run equilibrium position reached? The adjustments that take place can be described in terms of changes in the dd' demand curve and in the DD' demand curve. The DD' demand curve shifts in response to the entry of new firms and the exit of old firms. Increases in the number of firms in the industry shift the DD' demand curve facing the representative firm to the left, because the market (which is relatively fixed) must be divided among more firms. Reductions in the number of firms shift the DD' demand curve facing the representative firm to the right, because the market must be divided among fewer firms. As a result of entry and exit, the DD' demand curve is pushed toward the equilibrium position, where it intersects the dd' demand curve at the point at which the dd' demand curve is tangent to the long-run average cost curve.

Consider Figure 11.6, where D_1D_1' is the initial DD' demand curve. This firm (and the others in the group) is making an economic profit since the current price is OP_0. Thus, it follows that entry is encouraged and the DD' demand curve shifts to the left. Simultaneously, the dd' demand curve also moves to the left from d_1d_1'. As entry continues, the DD' demand curve may shift to D_2D_2'. If so, one might think that point A would be a long-run equilibrium position, since the DD' demand curve, D_2D_2', intersects the long-run average cost curve at point A. However,

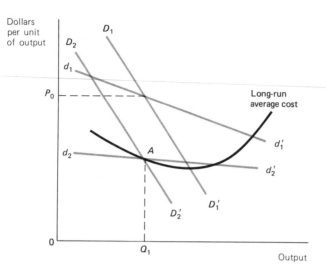

Figure 11.6   Movement toward long-run equilibrium

this is not the case, since the dd' demand curve, d_2d_2', lies above the long-run average cost curve for a range of outputs above OQ_1. Thus each firm believes that it is profitable to expand.

Only when at last the situation in Figure 11.5 is reached will a long-run equilibrium be established. At point B in Figure 11.5, the DD' demand curve intersects the long-run average cost curve, with the result that there is no incentive for entry or exit, since economic profits are nonexistent. Moreover, at point B, the dd' demand curve is always below the long-run average cost curve, except at point B where the two curves intersect. Thus the firm has no incentive to change its price or output, since any such change appears to be unprofitable.

6. Product Variation

In his theory Chamberlin recognizes that firms can change the characteristics of their products as well as change their prices. With regard to product variation, we can begin to find the optimal strategy for the representative firm by assuming that the price and product characteristics of its competitors are fixed. Then we can take each possible variant of the firm's product; and, after calculating the effect on profits of alternative prices, we can find the most profitable price for each variant of the product, given the prices and product characteristics of competitors. Next, we can compare the (maximum) profits that can be made with each variant of the product, and we can find the most profitable of all the variants of the product. The representative firm will choose this variant of the product and charge the price that renders it most profitable.

Of course, this change in the characteristics and price of the firm's product may have repercussions on the product characteristics and

Example 11.1   Dress Shops and Monopolistic Competition

Suppose that dress shops are a monopolistic-competitive industry, and that each dress shop's dd' demand curve, DD' demand curve, and long-run average cost curve are shown below:

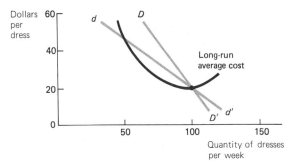

(a) If each dress shop earns no economic profit, what is its price and output? (b) Is each dress shop in long-run equilibrium under these circumstances? (c) Does the individual dress shop believe it is possible to earn positive economic profits under these circumstances? (d) If some dress shops leave the industry, will this shift the DD' demand curve to the left? (e) Will the long-run average cost curve of the individual dress shop be increasing, decreasing, or horizontal at the long-run equilibrium point?

Solution

(a) Price is $20, and output is 100 dresses per week, because this is the point where the dd' and DD' demand curves intersect the long-run average cost curve. Thus no economic profits are being earned. (b) No, because the dd' demand curve is not tangent to the long-run average cost curve. Since the dd' demand curve lies above the long-run average cost curve, when output per week is between 50 and 100 dresses, each shop believes that it can earn economic profits by reducing its output rate. (c) As pointed out in the previous sentence, the individual dress shop believes that it can earn positive economic profits if it reduces its output rate to between 50 and 100 dresses per week. (d) No, the exit of some firms will shift the DD' demand curve to the right. (e) Average cost will be decreasing. This is always the case (at least to some extent) in monopolistically competitive firms in long-run equilibrium. (More will be said on this score in Section 8.)

prices of other firms in the product group; and the change in the product characteristics and prices of other firms is likely to make further change on the part of this firm profitable. Eventually, however, an equilibrium position is reached. In terms of Figure 11.5, changes in the firm's product characteristics result in changes in all three curves (the long-run average cost curve, the DD' demand curve, and the dd' demand curve), since changes in a product generally mean changes in its costs and demand. In long-run equilibrium, however, the relationships among the curves must be like those in Figure 11.5, regardless of which product characteristics are chosen by the firm and its rivals. In other words, the position of the long-run average cost curve, the DD' demand curve, and the dd' demand curve will vary with the product characteristics that are chosen, but it will always be true that the equilibrium point occurs where the long-run average cost curve is tangent to the dd' demand curve and where, at the same time, the DD' demand curve intersects the dd' demand curve and the long-run average cost curve at the tangency point. This follows from the fact that the analysis in Section 5 is applicable regardless of which variant of the product is picked.

Monopolistic competition, as visualized by Chamberlin and others, is characterized by considerable product variety. Some firms may decide to cater to the portion of the market that is very price-conscious, with the result that their product is inexpensive and of relatively low quality. Other firms may decide to cater to the portion of the market that is quality-conscious, with the result that their product is of high quality but costly. Still other firms may attempt to add stylish gimmicks to their product, in the hope that they will attract sales. Whether this proliferation of product varieties is worth its cost is a very important question which, as we shall see below, is unsettled.

7. Selling Expenses

Besides varying price and the characteristics of their products, firms can also vary the extent of their selling expenses. To determine the optimal selling expense for the representative firm, it is convenient to begin by assuming that price and the characteristics of the firm's product are already determined. Suppose that Figure 11.7 represents the situation faced initially by the representative firm. The ZZ' curve is the long-run average cost curve when production, but not selling, costs are considered. The TT' curve is the ZZ' curve plus the amount of selling expenses (per unit of output) necessary to sell the relevant output, given that the other firms in the product group hold constant their selling expenses. For example, to sell an output of OQ_1, the total selling expenses by this firm must be $OQ_1 \times BA$; thus the average total cost—of both production and selling—of OQ_1 units is OA, OB being the average cost of production and BA being the average cost of selling.

For the representative firm in Figure 11.7, we assume that the initial price is OP_0 and that output is OQ_0, with the result that the firm is incurring a loss of P_0W per unit. This does not appear to be the most profitable output level for the firm. The UU' curve is the marginal curve corresponding to the TT' average cost curve; that is, it shows the total additional cost—both of production and selling—required to make and market the last unit sold. More specifically, if $V(q)$ is the total cost of

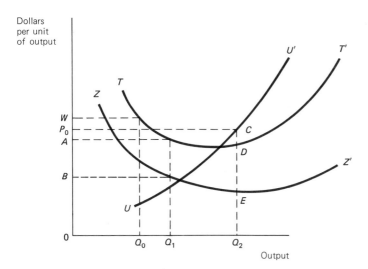

Figure 11.7   Initial choice of selling expense

producing and selling q units of output, the UU' curve shows $[V(q) - V(q-1)]$ between each value of q and $(q-1)$. Since we assume that price is given (and fixed), marginal revenue is constant and equal to the price, OP_0. Consequently, the most profitable output for this firm seems to be OQ_2 units, since this is the output at which the total marginal cost curve, UU', intersects the marginal revenue curve, P_0C. To sell this output, the firm's selling expenses per unit of output must be increased to ED.

However, the firm may not be able to earn the expected profits by this course of action. For example, if greater selling expenses do not raise the market demand curve, and if all firms attempt to increase their selling expenses in this way, the sales of the representative firm will remain OQ_0, but the firm's average total costs will rise because of the higher selling costs. Eventually, the TT' curve will rise to the point where it is tangent to the price line, and the firm will then have no reason to alter its selling costs. In the long run, when firms can enter or leave the product group, changes in the number of firms will go on until economic profits or losses are eliminated. Long-run equilibrium will be attained when economic profits are zero and when, if other firms' selling expenses remain constant, there is no apparent gain from any firm's altering its own selling expenses.

Thus Figure 11.8 shows the full long-run equilibrium when the firm is allowed to manipulate all variables: price, product characteristics, and selling expenses. The SS' curve shows the average total costs of the firm, assuming that the actual selling expense currently being incurred will be maintained at each output level. At the equilibrium solution, the dd' demand curve is tangent to the SS' curve at a price of OP and an output of OQ, and the DD' demand curve intersects the dd' demand curve and the TT' curve at the tangency point. This is the full long-run equilibrium

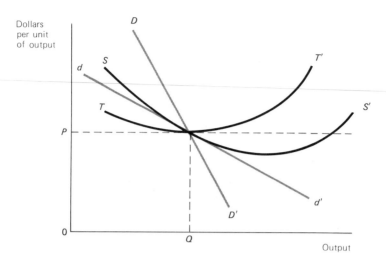

Figure 11.8   Long-run equilibrium: Price, product characteristics, and selling expense

because no incentive exists for entry or exit since economic profits are zero, and because there is no apparent advantage to be achieved by any firm from changing its price, product characteristics, or selling expense, as long as other firms in the product group make no such changes.

8. Excess Capacity in Monopolistic Competition

Economists[3] have generally regarded the *ideal output* of a firm to be the output where long-run average cost is a minimum. For example, in Figure 11.9, the ideal output is OQ_0. Similarly, the *ideal plant* is the one with the short-run average cost curve which is tangent to the long-run average cost curve at the ideal output. *Excess capacity* is the difference between the ideal output and the actual output in long run equilibrium. For example, if the firm's output in long-run equilibrium is OQ_1, excess capacity in Figure 11.9 is $(OQ_0 - OQ_1)$.

A famous and somewhat controversial conclusion of the theory of monopolistic competition is that firms under this form of market organization will tend to operate with excess capacity. In other words, the firm will not construct the minimum-cost size of plant or operate the one it does construct at the minimum-cost rate of output. This conclusion can be deduced from Figure 11.5 (p. 317). The firm will not produce the ideal output or build the ideal plant because average cost at the ideal output would be greater than price, with the result that the firm would

3. For example, see J. Cassels, "Excess Capacity and Monopolistic Competition," *Quarterly Journal of Economics,* 1936–37; and R. Harrod, "Doctrines of Imperfect Competition," *Quarterly Journal of Economics,* 1934–35.

Example 11.2   Advertising and Product Differentiation

According to a survey conducted by the Conference Board, many firms determine the total amount they spend on advertising by multiplying their anticipated sales by some historical percentage. For example, the marketing vice-president of a consumer products firm said, "Our [advertising] budget is generally established as a percentage of our targeted sales goal. Each product line is considered on its own, and different percentage factors are used for them." These percentages remain relatively constant from year to year and are based on past performance. (a) Is this procedure in accord with Chamberlin's theory? If not, how can it be reconciled with this theory (if at all)? (b) Can advertising result in heightened product differentiation? (c) What are some of the social benefits and costs of advertising?

Solution

(a) Advertising is a form of selling expense. As indicated in Section 7, Chamberlin's theory says that firms will choose the level of their selling expenses so as to maximize their profit. To the extent that they can estimate the effects of variation in advertising costs on their profits, firms often do try to set their advertising budgets so as to maximize their profits. But some firms find it so difficult to estimate the effects of variation in their advertising expenses on their profit levels that they feel the best they can do is to formulate their advertising budgets by taking a relatively fixed percentage of sales. If such firms could obtain more and better information concerning the effects of variation in their advertising expense on their profits, they probably would not adhere to this policy. But given their ignorance, they feel that this policy is about as likely as any other to maximize their profits. (b) Yes. Products are differentiated by the subjective image they impress on the consumer's mind. If an advertising campaign convinces the consumer that product X is better for some purposes than product Y, this will serve to differentiate product X from product Y even if there is no essential difference between them. (c) Perhaps the primary social benefit is that advertising informs buyers of what is available; however, a major social cost is that it sometimes misleads them as well.*

* For further discussion, see N. Buchanan, "Advertising Expenditure: A Suggested Treatment," *Journal of Political Economy,* August 1942; M. McNiven, *How Much to Spend for Advertising?,* Association of National Advertisers, 1969; and F. M. Scherer, *Industrial Market Structure and Economic Performance,* 2d ed. (Chicago: Rand McNally, 1980).

incur losses at this output. In long-run equilibrium, the firm will produce that quantity of output at which the dd' demand curve is tangent to the long-run average cost curve. But since the dd' demand curve slopes

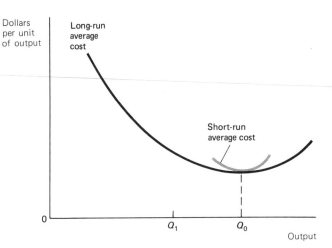

Figure 11.9   Ideal output of the firm

downward, the long-run average cost curve must also be downward sloping at the output the firm produces in long-run equilibrium. Thus, since the long-run average cost curve slopes downward only at outputs that are less than the ideal output, it follows that the output produced by the firm in long-run equilibrium must be less than the ideal output. In other words, there is excess capacity.

Since each firm builds a smaller than ideal plant and produces a smaller than ideal output, more firms can exist under these circumstances than if there were no excess capacity. Thus there is likely to be some "overcrowding" of the industry. It is difficult to know whether particular industries in the real world that are close to the monopolistic competitive model are in fact overcrowded in this sense. To be sure that such overcrowding occurred, one would have to know the ideal output of firms in each industry. However, on the basis of relatively casual empiricism, it is often asserted that a number of cases of this sort exist. For example, in the case of gas stations and grocery stores, both of which bear some resemblance to monopolistic competition, it is sometimes asserted that there are too many firms.

9. Comparisons with Perfect Competition and Monopoly

Frequently, attempts are made to compare the long-run equilibria that result from various market organizations. If we suppose that an industry were monopolistically competitive, rather than purely competitive or purely monopolistic, what difference would it make in the long-run behavior of the industry? It is difficult to interpret this question in a meaningful way, let alone answer it, since the output of the industry would be heterogeneous in one case and homogeneous in the other, and since the cost curves of the industry would probably vary with its organization. Nevertheless, many economists seem to believe that differences of the following kinds can be expected.

First, the firm under monopolistic competition is likely to produce less, and set a higher price, than under perfect competition. The demand curve confronting the monopolistic competitor is not perfectly elastic, as it is in perfect competition. Since marginal revenue is less than price in monopolistic competition, the firm will produce less than the amount at which price equals marginal cost, the consequence being that it will produce less than under perfect competition. However, the difference may not be very great, since the demand curve facing the firm under monopolistic competition may be very close to perfectly elastic.

Second, relative to pure monopoly, monopolistically competitive firms are likely to have lower profits, greater output, and lower prices. The firms in a product group might obtain economic profits if they were to collude and behave as a monopolist. For example, in Figure 11.5, the DD' demand curve is above the long-run average cost curve for outputs less than OQ. Of course, the increase in profits resulting from the monopoly would make the producers better off, but consumers would be worse off because of higher prices and a smaller output of goods.

Third, as noted in the previous section, firms in monopolistic competition may be somewhat inefficient because they tend to operate with excess capacity. Of course, inefficiences of this sort would not be expected under perfect competition. However, these inefficiencies may not be very great, since the demand curve confronting the monopolistically competitive firm is likely to be highly elastic; and the more elastic it is, the less excess capacity the firm will have.

A good deal of effort has been devoted by economists to determine the effects on social welfare of monopolistic competition. Thus far these efforts have not been very successful, and little or nothing can be said concerning the social desirability or undesirability of monopolistic competition. On the one hand, some economists are impressed by the apparent waste in monopolistic competition. They think it results in too many firms, too many brands, too much selling effort, and too much spurious product differentiation. On the other hand, if the differences among products are real and are understood by consumers, the greater variety of alternatives available under monopolistic competition may be worth a great deal to consumers. The unfortunate truth is that economics is not yet in a position to tell whether the market imperfections associated with product differentiation decrease or enhance the welfare of consumers.[4]

4. However, progress has been made in this area in recent years. See K. Lancaster, "Socially Optimal Product Differentiation," *American Economic Review,* September 1975; H. Leland, "Quality Choices and Competition," *American Economic Review,* March 1977; A. Dixit and J. Stiglitz, "Monopolistic Competition and Optimum Product Diversity," *American Economic Review,* June 1977; F. M. Scherer, "The Welfare Economics of Product Variety: An Application to the Ready-to-Eat Cereals Industry," *Journal of Industrial Economics,* 1979; and M. Spence, "Product Selection, Fixed Costs, and Monopolistic Competition," *Review of Economic Studies,* June 1976.

10. Criticisms of the Theory of Monopolistic Competition

According to some social philosophers (mostly very young or very old), life begins at forty. Chamberlin's theory of monopolistic competition celebrated its fortieth birthday not long ago, but there is still a good deal of argument concerning its significance. A number of important criticisms have been made of the theory. For example, Chicago's George Stigler and others have argued that the definition of the group of firms included in the product group is extremely ambiguous. It may contain only one firm or all of the firms in the economy. Moreover, in Stigler's view, the concept of the group is not salvaged by the assumption that each firm neglects the effects of its decisions on other firms in the group, and that each firm has essentially the same demand and cost curves.

Indeed, according to Stigler, the firms in the group must be selling homogeneous commodities if the assumption of similar demand and cost curves for all firms in the group is to be at all realistic. But if the commodities are homogeneous, there is no reason why firms should have downward-sloping demand curves. If one loosens the assumption that the demand and cost curves are the same for all firms, other criticisms can be made of the analysis. Stigler states that "in the general case we cannot make a single statement about economic events in the world we sought to analyze ... [although] many such statements are made by Chamberlin."[5]

In addition, a number of economists have questioned the conclusion that excess capacity will be present under monopolistic competition. For example, Oxford's Sir Roy Harrod believed that the argument leading to this conclusion contains inconsistencies since the firm uses a short-run marginal revenue curve and a long-run marginal cost curve to determine its output and size of plant. Thus the firm sets the price at a level that attracts the entry of other firms, which in turn shifts its marginal revenue curve downward. The supposedly rational entrepreneur is unaccountably shortsighted. Harrod's own analysis, which attempts to eliminate this inconsistency, results in the conclusion that excess capacity will be less, if existent at all, than Chamberlin suggests.

Still other economists claim that there are relatively few markets in the real world where the model of monopolistic competition is really relevant. There certainly is a great deal to be said for this view, since the assumptions underlying the theory are quite stringent.

In conclusion, it must be granted that these criticisms have a considerable amount of merit. Although there was a good deal of enthusiasm for the theory soon after its development, the passage of time seems to have pushed the theory farther and farther from the center of the stage. However, it remains a standard part of most courses in microeconomic theory, perhaps partly in the hope that it will lead to more adequate models of the middle ground between perfect competition and pure monopoly. Incipient economic theorists take note.[6]

5. G. Stigler, *Five Lectures on Economic Problems* (London: Longmans Green, 1949), pp. 18–19.

6. For an excellent brief discussion of the criticisms of Chamberlin's theory, see K.

11. Summary

The theory of monopolistic competition is based on the following assumptions. First, there is assumed to be a large number of firms producing a differentiated product, with each firm's product being a close substitute for the product of every other firm in the product group. Second, the number of firms in the product group is assumed to be sufficiently large so that each firm expects its actions to go unheeded by its rivals and to be unimpeded by any retaliatory measures on their part. Third, it is assumed that both demand and cost curves are the same for all of the firms in the group.

In the theory of monopolistic competition, there are two kinds of demand curves. On the one hand, there is the dd' demand curve, which shows how much the firm will sell if it varies its price from the going level and if other firms maintain their existing prices. On the other hand, there is the DD' demand curve, which shows how much the firm will sell if all firms raise or lower their prices by the same amount as this firm. In discussing the pricing behavior of firms under monopolistic competition, it simplifies matters to assume that the firms have already decided on the characteristics of product and the extent of selling expenses that are most profitable.

In the short run, equilibrium price and output occur when marginal revenue based on the dd' demand curve equals marginal cost at the existing output, while the dd' demand curve intersects the DD' demand curve at the existing price (and output). In the long run, firms, as in perfect competition, are able to change the scale of their plant and to leave or enter the industry. The long-run equilibrium position is the point at which (1) the long-run average cost curve is tangent to the dd' demand curve, and (2) the DD' demand curve intersects the dd' demand curve and the long-run average cost curve at the tangency point.

Under monopolistic competition, firms can vary the characteristics of the products as well as price. It is assumed that they choose the product characteristics that appear most profitable. Firms also can vary their selling expenses. Long-run equilibrium will be attained when economic profits are zero and when, if other firms' selling expenses remain constant, there is no apparent gain from any firm's altering its own selling expenses.

A famous, and somewhat controversial, conclusion of the theory of monopolistic competition is that firms under this form of market organization will tend to operate with excess capacity. That is, the firm will not construct the minimum-cost size of plant or operate the one it does construct at the minimum-cost rate of output. There have been a number of attacks on this conclusion, as well as on other aspects of the theory. Attempts have been made to determine the effects on social welfare of monopolistic competition, but little or no success has been achieved.

Cohen and R. Cyert. *Theory of the Firm* (Englewood Cliffs, N.J.: Prentice-Hall, 1965), pp. 221–26.

QUESTIONS AND PROBLEMS

1. For a particular monopolistically competitive firm, the DD' demand curve intersects the dd' demand curve at a price of $10. Can the price of the firm's product be in equilibrium now at $12? Why or why not?

2. Explain in detail why you believe that each of the following industries can or cannot be represented by Chamberlin's model: (a) copper, (b) outboard motors, (c) airlines, (d) cement.

3. Explain why the extent of the excess capacity in a particular monopolistically competitive firm is inversely related to the price elasticity of demand of its product.

4. How damaging do you consider the criticisms of Stigler, Harrod, and others to be to Chamberlin's theory?

5. The situation facing a particular monopolistically competitive firm is the following:

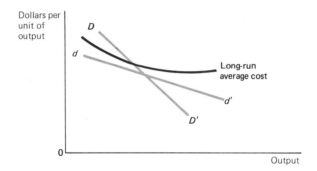

Is this situation a long-run equilibrium? Will entry occur in the industry? Will exit occur in the industry?

6. Would you expect that increases in advertising expenditures will increase a monopolistically competitive firm's sales, regardless of the size of these expenditures? Would you expect advertising to be subject to the law of diminishing marginal returns? Why or why not?

7. Give five real-world examples of industries in which there is product differentiation.

8. According to Paul Samuelson, "Chicago economists can continue to shout until they are blue in the face that there is no elegant alternative to the theory of perfect competition. If not, the proper moral is, 'So much the worse for elegance.'" What does he mean? Do you agree? Why or why not?

9. According to some economists, there are too many gas stations and grocery stores. Is this in keeping with the theory of monopolistic competition?

10. Suppose that you were given the job of determining whether there were too many clothing stores in your town or city. How would you go about testing this hypothesis? What kinds of data would you need? How would you go about getting these data? (And what does "too many" mean?)

SELECTED REFERENCES

CHAMBERLIN, EDWARD. *The Theory of Monopolistic Competition.* Cambridge, Mass.: Harvard University Press, 1933.

ROBINSON, JOAN. *The Economics of Imperfect Competition.* London: Macmillan, 1933.

SAMUELSON, PAUL. "The Monopolistic Competition Revolution." Reprinted in E. Mansfield, *Microeconomics: Selected Readings.* 4th ed. New York: Norton, 1982.

SCHERER, F. M. *Industrial Market Structure and Economic Performance.* 2d ed. Chicago: Rand McNally, 1980.

STIGLER, GEORGE. *Five Lectures on Economic Problems.* London: Longmans Green, 1949.

TRIFFIN, ROBERT. *Monopolistic Competition and General Equilibrium Theory.* Cambridge, Mass.: Harvard University Press, 1949.

12 Price and Output under Oligopoly

1. Oligopoly: Definition, Causes, and Classification

Oligopoly, in contrast to perfect competition or monopoly, is very often encountered in the modern economy. Oligopoly is a market structure characterized by a small number of firms and a great deal of interdependence, actual and perceived, among them. Each oligopolist formulates its policies with an eye to their effect on its rivals. Since an oligopoly contains a small number of firms, any change in the firm's price or output influences the sales and profits of competitors. Moreover, since there are only a few firms, each firm must recognize that changes in its own policies are likely to elicit changes in the policies of its competitors as well.

A good example of an oligopoly is the American petroleum industry where eight firms have accounted in recent years for about 60 percent of the industry's refining capacity. Each of the major oil firms must take account of the reaction of the others when it formulates its price and output policy, since its policy is likely to affect theirs. Thus, when Exxon and other leading oil companies raised their prices of home heating oil and diesel fuel by 1 or 2 cents per gallon in early 1981, they had to anticipate what the reaction of other firms in the industry would be. Had their rivals decided against such a price increase, it is likely that the price increase would have had to be rescinded.

Oligopoly is a common market structure in the United States, where many industries are dominated by a few firms. The automobile industry is dominated by three firms—General Motors, Ford, and Chrysler.

Many parts of the electrical equipment industry are dominated by General Electric and Westinghouse. The can industry has been dominated by two firms: American Can and Continental Can. And these are only a few highly visible examples. Not all oligopolists are large firms. If two grocery stores exist in an isolated community, they are oligopolists, too; the fact that they are small firms does not change this situation.

There are many reasons for oligopoly, one being economies of scale. In some industries, low costs cannot be achieved unless a firm is producing an output equal to a substantial percentage of the total available market, with the consequence that the number of firms will tend to be rather small. In addition, there may be economies of scale in sales promotion as well as in production, and this too may promote oligopoly. Further, there may be barriers that make it very difficult to enter the industry. A variety of such barriers are discussed in Section 15. Finally, of course, the number of firms in an industry may decrease in response to the desire to weaken competitive pressures.

Oligopolistic industries can be classified in various ways. If the firms produce a homogeneous product, like steel or cement, the industry is called a *pure oligopoly*. If the firms produce a differentiated product, like automobiles, the industry is called a *differentiated oligopoly*. Throughout most of this chapter, we shall deal with the case of pure oligopoly. Also, oligopolistic industries may be marked by *collusion* or *independent action*. In Sections 2 to 8, we take up cases where oligopolists act independently. In Sections 9 to 12, we take up cases of collusion, perfect and imperfect.

2. The Cournot Model

To begin with, we consider a theory put forth by Augustin Cournot[1] almost a hundred fifty years ago. Although this theory is too simple to capture much of the richness of the oligopolistic situation, it has attracted considerable attention and is still cited. Cournot considers the case in which there are two sellers, that is, the case of *duopoly;* but his model can easily be generalized to include the case of three or more sellers. To describe his model, it is convenient to assume that the two firms, firm I and firm II, produce the same product, have the same cost functions, and are perfectly aware of the demand curve for their product, which is supposed to be linear. More specifically, Cournot discusses the case of two firms selling spring water, with the cost of production being zero for each firm.

Turning to behavioral assumptions, both firms are supposed to maximize profits. Each assumes that, regardless of what output it produces, the other will hold its output constant at the existing level. Taking the other firm's output level as given, each firm chooses its own

---

1. A. Cournot, *Recherches sur les Principes Mathématiques de la Théorie des Riches,* translated by Nathaniel Bacon (New York: Macmillan, 1897). He first published his model in 1838.

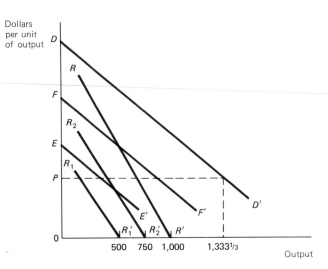

Figure 12.1   The Cournot model

output level to maximize profit. Suppose that firm I is the first to act. It sells the monopoly output, 1,000 units, according to the situation in Figure 12.1. It chooses this output level because it assumes that firm II will continue to produce nothing. If this is the case, firm I's marginal revenue (RR') equals its marginal cost (which is zero) at 1,000 units if the demand curve for the product is DD'.

Now it is firm II's turn to act. Contrary to firm I's expectation, firm II is seriously considering changing its current output level, which is zero. Taking firm I's output level (of 1,000) as given, firm II believes that the demand curve for its product is the total market demand curve less 1,000, or EE' in Figure 12.1. Thus firm II chooses an output level of 500, where the marginal revenue, R_1R_1', based on the demand curve EE' equals its marginal cost, which is zero.

The spotlight now moves back to firm I, which is assumed to have the next move. Again, firm I assumes that firm II has chosen an output level that will be maintained regardless of what it, firm I, does. Consequently, firm I believes that the demand curve for its product is the total demand curve less 500, or FF' in Figure 12.1. Thus firm I chooses an output level of 750, where marginal revenue (R_2R_2') based on the demand curve FF' equals the firm's marginal cost, which is zero.

This process goes on indefinitely, each firm taking the other firm's output as given and choosing the output that maximizes its own profits. Firm I's output is 1,000, then 750, then $22,000 \div 32, \ldots$[2] Firm II's output is 0, then 500, then $20,000 \div 32, \ldots$[3] Ultimately, it can be shown that the

2. How do we get 22,000/32? It can be shown that firm I will produce $C/2$, $3C/8$, $11C/32$, $\cdots$, where C is the competitive output (2,000 in this case). Try to prove this as an exercise.

3. It can be shown that firm II will produce 0, $C/4$, $5C/16$, $\cdots$, where C is the competitive output (2,000 in this case). Prove this as an exercise. See Footnote 2.

output of each firm tends to $666\frac{2}{3}$.[4] Thus the price that eventually is maintained is OP. If price were set equal to marginal cost, it would equal zero and the industry's output would be 2,000. This is the perfectly competitive solution. Thus the equilibrium output under duopoly in the Cournot model is $\frac{2}{3}$ of the competitive output. Since the monopoly output would be 1,000, it is $\frac{4}{3}$ of the monopoly output.[5]

3. The Edgeworth Model

Cournot's model was criticized by Joseph Bertrand and F. Y. Edgeworth,[6] who believed that it was better to assume that firms think that their rivals will hold price, rather than quantity, constant. In his model, Edgeworth followed Cournot in assuming that the industry is composed of two firms that sell a homogeneous product at zero marginal cost. In addition, he assumed that each firm has a maximum output rate.

4. Firm I's output in the limit can be represented as
$$C[1 - (\tfrac{1}{2} + \tfrac{1}{8} + \tfrac{1}{32} + \cdots)] = C[1 - \tfrac{1}{2}(1 + \tfrac{1}{4} + (\tfrac{1}{4})^2 + \cdots)]$$
which equals
$$C\left[1 - \frac{1}{2}\left(\frac{1}{1 - \frac{1}{4}}\right)\right] = C(1 - \tfrac{2}{3}) = \frac{C}{3}$$
Firm II's output in the limit can be represented as
$$C(\tfrac{1}{4} + \tfrac{1}{16} + \tfrac{1}{64} + \cdots)$$
which equals
$$\tfrac{1}{4}C[1 + \tfrac{1}{4} + (\tfrac{1}{4})^2 + \cdots] = \frac{1}{4} C \left(\frac{1}{1 - \frac{1}{4}}\right) = \frac{C}{3}.$$
C is the competitive output.

5. Another way to describe the Cournot model is as follows: There is a demand curve for the industry's product, $p = f(q_1 + q_2)$, where q_1 is the output of firm I, q_2 is the output of firm II, and p is the price of the product. The total cost function of firm I is $C_1(q_1)$ and the total cost function of firm II is $C_2(q_2)$. Thus the profit of firm I is
$$\Pi_1 = q_1 f(q_1 + q_2) - C_1(q_1)$$
and the profit of firm II is
$$\Pi_2 = q_2 f(q_1 + q_2) - C_2(q_2)$$
If each firm takes the other firm's output as given and maximizes profit
$$\frac{\partial \Pi_1}{\partial q_1} = f(q_1 + q_2) + q_1 \frac{\partial f(q_1 + q_2)}{\partial q_1} - \frac{\partial C_1}{\partial q_1} = 0$$
$$\frac{\partial \Pi_2}{\partial q_2} = f(q_1 + q_2) + q_2 \frac{\partial f(q_1 + q_2)}{\partial q_2} - \frac{\partial C_2}{\partial q_2} = 0$$
Solving these two equations simultaneously, we obtain the equilibrium q_1 and q_2, which in turn tells us what the equilibrium value of p will be.

6. J. Bertrand, "Théorie Mathématique de la Richesse Sociale," *Journal des Savants,* Paris, 1883; and F. Edgeworth, "La Teoria Pura del Monopolio," *Giornale degli Economisti,* 1897.

Suppose once again that firm I is the first to act and that it chooses the price that it believes will maximize its profit. It is then firm II's turn to act. Expecting that firm I will maintain its price, firm II decides to set a price slightly below that set by firm I, since by doing so it will take much of the market away from firm I. This is not the only action that firm II could have taken. It could have focused its attention on consumers that firm I could not accommodate (because firm I's output is limited), and it could have charged these consumers the monopoly price. But if firm I maintains its price, this is less profitable to firm II than the action it takes.

Firm I acts next. Assuming that firm II will maintain its price, firm I sets a price somewhat below that set by firm II, firm I's expectation being that it will take much of the market away from firm II. This is not the only action firm I could have taken. It too could have focused its attention on consumers that firm II could not accommodate (because firm II's output is limited), and it could have charged these consumers the monopoly price. But if firm II maintains its price, this is less profitable to firm I than the action it takes.

According to Edgeworth, this process of successive price cutting goes on until price reaches a certain minimum level. At this level, one of the firms, according to Edgeworth, notes that if the other firm maintains its price at this level, it is profitable for this firm to raise its price to the monopoly level originally set by firm I. Why is this profitable? Because at this point more money can be made by charging the monopoly price to consumers that the other firm cannot accommodate (because its output is limited) than by cutting price in an attempt to take away the other firm's customers. Since the price of the product is relatively low, each consumer purchases a relatively large amount of it,[7] and relatively few consumers can be accommodated by the other firm. The portion of the market that cannot be accommodated by the other firm—and that can be charged the monopoly price by this firm—is substantial.

Thus, this firm, say firm I, raises its price to the monopoly level, assuming that the other firm, firm II, will maintain its price at the minimum level. But once firm I raises its price to the monopoly level, firm II sets a price somewhat below this level, firm I sets a somewhat lower price, and the process is repeated. Consequently, price moves continually between the monopoly level and the minimum level, according to Edgeworth.

Both the Cournot and Edgeworth models are extremely naïve. They make the unrealistic assumption that a firm continually makes the mistake of assuming that its rivals will not alter their output or price in response to the firm's own changes in output and price. In addition, the Edgeworth model makes the assumption that firms have maximum output levels, whereas output in the long run is generally augmentable. The Cournot and Edgeworth models are worth studying, because they are

---

7. It is assumed that the number of consumers is constant and that each consumer has an identical demand curve for the product.

important forerunners of more realistic models, but taken by themselves they have very limited use.

4. The Chamberlin Model

A more realistic model was put forth by Edward Chamberlin of Harvard University.[8] He makes the same basic assumptions as Cournot: There are two firms, each selling water at zero marginal cost, and the demand curve for their combined output is DD' in Figure 12.2. Firm I is the first to act, and it chooses the monopoly output, 1,000 units. Firm II, taking firm I's output as given, faces a demand curve of EE', and thus decides to produce 500 units. All of this is precisely the same as the Cournot model.

But Chamberlin takes a different path at the next step in the process. Firm I does not assume that firm II will maintain its output rate at 500 units, regardless of what firm I does. Instead of making this naïve assumption, which is characteristic of the Cournot model, firm I recognizes that firm II will react to firm I's actions. After some deliberation, firm I concludes that the best thing that it and firm II can do is to share the monopoly profit—the profit of $OR'AP_0$. Firm II reaches the same conclusion. Thus firm I reduces its output to 500 units, and firm II keeps its output at 500 units, with the result that total output in the industry is 1,000 units, price is OP_0, and the two firms share the monopoly level of profits.

An important thing to note regarding Chamberlin's model is the fact

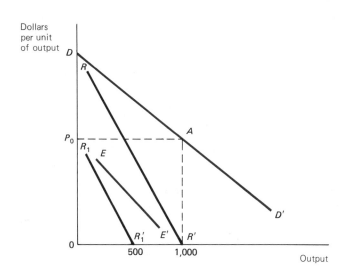

Figure 12.2   The Chamberlin model

8. E. Chamberlin, *The Theory of Monopolistic Competition* (Cambridge, Mass.: Harvard University Press, 1933).

that the solution is quite stable. In contrast to Edgeworth's model, and to some extent Cournot's, price will not tend to fluctuate a great deal in Chamberlin's model. This is an advantage of Chamberlin's model, because the facts seem to indicate that prices in oligopolistic markets tend to be quite stable. For example, as we shall see in the following section, the price of one oligopolistic product, steel rails, remained essentially fixed for over a decade. Although this may be an extreme case, it illustrates the stability of prices in oligopolistic industries.

Chamberlin's model showed how firms may decide to set identical prices and maximize their joint profits, even though there is no collusion among them. They may do so, according to the Chamberlin model, without any form of agreement. Whether or not their profits are large or small depends, of course, on the individual case. Just as a monopolist may earn little or no profit, so may a Chamberlin type of oligopoly. It is difficult to know how often noncollusive behavior of this sort occurs, but it is a reasonable possibility in at least some oligopolistic markets.

5. The Kinked Demand Curve

In the previous section, we noted that empirical studies of pricing in oligopolistic markets have often concluded that prices in such markets tend to be rigid. A classic example occurred in the steel industry. From 1901 to 1916, the price of steel rails remained at $28 a ton, and from 1922 to 1933, it remained at $43 a ton. These were periods when considerable shifts occurred in demand and cost; yet the industry's price remained constant. This example is somewhat extreme, but it illustrates the basic point, which is that prices in oligopolistic industries commonly remain unchanged for fairly long periods.[9]

Of course, one would not expect prices always to respond quickly to small changes in demand and cost. It costs money for a firm to change prices, and it costs the consumer time and trouble—and perhaps money, too—to learn about them. Moreover, although quoted prices may not vary very much, this does not necessarily imply that actual prices do not vary considerably. For example, in periods when demand is low, concessions (secret or fairly open) from the quoted prices may be made to buyers. Nevertheless, taking these things into account, it is frequently concluded that prices in oligopolistic markets tend to be rigid.

A well-known theory designed to explain the rigidity of prices in oligopolistic markets was advanced by Paul Sweezy[10] in 1939. He asserted that, if an oligopolist cuts its price, it can be pretty sure that its rivals will meet the reduction. On the other hand, if an oligopolist increases its price, it is likely to find that its rivals will not change their prices. In such

9. H. Purdy, M. Lindahl, and W. Carter, *Corporate Concentration and Public Policy* (Englewood Cliffs, N.J.: Prentice-Hall, 1950), p. 646.

10. P. Sweezy, "Demand under Conditions of Oligopoly," *Journal of Political Economy,* August 1939.

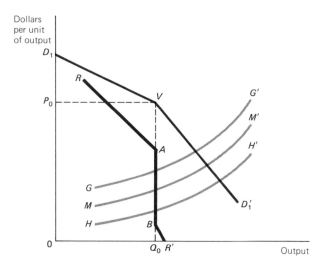

Figure 12.3   The Sweezy model

a case, the demand curve for the oligopolist's product would be much more elastic for price increases than for price decreases.

Figure 12.3 shows the situation, the oligopolist's demand curve being represented by $D_1 V D_1'$ and the current price being OP_0. Because of the "kink" in the demand curve, the marginal revenue curve is not continuous: It consists of two segments RA and BR'. Given that the firm's marginal cost curve is MM', marginal revenue does not equal marginal cost at any level of output. But it can be shown that OQ_0 is the most profitable output of the firm. Moreover, OQ_0 remains the most profitable output—and OP_0 the most profitable price—even if the marginal cost curve changes considerably. For example, it remains the most profitable output if the marginal cost curve shifts to GG' or HH'. Also, OQ_0 remains the most profitable output—and OP_0 the most profitable price— for some changes in demand, as long as the kink remains at the same price level. Thus, under these circumstances, one might expect price to be quite rigid.

Soon after Sweezy's theory first appeared, it was regarded by some economists as a general theory of oligopoly. However, subsequent research has cast doubt on its general usefulness. For example, George Stigler found that in seven oligopolistic industries there was little indication that an increase in price by one firm would not be matched, in general, by other firms.[11] Thus, in these industries at least, there seemed to be little evidence for the existence of a kink in the demand curve. Moreover, although this theory may be useful under some circumstances

11. G. Stigler, "The Kinky Oligopoly Demand Curve and Rigid Prices," *Journal of Political Economy,* 1947. Also see W. Primeaux, Jr., and W. Smith, "Pricing Patterns and the Kinky Demand Curve," *Journal of Law and Economics,* April 1976; and J. Simon, "A Further Test of the Kinky Oligopoly Demand Curve," *American Economic Review,* December 1969.

Example 12.1   Pricing under Oligopoly

Suppose that an oil company's perceived demand curve is DVD', its marginal revenue curve is RAR', and its marginal cost curve is MM' in panel A below:

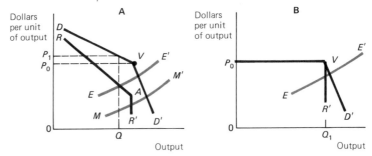

Suppose further that, because of developments in the Middle East, the firm's costs increase sharply, with the result that the marginal cost curve rises from MM' to EE'. (a) An oil economist says that, because the firm's demand curve is kinked, this will not increase its price. Is he correct? (b) Fearful that the cost increase will result in a price hike, Congress passes a bill saying that the firm's price must not exceed OP_0. What effect does this have on the firm's demand curve? Marginal revenue curve? Output?

Solution

(a) No. As shown in panel A above, the new marginal cost curve (EE') intersects the marginal revenue curve at an output of OQ, which means that the profit-maximizing price is OP_1, not OP_0. Thus, if the firm maximizes profit, it will increase its price to OP_1. (b) Its demand curve now is P_0VD', as shown in panel B above. In contrast to the situation before Congress acted, the firm now cannot sell anything at a price exceeding OP_0. Its marginal revenue curve now is P_0VR'. Since its demand curve is horizontal for outputs less than OQ_1, so is its marginal revenue curve. Its output now is OQ_1, since this is the output where the marginal revenue curve (P_0VR') intersects the new marginal cost curve (EE').*

---

* In both panels of the above graph, only parts of the marginal revenue curves are shown, but these parts are sufficient for present purposes.

in explaining why price tends to remain at a certain level (OP_0 in Figure 12.3), it is of no use in explaining why this level, rather than another, currently prevails. For example, it simply takes as given that the current price is OP_0 in Figure 12.3; it does not explain why the current price is OP_0. Thus this theory is an incomplete model of oligopolistic pricing.

6. The Theory of Games

As we have seen in previous sections, a basic feature of oligopoly is that each firm must take account of its rivals' reactions to its own actions. For this reason an oligopolistic firm cannot tell what effect a change in its output will have on the price of its product and on its profits, unless it can guess how its rivals will respond to this change in its output. Thus oligopolistic behavior has some of the characteristics of a game. One of the most interesting developments in the theory of oligopoly in the post-war period was the appearance of the *Theory of Games and Economic Behavior,* by John von Neumann and Oskar Morgenstern.[12] Although the theory of games has not shed as much light on oligopolistic behavior as was originally hoped, it has enriched oligopoly theory considerably. In this section, we provide a basic description of the objectives and concepts of game theory, as well as a very simple example of a two-person constant-sum game.

Game theory attempts to study decision-making in conflict situations. A game is a competitive situation where two or more persons pursue their own interests and no person can dictate the outcome. For example, poker is a game, and so is a situation in which two firms are engaged in competitive advertising campaigns. A game is described in terms of the players, the rules of the game, the payoffs of the game, and the information conditions that exist during the game. These elements, common to all conflict situations, are the fundamental characteristics of a game.

More specifically, a *player,* which may be a single person or an organization, is a decision-making unit. Each player has a certain amount of resources; the *rules of the game* describe how these resources can be used. For example, the rules of poker indicate how bets can be made and which hands are better than other hands. A *strategy* is a complete specification of what a player will do under each contingency in the playing of the game. For example, a corporation president might tell his subordinates how he wants an advertising campaign to start, and what should be done at subsequent points in time in response to various actions of competing firms.

The game's outcome clearly depends on the strategies used by each player. A player's *payoff* varies from game to game: It is win, lose, or draw in checkers, and various sums of money in poker. For simplicity we restrict our attention to *two-person games,* games with only two players. Moreover, we restrict our attention to *zero-sum games,* games in which the amount that one player wins is exactly equal to the amount that the other player loses. Duopoly situations are frequently not of this type (although some are), but zero-sum games are the simplest sort, and thus we will describe them here.

The relevant features of a two-person, zero-sum game can be shown by constructing a *payoff matrix.* To illustrate, suppose that two firms are

---

12. J. von Neumann and O. Morgenstern, *Theory of Games and Economic Behavior* (Princeton, N.J.: Princeton University Press, 1944).

about to stage rival advertising campaigns and that each firm has a choice of strategies. Firm I can choose strategy A or B, and firm II can choose strategy 1, 2, or 3. The payoff, expressed in terms of profits for firm I, is shown in Table 12.1 for each combination of strategies. For example, if firm I adopts strategy A and firm II adopts strategy 2, firm I makes a gain of $2 million. And since it is a zero-sum game, firm II loses $2 million. If firm I adopts strategy B and firm II adopts strategy 1, firm I gains $1 million and firm II loses $1 million.

This game is *strictly determined* because, upon examination of the payoff matrix, there is a definite optimal choice for each firm. To see that this is the case, suppose that firm I is allowed to select its strategy first and it chooses strategy B. Firm II would respond by choosing strategy 1 to minimize its losses. Assuming that each firm knows the payoff matrix, this would therefore be a foolish move on firm I's part. Firm I knows that, whatever strategy it chooses, firm II will choose its strategy so as to minimize firm II's losses—and minimize firm I's gains. Consequently, firm I focuses its attention on the row minima, shown in the last column of Table 12.1. Thus firm I will choose strategy A, since it provides firm I

Table 12.1   Payoff matrix

POSSIBLE STRATEGIES
FOR FIRM I

POSSIBLE STRATEGIES FOR FIRM II

	1	2	3	Row minimum
	[PROFITS FOR FIRM I, OR LOSSES FOR FIRM II]			
A	$3 million	$2 million	$4 million	$2 million
B	$1 million	$1.5 million	$3 million	$1 million
Column maximum	$3 million	$2 million	$4 million	

with the greatest gain. Similarly, firm II focuses its attention on the column maxima, since it knows that firm I's response to its strategy will be to pick a strategy that maximizes the payoff to firm I. Thus firm II will choose strategy 2, since it provides firm II with the smallest loss.

Consequently, it turns out that the solution to this game is quite simple. Firm I chooses strategy A, and firm II chooses strategy 2. Firm I adopts a *maximin* policy: It maximizes the row minima. Firm II adopts a *minimax* policy: It minimizes the column maxima. Firm I gains $2 million, and firm II loses $2 million. This game is strictly determined, since there is a unique strategy that each player chooses. The maximum of the row minima equals the minimum of the column maxima. Consequently, firm I can guarantee itself a gain of $2 million, and firm II can guarantee that firm I's gain, which is at firm II's expense, will not exceed $2 million. This is the best that either player—that is, either firm—can do.

Table 12.2   Payoff matrix: Game not strictly determined

POSSIBLE STRATEGIES
FOR FIRM I   POSSIBLE STRATEGIES FOR FIRM II

	1	2	3	Row minimum
	[PROFITS FOR FIRM I, OR LOSSES FOR FIRM II]			
A	−$5 million	$3 million	$6 million	−$5 million
B	$6 million	$3 million	−$5 million	−$5 million
Column maximum	$6 million	$3 million	$6 million	

7. Mixed Strategies

Not all games are strictly determined. For example, suppose that the payoff matrix is the one shown in Table 12.2 rather than that in Table 12.1. If so, firm I is in bad shape if it chooses strategy A, since firm II can impose a $5 million loss on firm I by adopting strategy 1. It is also in bad shape if it chooses strategy B, since firm II can impose a $5 million loss on firm I by adopting strategy 3. What can firm I do? According to von Neumann and Morgenstern, the answer lies in the concept of a *mixed strategy*. Firm I can assign probabilities to the two pure strategies (A and B) and choose a strategy in accord with these probabilities.

Suppose that firm I chooses strategy A with probability x_1 and strategy B with probability $(1 - x_1)$. Suppose that firm II chooses strategy 1 with probability y_1, strategy 2 with probability y_2, and strategy 3 with probability $(1 - y_1 - y_2)$. Because of the uncertainty of the outcome, the firms can no longer try to maximize or minimize the particular payoff, since this payoff has no unique value. Instead they are assumed to maximize the *expected value* of the game, which can be derived from the payoff matrix by multiplying each payoff in the matrix by the probability that it occurs and summing these products for all entries in the payoff matrix.

Thus, in the case at hand, the expected gain for firm I is

$$-5x_1 + 6(1 - x_1) = 6 - 11x_1,$$

if firm II uses strategy 1. It is $3x_1 + 3(1 - x_1) = 3$, if firm II uses strategy 2. And it equals $6x_1 - 5(1 - x_1)$ if firm II uses strategy 3. Given whatever value of x_1 it chooses, firm I can be sure that its expected gain will be no less than the lowest of these three values.

Figure 12.4 shows firm I's expected gain if it adopts various values of x_1 and if firm II adopts strategies 1, 2, or 3. Suppose that firm I is interested in choosing x_1 so as to put the highest possible floor under its expected gain. It is clear from Figure 12.4 that, if firm I chooses a value of x_1 that is less than $\frac{1}{2}$, the worst thing that can happen to it is if firm II

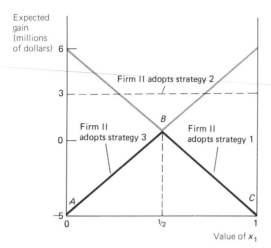

Figure 12.4 Firm I's expected gain, given its choice of x_1

M. Shubik, "The Uses of Game Theory in Management Science," reprinted in E. Mansfield, *Microeconomics: Selected Readings,* 4th ed. (New York: Norton, 1982).

adopts strategy 3. Similarly, it is clear that, if firm I chooses a value of x_1 that is more than $\frac{1}{2}$, the worst thing that can happen to it is if firm II adopts strategy 1. Thus, if firm II adopts the strategy that from firm I's point of view is worst, the expected gain to firm I corresponding to each value of x_1 is given by ABC.

Consequently, if firm I puts the highest possible floor under its expected gain, it will choose $x_1 = \frac{1}{2}$. That is, it will attached a probability of $\frac{1}{2}$ to strategy A and a probability of $\frac{1}{2}$ to strategy B. It can then be sure that its expected gain is at least \$500,000. This is termed an *optimal mixed strategy* for firm I. It can be shown that the optimal mixed strategy for firm II is $y_1 = \frac{1}{2}$ and $y_2 = 0$. That is, firm II will attach a probability of $\frac{1}{2}$ to strategy 1, a probability of 0 to strategy 2, and a probability of $\frac{1}{2}$ to strategy 3.[13]

Von Neumann and Morgenstern proved that a pair of mixed strategies will always exist which are an equilibrium pair insofar as neither player can improve his position when each uses his optimal mixed strategy. It is easy to see that there is an equilibrium of this sort in the case just described. By choosing $x_1 = \frac{1}{2}$, firm I can guarantee itself an expected gain of \$500,000. No other value of x_1 can guarantee firm I more. By choosing $y_1 = \frac{1}{2}$ and $y_2 = 0$, firm II can guarantee that its expected loss is

13. The payoff matrix and solution of this example are taken from M. Shubik, "The Uses of Game Theory in Management Science," reprinted in E. Mansfield, *Microeconomics: Selected Readings,* 4th ed. (New York: Norton, 1982). The payoff matrix in Table 12.2 is also similar to one in Shubik's article.

$500,000. No other values of y_1 and y_2 can guarantee firm II more. The fact that such an equilibrium always exists in two-person zero-sum games is remarkable, indeed.[14]

8. More Complicated Games and Limitations of Game Theory

Thus far the discussion has dealt only with two-person constant-sum[15] games. Most economic problems are not of the constant-sum variety. For example, two firms can often increase their total profits by collusion; it is not necessary for one to gain only at the expense of the other. Although the theory is not so well developed when we leave the realm of constant-sum games, a considerable literature exists concerning both *nonco-operative* games (where collusion does not occur) and *cooperative* games (where collusion does occur) that are not constant-sum. In the case of cooperative games, it is often claimed that the players will wind up on the contract curve discussed in Chapter 15. When we consider games with more than two players, added difficulties are encountered and fewer results are available.

Game theory has been criticized on several grounds, one being that the minimax principle is too conservative. According to the minimax principle, which is fundamental to the theory, a player maximizes his or her payoff under the assumption that his or her opponent will adopt the strategy that is most damaging to him or her. Many economists feel that this is an unnecessarily pessimistic outlook for the player, and they wonder whether such an attitude is a realistic representation of how firms actually do view competitive situations. If a player adopts a mini-max strategy and his or her competitor does not, the former is likely to forgo considerable extra profit. Despite this limitation and others, the theory of games is a useful addition to the tool kit of the microeconomist. It is useful as a suggestive framework for analysis. One can structure formerly intractable problems and think about them in terms of this theory. However, in its present state, game theory cannot be used to derive specific predictions of the behavior of oligopolists, and despite the high hopes of thirty-five years ago, it has permitted only a modest advance in oligopoly theory.

---

14. Note that there is a relationship between games and linear programming. See, for example, R. Dorfman, P. Samuelson, and R. Solow, *Linear Programming and Economic Analysis* (New York: McGraw-Hill, 1958); and W. Baumol, *Economic Theory and Operations Analysis* 4th ed. (Englewood Cliffs, N.J.: Prentice-Hall, 1977).

15. Strictly speaking we have dealt only with *zero-sum games,* but there is no problem in extending the analysis to include *constant-sum games.* A constant-sum game is a case where the sum of the winnings and losses of the players is a constant, but not necessarily zero. For example, if the gambling house takes a certain amount out of each pot, the sum of winnings and losses will be a negative constant equal to the gambling house's take.

9. Collusion and Cartels

In previous sections we have presented theories of oligopolistic behavior based on the assumption that oligopolists do not collude.[16] However, conditions in oligopolistic industries tend to promote collusion, since the number of firms is small and the firms recognize their interdependence. The advantages to the firms of collusion seem obvious: increased profits, decreased uncertainty, and a better opportunity to prevent entry. However, collusive arrangements are often hard to maintain, since once a collusive agreement is made, any of the firms can increase its profits by cheating on the agreement. Moreover, collusive arrangements generally are illegal, at least in the United States.

When a collusive arrangement is made openly and formally, it is called a *cartel*. In many countries in Europe, cartels have been common and legally acceptable. In the United States, most collusive agreements, whether secret or open cartels, were declared illegal by the Sherman Antitrust Act, which dates back to 1890. However, this does not mean that such agreements do not exist. For example, as we shall see in Section 11, there was widespread collusion among American electrical equipment manufacturers during the 1950s. Moreover, trade assocations and professional organizations may sometimes perform functions somewhat similar to a cartel. In addition, some types of cartels have the official sanction of the United States government.[17]

Suppose that a cartel is established to set a uniform price for a particular (homogeneous) product. What price will it charge? To begin with, the cartel must estimate the marginal cost curve for the cartel as a whole. If input prices do not increase as the cartel expands, this marginal cost curve is the horizontal sum of the marginal cost curves of the individual firms. Suppose that the resulting marginal cost curve for the cartel is as shown in Figure 12.5. If the demand curve for the industry's product and the relevant marginal revenue curve are as shown there, the output that maximizes the total profit of the cartel members is OQ_0. Thus, if it maximizes cartel profits, the cartel will choose a price of OP_0. This, of course, is the monopoly price.

Another important task of a cartel is to distribute the industry's total sales among the firms belonging to the cartel. If the aim of the cartel is to maximize cartel profits, it will allocate sales to firms in such a way that the marginal cost of all firms is equal. Otherwise the cartel could make more money by reallocating output among firms so as to reduce the cost of producing the cartel's total output. For example, if the marginal cost at firm I was higher than at firm II, the cartel can increase its total profits by transferring some production from firm I to firm II.

16. Of course, the theory of cooperative games is concerned with collusion. This is an exception to the statement in the text.

17. For example, airlines flying transatlantic routes are members of the International Air Transport Association, which can agree on uniform prices for transatlantic flights.

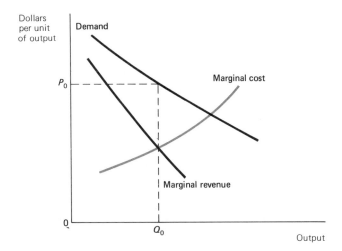

Figure 12.5 Price and output determination by a cartel

However, this allocation of output—sometimes called the ideal allocation by economists—is unlikely to occur, since allocation decisions are the result of negotiation between firms with varying interests and varying capabilities. This is a political process in which various firms have different amounts of influence. Those with the most influence and the shrewdest negotiators are likely to receive the largest sales quotas, even though this increases total cartel costs. Moreover, high-cost firms are likely to receive larger sales quotas than cost minimization would dictate, since they would be unwilling to accept the small quotas dictated by cost minimization. In practice, there is some evidence that sales are often distributed in accord with a firm's level of sales in the past, or the extent of its productive capacity. Also, a cartel sometimes divides a market geographically, with some firms being given certain regions or countries and other firms being given other regions or countries.

10. The Instability of Cartels

We have already noted that collusive agreements tend to break down. Of course, the difficulty in keeping a cartel from breaking down increases with the number of firms in the cartel. To see why firms are tempted to leave the cartel, consider the case of the firm in Figure 12.6. If this firm were to leave the cartel, it would be faced with a demand curve of DD' as long as the other firms in the cartel maintain a price of OP_0. This demand curve is very elastic; the firm is able to expand its sales considerably by small reductions in price. Even if the firm were not to leave the cartel, but if it were to grant secret price concessions, the same sort of demand curve would be present.

Under these circumstances the firm's maximum profit if it leaves the

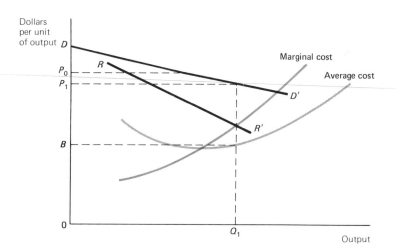

Figure 12.6   The instability of cartels

cartel or secretly lowers price will be attained if it sells an output of OQ_1, at a price of OP_1, since this is the output at which marginal cost equals marginal revenue. (RR' is the firm's marginal revenue curve). This price would result in a profit of $OQ_1 \times BP_1$, which is higher than if the firm conforms to the price and sales quota dictated by the cartel. A firm that breaks away from a cartel—or secretly cheats—can increase its profits as long as other firms do not do the same thing and as long as the cartel does not punish it in some way. But if all firms do this, the cartel breaks down.

Consequently, as long as a cartel is not maintained by legal provisions, there is a constant threat to its existence. Its members have an incentive to cheat, and once a few do so, others may follow. Price concessions made secretly by a few "chiselers" or openly by a few malcontents cut into the sales of cooperative members of the cartel who are induced to match them. Thus the ranks of the unfaithful are expanded; and ultimately the cartel may break down completely.

11. Collusion in the Electrical Equipment Industry

In early 1960 the Department of Justice charged that a large number of companies and individuals in the electrical equipment industry were guilty of fixing prices and dividing up the market for circuit breakers, switchgears, and other important products. Most of the defendants were found guilty; the companies, including General Electric and Westinghouse, received fines; and some of the guilty executives were sent to prison. This was a very interesting and instructive modern example of collusive oligopoly behavior.

The price-fixing agreements were reached in various ways. Many of the meetings occurred at conventions of the National Electrical Manufacturers Association and other trade groups. Some agreements were made through telephone calls and written memoranda transmitted from one sales executive to another. Efforts were made to keep the meetings and agreements secret. For example, codes were used, and the participants at meetings sometimes disguised their records and did not use their companies' names when registering at hotels. The executives recognized that these agreements were illegal.

To see how these agreements worked, consider the case of circuit breakers. In 1958 there were only five manufacturers of circuit breakers, and it was decided that General Electric would receive about 40 percent of the sealed-bid business; Westinghouse, about 31 percent; Allis-Chalmers, about 9 percent; Federal Pacific, about 16 percent; and I-T-E, 4 percent. According to a statement to the court, this is how it worked:

> At a working level meeting where a particular job was up for discussion, the percentages initially would be reviewed in light of what was known on the ledger list, which had on it recent sealed-bid jobs given to the other defendants. In light of that ledger list it was decided which of the companies, to keep the percentages constant, would get the job. Now if that company was prepared to say the price at which it was going to bid, then the other companies could discuss among themselves what they would bid, add on for accessories, to make sure to give ... the company ... whose turn it was to get the job, the best shot at it. ... If the company whose job the particular rigged job was supposed to be did not know the price, there would be later communications, either by phone to homes with just the first names used, or by letter to homes with just first names of senders, with no return address, and ... [using] code. [18]

In view of the discussion in the previous section, it is interesting to note that many of these agreements tended to be unstable. In the early and mid-fifties, as well as in the period after 1958, there were agreements of this sort, but eventually overcapacity in the industry led to "chiseling" by various firms. For example, price-cutting in sales of power switching machinery to government agencies was regarded as a major problem in late 1958. One collusive agreement after another was drawn up, but after a while some firms began in each case to pursue an independent price policy.

12. The OPEC Oil Cartel: Another Application

To illustrate the nature and behavior of international cartels, as distinct from purely national ones, consider the Organization of Petroleum Exporting Countries (OPEC) cartel. This cartel first hit the headlines in late 1973 when its Arab members precipitated a crisis in the United States by announcing a cutback in oil exports to us. Then it attracted further attention by taking a series of actions resulting in very large increases in the price of crude oil. For example, the price of Saudi Arabian crude oil (delivered to the United States East Coast) jumped from $4 in

18. *Wall Street Journal*, 1961, reprinted in E. Mansfield, *Microeconomics: Selected Readings*.

1973 to over $10 in early 1974. Again in 1979, in the wake of the Iranian revolution, OPEC raised the price enormously, to over $30 a barrel. In view of its impact on subsequent economic events, it is important that we understand something about the nature and workings of the OPEC cartel.

OPEC consists of twelve major oil-producing countries, including Saudi Arabia, Iran, Venezuela, Libya, and Nigeria. The OPEC countries impose an excise tax of so many cents per barrel on each barrel of oil produced in their countries. These taxes are well publicized and, like any excise tax, they are treated as a cost of production by any of the international oil companies operating in these countries. Thus, by increasing these taxes, the OPEC countries can increase the price of crude oil, since no company can afford to sell oil for less than its production costs plus the tax. How far are they likely to increase the price? According to the model discussed in Section 9, one would expect the OPEC cartel to push the crude oil price up toward the monopoly level, since this would increase their tax revenues. In fact, this seems to have been exactly what has occurred.

Experts estimate that hundreds of billions of dollars have been transferred by this means from oil consumers to OPEC. What can the oil-consuming nations do to break the hold of this cartel? According to MIT's Morris Adelman, one possibility is to get the multinational firms (like Exxon, Mobil, and Shell) out of crude oil marketing and to make the OPEC countries sell their own crude oil. He argues that the oil-producing countries cannot fix prices without using the multinational companies. As we have observed in previous sections, a cartel must either control output or detect and prevent "cheating" in the form of under-the-counter price reductions. The OPEC tax system results in the publication by every important OPEC nation of its level of taxes per barrel. Since they are a matter of public record, the price floor of taxes-plus-cost is safe, once the taxes are approved by the companies and the government.

Adelman argues that the oil companies' role as crude oil marketers is essential to the cartel. If the producing nations had to sell their own crude oil, and had to pay the oil firms in cash or oil for their services, he believes that the cartel would disintegrate. Why? Because the floor to price would be not the tax-plus-cost, but only bare cost. Unless the producing nations established (and obeyed) production quotas, "chiseling" would result. Each nation would be likely to reduce prices to retain its markets because the collaboration of all the other sellers would no longer be certain. Based on this line of reasoning, Adelman concludes that "every cartel has in time been destroyed by one then some members chiselling and cheating; without the instrument of the multinational companies and the cooperation of the consuming countries, OPEC would be an ordinary cartel. And national companies have always been and still are price cutters."[19]

---

19. Morris Adelman, "Is the Oil Shortage Real?" *Foreign Policy,* 1972.

13. Price Leadership

Another model of oligopolistic behavior is based on the supposition that one of the firms in the industry is the price leader. This form of behavior seems to be quite common in oligopolistic industries, where one or a few firms apparently set the price and the rest follow their lead. Examples of industries that have been characterized by price leadership, according to various studies, are steel, nonferrous alloys, agricultural implements, and retail groceries.[20] Two forms of price leadership are discussed in this section, the dominant-firm model and the barometric-firm model.

The *dominant-firm* model applies to industries in which there is a single large dominant firm in the industry and a number of small firms. It is assumed that the dominant firm sets the price for the industry, but that it lets the small firms sell all they want at that price. Whatever amount the small firms do not supply at that price is supplied by the dominant firm. If this model holds, it is easy to derive the price that the dominant firm will set if it maximizes profits. Since each small firm takes the price as given, it produces the output at which price equals marginal cost. Thus a supply curve for all small firms combined can be drawn by summing horizontally the marginal cost curves of the small firms. This supply curve is labeled SS' in Figure 12.7. The demand curve for the dominant firm can be derived by subtracting the amount supplied by the small firms at each price from the total amount demanded at that price.

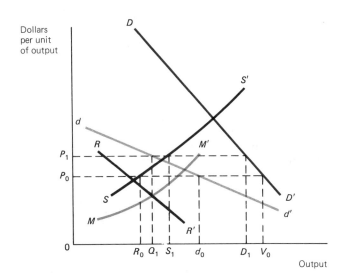

Figure 12.7 The dominant-firm model

20. See A. Kaplan, J. Dirlam, and R. Lanzillotti, *Pricing in Big Business* (Washington, D.C.: Brookings Institution, 1958); M. Colberg, D. Forbush, and G. Whitaker, *Business Economics* (Homewood, Ill.: Irwin, 1964); and C. Wilcox, *Competition and Monopoly in American Industry,* TNEC Monograph 21 (Washington, D.C., 1940).

Consequently, if DD' is the demand curve for the industry's product, the demand curve for the output of the dominant firm, dd', can be determined by finding the horizontal difference at each price between the DD' curve and the SS' curve.

To illustrate the derivation of dd', suppose that the dominant firm sets a price of OP_0. The SS' curve shows that the small firms will supply OR_0, and the DD' curve shows that the total amount demanded will be OV_0. Thus the amount to be supplied by the dominant firm is $OV_0 - OR_0$, which is the quantity on the dd' curve at price OP_0. In other words, Od_0 is set equal to $OV_0 - OR_0$. The process by which the other points on the dd' curve are determined is exactly the same; this procedure is repeated at various price levels.

Given the demand curve for the output of the dominant firm, dd', and the dominant firm's marginal cost curve, MM', it is a simple matter to determine the price and output that will maximize the profits of the dominant firm. The dominant firm's marginal revenue curve, RR', can be derived from the dominant firm's demand curve, dd', in the usual way. The optimal output for the dominant firm is the output, OQ_1, where its marginal cost equals its marginal revenue. This output will be achieved if the dominant firm sets a price of OP_1. The total industry output will be OD_1, and the small firms will supply $OS_1 (= OD_1 - OQ_1)$.

The *barometric-firm* model applies to another form of price leadership in which one firm usually is the first to make changes in price that are generally accepted by other firms in the industry. The barometric firm may not be the largest, or most powerful firm. Instead it is a reasonably accurate interpreter of changes in basic cost and demand conditions in the industry as a whole. According to Kaplan, Dirlam, and Lanzillotti, barometric price leadership frequently occurs as a response to a period of violent price fluctuation and cutthroat competition in an industry, during which many firms suffer and greater stability is widely sought. The gasoline market in Ohio is often cited as an example of barometric price leadership. Standard Oil of Ohio has generally initiated price changes which have been accepted, wholly or in part, by other producers. Studies suggest that Standard Oil of Ohio has acted as a barometer of market conditions, lowering the list price when market conditions have been depressed, and raising it successfully only when demand and cost conditions permit.[21]

14. Cost-Plus Pricing

Empirical studies have often suggested that cost-plus pricing is used by many oligopolists. There are two basic steps in this approach to pricing. First, the firm estimates the cost per unit of output of the product. Since

21. See F. M. Scherer, *Industrial Market Structure and Economic Performance* 2d ed. (Chicago: Rand McNally, 1980). For an influential early article on this topic, see J. Markham, "The Nature and Significance of Price Leadership," *American Economic Review,* December 1951.

this cost will generally vary with output, the firm must base this computation on some assumed output level. Usually, firms seem to use for this purpose some percentage, generally between two-thirds and three-quarters, of capacity. Second, the firm adds a *markup* (generally put in the form of a percentage) to the estimated average cost. This markup is meant to include certain costs that cannot be allocated to any specific product and to provide a return on the firm's investment. The size of the markup depends on the rate of profit that the firm believes it can earn. Some firms have set up a *target return* figure that they hope to earn, which determines the markup. For example, General Electric and General Motors have established a target rate of return of 20 percent.

There is considerable controversy over the extent to which cost-plus pricing is compatible with profit maximization. At first glance, it seems extremely unlikely that this form of pricing can result in the maximization of profits. Indeed, this pricing technique seems naive, since it takes no account, explicitly at least, of the extent or elasticity of demand or of the size of marginal, rather than average, costs. Nevertheless, some economists believe that cost-plus pricing may result in firms, under oligopolistic circumstances, coming close to maximum profits. They argue that cost-plus pricing is used to "stabilize" competition and lessen uncertainty. Moreover, if average variable costs are relatively constant over the relevant range, and if the elasticity of demand remains relatively constant, cost-plus pricing could result in something approaching profit maximization.

Unquestionably, many firms do compute prices on the basis of this sort of procedure. However, a model of this sort is incomplete unless it specifies more precisely the determinants of the size of the markup. Although firms may construct these markups to yield a certain target rate of return, it is clear that these markups frequently do not prevail, since the firm's actual rates of return frequently vary considerably from the target rates of return. The simple cost-plus pricing model is silent on this score.

15. The Long Run and Barriers to Entry

So far we have been concerned primarily with oligopolistic behavior in the short run. In the long run it may be possible for entry or exit of firms to occur. We are already familiar, of course, with the in-migration and out-migration of firms from our discussions of other market structures in Chapters 9 to 11. However, the importance of entry of new firms—and the exit of old firms—in modifying the structure of an industry should be noted once more. In particular, an oligopolistic industry may not be oligopolistic for long if every Tom, Dick and Harry can enter.

Whether or not the industry remains oligopolistic in the face of relatively easy entry depends on the size of the market for the product relative to the optimum size of firm. Above-average profits will attract new firms. If the market is small relative to the optimum size of firm in this industry, the number of firms will remain sufficiently small so that the industry will still be an oligopoly. If the market is large relative to the optimum size of the firm, the number of firms will grow sufficiently large so that the industry will no longer be an oligopoly.

Ease of entry also tends to erode collusive agreements. We saw in Section 10 that existing firms are tempted continually to "cheat" on a collusive agreement, since they can attract business from their rivals by lowering prices. The situation is similar for entrants. They, too, are faced by a relatively elastic demand curve as long as existing firms adhere to collusive agreements to maintain price at its existing level. As long as profits exist in the industry, firms will be tempted to enter and take business away from the collusive group by lowering the price a bit. Once entry of this sort occurs, it becomes more and more difficult to keep a cartel together.

Since it may not be possible to maintain an oligopoly for long if firms can enter the industry, it is important that we discuss the various kinds of barriers to entry. The first barrier to entry, already noted, is smallness of the market relative to the optimum size of firm. For example, suppose that the industry demand curve is DD' in Figure 12.8. Thus, if the industry is composed of two identical duopolists producing a homogeneous product, each firm faces a demand curve of EE', which is half of DD' at each price. On the other hand, if the industry is composed of three identical oligopolists producing a homogeneous product, each firm faces a demand curve of FF', which is one-third of DD' at each price. If the average cost curve of a firm in this industry is as shown in Figure 12.8, only two firms can exist in this industry; once there are two firms, there is an effective barrier to entry.

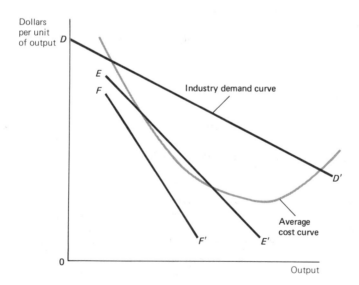

Figure 12.8 Size of market as a barrier to entry

Another barrier to entry is the requirement in some industries that a firm build and maintain a large, complicated, and expensive plant. It is difficult to obtain the funds required to build a modern automobile or steel plant, which may cost hundreds of millions of dollars. Also, skilled personnel must be acquired, distribution channels must be established, and various types of productive and repair facilities must be set up. Because of the scale of the undertaking, as well as for other reasons, there has been little entry in recent years in industries like steel and autos.

Still another barrier to entry is the unavailability of natural resources. This factor is often cited in the case of nickel, sulfur, diamonds, and bauxite. A further barrier to entry is the existence of important patents. The holder of these patents, which may relate to the product itself or key processes by which the product is made, may license only a few firms to produce the product. Moreover, the firms in an industry may allow one another to use their patents but refuse to permit any outsider to use them. Finally, the government is sometimes responsible for other important barriers to entry. For example, taxicabs and buses must obtain franchises, and local licensing laws may be used to limit the number of plumbers, barbers, and so on.

In some oligopolistic industries it is sometimes asserted that firms set price so as to bar entry. This is called *limit pricing.* A limit price is a price that discourages or prevents entry. Firms that practice limit pricing give up short-run profits in order to earn larger longer-term profits. The limit price must lie somewhere below the price that would maximize profits if entry were impossible regardless of price. The exact level of the limit price will depend on how difficult it is to enter the industry. Of course, the firms already in the industry must agree, at least within certain bounds, concerning the advisability and proper level of a limit price.

16. Nonprice Competition

In many oligopolistic industries, firms tend to use advertising and variation in product characteristics, more than price, as competitive weapons. They seem to view price cutting as a dangerous tactic, since it can start a price war that may have grave consequences. On the other hand, advertising and product variation are viewed as less risky ways of wooing customers away from competitors.

When a firm advertises, it attempts to shift the demand curve for its product to the right. An effective advertising campaign will make it possible for a firm to sell more at the same price. Firms use advertising to differentiate their product from those of their competitors. In this way customers may be induced to stick with a particular brand name, even though the products of all firms in the industry are much the same. For example, various brands of cigarettes are quite similar, although not identical. The cigarette industry has spent over $200 million a year on

Example 12.2   Oligopoly and the Antitrust Laws

In the United States agreements to fix prices and restrict output are illegal. Section 1 of the Sherman Antitrust Act says, "Every contract, combination . . . , or conspiracy in restraint of trade or commerce among the several states, or with foreign nations, is hereby declared to be illegal." (a) Does this mean that oligopoly is illegal? (b) Is any formal agreement among firms necessary to constitute an unlawful conspiracy? (c) For decades, the Big Three of the cigarette industry—American Tobacco, Liggett and Myers, and Reynolds—followed a pattern of setting the same price. Even at the pit of the Great Depression, the other two firms matched a price increase by Reynolds. Also, they behaved in such a way as to make it likely that each would pay much the same price for tobacco. Can such parallel action be used in court as convincing circumstantial evidence of illegal collusion? (d) Is mere recognition of mutual interdependence and parallel behavior by a group of firms sufficient to make conspiracy charges against them stick?

Solution

(a) No, oligopoly by itself is perfectly legal. (b) No. In its 1946 decision in *American Tobacco Co. et al.* v. *U. S.,* the Supreme Court said, "No formal agreement is necessary to constitute an unlawful conspiracy. . . . Where the circumstances are such as to warrant a jury in finding that the conspirators had a unity of purpose or a common design and understanding, or a meeting of minds in an unlawful arrangement, the conclusion that a conspiracy is established is justified." (c) Yes, in the *Tobacco* case cited above, a jury found the cigarette companies guilty of price-fixing and other Sherman Act violations on the basis of such evidence. Moreover, the Court of Appeals, in reviewing the case, found this circumstantial evidence sufficent to sustain the charges. (d) No. As the Supreme Court said in its 1954 decision in *Theater Enterprises* v. *Paramount Film Distributing Corporation,* "This court has never held that proof of parallel business behavior conclusively established agreement or, phrased differently, that such behavior itself constitutes a Sherman Act offense."*

* For further discussion, see F. M. Scherer, *Industrial Market Structure and Economic Performance,* 2d ed. (Chicago: Rand McNally, 1980).

advertising to impress their brand names, and whatever differences exist among brands, on the consumer.[22]

Sometimes advertising expenditures only have the effect of raising

22. Other industries that spend very heavily on advertising are department stores, retail food stores, drugs and medicines, and beer. See L. Telser, "Advertising and Cigarettes," *Journal of Business,* 1963; and W. Comanor and T. Wilson, *Advertising and Market Power* (Cambridge, Mass.: Harvard University Press, 1974).

the costs of the entire industry, since one firm's advertising campaign causes other firms to increase their advertising. The total market for the industry's product may not increase in response to the increased advertising, and the effects on the sales of individual firms may be small, since the effects of the advertising may cancel out. However, once every firm has increased its advertising expenditures, no single firm can reduce them to their former size without losing sales. Thus the cost curves—including both production and selling costs—of the firms in the industry are pushed upward.

Frequently a firm varies the characteristics of its product as well as advertises in order to differentiate its product from those of its competitors. Like advertising, one purpose of varying the firm's product is to manipulate the firm's demand curve. Of course, changes in product, like other competitive tactics, often result in retaliatory moves by competitors. Successful changes in product design or product quality tend to be imitated by competitors, although with a lag of varying length. The costs of competition through style and quality of product can be very great. For example, the automobile industry has been engaged for many years in intense competition of this sort; the cost of model changes during the 1950s was approximately $5 billion per year.[23]

17. Effects of Oligopoly

This chapter has taken up some of the oligopoly models that economists have constructed. Since there is no agreement that any of these models is an adequate general representation of oligopolistic behavior, it is difficult to estimate the effects of an oligopolistic market structure on price, output, and profits. Nevertheless, a few things can be said.

First, the models we have discussed usually indicate that price will be higher than under perfect competition. The difference between the oligopoly price and the perfectly competitive price will depend, of course, on the number of firms in the industry and the ease of entry. The larger the number of firms and the easier it is to enter the industry, the closer the oligopoly price will be to the perfectly competitive level. Also, prices will tend to be more inflexible under oligopolistic conditions than under perfect competition.

Second, if the demand curve is the same under oligopoly as under perfect competition, it also follows that output will be less under oligopoly than under perfect competition. However, it is not always reasonable to assume that the demand curve is the same under oligopoly as under perfect competition, since the large expenditures for advertising and product variation that are incurred by some oligopolies may tend to shift the demand curve to the right. Consequently in some cases both

23. F. Fisher, Z. Griliches, and C. Kaysen, "The Cost of Automobile Model Changes since 1949," *Journal of Political Economy,* October 1962. For more recent data, see L. White, *The Automobile Industry Since 1945* (Cambridge, Mass.: Harvard University Press, 1971).

price and output may tend to be higher under oligopoly than under perfect competition.

Third, we have already noted that oligopolistic industries tend to spend large amounts on advertising and product variation. The use of some resources for these purposes is certainly worthwhile, since advertising provides buyers with information, and product variation allows greater freedom of choice. Whether or not oligopolies spend too much for these purposes is by no means obvious. However, there is a widespread feeling among economists, based largely on empirical studies (and hunch), that in some oligopolistic industries such expenditures have been expanded beyond the levels that are socially optimal.[24]

Fourth, one would expect on the basis of the models presented in this chapter that the profits earned by oligopolists should be higher, on the average, than the profits earned by perfectly competitive firms. This conclusion is supported by statistical evidence. For example, Joe Bain, of the University of California, has found that firms in industries in which the largest few firms had a high proportion of total sales tended to have higher rates of return than firms in industries in which the largest few firms had a small proportion of total sales.[25]

18. Summary

Oligopoly is characterized by a small number of firms and a great deal of interdependence, actual and perceived, among them. A good example of an oligopoly is the American oil industry, where a small number of firms accounts for the bulk of the industry's capacity. Oligopolistic industries may be marked by independent action or collusion. Two early models based on the supposition that firms act independently are the Cournot and Edgeworth models, both of which make naïve assumptions concerning the ability (or inability) of firms to learn. Somewhat more realistic models are those put forth by Chamberlin and Sweezy. An interesting development of the postwar period was the theory of games, which enriched oligopoly theory considerably, although it has not yet lived up to early expectations. One can structure formerly intractable problems and think about them in terms of game theory, but in its present state game theory cannot be used to derive specific predictions of the behavior of oligopolists.

24. Note that we are not talking here about expenditures on relatively fundamental research and development, when we talk about product variation. A great deal of existing product variation is based on relatively superficial differences among products. For some discussion of research and development, see Chapter 18.

25. J. Bain, "Relation of Profit Rate to Industry Concentration: American Manufacturing, 1936–1940," *Quarterly Journal of Economics,* August 1951. However, there has been much disagreement on this score. See L. Weiss, "The Concentration-Profits Relationship and Antitrust," in H. Goldschmid, H. M. Mann, and J. F. Weston, *Industrial Concentration: The New Learning* (Boston: Little Brown, 1974); and J. Kwoka, "The Effect of Market Share Distribution on Industry Performance," *Review of Economics and Statistics,* February 1979.

Conditions in oligopolistic industries tend to promote collusion, since the number of firms is small and firms recognize their interdependence. The advantages to be derived by the firms from collusion seem obvious: increased profits, decreased uncertainty, and a better opportunity to control the entry of new firms. However, collusive arrangements are often hard to maintain, since once a collusive agreement is made, any of the firms can increase its profits by "cheating" on the agreement. Also, such arrangements are illegal in the United States. An interesting example of collusion took place in the electrical equipment industry during the fifties. In addition, we looked at the operation of the OPEC cartel, which has played so important a role in the oil crisis of the 1970s and 1980s.

Another model of oligopolistic behavior is based on the supposition that one of the firms in the industry is a price leader, either because it is a dominant firm or a barometric firm. Still other models assume that oligopolists use cost-plus pricing or limit pricing. The effects of oligopoly are difficult to predict, but it appears that price and profits will be higher than under perfect competition. Also, oligopolists engage in nonprice competition, perhaps excessively in some cases from the point of view of social welfare.

QUESTIONS AND PROBLEMS

1. Suppose that two firms are producers of spring water, which can be obtained at zero cost. The marginal revenue curve for their combined output is

    $MR = 10 - 2Q$,

    where MR is marginal revenue and Q is the number of gallons per hour of spring water sold by both together. If the two producers act in accord with Chamberlin's model, how much will be their combined output? Why?

2. Five men play poker every Thursday. A dime is taken out of every pot by the owner of the apartment where they play. The owner of the apartment is not one of the players. Is this a zero-sum game?

3. Suppose that a cartel is formed by three firms. Their total cost functions are as follows:

Units of output	TOTAL COST		
	Firm 1	Firm 2	Firm 3
0	20	25	15
1	25	35	22
2	35	50	32
3	50	80	47
4	80	120	77
5	120	160	117

    If the cartel decides to produce 11 units of output, how should the output be distributed among the three firms, if they want to minimize cost?

4. A firm chooses strategy L with probability $\frac{1}{6}$ and strategy M with probability $\frac{5}{6}$. If it chooses strategy L, the gain is $10 million. If it chooses strategy M, the

gain is $6 million. Is this a mixed strategy? What is the expected value to the firm?

5. A firm estimates its average total cost to be $10 per unit of output when it produces 10,000 units, which it regards as 80 percent of capacity. Its goal is to earn 20 percent on its total investment, which is $250,000. If it uses cost-plus pricing, what price should it set? Can it be sure of selling 10,000 units if it sets this price?

6. Describe how advertising expenses can be an important barrier to entry in some industries. What are some industries where this is the case? Describe how large research and development expenses can be an important barrier to entry. What are some industries where this is the case?

7. Suppose the pay-off matrix is as given below. What strategy will firm I choose? What strategy will firm II choose?

POSSIBLE STRATEGIES FOR FIRM I	POSSIBLE STRATEGIES FOR FIRM II		
	1	*2*	*3*
	[*Profits for firm I, or losses for firm II, in millions of dollars*]		
A	10	9	11
B	8	8.5	10

8. According to the Senate Subcommittee on Antitrust and Monopoly, there has been a long history of international cartels that have controlled the price and output of quinine. What do you think the effects of the cartels have been? Do you think that such cartels should be broken up? If so, how can individual governments go about doing this?

9. Suppose that you are on the board of directors of a firm which is the dominant firm in the industry. That is, it lets all of the other firms, which are much smaller, sell all they want at the existing price. In other words, the smaller firms act as perfect competitors. Your firm, on the other hand, sets the price, which the other firms accept. The demand curve for your industry's product is $P = 300 - Q$, where P is the product's price (in dollars per unit) and Q is the total quantity demanded. The total amount supplied by the other firms is equal to Q_r, where $Q_r = 49\ P$. If your firm's marginal cost curve is $2.96\ Q_b$, where Q_b is the output of your firm, at what output level should you operate to maximize profit? What price should you charge? How much will the industry as a whole produce at this price? (Q, Q_b, and Q_r are expressed in millions of units.)

10. According to the *Wall Street Journal,* "The climate in which the individuals and companies in the heavy electrical equipment industry operated was loaded with potentials for trouble [i.e., with potentials for illegal collusion]." What characteristics of this industry made it likely that collusion might arise? What other industries have these characteristics? How difficult is it to determine the amount and extent of collusion among the firms in an industry?

SELECTED REFERENCES

FEDERAL TRADE COMMISSION. "The Petroleum Industry: Structure and Conduct." Reprinted in E. Mansfield, *Microeconomics: Selected Readings,* 4th ed. New York: Norton, 1982.

FEDERAL TRADE COMMISSION. "Pricing Behavior in the American, European, and Japanese Steel Industries." Reprinted in *Microeconomics: Selected Readings.*

FELLNER, WILLIAM. *Competition Among the Few.* New York: Knopf, 1949.

MANSFIELD, EDWIN. *Monopoly Power and Economic Performance.* 4th ed. New York: Norton, 1978.

MODIGLIANI, FRANCO. "New Developments on the Oligopoly Front." *Journal of Political Economy,* June, 1958.

SCHERER, F. M. *Industrial Market Structure and Economic Performance.* 2d ed. Chicago: Rand McNally, 1980.

SENATE SUBCOMMITTEE ON ANTITRUST AND MONOPOLY. "Quinine: An International Cartel." Reprinted in *Microeconomics: Selected Readings.*

SHUBIK, MARTIN. *Strategy and Market Structure.* New York: Wiley, 1959.

13 Price and Employment of Inputs under Perfect Competition

1. Incomes: Distribution and Inequality

No one needs to be convinced that income is an interesting topic. Both a struggling member of the working class and a dowager whose labor is confined to endorsing dividend checks recognize the significance of income. Moreover, no one has to be intimately acquainted with government statistics to know that there are enormous differences in the amounts of money that people make. For example, a stroll through midtown Manhattan will provide plenty of evidence of abject poverty and great affluence existing almost side by side.

Why do these differences in income exist? Why is it that one person receives so much more income than another? As we pointed out in Chapter 1, a person's income depends partly on the quantity of resources owned. Some people own lots of land; others own none. Some people have unusual skills and talents; others do not. Some people own equipment and factories; others own little beyond their clothes (and even their clothes may not be completely paid for).

But the quantity of resources a person owns is by no means the only determinant of income. The other important determinant is the price received for the services of each type of resource. For example, if a man is a landowner with 100 acres of land, he will receive $10,000 per year if the price he obtains from the farmers who work his land is $100 per acre (annually); however, if the price goes down to $50 per acre, he will receive only $5,000 per year. Similarly, a laborer's income will obviously depend on the price received for the services performed.

Thus, to understand why differences in income exist, we must understand why the prices of the services of each type of resource are what they are. We must ask questions like: Why is the wage rate for physicians frequently in the neighborhood of $100 an hour while the wage rate for secretaries is often about $7 an hour? Why is the wage rate for mathematicians so much higher than it was several decades ago? Why is it that land of one kind yields a higher financial return than land of another kind?

In other words, we must try to understand the determinants of input prices. In a free-enterprise economy, input prices are important determinants of the incomes of consumers. In the typical household, the breadwinner sells his or her services to a firm; the wage that the worker receives is an input price from the viewpoint of the firm. Wages are a cost to the firm but to the worker they are an important determinant of income, which (as we saw in Chapter 3) helps to determine the worker's choice of consumers' goods. The distribution of income among individuals in the economy is determined to a considerable extent by the configuration of input prices.

2. Price and Employment of Inputs

The previous four chapters were concerned with the analysis of the pricing and output of consumers' goods. We turn now to the determinants of the price and employment of inputs, which will be the topic of the present chapter as well as Chapter 14. This chapter assumes that there is perfect competition in both commodity and input markets; the next chapter relaxes these assumptions.

At the outset, two points should be noted. First, a good deal of the theory presented in the previous four chapters is applicable to inputs as well as commodities; for example, the price of inputs as well as commodities is determined by the interaction of supply and demand. However, the demand for inputs differs in important respects from the demand for commodities, and the supply of inputs differs in important respects from the supply of commodities. These differences stem largely from the fact that inputs are demanded by firms, not consumers; and that some important inputs, like labor, are supplied by consumers, not firms.

Second, in the nineteenth century it was customary for economists to classify inputs into three categories: land, labor, and capital. The theory of input pricing was therefore a theory of the distribution of income among landowners, wage earners, and capitalists, three important economic and social classes. (The incomes of these classes were rent, wages, and profits, respectively.) A disadvantage of this simple classification of inputs is that each category contains such an enormous amount of variation. For example, labor includes the services of a Nobel-Prize-winning biochemist and the services of a secretary whose typing is strictly hunt-and-peck. In this chapter we shall seldom use this tripartite classification;[1] instead we shall present our results in general terms so that the user of the model can classify inputs to fit any particular problem.

3. Profit Maximization and Input Employment

Fortunately, we do not have to start from scratch in constructing a model of input pricing and utilization under perfect competition. We learned a great deal that is relevant and useful in Chapters 7 and 8 when we analyzed the firm's decisions concerning input combinations and output level. A moment's reflection should convince you that, when we determined how much the firm would produce and the input combination it would use to produce this output, we in effect determined how much of each input the firm would demand under various sets of circumstances. This, of course, is an important beginning.

To make sure that the implications of our findings in Chapter 7 are clear, we shall review a few of these findings. In particular, recall the way in which a firm combines inputs in order to minimize costs. We showed that the firm will pick a combination of inputs where the ratio of each input's marginal product to its price is equal. That is, it will set

$$\frac{MP_x}{P_x} = \frac{MP_y}{P_y} = \cdots = \frac{MP_z}{P_z} \qquad\qquad 13.1$$

where MP_x is the marginal product of input x, P_x is the price of input x, MP_y is the marginal product of input y, P_y is the price of input y, and so on. If Equation 13.1 does not hold, the firm can always reduce costs by changing the utilization of certain inputs. For example, if the marginal product of a unit of input x is 2 units of output, the price of a unit of input x is \$1, the marginal product of a unit of input y is 6 units of output, and the price of a unit of input y is \$2, the firm can reduce its costs by using 1 unit less of input x—which reduces output by 2 units and cost by \$1—and by using $\frac{1}{3}$ unit more of input y—which increases output by 2 units and cost by \$0.67. This substitution of input y for input x has no effect on output but reduces the cost by \$0.33.

Going a step further, it can be shown that, if a firm minimizes cost, each of the ratios in Equation 13.1 equals the reciprocal of the firm's marginal cost. In other words,

$$\frac{P_x}{MP_x} = \frac{P_y}{MP_y} = \cdots = \frac{P_z}{MP_z} = MC \qquad\qquad 13.2$$

where MC is its marginal cost. To prove this, consider input x. What is the cost of producing an extra unit of output if this extra unit of output is achieved by increasing the utilization of input x, while holding constant the utilization of other inputs? Since an extra unit of input x results in

---

1. Toward the end of the nineteenth century, a fourth "factor of production"—or type of input—was recognized: entrepreneurship. Then profits were viewed as the return to the entrepreneur, and interest was viewed as the return to the owner of capital.

MP_x extra units of output, $(1/MP_x)$ units of input x will result in one unit of extra output. Since $(1/MP_x)$ units of input x will cost $(1/MP_x)P_x$, $P_x \div MP_x$ equals marginal cost. This same type of reasoning can be used for any input, not just input x, with the consequence that Equation 13.2 holds.[2]

As an illustration, suppose that there are only two inputs, input x and input y. Suppose that the marginal product of a unit of input x is 2 units of output, the price of a unit of input x is \$1, the marginal product of a unit of input y is 4 units of output, and the price of a unit of input y is \$2. The extra cost of producing an extra unit of output, if the extra production occurs by increasing the use of input x, is \$0.50, since an extra $\frac{1}{2}$ unit of input x—at \$1 a unit—will result in an extra unit of output. Similarly, the extra cost of producing an extra unit of output, if the extra production comes about by increasing the use of input y, is \$0.50, since an extra $\frac{1}{4}$ unit of input y—at \$2 a unit—will result in an extra unit of output. Thus the ratio of the price of each input to its marginal product equals marginal cost, which is \$0.50.

Going another step further, the firm, if it maximizes profit, must be operating at a point at which marginal cost equals marginal revenue.

2. Let $Q = f(X_1, \cdots, X_n)$, where Q is the firm's output, X_1 is the amount of the first input used by the firm, X_2 is the amount of the second input used by the firm, and so on. To minimize cost subject to the constraint that output equals Q^*, we form the Lagrangian function

$$L = \sum_{i=1}^{n} P_i X_i - \lambda[f(X_1, \cdots, X_n) - Q^*]$$

where P_i is the price of the ith input and λ is a Lagrange multiplier. Setting $\partial L/\partial X_i = 0$, we have

$$P_i - \frac{\lambda \partial f}{\partial X_i} = 0 \qquad\qquad (i = 1, \cdots, n)$$

Or

$$P_i \div \frac{\partial f}{\partial X_i} = \lambda \qquad\qquad (i = 1, \cdots, n)$$

The point in the text is that λ equals marginal cost. To prove this, note that

$$dC = \sum_{i=1}^{n} P_i dX_i$$

$$dQ = \sum_{i=1}^{n} \frac{\partial f}{\partial X_i} dX_i$$

where dC is a small change in cost, dQ is a small change in output, and dX_i is a small change in X_i. Since marginal cost equals $dC \div dQ$, it follows that marginal cost equals

$$\frac{\sum_{i=1}^{n} P_i dX_i}{\sum_{i=1}^{n} (\partial f/\partial X_i) dX_i} = \frac{\sum_{i=1}^{n} \lambda(\partial f/\partial X_i) dX_i}{\sum_{i=1}^{n} (\partial f/\partial X_i) dX_i} = \lambda$$

This proves the point in the text.

Thus it follows that

$$\frac{P_x}{MP_x} = \frac{P_y}{MP_y} = \cdots = \frac{P_z}{MP_z} = MR \qquad \text{13.3}$$

where MR is the firm's marginal revenue. Rearranging terms,

$$MP_x \cdot MR = P_x \qquad \text{13.4a}$$
$$MP_y \cdot MR = P_y \qquad \text{13.4b}$$
$$\vdots$$
$$MP_z \cdot MR = P_z \qquad \text{13.4c}$$

Thus we conclude that the profit-maximizing firm employs each input in an amount such that the input's marginal product multiplied by the firm's marginal revenue equals the input's price. This result, as we shall see in the following section, provides the basis for the firm's demand curve for an input.

4. The Firm's Demand Curve: The Case of One Variable Input

Our first step in analyzing the demand for an input is to consider the demand curve of an individual firm for an input, assuming that this input is the only variable input in the firm's production process. In other words, the quantities of all other inputs are fixed. This assumption is relaxed in the next section. The demand curve of a firm for this input— call it input x—shows the quantity of input x that the firm will demand at each possible price of input x. Assuming that the firm maximizes its profits, it will demand that amount of input x at which the value of the extra output produced by an extra unit of input x is equal to the price of input x. This is the meaning of Equation 13.4a.

To make this more concrete, suppose that we know the firm's production function, from which we deduce that the marginal product of input x (at each level of utilization of input x) is as shown in Table 13.1. Suppose that the price of the product is $3. Since the product market is perfectly competitive, the marginal revenue is also $3. The value to the firm of the extra output resulting from its increasing its utilization of input x by one unit is shown in the last column of Table 13.1. This is called the *value of the marginal product* of input x, and equals $MP_x \cdot P$, where P is the price of the product. Since $P = MR$ in perfect competition, the value of the marginal product is the left-hand side of Equation 13.4a.

How many units of input x should the firm use if input x costs $10 a unit? A one-unit increase in the utilization of input x adds to the firm's revenues the amount shown in the last column of Table 13.1, and it adds $10 to the firm's costs. (Since the input markets are perfectly competitive, the firm cannot influence the price of any input.) Thus the firm should increase its utilization of input x as long as the increase in revenues exceeds the increase in costs; in other words, as long as the figure in

Table 13.1   Value of marginal product of input x

Quantity of x	Marginal product*	Value of Marginal product* (dollars)
3	8	24
4	7	21
5	6	18
6	5	15
7	4	12
8	3	9
9	2	6

* The figures pertain to the interval between the indicated quantity of input x and one unit less than the indicated quantity of input x.

the last column of Table 13.1 exceeds $10. For example, if the firm is using 5 units of input x, the use of an extra unit will increase revenues by $15 and increase costs by $10; consequently, the extra unit should be used. What about adding still another unit? If the firm is using 6 units of input x, the use of an extra unit will increase revenue by $12 and increase costs by $10; thus it too should be added. Increases in the utilization of input x are profitable up to 7 units; beyond this point, an extra unit of input x increases costs more than revenues. Thus the firm should use 7 units of input x.

The optimal number of units of input x is the number at which the value of the marginal product of input x equals the price of input x.[3] This, of course, is just another way of stating the result in Equation 13.4a, since under these circumstances the value of the marginal product of input x is equal to the left-hand side of the equation and the price of input x is the right-hand side of the equation.

If the firm demands the optimal amount of input x at each price of input x, its demand schedule for input x must be the value-of-marginal-product schedule in the last column of Table 13.1. For example, if the price of input x is between $6 and $9, the firm will demand 8 units of input x; if the price of input x is between $9 and $12, the firm will demand 7 units of input x. Thus the firm's demand curve for input x is the value-of-marginal-product curve, which shows the value of input x's marginal product at each quantity of input x used. This curve will slope downward and to the right, because it is proportional to the curve showing the input's marginal productivity.

3. This assumes that the quantity of the input can be varied continuously, which is often the case. However, it is not the case in Table 13.1. Since only integer values can be used, according to Table 13.1, this rule must be changed somewhat here. In this case, the optimal number of units of input x is the largest integer at which the value of the marginal product of input x is greater than or equal to the price of input x.

5. The Firm's Demand Curve: The Case of Several Variable Inputs

Suppose now that the firm uses a number of inputs that can be varied in quantity and input x is only one of them. Under these circumstances, the firm's demand curve for input x is no longer the value-of-marginal-product curve. This is because a change in the price of input x will result in a change in the quantities of the other variable inputs used, and these changes in the quantities of the other variable inputs used will affect the quantity of input x used.

As an example, suppose that the price of input x is initially $10 and the quantity of input x used is 100 units. Holding constant the use of other inputs, suppose that the value-of-marginal-product curve is $V_1 V_1'$ in Figure 13.1. If none of the other inputs were variable, this would be the demand curve for input x. In fact, however, a number of other inputs are variable. Suppose that the price of input x falls to $6. What will happen to the quantity of input x demanded by the firm? Since the value of its marginal product exceeds its new price, the firm will tend to expand its use. But the increase in its use will shift the value-of-marginal-product curves of other inputs. For example, if another variable input is complementary to input x, its value-of-marginal-product curve will shift to the right. These shifts in the value-of-marginal-product curves of other variable inputs will result in changes in the amounts used of them. And the changes in the amounts used of other inputs will in turn shift the value-of-marginal-product curve of input x.

When all of these effects have occurred, the firm will be on another value-of-marginal-product curve for input x, say $V_2 V_2'$ in Figure 13.1. And the amount demanded of input x will be such that the value of its marginal product will be equal to its new price. Thus the firm will de-

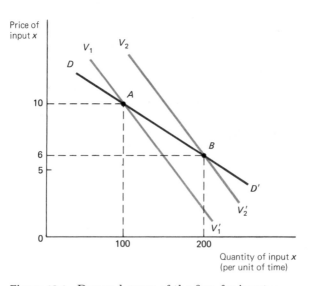

Figure 13.1 Demand curve of the firm for input x

mand 200 units of input x. Points A and B are both on the firm's demand curve for input x. Other points can be determined in a similar fashion; the complete demand curve is DD'. It can be shown that all demand curves of this type slope down and to the right, as would be expected.[4]

6. The Market Demand Curve

When we derived a market demand curve for a commodity in Chapter 5, we summed horizontally over the demand curves of individual consumers of the commodity. At first glance it may seem that we can derive the market demand curve for an input by simply summing horizontally over the demand curves of individual firms for the input. Although this would provide a first approximation, it would not yield the correct result because it neglects the effect of changes in the input price on the product price.

Each firm's demand curve for the input is based on the supposition that the firm's decisions cannot affect the price of its output. For example, in Table 13.1, the firm assumes that the price of its product will be $3, regardless of how it alters its utilization of input x in response to changes in the price of input x. This is a perfectly reasonable assumption for the firm to make, because it is only a very small portion of the industry. But

---

4. In passing, we should note that economists of the past were bothered by the question of whether or not, if each input was paid the value of its marginal product, the total amount paid by firms for inputs would be equal to the firm's revenues. Much of the discussion of this question was beside the point, and need not concern us here (see P. Samuelson, *Foundations of Economic Analysis* [Cambridge, Mass.: Harvard University Press, 1947], pp. 81–87). However, it may be worth noting that, if the production function exhibits constant returns to scale, Euler's theorem states that the total physical output of a firm will be identically equal to the sum of the amount of each input used multiplied by the input's marginal product:

$$Q = X_1 MP_1 + X_2 MP_2 + \cdots + X_n MP_n \qquad \text{13.5}$$

where Q is the firm's output level, X_1 is the amount of the first input used by the firm, X_2 is the amount of the second input used by the firm, X_n is the amount of the nth input used by the firm, MP_1 is the marginal product of the first input, MP_2 is the marginal product of the second input, MP_n is the marginal product of the nth input, and n is the number of inputs used by the firm. Thus, multiplying both sides of Equation 13.5 by P, the price of the product, we have

$$PQ = X_1 P(MP_1) + X_2 P(MP_2) + \cdots + X_n P(MP_n) \qquad \text{13.6}$$

If each input is paid the value of its marginal product, if follows that

$$PQ = X_1 P_1 + X_2 P_2 + \cdots + X_n P_n \qquad \text{13.7}$$

where P_1 is the price of the first input, P_2 is the price of the second input, and P_n is the price of the nth input. The left-hand side of Equation 13.7 is the firm's receipts. The right-hand side of Equation 13.7 is the total amount paid by the firm to inputs. Thus, if there are constant returns to scale, the firm's total receipts will be identically equal to the amount necessary to pay all inputs the value of their marginal products. Finally, note that Equation 13.7 is an identity under these circumstances. In general, Equation 13.7 holds as a condition of long-run competitive equilibrium (see Samuelson, ibid.).

this is not the situation underlying the market demand curve. The market demand curve shows the total amount of the input demanded at various possible prices of the input. Thus it shows the effect of changes in input price on the utilization of the input *when all firms in the industry respond at the same time.*

Suppose that the price of input *x* decreases substantially. This will result in increased utilization of input *x* by all firms in the industry and in increased output by all members of the industry. Although the increased output by any single firm cannot affect the price of the industry's product, the combined expansion of output by all firms results in a decrease in the price of the product. This decrease in the price of the product shifts each firm's value-of-marginal-product curve, and consequently it shifts each firm's demand curve for input *x*.

To derive the market demand curve for input *x,* suppose that its initial price is $8 and that each firm in the market is in equilibrium, with its demand curve for input *x* being *dd'* in Figure 13.2. Each firm uses *Oq* units of input *x*. Multiplying *Oq* by the number of firms in the market we get *OQ*, the total amount taken off the market at a price of $8. Thus *A* is a point on the market demand curve.

Suppose that the price of input *x* falls to $6. Each firm will increase its use of input *x* and increase output, with the consequence that the price of the product will fall and the individual firm demand curves for input *x* will shift toward *ee'*. When all adjustments have been made, each firm will be using *Or* units of input *x*. This is less than the *Os* units that each would have used if it had remained on the demand curve, *dd'*. Multiplying *Or* by the number of firms in the market, we get *OR*, the total amount taken off the market at a price of $6. Thus *B* is another point on the market demand curve. Other points on the market demand curve can be obtained in similar fashion; the complete market demand curve for input *x* is *DD'*.   The Market Demand Curve   371

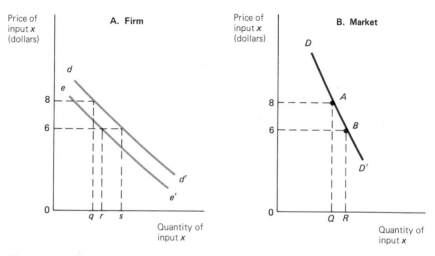

Figure 13.2   Derivation of market demand curve for input *x*

7. Determinants of the Price Elasticity of Demand for an Input

In Chapter 5 we pointed out that, in the case of commodities, the price elasticity of market demand varies enormously, the quantity demanded of some commodities being very sensitive to price changes, and the quantity demanded of other commodities being quite insensitive to price changes. This is true of inputs as well. The quantity demanded of some inputs is very sensitive to price changes, whereas the quantity demanded of other inputs is not at all sensitive to price changes. Why is this the case? What determines whether the price elasticity of demand for a particular input will be high or low? Several rules are important.

First, the more easily other inputs can be substituted for a certain input, say input x, the more price elastic is the demand for input x. This certainly makes sense. If the technologies of the firms using input x allow these firms to substitute other inputs readily for input x, a small increase in the price of input x may result in a substantial decrease in its use. But if these firms cannot substitute other inputs readily for input x, a large increase in the price of input x may result in only a small decrease in its use.

Second, the larger the price elasticity of demand for the product that input x helps to produce, the larger the price elasticity of demand for input x. This, too, seems clear enough. The demand for an input is prompted by the demand for the product it produces; in other words, the demand for an input is a *derived demand*. The greater the price elasticity of demand of the product, the more sensitive is the output of the commodity to changes in its price that occur in response to changes in the price of input x.

Third, the greater the price elasticity of supply of other inputs, the greater is the price elasticity of demand for input x. The supply curve for an input is the relationship between the amount of the input that is supplied and the input's price. The price elasticity of supply of an input is the percentage increase in the quantity supplied of the input resulting from a 1 percent increase in the price of the input.[5] Thus, if small increases in price bring forth large increases in the quantity of other inputs supplied, this will mean that the demand for input x will be more price elastic than if large increases in price are required to bring forth small increases in the quantity supplied of other inputs.

Finally, the price elasticity of demand for an input is likely to be greater in the long run than in the short run. The reasoning here is like that underlying the similar proposition in Chapter 5 concerning the demand for commodities. Basically, the point is that it takes time to adjust fully to a price change. For example, if the price of skilled labor increases, it may not be possible for many plants to reduce very greatly the quantity of skilled labor demanded in the short run, since their plants are built to use fairly rigidly defined amounts of this input. But in

---

5. More accurately, the price elasticity of supply is $dQ/dP \div Q/P$, where Q is the quantity supplied of the input and P is its price.

the long run, firms can build new plants to reduce their utilization of skilled labor.[6]

8. The Market Supply Curve

Under perfect competition, the supply of an input to an individual firm is infinitely elastic. In other words, the firm can buy all it wants without influencing the price of the input. When we consider the market supply curve, which is the relationship between the price of the input and the total amount of the input supplied in the entire market, it is often untrue that the supply is infinitely elastic. In many cases, the total amount of the input supplied in the entire market will increase only if the price of the input is increased. Indeed, in some cases it is alleged that the market supply curve is perfectly inelastic, that is, the total amount of the input supplied in the entire market is fixed and unresponsive to the price of the input.

There is, of course, no contradiction between the assertion that the supply of an input *to an individual firm* is perfectly elastic under perfect competition and the assertion that the *market* supply curve may not be perfectly elastic under perfect competition. For example, arable land might be available to any one farmer in as great an amount as he could possibly use at a given price; yet the aggregate amount of arable land available to all farmers may increase little with increases in the price per acre. The situation is similar to the sale of commodities: We saw in Chapter 9 that any firm under perfect competition believes that it can sell all it wants at the existing price; yet the total amount of a commodity sold in a given market can usually be increased only by reducing price.

There is sometimes a tendency to underestimate the extent to which the market supply of an input will be increased in response to an increase in the price of the input. For example, it is sometimes argued that the nation is provided with a certain amount of land and mineral resources, and that there is no way to change these amounts. For this reason, it is assumed that their market supply is perfectly inelastic, the available supply being completely unresponsive to price. But this can be quite wrong. For present purposes, what is important is the amount of land and mineral resources that is used, not the amount in existence. A large increase in price generally will increase the amount of these resources in use. This will occur because a higher price will result in more exploration

---

6. Another proposition that is frequently advanced is that the demand for an input will be less elastic if the payments to this input are a small, rather than a large, proportion of the total cost of the product. There is good deal of truth in this proposition, but it does not always hold. See M. Bronfenbrenner, "Note on the Elasticity of Derived Demand," *Oxford Economic Papers,* October 1961, as well as the accompanying note by J. Hicks.

For a recent study of the price elasticity of demand for labor, see K. Clark and R. Freeman, "How Elastic is the Demand for Labor?" *Review of Economics and Statistics,* November 1980.

for resources, in the reopening of high-cost mines and farms, and in the irrigation and upgrading of poorer land.

9. The Market Supply Curve: The Backward-Bending Case

Most inputs are *intermediate goods,* goods that are bought from other business firms. For example, an important input in the electric power industry is coal, which is bought from the coal industry. The supply curve for inputs of this kind is already familiar, and there is no need to discuss once again the determinants of the nature and shape of the market supply curve in these cases.

However, not all inputs are supplied by business firms. One of the most significant inputs—labor—is provided by individuals. (In addition, individuals provide other inputs like savings.) When individuals supply an input like labor, they are supplying something that they themselves can use, since the time that they do not work can be used for leisure activities. Thus sellers of these inputs want to keep some of them for themselves. And the amount of these inputs that is supplied to firms depends on the quantities of these inputs that are produced and the quantities that the suppliers want to keep for themselves.

In Chapter 9, we saw that the market supply curve for inputs supplied by business firms will generally slope upward and to the right. In other words, higher prices generally are required to bring forth an increased supply. An interesting feature of the market supply function for inputs supplied by individuals is that it, unlike the supply function for inputs supplied by business firms, may be backward-bending. That is, increases in price may result in smaller amounts of the input being supplied. An example of a backward-bending supply curve is SS' in Figure 13.3.

To see how such a case can occur, consider the labor time supplied

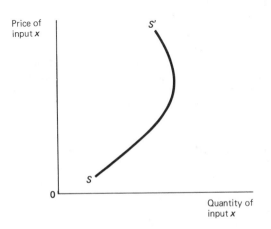

Figure 13.3   Backward-bending supply curve

by a single worker, Bill Jones. Jones has twenty-four hours a day to allocate between work and leisure. To him leisure time is a commodity he desires, and its price is the hourly wage rate—the amount of money he gives up to enjoy an hour of leisure time. What will be the effect of an increase in the wage rate on the amount of leisure time that Jones will demand? Clearly, this is a problem of consumer choice, since the question can be restated: What is the effect of an increase in the price of leisure time on the quantity of leisure time that Jones demands? The theoretical tools discussed in Chapter 4 can help us to answer this question.

As we learned in Chapter 4, we can divide the effect of the price increase into two parts: the substitution effect and the income effect. The substitution effect is the effect of the increase in the cost of leisure relative to other commodities. Since other consumer goods will become relatively less expensive, the substitution effect will result in his reducing his leisure time and increasing his purchase of other consumer goods. Thus the substitution effect will result in his increasing the amount of labor time he puts forth.

In addition, there is an income effect, which is quite different from the income effect in the case of the purchase of most consumer products. In the first place, the income effect here works in the opposite direction from the income effect in the case of the purchase of the typical consumer product. As we saw in Chapter 4, the income effect of a price increase of a good is generally to reduce the consumption of the good, since the price increase reduces the consumer's real purchasing power. But this is not the case here. An increase in the price of his leisure time due to an increase in his wage makes Jones more affluent and better able to afford the things he wants, including leisure. Thus the income effect of an increase in the price of leisure is likely to be an increase in the demand for leisure.

The income effect in this case differs from the income effect for most consumer products in another important respect: It is likely to be much stronger than for most consumer products. In general, the consumer spends only a small percentage of his budget on the product in question, with the result that an increase in its price has only a small impact on his real income. However, in the case of leisure, an increase in its price will almost certainly have a great effect on his real income, since most of his income is likely to stem from the sale of his labor. (Remember that the price of leisure time is equal to the wage rate.) Thus an increase in the price of leisure time is likely to have a great effect on Jones's income and on his consumption pattern.

The income effect may offset the substitution effect, with the result that an increase in the wage rate may reduce the supply of labor. In other words, an increase in the price of leisure time may increase the quantity demanded of leisure time. Of course, institutional constraints often prevent workers from choosing their own working hours; for example, the 40-hour week is commonly worked in industry. But the typical, or average, work week responds to the shape of the supply curve for labor. Thus, in the United States, as workers have become more affluent the average

Example 13.1 The Supply Curve for Physicians' Services

Martin Feldstein estimated that physicians have a backward-bending supply curve for labor. He found that the price elasticity of supply of physicians' services was about -0.91. (a) Draw a graph where hours per week devoted to leisure are plotted along the horizontal axis, and income derived from working is plotted along the vertical axis. Letting leisure be one good and income derived from working be the other, construct an individual physician's budget line and indifference curves. (b) Using the graph constructed in (a), show how the physician's desired amount of leisure is influenced by a decrease in his or her wage rate, if his or her supply curve for labor is backward-bending. (c) The American Medical Association has argued that any legislation that reduces the fees that physicians can charge will cut the supply of physicians' services. Does this appear to be true?

Solution

(a) Such a graph is shown in panel A below. The budget line here is CD. To derive this budget line, note that a physician who devoted every hour in the week to leisure would receive no income from working. That there are 168 hours in a week explains why the budget line passes through point D. If the physician devotes no time to leisure, the amount of income received from working is OC (which equals $168W$, where W is the physician's hourly wage rate). This explains why the budget line passes through point C. Note that the slope of the budget line equals -1 times the physician's hourly wage rate, because every extra hour devoted to leisure reduces the amount of income received from working by an amount equal to the hourly wage rate. Panel A also shows the physician's indifference curves. Given these indifference curves and the budget line, the physician will maximize utility by choosing OX hours of leisure and by obtaining OY dollars of income from working.

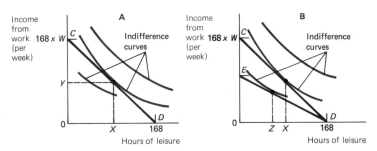

(b) A decrease in the physician's hourly wage rate reduces the amount that he or she can earn if no time is devoted to leisure from OC to OE in panel B. Thus the budget line is no longer CD, but ED, and the physician will maximize utility by choosing OZ rather than OX hours of leisure. Since he or she is in the backward-bending portion of the supply curve, OZ is less than OX. (c) If the price elasticity of supply for physicians' services is negative, this does not appear to be true.[*]

*For further discussion, see M. Feldstein, "The Rising Price of Physicians' Services," *Review of Economics and Statistics*, May 1970.

work week has tended to decrease. For example, the average work week in 1850 was almost 70 hours, as contrasted with about 40 hours at present.[7]

10. Determination of Price and Employment of an Input

The market demand and supply curves for an input determine the input's equilibrium price. The price of the input will tend in equilibrium to the level at which the quantity of the input demanded equals the quantity of the input supplied. Thus, in Figure 13.4, the equilibrium price of the input is OP_0. If the price were higher than OP_0, the quantity supplied would exceed the quantity demanded, and there would be downward pressure on the price. If the price were lower than OP_0, the quantity supplied would fall short of the quantity demanded, and there would be upward pressure on the price.

The equilibrium amount of the input that is employed is also given by the intersection of the market demand and supply curves. For example, in Figure 13.4, OQ_0 units of the input will be employed in equilibrium. In equilibrium the value of the marginal product of an input will be equal in each and every place where the input is used. In all uses the value of the marginal product of an input will equal the price of the input—and the price of the input will, of course, be the same to all firms under perfect competition.

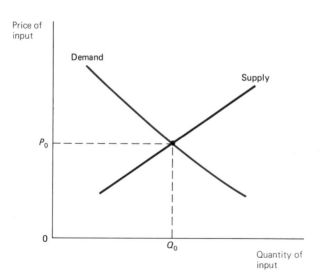

Figure 13.4 Determination of equilibrium price and quantity of input

7. For a relevant empirical study, see L. Dunn, "An Empirical Indifference Function for Income and Leisure," *Review of Economics and Statistics,* November 1978.

11. The Market for Engineers: An Application

At this point, it is advisable to pause for a moment and illustrate how the theory we have been discussing has been put to use. During much of the period since World War II, top government policy-makers have been concerned with the adequacy of the national supply of engineers. During the 1950s and early 1960s, there was a widespread fear among government officials and senior scientists that a serious shortage of engineers existed in the United States. Then during the late 1960s and early 1970s, there was a feeling that too many engineers were being turned out by the nation's colleges and universities. Both during the period of apparent shortage and that of apparent surplus, questions were repeatedly raised by knowledgeable people concerning the workings of the market for engineers. In particular, it was asked whether the sort of model described in previous sections of this chapter really explained the quantity of engineers graduated in a particular period and the level of their salaries.

To help answer this question, Richard Freeman of Harvard University gathered detailed data concerning the annual number of freshmen enrolling in engineering, the annual number of engineers graduating and seeking work, and the annual level of starting salaries of engineers (with a bachelor's degree) during 1948–67.[8] Based on careful statistical analysis, he estimated the supply and demand curves for engineers during this period. In the case of the supply curve, he divided the analysis into two parts. First, he estimated the effect of the level of engineering starting salaries on the number of freshmen enrolling in engineering. Holding other factors (like the total number of freshmen in all fields and the previous levels of salaries and enrollments) constant, he found that the relationship between the number of freshmen enrolling in engineering and the level of engineering starting salaries was as shown in panel A of Figure 13.5. Specifically, a 1 percent increase in starting salaries results in a 2.9 percent increase in freshmen enrollment in engineering.

Next, taking the freshman enrollment in engineering as given, he estimated the effect of the level of engineering starting salaries on the number of engineers graduating four years later and seeking work. Holding the freshman enrollment (and other factors) constant, he found that the relationship between the number of engineers graduating (and seeking work) and the level of starting salaries[9] was as shown in panel B of Figure 13.5. Specifically, a 1 percent increase in starting salaries results in about a 1 percent increase in the number of graduate engineers. In other words, more students switched to engineering or stayed in engineering when engineering salaries were relatively high than when they were relatively low. But as one would expect, the quantitative impact of salaries was smaller here than on freshmen enrollment in engineering.

Together, the two panels of Figure 13.5 provide some interesting insights concerning the supply curve for engineers in the United States.

8. Richard B. Freeman, *The Market for College-Trained Manpower* (Cambridge, Mass.: Harvard University Press, 1971).

9. Starting salaries here refer to a couple of years before graduation.

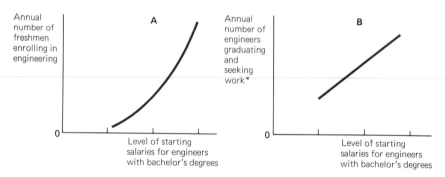

Figure 13.5 Estimated relationship between number of people going into engineering and the level of engineering salaries, United States, 1948–67

* Holding constant the number of freshmen enrolled in engineering four years earlier.

To government policy-makers, information of this sort is of great importance. For example, if national goals seem to require a certain number of engineers, the information such as that in Figure 13.5 can be used to indicate the level of starting salaries that, in the absence of other measures, would be required to call them forth. Further, Freeman's results shed valuable light on the extent to which the theory presented in previous sections can explain the workings of the market for engineers. He concludes that "traditional market forces—shifts in supply and demand—explain changes in engineering starting salaries, though with a lag due to sluggish adjustment to unexpected supply conditions."[10]

12. The Concept of Rent

In Section 8, we stated that there is sometimes a tendency to underestimate the extent to which the market supply of an input will be increased in response to an increase in the price of the input. Nevertheless, some inputs, like certain types of land, may be in relatively fixed supply. Suppose that the supply of an input is completely fixed: Increases in its price will not increase its supply and decreases in its price will not decrease its supply. Following the terminology of the classical economists of the nineteenth century, the price of such an input is rent. This use of the word *rent* is quite different from everyday usage, according to which *rent* is the price of using an apartment or a car or some other object owned by someone else.

If the supply of an input is fixed, its supply curve is a vertical line, as shown in Figure 13.6. Thus the price of this input, that is, its rent, is determined entirely by the demand curve for the input. For example, if the demand curve is DD', the rent is OP; if the demand curve is $D_0 D_0'$, the rent is OP_0. Since the supply of the input is fixed, the price of the input can be lowered without influencing the amount of the input that is

10. Freeman, p. 72.

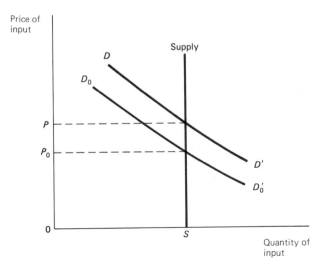

Figure 13.6   An input in completely fixed supply

supplied. Thus a rent is a payment above the minimum necessary to attract this amount of the input.[11]

In recent years, there has been a tendency among economists to extend the use of the word *rent* to encompass all payments to inputs that are above the minimum required to make these inputs available to the industry or to the economy. To a great extent these payments are costs to individual firms, since these firms must make such payments in order to attract and keep these inputs, which are useful to other firms in the industry. But, if the inputs have no use in other industries, these payments are not costs to the industry as a whole (or to the economy as a whole) because the inputs would be available to the industry whether or not these payments are made.

Why is it important to know whether or not a certain payment for inputs is a rent? Because a reduction of the payment will not influence the availability and use of the inputs if the payment is a rent; whereas, if it is not a rent, a reduction of the payment is likely to change the allocation of resources. For example, if the government imposes a tax on rents, there will be no effect on the supply of resources to the economy.

13. Quasi-Rents

The payment to any input in temporarily fixed supply is called a quasi-rent. In previous chapters, we have seen that many inputs are in fixed

11. Note that whether rent is or is not price-determined depends on whether we are looking at the matter from the point of view of a firm, a small industry, a large industry, or the whole economy. Although a payment to an input that is in fixed supply to the whole society or a large industry may be a rent from the point of view of the society or the industry, it may appear to be a price-determining cost to an individual small firm or a small industry.

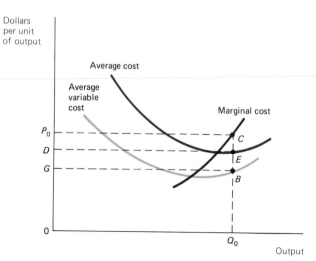

Figure 13.7   Quasi-rent

supply to a firm in the short run. For example, a firm's plant cannot be changed appreciably. In the short run, fixed inputs cannot be withdrawn from their current use and transferred to a use where the returns are higher. Also, fixed inputs cannot be supplemented with other similar inputs in the short run. Thus the payments to the fixed inputs are determined differently from the payments to the variable inputs. Whereas inputs that are variable in quantity are free to move where the returns are highest, fixed inputs are stuck where they are, at least in the short run. Consequently, firms must pay the variable inputs as much as they can earn in alternative uses, and the fixed inputs receive whatever is left over.

The return to the fixed inputs is a quasi-rent. It is a residual. To understand its nature, it is useful to consider the diagram in Figure 13.7, which shows a firm's short-run cost curves. Suppose that the price is OP_0, with the result that the firm will produce OQ_0 units and its total variable costs will be $OGBQ_0$ (since OG equals its average variable cost). This area, $OGBQ_0$, represents the amount that the firm must pay in order to attract and keep the amount of variable inputs corresponding to an output of OQ_0. It cannot pay less and expect to keep them. The fixed inputs get the residual, which is GP_0CB. This is the quasi-rent.

The short-run average total cost curve includes both the average variable costs and the average fixed costs. To determine the average fixed costs, we see what the returns on the firm's fixed assets would be if the rate of return were equal to that available elsewhere in the economy. Thus, since the firm's average total cost curve is as shown in Figure 13.7, the total fixed costs of the firm are equal to $GDEB$. Consequently, this amount of the quasi-rent is not pure economic profit; only DP_0CE is economic profit. Needless to say, quasi-rent need not be greater than total fixed costs. Firms with pure economic losses do not have quasi-rents that are large enough to cover total fixed costs.

14. Qualitative Differences in Inputs

In previous sections we have dealt with inputs that have been assumed to be homogeneous. In this section, we take account of the fact that inputs may differ in productive capacity. For example, some carpenters may be more skillful than others. Suppose that there are two types of carpenters: skilled and unskilled. Then the firm, if it maximizes profit, should hire each type of carpenter up to the point at which

$$MP_s \cdot MR = P_s \tag{13.8a}$$

$$MP_u \cdot MR = P_u \tag{13.8b}$$

where MP_s is the marginal product of skilled carpenters, MP_u is the marginal product of unskilled carpenters, P_s is the wage rate for skilled carpenters, P_u is the wage rate for unskilled carpenters, and MR is marginal revenue. This follows directly from Equations 13.4a to 13.4c. Equations 13.8a and 13.8b show that the differential in wages between skilled and unskilled carpenters will equal the differential in their marginal products, that is, $P_s \div P_u = MP_s \div MP_u$.

Suppose that we can no longer divide workers into two groups, since each worker differs from the next in the value of his or her output. Then the difference in wages paid to workers will equal the difference in the total value of their output. For example, suppose that Joe (together with the appropriate tools and materials) produces output worth $1,000 per month and Bill (with the same tools and materials) produces output worth $900 per month. In equilibrium, Joe will earn $100 more per month than Bill. If the difference in wages were less than $100, Bill's employer would find it profitable to replace Bill with Joe, since this would increase the value of output by $100 and cost less than $100. If the difference were more than $100, Joe's employer would find it profitable to replace Joe with Bill; although this would reduce the value of output by $100, it would reduce costs by more than $100.

This kind of analysis has been applied repeatedly to explain differences in land rents. According to the classical discussions of this subject, only the better tracts of land will be used at a given point in time; the less productive lands will not be in use because they are not sufficiently productive to earn a profit. The least productive lands in use earn neither a profit nor a loss; consequently their price is zero, since no one would be willing to pay more for them. The rent of any other tract of land in use will equal the difference between its value yield and the value yield of this zero-priced *marginal land,* when the area of the plot is held constant. Thus the tracts of land (that are worked) will rent at a variety of levels, but after subtracting rental costs they will earn an equal net profit for those who work them.

15. Wage Differentials among Labor of Similar Quality

In previous sections we pointed out that variable inputs will be transferred from one use to another in response to differences in the return

Example 13.2   The Effects of Minimum Wage Laws

Congress has passed round after round of minimum-wage legislation. The minimum wage, which was only 25 cents per hour in 1938,
reached $3.35 in early 1981. Suppose that a minimum wage, OP_m, is
instituted in a competitive labor market, with the demand and supply curves for labor as follows:

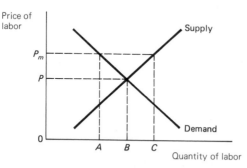

(a) Will the minimum wage affect the level of employment? If so,
how big will its effect be? (b) How may employers (and workers) get
around the minimum wage? (c) Are certain types of workers affected more than others by the minimum wage? If so, which types
are affected most?

Solution

(a) Yes. The minimum wage will cause employment to fall from OB
to OA workers; thus AB workers will be laid off. Note that this is
less than the excess supply of workers (the difference between the
quantity of workers supplied and the quantity demanded), which
equals AC. The excess supply of workers is the total number that
would like to work at the minimum wage, but cannot do so. (b)
Sometimes employers can provide less in-kind benefits, such as
meals, or employees are willing to pay for items that normally would
be the responsibility of the employer. In this way, the *net* amount
paid by the employer is below the minimum wage, although the
wage appears to be above it. (c) Unskilled workers and occupations
are affected much more than skilled workers and occupations, because only in unskilled labor markets does the minimum wage exceed the equilibrium wage. There is a strong effect on teen-agers,
particularly black teen-agers. One study indicated that the unemployment rate for black teen-agers increases about 1.8 percentage
points for each percentage point rise in the ratio of the minimum
wage to the average hourly earnings of production workers in private nonagricultural employment.*

* For further discussion, see Y. Brozen, "The Effect of Statutory Minimum
Wage Increases on Teen-Age Unemployment," *Journal of Law and Economics,* April 1969; and T. Moore, "The Effect of Minimum Wages on Teen-
age Unemployment Rates," *Journal of Political Economy,* July 1971.

they can yield. Thus labor will move from uses in which its wages are low to uses in which its wages are high. This migration from low-wage uses to high-wage uses tends to equalize the wage level for labor of comparable quality, but it does not eliminate all wage differentials among such labor. Even if all workers were identical, even to their fingerprints (a criminal's paradise), some wage differentials would still be required to offset differences in the characteristics of various occupations and areas.[12]

For example, some occupations require large investments in training, while other occupations require a much smaller investment in training. Consider John Sharp, a physicist who spends about eight years in undergraduate and graduate education. During each year of his training, he incurs direct expenses for items like books and tuition, and he loses the income that he could make if he were to work rather than go to school. Clearly, if his net remuneration is to be as high in physics as in other jobs he might take, he must make a greater wage when he gets through than a comparable person whose job requires no training beyond high school; the difference in wages must be at least sufficient to compensate for his investment in extra training.

Similarly, members of some occupations incur larger occupational expenses than others. For example, a psychologist may have to buy testing materials and subscribe to expensive journals. In order for net compensation to be equalized, such workers must be paid more than others. Also, some jobs are more unstable than others. For example, some types of workers may be subject to frequent layoffs and have little job security, whereas others may be assured stable and secure employment. If the former jobs are to be as attractive as the latter, they must pay more than the latter.

In addition, there are other differences among jobs that must be offset by wage differentials if the net remuneration is to be equalized. For instance, there are differences among regions and communities in the cost of living. (Living costs generally are lower in small towns than in big cities.) Also, some jobs are more prestigious than others, with the result that people would be willing to accept them even though they paid less than others. (However, the high-paying jobs frequently tend to be the more prestigious ones.)

16. The Elasticity of Substitution and the Distribution of Income

The elasticity of substitution measures the extent to which the capital-labor ratio changes in response to changes in the ratio of the price of capital to the price of labor. More precisely, the elasticity of substitution equals

$$S = - \left(\frac{\Delta(X_K/X_L)}{X_K/X_L} \div \frac{\Delta(P_K/P_L)}{P_K/P_L} \right) \qquad 13.9$$

12. In addition, of course, such wage differentials may arise because of less than perfect mobility of inputs and frictions of various kinds.

where X_K is the quantity of capital employed, X_L the quantity of labor employed, P_K the price of capital, and P_L the price of labor. The level of output is held constant.

The elasticity of substitution is an important determinant of how a change in the price of labor or in the price of capital will alter the share of total income going to labor or capital. Since capital's total income is $X_K P_K$ and labor's total income is $X_L P_L$, the ratio of capital's share of total income to labor's share is

$$X_K P_K \div X_L P_L \qquad \text{or} \qquad \frac{X_K}{X_L} \times \frac{P_K}{P_L}$$

Suppose that P_K/P_L decreases by 1 percent. Then, if $S > 1$, this decrease in the price of capital relative to the price of labor results in a more than 1 percent increase in the capital-labor ratio. If $S = 1$, it results in a 1 percent increase in the capital-labor ratio. If $S < 1$, it results in less than a 1 percent increase in the capital-labor ratio.

Given the value of S, one can determine the effect of a change in the price of labor or in the price of capital on the ratio of capital's total income to labor's total income. For example, suppose that the price of labor increases relative to the price of capital. If $S < 1$, the relative increase in X_K/X_L is less than the relative decrease in P_K/P_L, with the result that $X_K/X_L \times P_K/P_L$ must decrease. If $S = 1$, the relative increase in X_K/X_L is just equal to the relative decrease in P_K/P_L, with the result that $X_K/X_L \times P_K/P_L$ does not change. If $S > 1$, the relative increase in X_K/X_L is greater than the relative decrease in P_K/P_L, with the result that $X_K/X_L \times P_K/P_L$ must increase. Thus, when the price of labor increases relative to that of capital, if $S < 1$, the ratio of capital's share to labor's share will decrease; if $S = 1$, it will stay the same; and if $S > 1$, it will increase.

According to many observers, the share of income going to labor and capital has been relatively constant in the United States. Over the past seventy-five years, labor has received about 70 to 85 percent of the total real income; the exact number varies with the definition of labor income that is used. Some economists have tried to explain this phenomenon by asserting that the aggregate production function exhibits an elasticity of substitution of one. For example, former Senator Paul Douglas conjectured that the appropriate production function might be the Cobb-Douglas function (discussed in Chapter 6), which exhibits an elasticity of substitution of one. Three points should be noted in this regard. First, not all observers are impressed by the constancy of shares. Second, technological change as well as the elasticity of substitution influences the ratio of capital's share to labor's share. Third, we have relatively little evidence concerning the value of the elasticity of substitution.[13]

13. For a survey of empirical studies of the elasticity of substitution, see M. Nerlove, "Recent Empirical Studies of the CES and Related Production Functions," in M. Brown, *The Theory and Empirical Analysis of Production* (New York: National Bureau of Economic Research, 1967); E. Berndt, "Reconciling Alternative Estimates of the Elasticity of Substitution," *Review of Economics and Statistics*, February 1976; and C. Paraskevopoulos, "Alternative Estimates of the Elasticity of Substitution," *Review of Economics and Statistics*, August 1979.

17. The Shortage of Nurses: Another Application

During the past thirty years, there have been chronic complaints of a shortage of professional nurses. According to Donald Yett of the University of Southern California,

> In recent years, 10 to 20 percent of all budgeted positions for hospital registered nurses ... have been reported vacant.... Reported hospital vacancies were higher for general duty nurses than for directors, supervisors, and head nurses.... Nursing and hospital leaders agree that teaching and supervisory positions should be filled by college-trained nurses, but the existing supply is not sufficient. Consequently, many of these positions have been filled by nurses who otherwise would have been assigned to general duty, an area in which, as a result, the shortage appears to be concentrated.[14]

How can such a shortage persist? A simple model devised by Stanford's Nobel laureate Kenneth Arrow and William Capron seems to explain the situation, at least partly.[15] According to many authorities, the demand curve for nurses has shifted to the right in the past thirty years, as population and demand for hospital care have increased. In particular, suppose that the demand curve for nurses shifted from D_1D_1', to D_2D_2', in Figure 13.8. Under these circumstances, the wage for nurses that would bring supply and demand into balance is OP_2. But as Arrow and Capron point out, it will take time for the wage to move from OP_1 to OP_2. During the transition period—the period when the wage is moving from OP_1 to OP_2—the organizations hiring nurses will experience a "shortage" in the sense that they will not be able to hire as many nurses as they would like at the going wage. For example, when the wage is OP_3, they would like to hire OQ_3 nurses, but they will be able to hire only OQ_2 nurses.

A shortage of this sort can persist for a number of years if the demand curve continues to shift to the right (as it seemed to for nurses during this period) and if the wage rate tends to be "sticky" and to increase slowly in response to the excess demand. Among the reasons why the wage may be sticky is "the prevalence of long-term contracts, the influence of the heterogeneity of the market in slowing the diffusion of information, and the dominance of a relatively small number of [employers]."[16] Such a shortage will be over when the necessary wage increases occur. For example, when the wage rate increases to OP_2 in

14. D. Yett, "The Chronic Shortage of Nurses," in Herbert Klarman, ed., *Empirical Studies in Health Economics* (Baltimore: Johns Hopkins University Press, 1970). See, also his *An Economic Analysis of the Nurse Shortage* (Lexington, Mass.: Lexington Books, 1975).

15. K. Arrow and W. Capron, "Dynamic Shortages and Price Rises: The Engineer-Scientist Case," *Quarterly Journal of Economics,* May 1959. This paper had a considerable influence in clarifying issues and helping to guide policy regarding the market for scientists and engineers. The fact that the model was designed to deal with the market for scientists and engineers in the late 1950s does not mean, of course, that it is not applicable to nurses (or other groups).

16. Ibid., p. 303.

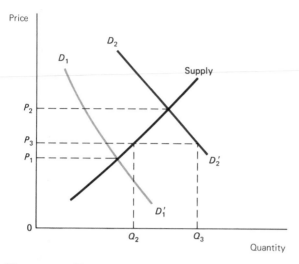

Figure 13.8   Shortage of nurses

Figure 13.8, the quantity demanded equals the quantity supplied.

This model sheds useful light on the nurse shortage, a problem which has commanded the attention of the Congress; the Department of Health and Human Services; and other groups. But according to Donald Yett, this is not the whole story. He points out that the labor market for nurses is not perfectly competitive, and that the imperfections in the labor market may also be responsible for the apparent shortage. (The discussion of the price and employment of inputs under imperfect competition is reserved for the next chapter.) Nonetheless, the simple concepts put forward in this example can take us a substantial way toward understanding the nature of this complex problem.

18. Summary

The importance of understanding the determinants of input prices is obvious. In a free-enterprise economy, input prices are an important determinant of any consumer's income. Our first step in analyzing the demand for an input is to consider the demand curve of an individual firm. If there is only one variable input, the firm's demand curve is the same as the value-of-marginal-product schedule. If there is more than one variable input, the situation is somewhat more complicated. The market demand curve for the input can be derived from the demand curves of the individual firms in the market; however, it cannot be derived by simply taking their horizontal sum.

Under perfect competition, the supply of an input to an individual firm is infinitely elastic. However, when we consider the market supply curve, which is the relationship between the price of the input and the amount of the input supplied in the entire market, it is often not true that supply is infinitely elastic. Many inputs are supplied by business firms, and the factors influencing their supply have been discussed in previous chapters. But other inputs—notably labor—are supplied by individuals, not business firms. For inputs supplied by individuals, the supply curve may be backward bending; that is, increases in input price may result in a smaller supply of the input, at least over some range of variation of input price.

Given the market demand and supply curves for an input, the price of the input will tend in equilibrium to the level at which the quantity of the input demanded equals the quantity of the input supplied. The equilibrium amount of the input that is utilized is also given by the intersection of the market demand and supply curves. To illustrate how these concepts can be used to help solve important problems of public policy, we described how economists have used these concepts to analyze the market for engineers and the shortage of nurses.

The payment to an input that is completely fixed in supply is called a rent; and the payment to an input in temporarily fixed supply is a quasi-rent. One can extend the analysis to take account of qualitative differences among inputs. Wage differentials are due to such differences, as well as differences among jobs in training required, occupational expenses, security, and other factors. Finally, the elasticity of substitution, which measures the extent to which the capital-labor ratio changes in response to changes in the ratio of the price of capital to the price of labor, is an important determinant of how a change in the price of labor or capital affects the share of total income going to labor or capital.

QUESTIONS AND PROBLEMS

1. A textile mill uses labor and capital. The price of a unit of labor is $5 and the price of a unit of capital is $6. The marginal product of a unit of labor is the same as the marginal product of a unit of capital. Is this firm (which is a perfect competitor) maximizing its profit? Explain.

2. Describe how the cobweb model (described in Chapter 9, Section 12) can be applied to the market for engineers. (In fact, this model has been used by some economists to represent the workings of this market.)

3. A perfectly competitive firm can hire labor at $30 per day. The firm's production function is as follows:

Number of days of labor	Number of units of output
0	0
1	8
2	15
3	21
4	26
5	30

If each unit of output sells for $5, how many days of labor should the firm hire?

4. A firm sells its product for $10 per unit. It produces 100 units per month, and its average variable cost is $5. What is its quasi-rent? If its average fixed cost is $4, does its quasi-rent equal its economic profit?

5. Suppose that the ratio of the price of capital to the price of labor decreases by 1 percent in 1982, with the result that the capital-labor ratio increases by 0.5 percent. What is the elasticity of substitution? If the elasticity of substitution remains at this value, and if the ratio of the price of capital to the price of labor decreases by 1 percent again in 1983, will the ratio of capital's total income to labor's total income rise in 1983? Or will it fall? Explain.

6. William Moran, a (hypothetical) bricklayer who suffers from a disability, is $\frac{1}{4}$ as productive as the typical bricklayer; that is, his marginal product is $\frac{1}{4}$ of that of the typical bricklayer. If the going wage for typical bricklayers is 3 times the minimum wage, will Mr. Moran find work? Explain.

7. Using the conventional supply and demand apparatus, show why nonwhite labor receives lower wages than white labor. What would happen to nonwhite wages, white wages, and total output if discrimination were to cease?

8. Using the concepts presented in this chapter, describe the effect on the market for unskilled labor if the existing minimum wage was abolished.

9. (Advanced) Suppose that a textile firm's production function is $Q = L^8 K^2$, where Q is output, L is the amount of labor used, and K is the amount of capital used. If the firm takes the product price and the input prices as given, show that total wages paid by the firm will equal 80 percent of its revenues.

10. According to 1981 Nobel Laureate James Tobin, "When there are only a few people left in the population whose capacities are confined to garbage-collecting, it will be a high-paid calling. The same is true of domestic service and all kinds of menial work." Do you agree? Using the concepts presented in this chapter, explain why you agree or disagree.

SELECTED REFERENCES

AMERICAN ECONOMIC ASSOCIATION. *Reading in the Theory of Income Distribution.* New York: Blakiston, 1946.

HICKS, JOHN. *The Theory of Wages.* New York: Macmillan, 1932.

KALDOR, NICHOLAS. "Alternative Theories of Distribution," *Review of Economic Studies,* 1955–56.

SAMUELSON, PAUL. *Foundations of Economic Analysis,* Cambridge, Mass.: Harvard University Press, 1947. (Advanced)

SCITOVSKY, TIBOR. *Welfare and Competition,* 2d ed. Homewood, Ill.: Irwin, 1971.

STIGLER, GEORGE. *Production and Distribution Theories.* New York: Macmillan, 1941.

14 Price and Employment of Inputs under Imperfect Competition

1. Introduction

In some parts of the economy, perfect competition is clearly not the best model. In this chapter, we continue our discussion of the determinants of the price and employment of inputs, but we relax the assumption that there is perfect competition. More specifically, this chapter is divided into three parts. In the first part, we consider the case in which there is perfect competition in the market for the input, but imperfect competition (that is, monopoly, oligopoly, or monopolistic competition) in the relevant product markets. In other words, we allow some of the firms that are potential buyers of the input to have some monopoly power in the sale of their products. In the second part, we take up the case in which there is only a single buyer of an input. In the third part, we discuss an important and highly visible form of market imperfection in the market for labor—the labor union.[1]

2. Profit Maximization and Input Employment: Imperfect Competition in the Product Market

In Section 3 of the previous chapter we showed that a firm, if it maximizes profit, will employ inputs in

---

1. Of course, this is only a brief introduction to the economics of collective bargaining; readers with a particular interest in this field should take a specialized course in labor economics. The material presented here is chosen and viewed from the vantage point of microeconomic theory. Some of the leading texts in labor economics are listed at the end of this chapter.

such a way that each input's marginal product multiplied by the firm's marginal revenue will equal the price of the input. Put in symbols, this condition for profit maximization is

$$MP_x \cdot MR = P_x \qquad\qquad \text{14.1a}$$

$$MP_y \cdot MR = P_y \qquad\qquad \text{14.1b}$$
$$\vdots$$

$$MP_z \cdot MR = P_z \qquad\qquad \text{14.1c}$$

where MP_x is the marginal product of input x, MP_y is the marginal product of input y, MP_z is the marginal product of input z, P_x is the price of input x, P_y is the price of input y, P_z is the price of input z, and MR is the marginal revenue of the firm's output.

Suppose that the firm is a monopolist or an oligopolist or a monopolistic competitor, rather than a perfect competitor as assumed in the previous chapter. Will the firm still employ inputs in the way described by Equations 14.1a, 14.1b, $\cdots$, 14.1c if it maximizes profit? The answer is yes. As long as the market for the input is perfectly competitive and the firm cannot influence the price of the input by its purchases, it must conform to Equations 14.1a, 14.1b, $\cdots$, 14.1c if it maximizes profit. It is a simple matter to prove to yourself that this is the case: Merely turn back to Section 3 of Chapter 13 and work through the derivation of the conditions in Equations 13.4a, 13.4b, $\cdots$, 13.4c. Nowhere in that derivation is it assumed that the firm's product is sold in a perfectly competitive market. Thus the results hold whether the firm is a perfect competitor or an imperfect competitor in the product market.

3. The Firm's Demand Curve: The Case of One Variable Input

Equations 14.1a, 14.1b, $\cdots$, 14.1c are the basis for the theory of input demand under imperfect competition in the product market (just as they are under perfect competition in the product market). As in the previous chapter our first step in analyzing the demand for an input is to consider the demand of an individual firm for an input, assuming that this input is the only variable input in the firm's production process. In other words, the quantities of all other inputs are fixed. This assumption is relaxed in the next section. In Section 5 we discuss the market demand for the input and the determination of input price and employment.

Suppose that the only variable input is input x. The demand curve of a firm for this input shows the quantity of input x that the firm will take at various possible prices of input x. Assuming that the firm maximizes its profits, it will take that amount of input x at which the value of the extra output produced by an extra unit of input x is equal to the price of a unit of input x. This is the meaning of Equation 14.1a.

To be more specific, suppose that the marginal product of input x at various levels of utilization of input x is that shown in Table 14.1; the total amount of output that can be derived from each number of units of input x is shown in the third column of Table 14.1. Because the firm is an

Table 14.1   Marginal revenue product of input x

Quantity of x	Marginal product of x*	Total output	Price of good (dollars)	Total revenue (dollars)	Marginal revenue product of x* (dollars)
3	10	33	20.00	660.00	—
4	9	42	19.50	819.00	159.00
5	8	50	19.00	950.00	131.00
6	7	57	18.50	1,054.50	104.50
7	6	63	18.00	1,134.00	79.50
8	5	68	17.50	1,190.00	56.00
9	4	72	17.00	1,224.00	34.00

* These figures pertain to the interval between the indicated amount of input x and one unit less than the indicated amount of input x.

imperfect competitor, the price of its product will vary with the amount it sells; the fourth column of Table 14.1 provides the price that corresponds to each output in the third column. Multiplying the output in the third column by the price in the fourth column, we get the total revenue corresponding to each number of units of input x used; this is shown in column 5.

Finally, in column 6 of Table 14.1 we show the increase in total revenue that stems from the use of each additional unit of input x. For example, the fifth unit of input x (that is, going from 4 units to 5 units of input x) increases the firm's total revenue by $131. Similarly, the seventh unit of input x (that is, going from 6 units to 7 units of input x) increases the firm's total revenue by $79.50. The increase in total revenue due to the use of an additional unit of input x is called the *marginal revenue product* of input x, which explains the heading of column 6. The marginal revenue product of input x is equal to the marginal physical product of input x times the firm's marginal revenue.[2] Thus it is equal to the left-hand side of Equation 14.1a.

If the firm maximizes profit it sets the marginal revenue product of input x equal to the price of input x. This is the meaning of Equation 14.1a. Thus the firm's demand schedule for input x must be the mar-

2. It is easy to prove that the marginal revenue product (MRP) is the product of the marginal product (MP) and marginal revenue (MR). By definition,

$$MRP = \frac{\Delta R}{\Delta I}$$

where ΔR is the change in total revenue and ΔI is the change in the quantity of the input. Since $MR = \Delta R \div \Delta Q$, where ΔQ is the change in output, it follows that

$$MRP = \frac{MR\Delta Q}{\Delta I}$$

But since $MP = \Delta Q \div \Delta I$, it also follows that

$$MRP = MR \times MP$$

which is what we set out to prove.

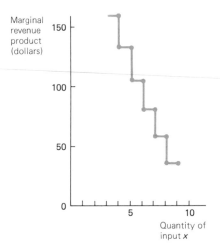

Figure 14.1   Marginal-revenue-product
curve for input x

ginal-revenue-product schedule in column 6 of Table 14.1. For example, suppose that the price of input x is $56. Then according to Equation 14.1a the firm will set the marginal revenue product of input x equal to $56, which means that it will demand 8 units of input x. Or suppose that the price of input x is $34. Then the firm will set the marginal revenue product of input x equal to $34, which means that it will demand 9 units of input x. Thus the number of units of input x that the firm will demand at any price is given by the marginal-revenue-product curve, which shows the marginal revenue product of input x at various quantities of input x used. This curve is shown in Figure 14.1.

Two points should be noted concerning the marginal-revenue-product curve. First, it will slope downward and to the right (as a demand curve should for an input) for two reasons: the input's marginal product will decrease as more of it is used, and the firm's marginal revenue will decrease as its output increases. Since the marginal revenue product is the product of the input's marginal product and the firm's marginal revenue, it will decrease for both reasons as more of the input is used. Second, the value-of-marginal-product schedule in the previous chapter can be regarded as a special case of the marginal-revenue-product schedule. If marginal revenue is equal to price (as it is in perfect competition), the marginal-revenue-product schedule becomes precisely the same as the value-of-marginal-product schedule.

4. The Firm's Demand Curve: The Case of Several Variable Inputs

Suppose that the firm uses a number of inputs that can be varied in quantity, with input x being only one of them. As in the case of perfect competition, the firm's demand curve for input x is no longer its marginal-revenue-product curve. This is because a change in the price of

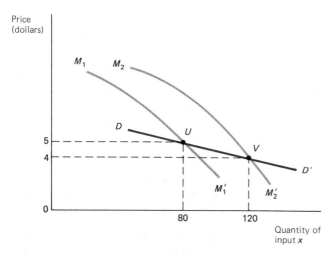

Figure 14.2   Firm's demand curve for input x

input x will result in changes in the quantities used of other variable inputs, and these changes in the quantities used of other inputs will affect the quantity used of input x.

For example, suppose that the price of input x is initially \$5 and that 80 units of input x are used at this price. Holding constant the use of other inputs, the marginal-revenue-product curve is assumed to be M_1M_1' in Figure 14.2. This would be the demand curve for input x if the other inputs were not variable. Suppose that the price of input x falls to \$4. Since the marginal revenue product of input x exceeds its new price, the firm will tend to increase its use of input x. But this will shift the marginal-revenue-product curves of other variable inputs, which in turn will change the amount used of them, which in turn will shift the marginal-revenue-product curve of input x.

When all of these effects have taken place, the firm will be on another marginal-revenue-product curve for input x, say M_2M_2' in Figure 14.2. Since the amount demanded of input x will be such that the marginal revenue product of input x will equal its new price, the firm will demand 120 units. Points U and V are both on the firm's demand curve for input x. Other points can be determined in similar fashion; the complete demand curve is DD'.

5. The Market Demand Curve and Input Price

The previous sections derived the demand curve of an individual firm for an input. The next step is to combine the demand curves of the individual firms in the market (for the input) into a single market demand curve for the input. This step can be accomplished in different ways, depending on whether the firms are all monopolists or whether some are oligopolists or monopolistic competitors. If all firms are monopolists in their product markets, the market demand curve for the input would simply be the horizontal summation of the demand curves of the individual firms.

On the other hand, if some of the firms are oligopolists or monopolistic competitors, one cannot simply sum (horizontally) the demand curves of the individual firms to derive the market demand curve. This will not work for the same reason that it would not work in the case of perfect competition (discussed in the previous chapter): A change in the price of the input will affect both the output of the individual firm and the outputs of its competitors. Because of the change in its competitors' outputs, the demand curve for its own product will change, and this in turn will change its demand curve for the input. In a case of this sort, the market demand curve for the input can be determined only by finding at each price the amount of the input that will maximize the profits of each firm in the market, and by summing these amounts over all firms in the market.

Given the market demand curve for the input, the equilibrium price of the input will be the price at which this demand curve intersects the input's market supply curve. Moreover, the total amount of the input that will be used in equilibrium in this market is also determined in the usual way by the intersection of this demand curve and this supply curve. The nature and determinants of an input's market supply curve, discussed in the previous chapter, need not be altered by the existence of imperfect competition in the product market.

6. Monopsony

Up to this point we have assumed that there is perfect competition in the input market. Now we change this assumption. We begin by considering the case of monopsony. Monopsony is a situation in which there is a single buyer. For example, a group of small firms may be set up to provide tooling, supplies, or materials for a single large manufacturing firm, and because this large firm is the only one of its type in the area and its requirements are highly specialized, this large firm may be the only buyer for the product of the small firms. This is a case of monopsony.

Note the difference between monopsony and monopoly: Monopsony is a case of a single buyer; monopoly is a case of a single seller. Other market situations that could also be studied are oligopsony (where there are a few buyers) and monopsonistic competition (where there are many buyers but the inputs are not homogeneous and some buyers prefer some sellers' inputs to other sellers' inputs). However, it is sufficient for present purposes to limit our attention to monopsony.

Monopsony can occur for various reasons. In some cases, a particular type of input is much more productive in one kind of use than in others. For example, some land that is rich in iron ore may be much more profitably devoted to iron mining than to any other use. Or a person with certain specialized skills may be much more profitably employed using these skills than working at other jobs. If there is only one firm that rents such land or hires such labor, the result is a monopsonistic situation.

The classic case of monopsony is the company town in which a single firm is the sole buyer of labor services. Many "mill towns" and "mining towns" have been dominated by a single firm. As long as workers are unable or unwilling to move elsewhere to work, this firm is a monopsonist. If the mobility of labor can be increased, the monopsony can be broken, at least partially. However, the difficulties in increasing the mobility of labor should not be underestimated: Workers become emotionally attached to a particular area and to their friends and family located there; they often are ignorant of opportunities elsewhere; and they sometimes lack the money and skills that are required to move.

7. Input Supply Curves and Marginal Expenditure Curves

The supply curve of the input facing the monopsonist is the market supply curve: This is the key feature of monopsony. The reason why the monopsonist faces the market supply curve of the input is that the monopsonist is the entire market for the input: It is the sole buyer. Since the market supply curve of an input is generally upward sloping, as we saw in the previous chapter, this means that the supply curve for the input that the monopsonist faces is upward sloping. In other words, the monopsonist is forced to increase the price of the input if it wishes to use more of it, and it can reduce the input's price if it chooses to use less of it.

The contrast between this situation and the situation under perfect competition in the input market should be noted. In the case of perfect competition in the input market, each firm buys only a very small proportion of the total supply of any input, the consequence being that each firm faces a perfectly elastic supply curve for the input. In other words, each firm can buy all it wants of an input without affecting the input's price.

The situation under monopsony is illustrated by the case in Table 14.2. Suppose that a firm is a monopsonist with respect to input x. Suppose that the market supply schedule for input x is that shown in col-

Table 14.2. Marginal expenditure for input x

Quantity of x	Price of x (dollars)	Total cost of x (dollars)	Marginal expenditure for x* (dollars)
8	10.00	80.00	—
9	10.50	94.50	14.50
10	11.00	110.00	15.50
11	11.50	126.50	16.50
12	12.00	144.00	17.50
13	12.50	162.50	18.50
14	13.00	182.00	19.50

* Each figure pertains to the interval between the indicated amount of input x and one unit less than the indicated amount of input x.

umns 1 and 2. For example, 8 units of input x will be supplied if the price of input x is \$10.00; 9 units of input x will be supplied if the price of input x is \$10.50; and so forth. Column 3 shows the total cost to the firm of buying the quantities of input x in column 1. For example, the total cost of 8 units of input x is \$80.00; and the total cost of 9 units of input x is \$94.50. Of course, column 3 is simply the product of the figures in column 1 and column 2.

Column 4 shows the additional cost to the firm of increasing its utilization of input x by one unit. This is called the *marginal expenditure* for input x. For example, the marginal expenditure for the 9th unit of input x is \$14.50; and the marginal expenditure for the 10th unit of input x is \$15.50. When the market supply curve for the input is upward sloping, the marginal expenditure for the input will be greater than the input price. The reason for this is simple. Suppose, for example, that the firm in Table 14.2 increases its use of input x from 8 units to 9 units. If it did not have to increase the price of input x in order to expand the supply of the input, it would have to pay only the price, \$10, of another unit. But because the supply curve *is* upward sloping, the firm *will* have to increase the price of input x in order to increase the supply. *Moreover, this will mean paying all 9 units the higher price, not just paying more for the 9th unit.* Consequently, the marginal expenditure will exceed the input's price.

Figure 14.3 shows input x's supply curve, SS'. If the input is bought by a single buyer, the monopsonist's marginal expenditure curve, which shows the marginal expenditure for the input at various quantities used of the input, is EE'. Since the supply curve is upward sloping, the marginal expenditure curve lies above it.

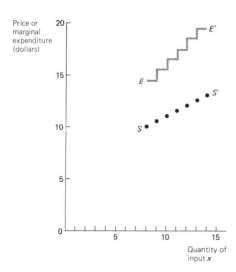

Figure 14.3   Supply curve and marginal expenditure curve for input x

Table 14.3 Optimal employment of input x: Monopsony

Quantity of input x used by monopsonist	Price of x (dollars)	Marginal revenue product of x* (dollars)	Marginal expenditure for input x* (dollars)
5	9	40	—
6	10	38	15
7	11	35	17
8	12	30	19
9	13	24	21
10	14	18	23
11	15	10	25
12	16	2	27

*These figures pertain to the interval between the indicated amount of input x and one unit less than the indicated amount of input x.

8. Price and Employment: A Single Variable Input

Suppose that there is only one variable input. If the monopsonist maximizes profit, it will purchase larger amounts of the input as long as the extra revenues derived from the additional quantity of input are at least as large as the extra cost of the additional quantity of input. When this is no longer the case, the monopsonist will no longer increase its employment of the input. Indeed, if the extra revenues derived from an additional quantity of input are less than the extra cost of the additional quantity of input, the monopsonist will cut back its employment of the input.

More specifically, consider the case in Table 14.3. Column 3 shows the marginal revenue product of the input, that is, the additional revenue derived from an additional unit of the input. For example, the addition of the 6th unit of the input results in $38 of additional revenue. Column 4 shows the marginal expenditure for the input, that is, the additional cost of an additional unit of the input. For example, the addition of the 6th unit of the input results in $15 of additional costs.

Clearly, the monopsonist, if it maximizes profit, will employ additional units of the input as long as the marginal revenue product of the input exceeds the marginal expenditure. When the marginal revenue product no longer exceeds the marginal expenditure, it will stop adding further units of the input. Thus, in Table 14.3, the monopsonist will employ 9 units of the input. Also, in Figure 14.4, if the marginal-revenue-product curve is DD' and the marginal expenditure curve is EE', the firm will hire OQ units of the input.

Note the difference between the condition for profit maximization under monopsony and the condition for profit maximization when there is perfect competition in the input market. Under perfect competition in the input markets, we saw in the previous chapter and in Equation 14.1a of this chapter that the firm must set

$$MP_x \cdot MR = P_x \tag{14.2}$$

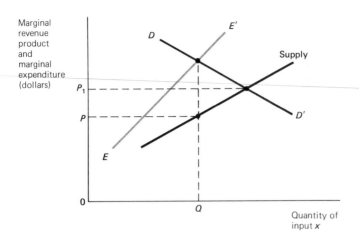

Figure 14.4   Optimal employment of input x: Monopsony

However, if the firm is a monopsonist, it must set

$$MP_x \cdot MR = ME_x \qquad\qquad 14.3$$

where ME_x is the marginal expenditure for input x.

The difference between Equation 14.2 and 14.3 lies in the quantities on the right-hand side: P_x in one case and ME_x in the other. Since ME_x is greater than P_x if the input's supply curve is upward sloping (see Section 7) and since the marginal revenue product of input x (which equals $MP_x \cdot MR$) decreases as more of input x is used, it follows that less of input x is used if Equation 14.3 is met than if Equation 14.2 is met. Thus the monopsonist will employ less of the input than would be used if the input market were perfectly competitive.

The monopsonist sets the input's price at the level at which the quantity it demands—the quantity at which marginal revenue product equals marginal expenditure—will be supplied. Thus, in Table 14.3, it sets a price of $13. And in Figure 14.4 it sets a price of OP, if the supply curve for input x is as shown there. Note that the price set by the monopsonist is lower than would be set in a competitive market for the input. For example, in Figure 14.4, if DD' were the demand curve for the input in a competitive market, the equilibrium price of the input would be OP_1 rather than OP.

9. Price and Employment: Several Variable Inputs

The previous section dealt with the case where the monopsonist uses only one variable input. It is easy to generalize our results to the case in which it uses more than one variable input. For example, suppose that there are a number of variable inputs: input x, input $y \cdots$, input z. For each of these inputs, it will pay the monopsonist to increase its use of the input only as long as the extra revenue derived from the additional

Example 14.1   The Market for Schoolteachers

Studies by John Landon and Robert Baird indicate that, when other factors are held equal, the level of teachers' salaries in a school district depends on the number of other school districts in the county containing the district in question. (a) If there are a relatively large number of other districts in the county containing a particular school district, would you expect the salary level of teachers in this district to be relatively high or relatively low? Why? (b) Suppose that teachers could move costlessly to school districts outside the county. Would this influence your answer to question (a)? (c) In recent years, there has been a tendency for large metropolitan school districts to decentralize into a number of autonomous districts, each of which makes its own hiring and firing decisions. What effect, if any, do you think that such decentralization will have on teachers' salaries? (d) What are some of the arguments put forth by those who favor such decentralization?

Solution

(a) Based on the theory of monopsony, one might expect school districts that are the only buyers of teachers' services in a particular area to pay less than those that must compete with other school districts in the area. (b) If teachers could move costlessly to school districts outside the county, a school district that was the sole buyer of teacher's services within a county would have much less monopsonistic power, and would be less able to pay lower salaries than is now the case. (c) It will probably tend to increase teachers' salaries, because there will be more competition among school districts for teachers. (d) One major argument is that decentralization allows educational curricula to be tailored more closely to the differences among communities in preferences.*

* For further discussion see J. Landon and R. Baird, "Monopsony in the Market for Public School Teachers," *American Economic Review,* December 1971.

quantity of input is at least as large as the extra cost of the additional quantity of input. Thus the monopsonist will increase its use of each input as long as the marginal revenue product of the input exceeds its marginal expenditure for the input. The firm will stop increasing its use of each input when the input's marginal revenue product equals the marginal expenditure for the input.

Thus, since an input's marginal revenue product equals its marginal product times the firm's marginal revenue, it follows that the monopsonist will hire inputs so that

$$MP_x \cdot MR = ME_x \qquad \text{14.4a}$$

$$MP_y \cdot MR = ME_y \qquad \text{14.4b}$$

$$\vdots$$

$$MP_z \cdot MR = ME_z \qquad \text{14.4c}$$

where ME_x is the marginal expenditure for input x, ME_y is the marginal expenditure for input y, and ME_z is the marginal expenditure for input z.

These equations are the basic conditions for profit maximization under monopsony. Note that Equations 14.1a $\cdots$ 14.1c can be regarded as a special case of Equations 14.4a $\cdots$ 14.4c. If the markets for the inputs are perfectly competitive, the marginal expenditure for each input is simply equal to the price of each input, since a firm can buy all it wants of each input without affecting its price. Thus, Equations 14.1a $\cdots$ 14.1c are special cases of Equations 14.4a $\cdots$ 14.4c that hold under perfect competition in the input markets.

It is often stated that a monopsonist will hire inputs so that

$$\frac{MP_x}{ME_x} = \frac{MP_y}{ME_y} = \cdots = \frac{MP_z}{ME_z} \qquad \text{14.5}$$

To see that Equation 14.5 follows from Equations 14.4a, 14.4b, $\cdots$, 14.4c, note that Equations 14.4a, 14.4b, $\cdots$, 14.4c imply

$$MP_x \div ME_x = \frac{1}{MR}$$

$$MP_y \div ME_y = \frac{1}{MR}$$

$$\vdots$$

$$MP_z \div ME_z = \frac{1}{MR}$$

Thus Equations 14.4a, 14.4b, $\cdots$, 14.4c imply that Equation 14.5 is true. Note also that Equation 14.5 is equivalent to the standard condition for cost minimization under perfect competition,

$$\frac{MP_x}{P_x} = \frac{MP_y}{P_y} = \cdots = \frac{MP_z}{P_z}$$

if there is perfect competition in the input markets. This follows from the fact, noted previously, that the marginal expenditure for an input equals its price under perfect competition.

10. Baseball: A Case Study

Before leaving the subject of monopsony, sports fans (and others) may be interested to note that the labor market in professional baseball has had many monopsonistic characteristics. There is a tight set of rules governing contractual arrangements between players and teams. Until the mid-1970s, once a player signed his first contract, the club could renew his contract for the following year at a price that the club could set (as long as it was not less than about 75 percent of his current salary). Another stipulation was that the team had exclusive rights to the use of the player's services. He could not play baseball for anyone else without the team's consent.

Consequently, once a player had signed his first contract in organized baseball, he was no longer able to sell his services in any way he chose. He could not move freely from one team to another. He could, of

course, drop out of organized baseball and take up some other occupa-
tion. But if he stayed in organized baseball, he had to do what the team
with his contract said. If the team assigned his contract to another team,
the player had to work for the assignee team. No other team in organized
baseball could hire him.

Given these rules, one would expect, on the basis of the analysis in
the previous four sections, that baseball players would receive less than
they would if the labor market for baseball players were perfectly competitive. It may seem hard to believe that baseball stars making very
large salaries were being exploited—in the sense that their salaries were
less than they would have received in a free labor market. But leading
labor economists like Simon Rottenberg of the University of Massachusetts reached this conclusion after careful study of the market for baseball players.

According to some observers, the situation could be represented (in
simplified form) by Figure 14.5, which shows the club owners' demand
curve for baseball players and the supply curve for baseball players.
Assuming that the club owners did not compete among themselves for
players, but acted as a monopsonist, they would hire players up to the
point where the marginal expenditure curve (*EE'*) intersected the demand curve. That is, they would hire *OU* players and pay a wage of *OX*
thousands of dollars per year. On the other hand, if the market for
players was competitive, the club owners would hire *OV* players and pay

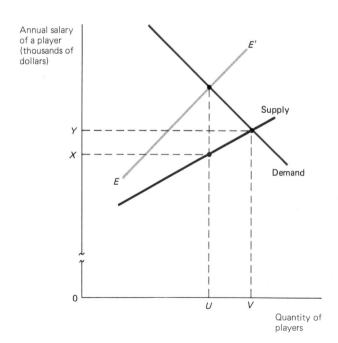

Figure 14.5   The market for baseball players: A simple
monopsony model

a wage of OY thousands of dollars per year. In this highly simplified situation, it is clear that the wage was lower in the former case than in the latter.[3]

A number of reasons were given for the restrictive rules built into contracts for professional athletes. For example, it was frequently asserted that they were necessary to maintain a relatively equal distribution of playing talent among the various teams. Without these rules, it was claimed that the wealthier clubs would buy up most of the best players, with the result that games would be uneven and attendance would drop. This argument was challenged by many observers. According to Rottenberg and others, a free market for players would produce better results: "It appears that free markets would give as good aggregate results as any other kind of market for industries, like the baseball industry, in which all firms must be nearly equal if each is to prosper. On welfare criteria, . . . the free market is superior to the others, for in such a market each worker receives the full value of his services and exploitation does not occur."[4]

In the mid-1970s, after protracted legal battles, the rules governing the hiring of baseball players were changed. Players were allowed to declare themselves free agents, and other teams were allowed to bid for their services. These and other such changes (some of which were factors in the baseball strike of 1981) meant a reduction in the monopsonistic power of the baseball clubs.

11. Labor Unions

One of the most important inputs is, of course, labor, and an important feature of the labor market is the existence of unions. About 1 in 4 nonfarm workers in the United States belongs to a union. The four largest unions are the Teamsters, the Auto Workers, the National Education Association, and the Steel Workers. Until the 1930s, there was strong opposition to unions, but since the passage of the Wagner Act in 1935, most manufacturing industries have become unionized. In the remainder of this chapter, we discuss briefly the ways in which unions can

3. The material in this section is based largely on S. Rottenberg, "The Baseball Players' Labor Market," *Journal of Political Economy,* June 1956; and D. North and R. Miller, *The Economics of Public Issues* (New York: Harper and Row, 1973). Note that Figure 14.5 is highly simplified. For one thing, it assumes that the players do not band together to try to counteract the monopsony power of the club owners. In fact, the players have formed an association and have carried out strikes on occasion. Thus there is a strong element of bilateral monopoly, discussed in Chapter 10. For further discussion, see R. Noll and B. Okner, *The Economics of Professional Baseball* (Washington, D.C.: Brookings Institution, 1973); and J. Quirk and M. El Hodiri, "Model of a Professional Sports League," *Journal of Political Economy,* December 1971. I am indebted to Edward D. Mansfield for sharing his extensive knowledge of this subject with me, and for doing his best to keep me from error.

4. S. Rottenberg, ibid.

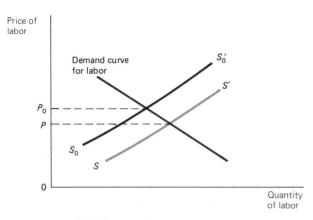

Figure 14.6   Shift in supply curve for labor

try to increase wages, the nature of union objectives, tactical considerations in collective bargaining, and the economic effects of unions.

For the moment, let us suppose that a union wants to increase the
wage rate paid its members. How might it go about accomplishing this
objective? First, the union might try to shift the supply curve of labor to
the left. For example, it might shift the supply curve from SS' to $S_0 S'_0$ in
Figure 14.6, with the result that the price of labor will rise from OP to
OP_0. To cause this shift in the supply curve, the union might restrict
entry into the union, or it might not let nonunion workers obtain jobs, or
it might restrict the labor supply in other ways.

Second, the union might try to get the employers to pay a higher
wage, while allowing some of the supply of labor forthcoming at this
higher wage to find no opportunity for work. For example, in Figure 14.7,
the union might exert pressure on the employers to get them to raise the

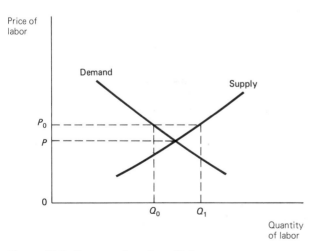

Figure 14.7   Increase in price of labor

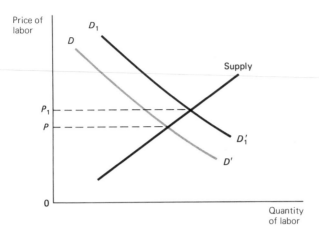

Figure 14.8 Shift in demand curve for labor

price of labor from OP to OP_0. At OP_0, not all of the available supply of labor can find jobs, because the quantity of labor supplied is OQ_1, while the amount of labor demanded is OQ_0. The effect is the same as in Figure 14.6, but in this case the union does not limit the supply directly: It lets the higher wage reduce the opportunity for work.

Third, the union might try to shift the demand for labor upward and to the right. For example, in Figure 14.8 it might shift the demand curve from DD' to D_1D_1', with the result that the price of labor will increase from OP to OP_1. To cause this shift in the demand curve for labor, the union might help the employers advertise their products; it might help them to be more efficient and better able to compete against other industries, or it might try to get Congress to pass legislation to protect the employers from foreign competition. Also, it might try to force employers to hire more workers than are needed for particular jobs.

12. Collective Bargaining and Bilateral Monopoly

In the previous section, we described various ways in which unions might influence the price of labor. But this does not tell us what the price of labor will be. Can we predict the equilibrium wage level in a unionized labor market? For simplicity, suppose that the union is confronted by a single group representing the employers. For example, the Steel Workers might be confronted by a single group representing the steel firms. To some extent, the union can be viewed as a labor monopoly in a case of this sort, and the process of wage negotiation can be viewed as a case of bilateral monopoly, the union on the one side, management on the other.

Figure 14.9 shows the demand curve for labor and the union's supply curve for labor.[5] If RR' is the marginal revenue curve corresponding to

5. See Footnote 9, Chapter 10 (p. 293).

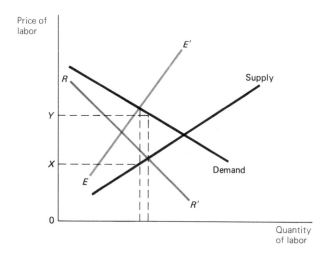

Figure 14.9   Bilateral monopoly in the labor market

this demand curve, and *EE'* is the curve showing the firms' marginal expenditure for labor, it will be recalled from Chapter 10 that, according to the theory of bilateral monopoly, the employers will want to set a wage rate of *OX* and the union will want to set a wage rate of *OY*. Since the wage that will result in such a situation is indeterminate, we cannot go any further toward predicting the wage level. The result depends on the relative bargaining power and negotiating skill of the two parties. For example, the industry may feel that it is not in a position to withstand a strike, while the workers may feel that they can easily weather a strike. The result also depends on public opinion and political action. For example, some government unions, like the letter carriers, have obtained wage increases through congressional influence, and some strikes result in government intervention to try to protect vital public services.

Note an important problem in applying the theory of bilateral monopoly to this situation: The theory assumes that the union wants to maximize the difference between the total wages that are paid to (employed) workers and the amount of money required to bring this amount of labor onto the market if each unit of labor were paid only the price necessary to induce it to work. It is by no means obvious that this is what unions are trying to do. Indeed, a number of other assumptions concerning the objectives of unions are equally plausible, as we shall see in the next section.

13. The Nature of Union Objectives

What are the objectives of unions? This is a difficult matter to settle, since unions, like firms, have diverse goals that are not easy to encapsulate and measure. Indeed, the problem is even more difficult for unions than for firms, because there is less agreement that any relatively simple

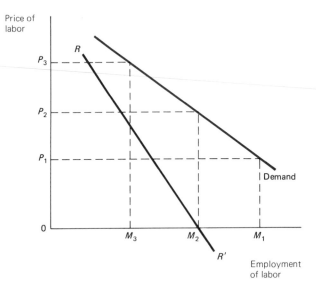

Figure 14.10   Three types of union behavior

objective like profits is a reasonable first approximation. Nevertheless, it is worthwhile discussing the implications of some simple hypotheses concerning union motivation that have been put forth. Three possible union objectives that are often considered are: (1) The union wants to keep its members fully employed; (2) the union wants to maximize the aggregate income of its members; and (3) the union wants to maximize the wage rate subject to the condition that a certain minimum number of its members be employed. All three hypotheses concerning union motivation have a certain amount of plausibility. It is easy to show, however, that they lead to quite different conclusions regarding union behavior.

Suppose that the demand curve for labor that faces the union is as shown in Figure 14.10. If the union has objective 1 and if it contains OM_1 members, it will have to accept a wage of OP_1, since this is the highest wage that will enable all of its members to find work.

But suppose that it has objective 2. Then it will choose OP_2, since this is the wage that maximizes the total wage bill of the union. To prove this, note that the wage bill is the union's total revenue from its product, labor; and that consequently the wage bill is maximized when the union's marginal revenue is zero. Using the techniques described in Chapter 5, one can derive the union's marginal revenue curve from the demand curve; the result is RR'. Since this marginal revenue curve intersects the horizontal axis at OM_2, the union's wage bill is maximized when OM_2 workers are employed, which means that the wage must be OP_2. Note that, if the union has objective 2, it must be prepared to see a great many of its members out of work.[6]

6. And there is the difficult question of which members should be unemployed and which members should work.

On the other hand, suppose that the union has objective 3. Specifically, suppose that it wants to maximize the wage rate subject to the condition that OM_3 of its members are employed, these members being perhaps those with considerable seniority. If this is its objective, it will choose a wage of OP_3, since this is the highest wage at which the employment level is at least OM_3.

It is clear that the wage desired by the union—and the supply of labor—will vary considerably, depending on which of these objectives is pursued. After all, OP_1, OP_2, and OP_3 are quite different wage levels, and OM_1, OM_2, and OM_3 are quite different labor supplies. Moreover, it is also perfectly clear that the three objectives stated above are only three possibilities out of a very large number. For example, the union leadership obviously has as one objective the maintenance of its own position in the union.[7]

14. Tactical Considerations in Collective Bargaining

The wage demands made by unions depend on tactical considerations, as well as on the union's basic objectives. The initial asking figure put forth by the union is likely to be higher than the union's real expectations. The difference between the initial asking figure and the union's real expectation is governed by what the union regards as the best tactics. In most cases the union refrains from making the difference so large that the initial asking figure seems ridiculously large. On the other hand, the union often considers it unwise to make the difference so small that there is little room for compromise.

The union's basic demand, the one for which it fundamentally is striving, is likely to be influenced considerably by what other unions are obtaining for their memberships. If other unions are getting increases of 60 cents an hour, the union may feel that it must do at least this well in order to show the membership that it can produce for them. Thus wage negotiations in a few major industries like automobiles and steel may set a pattern for other industries. Also, the union's basic wage demands will depend on the size of the industry's profits (its "ability to pay"), the mood and militancy of the membership, and the extent of the union's nonwage demands (work rules, pensions, union shop, etc.).

The employer tries, of course, to pay only what it must for what it regards to be the optimal number of employees. Like the union, it is influenced by tactical considerations in bargaining with the union concerning wages. For example, it may adopt a hard bargaining position when it thinks the union is in a relatively weak position, or an easy bargaining position when it wants to maintain a friendly group of union officials in office. It may adopt a hard bargaining position when it thinks that the union needs to be "put in its place," or an easy bargaining

---

7. For an excellent discussion of this topic, see J. Dunlop, *Wage Determination Under Trade Unions,* Reprints of Economic Classics (New York: Augustus M. Kelley, 1966). This section is based largely on Dunlop's book.

Example 14.2   Economic Effects of Unions

Suppose that the economy can be divided into a unionized sector and a nonunion sector. The demand curve for labor in the union sector is D_u, the demand curve for labor in the nonunion sector is D_n, and the demand curve for labor in both sectors combined is D_c. The supply curve for labor in the economy as a whole is shown below.

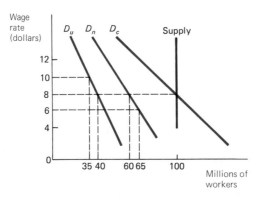

(a) Before the entry of the union, what will be the wage rate? (b) If the union raises the wage rate to $10 in the unionized sector, how many workers will the union sector lay off? (c) If all of these workers get jobs in the nonunion sector, what will be the effect on the wage rate in the nonunion sector? (d) Unions sometimes engage in featherbedding, which requires employers to hire more workers than they would otherwise. For example, railroads often have been required to hire more operating employees per train than they deemed necessary (or profitable). In the short run, such practices often increase the employment of union members. Does this effect persist in the long run as well?

Solution

(a) $8, since this is where the combined demand curve, D_c, intersects the supply curve. (b) Its employment will fall from 40 million to 35 million, so 5 million will be laid off. (c) The wage rate in the nonunion sector will have to fall to $6 if an additional 5 million workers are to be hired there. (d) In the long run, the effect is unpredictable since the increase in the labor costs may accelerate types of substitution that the union cannot block. For example, new technologies utilizing fewer or other types of labor may be developed more quickly, or the product (made more expensive by featherbedding) may lose some of its markets to competing products or to imports.*

* For further discussion, see A. Rees, "The Effects of Unions on Resource Allocation," *Journal of Law and Economics,* October 1963.

position when it wants to persuade the union to reduce its nonwage demands.

Given the basic objectives of the union and the employer in a particular case, the wage level that actually is negotiated is determined by the relative bargaining strength of the two parties and by their relative skill at negotiation. The strength of the employer depends on its ability to withstand a strike and to keep its head above water. The strength of the union depends on the extent of its membership, its ability to keep out nonunion workers and to enlist the support of other unions, and the size of its financial reserves.

15. Effects of Unions on Wages

Given the apparent importance of labor unions in the American economy, it may seem that we should be able to describe the effects of unions on wages with relative ease. Unfortunately, we are not able to do so. Although a considerable amount of research has been carried out, there is a great deal of uncertainty concerning the effects of unions. Of course, if unions provide labor with a relative bargaining advantage—or counterbalance monopsonistic pressures by employers—it would seem that the wage rate should be higher with unions than without them. But it is very difficult to isolate and measure this effect.

Empirical studies of the effect of unions on wages have generally been based on comparisons of wage increases in unionized industries with those in nonunion industries. Using such methods, H. G. Lewis has concluded that unions increased wages by about 15 percent during the 1950s.[8] Similarly, Weiss finds that "unions that organize entire jurisdictions seemed to raise earnings by 7 to 8 percent for craftsmen and 6 to 8 percent for operatives, compared with poorly organized industries."[9] However, the results vary considerably from time period to time period. Moreover, comparisons of this sort are difficult to interpret because increases in union wages may prompt increases in nonunion wages, with the result that the difference in wage increases between union and nonunion fields underestimates the effect of unions on wages.

Besides influencing the general wage level, unions may influence the size of wage differentials among firms, jobs, and regions. With respect to wage differentials among firms or regions, it seems quite likely that unionization will reduce such differentials, particulary if industry-wide bargaining develops. However, if some firms or regions become unionized and others do not, differentials may increase. With respect to wage dif-

8. H. G. Lewis, *Unionism and Relative Wages in the United States* (Chicago: University of Chicago Press, 1963).

9. L. Weiss, "Concentration and Labor Earnings," *American Economic Review,* March 1966.

ferentials among occupations, the available evidence seems to suggest that unions have tended to reduce wage differentials between high-paid and low-paid occupations. This is probably due in part to the tendency of unions to seek larger percentage increases for the least-skilled workers.

16. Summary

If there is imperfect competition in product markets but perfect competition in the market for an input, a firm will use an input in such a way that the marginal revenue product of the input equals the price of the input. Thus, if there is only one variable input, the firm's demand curve for the input is the same as the marginal-revenue-product curve. If there are several variable inputs, the firm's demand curve for an input is no longer the same as the marginal-revenue-product curve, since a change in the price of one input will result in changes in the quantity used of other inputs. The market demand curve for an input can be derived by finding at each price the amount of the input that will maximize the profits of each firm in the market, and by summing these amounts over all firms in the market. The equilibrium price of the input is given by the intersection of the market demand and supply curves for the input.

Monopsony is a situation in which there is a single buyer. The supply curve of the input facing the monopsonist is the market supply curve. If the monopsonist maximizes profit, it sets the marginal expenditure for the input equal to the marginal revenue product of the input. The monopsonist will employ less of the input than would be used if the input market were perfectly competitive. Also, the monopsonist will set a lower price for the input than if the input market were perfectly competitive. The market for baseball players has had some monopsonistic aspects.

An important feature of the market for labor is the existence of labor unions. To some extent, unions can be viewed as labor monopolies. However, it is difficult to know what the objectives of the union are. Under certain circumstances the union might want to keep its members fully employed. Under other circumstances, a union might want to maximize the aggregate income of its members. And these two objectives are only two possibilities out of a very large number. The wage demands made by unions depend on tactical considerations, as well as the union's basic objectives. The initial asking figure put forth by the union is likely to be higher than the union's real expectations. The wage that actually results from collective bargaining is indeterminate: It is likely to depend on the relative bargaining strength and negotiating skill of the two parties, as well as on public opinion and other factors. If unions provide labor with a relative bargaining advantage—or counterbalance monopsonistic pressures by employers—it would seem that the wage rate should be higher with unions than without them. Empirical studies seem to indicate such an effect, but they are subject to many limitations.

QUESTIONS AND PROBLEMS

1. Suppose that a firm's demand curve for its product is as follows:

Output	Price of good (dollars)
23	5.00
32	4.00
40	3.50
47	3.00
53	2.00

Also, suppose that the marginal product and total product of labor (the only variable input) is:

Amount of labor	Marginal product of labor	Total output
2	10	23
3	9	32
4	8	40
5	7	47
6	6	53

(Note that the figures regarding marginal product pertain to the interval between the indicated amount of labor and one unit less than the indicated amount of labor.) Given these data, how much labor should the firm employ if labor costs $12 a unit?

2. The Chicago local of the musicians' union once required that an orchestra must consist of at least 18 men. Analyze the effects of this requirement on the number of musicians hired in the Chicago area.

3. According to Allan Cartter and F. Ray Marshall, former President Carter's Secretary of Labor, the impact of unionism on wage levels of organized workers is most noticeable during periods of recession. Why?

4. According to Albert Rees, there is evidence that agreements sometimes exist "among employers not to raise wages individually or not to hire away each other's employees. . . . Except in the unusual case of professional sports, however, these agreements must be very difficult to enforce." Using the concepts presented in this chapter, analyze the effects on wages and employment of such agreements. Also, indicate some of the reasons why they may be difficult to enforce.

5. Suppose that the market supply schedule for input Y is as follows:

Quantity of Y	Price of Y (dollars)
10	1
11	2
12	3

Plot the marginal expenditure curve for Y in the relevant range. (Assume that input Y must be used in integer amounts.)

6. If the market supply curve for an input is a horizontal line, will the marginal expenditure curve for this input differ from the market supply curve? Explain.

7. A craft union is formed, which forces employers to hire only union members. The union membership is restricted by high initiation fees and a variety of other devices. What are the effects on the demand curve, supply curve, and price of labor?

8. What would be the effect of a union on a monopsonistic labor market? Would it necessarily lead to unemployment?

9. What would be the effect of a minimum wage on a monopsonistic labor market? Would it necessarily reduce employment?

10. An input is said to be "exploited" when it receives less than the value of its marginal product. Is labor exploited under (a) perfect competition, (b) unions, (c) monopsony?

SELECTED REFERENCES

BECKER, GARY. *The Economics of Discrimination.* Chicago: University of Chicago Press, 1957.

DUNLOP, JOHN. *Wage Determination Under Trade Unions.* Reprints of Economic Classics. New York: Augustus M. Kelly, 1966.

NORTHRUP, HERBERT, AND GORDON BLOOM. *Economics of Labor Relations.* 8th ed. Homewood, Ill.: Irwin, 1977.

REYNOLDS, LLOYD. *Labor Economics and Labor Relations.* 6th ed. Englewood Cliffs, N.J.: Prentice-Hall, 1974.

REES, ALBERT. *The Economics of Work and Pay.* New York: Harper and Row, 1973.

RIMA, INGRID H. *Labor Markets, Wages, and Employment.* New York: Norton, 1981.

15 General Equilibrium Analysis and Resource Allocation

1. Interrelationships among Microeconomic Units

At the beginning of this book we said that microeconomics is concerned with the economic behavior of individual decision-making units like consumers, resource owners, and firms. At first glance one might interpret this statement to mean that microeconomics views the behavior of such individual units and the workings of individual markets in isolation, with each unit or market being considered separately. Such an interpretation would be quite wrong. Microeconomics is also concerned in an important way with how these units and these markets fit together. Indeed, some of the intellectually most exciting, and practically most significant, aspects of microeconomics deal with the interrelations among individual units and among various markets.

In previous chapters we looked in detail at the behavior of individual decision-making units and the workings of individual markets. Our approach has been like that of a movie-maker who, sitting with a camera in a helicopter, depicts a battle by zooming in to get a close-up picture of what the infantry is doing, then by zooming in to get a picture of what the artillery is doing, then by zooming in to get a picture of what the commanding generals are doing, and so on. After taking these pictures, the movie-maker has the problem, of course, of showing how the pieces fit together.

At this point, we face the same kind of problem. We, like the movie-maker, have zoomed in to study the behavior of people acting as consumers; then we have zoomed in to study the behavior of people acting as managers and as workers. And we have zoomed in to look at the workings of various kinds of markets, each considered separately. Now we must show how economists have attempted to form an integrated model of the economy as a whole. This clearly is an important task: Every schoolchild knows that it is important not to get so engrossed in the trees that one loses sight of the forest.

In this chapter, we provide a brief introduction to general equilibrium analysis, the branch of microeconomics that deals with the interrelations among various decision-making units and various markets. After defining general equilibrium analysis, we see whether we can be reasonably sure that a state of general equilibrium can exist in a perfectly competitive economy. Then we build a simple general equilibrium model and describe input-output analysis, an important application and extension of this type of model. Finally, we take up some questions concerning the optimal allocation of resources.

2. Partial Equilibrium Analysis vs. General Equilibrium Analysis

As stressed in the last section, our analysis in previous chapters has focused on a single market, viewed in isolation. According to the models we have used, the price and quantity in each such market are determined by supply and demand curves, and these supply and demand curves are drawn on the assumption that other prices are given. Each market is regarded as independent and self-contained for all practical purposes. In particular, it is assumed that changes in price in this market do not have significant repercussions on the prices existing in other markets.

But this assumption in reality may be seriously wrong. No market can adjust to a change in conditions without there being a change in other markets, and in some cases the change in other markets may be substantial. For example, suppose that a shift to the left occurs in the demand for pork. In previous chapters, it was assumed that when the price and output of pork changed in response to this change in conditions, the prices of other products would remain fixed. However, the market for pork is not sealed off from the markets for lamb, beef, and other meats.[1] (For that matter, it is not completely sealed off from the markets for other food products or from the markets for other less similar products, like washing machines and autos.) Thus the market for pork cannot adjust without disturbing the equilibrium of other markets *and without having these disturbances feed back on itself.*

An analysis that assumes that changes in price can occur without causing significant changes in price in other markets is called a *partial*

---

1. Quantitative evidence on this point was presented in Table 5.4, where the cross-elasticity of demand for beef with respect to the price of pork was given.

equilibrium analysis. This is the kind of analysis we carried out in previous chapters. An analysis that takes account of the interrelationships among prices is called a *general equilibrium analysis.* Both kinds of analysis are very useful, each being valuable in its own way. Partial equilibrium analysis is perfectly adequate in cases in which the effect of a change in market conditions in one market has *little* repercussion on prices in other markets. For example, in studying the effects of a proposed excise tax on the production of a certain commodity, the assumption that prices of other commodities are fixed may be a good approximation to the truth. However, if the effects of a change in market conditions in one market result in *important* repercussions on other prices, a general equilibrium analysis may be required.

3. The Nature and Existence of General Equilibrium

General equilibrium analysis, like partial equilibrium analysis, can be used to solve problems of many kinds. One of the most fundamental problems that general equilibrium analysis has been used to help solve is as follows: If we could somehow establish a perfectly competitive economy, would it be possible for equilibrium to occur simultaneously in all markets? That is, does a set of prices exist such that all of the markets would be in equilibrium simultaneously?

Approaching this problem somewhat differently, let us define a state of *general equilibrium* as a state of the economy in which the following conditions hold: (1) Every consumer chooses his or her preferred market basket subject to his or her budget line, which is determined by the prices of inputs and the prices of products; (2) every consumer supplies whatever amount of inputs he or she chooses, given the input and product prices that prevail; (3) every firm maximizes its profits subject to the constraints imposed by the available technology, the demand for its product, and the supply of inputs; but in the long run profits are zero; and (4) the quantity demanded equals the quantity supplied at the prevailing prices in all product and input markets.

Given this definition of a state of general equilibrium, the problem is: Can we be sure that a state of general equilibrium can be achieved? It is evident from the definition of general equilibrium that a great many conditions must be satisfied simultaneously if a state of general equilibrium is to be achieved. Can we be sure that all of these conditions can always be satisfied at the same time? Or can they all be satisfied only under certain conditions? And if so, what are these conditions? This is an important question that has received considerable attention from economic theorists.

4. The Conditions for the Existence of General Equilibrium

Work by Kenneth Arrow, Gerard Debreu, Lionel McKenzie, and others has established that in a perfectly competitive economy a general equilibrium can be achieved under a fairly wide set of conditions. As Robert Kuenne has put it,

> Judged ... against the characteristics of our abstract economic models [of consumption and production], the pragmatic assertion of a faith that our data would need to be constrained in wholly acceptable ways to guarantee a solution under all allowable conditions of their initial values seems to be well justified on the whole.[2]

But are the prices and outputs that make up a general equilibrium unique? That is, is there only one set of prices and outputs at which supply equals demand in all markets? Clearly the answer is no. Only relative prices affect the decisions of consumers, firms, and resource owners. Thus, if all markets are in equilibrium at one set of prices, they will also be in equilibrium if all prices are increased or decreased in the same proportion. Whether there is more than one set of *relative* prices that can result in equilibrium is a more difficult question that is taken up in advanced texts but is beyond the scope of this book.

It is important to know that general equilibrium can be achieved under a wide set of conditions in a perfectly competitive economy. As we shall see in the next chapter, economists have concluded that, under certain circumstances, a perfectly competitive economy has a variety of desirable characteristics; for this reason, a perfectly competitive economy is sometimes held up as an ideal. For those who put forth this view, it would be embarrassing to find that this kind of economy is based on behavioral assumptions and market mechanisms that are incompatible in the sense that general equilibrium cannot be achieved. Fortunately, no such embarrassment is necessary.

5. A Simple Model of General Equilibrium

In the next three sections, we present in somewhat more detail a simple general-equilibrium model of the economy.[3] This model shows more

2. R. Kuenne, *The Theory of General Economic Equilibrium* (Princeton, N.J.: Princeton University Press, 1963), p. 566. Also see K. Arrow and G. Debreu, "Existence of an Equilibrium for a Competitive Economy," *Econometrica*, July 1954; G. Debreu, *Theory of Value* (New York: Wiley, 1959); L. McKenzie, "On the Existence of General Equilibrium for a Competitive Market," *Econometrica*, January 1959; J. Quirk and R. Saposnik, *Introduction to General Equilibrium Theory and Welfare Economics* (New York: McGraw-Hill, 1968); and K. Arrow and F. Hahn, *General Competitive Analysis* (San Francisco: Holden-Day, 1971).

To be more specific, Arrow and Debreu show that a general equilibrium exists if increasing returns to scale exist for no firm, at least one primary input must be used to produce each commodity, the quantity of a primary input supplied by a consumer must not be greater than his or her initial stock of the input, each consumer can supply all primary inputs, each consumer's ordinal utility function is continuous, his or her wants cannot be satiated, and his or her indifference curves are convex. Of course, these conditions are sufficient but not necessary.

3. This model is similar to ones presented in J. Due and R. Clower, *Intermediate Economic Analysis* (Homewood, Ill.: Irwin, 1966), pp. 391–97; and R. G. D. Allen, *Mathematical Economics* (London: Macmillan, 1960), pp. 317–19. Also see H. Varian, *Microeconomic Analysis* (New York: Norton, 1978).

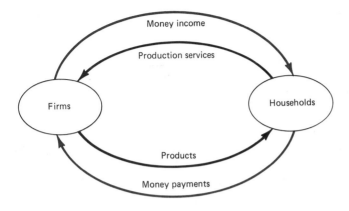

Figure 15.1   Flows in a two-sector economy

completely the nature of general equilibrium in a perfectly competitive economy. The nature of the analysis being such that it is necessary for the reader to be familiar with the idea of, and notation for, a set of equations, readers who do not have this familiarity can skip to Section 8 without losing the thread of the argument.

For simplicity, we assume in this model that the economy is composed of two sectors, a business sector and a consumer sector. A diagram describing the flows of income, payments, products, and services in such an economy is shown in Figure 15.1. Note that there is no government sector or foreign sector. Although they could be added, the essential features of general equilibrium can be described without them. We assume that all production is done by firms (not consumers) and that all inputs come from consumers (not firms). This means that there are no intermediate goods—goods made by one firm to be used by another firm.

In addition, we assume that consumers obtain their incomes only from the sale of inputs to firms, and that this income is spent entirely on the products of these firms. Moreover, we assume that the amount of inputs supplied by each consumer is fixed and independent of the level of input prices. This assumption is made because it simplifies the analysis, not because of necessity or realism; it can easily be relaxed in more advanced treatments of this topic. Finally, we also assume that there are fixed coefficients of production. This assumption too can easily be relaxed.

When this simple two-sector model is in equilibrium, the total flow of money income from firms to households is equal to the flow of payments from households to firms. We shall be concerned here with the characteristics of this simple economy in equilibrium, not with the path by which it moves from one equilibrium to another. Let the economy consist of A consumers, C consumer products, and D types of inputs. Thus, if there are 2 million consumers, 500 consumer products, and 1,000 types of inputs, A equals 2 million, C equals 500, and D equals 1,000. We assume that all markets are perfectly competitive.

6. Equations of the Model

There are three kinds of equations in this simple model of general equilibrium. First, there are equations representing the demand by consumers for commodities. Let r_{ca} be the amount of the cth commodity demanded by the ath consumer. We know from Chapter 5 that r_{ca} will depend on the prices of all commodities and on the tastes of the ath consumer. Also, r_{ca} will depend on the prices of all of the inputs, since they (together with the amount of each input supplied by the consumer) determine the consumer's income. Thus, there are AC equations of the form:

$$r_{ca} = r_{ca}(p_1, \cdots, p_C, W_1, \cdots, W_D) \qquad \begin{matrix} (c = 1 \cdots C) \\ (a = 1 \cdots A) \end{matrix} \qquad \text{15.1}$$

where p_c is the price of the cth commodity, and W_d is the price of the dth input. The consumer's tastes (and his or her supply of inputs) determine the functional form of each of these equations.

Letting R_c be the total quantity demanded by consumers of the cth commodity, it is obvious that

$$R_c = r_{c1} + r_{c2} + \cdots + r_{cA} \qquad (c = 1 \cdots C) \qquad \text{15.2}$$

Consequently, it follows from the equations in (15.1) that

$$R_c = R_c(p_1, \cdots, p_C, W_1, \cdots, W_D) \qquad (c = 1 \cdots C) \qquad \text{15.3}$$

In other words, the total quantity demanded of each commodity depends on all commodity and input prices, with the form of the relationship differing from commodity to commodity.

Second, there are equations that insure that the total amount of each input employed by firms is equal to the total amount of the input supplied by consumers. That is, firms cannot use more inputs than are supplied, and there is no unemployment of inputs. If u_{cd} is the amount of the dth type of input used to produce one unit of the cth consumer good, this means that

$$X_d = u_{1d} R_1 + u_{2d} R_2 + \cdots + u_{Cd} R_C \qquad (d = 1 \cdots D) \qquad \text{15.4}$$

where X_d is the total amount of the dth type of input supplied by consumers.

Third, there are equations that insure that the long-run conditions of perfect competition are met, with neither profit nor loss in the production of each commodity. In other words, price must equal average cost for each commodity. And since there are fixed coefficients of production, the average cost of producing the cth commodity is

$$A_c = u_{c1} W_1 + u_{c2} W_2 + \cdots + u_{cD} W_D \qquad (c = 1 \cdots C) \qquad \text{15.5}$$

where W_1 is the price of the first input, W_2 is the price of the second input, and so on. Consequently, if the price of the cth commodity equals its average cost,

$$p_c = u_{c1} W_1 + u_{c2} W_2 + \cdots + u_{cD} W_D \qquad (c = 1 \cdots C) \qquad \text{15.6}$$

7. Existence of a Solution

We have constructed a simple general equilibrium model composed of equations in 15.3, 15.4, and 15.6.[4] However, the fact that we have written down these equations does not insure that a solution exists. In other words, it does not insure that at least one consistent and feasible set of numbers can be assigned to all the variables so that all these equations are satisfied. One step in telling whether a solution exists is to compare the number of equations in the model with the number of variables to be determined. Table 15.1 shows the number of equations in the model and the number of variables to be determined. Note that the number of equations in 15.4 is given as $(D - 1)$, rather than D. This is because one of the equations in 15.4 is not independent. If all the other equations in the model hold, it can be shown that this equation must hold too. Thus there are only $(D - 1)$ independent equations in 15.4.[5]

Table 15.1 shows that the number of equations is one less than the number of variables. This means that the model cannot determine values for each of the variables to be determined. The situation is similar to having one equation and two variables to be determined: Although only

4. This is an extremely simple model. For more complete accounts of general equilibrium analysis, see R. G. D. Allen, *Mathematical Economics;* and J. Quirk and R. Saposnik, *Introduction to General Equilibrium Theory and Welfare Economics;* as well as R. Kuenne, *The Theory of General Economic Equilibrium.*

5. Suppose that each of the equations in 15.6 holds and that all but one of the equations in 15.4 hold. That is, assume that

$$p_c = \sum_d u_{cd} W_d \qquad\qquad (c = 1 \cdots C)$$

$$X_d = \sum_c u_{cd} R_c \qquad\qquad (d = 1 \cdots (D - 1))$$

It is easy to show that the remaining equation in 15.4 must hold too. Since the total amount spent by consumers must equal their total income,

$$\sum_c R_c p_c = \sum_d X_d W_d$$

And since $p_c = \sum_d u_{cd} W_d$, it follows that

$$\sum_d X_d W_d = \sum_c R_c \sum_d u_{cd} W_d$$

Moreover, since $\sum_{d=1}^{D-1} X_d W_d = \sum_{d=1}^{D-1} \sum_c u_{cd} R_c W_d$,

$$X_D W_D = \sum_c R_c \sum_d u_{cd} W_d - \sum_{d=1}^{D-1} \sum_c u_{cd} R_c W_d$$

$$= \sum_c R_c \sum_d u_{cd} W_d - \sum_c R_c \sum_{d=1}^{D-1} u_{cd} W_d$$

$$= \sum_c R_c u_{cD} W_D$$

Therefore, since $W_D > 0$, $X_D = \sum_c u_{cD} R_c$, which is what we set out to prove.

Table 15.1   Number of equations versus number of variables

EQUATIONS		VARIABLES	
Equation	*Number*	*Variable*	*Number*
15.3	C	R_c	C
15.4	$D - 1$	W_d	D
15.6	C	p_c	C

certain pairs of numbers can be solutions, there is no single solution. However, we can obtain a solution if we take the price of one commodity or input as being given: If we arbitrarily select one commodity or input as the *numeraire* and assign this commodity or input a price of 1, we have an exactly determined system. This is just like setting one variable equal to 1 and solving for the other variable in a case where there are two variables and one equation. In effect, the prices of all commodities and inputs are expressed in terms of the price of the numeraire. For example, if $p_3 = 3$, this means that the price of the third commodity is 3 times the price of the numeraire.

We stated above that one step in telling whether a solution exists is to compare the number of equations in the model with the number of variables to be determined. However, for reasons that are too technical to concern us here, the equality of the number of variables and the number of equations does not always guarantee that a solution exists. Whether or not it does depends on the functional form of the equations; and whether the solution is economically meaningful depends on the solution's satisfying various nonnegativity constraints.[6] But as we saw in Section 4, it can be shown that a meaningful state of general equilibrium exists under a fairly wide set of conditions.

8. Input-Output Analysis: An Extension and Application

Léon Walras,[7] a nineteenth-century French economist, was the first to construct a model of the general equilibrium of a perfectly competitive economy. His model has been modified in subsequent years but the general formulation remains much the same. Vilfredo Pareto[8] was another great nineteenth-century figure in the development of this field. In the period since these men did their pioneering work, many improvements and extensions have been made in general equilibrium analysis, some of which have been cited in previous sections. In more recent years, a dominant figure in general equilibrium analysis has been Wassily Leontief,[9] a Nobel laureate and the father of input-output analysis.

6. These nonnegativity constraints are like those discussed in Chapter 8; it makes no sense for some variables, like the production of corn, to be negative.

7. L. Walras, *Elements of Pure Economics,* translated by W. Jaffé (New York: Allen and Unwin, 1954). It originally appeared in French in 1874.

8. V. Pareto, *Cours d'Economie Politique* (F. Rouge, 1897).

9. W. Leontief, *The Structure of the American Economy* (New York: Oxford University Press, 1951).

Input-output analysis puts general equilibrium analysis in a form that is operationally useful to governments and firms faced with a variety of important practical problems. An important feature of input-output analysis is its emphasis on the interdependence of the economy. Each industry uses the outputs of other industries as its inputs, and its own output may be used as an input by the same industries whose output it uses.[10] Recognizing this interdependence, input-output analysis attempts to determine the amount that each industry must produce in order that a specified amount of various final goods can be consumed. It has been applied to help predict production requirements to meet estimated demands; for example, it has been applied by economic planners to estimate capacity requirements in various industries.

To put general equilibrium analysis in a form that is operationally useful, input-output analysis makes a number of simplifying assumptions. To begin with, it uses as variables the *total* quantity of a particular good demanded or supplied, rather than the quantity demanded by a particular consumer or the quantity supplied by a particular firm. This reduces enormously the number of variables and the number of equations that are included. Also, it is assumed that consumer demand for all commodities is given. This assumption, together with the assumption (discussed in the following paragraph) that inputs are used in fixed proportions, means that demand theory does not play an important part in input-output analysis.[11] Input-output analysis attempts to find out what can be produced, and the amount of each input and intermediate good that must be employed to produce a given output. The question is viewed as being largely a matter of technology.

Finally, it is assumed that inputs are used in fixed proportions in producing any product and that there are constant returns to scale. This is a key assumption of Leontief's input-output system. For example, in the production of steel, Leontief would assume that, for every ton of steel produced, a certain amount of iron ore, a certain amount of coke, a certain amount of fuel, and so on would be required. The amount of each input required per unit of output is assumed to be the same, regardless of the level of output. For example, if a certain amount of iron ore is required to produce 1 million tons of steel, it is assumed that 10 times that amount is required to produce 10 million tons of steel.[12]

---

10. Note that this is in contrast to the model in Sections 5 to 7 where it was assumed that there were no intermediate goods.

11. Strictly speaking, this is true only in Leontief's open model, which is all that is described here. In his closed model, at least some attention must be given to the determinants of demand. See W. Leontief, *Input-Output Economics* (New York: Oxford University Press, 1966); and H. Chenery and P. Clark, *Interindustry Economics* (New York: Wiley, 1959).

12. In Chapter 6, we said that the proportion in which inputs are combined can generally be altered. This, of course, is a direct contradiction of the assumption of fixed proportions in input-output analysis. But it often takes a fair amount of time for changes to be made and they are often gradual, with the result that Leontief's assumption of fixed proportions may work reasonably well in the short run despite this fact.

9. A Simple Input-Output Model

Anyone with a rudimentary understanding of the solution of simultaneous linear equations can quickly grasp the essentials of input-output analysis. For example, suppose that the economy consists of only three industries: coal, chemicals, and electric power. Suppose that each industry uses the products of the other industries in the proportions shown in Table 15.2. For instance, the second column of Table 15.2 states that every dollar's worth of coal requires 20 cents worth of electric power, 10 cents worth of coal, and 70 cents worth of labor.[13]

Suppose that this economy has set consumption targets of $100 million of electric power, $30 million of coal, and $40 million of chemicals. Input-output analysis is concerned with the question: How much will have to be produced by each industry in order to meet these targets? To begin to solve this problem, consider the case of coal. If electric power output is E, chemical output is C, and coal output is X (E, C, and X are measured in millions of dollars), it follows from Table 15.2 that

$$X = .4E + .1X + .2C + 30 \qquad \text{15.7}$$

if the target is met. Why? Because an amount of coal equal in value to $.4E$ must be produced to meet the needs of the electric power industry, an amount of coal equal in value to $.1X$ must be produced to meet the needs of the coal industry, an amount of coal equal in value to $.2C$ must be produced to meet the needs of the chemical industry, and an amount of coal equal in value to 30 must be produced for consumption. Thus the total output of coal must be equal to the sum of these four terms, as shown in Equation 15.7.

If we construct similar equations for electric power output and chemical output, we find that

$$E = .2E + .2X + .2C + 100 \qquad \text{15.8}$$

$$C = .2E + .1C + 40 \qquad \text{15.9}$$

if the targets are to be met. For example, Equation 15.9 must hold because chemical output must equal the amount needed by the electric power industry ($.2E$) plus the amount needed by the chemical industry itself ($.1C$) plus 40 for consumption.

Equations 15.7 to 15.9 are three simultaneous linear equations in three variables, X, E, and C. It is a simple matter to solve for these unknowns; the solution is $X = 131$, $E = 178$, and $C = 84$. This provides the answer to our question: $131 million of coal, $178 million of electric power, and $84 million of chemicals must be produced if the consumption targets are to be met. Also, we can find out how much labor will be required to meet these targets, since (according to Table 15.2) the total value of labor required equals

$$.2E + .7X + .5C$$

13. In some cases, outputs and inputs are measured in physical units rather than dollars. For example, coal output and coal input might be measured in tons per year, and labor input might be measured in man-hours per year. Clearly, one can carry out the analysis in either way.

Table 15.2   Amount of each input used per dollar of output

TYPE OF INPUT	TYPE OF OUTPUT		
	Electric power (dollars)	Coal (dollars)	Chemicals (dollars)
Electric power	0.2	0.2	0.2
Coal	0.4	0.1	0.2
Chemicals	0.2	0.0	0.1
Labor	0.2	0.7	0.5
Total	1.0	1.0	1.0

Substituting the 131, 178, and 84 for X, E, and C, respectively, we find that $169 million of labor are required. If this is within the available labor supply, the solution is feasible; otherwise the targets must be scaled downward.

This simple example illustrates the fundamentals of input-output analysis. It also suggests why the assumption that inputs are used in fixed proportions is so convenient. Without this assumption, the input-output table in Table 15.2 would not hold for each output level of the industries; instead the numbers in the table would vary depending on how much of each commodity was produced. The added complexity that would arise if this assumption were relaxed is obvious. Even with this assumption, the computational difficulties and problems of estimation involved in obtaining solutions to large input-output models can be substantial. Although a model involving 450 industries has been constructed for the United States, usually far fewer industries are included in such models.

10. Applicability of Input-Output Analysis

Whether or not input-output analysis can be applied fruitfully in a particular situation depends in part on whether the *production coefficients*—the numbers in Table 15.2, for example—remain constant (see footnote 12). There are at least two important factors that might cause changes over time in such coefficients: First, changes in technology may result in smaller amounts of certain inputs, and more of other inputs, being used. For example, the amount of coal required to produce many goods decreased considerably in the period since World War II. Second, changes in the relative prices of inputs may result in changes in production coefficients as cheaper inputs are substituted for more expensive ones.

In the previous section we showed how input-output analysis can be used to determine the output level of each industry, and the total amount of labor, required to meet specified target consumption levels. It is also possible to determine long-run equilibrium prices in an input-output model. In the long run, there will be no economic profits; the total

Example 15.1   The Economics of Gasohol

Gasohol is a blend of 10 percent ethanol and 90 percent regular gasoline. Ethanol can be made from corn. In late 1979, the cost of a gallon of ethanol made from corn was estimated at $1.20. The refinery price of regular gasoline was 85 cents per gallon. To encourage the production of gasohol, the federal government exempted gasohol from the federal gasoline tax, worth 40 cents on the 10 percent ethanol content of gasohol. And many states exempted it from their motor fuel taxes, worth another 40 cents to $1 per gallon of ethanol. (a) Will each gallon of ethanol used in gasohol result in a one-gallon reduction in the amount of regular gasoline (or other fuels) used in the United States? (b) In what way would an input-output table (like Table 15.2) be useful in answering part (a)? (c) Given the above tax incentives, is it profitable to produce gasohol? If so, does this mean that gasohol will displace regular gasoline completely? (d) What will be the effect of these tax exemptions on corn prices? On the value of corn-producing land? Can a partial equilibrium analysis answer these questions?

Solution

(a) No, because fuel must be used to produce and transport the corn required to produce the ethanol. (b) It would indicate how much fuel is required to produce a gallon of ethanol. (c) Yes. Although the cost of a gallon of ethanol is 35 cents higher (that is, $1.20 minus 85 cents) than a gallon of gasoline, exemption from the federal gasoline tax is worth 40 cents per gallon and exemption from state taxes is often worth at least 40 cents more per gallon. Thus the tax exemptions more than offset the higher cost of production of ethanol. However, some very optimistic forecasts in the late 1970s of gasohol sales have yet to be achieved. Gasohol will never displace regular gasoline completely, because as more and more gasohol is produced, the price of corn will be bid up, and eventually, despite the tax exemptions, it will no longer be profitable to substitute more gasohol for regular gasoline. (d) Corn prices and the value of corn-producing land will tend to rise. A general equilibrium analysis can handle these questions more adequately than a partial equilibrium analysis.*

* For further discussion, see Fred Sanderson, "Gasohol: Boon or Blunder," *The Brookings Bulletin,* Winter 1980; and "Gasohol Fails to Live Up to Its Advance Billings, But Still Manages to Attract Its Share of Schemers," *Wall Street Journal,* March 10, 1981.

revenue received by each industry will be equal to its total costs. Using this proposition, it is possible to determine the level of long-run equilibrium price in each industry.[14]

14. Suppose that we have an input-output table like Table 15.2, but suppose that the production coefficients are expressed in physical units (see footnote 13). If we have

The postwar period has seen a great deal of work carried out to implement and extend input-output analysis. Some of it has been basic research carried out by academic economists interested in the quantitative significance of various types of economic interdependence. Some of it has been research aimed at the formulation of techniques that would be useful in decision-making in government and business. For example, a large government-sponsored program in the United States in the early fifties was carried out to analyze problems of defense and mobilization. In other countries, programs have been carried out to determine the relationship of imports and exports to domestic production, as well as to analyze various problems of economic development.[15]

With regard to our energy crises, input-output analysis has been used in a variety of ways. Anne Carter of Brandeis University and Clopper Almon of the University of Maryland used this technique to estimate the effect of the Arab oil embargo on the level of unemployment in various industries. The Department of Commerce used it to estimate the effect of increases in oil prices on industrial and consumer prices. And a number of research groups used it to forecast the economic effects of possible new technologies in the energy field.

11. Resource Allocation and the Edgeworth Box Diagram

We now turn our attention to a somewhat different, but related, topic. In previous chapters, we have stated repeatedly that microeconomics is concerned with the way in which resources should be allocated. Once we consider more than a single market, it becomes possible to consider many interesting questions concerning the optimal allocation of resources. The rest of this chapter is devoted to a discussion of some of these questions.

In the simple models that we shall take up, the Edgeworth box diagram finds extensive use. The Edgeworth box diagram shows the interaction between two economic activities when the total amount of commodities consumed or inputs used by these activities is fixed in quantity. To see how the Edgeworth box diagram is constructed, and how it should be interpreted, see Figure 15.2. We assume that there are two goods, food and medicine, and two consumers, Tom and Harry. The total amount of food that they have is OF and the total amount of medicine that they have is OM.

The amount of food that Tom has is measured horizontally from the origin at O. The amount of medicine that Tom has is measured vertically from O. Thus any point in the box diagram indicates a certain amount of food and a certain amount of medicine consumed by Tom. For example, the point, P, indicates that Tom consumes OR of food and OS of medi-

---

the price of each input, we can determine the long-run equilibrium price in each industry by solving a set of simultaneous equations. See R. Dorfman, *The Price System* (Englewood Cliffs, N.J.: Prentice-Hall, 1964).

15. H. Chenery and P. Clark, *Interindustry Economics;* and Leontief, *Input-Output Economics.*

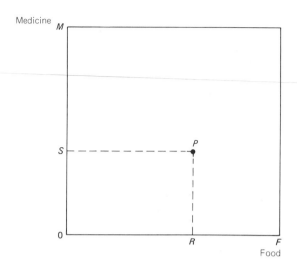

Figure 15.2   Edgeworth box diagram

cine. The amount of food that Harry consumes is measured by the horizontal distance to the left of the upper right-hand corner of the box diagram. And the amount of medicine that Harry consumes is measured by the vertical distance downward from the upper right-hand corner of the box diagram. Thus every point in the diagram indicates an amount of food and medicine consumed by Harry. For example, the point P indicates that Harry consumes $(OF - OR)$ of food and $(OM - OS)$ of medicine.

The important points to remember about the Edgeworth box diagram are that its length and width represent the total amounts of the two commodities that both consumers together have, and that each point in the box represents an allocation of the total supplies of the two goods between the two consumers.

The Edgeworth box diagram can be used for production problems, as well as consumption problems. For example, suppose that there are two industries, industry A and industry B, and that there are two inputs, labor and capital. Suppose that the total amount of labor available to the two industries is OL and the total amount of capital available to the two industries is OK. Figure 15.3 shows the relevant Edgeworth box diagram, the height of which equals the total amount of labor, OL, and the width of which equals the total amount of capital, OK.

Any point in the box represents an allocation of this total supply of labor and total supply of capital between the two industries. The amount of labor allocated to industry A is represented by the vertical distance upward from the origin, and the amount of capital allocated to industry A is represented by the horizontal distance to the right of the origin. For example, point Q indicates that industry A has OU of labor and OV of capital. The amount of labor allocated to industry B is represented by the distance downward from the upper right-hand corner of the box diagram, and the amount of capital allocated to industry B is

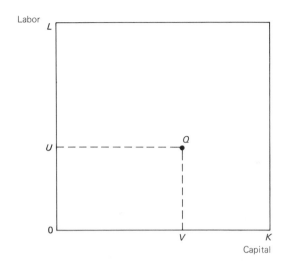

Labor

Figure 15.3 Edgeworth box diagram: Production

represented by the distance leftward from the upper right-hand corner of
the box diagram. Thus point Q indicates that industry B receives $(OL -
OU)$ of labor and $(OK - OV)$ of capital.

12. Exchange

Let's return now from production to consumption, and discuss the process of exchange. To begin with, consider an economy of the simplest
sort. There are only two consumers, Tom and Harry, and only two
commodities, food and medicine. There is no production; the only economic problem is the allocation of a given amount of food and medicine
between the two consumers. If it helps, you may regard Tom and Harry
as two shipwrecked sailors marooned on a desert island with a certain
amount of food and medicine that they rescued from their ship.

The amount of food and medicine brought by Tom to the island is
indicated in the Edgeworth box diagram in Figure 15.4: He arrives with
OH units of food and OI units of medicine. The amount of food and
medicine brought by Harry to the island is also indicated in Figure 15.4:
He arrives with $(OF - OH)$ units of food and $(OM - OI)$ units of
medicine. The total amount of food brought to the island by both men is
OF, and the total amount of medicine brought to the island by both men
is OM.

If the two men are free to trade with one another, what sort of
trading will take place? What can be said about the optimal allocation of
the commodities between the two men? To find out, we must insert the
indifference curves of Tom and Harry into the Edgeworth box diagram in
Figure 15.4. Three of Tom's indifference curves are T_1, T_2, and T_3. The
highest indifference curve is T_3; the lowest is T_1. Three of Harry's indifference curves are H_1, H_2, and H_3. The highest indifference curve is H_3;

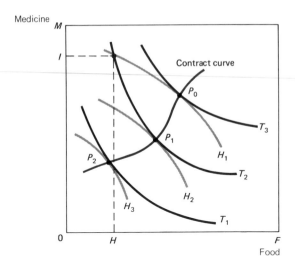

Figure 15.4 Exchange

the lowest is H_1. In general, Tom's satisfaction is increased as we move from points close to the origin to points close to the upper right-hand corner of the box. Conversely, Harry's satisfaction is increased as we move from points close to the upper right-hand corner of the box to points close to the origin.

Given the initial allocation of food and medicine, we find that Tom is on indifference curve T_2 and Harry is on indifference curve H_1. At this point, Tom's marginal rate of substitution of food for medicine is much higher than Harry's, as shown by a comparison of the slope of T_2 with the slope of H_1 at this point. Thus, if both men are free to trade, Tom will trade some medicine to Harry in exchange for some food. The exact point to which they will move cannot be predicted, however. If Tom is the more astute bargainer, he may get Harry to accept the allocation at point P_0, where Harry is no better off than before (since he is still on indifference curve H_1) but Tom is much better off (since he has moved to indifference curve T_3). On the other hand, if Harry is the better negotiator, he may be able to get Tom to accept the allocation at point P_1, where Tom is no better off than before (since he is still on indifference curve T_2) but Harry is much better off (since he has moved to indifference curve H_2). The ultimate point of equilibrium is very likely to be between P_0 and P_1.

One thing is certain. If the object is to make the men as well off as possible, the optimal allocation of the commodities is one in which the marginal rate of substitution of food for medicine will be the same for both men. Otherwise one man can be made better off without making the other worse off. In other words, the optimal allocation is a point at which Tom's indifference curve is tangent to Harry's. The locus of points at which such a tangency occurs is called the *contract curve*. This curve, shown in Figure 15.4, includes all points, like P_0, P_1, and P_2, where the marginal rates of substitution are equal for both consumers. The contract curve is an optimal set of points in the sense that, if the consumers are at a point *off* the contract curve, it is always preferable for them to move to a point *on* the contract curve, since one or both can gain from the move while neither incurs a loss.

13. Production[16]

In the previous section we discussed the case in which consumers exchange quantities of commodities, when there is no production. In this section and the next, we take up a simple case in which there is production but no consumption. Then, in Section 15, we combine the results and consider a case in which there is both consumption and production.

Consider a simple economy in which only two goods are being produced, the production sector of the economy being composed of a food industry and a medicine industry. Suppose that there are two inputs, labor and capital, and that the total amount of labor to be allocated between the two industries is OL and the total amount of capital to be allocated between the two industries is OK. Suppose that the initial allocation of labor and capital is that represented by point Z in the Edgeworth box diagram in Figure 15.5. That is, the food industry has OA units of labor and OB units of capital, and the medicine industry has ($OL - OA$) units of labor and ($OK - OB$) units of capital.

On the basis of the production functions for food and medicine one can insert isoquants for both food production and medicine production in Figure 15.5. Three isoquants for food production are F_1, F_2, and F_3. The

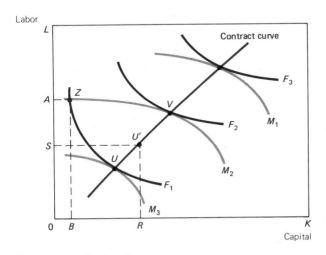

Figure 15.5   Production

16. The following sections are based to some extent on F. Bator, "The Simple Analytics of Welfare Maximization," *American Economic Review*, March 1957.

Example 15.2   Can Boretania's Targets Be Met?

Boretania, a hypothetical country with a very simple economy, produces only two goods: food and machinery. The amount of each input used per dollar of output is shown below.

TYPE OF OUTPUT

TYPE OF INPUT	Food (dollars)	Machinery (dollars)
Food	0.10	0.20
Machinery	0.40	0.70
Labor	0.50	0.10
Total	1.00	1.00

The Boretania government has set consumption targets of $100 million of food and $50 million of machinery. There is available in the Boretania economy sufficient capacity to produce $200 million of food and $400 million of machinery, but no more. Can the consumption targets be met?

Solution

No. To meet these targets,

$$F = 100 + 0.1\,F + 0.2\,M$$
$$M = 50 + 0.4\,F + 0.7\,M,$$

where F is the food output and M is the machinery output needed to meet the targets (both F and M are expressed in millions of dollars). Solving these two equations simultaneously, we find that $F = 211$ and $M = 448$; so, to meet these targets, $211 million of food and $448 million of machinery would have to be produced.

---

isoquant pertaining to the highest output level is F_3; the isoquant pertaining to the lowest output is F_1. Three isoquants for medicine production are M_1, M_2, and M_3. The isoquant pertaining to the highest output level is M_3; the isoquant pertaining to the lowest output level is M_1.

What will be the optimal allocation of inputs between the two industries? At the original allocation at point Z, the marginal rate of technical substitution of capital for labor in producing food is higher than in producing medicine. This is indicated by the fact that the slope of F_1 is steeper than the slope of M_2 at point Z. The fact that the marginal rates of technical substitution are unequal means that the inputs are not being allocated efficiently. For example, suppose that at point Z the food industry can substitute 2 units of labor for 1 unit of capital without changing its output level, while the medicine industry must substitute 1 unit of labor for 2 units of capital to maintain its output level. In this case if the medicine industry uses more labor and less capital and if the food industry uses less labor and more capital, it will be possible for one industry to expand its output without any reduction in the other industry's output. Specifically, it is possible to move to point U, where the output of food is the same as at Z but the output of medicine is at the level corresponding to M_3. It is also possible to move to point V, where the output of medicine is the same as at Z but the output of food is at the level corresponding to F_2. Or it is possible to move to a point between U and V.

Regardless of which point is chosen, production should occur at a point at which the marginal rate of technical substitution between inputs is the same for all producers, if the allocation of inputs is to be efficient in the sense that an increase in the output of one commodity can be achieved only by reducing the output of the other commodity. Thus the optimal allocation of inputs will lie somewhere along the locus of points, where the marginal rates of technical substitution are equal—and consequently where a food isoquant is tangent to a medicine isoquant. This locus of points, like the analogous set in the previous section, is called the *contract curve*,[17] and is shown in Figure 15.5. This curve is an optimal set of points in the sense that, if producers are at a point *off* the contract curve and if society is interested in producing as much as possible of each good, it is always socially desirable for them to move to a point *on* the contract curve, since output in one industry or the other can be increased without a reduction in the other's output.

Note that this analysis of production is entirely analogous to the analysis of exchange in the previous section. The total amounts of the two inputs determine the dimensions of the Edgeworth box in this section; the analogous quantities in the previous section are the total amounts of the two commodities. The isoquant maps play an analogous role to the indifference maps in the previous section.

14. The Product Transformation Curve

The contract curve in Figure 15.5 shows the various allocations of inputs that are optimal. Corresponding to each point on this contract curve is a level of output of food and a level of output of medicine. For example, consider U. If the level of output of food corresponding to isoquant F_1 is 100 and if the level of output of medicine corresponding to isoquant M_3 is 200, then an output of 100 units of food and 200 units of medicine corresponds to the point U. Similarly, if the level of output of food corresponding to isoquant F_2 is 200 and if the level of output of medicine corresponding to isoquant M_2 is 100, then an output of 200 units of food and 100 units of medicine corresponds to the point V.

Proceeding in this way, we can find the pair of outputs corresponding to each point on the contract curve. Then we can plot each such pair

17. Other terms could be used as well, but this is the term that is often applied.

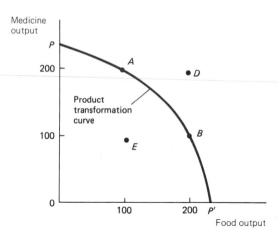

Figure 15.6   Product transformation curve

of points in a graph like Figure 15.6, where the amount of food produced is shown on the horizontal axis and the amount of medicine produced is shown on the vertical axis. For example, the pair of outputs corresponding to point U on the contract curve are plotted as point A in Figure 15.6, and the pair of outputs corresponding to point V on the contract curve are plotted as point B in Figure 15.6. The curve, PP', which results when all of these points are plotted in Figure 15.6, is called the product transformation curve.

The product transformation curve shows the various combinations of food output and medicine output that can be derived from the economy's input base (which is OL units of labor and OK units of capital). More specifically, it shows the maximum output of one good that can be produced, holding fixed the output of the other good. Given the economy's input base, it is impossible, given existing technology, to attain a point (like D) that is outside the product transformation curve. It is possible to attain a point like E that is inside the product transformation curve, but it would be inefficient to do so. As long as production is efficient, production occurs at some point along the product transformation curve.

15. Production and Exchange

In this section, we take up a simple model that includes both production and exchange. Our simple economy contains two consumers, Tom and Harry, and two commodities, food and medicine, and two inputs, labor and capital. As in Sections 13 and 14, this economy can use a total of OL units of labor and OK units of capital. If the input base, the utility functions of the consumers, and the production functions in the two industries are given, how should these inputs be allocated between industries, and how should the output of goods be allocated between the consumers?

Example 15.3 The Allocation of Fissionable Material

During the early 1950s, a key U.S. defense problem was how to allocate fissionable material between our tactical and strategic forces. There were a fixed total number of aircraft (OA) and a fixed supply of fissionable materials (OM) in the short run. Every point in the Edgeworth box diagram shown below indicates an allocation of fissionable material and airplanes to the tactical and strategic forces. For example, point P represents a case where our strategic forces get OU units of aircraft and OV units of fissionable material, and our tactical forces get ($OA - OU$) units of aircraft and ($OM - OV$) units of fissionable material. Within limits, it was possible to substitute airplanes for fissionable material and vice versa. For example, fewer aircraft would be required to destroy a certain number of targets if atomic weapons, rather than conventional weapons were used. Curve T_1 contains combinations of aircraft and fissionable material that result in equal effectiveness of the tactical forces. Curve T_0 also contains combinations that result in equal effectiveness of the tactical forces—but at a lower level than curve T_1. Curve S_2 contains combinations of aircraft and fissionable material that result in equal effectiveness of the strategic forces. Curve S_3 also contains combinations that result in equal effectiveness of the strategic forces—but at a higher level than curve S_2. The allocation at that time was represented by point W. Was this an optimal choice?

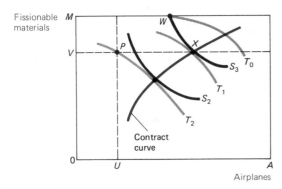

Solution

No, because point W is not on the contract curve. The Defense Department could increase the effectiveness of either the tactical or strategic forces without reducing the effectiveness of the other by moving to a point on the contract curve. For example, point X results in the same effectiveness of our strategic forces as point W, since both points are on curve S_3. But point X results in more effectiveness of our tactical forces than point W. In fact, this simple kind of economic analysis was used to help solve this important policy problem.[*]

---

[*] For further discussion, see S. Enke, "Using Costs to Select Weapons," *American Economic Review,* May 1965; and "Some Economic Aspects of Fissionable Materials," *Quarterly Journal of Economics,* May 1964.

If the isoquant map in each industry is that shown in Figure 15.5, we know from the previous section that the various combinations of food output and medicine output that can be derived from this input base are given by the product transformation curve, PP', in Figure 15.6. This curve, PP', is reproduced in Figure 15.7. Suppose that we know the composition of output in the economy, that is, the amount of food and medicine that will be produced. Then we can insert an Edgeworth box diagram similar to Figure 15.4 in Figure 15.7, the upper right-hand corner of the box being the point on the product transformation curve corresponding to the composition of output.

More specifically, suppose that we know that the composition of output in the economy will be represented by point A', where the quantity of food produced is OQ and the quantity of medicine produced is ON. Then we can draw a box diagram with OQ as its width and ON as its height. Since OQ is the total amount of food to be distributed to Tom and Harry, and ON is the total amount of medicine to be distributed to them, this box diagram can be used to see how much of the total output of each good will go to each consumer. Figure 15.7 shows the indifference curves of each consumer (T_1', T_2', and T_3' for Tom and H_1', H_2', and H_3' for Harry) within the box, $OQ A'N$. It also shows the contract curve, $C_1 C_1'$, the locus of points where Tom's indifference curves are tangent to Harry's.

We know from Section 12 that the distribution of output between the two consumers should be such that they will be on the contract curve, $C_1 C_1'$. But at what point on the contract curve should they be? We show in the following section that, if the economy's output is allocated so that consumer satisfaction is maximized, the marginal rate of transformation—the negative of the slope of the product transformation curve—must equal the marginal rate of substitution. Thus, if the economy's output is allocated to maximize consumer satisfaction, the consumers should be at the point on the contract curve at which the common slope

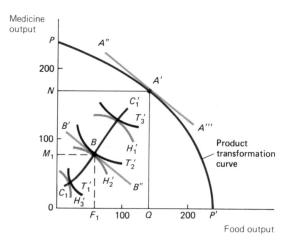

Figure 15.7   Production and exchange

of their indifference curves equals the slope of the product transformation curve at A'.

At what point on the contract curve does the common slope of their indifference curves equal the slope of the product transformation curve at A'? An examination of Figure 15.7 shows that this condition is fulfilled at point B on the contract curve, where Tom gets OF_1 units of food and OM_1 units of medicine and Harry gets $(OQ - OF_1)$ units of food and $(ON - OM_1)$ units of medicine. The slope of the indifference curves at point B equals the slope of the product transformation curve at point A', as demonstrated by the fact that the tangents, $B'B''$ and $A''A'''$ are parallel. Thus, given the amount to be produced of each commodity, we can find in this way the amount of each commodity that should be allocated to Tom and Harry.

In addition, we can find the amount of labor and capital that should be allocated to the production of each commodity by consulting the Edgeworth box diagram in Figure 15.5 that underlies the product transformation curve. Recall from Section 14 that each point on the product transformation curve corresponds to a point on the contract curve in Figure 15.5, and that each point on the contract curve in Figure 15.5 corresponds to a particular allocation of labor and capital between the production of the two commodities. For example, point A' on the product transformation curve corresponds to point U' on the contract curve in Figure 15.5. Thus, given that the composition of output in the economy will be given by point A', we know that OS units of labor will be devoted to the production of food, $(OL - OS)$ units of labor will be devoted to the production of medicine, OR units of capital will be devoted to the production of food, and $(OK - OR)$ units of capital will be devoted to the production of medicine.

To sum up, we have answered the two questions set forth at the beginning of this section. Given the amount of each commodity to be produced, we have shown how this output should be distributed between consumers and how the available inputs should be distributed between industries if production is to be efficient and if consumer satisfaction is to be maximized. However, it is important to note that our model is incomplete even for this simple two-commodity, two-consumer, two-input economy, since we take as given the amount of each commodity to be produced. In the next chapter, we shall describe one way that economists have attempted to complete the model.

16. The Marginal Rate of Product Transformation, the Marginal Rate of Substitution, and Consumer Satisfaction

In the previous section, it was asserted that consumer satisfaction will not be maximized unless the marginal rate of product transformation between two goods is equal to the marginal rate of substitution between the two goods. The purpose of this section is to demonstrate that this is the case. For simplicity, suppose that firm A produces both food and medicine and that it supplies all of these commodities consumed by Tom.

Suppose, too, that Tom initially consumes M_T units of medicine and F_T units of food, and that his marginal rate of substitution of medicine for food is X. Finally, suppose that firm A produces M units of medicine and F units of food and that the marginal rate of product transformation between food and medicine is Y.

The first thing we shall show is that consumer satisfaction is not being maximized if X is less than Y. If X is less than Y, suppose that we decrease the amount of medicine produced by firm A and the amount of medicine consumed by Tom by 1 unit. For Tom to maintain the same level of satisfaction, he can be given X additional units of food to offset the loss of the 1 unit of medicine. (This follows from the definition of the marginal rate of substitution, given in Chapter 3.)

Suppose that firm A gives him the extra X units of food. By decreasing its production of medicine by 1 unit, firm A can make an additional Y units of food. (This follows from the definition of the marginal rate of product transformation, given in Chapter 8.) After decreasing its output of medicine, firm A supplies Harry just as much medicine as before, since both its total output of medicine and Tom's consumption of medicine are reduced by 1 unit. But it can supply Harry with an extra ($Y - X$) units of food (the extra Y units it can produce less the X units it has given Tom). Consequently, Harry can be made better off without hurting Tom, if X is less than Y. Thus consumer satisfaction is not being maximized if X is less than Y.[18]

The next thing we shall show is that consumer satisfaction is not being maximized if X is greater than Y. If X is greater than Y, suppose that we increase the amount of medicine produced by firm A and the amount of medicine consumed by Tom by 1 unit. For Tom to maintain the same level of satisfaction, he must give up X units of food. Suppose that he gives them to firm A. By increasing its output of medicine by 1 unit, firm A can make Y fewer units of food. Firm A can supply Harry with as much medicine as before but it can supply him with an extra ($X - Y$) units of food (the X units Tom has given up minus the Y units by which its output of food has fallen). Consequently Harry can be made better off without hurting Tom if X is greater than Y. Thus consumer satisfaction is not being maximized if X is greater than Y.[19]

18. A numerical example may help make this easier. If Tom's marginal rate of substitution of medicine for food is 1 and if the marginal rate of product transformation between food and medicine is 2, firm A can reduce its output of medicine by 1 unit and provide Tom with 1 less unit of medicine. Firm A can also increase its production of food by 2 units and give Tom 1 extra unit of food to compensate for his loss of medicine. There is 1 unit of food left over, which can make Harry better off without hurting Tom.

19. A numerical example may help make this easier. If Tom's marginal rate of substitution of medicine for food is 2 and if the marginal rate of product transformation between food and medicine is 1, firm A can increase its output of medicine by 1 unit and provide Tom with 1 extra unit of medicine. Firm A can also obtain 2 units of food from Tom to compensate for the extra unit of medicine, but to produce the extra unit of medicine, firm A had to produce 1 less unit of food. Thus firm A has 1 unit of food left over, which can make Harry better off without hurting Tom.

If consumer satisfaction is not being maximized if X is less than Y, and if it is not being maximized if X is greater than Y, it follows that consumer satisfaction can be maximized only if X is equal to Y. This, of course, is what we set out to prove.

17. Summary

Previous chapters have been concerned with partial equilibrium analysis, which assumes that changes in price can occur in whatever market is being studied without causing significant changes in price in other markets, which in turn affect the market being studied. An analysis that takes account of the interrelationships among prices in various markets is called a general equilibrium analysis. One of the most fundamental problems that general equilibrium analysis has been used to help solve is whether or not it is possible for equilibrium to occur simultaneously in all markets in a perfectly competitive economy. Modern work has established that in a perfectly competitive economy a state of general equilibrium can be achieved under a fairly wide set of conditions.

General equilibrium analysis provides a framework of price and output relations for both commodities and inputs for the economy as a whole. Its purpose is to show what the equilibrium configuration of prices, outputs, and inputs will be in various markets, given a certain set of consumer preferences, production functions, and input supply functions. In the simple model studied in Sections 5 to 7, there are three kinds of equations. This model is extremely simple, since it assumes that the supply of inputs is given (and independent of prices) and that production coefficients are fixed. However, it illustrates the nature of general equilibrium models.

Input-output analysis attempts to make the general equilibrium model empirically useful. It assumes that inputs are used in fixed proportions in producing any product, that there are constant returns to scale, and that consumer demand for all commodities is given. An important feature of input-output analysis is its emphasis on the interdependence of the economy. Input-output analysis involves the solution of a number of simultaneous linear equations. A typical problem handled by input-output analysis is: If consumption targets for each of a number of industries are given, how much will have to be produced by each industry to meet these targets? Can these production levels be achieved with the available resources?

Once we consider more than a single market, it becomes possible to consider many interesting questions concerning the optimal allocation of resources. Using the Edgeworth box diagram, we showed that the optimal allocation of commodities between consumers lies on the contract curve. We also showed that the optimal allocation of inputs between industries lies on an analogous contract curve and that a production transformation curve can be constructed from the latter contract curve. Finally, we studied a simple model that included both production and exchange. It was shown that consumer satisfaction will not be maximized unless the marginal rate of product transformation between two goods is equal to the marginal rate of substitution between them.

QUESTIONS AND PROBLEMS

1. John takes a date, Joan, to a Chinese restaurant, and they order a portion of lemon chicken and a portion of sweet and sour pork. When the food arrives, they divide each portion between them. Indicate how the Edgeworth box diagram might be used to analyze the way in which they should divide the food. Is it reasonable to assume that John's satisfaction depends only on the amount of food he consumes and not on the amount Joan consumes too?

2. If the assumptions underlying input-output analysis are correct, what is the shape of isoquants?

3. Suppose that you have 6 bottles of beer (and no potato chips) and your roommate has 4 bags of potato chips (and no beer). It is late at night, and the stores are closed. You decide to swap some of your beer for some of her potato chips. The Edgeworth box diagram is the following:

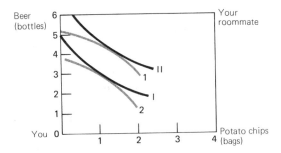

Your indifference curves are labeled I and II; hers are labeled 1 and 2. Label the point on the diagram which represents your pretrade situation.

4. In the previous question, suppose that you decide to swap 3 bottles of your beer for 1 bag of your roommate's potato chips. Is this a rational offer? That is, will it make you better off? Explain.

5. In Question 3, suppose that you offer to swap 2 bottles of your beer for 1½ bags of your roommate's potato chips. Will your roommate agree to this? Is this a rational offer for you to make? That is, will it make you better off?

6. In Example 15.2, suppose that $150 million worth of labor is available in the economy. Would this be enough to permit the consumption targets (given there) to be met, if the required capacity for food and machinery production were available?

7. Suppose that the following table shows the amount of each type of input used per dollar of output:

TYPE OF INPUT	OUTPUT		
	Electric power (dollars)	*Coal (dollars)*	*Chemicals (dollars)*
Electric Power	0.1	0.3	0.0
Coal	0.5	0.1	0.0
Chemicals	0.2	0.0	0.9
Labor	0.2	0.6	0.1
Total	1.0	1.0	1.0

Express the value of electric power output as a function of the value of coal output and the value of chemical output.

8. In Question 7, express the value of coal output as a function of the value of electric power output and the value of chemical output.

9. Describe how a product transformation curve can be derived from an Edgeworth box diagram representing production of two goods.

10. According to Bertrand de Jouvenel, "In an economic policy-making committee I recently happened to suggest that the Parthenon was an addition to the wealth of Athenians, and its enjoyment an element of their standard of life. This statement was regarded as whimsical." Do you agree with this statement? Why or why not?

SELECTED REFERENCES

CASSEL, GUSTAV. *The Theory of Social Economy.* New York: Harcourt, Brace and World, 1924.

DEBREU, GERARD. *Theory of Value.* New York: Wiley, 1959.

HENDERSON, JAMES, AND RICHARD QUANDT. *Microeconomic Theory.* 3d ed. New York: McGraw-Hill, 1980.

LEONTIEF, WASSILY. *The Structure of the American Economy.* New York: Oxford University Press, 1951.

VARIAN, HAL. *Microeconomic Analysis.* New York: Norton, 1978.

WALRAS, LÉON. *Elements of Pure Economics.* Translated by William Jaffé, Homewood, Ill.: Irwin, 1954.

16 Welfare Economics

1. Optimal Resource Use

At the beginning of this book, we made the claim that microeconomics is of use in clarifying public-policy issues. Having made this claim, we hastened to add that microeconomics alone is seldom able to provide a clear-cut solution to such issues, but that, in combination with other relevant disciplines, it frequently can provide useful ways of structuring and analyzing these issues. The purpose of this chapter is to provide an introduction to welfare economics, the branch of microeconomics that is concerned with the nature of the policy recommendations that economists can make.

To prevent confusion, note that welfare economics is not concerned with the various government "welfare" programs you read about in the newspapers. Instead, welfare economics covers a much broader set of questions; its primary concern is with policy issues concerning the allocation of resources. In other words, it deals mainly with questions concerning the optimal allocation of inputs among industries and the optimal distribution of commodities among consumers. These are general equilibrium problems, since the optimal usage of any input cannot be determined by looking at the market for this input alone, and the optimal output of any commodity cannot be determined by looking at the market for this commodity alone. On the contrary, the optimal allocation of resources between two products depends on the relative strength of the demands for the products and their relative production costs.

We have already begun the study of welfare economics, although we have not called it by that name. The latter part of the previous chapter, devoted to resource allocation, was concerned with welfare economics in the very simple case of a two-commodity, two-consumer, two-input economy. This chapter provides a further introduction to the fundamental principles of welfare economics. We begin by considering interpersonal comparisons of utility and by taking up the conditions that must be satisfied by an optimal allocation of resources. Then we deal with the role of perfect competition, as well as rules for government planning, in promoting an optimal allocation of resources. Finally, we discuss the nature and effects of external economies and diseconomies, various criteria for welfare judgments, Arrow's impossibility theorem, and the theory of the second best.

2. Interpersonal Comparisons of Utility and Pareto Efficiency

At the outset it is important to recognize an important limitation of welfare economics: *There is no scientifically meaningful way to compare the utility levels of various individuals.* The reader will recall that in our previous discussion of utility and demand theory in Chapters 3 and 4 we were not required to make any such interpersonal comparisons.[1] This was fortunate, and intentional. There is no way that one can state scientifically that a piece of Aunt Mary's apple pie will bring you more satisfaction than it will me, or that your headache is worse than mine. This is because there is no scale on which we can measure pleasure or pain in such a way that interpersonal comparisons can be made validly.

Because we cannot make interpersonal comparisons of utility, we cannot tell whether one distribution of income is better than another. For example, suppose you receive twice as much income as I do. Economics cannot tell us whether this is a better distribution of income than if I receive twice as much income as you do. This is a value judgment, pure and simple. However, most problems of public policy involve changes in the distribution of income. For example, even a decision to increase the production of numerically controlled machine tools and to reduce the production of conventional machine tools may mean that certain stockholders and workers will gain, while others will lose (since some machine tool firms specialize more heavily than others in the production of numerically controlled tools). Because it is so difficult to evaluate the effects of such a decision on the distribution of income, it is correspondingly difficult to come to any conclusion as to whether or not such a decision is good or bad.

1. However, there were two exceptions. In the treatment of the water problem in Chapter 4, we simply added the areas under the demand curves of various consumers to get an aggregate measure of the loss to consumers due to the curtailment of their use of water. We noted that this treatment, although sometimes adopted in applied work, suffers from difficulties. In this chapter, these difficulties are explained at length. Also, in Chapter 10, when we computed the welfare loss due to monopoly, we simply added up the areas under the demand curves of various persons. We indicated that this entailed problems which are discussed here in detail.

Faced with this problem, economists have adopted a number of approaches, all of which have important difficulties. Some economists simply have paid no attention to the effects of proposed policies on the income distribution. Others have taken the existing income distribution as optimal, while still others have asserted that income distributions exhibiting less inequality of income are preferable to those exhibiting more inequality of income. Purists have argued that we really cannot be sure a change is for the better unless it hurts no member of society. Others have suggested that we must accept the judgment of Congress (or the public as a whole) as to what is an optimal distribution of income.[2]

Much more will be said about these approaches when we discuss criteria for welfare judgments later in this chapter. For the moment, the important thing to note is that practically all economists accept the proposition that a change that harms no one and improves the lot of some people (in their own eyes) is an improvement. This criterion, put forth by Vilfredo Pareto at about the turn of the century and often called the *Pareto criterion*,[3] evades the question of income distribution. If a change benefits one group of people and harms another group, this criterion is not applicable. Nonetheless, this criterion is by no means useless, as we shall see below, and most economists would agree that all changes that satisfy this criterion should be carried out. That is, they believe that society should make any change that harms no one and improves the lot of some people. If all such changes are carried out—and thus no opportunity to make such changes remains—the situation is termed *Pareto-optimal* or *Pareto-efficient*. In Sections 3 and 4, we describe and discuss the marginal conditions for a Pareto-optimal allocation of resources. In Section 5, we take up one approach to the income-distribution problem.

3. Marginal Conditions for Optimal Resource Allocation

Fundamentally, there are three necessary conditions for optimal resource allocation. The first pertains to the optimal allocation of commodities among consumers. It states that *the marginal rate of substitution between any two commodities must be the same for any two consumers.* The proof that this condition is necessary to maximize consumer satisfaction is quite simple. All that needs to be noted is that, if the marginal rates of substitution were unequal, both consumers could benefit by trading. For example, suppose that the first consumer regards an additional unit of product A as having the same utility as 2 extra units of product B, whereas the second consumer regards an additional unit of

2. One contribution to this literature that has received considerable attention is J. Rawls, *A Theory of Justice* (Cambridge, Mass.: Harvard University Press, 1971). Rawls argues that "all social values ... are to be distributed equally unless an unequal distribution ... is to everyone's advantage." Needless to say, this proposition has aroused much controversy.

3. V. Pareto, *Manuel d'Economie Politique* (1909).

product A as having the same utility as 3 extra units of product B. Then, if the first consumer trades 1 unit of product A for 2.5 units of product B from the second consumer, both consumers are better off.

This condition implies that commodities should be distributed in such a way that consumers are on their contract curve, since the contract curve is composed of points where the marginal rates of substitution are equal for the consumers. In the case of only two commodities and two consumers, we showed in the previous chapter (Section 12) that this condition must be met if consumer satisfaction is to be maximized. We are now stating the more general proposition that this condition must also be met in the more realistic case in which there are more than two commodities and two consumers.

The second condition pertains to the optimal allocation of inputs among producers. It states that *the marginal rate of technical substitution between any two inputs must be the same for any pair of producers.* If this condition does not hold, it is possible to increase total production merely by reallocating inputs among producers. For example, suppose that, for the first producer, the marginal product of input 1 is twice that of input 2, whereas for the second producer the marginal product of input 1 is 3 times that of input 2. Then, if the first producer gives 1 unit of input 1 to the second producer in exchange for 2.5 units of input 2, both firms can expand their output.

To see this, suppose that the marginal product of input 1 is M_1 for the first producer and M_2 for the second producer. Then the output of the first producer is reduced by M_1 units because of its loss of the unit of input 1, but it is increased by $2.5 \times M_1/2$ units because of its gain of the 2.5 units of input 2, with the consequence that, on balance, its output increases by $M_1/4$ units because of the trade. Similarly, the output of the second producer is increased by M_2 units because of its gain of the one unit of input 1, but it is decreased by $2.5 \times M_2/3$ units because of its loss of the 2.5 units of input 2, with the consequence that, on balance, its output increases by $M_2/6$ units because of the trade.

This condition implies that inputs should be allocated so that producers are on their contract curve, since the contract curve is made up of points at which the marginal rates of technical substitution are equal for producers. In the case of only two inputs and two producers, we showed in the previous chapter (Section 13) that this condition must be met if the output of each producer is maximized, holding constant the output of the other producer. We are now stating the more general proposition that this condition must also be met in the more realistic case in which there are more than two inputs and two producers.

The third condition pertains to both the optimal allocation of inputs among industries and the optimal allocation of commodities among consumers. It states that *the marginal rate of substitution between any two commodities must be the same as the marginal rate of product transformation between these two commodities for any producer.* Suppose that PP' in Figure 16.1 is the product transformation curve, the curve that shows the maximum amount of good X that can be produced, given various output levels for good Y. The marginal rate of product transfor-

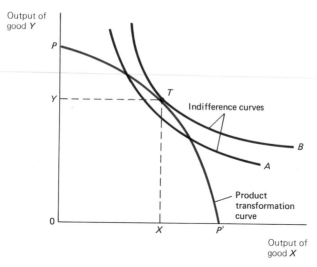

Figure 16.1   Product transformation curve and
indifference curves

mation is the negative of the slope of the product transformation curve;
it shows the number of units of good Y that society must give up in order
to get an additional unit of good X.

Suppose that curves A and B in Figure 16.1 represent the indifference curves of a consumer who, for simplicity, is assumed to be the
only consumer in the economy. To maximize the consumer's satisfaction,
production must take place at point T, where the output of good X is OX
and the output of good Y is OY. Clearly, T is the point on the product
transformation curve that is on the consumer's highest indifference
curve. Since the product transformation curve is tangent to the indifference curve at point T, it follows that the marginal rate of product
transformation equals the marginal rate of substitution at point T. Thus
the marginal rate of product transformation equals the marginal rate of
substitution if consumer satisfaction is maximized. This result will hold
for any number of consumers, not just for one.

In the case of two products and two consumers, we showed in the
previous chapter (Section 16) that this condition must hold if the satisfaction of one consumer is maximized, holding constant the other consumer's satisfaction. We are now stating the more general proposition
that this condition must also be met in the more realistic case in which
there are more than two commodities and two consumers.

4. Agricultural Price Supports: An Application

We can use these three conditions for optimal resource allocation to
analyze many interesting questions, such as the choice among alternative agricultural price support schemes. From Chapter 9 it will be re-

called that in the past such schemes have commonly specified that each farm can produce a certain quota, represented by OX in panel A of Figure 16.2. The total quota for the entire industry is OY in panel B of Figure 16.2. Also, a support price has frequently been set by the government, which is OP in this case. Since the demand curve for the product is as shown in panel B of Figure 16.2, consumers will purchase OQ_1 units of the product, and the government will buy $(OY - OQ_1)$ units of the product. This is in contrast to the situation that would prevail if there were no quotas and price supports; under these circumstances, price would be OP_1 and the total output of the product would be OQ_2. The purpose of the quotas and price supports is to increase the income of farmers.

Unfortunately, this type of support scheme leads to inefficiencies of various kinds in the use of resources. First, because the marginal cost at OX will certainly vary from farm to farm, the industry's total output will be produced inefficiently. That is, the total cost of producing the total output could be decreased by reducing the output of farms with high marginal cost at OX and increasing the output of farms with low marginal cost at OX. Since the industry's total output is being produced inefficiently, it is clear that the second condition in the previous section is being violated. Second, part of the industry's output is unnecessary, and is taken off the market by the government. Third, since price is above marginal cost for this product (see panel A of Figure 16.2), the third condition in the previous section is also violated, if the prices of other goods equal marginal cost (as they would in a perfectly competitive economy). The reasoning underlying this statement is explained in some detail in Section 6. For the moment, it is sufficient to accept it on faith.

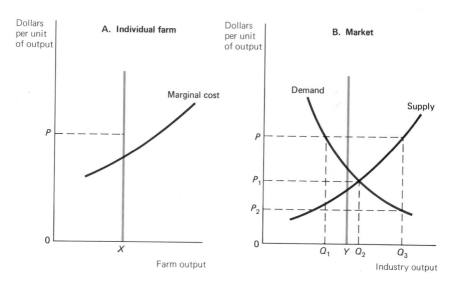

Figure 16.2 Agricultural price supports

On the other hand, suppose that the government adopts a different sort of scheme, one closer to that adopted in 1973. Suppose that the government guarantees each farmer a price of OP, with the result that the industry produces OQ_3 units of the product. But then suppose that it lets the free market alone, with the result that the OQ_3 units of the agricultural product command a price of only OP_2 in the market and the government pays each farmer $(OP - OP_2)$ per unit. The first type of inefficiency would be eliminated because each farmer would set marginal cost equal to OP, with the result that the marginal cost for each farm would be the same. The second type of inefficiency would be eliminated because the government no longer would take part of the industry's output off the market. The third type of inefficiency remains, since the price to consumers would be less than marginal cost.[4]

However, this does not mean that this scheme is necessarily an improvement. For instance (as noted in Section 2), any choice among policies must take into account their effects on the income distribution. This kind of plan would result in a different distribution of benefits and costs among consumers and farmers. For example, the abandonment of the quota system would hurt farmers who possess quotas. These aspects of the choice may outweigh all others in many people's minds. (Congressmen in particular may be sensitive to the question of whose ox is gored.) More will be said on this score in the next section.

5. The Utility-Possibility Curve and the Social Welfare Function[5]

In Section 2, we stated that the three conditions described in Section 3 are incomplete guides to an optimal allocation of resources, since they say nothing concerning the question of income distribution. In this section we show more explicitly how these conditions are incomplete, and we describe one way that economists have attempted to get around this problem. To do these things, it is convenient to return to the two-commodity, two-consumer, two-input case discussed at the end of the previous chapter. There are two consumers, Tom and Harry; two commodities, food and medicine; and two inputs, labor and capital. There are a total of OL units of labor and OK units of capital.

Given that the production functions are as shown in Figure 15.5 (p. 427), the previous chapter (Section 14) shows that the product transformation curve is that shown in Figure 15.6 (p. 430). This curve, PP', is reproduced in Figure 16.3. At any point on this curve, inputs are allocated so that the second condition in Section 3 is met (see Sections 13 and 14 of Chapter 15). If we know the amount of food and the amount of

---

4. See G. Stigler, *The Theory of Price* (New York: Macmillan, 1966), pp. 187–90. However, note that piecemeal attempts to induce fulfillment of the marginal conditions may not improve matters. See Section 15.

5. This section is based to a considerable extent on F. Bator, "The Simple Analytics of Welfare Maximization," *American Economic Review*, March 1957.

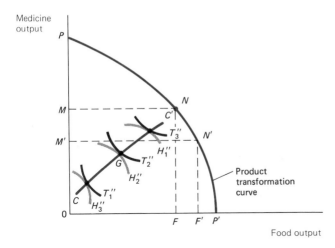

Figure 16.3   Production and exchange

medicine that will be produced, we can construct an Edgeworth box diagram for the two consumers. For example, if the total quantity of food produced is OF and the total amount of medicine produced is OM, the Edgeworth box diagram has OF as its width and OM as its height. Figure 16.3 also shows the indifference curves of Tom and Harry (T_1'', T_2'', and T_3'' for Tom; and H_1'', H_2'', and H_3'' for Harry) and the contract curve, CC'. At any point on this contract curve, commodities are allocated so that the first condition in Section 3 is met (see Section 12 of Chapter 15).

If the total quantity of food produced is OF and the total quantity of medicine produced is OM, the third condition in Section 3 dictates that the commodities be distributed between the consumers so that they are at point G. Only at point G does the common slope of their indifference curves (the negative of the marginal rate of substitution) equal the slope of the product transformation curve at point N (the negative of the marginal rate of product transformation). The distribution of commodities at point G between Tom and Harry means that Tom achieves a certain level on his (ordinal) utility function and Harry achieves a certain level on his (ordinal) utility function. Suppose that this pair of utility levels corresponds to point R in Figure 16.4.

Now suppose that we take another point on the product transformation curve in Figure 16.3, say N'. On the basis of this amount of food output and this amount of medicine output, a new Edgeworth box diagram can be drawn; its width is OF' and its height is OM'. Drawing Tom's and Harry's indifference curves in this new Edgeworth box diagram, we can find the contract curve for this new box diagram, and we can find the point on this contract curve at which the common slope of the indifference curves (the negative of the marginal rate of substitution) equals the slope of the product transformation curve at point N' (the negative of the marginal rate of product transformation). Then we can see what levels of Tom's utility and Harry's utility correspond to this

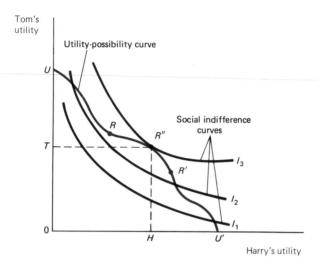

Figure 16.4   Utility-possibility curve and social
indifference curves

point and we can plot these utility levels in Figure 16.4, the result being
point R'.

If we repeat this process for all points on the product transformation
curve, we shall obtain a locus of points, UU', that shows the various
possible pairs of utility levels of Tom and Harry if the three conditions in
Section 3 are met. This locus of points is called the *utility-possibility
curve*. As would be expected, UU' is negatively sloped: If these conditions are met, the greater satisfaction obtained by Tom, the less satisfaction obtained by Harry. Some point on UU' must be chosen. Basically, the choice of a point on the utility-possibility curve is the choice of
an income distribution. If this choice is made, the problem of finding an
optimal allocation of resources in this case is solved.

But how can a choice be made among the points on UU'? One
approach is to posit the existence of a *social welfare function,* a function
that is an aggregate measure of national, or social, well-being. This function is assumed to depend solely on where Tom and Harry are on their
own utility functions. It summarizes and takes into account the "de-
servingness" of Tom and Harry, as seen by society as a whole, or by the
dictator if one exists. In a democracy it is possible under certain circumstances that such a function could be developed by voting. However, as
we shall see in subsequent sections, the construction of a social welfare
function is an extremely difficult business.

For present purposes, it is sufficient simply to assume that a social
welfare function exists and is represented by the social indifference
curves, I_1, I_2, and I_3, in Figure 16.4. Each social indifference curve includes a locus of points at which social welfare is the same. Of course, I_2 is
a higher indifference curve than I_1 because both Tom's and Harry's
utility levels are higher at points on I_2 than at points on I_1. Clearly, the

highest attainable social indifference curve is I_3, and the optimum point in Figure 16.4 is R''. This is the chosen distribution of income, at which Tom's utility level is OT and Harry's utility level is OH. Thus, if there exists a social welfare function, one can obtain a complete solution to the problem of resource allocation in this case. Note that this solution answers the question left unanswered in Chapter 15: How much of each commodity should be produced? To answer this question, we need only find out what point on the product transformation curve corresponds to R''.[6]

6. Perfect Competition and Economic Efficiency

One of the most important, and most fundamental, findings of microeconomics is that a perfectly competitive economy satisfies the three sets of conditions for welfare maximization set forth in Section 3. The argument for competition can be made in various ways. For example, some people favor competition simply because it prevents the undue concentration of power and the exploitation of consumers. But to the economic theorist, the basic argument for a perfectly competitive economy is the fact that such an economy satisfies these conditions. In this section we prove that this is indeed a fact. In Sections 7 and 8, we discuss how prices can be used in planned economies and by regulated industries to achieve the same kinds of results.

The first condition in Section 3 is that the marginal rate of substitution between any pair of commodities must be the same for all consumers. To see that this condition is met under perfect competition, we must recall from Chapter 4 that, under perfect competition, consumers choose their purchases so that the marginal rate of substitution between any pair of commodities is equal to the ratio of the prices of the pair of commodities. Since prices, and thus price ratios, are the same for all buyers under perfect competition, it follows that the marginal rate of substitution between any pair of commodities must be the same for all consumers. For example, if every consumer can buy bread at 50 cents a loaf and butter at $1 a pound, each one will arrange his or her purchases so that the marginal rate of substitution of butter for bread is two. Thus the marginal rate of substitution will be the same for all consumers: two for everyone.

The second condition in Section 3 is that the marginal rate of technical substitution between any pair of inputs must be the same for all producers. To see that this condition is met under perfect competition, we must recall from Chapter 7 that, under perfect competition, producers will choose the quantity of each input so that the marginal rate of technical substitution between any pair of inputs is equal to the ratio of

6. Note that this section as well as Sections 11 to 16 of Chapter 15 specify nothing about the institutional context. All that we have done is to figure out how resources should be allocated in this situation. We have not said anything about the sorts of institutional arrangements that will result in such an allocation of resources. The next few sections deal with the latter subject.

the prices of the pair of inputs. Since input prices, and thus price ratios, are the same for all producers under perfect competition, it follows that the marginal rate of technical substitution must be the same for all producers. For example, if every producer can buy labor services at $4 an hour and machine tool services at $8 an hour, each one will arrange the quantity of its inputs so that the marginal rate of technical substitution of machine tool services for labor is two. Thus the marginal rate of technical substitution will be the same for all producers: two for each of them.

The third condition in Section 3 is that the marginal rate of product transformation must equal the marginal rate of substitution for each pair of goods. The proof that this condition is met under perfect competition is somewhat lengthier than in the case of the other conditions. To begin with, we must note that the marginal rate of product transformation is the number of units of good A that must be given up to produce an additional unit of good B. The additional cost of producing the extra unit of good B is, of course, the marginal cost of good B. To see how many units of good A must be given up to get this extra unit of good B, we must divide the marginal cost of good B by the marginal cost of good A. This will tell us how many extra units of good A cost as much as one extra unit of good B. Thus the marginal rate of product transformation under perfect competition equals the ratio of the marginal cost of good B to the marginal cost of good A.

From Chapter 8 it will be recalled that price equals marginal cost under perfect competition. Consequently, the ratio of the marginal cost of good B to the marginal cost of good A equals the ratio of the price of good B to the price of good A under perfect competition. Coupled with the result of the previous paragraph, this means that the marginal rate of product transformation is equal to the ratio of the price of good B to the price of good A under perfect competition. But, as we noted in connection with our discussion of the first condition, the marginal rate of substitution is equal to the ratio of the price of good B to the price of good A under perfect competition. Consequently, it follows that the marginal rate of product transformation equals the marginal rate of substitution for any pair of products under perfect competition.

Referring back to Section 4 for a moment, it is obvious now why the agricultural price supports violated the third condition for optimality. Since the price of the agricultural good does not equal marginal cost (see Figure 16.2), the third condition must be violated if the prices of other goods equal marginal cost. For example, take some other good with marginal cost, MC_x, and price, P_x. The marginal rate of product transformation between this good and the agricultural product is $MC_A \div MC_x$, where MC_A is the marginal cost of the agricultural good. Moreover, if consumers maximize satisfaction, the marginal rate of substitution between the two goods is $P_A \div P_x$, where P_A is the price of the agricultural product. However, since $P_x = MC_x$ and $MC_A \neq P_A$, it follows that the marginal rate of substitution does not equal the marginal rate of product transformation.

Returning to the original topic of this section, we find that all three conditions for optimal resource allocation are satisfied under perfect

Example 16.1   Water Pricing and Resource Allocation

In some cities (for example, Los Angeles), the price of water is lower for some water uses—irrigation, for example—than for others. Will this result in a malallocation of resources? If so, how? What may be a preferable water pricing system?

Solution

This will result in a malallocation of resources because the marginal rate of technical substitution between any two inputs will *not* be the same for any two firms using water. For example, suppose that a farm (which pays a low water price) pays 10 times as much for an hour of unskilled labor as for 100 cubic feet of water, whereas a steel plant (which pays a high water price) pays 5 times as much for an hour of unskilled labor as for 100 cubic feet of water. Then the farm will choose the quantity of its inputs so that the marginal rate of technical substitution of labor for water is 10, whereas the steel plant will choose its inputs so that the marginal rate of technical substitution is 5 (see Chapter 7). As emphasized in Section 3, inputs are not allocated optimally when marginal rates of technical substitution are unequal in this way. In general, we would expect farms to use too much water and steel mills to use too little. To bring about a better allocation, the price of water should be equal for all producers—and equal to its marginal cost.*

* For further discussion, see J. Hirschleifer, J. Milliman, and J. De Haven, *Water Supply,* (Chicago: University of Chicago Press, 1960).

competition. This is one of the principal reasons why economists are so enamoured of perfect competition and so wary of monopoly. If a formerly competitive economy is restructured so that some industries become monopolies, these conditions for optimal resource allocation are no longer met. As we know from Chapter 10, each monopolist produces less than the perfectly competitive industry that it replaces would have produced. Thus too few resources are devoted to the industries that are monopolized, and too many resources are devoted to the industries that remain perfectly competitive. This is one of the economist's chief charges against monopoly. It wastes resources because its actions result in an overallocation of resources to competitive industries and an underallocation of resources to monopolistic industries. Society is then less well off.[7]

7. In evaluating this result and judging its practical relevance, it is important to note that it stems from a very simple model that ignores such things as technological change and other dynamic considerations, risk and uncertainty, and externalities. Some of these factors are taken up in subsequent sections of this chapter and in Chapters 17-19. The reader should be very careful to note the qualifications and assumptions that must be made. Sometimes the argument for perfect competition is made without full recognition of these qualifications.

7. Economic Planning and Marginal Cost Pricing

The previous section showed that the three conditions for optimal resource allocation are satisfied under perfect competition. Economists interested in the functioning of planned, or socialist, economies have pointed out that a price system could be used in a similar way to increase social welfare in such economies. According to economists like Abba Lerner,[8] rational economic organization could be achieved in a socialist economy that is decentralized, as well as under perfect competition. For example, the government might try to solve the system of equations that is solved automatically in a perfectly competitive economy, and obtain the prices that would prevail under perfect competition. Then the government might publish this price list, together with instructions for consumers to maximize their satisfaction and for producers to maximize profit. (Of course, the wording of the instructions to consumers might be a bit less heavy-handed than "Maximize your satisfaction!")

An important advantage claimed for planning and control of this sort is that the government does not have to become involved in the intricate and detailed business of setting production targets for each plant. It need only compute the proper set of prices. As long as plant managers maximize "profits," the proper production levels will be chosen by them. Thus decentralized decision-making, rather than detailed centralized direction, could be used, with the result that administrative costs and bureaucratic disadvantages might be reduced.

The prices that the government would publish, like those prevailing in a perfectly competitive economy, would equal marginal cost. Many economists have recommended that government-owned enterprises in basically capitalist economies also adopt *marginal cost pricing*, that is, that they set price equal to marginal cost. For example, Harold Hotelling argued that this should be the case.[9] Taking the case of a bridge where the marginal cost (the extra cost involved in allowing an additional vehicle to cross) is zero, he argued that the socially optimal price for crossing the bridge is zero, and that its cost should be defrayed by general taxation. If a toll is charged, the conditions for optimal resource allocation are violated.

Marginal cost pricing has fascinated economists during the more than forty years that have elapsed since Hotelling's article.[10] But there are a number of important problems in the actual application of this idea. One of the most important is that, if (as is frequently the case in public utilities) the firm's average costs decrease with increases in its scale of output, it follows from the discussion in Chapter 7 that marginal cost must be less than average cost, with the consequence that the firm will not cover its costs if price is set equal to marginal cost. This means that marginal cost pricing must be accompanied by some form of subsidy if the firm is to stay in operation. However, the collection of the funds

8. A. Lerner, *The Economics of Control* (New York: Macmillan, 1944).

9. See H. Hotelling, "The General Welfare in Relation to Problems of Taxation and of Railway and Utility Rates," *Econometrica*, July 1938.

required for the payment of the subsidy may also violate the conditions for optimal resource allocation. Moreover, this subsidy means that there is a change in the income distribution favoring users of the firm's output and penalizing nonusers of its output. Whether or not marginal cost pricing results in improved economic welfare depends on how one views this change in the income distribution.

8. Marginal Cost Pricing: A Case Study

During the mid-fifties, Électricité de France, the French nationalized electricity industry, introduced marginal cost pricing for its high-tension service. The ultimate goal of the new pricing scheme was that the price paid for a kilowatt-hour of electricity at a given time of day in a given season of the year in a given region was to approximate the cost of an additional kilowatt-hour at this time in this season in this region.

Of course, a great many simplifications had to be made in computing the new price schedule. First, consider price differences at various times of day. In the winter, the day is divided into three periods: the peak daytime hour, the other daytime hours, and the night. In the summer, it is divided into two periods: day and night. A consumer in a given region must pay a different price for kilowatt-hours in each period, with the differences reflecting differences in marginal costs. Next, consider price differences among regions. To estimate the marginal costs in each region, a pattern of movements of electricity from generating stations to consumption areas is derived that meets estimated demands at minimum total cost given present capacity. The marginal costs corresponding to this pattern are used to determine prices in various regions.

Finally, consider price differences among seasons. Differences among seasons in demand curves, as well as differences in hydroelectric reservoir levels and river flows, are responsible for these differences in price. The seasonal differences in demand are assumed by the industry to be like those observed in the past. Average snow and rainfall levels in each season can be used in the calculations. Since water tends to be less abundant in the winter, peak demands for electricity have to be satisfied by using less efficient thermal plants than have to be used in the summer. Also, demand for electricity tends to be higher in the winter. Both of these factors clearly influence the level of the marginal cost of electricity.

What has the new pricing scheme achieved? According to Berkeley's Thomas Marschak, who made a careful study of the French experience, Électricité de France's marginal cost pricing had a number of important

10. For example, see J. Nelson, *Marginal Cost Pricing in Practice* (Englewood Cliffs, N.J.: Prentice-Hall, 1964); N. Ruggles, "Recent Developments in Marginal Cost Pricing," *Review of Economic Studies*, 1949–50; W. Vickrey, "Some Implications of Marginal Cost Pricing for Public Utilities," reprinted in E. Mansfield, *Microeconomics: Selected Readings,* 4th ed.(New York: Norton, 1982); and R. Turvey, "Practical Problems of Marginal-Cost Pricing in Public Enterprise," in A. Phillips and O. Williamson, eds., *Prices: Issues in Theory, Practice, and Public Policy* (Philadelphia: University of Pennsylvania Press, 1968).

beneficial results. In his view, a

> clear improvement over the [old] pricing scheme is very plausibly claimed. Preliminary observation suggests that a leveling of consumption between the daytime and the nighttime periods may be expected. One immediate result is a reduction by 5 percent in the capacity required to meet peak demands.... Another is a substantial saving of imported (American) coal in winter, since the flattening of peaks eliminates the need for some of the inefficient thermal output previously required.[11]

9. External Economies and Diseconomies

Up to this point, we have generally assumed implicitly that there is no difference between private and social benefits, or between private and social costs. For example, costs to producers have been assumed to be costs to society, and costs to society have been assumed to be costs to producers; benefits to producers have been assumed to be benefits to society, and benefits to society have been assumed to be benefits to producers. In fact, however, there are many instances in which these assumptions do not hold. Instead, producers sometimes confer benefits on other members of the economy but are unable to obtain payment for these benefits, and they sometimes act in such a way as to harm others without having to pay the full costs. In these cases, the pursuit of private gain will not promote the social welfare. The purpose of this section is to describe how differences between private and social returns are likely to arise and the ways in which these differences influence our results. The following sections apply this theory to two areas of the modern economy.

It is convenient, and customary, to classify these divergences into four types. First, there are *external economies of production.* An external economy occurs when an action taken by an economic unit results in uncompensated benefits to others; when such benefits are due to an increase in a firm's production, they are called external economies of production. The firm may benefit others directly. For example, it may train workers that eventually go to work for other firms that do not have to pay the training costs. Or the firm may benefit other firms indirectly because its increased output may make it more economical for firms outside the industry to provide services to other firms in the industry. For example, a great expansion in an aircraft firm may make it possible for aluminum producers to take advantage of economies of scale, with the result that other metal fabricating firms can also get cheaper aluminum. In either case, there is a difference between private and social returns; the gains to society are greater than the gains to the firm.

Second, there are *external economies of consumption,* which occur when an action taken by a consumer, rather than a producer, results in an uncompensated benefit to others. For example, if I maintain my house and lawn, this benefits my neighbors as well as myself. If I educate my

11. T. Marschak, "Capital Budgeting and Pricing in the French Nationalized Industries," *Journal of Business,* January 1960, p. 151.

children and make them more responsible citizens, this too benefits my neighbors as well as myself. The list of external economies from consumption could easily be extended, but the idea should be clear at this point.

Third, there are *external diseconomies of production.* An external diseconomy occurs when an action taken by an economic unit results in uncompensated costs to others; when such costs are due to increases in a firm's production, they are called external diseconomies of production. For example, a firm may pollute a stream by pumping out waste materials, or it may pollute the air with smoke or materials. Such actions result in costs to others; for instance, Chesapeake Bay's oyster beds and Long Island's clam beds continually are being threatened by water pollution. However, the private costs do not reflect the full social costs, since the firms and cities responsible for the pollution are not charged for their contribution to poorer quality water and their harm to industries dependent on good water. There are many cases of external diseconomies of production, such as traffic congestion and the defacement of scenery.

Fourth, there are *external diseconomies of consumption,* which occur when an action taken by a consumer results in an uncompensated cost to others. Some external diseconomies of consumption can be fairly subtle. For example, Mrs. White may be trying hard to keep up with the social leader in town, Mrs. Brown. If Mrs. Brown obtains a new mink coat, this may make Mrs. White worse off, since she may become dissatisfied with her old mink coat. Similarly, a family that feels that a three-year-old Ford is perfectly adequate may become dissatisfied with it after moving to a community where everyone drives a new Cadillac.

The foregoing are some of the most important cases where social and private costs and benefits differ. At first glance, these cases may not seem very important. But when all of these types of external economies and diseconomies are considered, their aggregate significance can be substantial. For example, the fact that environmental pollution of various kinds resulting from industrial output is important has been stressed repeatedly in the United States in recent years. The importance of various types of external economies of production is undeniable, and the fact that consumer tastes and well-being are determined by the tastes and well-being of other members of society is obvious as well.

How do these external economies and diseconomies alter the optimality of the allocation of resources under perfect competition? If a man takes an action that contributes to society's welfare but which results in no payment for him, he is certainly likely to take this action less frequently than would be socially optimal. The same holds true for firms. Thus, if the production of a certain good, say beryllium, is responsible for external economies, less than the socially optimum amount of beryllium is likely to be produced under perfect competition, since the producers are unlikely to increase output simply because it reduces the costs of other companies. By the same token if a man takes an action that results in costs that he is not forced to pay, he is likely to take this action more frequently than is socially desirable. The same holds true for firms. Thus, if the production of a certain good is responsible for external diseconomies, more of this good is likely to be produced under perfect competition than is socially optimal. Much more will be said about these and other effects of externalities in Chapter 17.[12]

10. Public Policy toward Basic Research: An Application

To illustrate how the theory of external economies and diseconomies, together with the other principles discussed in this chapter, can be used to throw light on problems of public policy, consider the nature of social policy toward basic research. One of the most fundamental questions in this area is: Why should the government support basic research? Why not rely on private enterprise to support sufficient basic research? Confronted with this and related questions, the Committee on Science and Astronautics of the House of Representatives asked the National Academy of Sciences to prepare a report on this topic.

The Academy's report, prepared in part by Carl Kaysen of the Massachusetts Institute of Technology and the late Harry Johnson of the University of Chicago, emphasizes the fact that basic scientific research is likely to generate substantial external economies. Important additions to fundamental knowledge often have an impact on a great many fields. If a firm produces an important scientific breakthrough, it generally cannot hope to capture the full value of the new knowledge it creates. It cannot go into the full range of activities in which the knowledge has use, and it is seldom able to capture through patent rights the full social value of the new knowledge. Indeed, fundamental discoveries, such as natural laws, cannot be patented at all.

Because of these external economies, there is likely to be a divergence between the private and social benefits from basic research, with the result that a perfectly competitive economy would be expected to devote fewer resources to basic research than is socially optimal. Consequently, there seems to be a good case on purely economic grounds for the government (or some other agency not motivated by profit) to support basic research. As stated in the Academy's report,

> There is good theoretical reason for expecting that, left to itself, the market would not only tend to allocate too few resources to research in general, but would also tend to bias the allocation against basic scientific research.... These defects of the market mechanism with respect to the allocation of resources toward and among investments in research imply that the market needs to be supplemented, and perhaps, with respect to basic scientific research, entirely replaced by social provision and allocation of resources for the support of scientific research.[13]

12. This section and Section 13 are based partly on the treatment in W. Baumol, *Economic Theory and Operations Analysis,* 3d ed. (Englewood Cliffs, N.J.: Prentice-Hall, 1972), pp. 392–95 and 399–404.

13. National Academy of Sciences, *Basic Research and National Goals,* Report to the Committee on Science and Astronautics of the United States House of Representatives (Washington, D.C.: U.S. Government Printing Office, 1965), p. 136.

Based on similar considerations, there is a strong argument for government support of fundamental research to extend the technological underpinnings of broad industrial areas. For example, the National Advisory Committee on Aeronautics carried out research and development concerning wind tunnels, aircraft fuels, aircraft design, and other fundamental matters regarding aviation. No individual firm had much incentive to do such work because it could appropriate only a small share of the benefits. But because the benefits to the economy as a whole were substantial, the government intervened to finance work of this sort. The simple principles of welfare economics help to indicate why such a policy was justified.[14]

11. Technology Transfer by Multinational Firms: The Cases of Australia and Canada

A remarkable economic development of the last thirty years has been the growth of multinational firms, firms which operate in a very significant way in many countries. The reasons why firms have become multinational are varied. In some cases, firms have established overseas branches to control foreign sources of raw materials. In other cases, firms have invested overseas for defensive reasons. But in a great many cases, firms have established foreign branches to exploit a technological lead. After exporting a new product (or a modified version of an existing product) to foreign markets, firms have decided to establish plants overseas to supply these markets. Once the foreign market was big enough to accommodate a plant of minimum efficient size, this decision did not conflict with scale economies. Moreover, freight costs and tariffs often hastened such a decision. Also, in some cases, the only way that a firm could introduce its innovation into a foreign market was through the establishment of overseas production facilities.

Multinational firms, by carrying their technology overseas, have played a very significant role in the international diffusion of innovations. Moreover, they have often been responsible for important external economies, since the new technology that they introduced into other countries often spread quickly to other firms in these countries. Thus the transfer of technology benefited other firms as well as the multinational firm that transferred the technology. For example, in the case of Australia, Donald Brash concludes that the technologies of multinational firms "tend to become disseminated throughout the economy in a variety of ways. Executives with experience in [multinational] companies often move to Australian-owned companies.... Often the mere example of

14. J. Hirshleifer has pointed out that, if new information provides an individual or firm with a competitive edge, there may be a tendency to overinvest in it. The kinds of information discussed in this section can seldom be translated into an important competitive advantage, for reasons discussed above. See J. Hirshleifer, "The Private and Social Value of Information and the Reward to Inventive Activity," *American Economic Review*, September 1971.

Example 16.2   The Paper Industry and Water Pollution

The paper industry has been a notable source of water pollution. Suppose that every ton of paper which is produced imposes costs on others (for example, to people using local rivers for recreation and fishing) of $5. The supply and demand curves for paper are given below.

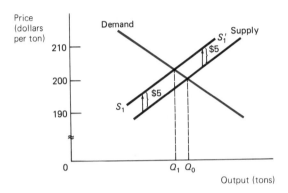

What will be the output of the paper industry? What is the socially optimal output of the paper industry?

Solution

The output of the paper industry will be OQ_0, since this is the point where the demand and supply curves intersect. To determine the socially optimal output, we construct curve S_1S_1', which shows the marginal *social* cost of producing each level of output. This equals the marginal *private* cost (given by the supply curve) plus the marginal *external* cost of $5 per ton. Assume that a product's price can be regarded as a reasonable measure of the social value of an extra unit of output. Then, since the socially optimal level of output is the one where the marginal social value of an extra unit of output equals its marginal social cost, the optimal level of output must be OQ_1. Why? Because under these assumptions, the demand curve shows the marginal social value of an extra ton of output, and $S_1 S_1'$ shows the marginal social cost, so the optimal output level is at the point where the demand curve (showing marginal social value) intersects the S_1S_1' curve (showing marginal social cost.)*

---

* For further discussion, see Chapter 17 which deals in much more detail with the economics of environmental pollution.

[multinational] firms is sufficient to induce a change in the operating methods of Australian firms."[15]

Of course, the fact that multinational firms result in such external economies does not mean that the activities of these firms always benefit the host country. As Canada's Watkins Committee has suggested, there may be considerable costs to the host country associated with its receipt of technology via the multinational firm. To the host countries, multinational firms are sometimes viewed as instruments of their parent country's policies. Also, the host country sometimes fears that the multinational firm, in pursuit of its own profits, may engage in activities that are contrary to the host country's interests and policies. A basic consideration here is the locus of control: Host countries do not feel comfortable about foreign control of much of their resources and capability.[16]

To illustrate the relevant considerations, take the case of MLW-Worthington, Ltd., of Montreal, a Canadian subsidiary of Studebaker-Worthington. The Trading with the Enemy Act specifies that it is against United States law for American individuals and corporations to deal directly or indirectly with enemies of the United States, unless with the license of the president. This law has prevented United States subsidiaries in other countries from trading with Cuba, North Korea, North Vietnam, and other such countries. In March 1974, MLW-Worthington announced that, despite this law, it would sell thirty locomotives to Cuba. In Canada, this decision was hailed as a victory for Canadian sovereignty. Many Canadians feel that Canadian companies like MLW-Worthington should not have policies of this sort dictated by what to them are foreign laws.[17]

12. Increasing Returns and Public Goods

If there are external economies or diseconomies, the simple conditions for optimal resource allocation in Section 3 are not valid. Other cases in which these conditions are not valid occur when some industries operate under increasing returns or when a good is a public good. First, consider the case of a good that is produced under increasing returns. In such a case the product transformation curve may look like that in panel A of Figure 16.5, rather than like that in panel B of Figure 16.5. Let curves 1 and 2 be the indifference curves of the sole consumer in our simple

15. Donald Brash, *American Investment in Australian Industry* (Cambridge, Mass.: Harvard University Press, 1966), pp. 178–79. Also see E. Mansfield and A. Romeo, "Technology Transfer by U.S.-Based Firms to Overseas Subsidiaries," *Quarterly Journal of Economics,* December 1980.

16. See R. Vernon, *Sovereignty at Bay* (New York: Basic Books, 1972); and C. Kindleberger, *The International Corporation* (Cambridge, Mass.: M.I.T. Press, 1970).

17. For further discussion of multinational firms in Canada, see A. F. Safarian and J. Bell, "Issues Raised by National Control of the Multinational Corporation," *Columbia Journal of World Business,* Winter 1973; and the Canadian government's *Foreign Direct Investment in Canada,* 1973.

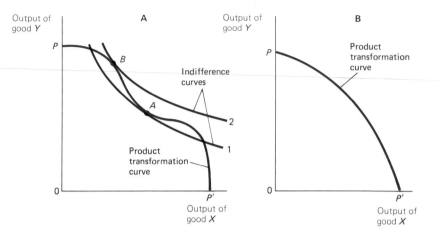

Figure 16.5   Product transformation curve with increasing returns

society. Then, if the marginal rate of product transformation is set equal to the marginal rate of substitution, in accord with the third condition in Section 3, the optimal allocation of resources may not be achieved, since this condition is fulfilled at point *A*, which is not the optimal point, as well as at point *B*, which is the optimal point. In cases like this, the price system, as well as the conditions in Section 3, can give faulty signals to producers and consumers.

Turning to public goods, it is important to recognize that one person can enjoy some goods without reducing the enjoyment they give others. The market mechanism does not work properly for such goods because excluding those who do not pay reduces their satisfaction and does not increase the satisfaction of others. Also, the consumer frequently cannot be made to pay a price for these commodities, either because a person cannot be barred from using them whether or not he or she pays or because it is obligatory for everyone to use them. Examples of such goods, called *public* or *collective goods,* are major items like national defense. Perfect competition will not result in an optimal allocation of resources to such goods. Instead, the government or private charities generally provide goods of this type. Indeed, much of government activity consists of the provision of public goods like national defense, fire and police protection, and the services of the courts. Much more will be said about public goods in Chapter 17.

13. When Is a Change an Improvement?[18]

There has been considerable controversy among economists over the circumstances under which economists, in their role as social scientists, can say that one policy is better for the welfare of society than another policy. This, of course, is an extremely fundamental question. Unless

18. See Footnote 12.

economists can tell whether one state of the world is better than another state of the world, they cannot legitimately make recommendations concerning public policy. In this section, we discuss various criteria that have been proposed as solutions to this problem. The following section discusses the relationships between individual and group decision-making.

Four criteria have been proposed to test whether a proposed change in policy is an improvement. The first is the Pareto criterion, which (as we know) says that a change that harms no one and improves the lot of some people (in their own eyes) is an improvement. This criterion is accepted by nearly everyone and is the basis for the rules in Section 3. However, there are many policy proposals that cannot be evaluated on the basis of this criterion. For example, a proposal that taxes be levied on the rich to help the poor cannot be judged on the basis of this criterion. Indeed, any change that benefits some people and harms others falls outside the scope of the Pareto criterion. As pointed out above, the Pareto criterion evades the question of income distribution. This, of course, is a serious limitation, since most proposed changes in the real world hurt at least one person.

The second criterion, proposed by Nicholas Kaldor,[19] is meant to surmount this limitation. According to Kaldor, a change is an improvement if the people who gain from the change evaluate their gains at a higher dollar figure than the dollar figure that the losers attach to their losses. For example, if a proposed change benefits Tom and harms Harry, and if Tom would be willing to pay up to $100 to see the change occur, while Harry would pay up to $50 to avoid the change, the change, according to the Kaldor criterion, is an improvement (even though no money is paid by Tom to Harry). However, an important problem in the criterion is that $50 may mean more to Harry than $100 does to Tom. This criterion makes money, together with the existing distribution of income, a measure of the relative strength of feeling of the individuals.

The third criterion, suggested by Tibor Scitovsky,[20] is intended to meet another weakness in the Kaldor criterion. Under certain circumstances the Kaldor criterion will indicate that a change is an improvement, but it will also indicate after the change that a change back to the original state of affairs is also an improvement. For example, it might happen that the Kaldor criterion would indicate that a tax increase was a good thing, but after the tax increase, the Kaldor criterion might also indicate that a reduction of taxes to their original level was a good thing. To avoid this possibility, Scitovsky proposed that a change is an improvement only if the move from the original point to the new point is an improvement (according to the Kaldor criterion) and if the move from the new point to the old point is not an improvement (according to the Kaldor criterion). Of course, this criterion, like Kaldor's, suffers from the fact that monetary units are used as a measure of pleasure or pain.

19. N. Kaldor, "Welfare Propositions in Economics and Interpersonal Comparisons of Utility," *Economic Journal*, 1939.

20. T. Scitovsky, "A Note on Welfare Propositions in Economics," *Review of Economic Studies*, November 1941.

The fourth criterion, put forth by Abram Bergson of Harvard University,[21] is based on an explicit social welfare function. Bergson argues that the problem can be solved only by formulating a set of explicit value judgments and incorporating them into a social welfare function of the sort discussed in Section 5. This social welfare function may represent the value judgments of the legislature, a dictator, the economist himself, or the general populace (as reflected by popular vote); regardless of which it is, an explicit social welfare function is required. Once such a social welfare function is formulated, a policy change can be judged an improvement or not on the basis of whether or not it moves the society to a higher point on the social welfare function. For example, a change that moves society from point R' to R'' in Figure 16.4 is an improvement, since R'' is on the higher social indifference curve.[22] Needless to say, the difficulty with this criterion is that social welfare functions are difficult to come by in the real world. Moreover, as we shall see in the following section, social welfare functions based on democratic decision-making do not always exist.

Finally, it is important to note that, while these controversies have been going on at the level of pure theory, economists operating at a practical level have had no choice but to make recommendations to policy-makers. Perhaps a good many of these recommendations really could not pass muster if the criteria of this section had been applied. However, in many cases, the desires of the community may have been so obvious that much of the discussion of this section may have been unnecessary. For example, in the Great Depression, it must have been pretty obvious that the community wanted to reduce unemployment. Of course, there could have been some disagreement about the extent of the sacrifices that should be made by various segments of the population in order to achieve this goal, but the disagreement may have been confined to a relatively narrow range.

14. Arrow's Impossibility Theorem

Can social choices be made in such a way as to reflect individual preferences? This question clearly bears on the existence and construction of social welfare functions. The seminal work in this area was done by

---

21. A. Bergson (Burk), "A Reformulation of Certain Aspects of Welfare Economics," *Quarterly Journal of Economics,* 1937–38.

22. Note that this social welfare function is of a special type: It assumes that the social welfare depends on the utility levels of the consumers. This implies the acceptance of an ethical norm regarding consumer sovereignty. Another approach might be to assume that the government (or some individual) can assert that society is better off in one situation than in another. This is a paternalistic or dictatorial approach. It is relatively straightforward, in contrast to the case in which social welfare depends on the utility levels of the consumers, but its limitations are obvious. See J. Rothenberg, *The Measurement of Social Welfare* (Englewood Cliffs, N.J.: Prentice-Hall, 1961).

Nobel laureate Kenneth Arrow,[23] who proposed the following four conditions that social choices must satisfy to reflect the preferences of the individuals comprising the society. First, social choices must be transitive. (If X is preferred to Y and Y is preferred to Z, Z cannot be preferred to X.) Second, social choices must not respond in an opposite direction to changes in individual choice. That is, an alternative that society would otherwise have picked must not be turned down because some individuals come to like it more. Third, social choices must not be dictated by anyone inside or outside the society. Fourth, the social preference between two alternatives must depend only on people's feelings regarding those two alternatives and not on their opinion of other alternatives.

Arrow showed that although these conditions may seem to be a sensible basis for democratic community decision-making, it is impossible to make a choice among all sets of alternatives without violating some of these conditions. This is a very disturbing conclusion, since it seems that, if social choice is to be consistent, it cannot be democratic. However, the moral to be drawn may not be quite as disturbing as at first it appears to be, since the fourth condition (in the preceding paragraph) is really more restrictive than it seems.

For example, suppose that opinion is split equally between citizens who believe that a billion dollars should be spent on space exploration rather than on aid to the poor and citizens who believe the opposite. According to the fourth condition, the government's choice must not be affected by the fact that the people who favor aid to the poor regard this as being the best use to which the money can be put, whereas the people who favor space exploration regard it as being less desirable than many other uses of the money. Also, the fourth condition does not allow for differences in the strength of feelings regarding various alternatives. The people who favor aid to the poor may feel that this alternative is much more desirable than space exploration, whereas the people who favor space exploration may feel that it is only slightly better than aid to the poor. Although there is no good way of measuring such differences in strength of feelings, it is hard to deny that they exist.

Arrow's work has led to a much clearer understanding of the relationship between individual preferences and social choice. There are many difficulties and traps in the analysis of decision-making by groups. Although the fourth condition may be too restrictive, it nevertheless is an eye opener to find that it is impossible to choose among all sets of alternatives without violating some of his conditions.

15. The Theory of the Second Best

Finally, we take up a very important part of welfare economics, the so-called theory of the second best. This theory has a fairly long history, although its name and general development are due considerably to

23. K. Arrow, *Social Choice and Individual Values* (New York: Wiley, 1951).

R. G. Lipsey and Kelvin Lancaster.[24] In previous sections, we have seen that, to attain a situation where no one can be made better off without making someone else worse off, it is necessary to fulfill all the conditions described in Section 3. The theory of the second best is concerned with a situation in which one or more of these conditions cannot be met. It asks whether, under these circumstances, it is still desirable to fulfill the other conditions that can be met.

For example, suppose that there are a number of monopolies in a particular economy and that these monopolies are not fulfilling the conditions in Section 3. Suppose that the country's antitrust authorities are in a position to break up some, but not all, of the monopolies and force them to fulfill the conditions. The theory of the second best asks: Can we be sure that this will increase welfare?

In general the answer is no. This is the principal conclusion of the theory of the second best: Since some of the conditions for efficiency remain unfulfilled, there is no assurance that the reduction in the number of unfulfilled conditions will result in increased welfare. This has important implications for welfare economics, since it means that, if some parts of the economy are misbehaving in the sense that they are not fulfilling the conditions described in Section 3, there is no reason to believe that welfare would be greater if other parts of the economy were to be convinced (or forced) to fulfill these conditions.

To repeat, the theory of the second best states that "it is *not* true that a situation in which more, but not all, of the optimum conditions are fulfilled is necessarily, or is even likely to be, superior to a situation in which fewer are fulfilled."[25] The widespread implications of the theory of the second best should be clear. It shows that piecemeal attempts to force fulfillment of the conditions in Section 3 can easily be a mistake. Unfortunately, many practical attempts to apply the principles of welfare economics have been, and are, piecemeal attempts of this sort.

16. Summary

Welfare economics is concerned with the nature of the policy recommendations that economists can make. An important limitation of welfare economics is that there is no scientifically meaningful way to compare the utility levels of different individuals, with the result that we cannot tell whether one distribution of income is better than another. Putting aside the question of income distribution, there are three conditions for a Pareto-optimal allocation of resources: (1) The marginal rate of substitution between any two commodities must be the same for any two consumers; (2) the marginal rate of technical substitution between any two inputs must be the same for any pair of producers; and (3) the marginal rate of substitution between any two commodities must be the

24. R. Lipsey and K. Lancaster, "The General Theory of Second Best," *Review of Economic Studies,* 1956–57.

25. Ibid., p. 12.

same as the marginal rate of transformation between these two commodities for any producer.

One of the most fundamental findings of microeconomics is that a perfectly competitive economy satisfies these three sets of conditions for welfare maximization. To the economic theorist, this is one of the basic arguments for a perfectly competitive economy. Economists interested in the functioning of planned, or socialist, economies have pointed out that a price system could be used in a similar way to increase welfare in such economies. The prices that would be set would equal marginal cost. There have been recommendations that government-owned enterprises in basically capitalist economies also adopt marginal cost pricing. The French electric industry has begun to do so with encouraging results.

Thus far, we have assumed that social costs do not differ from private costs and that social benefits do not differ from private benefits. In cases in which this assumption is false, perfect competition will not lead to an optimal allocation of resources. If the production of a certain good is responsible for external economies, less than the socially optimum amount of this good is likely to be produced under perfect competition. If the production of a certain good is responsible for external diseconomies, more of this good is likely to be produced under perfect competition than is socially optimal. Basic research is an example of a good that is likely to be underproduced in a perfectly competitive economy. Another area in which externalities are likely to be present is in the transfer of technology by multinational firms. Also, perfect competition will not result in an optimal allocation of resources in the presence of increasing returns or when a good is a public good.

There has been considerable controversy over the circumstances under which economists, in their role as social scientists, can say that one policy is better for society than another policy. At least four criteria have been proposed to test whether a proposed policy change is an improvement: Pareto's, Kaldor's, Scitovsky's, and Bergson's. Bergson's is based on an explicit social welfare function. In recent years, a considerable amount of attention has been devoted to the relationship between individual preferences and group choice; this topic is relevant to the existence and construction of a social welfare function. Finally, the theory of the second best shows that piecemeal attempts to force fulfillment of the optimality conditions can easily be a mistake. So long as some conditions remain unfulfilled there is no assurance that a reduction in the number of unfulfilled conditions will result in increased welfare.

QUESTIONS AND PROBLEMS

1. According to Milton Friedman, significant external economies are gained from the education of children: "The gain from the education of a child accrues not only to the child or its parents but also to other members of the society." Moreover, "It is not feasible to identify the particular individuals (or families) benefited and so to charge for the services rendered." What kind of government action is justified by these considerations?

2. Kenneth Arrow has pointed out that "two methods of social choice, dictatorship and convention, have in their formal structure a certain definiteness absent from voting or the market mechanism." What does he mean, and what is the economic significance of this proposition?

3. Suppose that two consumers, after swapping goods back and forth, have arrived at a point on the contract curve. In other words, neither can be made better off without making the other worse off. Does this mean that neither of them can find a point *off* the contract curve which is preferable to the point at which they have arrived? If it does not mean this, why do economists claim that points on the contract curve are to be preferred?

4. In recent years there has been considerable talk in government circles about tax reform. For example, former President Jimmy Carter suggested that lavish business lunches should no longer be completely tax deductible. If this suggestion were carried out, what segments of the population would it hurt? What segments might it help? Is there any way to tell whether, on balance, it would be good or bad for society?

5. A small private jet lands at Kennedy Airport in New York at the busiest time of day. It pays a nominal landing fee. What divergences may exist between the private and social costs of this plane's landing there at that time? What policies might help to eliminate such divergences?

6. Welfare economics is concerned largely with the determination of ways to satisfy human wants as best we can. But is this really a sensible goal? For example, suppose that people want the wrong things. Is it still sensible to try to satisfy these wants as completely as possible? Shouldn't welfare economics be concerned, too, with how wants are created?

7. Suppose that the market for men's neckties is in disequilibrium; that is, the actual price does not equal the equilibrium price. If all industries in the economy are perfectly competitive (including neckties), will the necessary conditions for optimal resource allocation be met?

8. In judging various social mechanisms and policies, welfare economics tends to emphasize the outcomes of these mechanisms and policies, as measured by the extent to which various human wants are satisfied. But shouldn't welfare economics be concerned with *means* as well as *ends?* For example, suppose that a particular policy resulted in an ideal allocation of resources, but that it was achieved by trickery or coercion. Doesn't this matter?

9. Suppose that Tom and Dick are the only consumers, and that the social welfare function is such that I_1, I_2, and I_3 in the graph below are social indifference curves. Explain in your own words the nature of the social welfare function.

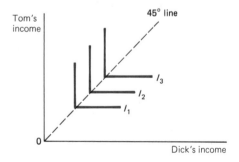

SELECTED REFERENCES

ARROW, KENNETH. *Social Choice and Individual Values.* New York: Wiley, 1951. (Advanced)

BATOR, FRANCIS. "The Anatomy of Market Failure," Reprinted in E. Mansfield, *Microeconomics: Selected Readings,* 4th ed. New York: Norton, 1982.

———. "The Simple Analytics of Welfare Maximization," *American Economic Review,* March 1957.

DE JOUVENEL, BERTRAND. "Efficiency and Amenity," Reprinted in *Microeconomics: Selected Readings.*

LERNER, ABBA. *The Economics of Control.* New York: Macmillan, 1944.

LITTLE, I. M. D. *A Critique of Welfare Economics,* 2d ed. Oxford, Eng.: Oxford University Press, 1957.

REDER, MELVIN. *Studies in the Theory of Welfare Economics.* New York: Columbia University Press, 1947.

ROTHENBERG, JEROME. *The Measurement of Social Welfare.* Englewood Cliffs, N.J.: Prentice-Hall, 1961.

SCITOVSKY, TIBOR. *Welfare and Competition.* 2d ed. Homewood, Ill.: Irwin, 1971.

17 Public Goods, Externalities, and the Role of Government

1. Introduction

A perfectly competitive economy, despite its attractive features, is unlikely to allocate resources efficiently in the production of public goods and of goods that are responsible for important external diseconomies and economies. This was one of the lessons of the previous chapter. Thus the government is charged with the responsibility for providing (but not necessarily producing) public goods and for trying to offset the distortions caused by externalities. In this chapter, we provide a more complete discussion of the nature of public goods, and of the amount of a public good that should be provided to promote economic efficiency. Also, using environmental pollution as a case study, we describe in more detail the effects of externalities on resource allocation and what the government can do to offset them. Further, we discuss Coase's theorem, which indicates circumstances under which a perfectly competitive economy will allocate resources optimally, even in the face of seemingly important external costs or benefits.

In addition, although a full discussion of the microeconomic analysis of government activities would take us too far afield, it is worthwhile considering two aspects of this subject. First, we discuss and illustrate the use of benefit-cost analysis, a technique frequently used by government agencies to help improve their decision-making. Second, we discuss some of the limitations of government agencies as allocators of resources. To obtain a balanced picture, it is essential to recognize that both competitive markets and government agencies can be quite imperfect in this respect.

2. The Nature of Public Goods

In Chapter 16 we learned that under the specified conditions, a perfectly competitive economy results in an optimal allocation of resources. Two assumptions, among others, were made there. First, it was assumed that the exclusion principle operates. That is, whether or not a person consumes a good depends on whether or not he or she pays the price. Those who pay for the good can consume it, while those who do not pay cannot consume it. Second, it was assumed that the benefits from a good flow to a particular consumer. Thus the consumption of a particular good is rival, in the sense that, if one person consumes a particular good, someone else cannot consume it too. For example, if one person drinks an entire bottle of beer, another person cannot drink the same bottle of beer as well. (Tavern owners and publicans the world over will pale at the thought that anything else might be true!)

But not all goods have both of these characteristics. Indeed, many very important goods, like the quality of the environment and national security, do not have them. Goods that do not have the second characteristic—rivalry in consumption—are called public goods. Such goods can be enjoyed by one person without reducing the enjoyment they give others. Consider an uncrowded bridge. If Mr. Smith crosses the bridge, this does not interfere with Mr. Jones's crossing it. Thus the use of this bridge is a public good.

It is important to note that the market mechanism will not work properly for a public good, even if it has the first characteristic—that is, even if it conforms to the exclusion principle. For example, in the case of the uncrowded bridge, it is perfectly feasible to charge a fee for crossing the bridge, and to prevent people who do not pay from crossing it. Nonetheless, it would be inefficient to do so. Why? Because excluding those who do not pay reduces their satisfaction and does not increase the satisfaction of others. Thus, although the market mechanism can be applied, it is not optimal to do so.[1]

Public goods will not be provided in the right amounts by the market mechanism. The market mechanism operates on the principle that those who do not pay for a good cannot consume it. However, as we have just seen, this principle is inefficient for public goods. Moreover, it frequently is impossible to prevent people from consuming a public good whether or not they pay for it. For example, there is no way to prevent someone from benefiting from national defense, regardless of whether or not he or she helps pay for it. Thus, in many cases, the market mechanism simply is not applicable.

1. Of course, if consumption is rival but the exclusion principle does not operate, this too may be in itself a cause of market failure.

3. The Optimal Quantity of a Public Good

If resources are to be allocated efficiently, how much should be produced of a public good? In this section, we analyze this question from the point of view of partial equilibrium analysis. Suppose for simplicity that there are only two consumers, the Adams family and the Brown family. Suppose that $D_A D_A'$ is the Adams family's demand curve for a good, $D_B D_B'$ is the Brown family's demand curve for the same good, and the supply curve for the good is as shown in Figure 17.1.

The left-hand panel of Figure 17.1 shows the optimal output of this good, assuming that it is a *private* good produced under perfect competition. Summing horizontally the demand curves of the two consumers, we obtain the market demand curve for the good, DD'. The optimal output is OQ, where this market demand curve intersects the market supply curve. Why is this optimal? Because at this output, the marginal benefit each consumer would obtain from an extra unit of the good equals its marginal cost. Assuming that the marginal benefit can be measured by the maximum amount that each family will pay for the extra unit, the marginal benefit for the Adams family would be CE, and the marginal benefit for the Brown family would be FG. The marginal cost of the extra unit is QH at an output of OQ. (Recall from Chapter 9 that the supply curve shows the marginal cost at each level of output.) Since $CE = FG = QH$, it follows that the marginal benefit to each consumer equals the marginal cost.

If, on the other hand, the good is a *public* good, the optimal output is shown in the right-hand panel of Figure 17.1. In this case, the market demand curve is obtained by summing the individual demand curves[2] *vertically*, not horizontally. This fundamental difference stems from the fact that both consumers consume the *total* amount of the good, and that the combined price paid by the two consumers is the sum of the prices paid by each one. The optimal output of the good is now OR, and the total price (the sum of the prices paid by each consumer) is OT.

To see why OR is the optimal output, recall (from page 291 of Chapter 10) that the optimal output is the one where marginal social benefit equals marginal social cost. Next, note that the marginal social benefit from an extra unit of output of a public good is obtained by adding vertically the distances under every consumer's demand curve. This is because all consumers share entirely in the consumption of whatever quantity of the good is available, and because the marginal social benefit is the sum of the marginal benefits to each consumer. (Also, if an extra unit of the good is worth to an individual the maximum amount that he or she is willing to pay for it, the marginal benefit to each consumer is the distance under his or her demand curve.) Thus, if output is OR, the marginal social benefit from an extra unit of output is the vertical sum of OL and ON, which equals OT. Since the marginal social cost of an extra unit of output is RM (as in the case of a private good),

---

2. These demand curves are sometimes called pseudo-demand curves or willingness-to-pay curves. See R. and N. Dorfman, *Economics of the Environment,* 2d ed. (New York: Norton, 1977).

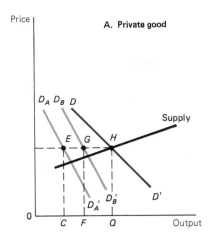

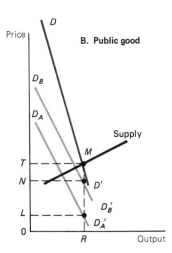

Figure 17.1 Determination of optimal output: Private good and public good

and since the optimal output is where marginal social benefit equals marginal social cost, it follows that OR must be the optimal output, since marginal social benefit (OT) and marginal social cost (RM) are equal at this output.

This analysis is illuminating. For example, Figure 17.1 shows the important fact that, whereas economic efficiency requires that each consumer's marginal benefit equal marginal cost for a private good, it requires that the sum of the marginal benefits of all consumers equal marginal cost for a public good. But despite its good points, this kind of analysis can take us only so far. For one thing, the demand curves in Figure 17.1 will not be revealed voluntarily if citizens believe that the amount they pay will be related to the preference they reveal. Consumers will find it worthwhile to be *free riders*. In other words, when consumers feel that the total output of the good will not be affected significantly by the action of any single person, they are likely to make no contribution to supporting the good, although they will use whatever output of the good is forthcoming.[3]

4. The Provision of Public Goods

If the number of people in a society is quite small, it may be worth while for people acting individually to provide some quantity of public goods. For example, consider a case where there are two families on an island that is infested with poisonous snakes. The reduction of the number of

3. In addition, a partial equilibrium analysis of this problem has obvious limitations. For a general equilibrium analysis, see P. Samuelson, "Diagrammatic Exposition of a Theory of Public Expenditure," *Review of Economics and Statistics,* November, 1955, reprinted in E. Mansfield, *Microeconomics: Selected Readings,* 4th ed. (New York: Norton, 1982).

such snakes is a public good, if there is no way of preventing the snakes from moving from one family's land to the other's, and if providing enhanced protection against the snakes for one family automatically provides it for the other family at no additional cost. Under these conditions, one of the families may well deem it worthwhile to engage in some activities to kill the snakes, even though this benefits the other family as well. Thus, when numbers are small, it is a mistake to say that no public goods will be produced unless the government does so. However, this does not mean that the proper amount of public goods will be produced, which brings us to the next point.

Even if there are few people in the society, there is a tendency for the provision of a public good to be too small, if its provision is left entirely up to the people acting individually in their own self-interest. To see why, suppose that a family lives alone for some time on the island cited above, and then is joined by a family that formerly lived alone on another island. Once the second family arrives, the first family will reduce its efforts to kill poisonous snakes because it will count on the other family to do some such work. Similarly, the other family will do less work of this sort than when it lived alone on the other island, for the same reasons. Both will cut back too much on their efforts because, whereas each family pays the full cost of devoting its time to this activity, it receives only part of the benefits, some of which accrue to the other family. Thus less will be produced of this public good than is socially optimal.

If there are few people in the society, there is a tendency for those who have the biggest interest in the outcome, or the biggest share of the resources, to provide a disproportionately large share of the amount of a public good that is supplied. For example, suppose that the first family in the previous paragraph owns 90 percent of the land (and other resources) on the island, and the second family owns 10 percent. Then the first family will recognize that whatever attempts are made to control the snake nuisance will rest largely on its shoulders, and it will act almost as if it were by itself on the island. On the other hand, the second family, recognizing that the first family has an incentive to do an effective job of this sort, is likely to reduce its efforts to a minimal level. Consequently, the first family is likely to do more than 90 percent of the snake-control work, and the second family is likely to do less than 10 percent.

The larger the number of people in the society, the farther it will fall short of producing an optimal amount of a public good. Thus, in large societies like the United States, the government must intervene in an attempt to assure the proper amount of public goods, unless, of course, the society is willing to rely on the selfless benevolence of the citizenry (a motive that is more often lauded than applied). There is general agreement that the government must provide public goods like national defense, and the provision of such goods unquestionably accounts for a significant portion of the government's expenditure. In democratic societies, the ballot box is used to determine the amount spent on various public goods. Each person votes for candidates that represent (often

Example 17.1 Economics of a Lighthouse

A lighthouse warns fishing boats away from a treacherous rock. Different levels of service can be provided by the lighthouse, resulting in different probabilities that a boat will be warned of its nearness to the rock. For example, the more powerful the beacon or signal emitted by the lighthouse, the higher the probability that a boat will receive the warning. The marginal cost of attaining various probabilities that a boat will be warned is as shown in the graph below. There are three boats in the area, owned by Captains Amos, Barnaby, and Columbus. The price that each captain is willing to pay for each level of service (that is, each probability that a boat will be warned) is shown by the individual demand curves in the graph below.

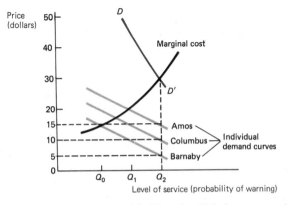

Level of service (probability of warning)

(a) Is the service provided by the lighthouse a private or public good? (b) What is the optimal level of service? That is, what should be the probability that a boat will be warned? (c) How much should each captain pay for this service? (d) Is it impossible for a lighthouse to be privately owned and operated?

Solution

(a) It is a public good because, if the service is provided for any fishing boat, it is available to all other boats at no extra cost. (b) To obtain the market demand curve for the service, we must sum the three individual demand curves vertically, the result being DD'. The optimal level of service is at the point where the marginal cost curve intersects the DD' curve; that is, the optimal level of service is OQ_2. (c) Barnaby should pay $5, Columbus should pay $10, and Amos should pay $15. (d) No. In England lighthouses were private for many years. They assessed the shipowners at the docks. Ordinarily only one ship was in sight of the lighthouse at a particular point in time. The light would not be shown if the ship (which was identified by its flag) had not paid.*

---

* For further discussion, see N. Singer, *Public Microeconomics* (Little, Brown, 1976); and R. Coase, "The Lighthouse in Economics," *Journal of Law and Economics,* October 1974.

imperfectly) the set of public expenditures and taxes that is closest to his or her own preferences.[4]

5. Externalities: The Case of Environmental Pollution

Besides providing public goods, the government sometimes intervenes in an attempt to offset distortions caused by external diseconomies and economies. In the previous chapter, we discussed briefly how considerations of this sort influence public policy. Now we look in more detail at a case of fundamental importance—the problem of environmental pollution—and discuss in what ways and to what extent the government should intervene. The pollution problem affects many vital aspects of our environment. To begin with, consider our water supplies. Many of our streams and lakes receive chemical wastes generated by industrial plants and mines, as well as pesticides, fertilizers, and detergents used by farms and homes. Also, municipal sewage plants sometimes discharge waste materials into rivers and other waterways, and animal and human wastes (in relatively untreated state) often are dumped into waterways. Water pollution is clearly a nuisance and perhaps a threat to health.

The fouling of our water supplies is one problem; in many of our major cities, air pollution is another. Automobiles are the prime source of many air pollutants. Also, factories generate particles of various kinds, often through the combustion of fossil fuels, that pollute the air. Among the more serious pollutants are sulfur dioxide, carbon monoxide, and various oxides of nitrogen. Although it is difficult to measure the costs of air pollution, many authorities believe that it is seriously detrimental to public health.

Besides water and air pollution, an enormous amount of solid waste—bottles, cans, junked cars, paper—is generated by our society. Also, in many of our cities, the noise level is annoying and perhaps dangerous. Further, there is thermal pollution. Water is used to cool machinery, particularly in electric power plants. In the process, the water is heated and when discharged raises the water temperature in the stream or lake into which it flows. Thus the solubility of certain substances may rise, the water may become more toxic and unable to hold as much oxygen, and the behavior patterns and reproductive capacities of fish may be altered.

Why does our economy tolerate such pollution of the environment? The answer lies largely in the concept of external diseconomies, discussed in Chapter 16. An external diseconomy, as you recall, occurs when one person's (or firm's) use of a resource damages other people who cannot obtain proper compensation. When this occurs, a competitive economy is unlikely to function properly. For market prices to produce an efficient allocation of resources, it is necessary that the full cost of

4. To a considerable extent, this section is based on M. Olson, *The Logic of Collective Choice*, rev. ed. (New York: Schocken, 1971). Also, see M. Olson and R. Zeckhauser, "An Economic Theory of Alliances," *The Review of Economics and Statistics*, August 1966.

using each resource is borne by the person or firm that uses it. If this is not the case, and if the user bears only part of the full costs, then the resource is not likely to be directed by the price system into the socially optimal use.

As we saw in Chapter 16, resources are used in their socially most valuable way in a perfectly competitive economy because they are allocated to the people and firms that find it worthwhile to bid most for them, assuming that prices reflect true social costs. Suppose, however, that because of the presence of external diseconomies, people and firms do not pay the true social costs for certain resources. In particular, suppose that some firms or people can use water or air for nothing, but that other firms or people incur costs as a consequence of this prior use. In this case, the private costs of using air and water differ from the social costs: *The price paid by the user of water and air is less than the true cost to society.* In a case like this, users of water and air are guided in their decisions by the private cost of water and air—by the prices they pay. Since they pay less than the true social costs, water and air are artificially cheap to them, so that they will use too much of these resources, from society's point of view.

Note that the divergence between private and social cost occurs if and only if the use of water or air by one firm or person imposes costs on other firms or persons. Thus, if a paper mill uses water and then treats it to restore its quality, there is no divergence between private and social cost. But when the same mill dumps untreated wastes into streams and rivers—and causes firms and towns downstream that use the water to incur costs to restore its quality—there is a divergence between private and social cost. The same is true of air pollution. When an electric power plant uses the atmosphere as a cheap and convenient place to dispose of wastes, but people living and working nearby incur costs (including poorer health) as a result, there is a divergence between private and social cost.

6. Optimal Pollution Control

In general, an industry can vary, at each level of output, the amount of pollution it generates. For example, it may install pollution control devices like scrubbers or electrostatic precipitators to reduce the amount of pollution it generates at each level of output. Holding the industry's output fixed, what is the socially optimal level of pollution control? At first blush, it may appear that this is a foolish question. Isn't it obvious that zero pollution is the optimal level? Strange as it may seem, the answer is no. Instead, the optimal solution for society is generally to tolerate a certain amount of pollution. This statement may not warm the hearts of some environmentalists, but it is true nonetheless, as we shall see.

Figure 17.2 shows the total social cost of each level of discharge of an industry's wastes, holding constant the industry's output. Clearly, the more untreated waste the industry dumps into the environment, the

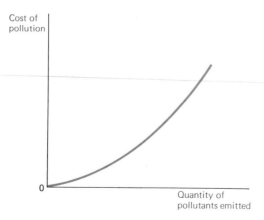

Figure 17.2 Cost of pollution

greater the total costs. Figure 17.3 shows the costs of pollution control at each level of discharge of the industry's wastes. Clearly, the more the industry cuts down on the amount of wastes it discharges, the higher are its costs of pollution control. Figure 17.4 shows the sum of these two costs—the cost of pollution and the cost of pollution control—at each level of discharge of the industry's wastes.

From the point of view of society as a whole, the industry should reduce its discharge of pollution to the point where the sum of these two costs—the cost of pollution and the cost of pollution control—is a minimum. Specifically, the optimal level of pollution in the industry is *OR* in Figure 17.4. Why is this the optimum level? Because if the industry discharges *less* than this amount of pollution, a one-unit increase in pollution will reduce the cost of pollution control by more than it will increase the cost of pollution, whereas if the industry discharges *more* than this amount of pollution, a one-unit reduction in pollution will

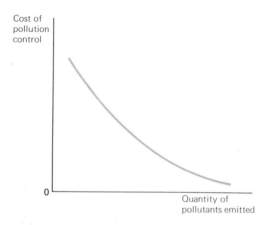

Figure 17.3 Cost of pollution control

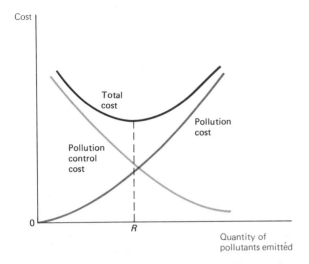

Figure 17.4 Sum of pollution cost and cost of pollution
            control

reduce the cost of pollution by more than it will increase the cost of
pollution control.

To make this more evident, Figure 17.5 shows the marginal cost of
an extra unit of discharge of ·waste, at each level of discharge of the
industry's wastes: This is designated by AA'. Figure 17.5 also shows the
marginal cost of reducing the industry's discharge of waste by one unit:
This is designated by BB'. The socially optimal level of pollution for the
industry is at the point where the two curves intersect. At this point, the
cost of an extra unit of pollution is just equal to the cost of reducing

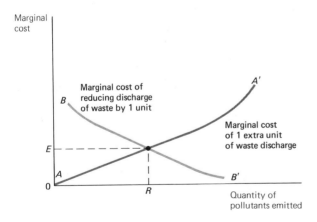

Figure 17.5 Marginal cost of pollution and marginal
            cost of pollution control

pollution by an extra unit. Regardless of whether we look at Figure 17.4 or 17.5, the answer is the same: *OR* is the socially optimal level of pollution.

Finally, let's return to our statement that the optimal level of pollution is generally not zero. Based on our discussion in previous paragraphs, it should be clear that this is true. Why? Because beyond some point, the cost of reducing pollution exceeds the benefits. In Figures 17.4 and 17.5, this point is reached at a pollution level of *OR*.[5]

7. Direct Regulation and Effluent Fees

Left to its own devices, the industry in Figure 17.5 will not reduce its pollution level to *OR,* because it does not pay all of the social costs of its pollution. This, as we saw in Section 5, is the heart of the problem. How can the government establish incentives that will lead to the optimal amount of pollution control? One way is by direct regulation. For example, the government may decree that this industry is to limit its pollution to *OR* units. Direct regulation of this sort is relied on in many sectors of the American economy, but most economists seem to prefer the use of effluent fees.

An effluent fee is a fee that a polluter must pay to the government for discharging waste. The idea behind the imposition of effluent fees is that they can bring the private cost of waste disposal closer to the true social costs. For example, in Figure 17.5, an effluent fee of *OE* per unit of pollution discharge might be charged. If so, the marginal cost of an additional unit of pollution discharge to the industry is *OE,* with the result that it will cut back its pollution to the socially optimal level, *OR* units. Why? Because it will be profitable to cut back pollution so long as the marginal cost of reducing pollution by a unit is less than *OE*—and, as you can see from Figure 17.5, this is the case so long as the pollution discharge exceeds *OR.* Thus, to maximize their profits, the firms in the industry will reduce pollution to *OR* units.[6]

Economists tend to favor effluent fees over direct regulation for at least two reasons. First, it obviously is socially desirable to use the cheapest way to achieve any given reduction in pollution. A system of effluent fees is more likely to accomplish this result than direct regulation. To see why this is the case, consider a particular polluter. Faced with an effluent fee—that is, a price it must pay for each unit of waste it discharges—the polluter will find it profitable to reduce its discharge of

---

5. For further discussion, see A. Freeman, R. Haveman, and A. Kneese, *The Economics of Environmental Policy* (New York: Wiley, 1973).

6. Another way for the government to intervene is to establish tax credits for firms that introduce pollution-control equipment. Such subsidies may not be very effective, since it still may be cheaper for the firms to continue polluting. Also, they may not be very efficient, since pollution-control equipment may not be the most economical means of reducing some kinds of pollution. Further, they are frequently attacked on the grounds that they are not equitable. Nonetheless, such subsidies are sometimes used.

waste to the point where the cost of reducing waste discharges by one unit equals the effluent fee. (Recall our discussion in the previous paragraph.)

It follows that, since the effluent fee is the same for all polluters, the cost of reducing waste discharges by one extra unit is then the same for all polluters. But if this is so, the total cost of achieving the resulting decrease in pollution must be a minimum. Why? Because the total cost of achieving a certain decrease in pollution is a minimum if the decrease is carried out so that the cost of reducing waste discharges by one extra unit is the same for all polluters. To see this, suppose that the cost of reducing waste discharges by an additional unit is *not* the same for all polluters. Then there is a cheaper way to reduce pollution to its existing level—by getting polluters whose cost of reducing waste discharges by an additional unit is low to reduce their waste disposal by an additional unit, and by allowing polluters whose cost of reducing waste discharges by an additional unit is high to increase their pollution commensurately.

Second, economists tend to favor effluent fees because this approach requires far less information in the hands of the relevant government agencies than does direct regulation. After all, when effluent fees are used, all the government has to do is meter the amount of pollution a firm or household produces (which admittedly is sometimes not easy) and charge accordingly. It is left to the firms and households to figure out the most ingenious and effective ways to cut down on their pollution and save on effluent fees.

Effluent fees have proven useful in practice as well as attractive in theory. For example, in West Germany's Ruhr Valley, a highly industrialized area with limited water supplies, effluent fees are used to help maintain the quality of the local rivers. The results have been highly successful. But this does not mean, of course, that direct regulation is not useful too. Some ways of disposing of certain types of waste are so dangerous that the only sensible thing to do is to ban them. Also, it sometimes is not feasible to impose effluent fees—for example, in cases where it is very difficult to meter the amount of pollutants emitted by various firms and households. In practice, public policy in the United States has tended to stress the regulatory approach.

8. Property Rights and Coase's Theorem

Under certain circumstances, a perfectly competitive economy will allocate resources optimally, even in the face of seemingly important external benefits or costs. For example, consider a firm that pollutes a stream by pumping out waste materials. Suppose that the downstream water users have well-defined property rights to water of a specified quality level, which means that they can sue the firm for damages if it passes water on to them that is below this quality level. In such a case, the firm can be required to pay for the pollution costs it imposes on others. Or consider a firm that upgrades the water in a stream, thus benefiting downstream water users. If this firm raises the water quality above the

Example 17.2 What Should Be Done with the Revenue from Effluent Fees?

The government is considering imposing an effluent fee on pollutants discharged by the chemical industry into local waterways. The revenue obtained from this effluent fee may be used to cut the taxes of the general public or it may be used to compensate water users for the industry's pollution of the water. The demand curve for chemicals is shown below. The supply curve for chemicals is SS' (assumed for simplicity to be horizontal). The pollution damage imposed on water users by each ton of chemical output is OH and the effluent fee for each ton of output is ST, where $ST = OH$. What is the effect of each way of using the revenue obtained from the effluent fee on the general public and on water users? Which way seems more equitable?

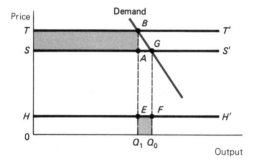

Solution

If the effluent fee is used to reduce the taxes of the general public, the general public gains an amount equal to $SABT$ (the shaded area) since this is the amount of the revenue from the effluent fee. And water users gain $Q_1 Q_0 FE$ (the other shaded area), since this is the reduction in the amount of pollution damage caused by the industry. But paper users suffer a loss since they must pay a higher price and use less paper. (Without the effluent fee, the industry's output is OQ_0, whereas it is OQ_1—because the supply curve is TT'—if the effluent fee is imposed.) If the effluent fee is used to compensate water users, they gain both $Q_1 Q_0 FE$ and $SABT$, while paper users again suffer the same loss as before. Thus the difference between the two ways of using the revenue from the effluent fees is that the amount formerly gained by the general public—equal to $SABT$—is now received instead by the water users. If one believes that water users are entitled to clean water, they are also entitled to compensation for its loss if such a loss occurs. Thus some observers believe it is more equitable to use the revenue from the effluent fee to compensate water users.*

* For further discussion, see R. and P. Musgrave, *Public Finance in Theory and Practice* (New York: McGraw-Hill, 1973), pp. 696–98. Of course, this simple example is meant only to illustrate some of the relevant considerations, not to provide general answers to the basic question of who should bear the costs of reducing pollution.

legally required level, it can seek compensation from the water users if property rights of this sort are well-defined.

If the costs of negotiating are not too large, the parties responsible for an external benefit or cost can negotiate with the parties affected by this externality. For example, if downstream water users are entitled to water of a particular quality, a firm may purchase from them the right to pollute the stream to a certain extent. Or the downstream users may purchase from the firm the right to water of better quality than they would otherwise be entitled to. In this way, the externality is brought into the calculations of the interested parties. Thus there is no divergence between social and private costs because a firm or individual that harms others must pay for this right, and a firm or individual that benefits others receives compensation.

According to Ronald Coase of the University of Chicago, a competitive economy will allocate resources efficiently, even in the face of seemingly important external effects, if it is possible to carry out such negotiations at little or no cost. In the course of these negotiations, the relevant parties will be led to take proper account of the effects of their actions on others. For example, if downstream water users are endowed with a property right to obtain water of a particular quality, a firm that wants to pollute a stream will be led to offer compensation to them, and, pursuing its own interest, it will not find it worthwhile to pollute beyond the socially optimal point. Moreover, Coase has shown that, *regardless of which party is endowed with the relevant property rights,* the outcome will be the same. That is, regardless of whether the downstream users are endowed with the right to obtain water of a particular quality or the firm is endowed with the right to emit a certain amount of pollutants into the stream, the parties will be led to buy or sell these rights so that the socially optimal amount of pollution results.[7]

This theorem, often referred to as Coase's theorem, is of considerable interest and importance. However, it is important to recognize that it assumes that the costs of negotiating and contracting by the interested parties are relatively small. For example, it assumes that the downstream water users can get together with the polluting firm and that they can negotiate effectively without prohibitive expense. In fact, however, when there are more than a relatively small number of interested parties, the costs of such negotiations may be so high that they are not feasible. Indeed, even if the costs are moderate, negotiations of this sort may not be practical. If the number of interested parties is large, it may not be possible to get the unanimity required to make the negotiations effective. And if the number of interested parties is small, the fact that mutually advantageous deals are possible does not mean that they will necessarily be consummated.

Nonetheless, Coase's theorem suggests that the assignment of well-defined property rights might help to promote economic efficiency. For example, to get around the difficulties caused by external diseconomies

---

7. R. Coase, "The Problem of Social Cost," *Journal of Law and Economics,* October 1960, reprinted in E. Mansfield, *Microeconomics: Selected Readings.*

arising from waste disposal, society might find it useful to try to establish more unambiguous property rights for individuals and firms with respect to environmental quality. Then, assuming that the relevant negotiations are feasible, the interested parties in a particular area might try to negotiate to determine how much pollution will occur. Note that if these negotiations are to be effective, property rights must be exchangeable, as well as unambiguous. That is, it must be possible for a person (or firm) to buy or sell his or her property rights of this sort.

9. Government Intervention and Benefit-Cost Analysis

The government intervenes in the economy in a wide variety of ways, ranging from the provision of public goods to the redistribution of income, and from the regulation of monopoly to the regulation of pollution. Government officials (and more fundamentally, the general public) must continually decide whether it is worthwhile for the government to carry out particular projects. Frequently, it is extremely difficult to make such decisions because it is so hard to measure the benefits and costs to society of the projects in question. But in some cases, these benefits and costs can be measured well enough so that benefit-cost analysis can be used to help guide these decisions. Although benefit-cost analysis is by no means a panacea, it has frequently proved useful in this context.

To understand how benefit-cost analysis operates, it is convenient to begin by assuming that a government agency has a fixed budget that limits the amount that it can spend and that it can carry out a number of alternative projects, each of which is relatively indivisible or lumpy. For example, suppose that the Department of Transportation has a fixed amount to spend on roads and that it is considering the construction of each of the roads in Table 17.1. Its problem is to decide which ones to build. As shown in Table 17.1, certain benefits accrue to the people from each of these projects, and each project entails costs.

The government agency tries to maximize the difference between total benefits and total costs. Since we are assuming (for the moment)

Table 17.1   Benefit-cost analysis, fixed budget

| Possible roads | Benefits | Costs | Benefits |
	(billions of dollars)		Costs
A to B	.30	.20	1.50
A to D	.30	.24	1.25
B to C	.10	.08	1.25
C to D	.18	.20	0.90
D to E	.70	.40	1.75
F to H	.40	.30	1.33
G to R	.40	.20	2.00
H to S	.36	.30	1.20
S to T	.35	.20	1.75

that its total costs are fixed, it follows that it will maximize this difference if it maximizes the total benefits obtained from this fixed expenditure. But how can it determine which projects will maximize the total
benefits? For example, in Table 17.1, if the Department of Transportation has $1 billion to spend on roads, which roads will maximize the total
benefits? The answer is simple. It should calculate the ratio of benefits to
costs for each project, and accept those projects with the highest values
of this ratio. Thus, in Table 17.1, the roads from A to B, D to E, G to R,
and S to T should be built. These projects have the highest benefit-cost
ratios (and together their costs sum to $1 billion).[8]

Up to this point, we have assumed that the government agency's
budget is fixed. But in reality, of course, the budget of most government
agencies is variable, not fixed. If its budget is variable, which projects
should it carry out? For example, if the Department of Transportation
can spend as much as it likes on the roads in Table 17.1, which ones
should it build? The answer is that all projects with a benefit-cost ratio
exceeding 1 should be carried out. Why? Because all projects where
benefits exceed costs (that is, where the benefit-cost ratio exceeds 1) are
assumed to be carried out in the private sector. Under perfect competition, this will be true, since spending in the private sector will be carried
to the point where the marginal benefit of an extra dollar of spending will
equal one dollar. Thus, so long as a public project has a benefit-cost ratio
exceeding 1, a transfer of resources from private to public use will result
in a social gain.[9]

10. The Measurement of Benefits and Costs

From our discussion so far, one could get the impression that benefit-cost
analysis involves little more than a straightforward calculation of the
benefit-cost ratio for each project and a simple comparison of these ratios.[10] Unfortunately, things are not so simple. The application of this

8. It is easy to see that this procedure will maximize the sum of the benefits received.
Looking at the benefits and costs columns of Table 17.1, it is clear that if only $.2
billion could be spent, the optimal choice would be the road from G to R; if $.4
billion could be spent, the optimal choice would be the road from G to R and the
road from S to T; and if $.8 billion could be spent, the optimal choice would be the
road from G to R, the road from S to T, and the road from D to E. In each case,
these same results can be gotten by picking the projects with the highest benefit-
cost ratios. (If you aren't convinced, try it in each case, and see.) Note, too, that we
are assuming that the costs and benefits of each project do not depend on whether
any of the other projects is carried out. Sometimes this assumption holds; but
sometimes it doesn't, and more advanced techniques may be required.

9. If projects are divisible, the government agency should allocate funds among projects so that the marginal benefit from an extra dollar of expenditure on each
project (carried out) is equal—and the same as the marginal benefit from an extra
dollar of expenditure in the private sector of the economy.

10. Although the basics are easy to master, the theory is not so straightforward once
one gets beyond fundamentals. There are a number of theoretical problems that

analysis is often marked by great difficulties in measuring the benefits and costs of each project. Although it would be inappropriate for us to dwell at length on the ways in which benefits and costs should be measured, two important principles should be borne in mind. First, it is important to distinguish between *real* benefits (and costs) and *pecuniary* benefits (and costs). Real benefits augment society's welfare; consequently, they should be weighed against the real costs of a project. Pecuniary benefits and costs, on the other hand, arise because of changes in relative prices that come about as the economy adjusts to the project. Pecuniary benefits and costs change the income distribution since some people gain from them, while others lose. But since the pecuniary gains of one individual are offset by the pecuniary losses of another, they are not benefits or costs to society as a whole.

To illustrate the distinction between real and pecuniary benefits (and costs), consider a dam that is built by the government. The construction of the dam may result in an increase in wage rates for construction workers in the locality. Although this is a benefit to them, it is offset by a reduction in relative wage rates somewhere else in the economy, due to reduced demand because of higher taxes. Thus this is a pecuniary, not a real, benefit. Or the dam may result in a higher price for food in restaurants near the dam site. Since such gains to the restaurant owners are offset by the losses to the restaurant patrons who pay the higher prices, they too are pecuniary, not real, benefits.

Second, in carrying out a benefit-cost analysis, one should try to estimate *all* of the benefits and costs of each public project. This is much easier said than done. One problem is that some benefits may accrue indirectly. For example, the dam may have indirect effects on consumers, laborers, investors, and firms in many parts of the nation. Another problem is that many benefits and costs are intangible. For example, one of the costs of the dam may be that it will mar the scenery, an intangible effect that cannot be valued in the marketplace. The situation has been described very well by Roland McKean:

> Needless to say, in reaching decisions, one should attempt to take into account all gains and all costs. Some people feel that there are two types of gain or cost, economic and noneconomic, and that economic analysis has nothing to do with the latter. This distinction is neither very sound nor very useful. People pay for—that is, they value—music as well as food, beauty or quiet as well as aluminum pans, a lower probability of death as well as garbage disposal. The significant categories are not economic and noneconomic items but (1) gains and costs that can be measured in monetary units (for example, the use of items like typewriters that have market prices reflecting the marginal evaluations of all users); (2) other commensurable effects (impacts of higher teacher salaries, on the one hand, and of teaching machines, on the other hand, on students' test scores); (3)

---

we have not taken up, since they would take us too far afield. In particular, a great deal of attention has been devoted in the literature to the question of what is the proper discount rate. For a good discussion, see R. and P. Musgrave, *Public Finance in Theory and Practice.*

incommensurable effects that can be quantified but not in terms of a common denominator (capability of improving science test scores and capability of reducing the incidence of ulcers among students); and (4) nonquantifiable effects. Examples of the last category are impacts of alternative policies on the morale and happiness of students, on the probability of racial conflicts, and on the probability of protecting individual rights. In taking a position on an issue, each of us implicitly quantifies such considerations. But there is no way to make quantifications that would necessarily be valid for other persons. This sort of distinction between types of effects does serve a useful purpose, especially in warning us of the limitations of cost-benefit analysis.[11]

11. The Middle Snake River Power Project: An Application

Benefit-cost analysis is not new; the Corps of Engineers (and others) have used benefit-cost analysis for many years. With regard to water-resource projects, the Flood Control Act of 1936 resulted in increased utilization of benefit-cost analysis. More recently, an enormous amount of attention has been devoted by economists to benefit-cost analysis, and government agencies have relied to an increased extent on such analysis to help them arrive at better decisions. Among the diverse areas in which benefit-cost analyses have proven useful are water-resource, power, transportation, health, education, and recreation projects.

Let us examine how benefit-cost analysis has been used in connection with a proposed hydroelectric dam on the Middle Snake River in Idaho. The Middle Snake, an undeveloped stretch of about 150 miles between Hells Canyon Dam and Lewiston, is a wild, white-water river flowing through one of the country's deepest gorges. Conservationists have strongly opposed the construction of a dam in this area. As Dartmouth's Lawrence Hines puts it, "A power dam in the Middle Snake will not only turn a river into a pond and endanger or eliminate the migratory and resident game fish in the Snake; it will destroy a semiwilderness area and its wildlife."[12] Nonetheless, because the demand for power in the Pacific Northwest has been growing rapidly, many private citizens and government agencies have favored construction of such a dam.

In 1968, the Department of the Interior made a benefit-cost study of four alternative dam sites on the Middle Snake. The principal benefit was power production, although some other benefits (such as recreation and flood control) were estimated as well. As shown in Table 17.2, the benefit-cost ratio in each case exceeded 1, with the highest ratio achieved at the Appaloosa (and Low Mountain Sheep) site. Thus, based on these

11. R. McKean, "The Nature of Cost-Benefit Analysis," reprinted in E. Mansfield, *Microeconomics: Selected Readings.*

12. L. Hines, *Environmental Issues* (New York: Norton, 1973), p. 137. Also, see A. Fisher, J. Krutilla, and C. Cicchetti, "The Economics of Environmental Preservation," *American Economic Review,* September 1972.

Table 17.2   Benefit-cost analysis by the Department of Interior: Four
alternative sites for hydroelectric project on the Middle Snake
River

ALTERNATIVE SITES

	Appaloosa and Low Mountain Sheep	High Mountain Sheep and China Gardens	High Mountain Sheep only	Pleasant Valley and Low Mountain Sheep
		(millions of dollars)		
BENEFITS				
Power	49.3	60.7	35.9	44.2
Fish and Wildlife	6.6	None	None	None
Recreation	.4	.3	.3	.3
Flood Control	.2	.2	.2	.1
Total*	56.5	61.3	36.5	44.5
COSTS				
Total	20.8	24.3	13.6	19.0
BENEFIT-COST RATIO	2.72	2.53	2.69	2.35

* Individual figures may not sum to total because of rounding errors.
SOURCE Lawrence Hines, *Environmental Issues* (New York: Norton, 1973).

figures, it would appear that a dam should be built at one of these sites.
After all, as you will recall from Section 9, projects with benefit-cost
ratios exceeding 1 seem worthwhile if the budget is variable.

But before jumping to conclusions, it is important to recognize, as
stressed in the previous section, that all costs and benefits should be
included (to the extent possible). According to a number of conservationists and economists, the Department of Interior's benefit-cost analysis was faulty because it took no account of fish and wildlife destruc-
tion. For example, the staff of the Federal Power Commission (now the
Federal Energy Regulatory Commission) prepared a benefit-cost analysis for each of these projects, and concluded that when environmental
and other such costs are included, the benefit-cost ratio for none of the
sites exceeds 1 and thus none of the projects was economically justified.
In early 1971, despite these conclusions, the Federal Power Commission
examiner recommended that a license be granted to build a hydroelectric
dam on the Middle Snake. However, in 1976, the Federal Power Commission rejected the proposal. Of course, benefit-cost analysis was only
one of many factors that influenced the outcome, but it seemed to play a
consequential role.

12. Limitations of Government Effectiveness

Before concluding this brief discussion of selected aspects of government
activity, we should point out that government intervention need not
always be beneficial. Although we cannot do more than scratch the
surface of this topic in the available space, certain salient points should

be recognized. For one thing, the political process is characterized by the existence of various pressure groups, which are groups of citizens who band together to advocate certain policies to the people's representatives. These groups usually contain only a small proportion of the population, but they may be successful in getting enough representatives on their side to push through measures that benefit them at the expense of the general public. For example, industry groups lobby for and get special tax breaks and tariffs or subsidies. Because these groups have a great deal to gain from such measures, they have the incentive to spend large amounts to influence legislation. Also, because they contain relatively few members, the free-rider problem is not as great for them as if they had a larger number of members. (Recall Section 4.) Further, the general public, which frequently loses more than the pressure group gains through such measures, is often unaware of its losses because the amount each individual loses is small and hard for the individual to identify, let alone measure. For these and other reasons, pressure groups are sometimes successful in persuading the people's representatives to adopt the policies they support, even though these policies may be detrimental to the welfare of the public at large.

Our understanding of the determinants of the behavior of civil servants is limited, but, according to some economists, two of their principal goals are tenure of office and agency growth. Certainly, it is not surprising that they should be interested in tenure of office. Without the sorts of civil-service regulations that currently exist, it would be relatively easy for an incoming administration to replace hordes of civil servants with deserving cronies (and their deserving relatives and loved ones). Without these regulations, it would also be very difficult for civil servants to withstand any serious pressure from elected officials or pressure groups. As for the goal of agency growth, it has been pointed out repeatedly that there are many reasons why civil servants may want their agencies to expand, not contract. For one thing, the prestige (as well as pay and perquisites) of a bureau chief is related to the size of the bureau. Also, a bureaucrat's power tends to increase with the size and rate of growth of the bureau he or she heads. For example, if the bureau has lots of building funds, the chief has some latitude in choosing which congressional districts will receive new facilities, a fact which few congressmen are likely to ignore. Also, if the bureau has lots of jobs to keep filled, the chief has some latitude in choosing who will fill them, a fact which few jobseekers and ambitious junior bureaucrats are likely to ignore.

It is also alleged that civil servants have too little incentive to do away with activities and personnel that are not worth their costs. For instance, the Department of Defense has repeatedly been charged with "gold-plating"—that is, with the development of increments of technical performance and other features of weapons systems that are not worth their cost. Since there are strong incentives for agency growth and weak ones for reduced scope and expenditure, some observers believe that there is a built-in tendency for government agencies to grow regardless of whether their responsibilities and work load expand at all. For example, C. Northcote Parkinson claims that in public administration, "there need be little or no relationship between the work to be done and the size of the staff to which it may be assigned."[13] (For a sampling of Parkinson's reasoning and wit, see his "Parkinson's Law."[14])

Although these allegations should be taken seriously, it is difficult to know how much truth they contain, because of the lack of reasonably reliable measures of how efficient (or inefficient) various agencies are and of how much each of their various services is worth. Perhaps the most important lesson to be derived from this section is that *one cannot justify government intervention in a particular area of the economy merely by showing that market forces work imperfectly there.* Why? Because it is necessary to show (or to have substantial reason to expect) that government intervention will do more good than harm. Just as the private sector cannot be trusted to work in all instances for the public good (because of monopoly, external diseconomies, and other factors discussed above), so government agencies cannot be trusted always to do so either (because politicians may not represent the people's preferences and interests properly, civil servants may build empires and pursue their own interests, and so on). Further economic analysis of the behavior of government agencies is badly needed to indicate more clearly the circumstances under which government intervention of various sorts will be

13. C. N. Parkinson, "Parkinson's Law," reprinted in E. Mansfield, *Managerial Economics and Operations Research,* 4th ed. (New York: Norton, 1980), p. 20. Apparently international organizations are not free of these problems either. According to the *New York Times*'s United Nations bureau chief, Parkinson's observations apply remarkably well to the U.N., as reflected in the old saw, "How many people work at the United Nations?" Answer: "About half." See "Parkinson's Law at the U.N.," *New York Times Magazine,* November 23, 1980.

14. "Picture a civil servant called A who finds himself overworked.... For this real or imagined overwork there are, broadly speaking, three possible remedies: (1) He may resign. (2) He may ask to halve the work with a colleague called B. (3) He may demand the assistance of two subordinates to be called C and D. There is probably no instance in civil service history of A choosing any but the third alternative. By resignation he would lose his pension rights. By having B appointed, on his own level in the hierarchy, he would merely bring in a rival for promotion to W's vacancy when W (at long last) retires. So A would rather have C and D, junior men, below him. They will add to his consequence; and, by dividing the work into two categories, as between C and D, he will have the merit of being the only man who comprehends them both.

It is essential to realize, at this point, that C and D are, as it were, inseparable. To appoint C alone would have been impossible. Why? Because C, if by himself, would divide the work with A and so assume almost the equal status which has been refused in the first instance to B; a status the more emphasized if C is A's only possible successor. Subordinates must thus number two or more, each being kept in order by fear of the other's promotion. When C complains in turn of being overworked (as he certainly will) A will, with the concurrence of C, advise the appointment of two assistants to help C. But he can then avert internal friction only by advising the appointment of two more assistants to help D, whose position is much the same. With this recruitment of E, F, G and H, the promotion of A is now practically certain. Seven officials are now doing what one did before.... These seven make so much work for each other that all are fully occupied and A is actually working harder than ever" (ibid, pp. 21–22).

effective and worthwhile. Fortunately, economists in increasing numbers seem to be turning their attention to this topic.[15]

13. Summary

In previous chapters, it was generally assumed that the benefits from a good flowed to a particular consumer, and that the consumption of a particular good is "rival" in the sense that if one person consumes the good, someone else cannot consume it too. The hallmark of a public good is that the latter assumption does not hold. Instead, a public good can be enjoyed by one person without reducing the enjoyment it gives others. Even if the market mechanism can be applied to a public good, it is inefficient to do so, because the market mechanism cannot function except by excluding those who will not pay; but excluding them reduces their satisfaction and does not increase the satisfaction of others.

Whereas economic efficiency requires that each consumer's marginal benefit equal marginal cost for a private good, it requires that the sum of the marginal benefits of all consumers equal marginal cost for a public good. An important problem is to get people to reveal their true preferences since, if they can avoid paying, they can often get the benefits from public goods anyway. Nonetheless, if the number of people in a society is quite small, it may be worthwhile for people acting individually to provide some quantity of public goods. However, there is a tendency for the provision of a public good to be too small; the larger the number of people in the society, the farther it will fall short of providing an optimal amount of a public good. Thus the government tends to intervene in an attempt to assure the proper amount of such goods.

Besides providing public goods, the government sometimes intervenes in an attempt to offset distortions caused by external diseconomies and economies. An important example is the problem of environmental pollution. To a large extent, undesirably high levels of pollution are due to external diseconomies in waste disposal. The socially optimal level of pollution (holding output constant) is at the point where the marginal cost of pollution equals the marginal cost of pollution control. In general, this will be at a point where a nonzero amount of pollution occurs. To establish incentives that will lead to a more nearly optimal level of pollution, the government can establish effluent fees and enact direct regulations, among other things. Economists tend to prefer the use of effluent fees over direct regulation.

If the costs of negotiating are not too large, the parties responsible for an external benefit or cost can negotiate with the parties affected by this externality. Under these circumstances, a perfectly competitive economy can allocate resources optimally, even in the face of seemingly

15. For some work by economists concerning political processes, see A. Downs, *An Economic Theory of Democracy* (New York: Harper and Brothers, 1956); A. Hirschman, *Exit, Voice, and Loyalty* (Cambridge, Mass.: Harvard University Press, 1970); M. Olson, *The Logic of Collective Choice;* and G. Tullock, *Towards a Mathematics of Politics* (Ann Arbor: University of Michigan Press, 1967).

important externalities. Moreover, regardless of which party is endowed with the relevant property rights, the outcome is the same. However, it is important to recognize that the costs of negotiating and contracting by the interested parties may not be small and that negotiations of this sort may not be feasible in many situations.

The government intervenes in the economy in a wide variety of ways. Benefit-cost analysis is aimed at helping government agencies come to rational decisions concerning how much should be spent on various projects. If a government agency has a fixed amount to spend on projects of a certain kind (and the projects are indivisible), it should choose those projects with the highest benefit-cost ratios, if it wants to maximize social benefits. If its total budget is variable, it should accept all projects where the benefit-cost ratio exceeds 1, if it wants to maximize net social benefits. Although the basic theory underlying benefit-cost analysis is relatively simple, the application of this theory is often by no means straightforward, because of the difficulties in measuring the benefits and costs of each project.

Government intervention in a particular area of the economy cannot be justified merely by showing that market forces work imperfectly there. It is necessary to show (or have substantial reason to expect) that government intervention will do more good than harm. Just as the private sector cannot be trusted to work in all instances for the public good (because of such factors as monopoly and externalities), so government agencies cannot be trusted to do so either (because politicians may not represent the people's preferences and interests properly, civil servants may build empires and pursue their own interests, and so on).

QUESTIONS AND PROBLEMS

1. The 1972 amendments to the Federal Water Pollution Control Act required industries to use "best practicable" water-pollution-control technology by mid-1977 and "best available" technology by mid-1983. Do you think that this is proper public policy? Why or why not?

2. Suppose that the Department of Transportation has a budget of $5 billion to spend on roads, and that the costs and benefits from all roads under consideration are as follows:

Road	Benefits	Costs
	(billions of dollars)	
A	10	1
B	12	4
C	20	5

Which roads should the department finance, and why? If you were an adviser to the department, what questions would you ask concerning the derivation of these figures?

3. A. R. Prest and Ralph Turvey point out that the benefit-cost ratio for a cross-Florida barge canal was estimated to be 1.20 by the Corps of Engi-

neers, but only 0.13 by some consultants retained by the railroads. What factors might account for the difference in these results?

4. Education and health services can be provided by private enterprise on a fee basis. What is the rationale for government intervention in these areas? To what extent are education and health services public goods? In what ways can microeconomics help to shed light on proper public policy in these areas?

5. Suppose that there are only three citizens of a (very small) nation and that the amount of national defense each would demand (at various prices) is as follows:

Price of a unit of national defense	Citizen A	Citizen B	Citizen C
(dollars)	(number of units demanded)		
1	10	8	12
2	9	7	9
3	8	6	7
4	7	5	5

If the marginal cost of a unit of national defense is $9, what is the optimal amount of national defense for this nation?

6. In the previous question, suppose that the members of this small nation agree that if any citizen refuses to pay for national defense, his or her property and person will not be protected by the nation's defense forces. Under these circumstances, could a nongovernmental organization sell some of the services normally provided by the nation's defense forces? If so, will ordinary market forces result in the optimal amount of national defense being provided?

7. "All public goods must be provided by the government." Comment and evaluate.

8. In an oil field, each owner of a well is motivated to pump out the oil relatively fast, because this makes it more likely that the well owner can capture some oil under others' land and prevent others from capturing oil under his or her land. Are there externalities present in this situation? Do you think that they lead to inefficiencies? If so, what sorts of inefficiencies result?

9. C. N. Parkinson presents the following data concerning the British Admiralty in 1914 and 1928:

	1914	1928
Capital ships in commission	62	20
Officers and men in Royal Navy	146,000	100,000
Dockyard workers	57,000	62,439
Dockyard officials and clerks	3,249	4,558
Admiralty officials	2,000	3,569

Did the number of civil servants in the Admiralty vary in proportion to the size of the Royal Navy? What factors might have accounted for these results?

10. A steel plant is upstream from plant A. Plant A's costs reflect the fact that it has to clean up the water that the steel plant pollutes. The firm that owns the steel plant decides to buy plant A because it believes that the price of the product made by plant A will increase dramatically. Is it likely that the steel plant will emit the same amount of pollutants as before the purchase of plant A? What factors influence how much the steel plant will change the amount of pollutants it emits?

SELECTED REFERENCES

ARROW, KENNETH. "The Organization of Economic Activity: Issues Pertinent to the Choice of Market versus Nonmarket Allocation." Reprinted in E. Mansfield, *Microeconomics: Selected Readings,* 4th ed. New York: Norton, 1982.

BUCHANAN, JAMES. *The Demand and Supply of Public Goods.* Chicago: Rand McNally, 1969.

DORFMAN, ROBERT AND NANCY. *Economics of the Environment.* 2d ed. New York: Norton, 1977.

DOWNS, ANTHONY. *An Economic Theory of Democracy.* New York: Harper and Brothers, 1956.

FREEMAN, A.; R. HAVEMAN; AND A. KNEESE. *The Economics of Environmental Policy.* New York: Wiley, 1973.

HIRSCHMAN, ALBERT. *Exit, Voice, and Loyalty.* Cambridge, Mass,: Harvard University Press, 1970.

KNEESE, ALLEN, AND CHARLES SCHULTZE. *Pollution, Prices, and Public Policy.* Washington, D.C.: Brookings Institution, 1975.

MUSGRAVE, RICHARD AND PEGGY. *Public Finance in Theory and Practice.* New York: McGraw-Hill, 1973.

PREST, A., AND R. TURVEY. "Applications of Cost-Benefit Analysis." Reprinted in *Microeconomics: Selected Readings.*

SAMUELSON, PAUL. "Diagrammatic Exposition of a Theory of Public Expenditure." Reprinted in *Microeconomics: Selected Readings.*

18 Intertemporal Choice and Technological Change

1. Introduction

Many problems that are central to economics involve a choice between doing something now and doing it later. For example, consumers must decide whether they will consume all of their income now or save some for the future, and producers must decide whether they will devote some of their present resources to investment projects that will increase their future profits. These problems of intertemporal choice are of great practical importance. In this chapter, we describe some of the models that economists have devised to deal with them. These models are dynamic, in the sense that they focus attention on more than one time period. They enable (indeed, force) us to take up such major concepts as saving, investment, the interest rate, and present value.

Once we focus attention on dynamic considerations, we must reckon too with a very important force in the economy—technological change. Our discussion in previous chapters of the optimal allocation of resources was concerned largely with static conditions. We took as given the production functions in various industries and the utility functions of consumers, and attempted to determine the allocation of resources that, given these production functions and utility functions, would be optimal. Although an analysis of this kind is interesting, it is incomplete in important respects, since one of the most significant ways that economic welfare is increased is through the alteration of production functions due to technological change. In the latter part of this chapter, we discuss the microeconomics of technological change. First we take up the definition, measurement, and determinants of the rate of technological change. Then we discuss the limitations of static efficiency, the economics of the patent system, and the effects of market structure on the rate of technological change and the rate of productivity increase.

2. Intertemporal Choice: Consumption

Consumers try to maintain a desired balance between consumption in the present and consumption in the future. For example, if Frank Olcott receives a lump-sum payment of $50,000 upon retirement, he is likely to save much of it to tide him over in subsequent years. In this section, we take up the consumer's intertemporal choice with regard to consumption. To simplify matters, we assume that there is only a single commodity. Consumers must choose how much of this commodity they will consume at various points in time. In making this decision, they recognize that they can borrow or lend this commodity. To begin with, we consider only two periods: this year and next year. This assumption will be relaxed in Section 6.

The consumer's choice between the amount consumed this year and the amount consumed next year can be analyzed by the simple model of consumer behavior presented in Chapter 3. The consumer has preferences between consumption this year and consumption next year, just as he or she has preferences between meat and potatoes in a particular time period. (Recall Figure 3.2.) These preferences are represented by an indifference map like that shown in Figure 18.1. In addition, the consumer is confronted by a budget line, also shown in Figure 18.1, which indicates the combinations of present and future consumption that he or she can attain. The optimal choice for the consumer is represented by the point on the budget line that is on the highest indifference curve. In Figure 18.1, this optimal point is A, where OC_0 units are consumed this year and OC_1 units are consumed next year.

The position of the consumer's budget line is determined by his or her endowment position, which is represented by point B in Figure 18.1. The consumer's *endowment position* is the number of units of the good that the consumer will receive in each year. In Figure 18.1, the consumer knows that he or she will *receive* OC_2 units of the good this year and OC_3 units next year. Thus, in this case, this is the consumer's endowment position. Note that the consumer does not have to consume this amount each year, because the consumer can borrow or lend. By borrowing or lending, the consumer can move to other points on the budget line. If the consumer moves upward from B along the budget line, this represents *lending* (because less is consumed this year, and more is consumed next year). If the consumer moves downward from B along the budget line, this represents *borrowing* (because more is consumed this year, and less is consumed next year). In Figure 18.1, the consumer's optimal choice is to lend $(OC_2 - OC_0)$ units of the good this year. Whereas OC_2 units of

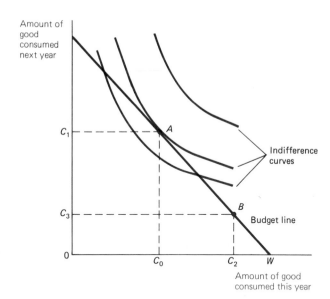

Figure 18.1   Equilibrium of the consumer

the good are received this year by the consumer, only OC_0 units are consumed, and the rest are lent out.

The slope of the budget line indicates the terms on which the consumer can borrow or lend. Recall from Chapter 3 that the slope of the budget line equals minus one times the extra number of units of the good on the vertical axis that can be consumed if the consumer gives up one unit of the good on the horizontal axis. Thus the slope of the budget line in Figure 18.1 must equal minus one times the extra number of units of the good that can be consumed next year if the consumer gives up (and lends) one unit of the good this year. The *rate of interest* is the premium received by the consumer one year hence if he or she lends a dollar for a year. In other words, if the consumer lends a dollar, and if the interest rate equals r, he or she receives $(1 + r)$ dollars a year hence. (Similarly, if the consumer borrows a dollar, he or she pays $(1 + r)$ dollars a year hence.) *The interest rate can be viewed as a price,* since $(1 + r)$ is the price of a dollar today in terms of dollars a year hence. For example, if the interest rate equals 0.10, a dollar today is worth \$1.10 a year hence. If the price of the good is the same next year as this year, it follows that the slope of the budget line in Figure 18.1 must equal $- (1 + r)$, since the number of units of the good that can be consumed next year if the consumer gives up (and lends) one unit of the good this year equals $(1 + r)$.

The intercept of the budget line on the horizontal axis in Figure 18.1 is called the consumer's *endowed wealth.* As noted above, the consumer's endowment position is at point B, which indicates that he or she will receive OC_2 units of the good this year and OC_3 units of the good next year. The consumer's endowed wealth will *not,* in general, be the same as his or her endowment position. The consumer's endowed wealth shows

Figure 18.2 Budget lines corresponding to wealth of W and W'

how much the consumer could consume this year if he or she borrowed against all of next year's receipts of the good. Clearly, the consumer's endowed wealth equals

$$W = OC_2 + \frac{OC_3}{1 + r} \qquad 18.1$$

because, besides the OC_2 units of the good that the consumer receives this year, he or she can consume an additional $OC_3/(1 + r)$ units of the good this year. Why? Because the consumer can borrow $OC_3/(1 + r)$ units of the good. This is the most that the consumer can borrow because, if he or she borrows this much, the amount (including interest) that must be paid next year is $OC_3/(1 + r)$ times $(1 + r)$, or OC_3, which is all the consumer will receive then.

Note that, if the interest rate is held constant, how much a person can consume is determined by his or her wealth. For example, Figure 18.2 shows that, if the consumer's wealth is reduced to W', the budget line is lower. (But its slope remains the same, since it equals $-[1 + r]$.) Just as the consumer's money income determined how high or low his or her budget line would be in the single-period model of consumer behavior in Chapter 3, so the consumer's wealth determines how high or low it will be in the present intertemporal model.

3. Intertemporal Choice: Production

Producers, like consumers, must make choices involving more than one time period. To make things as simple as possible, suppose that Mary

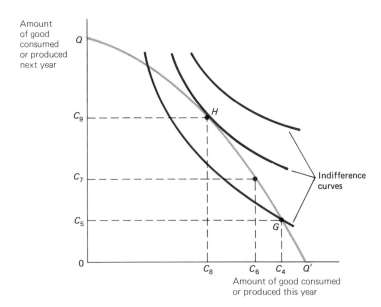

Figure 18.3   Equilibrium of the producer-consumer

McGann lives on an island and that she both produces and consumes the single good that exists. She is endowed with a certain amount of the good this year and next; this endowment is represented by point G in Figure 18.3. Specifically, she knows that she will produce OC_4 units of the good this year and OC_5 units of the good next year. Curve QQ' shows how much she can produce (and consume) next year if she saves some of the present year's output and invests it to increase next year's output.[1] By *saving,* we mean refraining from consumption. By *investment,* we mean the formation of new capital assets.

To illustrate the meaning of curve QQ', suppose that she consumes only OC_6 units of the good this year. Curve QQ' shows that, under these circumstances, she will produce OC_7 units of the good next year. That is, if she saves and invests $(OC_4 - OC_6)$ units of the good this year, she will receive $(OC_7 - OC_5)$ additional units next year. The reason for the extra output next year is that the investment pays off then. For example, if a farmer uses some corn for seed for next year's crop, rather than consuming it this year, this investment will add to next year's output.

To determine what is the optimal choice for this producer-consumer, we must consider her indifference curves, shown in Figure 18.3. Since all attainable combinations of present and future consumption are points on curve QQ', she will choose point H, the point on curve QQ' that lies on the highest indifference curve. Let's look at exactly what point H signifies. Clearly, this is the point where she consumes OC_8 units of the good this year and consumes OC_9 units of the good next year. But more can be

---

1. QQ' also indicates that she can dissave; that is, she can consume somewhat more than she produces this year, at the expense of next year's output. She does this if she chooses points along QQ' between G and Q'.

said than this. Since she knows that she will produce OC_4 units of the good this year, and yet she chooses to consume only OC_8 units of it, she is *saving* $(OC_4 - OC_8)$ units of the good. At the same time, she is also *investing* these $(OC_4 - OC_8)$ units of the good. That is, the $(OC_4 - OC_8)$ units of the good that she saves will be put to work to expand next year's output. Moreover, the amount by which this investment will expand next year's output can be determined from Figure 18.3. If she had invested nothing, her output next year would be OC_5 units, so this investment must increase next year's output by $(OC_9 - OC_5)$ units.

Since single life on an island can be dull, even for economists, it is time that we move on to somewhat more interesting (and realistic) circumstances. Suppose that another individual, James McBride, can both produce the good and lend or borrow it. His endowment, like Mary McGann's, is represented by point G. That is, he knows that he will produce OC_4 units of the good this year and OC_5 units of the good next year. Once again, QQ' shows how much he can produce (and consume) next year if he saves some of the present year's output and invests it to increase next year's output. But now, after he chooses a point on the QQ' curve, he can lend some (or all) of his current year's output to others, or he can borrow against some (or all) of his next year's output. For example, if he chooses point K on the QQ' curve in Figure 18.4, he can then borrow $(OC_{12} - OC_{10})$ units of the good from others, thus moving to point L. Clearly, his options are much richer than in Figure 18.3. What decision will he make?

As a first step toward answering this question, it is necessary to recognize that, corresponding to each choice of a point on QQ', there exists a *market line* which shows the various amounts of the good that he can consume in each period, if he lends or borrows various amounts. For example, if the producer-consumer chooses point K, he is then confronted with market line 1 when he subsequently decides how much to borrow or lend. This market line (like the budget lines in Figures 18.1 and 18.2) has a slope equal to $-(1 + r)$. It goes through the point that he chooses on QQ' because this point indicates how much of the good he will have in the present and next year. Since one of his options is to borrow (and lend) nothing, the market line must go through this point. The market line corresponding to his choosing point G on QQ' is market line 2 in Figure 18.4.

Each market line is associated with a particular level of *attained wealth,* which is equal to the market line's intercept on the horizontal axis. The producer-consumer's first step toward an optimal decision is to *choose the point on QQ' that is on the highest market line.* In other words, he should choose the point on QQ' that is associated with the maximum possible attained wealth. In Figure 18.4., this point is K. Next, *he should move along the market line corresponding to this point until he reaches the highest possible indifference curve.* In Figure 18.4, this point is L. In this way, he reaches the optimal decision. The opportunity to borrow or lend will usually result in the producer-consumer's being on a higher indifference curve than if he could not borrow or lend. For example, in Figure 18.4, he achieves a higher indifference curve at point L

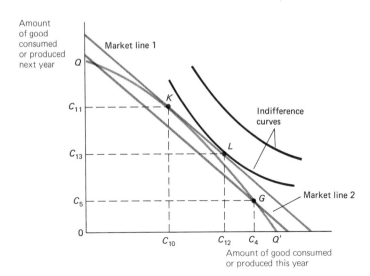

Amount of good consumed or produced next year

Amount of good consumed or produced this year

Figure 18.4   Equilibrium of the producer-consumer, with exchange possible

(which he can reach only by borrowing) than at point K (where he neither borrows nor lends).

In sum, the producer-consumer in Figure 18.4 should choose point K on QQ'. That is, he should invest ($OC_4 - OC_{10}$) units of his current year's output. This amount should be added to his capital assets. But he should not save this entire amount. Instead, he should borrow ($OC_{12} - OC_{10}$) units of this amount, thus moving along the market line to point L. This is his optimal decision. Of course, some other member of society must save enough to lend him the ($OC_{12} - OC_{10}$) units of the good. In the aggregate, the total amount that people desire to save must equal the total amount that people desire to invest, if equilibrium occurs. More will be said on this score in the next section.

4. The Interest Rate: Effects and Determinants

The choices made by individuals and firms are influenced by the rate of interest. To see that this is the case, suppose that the consumer in Figure 18.1 is confronted with a higher rate of interest. As shown in Figure 18.5, the increase in the interest rate will shift the budget line. Specifically, the budget line will be steeper after the increase in the interest rate, since the slope of the budget line equals $-(1 + r)$, as we know from Section 2. Thus, with the higher interest rate, the consumer will choose a different amount to consume each year than with the lower interest rate. Specifically, with the higher interest rate, the consumer will consume OC_{14} units of the good this year and OC_{15} units next year. With the lower interest rate, the consumer will consume OC_0 units this year and OC_1 units next year.

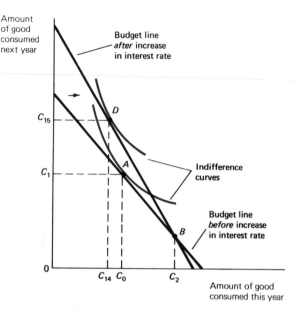

Figure 18.5 Effect of increase in the interest rate on the equilibrium of the consumer

The increase in the interest rate also affects the amount the consumer saves this year. With the higher interest rate, the consumer saves $(OC_2 - OC_{14})$ units. (Recall from Section 2 that the consumer receives OC_2 units this year. Since he or she decides to consume only OC_{14} units this year, it follows that $(OC_2 - OC_{14})$ units must be saved.) With the lower interest rate the consumer saves $(OC_2 - OC_0)$ units. (Since he or she consumes OC_0 units this year, it follows that $(OC_2 - OC_0)$ units are saved.)

Producers, like consumers, are also influenced by the rate of interest. For example, suppose that the producer-consumer in Figure 18.4 is confronted with a higher rate of interest. As shown in Figure 18.6, the increase in the interest rate will shift the market lines. Specifically, the market line in panel B of Figure 18.6 (which shows the situation when the interest rate is *higher*) is steeper than the market line in panel A of Figure 18.6 (which shows the situation when the interest rate is *lower*). This is true because the slope of a market line equals $-(1 + r)$, as we know from the previous section. As we also know from the previous section, the producer-consumer's first step toward an optimal decision is to choose the point on QQ' that is on the highest market line. In panel A of Figure 18.6, this point is K, whereas in panel B, it is M. Next, the producer-consumer should move along the market line corresponding to this point until he or she reaches the highest possible indifference curve. In panel A of Figure 18.6, this point is L; in panel B, it is N.

Thus the producer-consumer is led to make different investment and saving decisions when the interest rate is high than when it is low.

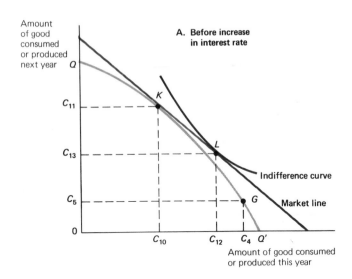

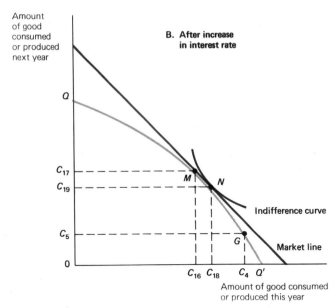

Figure 18.6   Effect of increase in the interest rate on the
equilibrium of the producer-consumer

Specifically, with the higher interest rate, $(OC_4 - OC_{16})$ units of the
current year's output are invested, whereas with the lower interest rate,
$(OC_4 - OC_{10})$ units are invested. With the higher interest rate, the
producer-consumer borrows $(OC_{18} - OC_{16})$ units and saves $(OC_4 -
OC_{18})$ units, whereas with the lower interest rate, he or she borrows
$(OC_{12} - OC_{10})$ units and saves $(OC_4 - OC_{12})$ units.

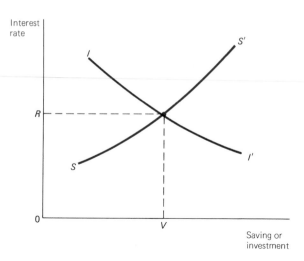

Figure 18.7   The equilibrium level of the interest rate

As pointed out in the previous section, aggregate saving must equal aggregate investment if equilibrium is to occur. That is, the total amount that consumers and producers want to save must equal the total amount that producers want to invest. The equilibrium level of the rate of interest is the level at which aggregate saving equals aggregate investment, as shown in Figure 18.7. SS' shows the total amount that will be saved at each level of the interest rate, and II' shows the total amount that will be invested at each level of the interest rate. The equilibrium level of the interest rate is OR, the level at which the total amount saved equals the total amount invested. If the interest rate is above this equilibrium level, the total amount people want to invest will be less than the total amount people want to save, with the result that the interest rate will tend to fall. If the interest rate is below this equilibrium level, the total amount people want to invest will exceed the total amount people want to save, with the result that the interest rate will tend to rise. Thus, assuming perfect competition, the interest rate, like any other price, is determined through the interaction of individuals and firms in the market.

5. The Present-Value Rule for Investment Decisions: Two Periods

The models of intertemporal choice presented in previous sections are highly simplified, and you may wonder whether they are of any practical significance. The fact is that they are the basis for some extremely valuable decision rules used by business firms and government agencies to determine which investment projects they should carry out. The typical firm or agency is confronted with a great many proposals for investment projects, far more than it can or should carry out. The economic health (perhaps even the survival) of the firm or agency depends on whether it accepts the right ones.

How do the models presented in previous sections provide a useful guide for investment decisions of this sort? As a first step toward answering this question, let's return to the case of the producer-consumer in Figure 18.4. It is clear from Figure 18.4 that *the optimal point on QQ' is unaffected by the producer-consumer's preferences.* That is, regardless of the shape or location of his indifference curves, the decision-maker should choose that point on QQ' that is on the highest market line—or, putting it differently, *he should choose that point that is associated with the maximum possible attained wealth.* The fact that this is the optimal decision, regardless of the decision-maker's preferences, is important, because it means that, to establish a rule to guide decisions of this sort, one does not have to worry about differences among decision-makers in preferences. Regardless of such differences, the same rule applies: *Maximize attained wealth.*[2]

To see how this rule can be applied, consider a particular investment project. Any such project can be characterized by an amount that the decision-maker gives up this year and an amount that he or she receives next year. In the case of this investment project, suppose that the decision-maker, if he or she gives up y_0 units of output this year, will gain y_1 units of output next year. The *present value* of this investment is defined to be

$$V = -y_0 + \frac{y_1}{1+r}.$$

18.2

Comparing this definition of present value with the definition of wealth in Section 2, it is clear that *the present value of this investment project is the change in the decision-maker's wealth resulting from carrying out the project.* To see this, suppose that the decision-maker, if he or she does not carry out the project, receives X_0 units of output this year and X_1 units of output next year, which means that his or her wealth equals $X_0 + \frac{X_1}{1+r}$. If the project is carried out, he or she receives $X_0 - y_0$ units this year and $X_1 + y_1$ units next year, which means that his or her wealth equals $X_0 - y_0 + \frac{X_1 + y_1}{1+r}$, or $\left(X_0 + \frac{X_1}{1+r}\right) + V$. The difference between his or her wealth if the project is carried out and his or her wealth if it is not carried out equals V, the present value of the project.

Since the decision-maker should maximize his or her wealth, and since the present value of an investment project is the change it effects in the decision-maker's wealth, it follows that *the decision-maker should carry out any investment project with a positive present value.* For ex-

2. The implicit assumption is made here that there are perfect and costless markets where borrowing and lending occur. If this is not (approximately) true, the analysis must be altered, as shown in more specialized texts concerning investment and capital budgeting.

ample, suppose that, if a decision-maker gives up 1 unit of output this year, he or she will receive 1.2 units of output next year. If the interest rate is .10, should he or she carry out this project? Since $y_0 = 1$, $y_1 = 1.2$, and $r = .10$,

$$V = -1 + \frac{1.2}{1+.10} = .09.$$

Since its present value is positive, this project should be carried out. Why? Because the decision-maker's wealth will be .09 units higher if the project is accepted than if it is rejected.

To see why the expression in Equation 18.2 is called the present value of the investment, note that *each unit of output received next year is worth only $1/(1 + r)$ units of output this year.* This is because, if one has $1/(1 + r)$ units of output this year, they can be lent out for a year; and because the rate of interest is r, they will return $(1 + r)$ times $1/(1 + r)$, or 1 unit next year. Since the value this year—that is, the *present* value—of each unit of output received next year is $1/(1 + r)$ units, the value this year—that is, the *present* value—of y_1 units received next year is $y_1 [1/(1 + r)]$ units. Subtracting the y_0 units that are given up this year from $y_1 [1/(1+ r)]$, we obtain the net value this year—that is, the *present* value—of the investment.

6. The Present-Value Rule: The Multiperiod Case

Since most investment projects extend over more than two periods, we must generalize the rule given in the previous section. To begin with, let's define the present value of a project as

$$V = z_0 + \frac{z_1}{1+r} + \frac{z_2}{(1+r)^2} + \cdots + \frac{z_n}{(1+r)^n} \qquad 18.3$$

where z_0 is the change (positive or negative) in the decision-maker's output this year, z_1 is the change in his or her output next year, z_2 is the change in his or her output 2 years hence, . . . , and z_n is the change in his or her output n years hence. Of course, Equation 18.2 is a special case of this equation, where $n = 1$, $z_0 = -y_0$, and $z_1 = y_1$. Equation 18.3 generalizes the earlier definition of present value (contained in Equation 18.2) to cases where more than two periods are relevant.

To see whether an investment project should be carried out, a decision-maker should determine whether the present value of the project is positive. If so, he or she should accept it. This is the rule to follow, regardless of the number of periods that must be included in the analysis. For example, suppose that a decision-maker is presented with the following investment opportunity: If he or she gives up 1 unit of output this year, he or she will receive 1 unit of output next year and $\frac{1}{2}$ unit of output in the following year. If the interest rate is .10, should he or she carry out this project? Since $z_0 = -1$, $z_1 = 1$, $z_2 = .50$, and $r = .10$,

$$V = -1 + \frac{1}{1+.10} + \frac{.50}{(1+.10)^2} = .32.$$

Thus, since the present value of the project is positive, the project should be carried out.

The reason why the decision-maker should accept a project if its present value is positive is the same as in the two-period case discussed in the previous section. Regardless of the number of periods that must be included in the analysis, the decision-maker's wealth will increase if he or she carries out a project whose present value is positive (and the decision-maker's wealth will decrease if he or she carries out a project whose present value is negative). In effect, the present value puts the outflows and inflows of output resulting from the investment in comparable form. Specifically, it converts these inflows and outflows (which occur in various periods) into their equivalent amounts in the *present* period. For example, the present value of the investment in the previous paragraph is .32, because the receipt of 1 unit next year is the equivalent of receiving 1 ÷ (1 + .10), or .91 units this year, and the receipt of $\frac{1}{2}$ unit two years hence is the equivalent of receiving $\frac{1}{2}$ ÷ (1 + .10)^2, or .41 units this year. Thus, since the investment entails giving up 1 unit this year, its present value is − 1 + .91 + .41, or .32 units.

Why is the receipt of 1 unit next year the equivalent of receiving 1 ÷ (1 + .10) units this year? Because, as pointed out in the previous section, each unit of output received next year is worth only $1/(1 + r)$ units this year. Why is the receipt of $\frac{1}{2}$ unit two years hence the equivalent of receiving $\frac{1}{2}$ ÷ (1 + .10)^2 units this year? Because, if one has $\frac{1}{2}$ ÷ (1 + .10)^2 units of output this year, they can be lent out for two years. Since the rate of interest is .10, they will return (1 + .10)^2 times $\frac{1}{2}$ ÷ (1 + .10)^2, or $\frac{1}{2}$ unit in two years. (At this point, it should be obvious that the receipt of 1 unit of output n years hence is the equivalent of receiving $1/(1 + r)^n$ units this year. Why? Because, if one has $1/(1 + r)^n$ units this year, they can be lent out for n years, and at that time they will be worth $(1 + r)^n$ times $1/(1 + r)^n$, or 1 unit, because of the accumulated interest.)

Finally, suppose that an investment yields a constant stream of output indefinitely into the future. Specifically, suppose that it yields z units of output next year, the following year, and every future year. What is the present value of this stream of output? Applying the principles described on the previous page, it is

$$\frac{z}{1+r} + \frac{z}{(1+r)^2} + \frac{z}{(1+r)^3} + \cdots = z\left[\frac{1}{1+r} + \frac{1}{(1+r)^2} + \frac{1}{(1+r)^3}\cdots\right]$$

which can be shown to equal z/r.[3] Thus, if the present value of this

3. If x is any number less than one,

$$1 + x + x^2 + x^3 + \cdots = 1/(1 - x).$$

Thus, since $\dfrac{1}{1 + r}$ is less than one,

$$\frac{1}{1 + r} + \left(\frac{1}{1 + r}\right)^2 + \left(\frac{1}{1 + r}\right)^3 + \cdots =$$

$$1/\left(1 - \frac{1}{1 + r}\right) - 1 = \frac{1 + r}{r} - 1 = \frac{1}{r}.$$

continued

investment is to be positive, the decision-maker must give up less than z/r units of output this year to get this stream of future output. For example, if an investment yields 1 unit of output next year, the following year, and so on, what is the most that a decision-maker should be willing to give up this year in order to obtain this stream of future output, if the interest rate is .05? The answer is $1 \div .05$, or 20 units of output, since $z = 1$ and $r = .05$.

7. The Investment Decision: An Example

The present-value rule, described in the previous two sections, has found widespread application throughout business and government. To illustrate its use, consider a firm that had to decide whether or not to purchase a machine which would reduce the firm's labor requirements.[4] The machine had a price of $2,200 and an anticipated life of five years with no salvage value at the end of that time. If the firm bought the machine, it would incur savings of labor costs in subsequent years, as shown in Table 18.1. If the interest rate was .10, should the firm have bought the machine? According to the present-value rule, the answer depends on whether the present value of the investment is positive. Using Equation 18.3, the present value of this investment was

$$V = -2,200 + \frac{200}{1+.10} + \frac{600}{(1+.10)^2} + \frac{800}{(1+.10)^3} +$$

$$\frac{1,200}{(1+.10)^4} + \frac{1,200}{(1+.10)^5} = \$644$$

because $z_0 = -2,200$, $z_1 = 200$, $z_2 = 600$, $z_3 = 800$, $z_4 = 1,200$, $z_5 = 1,200$, and $r = .10$. Since the present value of the investment was positive, the firm should have bought the machine.

In this case, the amount that the decision-maker gains or loses each year is expressed in terms of money, not output. This is because we no longer are making the assumption that only one good is present in the economy. The firm must estimate the effect of the investment—in this case, the new machine—on its cash inflow and outflow each year. The net change in its cash inflow (positive or negative) during each year is the value of z for this year. Thus, in this illustration, z_0 equals $-2,200$, since the machine reduces the firm's net cash inflow by $2,200 in the year when the machine is purchased (because the firm must spend this amount on

---

Consequently,

$$z \left[\frac{1}{(1+r)} + \left(\frac{1}{1+r} \right)^2 + \left(\frac{1}{1+r} \right)^3 + \cdots \right] = \frac{z}{r}$$

4. This case is taken from J. Dean, "Measuring the Productivity of Capital," in E. Mansfield, *Managerial Economics and Operations Research*, 4th ed. (New York: Norton, 1980).

Table 18.1 Effects of machine on firm's stream of cash inflows

Number of years hence	Effect on cash inflow* (dollars)
0	−2,200
1	200
2	600
3	800
4	1,200
5	1,200

* Positive numbers indicate cash savings; negative numbers indicate cash outflows.

the machine). And z_1 equals 200, since the machine increases the firm's net cash inflow by \$200 during the first year after the machine is purchased (because the firm spends \$200 less on labor than if it did not buy the machine).

Although the present-value rule is useful in guiding investment decisions, it sometimes cannot be applied in the straightforward way described here because of a variety of complications. For one thing, investment projects may be interdependent; that is, the stream of cash inflow or outflow from one project may depend on whether another project is undertaken. For another thing, there may be limitations on how many projects a firm can accept, perhaps because of limits on how much it is willing to borrow.[5] For still another thing, it is impossible to predict with certainty the stream of cash inflow or outflow from any investment project. One of the most difficult tasks facing any firm or agency is forecasting. In the present discussion, we have by-passed this problem and assumed that the firm's forecasts are correct. Techniques that help to deal with all of these complications are available in more advanced texts.[6]

8. Federal Water Projects and the Carter Administration: A Case Study

Government agencies, as well as business firms, use the present-value rule to determine whether investments should be carried out. For example, in evaluating a proposed water project (such as a dam), the present

5. In Chapter 17, we pointed out that a government agency's budget often is variable, but this is only within certain limits. Thus government agencies, too, must operate within limitations of this sort.

6. For example, see I. Fisher, *The Theory of Interest* (New York: Macmillan, 1930); J. Lorie and L. Savage, "Three Problems in Rationing Capital," reprinted in E. Mansfield, *Microeconomics: Selected Readings,* 4th ed. (New York: Norton, 1982); E. Solomon, "The Arithmetic of Capital Budgeting Decisions," *Journal of Business,* 1956; and F. Lutz and V. Lutz, *The Theory of Investment of the Firm* (Princeton: Princeton University Press, 1951).

Example 18.1 Evaluation of an Investment Project

A firm developed and introduced a new product used in connection with the drilling of wells. The product results in lower drilling costs because the drilling goes faster. This is an actual (not hypothetical) case. The effect of the investment in this new product on the firm's cash flow is shown below. (These figures, which were provided by the firm, have been rounded to make the computations simpler.)

Year	Effect on Cash flow (dollars)	Year	Effect on Cash flow (dollars)
1960	−100,000	1970	15,000
1961	−100,000	1971	200,000
1962	−100,000	1972	700,000
1963	−100,000	1973	700,000
1964	−100,000	1974	700,000
1965	−100,000	1975	700,000
1966	−100,000	1976	700,000
1967	15,000	1977	700,000
1968	15,000	1978	700,000
1969	15,000	1979	700,000

(a) Was the firm wise to make this investment if the interest rate was 10 percent? (b) If the effect of this investment on the firm's cash flow had been zero in 1967–71, would the firm have been wise to make this investment?

Solution

(a) If the interest rate is 10 percent, the present value of the investment is −$100,000

$$-\frac{\$100,000}{1.10} - \frac{\$100,000}{(1.10)^2} - \frac{\$100,000}{(1.10)^3} - \frac{\$100,000}{(1.10)^4}$$

$$-\frac{\$100,000}{(1.10)^5} - \frac{\$100,000}{(1.10)^6} + \frac{\$15,000}{(1.10)^7}$$

$$+\frac{\$15,000}{(1.10)^8} + \frac{\$15,000}{(1.10)^9} + \frac{\$15,000}{(1.10)^{10}}$$

$$+\frac{\$200,000}{(1.10)^{11}} + \frac{\$700,000}{(1.10)^{12}} + \frac{\$700,000}{(1.10)^{13}}$$

$$+\frac{\$700,000}{(1.10)^{14}} + \frac{\$700,000}{(1.10)^{15}} + \frac{\$700,000}{(1.10)^{16}}$$

$$+\frac{\$700,000}{(1.10)^{17}} + \frac{\$700,000}{(1.10)^{18}} + \frac{\$700,000}{(1.10)^{19}}$$

This is equal to −$100,000 (1 + .9091 + .8264 + .7513 + .6830 + .6209 + .5645) + $15,000 (.5132 + .4665 + .4241 + .3855) + $200,000 (.3505) + $700,000 (.3186 + .2897 + .2633 + .2394 + .2176 + .1978 + .1799 + .1635), or −$100,000 (5.3552) + $15,000 (1.7893) + $200,000

(.3505) + \$700,000 (1.8698). Thus the answer is − \$535,520 + \$26,840 + \$70,100 + \$1,308,860 = \$870,280. Since its present value was positive, the investment was worthwhile. It increased the firm's wealth. (b) If the effect on the firm's cash flow had been zero in 1967–71, the present value would have been − \$100,000 (5.3552) + \$700,000 (1.8698), or \$773,340. Since it is positive, the investment would still have been worthwhile.

value of the benefits is compared with the present value of the costs, and the project is supposed to be carried out only if the former exceeds the latter. Of course, the present value of both the benefits and the costs depends on the interest rate that is used. Increases in the interest rate decrease a project's chances of being accepted, because net costs occur early and net benefits occur late in the life of water projects. Ideally, the interest rate should be based on the alternative cost of public funds. That is, it should reflect the value of private alternatives forgone by the expenditure of public funds for water projects.

In 1977, there was a famous controversy at the highest levels of government over water projects. President Carter objected to eighteen water projects that had been approved when interest rates were lower. He said, "A more realistic interest rate must be used in calculating the cost and benefits of projects. Many of the projects reviewed were authorized at such low rates that even though we are building them today, we are pretending that the cost of capital is still the same as it was many years ago." Certainly, he was correct in believing that the interest rate should pertain to current conditions, not to conditions many years ago. However, he met very stiff opposition from congressional proponents of these water projects, and, according to some observers, he eventually softened his opposition to them.[7]

9. Technological Change[8]

In previous sections of this chapter, we have presented models pertaining to intertemporal choice by consumers and producers. Now we turn to another essentially dynamic phenomenon—technological change. Technology is society's pool of knowledge regarding the industrial and agricultural arts. The technology existing at a given point in time sets limits on how much can be produced with a given amount of inputs. Given the level of technology, there is generally a wide range of possible methods of

7. For further discussion, see W. Baumol, "On the Discount Rate for Public Projects," in E. Mansfield, *Microeconomics: Selected Readings;* and S. Hanke and J. Anwyll, "On the Discount Rate Controversy," *Public Policy,* Spring 1980.

8. For a much more extensive and detailed discussion of technological change, see E. Mansfield, *The Economics of Technological Change* (New York: Norton, 1968). Much of this chapter is based on parts of that book; in some cases material has been reprinted.

producing a given good or service. Some require little capital and much labor, some require much capital and little labor; some are old, some are new. Given a certain amount of various inputs, it is possible to determine which method results in the maximum output and what the maximum output is. We know from Chapter 6 that the production function shows, for a given level of technology, the maximum output rate that can be achieved from a given amount of inputs.

Technological change is the advance of technology; such advance often takes the form of new methods of producing existing products and new techniques of organization, marketing, and management. Technological change results in a change in the production function. If the production function were readily observable, a comparison of the production function at two points in time would provide the economist with a simple measure of the effect of technological change during the intervening period. For example, if there were only two inputs, labor and capital, and if there were constant returns to scale, the characteristics of the production function at a given date could be captured fully by a single isoquant.[9] Under these circumstances, one could simply look at the changing position of this isoquant to see the effects of technological change.

For example, if this isoquant shifted from position 1 to position 2 in Figure 18.8 during a certain period of time, technological change had less

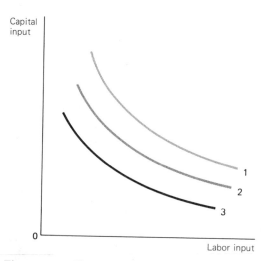

Figure 18.8   Change over a period of time in the position of an isoquant

9. Recall from Chapter 6 that, if there are constant returns to scale, an x percent increase in all inputs results in an x percent increase in output. Thus, if there are constant returns to scale, there is at á given point in time a unique relationship between capital input per unit of output and labor input per unit of output. This relationship holds for any output and completely summarizes the efficient input combinations.

impact during this period than if the curve shifted to position 3. As we shall see in subsequent sections, it is sometimes possible to estimate the average rate of movement of the production function by a single number, and economists often use this number to measure the rate of technological change. Of course, it is only an indirect measure but there is no way to measure the rate of technological change directly.

Technological change also results in the availability of new products. In many cases the availability of new products can be regarded as a change in the production function, since they are merely more efficient ways of meeting old wants if these wants are defined with proper breadth. This is particularly true in the case of new intermediate goods, which may result in little or no change in the final product. In other cases, however, the availability of new products cannot realistically be viewed as a change in the production function, since they entail an important difference in kind.[10]

10. Change in Technique

It is customary to distinguish between a technological change and a change in technique. Whereas technological change is an advance in knowledge, a change in technique is a change in the utilized method of production. Although technological change and a change in technique are two different things, they obviously are related to one another. Indeed, a technological change can have little economic impact unless it induces a change in techniques. The distinction between technological change and a change in technique is useful, but its sharpness should not be exaggerated. In this section, we show how changes in technology result in changes in techniques.

Suppose that the production function in a given industry is represented by the isoquant PP', in Figure 18.9. Assuming constant returns to scale, one isoquant fully represents the production function. To determine the minimum cost technique, isocost curves (A, B, C) can be drawn representing the combinations of quantities of labor and capital that can be purchased for various amounts. The minimum-cost technique corresponds to the point on the isoquant that is on the lowest isocost curve. In Figure 18.9, this point is point 1.

Now suppose that there is a change in technology in this industry which shifts the production function so that QQ' is the new isoquant. In this case the minimum-cost technique is no longer 1, but 2 instead. Thus

10. It is sometimes asserted that it is unrealistic to emphasize cost-reducing technological change, since firms report that only about 13 percent of their expenditures on research and development go for pure process improvement. But this is wrong because much of the research and development concerning new products and product improvements is devoted to new and improved intermediate goods and capital goods. In civilian industry, perhaps 80 percent of the reported research and development goes for new processes, new intermediate goods, and new capital goods. See E. Mansfield, J. Rapoport, J. Schnee, S. Wagner, and M. Hamburger, *Research and Innovation in the Modern Corporation* (New York: Norton, 1971).

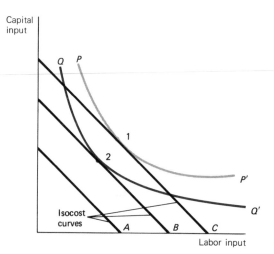

Figure 18.9   Effect of technological change on
minimum-cost technique

this change in technology will result in a change in technique. If output
is held constant, the amount of labor used by the industry will decrease;
so will the amount of capital used. But in actuality the industry's output
will probably change because, with the change in technique, the industry's supply curve will probably shift.[11]

Although technological change can result in a change in technique,
it need not always do so. For example, consider Figure 18.10. Suppose

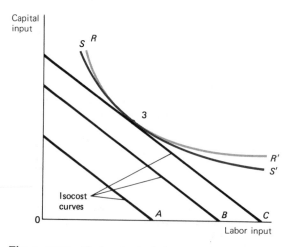

Figure 18.10   Technological change without change
in minimum-cost technique

11. Think back to the discussion in Chapter 9. What is likely to be the impact on
industry output of a shift to the right of the supply curve?

that the original production function is represented by the RR' isoquant and that a change in technology results in a new isoquant, SS'. In this case, although there has been a change in technology, there has been no change in technique; the minimum-cost technique before and after the change in technology is represented by point 3. This is because the shape of the isoquant has been changed in such a way that point 3 remains on the lowest isocost curve.

11. Productivity Growth and the Measurement of Technological Change

Economists have long been interested in productivity—the ratio of output to input. During the 1980s, American economists have shown a particular interest in this topic because there has been a well-publicized fall in the U.S. rate of productivity increase. The oldest and most commonly studied measure of productivity is labor productivity, output per man-hour of labor. One determinant of the rate of growth of labor productivity is the rate of technological change; a high rate of technological change is likely to result, all other things equal, in a high rate of growth of labor productivity. However, the rate of technological change is not the only determinant of the rate of growth of labor productivity, with the consequence that the latter is a very incomplete, though frequently used, measure of the rate of technological change.

To see how changes in labor productivity can produce false signals concerning the rate of technological change, consider Figure 18.11. Suppose that the relevant isoquant is II' and that input prices at the beginning of the period are such that the isocost curves are $A, B, C,$ and so on. The least-cost combination of inputs is OL_1 of labor and OK_1 of capital.

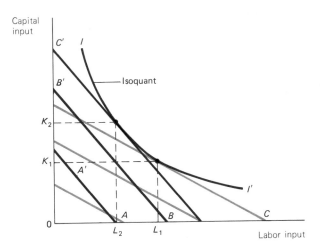

Figure 18.11   Labor productivity increase without technological change

Now suppose that input prices change, with labor becoming more expensive relative to capital; the result is that the isocost curves shift to A', B', C', and so on. Under these new circumstances, the least-cost combination of inputs to produce the same output is OL_2 of labor and OK_2 of capital. Since output remains constant and labor input decreases, labor productivity increases due to the change in input prices. But this productivity increase is not an indication of technological change, because there is no change at all in the production function.

A more adequate measure of the rate of technological change is the total productivity index, which relates changes in output to changes in both labor and capital inputs, not changes in labor inputs alone. Suppose that the production function is of the simple form:

$$Q = \alpha(bL + cK) \tag{18.4}$$

where Q is the quantity of output, L is the quantity of labor, K is the quantity of capital, b and c are constants, and α is a number that varies over time in response to technological change. Suppose that Q_0, L_0, K_0 and α_0 are the values of Q, L, K, and α in an early period and that Q_1, L_1, K_1, and α_1 are the values of Q, L, K, and α in a later period. To determine $\alpha_1 \div \alpha_0$, which is a measure of the rate of technological change, one can compute

$$\frac{Q_1}{Q_0} \div \left(U\frac{L_1}{L_0} + V\frac{K_1}{K_0} \right) \tag{18.5}$$

where $U = bL_0/(bL_0 + cK_0)$ and $V = cK_0/(bL_0 + cK_0)$. This is the total productivity index. It is equal to the relative increase in output divided by a weighted average of the relative increase in labor input and the relative increase in capital input.[12]

Of course, the production function in Equation 18.4 is a very special case. Economists have tried to devise better measures of the rate of movement of the production function than the total productivity index. These measures rest on somewhat different assumptions about the shape of the production function, with the Cobb-Douglas production function sometimes, but not always, being used. One of the pioneering studies of this type was carried out in 1957 by Robert Solow of the Massachusetts Institute of Technology.[13] The resulting estimates have proved useful in many contexts, but their limitations should be noted. In particular, since they equate the effects of technological change with whatever increase in output is unexplained by other inputs, they may not isolate the effects of technological change alone. In addition, they may contain the effects of

12. For comprehensive data concerning labor productivity and total productivity in the United States, see J. Kendrick, *Productivity Trends in the United States* (New York: National Bureau of Economic Research, 1961), and his more recent publications, as well as F. Gollup and D. Jorgensen, "U.S. Total Factor Productivity by Industry, 1947–73," in J. Kendrick and B. Vaccara, *New Developments in Productivity Measurement and Analysis* (Chicago: National Bureau of Economic Research, 1980).

13. R. Solow, "Technical Change and the Aggregate Production Function," *Review of Economics and Statistics*, August 1957.

whatever inputs may have been excluded from the analysis because of convenience, lack of data, ignorance, or some other reason.

12. Determinants of the Rate of Technological Change

What determines the rate of technological change? Existing theory is still in a relatively primitive state, for it is only recently that economists have begun to give this question the attention it deserves. It seems obvious, however, that an industry's rate of technological change depends to a large extent on the amount of resources devoted by firms, by independent inventors, and by government to the improvement of the industry's technology. The amount of resources devoted by the government depends on how closely the industry is related to defense, public health, and other social needs for which the government assumes major responsibility; on the extent of the external economies generated by the relevant research and development; and on more purely political factors.

The amount of resources devoted by private sources to improving an industry's technology is influenced by the anticipated profitability of the investment. From this it follows that the rate of technological change in a particular area is influenced by the same kinds of factors that determine the output of any good or service.[14] On the one hand, there are demand factors that influence the rewards for particular kinds of technological change. For example, if a prospective change in technology reduces the cost of a particular product, increases in the demand for the product are likely to increase the returns from effecting this technological change. Similarly, a growing shortage and a rising price of the inputs saved by a prospective change in technology are likely to increase the returns from effecting it. For example, increases in the eighteenth century in the demand for yarn, as well as increases in spinners' wages, raised the returns to various textile inventions and directly stimulated the work leading to the invention of the spinning jenny and the spinning mule.

On the other hand, there are also supply factors that influence the cost of making particular types of technological change. Obviously, whether people try to solve a given problem depends on whether they think it can be solved, and on how costly they think it will be, as well as on the expected payoff if they are successful. The cost of making science-based technological changes depends on the number of scientists and engineers in relevant fields and on advances in basic science; for example, advances in physics clearly reduced the cost of effecting

---

14. Needless to say, supply and demand are not the only factors that influence the rate of technological change. As emphasized in subsequent sections, there is considerable uncertainty in the research and inventive processes. Moreover, laboratories, scientists, and inventors are motivated by many factors other than profit. We have no intention of characterizing them as "economic men." See E. Mansfield, J. Rapoport, A. Romeo, E. Villani, S. Wagner, and F. Husic, *The Production and Application of New Industrial Technology* (New York: Norton, 1977).

changes in technology in the field of atomic energy. In addition, the rate of technological change depends on the amount of effort devoted to making modest improvements that lean heavily on practical experience. Although there is often a tendency to focus attention on the major, spectacular inventions, it is by no means certain that technological change in many industries results chiefly from these inventions, rather than from a succession of minor improvements.

Besides being influenced by the quantity of resources an industry devotes to improving its own technology, an industry's rate of technological change depends on the quantity of resources devoted by other industries to the improvement of the capital goods and other inputs it uses. Technological change in an industry that supplies materials, components, and machinery often prompts technological change among its customers. For example, technological change in electric power generation was an important stimulus to the commercial production of aluminum and to further technological change in the aluminum industry. In addition, there is another kind of interdependence among industries. Considerable spillover occurs because techniques invented for one industry sometimes turn out to be useful for others as well. Further, an industry's rate of technological change depends on the availability and usefulness of foreign technology. For example, for many years, Canada's Northern Electric based most of its designs on those of Western Electric.

Another factor that may influence an industry's rate of technological change is its market structure. Some attention will be devoted to this factor in Section 16.

13. Innovation

An invention, when applied for the first time, is called an innovation. Traditionally, economists have stressed the distinction between an invention and an innovation on the ground that an invention has little or no economic significance until it is applied. This distinction becomes somewhat blurred in cases like du Pont's nylon, where the inventor and the innovator are the same firm. Under these circumstances, the final stages of development may entail at least a partial commitment to a market test. However, in many cases, the inventor is not in a position to—and does not want to—apply his or her invention, because his or her business is invention, not production; or because he or she is a supplier, not a user, of the equipment embodying the innovation; or for some other reason. In these cases, the distinction remains relatively clear-cut.

Regardless of whether the break between invention and innovation is clean, innovation is a key stage in the process leading to the full evaluation and utilization of an invention. The innovator—the firm that is first to apply the invention—must be willing to take the risks involved in introducing a new and untried process, good, or service. In many cases these risks are high. Although research and development can provide a great deal of information regarding the technical characteristics and cost of production of the invention—and market research can provide considerable information regarding the demand for it—there are many areas of uncertainty that can be resolved only by actual production and marketing of the invention. By obtaining needed information regarding the actual performance of the invention, the innovator plays a vital social role.

The lag between invention and innovation seems to vary considerably, and is commonly ten years or more for major inventions. What factors does a firm consider in deciding whether or not to innovate? Clearly, the firm must begin by estimating how much profit it will realize by introducing the new product or process. If the expected profits from the introduction of the innovation do not exceed those obtainable from other investments by an amount that is large enough to justify the extra risks, the innovation will be rejected. If they do exceed those available elsewhere by this amount, the profitability and risks involved in introducing the innovation at present must be compared with the profitability and risks involved in introducing it at various future dates.

There are often considerable advantages in waiting, since improvements occur in the new product or process and more information becomes available regarding its performance and market. For example, in the case of new products, firms often employ test marketing to obtain additional information before making a full-scale commitment. However, there often are disadvantages, as well as advantages, in waiting; perhaps the most important is that a competitor may beat the firm to the punch or that the conditions favoring the innovation may become less benign. In the case of new products, there is often a considerable disadvantage in not being first; sales opportunities will be lost in the interval that competitors are in the market ahead of this firm, and part of the market may be lost for a considerable period after this firm makes its appearance.

If the expected profits exceed those obtainable from other investments by an amount that is large enough to justify the risks, and if the disadvantages of waiting seem to outweigh the advantages, the firm will introduce the innovation. Otherwise it will wait. Pioneering is a risky business; whether it pays off is often a matter of timing.

14. Technological Change in Energy Production: A Case Study

In recent years, there has been considerable emphasis in the United States on the development of new sources of clean fuel. Ever since the Arab oil embargo of late 1973, the nation has been engaged in a large program involving both the private and public sectors to develop new ways to power our economy. As applications of the concepts discussed in previous sections, consider three possible ways of producing energy: (1) shale oil, (2) oil from tar sands, and (3) coal gasification. Of course, these are only a sample of the new technologies currently being explored, but they are among the more important ones.[15]

Shale, found in large amounts in Colorado, Utah, and Wyoming, is a potentially important source of synthetic oil. But this source has not been used because others were cheaper. As conditions and prices change, this may no longer be the case. However, one problem with shale is that it involves a waste-disposal problem. The spent shale could fill an enormous volume, and the danger of environmental damage must be considered (see Example 9.1).

Another potentially important source of synthetic oil is the tar sands located in Alberta, Canada. Great Canadian Oil Sands, Ltd. (GCOS), 96 percent owned by Sun Oil Company, has invested about $750 million in learning how to obtain oil from these tar sands, which are estimated to be a potential source of as much as 30 billion barrels of synthetic crude oil. GCOS has been the innovator, and in accord with our discussion in Section 13, the risks have been high. (J. Howard Pew, chairman of Sun Oil, even went against the advice of his own engineers when he set the innovation in motion.) Based on its 45,000 barrel-a-day plant, opened in 1967, it has reported some success in reducing the cost of synthetic crude oil. One factor influencing the rate of adoption of this technique is the Canadian government's policies concerning the exploitation of this natural resource. In 1980, the Canadian government reduced the price that Sun was allowed to receive for its synthetic crude oil from $32 (the world oil price) to $14. In 1981, it allowed the price to rise somewhat.

Finally, coal gasification is another potentially important source of energy. The United States is endowed with huge deposits of coal (about 20 percent of the world's supply), but there is no commercially successful way of burning much of it cleanly. One way to get around the environmental problems involved in using coal as a fuel is to convert coal to a clean gas. At present, much of this work is still in the stage of research and development. A substantial portion of this R and D is being funded in part by the government. Since there is so much uncertainty concerning the relative merits of various processes, the government is helping to finance a number of parallel approaches to the problem. It will be some time before anyone can tell which of these processes, if any, is economically viable.

15. Static Efficiency and Economic Progress

In Chapter 16, we presented several conditions for economic efficiency: The marginal rate of substitution between any pair of commodities must be the same for all consumers, the marginal rate of technical substitution between any pair of inputs must be the same for all producers, and the

15. Among other new technologies are solar energy and the fusion reactor, both of which seem to be far in the future. When he was in office, President Carter favored an indefinite delay in the deployment of plutonium breeder technology because of the danger of proliferation of nuclear weapons capability.

marginal rate of product transformation must equal the marginal rate of substitution for each pair of goods. Given a fixed level of technology these conditions must be fulfilled (with certain qualifications discussed in Chapter 16) if consumer welfare is to be maximized.

It is important to note that these conditions result only in efficiency in a static sense. That is, they show how inputs and commodities must be allocated if welfare is to be maximized, *given a fixed level of technology.* It is possible that an allocation of inputs and commodities that violates these conditions might lead to a higher level of consumer welfare than any allocation that meets these conditions, because it might result in a faster rate of technological change and productivity increase.

Economists like Joseph Schumpeter and John Kenneth Galbraith of Harvard University[16] have argued that this is the case, and have gone on to suggest that a perfectly competitive economy is likely to be inferior in a dynamic sense to an economy including many imperfectly competitive industries (that is, monopolies, oligopolies, etc.). In their view, although (as we showed in Chapter 16) a perfectly competitive economy will satisfy the conditions for static economic efficiency, it will not result in as high a rate of technological change and productivity increase as an imperfectly competitive economy.

To illustrate what they have in mind, suppose that we compare the performance of two economies, one perfectly competitive, the other imperfectly competitive. Suppose that they start off with comparable technology in 1982, but that the rate of technological change is higher in the imperfectly competitive economy than in the perfectly competitive economy, with the result that the annual rate of productivity change is 3 percent in the imperfectly competitive economy and 2 percent in the perfectly competitive economy. Assuming that the quantity of inputs is the same in each economy and constant over time, it follows that

$$Q(t) = Q_0(1.02)^t \qquad\qquad 18.6$$

$$Q'(t) = Q_0'(1.03)^t \qquad\qquad 18.7$$

where $Q(t)$ is the output in year t in the perfectly competitive economy, $Q'(t)$ is the output in year t in the imperfectly competitive economy, and t is measured in years from 1982.

Suppose too that, because of the static inefficiencies due to its violation of the conditions in Chapter 16, the imperfectly competitive economy produces 98 percent as much as the perfectly competitive economy when their technology levels are the same. Thus $Q_0' = .98Q_0$, and

$$Q(t) = Q_0(1.02)^t \qquad\qquad 18.8$$

$$Q'(t) = .98Q_0(1.03)^t \qquad\qquad 18.9$$

16. J. Schumpeter, *Capitalism, Socialism, and Democracy* (New York: Harper & Row, 1947); J. K. Galbraith, *American Capitalism* (Boston: Houghton Mifflin, 1952); and H. Villard, "Competition, Oligopoly, and Research," *Journal of Political Economy,* December 1958. For a good review, see F. M. Scherer, *Industrial Market Structure and Economic Performance,* 2d ed. (Chicago: Rand McNally, 1980).

Example 18.2   Economic Effects of a Textile Innovation

J. P. Stevens, the large textile firm, devises a new production method which reduces the cost of making cloth. Other firms become aware of this development and imitate the new method. Suppose that the market demand curve for cloth in 1982 is as shown below. Because of this new method, the cost of producing a unit of cloth is OP_1, whereas it would have been OP_0 without the new method. Suppose that the market supply curve for cloth in 1982 is S_1; without this method, it would have been S_0. (a) During the period covered by the graph below, what is the social value of the extra output of cloth due to this new method? (b) What is the social value of the saving in resources due to this new method? (c) Prove that the social value of the extra output, which you found in question (a), plus the social value of the resource savings, which you found in question (b), equals the area $P_1 P_0 A B$. (d) Can the textile industry, which is highly competitive, appropriate all of the social benefits of the new method by keeping the price at OP_0?

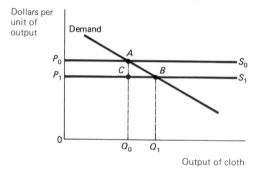

Dollars per unit of output — *Output of cloth*

Solution

(a) Output is OQ_1 with the new method, whereas it would have been OQ_0 without it. The social value of the extra output is the area under the demand curve from Q_0 to Q_1—that is, the area $Q_0 A B Q_1$. (Recall page 292.) (b) With the new method, OQ_1 units of cloth are produced, and each unit costs OP_1, so the total value of resources used is OQ_1 times OP_1, which equals the area $OP_1 B Q_1$. Without the new method, OQ_0 units of cloth would have been produced, and each unit would have cost OP_0, so that total value of resources used would have been OQ_0 times OP_0, which equals the area $OP_0 A Q_0$. Thus the saving equals the area $OP_0 A Q_0$ minus the area $OP_1 B Q_1$. Since these areas have in common the area $OP_1 C Q_0$, it follows that this saving equals the area $P_1 P_0 A C$ minus the area $Q_0 C B Q_1$. (c) From above, we know that the social value of the extra output equals the area $Q_0 A B Q_1$, and that the social value of the savings equals the area $P_1 P_0 A C$ minus the area $Q_0 C B Q_1$. Thus the sum of these social values must equal the area $Q_0 A B Q_1$ plus the area $P_1 P_0 A C$ minus the area $Q_0 C B Q_1$. Since the area $Q_0 A B Q_1$ minus the area $Q_0 C B Q_1$ equals the area $C A B$, it follows that the sum of these social values must equal the area $P_1 P_0 AC$ plus the area CAB, or the area $P_1 P_0 AB$. (d) No. Because of competition among producers, the price of cotton cloth falls to the new cost of production, OP_1. This competition arises because other firms imitate the new method.*

* For further discussion of this topic, see E. Mansfield, J. Rapoport, A. Romeo, S. Wagner, and G. Beardsley, "Social and Private Rates of Return from Industrial Innovations," *Quarterly Journal of Economics*, May 1977. This article shows how the benefits from an innovation can be related to the costs of developing it to determine the rate of return from the investment in the innovation. Also, it extends the results of this example to more complicated cases.

Thus it follows that

$$Q'(t) \div Q(t) = .98(1.03 \div 1.02)^t \qquad \text{18.10}$$

which implies that $Q'(t) \div Q(t)$ will be greater than one when t is greater than about two. Consequently, despite its being relatively inefficient in a static sense, the imperfectly competitive economy out-produces the perfectly competitive economy from about 1984 on, because it has the higher rate of technological change and productivity increase.

16. Imperfect Competition and Technological Change

This example shows that the static inefficiencies of an imperfectly competitive economy *can* be offset by its having a higher rate of technological change and productivity increase, but it does not tell us why we should expect the rate of technological change and productivity increase to be higher in an imperfectly competitive economy. This is a question that has been debated at great length. On the one hand, some economists, like Schumpeter and Galbraith, believe that there are a number of good reasons why the rate of technological change and productivity increase will be higher in an imperfectly competitive economy. On the other hand, other economists stick with the view of John Stuart Mill and J. B. Clark that this is not the case.[17]

Members of the Schumpeter-Galbraith group argue that firms under perfect competition have less resources to devote to research and experimentation than do firms under imperfect competition. Because profits are at a relatively low level, it is difficult for firms under perfect competition to support large expenditures on research and development. Moreover, it is argued that, unless a firm has sufficient control over the market to reap the rewards of an innovation, the introduction of the

17. J. S. Mill, *Principles of Political Economy* (London, 1852), Book IV, Ch. VII, p. 351; and J. B. Clark, *Essentials of Economic Theory* (New York, 1907), p. 374.

innovation may not be worthwhile. If competitors can imitate the innovation very quickly, the innovator may be unable to make any money from the innovation.

Defenders of perfect competition retort that there is likely to be less pressure for firms in imperfect markets to introduce new techniques and products, since such firms have fewer competitors. Moreover, such firms are better able to drive out entrants who, uncommitted to present techniques, are likely to be relatively quick to adopt new ones. (Entrants, unlike established producers, have no vested interest in maintaining the demand for existing products and the profitability of existing equipment.) Also, there are advantages in having a large number of independent decision-making units, since there is less chance that an important techological advance will be blocked by the faulty judgment of a few people.

It is difficult to obtain evidence to help settle this question, if it is posed in this way, since perfect competition is, of course, a hypothetical construct that does not exist in the real world. However, it does seem unlikely that a perfectly competitive industry (if such an industry could be constructed) would be able in many areas of the economy to carry out the research and development required to promote a high rate of technological change.[18] Moreover, if entry is free and rapid, firms in a perfectly competitive industry will have little motivation to innovate. Although the evidence is not at all clear-cut, this much can probably be granted the Schumpeter-Galbraith group.[19]

But it is one thing to grant that a certain amount of market imperfection may promote the rate of technological change, and another thing to say, as does Galbraith, that the "modern industry of a few large firms [is] an almost perfect instrument for inducing technical change."[20] If true, this is an extremely important point. But is it true? Does the evidence indicate that an industry dominated by a few giant firms is generally more progressive than one composed of a larger number of smaller firms?

Contrary to the allegations of Galbraith, there is little evidence that industrial giants are needed in all or even most industries to insure rapid technological change and rapid utilization of new techniques.[21] Of course, this does not mean that industries composed only of small firms would necessarily be optimal for the promotion and diffusion of new techniques either. On the contrary, there seem to be considerable advantages in a diversity of firm sizes; no single firm size is optimal in this

18. Even if supplier firms emerge that specialize in research and development, the members of the competitive industry must still carry out some technical work to be able to accept new technology rapidly. Moreover, there may have to be imperfect competition in the supplying industry if it is to be viable.

19. Also, technological change may result in a certain amount of market imperfection, although the extent of the market imperfection is likely to vary greatly from case to case.

20. J. K. Galbraith, *American Capitalism*, p. 91.

21. See the references in footnotes 10 and 14 and the final reference in footnote 16.

respect. Moreover, the optimal average size is likely to be directly related to the costliness and scope of the inventions that arise. However, in general, these factors do not make giantism necessary. To repeat, there is little evidence that industrial giants are needed in all or even most industries to promote rapid technological change and rapid utilization of new techniques.

17. The Patent System

Finally, we turn to the patent system, one of the major instruments of public policy regarding technology. The United States patent laws grant the inventor exclusive control over the use of his or her invention for seventeen years. In this section, we describe the role played by patents in a free-enterprise economy and some problems involved in the patent system. Needless to say, only a few aspects of the subject can be discussed in the available space.[22]

New technological knowledge differs from most other goods in an important way: It cannot be used up. A person or firm can use an idea repeatedly without wearing it out; and the same idea can serve many users at the same time. No one need be getting less of the idea because others are using it too. This property of knowledge creates an important problem for any firm that would like to make a business of producing knowledge. For an investment in research and development to be worth considering, a firm must be able to sell its results, directly or indirectly, for a price. But who would be willing to pay for a commodity that, once produced, becomes available to all in unlimited quantity? Why not let someone else pay for it, since then it would be available for nothing?

The patent laws are a way of handling this problem. They make it possible for firms to produce new knowledge and to sell or use it profitably. However, the patent system has the disadvantage that new knowledge is not used as widely as it should be, from the viewpoint of static efficiency. This is because the patent-holder, who attempts to make a profit, will set a price sufficiently high so that some people who could make productive use of the patented item will be discouraged from doing so. From the point of view of society, all people who can use the idea should be permitted to do so at a very low cost, since the marginal cost of their doing so is often practically zero. Another way of stating this is that the price of the information should, according to Chapter 16, be set equal to its marginal cost, which is often practically zero. But this, of course, would provide no incentive for invention.

A number of proposals have been made to alter the patent system so that this problem is met; one of the best-known is Michael Polanyi's suggestion that government grants, rather than patents, be awarded to

22. For a more thorough discussion, see F. Machlup, *An Economic Review of the Patent System,* Study 15 of the Senate Subcommittee on Patents, Trademarks, and Copyrights, 1958; and F. M. Scherer, *The Economic Effects of Compulsory Patent Licensing* (New York: New York University Press, 1977).

inventors.[23] Proposals for systems of prizes and bonuses to inventors are very old; for example, Alexander Hamilton favored such a system. From the point of view of welfare economics, Polanyi's suggestion has the advantage that there would be an optimal use of new knowledge (since it would be available without charge), as well as an incentive to produce new knowledge. However, this proposal has great practical disadvantages. The problem of selecting inventors and inventions to receive grants has limited the attention accorded this kind of scheme. It seems extremely unlikely that fundamental changes of this sort will be made.

18. Summary

The consumer has preferences between consumption this year and consumption next year, and these preferences can be represented by a set of indifference curves. The consumer is confronted by a budget line which indicates the combinations of present and future consumption that he or she can attain. The intercept of the budget line on the horizontal axis is called the consumer's endowed wealth. The slope of the budget line is $-(1 + r)$, where r is the interest rate. The rate of interest is the premium received by the consumer one year hence if he or she lends a dollar for a year. In other words, if the consumer lends a dollar, he or she receives $(1 + r)$ dollars a year hence. The optimal choice between the amount consumed this year and the amount consumed next year is represented by the point on the budget line that is on the highest indifference curve.

Suppose that a producer-consumer can both produce the good and lend or borrow it. He or she is confronted by a curve, QQ', showing how much he or she can produce (and consume) next year if he or she saves various amounts of the present year's output and invests it to increase next year's output. Corresponding to each point on this curve is a market line which shows the various amounts of the good that he or she can consume in each period, if he or she borrows or lends various amounts. A market line's intercept on the horizontal axis equals the level of attained wealth associated with this market line. To maximize his or her utility, the producer-consumer should choose the point on QQ' that corresponds to the market line with the highest level of attained wealth. Then he or she should move along this market line until he or she reaches the point that is on the highest possible indifference curve. For an equilibrium to occur in the economy as a whole, aggregate saving must equal aggregate investment. The equilibrium level of the interest rate is the level where aggregate saving equals aggregate investment.

The present value of an investment project is the change in the decision-maker's wealth resulting from carrying out the project. Clearly, the decision-maker should carry out any investment project with a positive present value. In calculating the present value of an investment, it is important to note that the receipt of a dollar n years hence is the equivalent of receiving $1/(1 + r)^n$ dollars now, since, if one has $1/(1 + r)^n$

23. M. Polanyi, "Patent Reform," *Review of Economic Studies,* Summer 1944.

dollars now, they can be lent out for n years, and at that time they will be worth $(1 + r)^n$ times $1/(1 + r)^n$, or \$1, because of the accumulated interest. The present-value rule—accept investment projects that have a positive present value—has found widespread application in business and government. Several examples of its uses were presented.

Technology is society's pool of knowledge concerning the industrial and agricultural arts. Technological change is the advance of technology, and such advance often results in a change in the production function for an existing product or in a new product. The rate of technological change is often measured by changes in total productivity indexes. The rate of technological change in an industry depends on the amount of resources devoted to the improvement of the industry's technology, which in turn depends in part on the rewards from particular kinds of technological change and on factors that determine their costs. An invention, when applied for the first time, is called an innovation. To illustrate these concepts, we discussed several potentially significant new technologies related to the current emphasis in the United States on developing new sources of clean fuel.

Schumpeter, Galbraith, and others have argued that, although a perfectly competitive economy will satisfy the conditions for static economic efficiency, it will not result in as high a rate of technological change and productivity increase as an imperfectly competitive economy. Although a certain amount of market imperfection may help to increase the rate of technological change and productivity increase, there is little evidence that giant firms are needed in all or even most industries to insure rapid technological change and rapid utilization of new techniques. One of the major instruments of public policy regarding technology is the patent system. Unfortunately, the patent system has the disadvantage that new knowledge is not used as widely as it should be, from the viewpoint of static efficiency. But no really practical alternative to the patent system has been proposed.

QUESTIONS AND PROBLEMS

1. Suppose that Mary Brown's situation is as follows, where AB is her budget line.

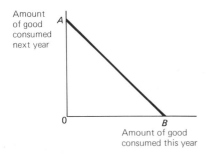

If $OA = 10$ units of the good, and the interest rate equals .08, what does OB equal? What is Mary Brown's endowed wealth?

2. John Brown is notified that his aunt has died and that she has willed him $5,000, which will be paid when her estate is settled in two years. If the interest rate is .10, what is the present value of his inheritance?

3. A government bond pays $10 per year, and has no due date. That is, the interest payment of $10 per year goes on forever. If the interest rate is .05, how much would you be willing to pay for the bond?

4. In Question 3, how much would you be willing to pay for the bond described there if the interest rate is .10?

5. Figures provided by the Bureau of Labor Statistics show that output per man-hour in blast furnaces using the most up-to-date techniques was about twice as large as the industry average in 1926. How can such large differences exist at a given point in time? Why don't all firms adopt the most up-to-date techniques at every point in time? Do you think that differences of this sort exist today?

6. Suppose that you were given the job of forecasting the rate of growth of sales of a new product to be introduced by du Pont. What factors would you expect to determine the rate of growth of sales? How would you go about measuring these factors?

7. According to Robert Solow, "Invention is the historical answer to the law of diminishing returns." Explain this statement.

8. What factors determine how much a particular development project will cost? Holding other factors constant, will development cost increase or decrease with how rapidly the development is carried out?

9. Technological change is called labor-saving if it results in a decrease in the marginal rate of technical substitution of labor for capital. Under these circumstances, does technological change result in a greater increase in the marginal product of capital than in the marginal product of labor (at a given capital-labor ratio)? Does it result in the firm's using more capital relative to labor?

10. An investment will have the following effect on a firm's annual cash inflow:

1982	− $5,000
1983	+ $2,000
1984	+ $2,000
1985	+ $1,000
1986	+ $1,000.

If the interest rate is .10, should this firm carry out this investment?

SELECTED REFERENCES

BAUMOL, WILLIAM. "On the Discount Rate for Public Projects." Reprinted in E. Mansfield, *Microeconomics: Selected Readings.* 4th ed. New York: Norton, 1982.

FISHER, IRVING. *The Theory of Interest.* New York: Macmillan, 1930.

LUTZ, FRIEDRICH, AND VERA LUTZ. *The Theory of Investment of the Firm.* Princeton: Princeton University Press, 1951.

SCHUMPETER, JOSEPH. *Capitalism, Socialism, and Democracy.* New York: Harper & Row, 1947.

MANSFIELD, EDWIN. *The Economics of Technological Change.* New York: Norton, 1968.

MANSFIELD, EDWIN; JOHN RAPOPORT; ANTHONY ROMEO; EDMOND VILLANI; SAMUEL WAGNER; AND FRANK HUSIC. *The Production and Application of New Industrial Technology.* New York: Norton, 1977.

MANSFIELD, EDWIN; ANTHONY ROMEO; MARK SCHWARTZ; DAVID TEECE; SAMUEL WAGNER; AND PETER BRACH. *Technology Transfer, Productivity, and Economic Policy.* New York: Norton, 1982.

NELSON, RICHARD; MERTON PECK; AND EDWARD KALACHEK. *Technology, Economic Growth, and Public Policy.* Washington, D.C.: Brookings Institution, 1967.

SCHMOOKLER, JACOB. *Invention and Economic Growth.* Cambridge, Mass.: Harvard University Press, 1966.

19 Decision-Making and Choice Involving Risk

1. Introduction

As we have seen, consumers, firms, and government agencies are constantly involved in decision-making. In previous chapters, we have made the simplifying assumption that certainty prevailed in the decision-making process. For example, consumers were assumed to know with certainty what present and future prices would be, and firms were assumed to know what their present and future demand curves and cost functions would be. Although this assumption seldom is entirely correct, it is good enough for many purposes. But in other cases, it is inadequate because risk is an important factor which should not be ignored.

Risk refers to a situation where the outcome is not certain, but where the probability of each possible outcome is known or can be estimated. Under such circumstances, one can apply the theory of decision-making and choice involving risk, which is the subject of this chapter. This theory has been developed (largely in the past forty years) by statisticians and mathematicians, as well as by economists. To understand the theory, it is essential to begin by defining what we mean by a probability, after which we take up expected monetary value, decision trees, and the expected value of perfect information. Procedures then are described for constructing a decision-maker's Neumann-Morganstern utility function and for determining the course of action that maximizes expected utility. Methods for determining the optimal amount of insurance are taken up as well. Finally, we discuss rules for decision-making when the probabilities of various outcomes are unknown.

2. Definitions of Probability

Suppose that a situation exists where one of a number of possible outcomes can take place. For example, if a gambler throws a single die, the number that comes up may be 1, 2, 3, 4, 5, or 6. A *probability* is a number that is attached to each outcome. It is the proportion of times that this outcome occurs over the long run if this situation exists over and over again. Thus, the probability that a particular die will come up a 1 is the proportion of times this will occur if the die is thrown many, many times; and the probability that the same die will come up a 2 is the proportion of times this will occur if the die is thrown many, many times; and so on.

Similarly, the probability that a forty-five-year-old American male will die before his forty-sixth birthday is the proportion of times that this outcome occurs. Detailed statistics are available concerning the proportion of people in a particular age group that die each year. Based on such statistics, one can calculate the proportion of forty-five-year-old American males that die before their forty-sixth birthdays. This proportion equals the probability in question.

In general, if a situation exists a very large number of times M, and if outcome U occurs m times, the probability of U is

$$P(U) = \frac{m}{M} \qquad\qquad\qquad 19.1$$

Thus, if a die is "true" (meaning that each of its sides is equally likely to come up when the die is rolled), the probability of its coming up a 1 is $\frac{1}{6}$, or 0.167, because if it is rolled many, many times, this will occur $\frac{1}{6}$ of the time. Moreover, even if the die is not true, this definition can be applied. Suppose, for instance, that a local mobster injects some loaded dice into a crap game, and that one of the players (who is suspicious) asks to examine one of them. If he rolls this die, what is the probability that it will come up a 1? To answer this question, we must imagine the die in question being rolled again and again. After many thousands of rolls, if the proportion of times that it has come up a 1 is 0.195, then this is the probability of its coming up a 1.

Based on our definition of a probability in Equation 19.1, the following three fundamental propositions must be true: First, the probability of an impossible outcome must be zero. If an outcome is impossible, the number of times the outcome occurs (that is, m) must equal zero. Second, the probability of an outcome that is certain must equal 1. If an outcome is certain, the number of times the outcome occurs (m) must equal the number of times the situation takes place (that is, M). Third, the probability of any outcome must be no less than zero and no greater than 1. Since the number of times any outcome occurs (m) cannot be negative, its probability cannot be less than zero. Since the number of times any outcome occurs cannot exceed the number of times the situation takes place (M), its probability cannot exceed 1.

The foregoing is the so-called *frequency definition of probability*. In some situations, this concept of probability may be difficult to apply because these situations cannot be repeated over and over. When Chrysler launched its new type of small, fuel-efficient car in October 1980, this was an "experiment" that could not be repeated over and over again under essentially the same set of circumstances. Market and other conditions vary from month to month. If Chrysler's car had not been introduced that month, the state of consumer expectations, the prices of other firms' cars, the advertising campaigns of other firms, and a host of other relevant factors would probably have been different.

In dealing with cases of this sort, economists and statisticians sometimes use a *subjective* or *personal definition of probability.* According to this definition, the probability of an event is the degree of confidence or belief on the part of the decision-maker that the event will occur. For example, if the decision-maker believes that outcome A is more likely to occur than outcome B, the probability of A is higher than the probability of B. If the decision-maker believes that it is equally likely that a particular outcome will or will not occur, the probability attached to the occurrence of this outcome equals 0.50. The important factor in this concept of probability is what the decision-maker believes.

3. Expected Monetary Value

Firms and individuals frequently are in situations where a variety of outcomes can occur, each of which results in a certain amount of money being gained or lost. If the probability of each outcome is known, it is possible to compute the *expected monetary value* in this situation, which is the sum of the amount of money gained (or lost) if each outcome occurs times the probability of occurrence of the outcome. For example, suppose that the Wilson Corporation, a producer of automobile tires, is thinking of raising the price of its product by $1 per tire. Based on the firm's estimates, such a price increase will result in an $800,000 increase in profit if its current advertising campaign is successful and a $500,000 decrease in profit if its current advertising campaign is not successful. The firm believes that there is a 0.5 probability that its current advertising campaign will be successful and a 0.5 probability that it will not be successful.

In this situation, the expected monetary value to the firm if it raises its price equals

($800,000) (0.5) + (−$500,000) (0.5) = $150,000.

As indicated above, the expected monetary value is the sum of the amount of money gained (or lost) if each outcome occurs times the probability of occurrence of the outcome. In this case, there are two possible outcomes: (1) the firm's current advertising campaign is successful or, (2) it is not successful. If we multiply the amount of money gained (or lost) if the first outcome occurs times its probability of occurrence, the result is ($800,000) (0.5). If we multiply the amount of money gained (or lost) if the second outcome occurs times its probability of occurrence, the result is (−$500,000) (0.5). Summing these two results, we get \$150,000, which is the expected monetary value if the firm raises its price.[1]

The expected monetary value is important because it is the mean amount that a decision-maker would gain (or lose) if he or she were to accept a gamble over and over again. For example, if the Wilson Corporation were to raise its price (under the above circumstances) repeatedly, sometimes its advertising campaign would be successful, and sometimes it would not. Over the long run, it would be successful in half of the cases and not successful in half of them. Thus the mean amount that the firm would make (per price increase) would be \$150,000.

What would be the expected monetary value if the Wilson Corporation did *not* increase its price? If it were certain that there would be no effect on its profit if it did not increase its price, the expected monetary value under these circumstances would be zero. (Since it would be certain that the effect would be no effect on profit, the expected monetary value would equal the amount of money gained if this outcome occurs [zero] times its probability of occurrence [one].) That is, the mean amount that the firm would make (per decision not to increase price) would be zero.

Under some circumstances, it is rational to choose the action or gamble that has the largest expected monetary value; under other circumstances, it is not. In Sections 4–6, we shall make the simplifying assumption that the decision-maker wants to maximize expected monetary value. Under such circumstances, the Wilson Corporation will increase its price, because the expected monetary value if it increases its price equals \$150,000, whereas the expected monetary value if it does not increase its price equals zero. In Sections 7–10, we shall discuss at length the circumstances under which it is rational to maximize expected monetary value—and how to proceed if it is not rational to do so.

4. Decision Trees

Any problem of decision-making under conditions of risk has the following characteristics. First, the decision-maker must make a choice, or perhaps a series of choices, among alternative courses of action. Second, this choice leads to some consequence, but the decision-maker cannot tell in advance the exact nature of this consequence because it depends on some unpredictable event, or series of events, as well as on the choice itself. For example, consider the case of the Wilson Corporation, which must decide whether or not to increase its price. In this case, the choice is between two alternatives: increase price or do not do so. And the consequence of increasing it is uncertain since the firm cannot be sure of whether or not its current advertising campaign will be a success.

1. The concept of the expected monetary value is not entirely new. In Chapter 12, we introduced the concept of the expected value of a game, or expected gain. A comparison of the present discussion with that in Chapter 12 will show that what we called expected gain in Chapter 12 is essentially the same as what we call expected monetary value here.

Example 19.1   The Economics of Parallel Development Efforts

Many development projects use parallel efforts to help cope with risk. For example, when the Manhattan Project to develop the atomic bomb was begun, there were several methods of making fissionable materials, and since no consensus existed among scientists as to which of these alternatives was most promising, all methods were pursued in parallel. In the case of coal gasification there are a number of possible approaches to developing an improved method. Suppose that each approach has a 0.5 probability of costing $2 million and a 0.5 probability of costing $1 million to achieve the desired result. (a) If a single approach is used, what is the expected total cost of development? In other words, what is the expected value of the monetary outflow? (b) If two approaches are run in parallel, and if C dollars are spent on each approach, after which the true cost of development using each approach is known, what is the expected total cost of development? (c) Under what circumstances is the expected total cost of development lower with the two parallel approaches than a single approach?

Solution

(a) The expected total cost of development is the sum of the total cost of development if each possible outcome occurs times the probability of the occurrence of this outcome. Thus the expected total cost equals 0.5 ($2 million) + 0.5($1 million) = $1.5 million, since there is a 0.5 probability that total cost with any single approach will be $2 million and 0.5 probability that it will be $1 million. (b) The expected total cost is 0.25 ($2 million) + 0.75 ($1 million) + C = $1.25 million + C. There is a 0.25 probability that total cost with both of the two approaches will be $2 million, in which case the cost is $2 million regardless of which approach is chosen. There is a 0.75 probability that total cost with the better of the two approaches will be $1 million. In addition, there is the certainty that a cost of C will be incurred for the approach that is dropped. The reason why there is a 0.25 probability that total cost with both approaches is $2 million is that this probability equals 0.5 × 0.5 = 0.25.* (c) From parts (a) and (b), we know that the expected total cost equals $1.5 million if a single approach is used, and it equals $1.25 million + C if two approaches are used (under these circumstances). Thus the expected total cost is lower with two parallel approaches than with a single approach if C is less than $250,000.

---

* When the probability of each of two independent events is 0.5, the probability that both events occur is 0.5 × 0.5 = 0.25. Thus, if two fair coins are flipped, the probability that both show heads is 0.25. And in this case, the probability that total cost is $2 million with both approaches is 0.25.

To represent any such problem, a decision tree is useful. A *decision tree* is a diagram that helps one visualize the relevant choices. It represents a decision problem as a series of choices, each of which is depicted by a fork (sometimes called a juncture or branching point). A *decision fork* is a juncture representing a choice where the decision-maker is in control of the outcome; a *chance fork* is a juncture where "chance" controls the outcome. To differentiate between a decision fork and a chance fork, we shall place a small square at the former juncture but not at the latter.

Figure 19.1 shows the decision tree for the problem facing the Wilson Corporation, which must decide whether or not to increase its price. Beginning at the left-hand side of the diagram, the first choice is up to the firm, which can either follow the branch representing a price increase or the branch representing no such increase. Since this fork is a decision fork, it is represented by a square. If the branch representing no price increase is followed, the consequence is certain: The firm will have no extra profits or losses. Thus, zero extra profit is shown at the end of this branch. If the branch representing a price increase is followed, we come to a chance fork since it is uncertain whether the firm's current advertising campaign is successful. The upper branch following this chance fork represents the consequence that it is successful, in which case the extra

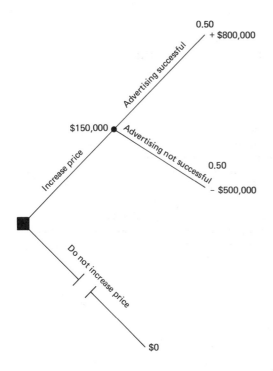

Figure 19.1 Decision tree for Wilson Corporation's problem of whether or not to increase price

profit to the firm is $800,000, shown at the end of this branch. The lower branch following this chance fork represents the consequence that it is not successful, in which case the outcome is $-$500,000 (a loss), shown at the end of this branch. The probability that "chance" will choose each of these branches is shown above the end of each branch.

Given such a decision tree, it is easy to determine which branch the firm should choose in order to maximize the expected monetary value. The process by which we solve this problem, known as *backward induction,* requires that we begin at the right-hand side of the decision tree, where the monetary payoff figures are located. The first step is to calculate the expected monetary value of being situated at the chance fork immediately to the left of these payoff figures. In other words, this is the expected monetary value to the firm given that "chance" will choose which subsequent branch will be followed. Since there is a 0.50 probability that the branch culminating in a profit increase of $800,000 will be followed, and a 0.50 probability that the branch culminating in a profit decrease of $500,000 will be followed, the expected monetary value of being situated at this chance fork is

$$0.50(\$800,000) + 0.50(-\$500,000) = \$150,000.$$

This number is written above the chance fork in question to show that this is the expected monetary value of being located at that fork. Moving further to the left along the decision tree, it is evident that the firm has a choice of two branches, one of which leads to an expected monetary value of $150,000, the other of which leads to a zero monetary value. If the firm wants to maximize the expected monetary value, it should choose the former branch. In other words, it should increase its price. Since the latter branch (Do not increase price) is nonoptimal, we place two vertical lines through it.

At this point, it is worth noting that this graphic procedure for analyzing the firm's problem amounts to precisely the same thing as the calculations we made in the previous section. Recall that we compared the expected monetary value if the price was increased ($150,000) with the expected monetary value if it was not increased ($0) and followed the course of action that resulted in the larger of the two. Our procedure in Figure 19.1 is exactly the same. Note, too, that the decision tree in Figure 19.1 is much simpler than those required to represent many practical problems. In many cases, decision trees have dozens of branches. But regardless of how complex they may be, decision trees are constructed and analyzed essentially in the way described in this section.

5. Drilling for Oil: A Case Study

One important area where the concepts presented in the previous sections have been applied is oil exploration. Huge amounts of money have been, and are being, invested in oil exploration. Due in large measure to the efforts of economists like C. Jackson Grayson,[2] oil firms have begun to use these analytical tools as an aid to decision-making. Of course, this does not mean that these tools are the only ones that are used, or that they are used by all firms. But they do seem to have played a role in this area, which is so important to both the oil firms and the nation as a whole (particularly since U.S. dependence on foreign sources of oil has increased).

To illustrate how these concepts can be applied to oil exploration, consider the case of the Beard Oil Company.[3] Suppose that this firm must decide whether or not to drill a well in a particular location. The firm has information concerning the cost of drilling and the price of oil, as well as geologists' reports concerning the likelihood of striking oil. Based on the geologists' reports, the firm believes that, if the well is drilled, there is a 0.60 probability that no oil will be found, a 0.10 probability that 50,000 barrels will be found, a 0.15 probability that 100,000 barrels will be found, a 0.10 probability that 500,000 barrels will be found, and a 0.05 probability that 1 million barrels will be found.

Based on these probabilities alone, the firm cannot decide whether or not to drill the well. In addition, information is needed concerning the profit (or loss) that will accrue to the firm if each of these outcomes occurs. Suppose that the firm believes that, if it drills the well, it will incur a $50,000 loss if it finds no oil, a $20,000 loss if it finds 50,000 barrels of oil, a $30,000 profit if it finds 100,000 barrels, a $430,000 profit if it finds 500,000 barrels, and a $930,000 profit if it finds 1 million barrels. Based on this information, should the firm drill the well?

If the firm wants to maximize the expected monetary value, it can answer this question by constructing the decision tree shown in Figure 19.2. Beginning at the left-hand side of the diagram, the first choice is up to the firm, which can follow the branch representing the drilling of the well or the branch representing not drilling. If the branch representing not drilling is followed, the expected monetary value is zero, which is shown at the end of this branch. If the branch representing the drilling of the well is followed, we come to a chance fork since it is uncertain whether the firm will strike oil and if so, how much oil it will find. The highest branch following this chance fork represents the consequence that no oil is found, in which case the firm loses $50,000, shown at the end of this branch. The second highest branch following this chance fork represents the consequence that 50,000 barrels are found, in which case the firm loses $20,000, shown at the end of this branch. Similarly, the middle, second lowest, and lowest branches following this chance fork represent respectively the consequences that 100,000, 500,000, and 1 million barrels are found; the number at the end of each of these branches is the corresponding profit to the firm.

2. C. Jackson Grayson, *Decisions under Uncertainty: Drilling Decisions by Oil and Gas Operators* (Boston: Harvard University Press, 1960).

3. The Beard Oil Company is an actual firm included in Grayson's study (ibid.). The situation described below is taken from Grayson.

Once this decision tree is constructed, the next step is to calculate the expected monetary value to the firm if it is situated at the chance fork immediately to the left of the profit (or loss) figures. If the firm is at this fork, there is a 0.60 probability that the branch culminating in a $50,000 loss will be followed, a 0.10 probability that the branch culminating in a $20,000 loss will be followed, a 0.15 probability that the branch culminating in a $30,000 profit will be followed, a 0.10 probability that the branch culminating in a $430,000 profit will be followed, and a 0.05 probability that the branch culminating in a $930,000 profit will be followed. To obtain the expected monetary value if the firm is situated at this fork, we must multiply each possible value of profit (or loss) by its probability, and sum the results. Thus, the expected monetary value if the firm is situated at this fork equals

$$0.60(-\$50,000) + 0.10(-\$20,000) + 0.15(+\$30,000) +$$
$$0.10(+\$430,000) + 0.05(+930,000) = +\$62,000.$$

In Figure 19.2, this result is written above the chance fork in question to show that this is the expected monetary value if the firm is located at that fork.

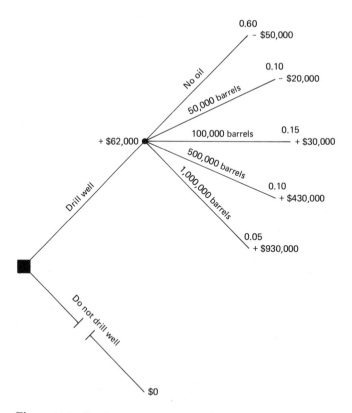

Figure 19.2   Decision tree representing the Beard Oil Company's problem of whether or not to drill a well.

Moving further along the decision tree to the left, the firm has a choice of two branches, one of which leads to an expected monetary value of $62,000, the other of which leads to a zero expected monetary value. If the firm wants to maximize the expected monetary value, it should choose the former branch. That is, it should drill the well.

6. The Expected Value of Perfect Information

In many cases, the decision-maker can obtain information that will dispel (at least some of) the relevant risk. If the decision-maker can get perfect information, how much is it worth? To answer this question, we define the expected value of perfect information as the increase in expected monetary value if the decision-maker could obtain completely accurate information concerning the outcome of the relevant situation (but if he or she does not yet know what this information will be). Thus, in the case of the Wilson Corporation (the firm in Section 3 that must decide whether or not to increase its tire price), this expected value is the increase in expected monetary value if the firm could obtain perfectly accurate information indicating whether or not its current advertising campaign will be successful.

To see how one can compute the expected value of perfect information, let's return to this case. To determine the expected value of perfect information, we carry out two steps, First, we evaluate the expected monetary value to the Wilson Corporation if it can obtain access to perfectly accurate information of this sort. Then we calculate the extent to which this expected monetary value exceeds the expected monetary value based on the information actually available to the firm.

Step 1: If the Wilson Corporation obtains perfect information, it will be able to make the correct decision, regardless of whether or not its current advertising campaign is successful. If it is successful, the firm will be aware of this fact, and will increase the price. If it is not successful, the firm will be aware of this fact also, and will not increase the price. Thus, given that the firm has access to perfect information, the expected monetary value is

0.5($800,000) + 0.5(0) = $400,000.

To see why this is the expected monetary value if the Wilson Corporation has access to perfect information, it is important to recognize that although it is assumed that the firm has access to perfect information, *it does not yet know what this information will be.* There is a .5 probability that this information will show that its advertising campaign is successful, in which case the Wilson Corporation will increase its price and the gain will be $800,000. There is also a .5 probability that the information will show that it is not successful, in which case the Wilson Corporation will not increase its price and the gain will be zero. Thus, as shown above, the expected monetary value if the firm has access to perfect information (that is not yet revealed to the firm) is $400,000.

Step 2: The expected monetary value if the firm bases its decision on existing information is $150,000 (as we saw in Section 3), not $400,000. The difference between these two figures—$400,000 minus $150,000 or $250,000—is the expected value of perfect information. It is a measure of the value of perfect information. *It shows the amount by which the expected monetary value increases as a consequence of the firm's having access to perfect information.* Put differently, *it is the maximum amount that the firm should pay to obtain perfect information.*

In many situations, it is very important that the decision-maker knows how much perfect information would be worth. Whether the decision-maker is a business executive, government official, or consumer, he or she is continually being offered information by testing services, research organizations, news bureaus, and a variety of other organizations. Unless the decision-maker knows how much particular types of information are worth, he or she will not be able to tell whether their worth exceeds their cost. Thus it will be difficult to decide rationally whether various types of information should or should not be bought. The sort of analysis presented in this section is useful in helping to guide such decisions.[4]

7. Is It Rational to Maximize the Expected Monetary Value?

In discussing both the pricing decision in Sections 3 and 4 and the oil-drilling decision in Section 5, we have assumed that the decision-maker wants to maximize the expected monetary value. In this and the following sections we will discuss how a more realistic criterion can be formulated. To understand why a decision-maker may not want to maximize the expected monetary value, consider a situation where you are given a choice between (1) receiving $1,000,000 for certain and (2) a gamble in which a fair coin is tossed, and you will receive $2,100,000 if it comes up heads or you will lose $50,000 if it comes up tails. The expected monetary value for the gamble is

$$0.50(\$2,100,000) + 0.50(-\$50,000) = \$1,025,000,$$

so you should choose the gamble over the certainty of $1,000,000 if you want to maximize the expected monetary value. However, it seems likely that many persons would prefer the certainty of $1,000,000 since the gamble entails a 50 percent chance that you will lose $50,000, a very substantial sum. Moreover, many people may feel that they can do almost as much with $1,000,000 as with $2,100,000, and therefore the extra amount is not worth the risk of losing $50,000.

Clearly, whether or not you will want to maximize the expected monetary value in this situation depends on your attitude toward risk. If

4. In this section, we have dealt only with the relatively simple case where information is perfect. If the only available information is less than perfect (that is, if it contains errors), can we determine whether its expected worth exceeds its cost? Under many circumstances, the answer is yes. To see how, consult the sections on preposterior analysis in any modern statistics text.

you are a widow of modest means, you will probably be overwhelmed at the thought of taking a 50 percent chance of losing $50,000. On the other hand, if you are the president of a big corporation, the prospect of a $50,000 loss may be not the least bit unsettling, and you may prefer the gamble to the certainty of a mere $1,000,000 profit. And if you are the sort of person who enjoys danger and risk, you may prefer the gamble even though a $50,000 loss may wipe you out completely.

Fortunately, there is no need to assume that the decision-maker wants to maximize the expected monetary value. Instead, we can construct a so-called *Neumann-Morgenstern utility function*[5] for the decision-maker which is based on his or her attitudes toward risk. From this, we can then go on to find the alternative that is best for the decision-maker, given his or her attitudes toward risk. The Neumann-Morgenstern utility function was named after John von Neumann and Oskar Morgenstern,[6] who developed this kind of utility function in their famous work on the theory of games (Chapter 12). A utility function of this sort should not be confused with the utility functions discussed in Chapter 3 (Section 12 discusses some of the differences between them). The procedure used to construct a Neumann-Morgenstern utility function is described in Section 9, but before proceeding to this discussion, we must present the axioms, or assumptions underlying such a utility function.

8. Axioms Underlying the Neumann-Morgenstern Utility Function

Basically there are four assumptions on which the Neumann-Morgenstern utility function is based. First, we must assume that the decision-maker's preferences are transitive. That is, if he or she prefers A to B, and B to C, he or she must therefore prefer A to C. The assumption of transitivity plays an important role in the theory of consumer behavior, and has already been discussed in Chapter 3.

Second, we must assume that if there are three outcomes, A, B, and C, and if the decision-maker prefers A to B and B to C, then there must be some probability P such that the decision-maker will be indifferent between the certainty of B and a gamble where there is a probability of P that A will occur and a probability of $(1-P)$ that C will occur. This probability may be big or small; that doesn't matter. What is important is that some value of P exists so that the decision-maker is indifferent between the gamble that A or C will occur and the certainty of B.

Third, we must assume that if the decision-maker is indifferent between two items, D and E, then he or she will be indifferent between two lottery tickets that are identical except that one offers item D as a prize while the other offers item E. This is known as the *independence axiom*.

---

5. John von Neumann and Oskar Morgenstern, *Theory of Games and Economic Behavior* (Princeton, N.J.: Princeton University Press, 1944).

6. Von Neumann was a famous mathematician at the Institute for Advanced Study; Morgenstern was an economist at Princeton University.

Fourth, we must assume that the decision-maker, faced with two lottery tickets for identical prizes, will always choose the one with the higher probability of winning. Also, we must assume that if the decision-maker is offered a lottery ticket whose prize is another lottery ticket, his attitude toward it will be the same as if he had computed the *ultimate* odds of winning or losing that are involved in this compound lottery ticket.

Although questions have been raised by some economists and statisticians concerning a few of these assumptions,[7] most people seem to regard them as quite reasonable foundations on which to build a theory of choice under conditions of risk. It is important to note, however, that we are not assuming that individuals always conform to all these assumptions in their actual decision-making processes. Even if a person agreed with all the axioms involved, he or she might make mistakes or act irrationally at times. But if these assumptions hold, the theory indicates how people should make choices if their decisions are to be in accord with their own preferences.

9. Construction of a Neumann-Morgenstern Utility Function

If the four assumptions listed in the previous section are met, it can be shown that *a rational decision-maker will maximize expected utility.* In other words, the decision-maker should choose the course of action with the highest expected utility. But what (in this context) is a *utility?* It is a number that is attached to a possible outcome of the decision. Each outcome has a utility. The decision-maker's Neumann-Morgenstern utility function shows the utility that he or she attaches to each possible outcome. This utility function, as we shall see, shows the decision-maker's preferences with respect to risk. What is *expected utility?* It is the sum of the utility if each outcome occurs times the probability of occurrence of the outcome. For example, if a situation has two possible outcomes, S and T, if the utility of outcome S is 5 and the utility of outcome T is 10, and if the probability of each outcome is 0.5, the expected utility equals

$$0.5(5) + 0.5(10) = 7.5.$$

To take a more complicated and realistic case, what is the expected utility if the Beard Oil Company drills the well under the circumstances described in Section 5? It equals

$$0.60 \ U(-50) + 0.10 \ U(-20) + 0.15 \ U(30) + 0.10 \ U(430) + 0.05 \ U(930),$$

where $U(-50)$ is the utility that the decision-maker attaches to a mone-

---

7. Suppose that there are three outcomes: (*A*) a gain of $1,000, (*B*) a zero gain, and (*C*) death. If there exists no value of *P* such that the decision maker is indifferent between the certainty of *B* and a gamble where there is a probability of *P* that *C* will occur and a probability of $(1-P)$ that *A* will occur, the second assumption will not hold. Or suppose that the decision-maker enjoys the process of gambling for its own sake. This can result in the violation of the fourth assumption.

tary loss of $50,000, $U(-20)$ is the utility attached to a loss of $20,000, $U(30)$ is the utility attached to a gain of $30,000, and so on. Since there is a 0.60 probability of a $50,000 loss, a 0.10 probability of a $20,000 loss, a 0.15 probability of a $30,000 gain, a 0.10 probability of a $430,000 gain, and a 0.05 probability of a $930,000 gain, this is the expected utility. What is the expected utility if the firm does not drill the well? It equals $U(0)$, since under these circumstances it is certain that the gain will be zero.

To determine the utility that the decision-maker attaches to each possible outcome, he or she must respond to a series of questions which indicate his or her preferences with regard to risk. The required utilities can be found in two steps. The first step is simple: *We set the utility attached to two monetary values arbitrarily.* The utility of the better consequence is set higher than the utility of the worse one. In the case of the decision-maker in the oil 'drilling problem, we might set $U(-50)$ equal to zero and $U(930)$ equal to 50. It turns out that the ultimate results of the analysis do not depend on which two numbers we choose, as long as the utility of the better consequence is set higher than the utility of the worse one. Thus, we could set $U(-50)$ equal to 1 and $U(930)$ equal to 10. It would make no difference to the ultimate outcome of the analysis.[8]

The second step is somewhat more complicated: *In this step we present the decision-maker with a choice between the certainty of one of the other monetary values and a gamble where the possible outcomes are the two monetary values whose utilities we set arbitrarily.* For example, in the oil-drilling problem, suppose that we want to find $U(-20)$. To do so, we ask the decision-maker whether he or she would prefer the certainty of a $20,000 loss to a gamble where there is a probability of P that the gain is $930,000 and a probability of $(1-P)$ that the loss is $50,000. We then try various values of P until we find the one where the decision-maker is indifferent between the certainty of a $20,000 loss and this gamble. Suppose that this value of P is 0.10.

If the decision-maker is indifferent between the certain loss of $20,000 and this gamble, it must be that the expected utility of the certain loss of $20,000 equals the expected utility of the gamble. (Why? Because under the assumptions of the previous section, the decision-maker maximizes expected utility.) Thus,

$$U(-20) = 0.10\ U(930) + 0.90\ U(-50).$$

And since we set $U(930)$ equal to 50 and $U(-50)$ equal to zero, it follows that

$$U(-20) = 0.10(50) + 0.90(0) = 5.$$

In other words, the utility attached to a loss of $20,000 is 5.

Similarly, we can find $U(30)$, $U(430)$, and $U(0)$, the other utilities

8. It is important to note that the utility function that we construct is not unique. Since we set two utilities arbitrarily, the results will vary, depending on the values of the utilities that are chosen. If $X_1, X_2, \ldots, X_n$ are the utilities attached to n possible monetary values, $(\alpha + \beta X_1), (\alpha + \beta X_2), \ldots, (\alpha + \beta X_n)$ can also be utilities attached to them (where α and β are constants, and $\beta > 0$).

required to calculate the expected utility if the oil company drills the well and the expected utility if it does not drill it. For example, to obtain $U(30)$, we ask the decision-maker whether he or she would prefer the certainty of a $30,000 gain to a gamble where there is a probability of P that the gain is $930,000 and a probability of $(1-P)$ that the loss is $50,000. Then we try various values of P until we find the one where the decision-maker is indifferent between the certainty of a $30,000 gain and this gamble. Suppose that this value of P is 0.20. Then the expected utility of a certain gain of $30,000 must equal the expected utility of this gamble, which means that

$$U(30) = 0.20 \ U(930) + 0.80 \ U(-50).$$

And since $U(930)$ equals 50 and $U(-50)$ equals zero, it follows that $U(30)$ equals 10.

The decision-maker's utility function is the relationship between his or her utility and the amount of his or her monetary gain (or loss). Based on our evaluation of $U(-50)$, $U(-20)$, $U(30)$, and $U(930)$ in previous paragraphs, we can identify four points on the decision-maker's utility function, as shown in Figure 19.3. Through the repeated use of the procedure described above, we can obtain as many such points as we like—or as the decision-maker's patience permits.

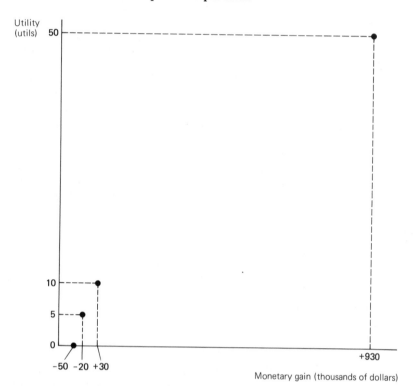

Figure 19.3   Four points on Neumann-Morgenstern utility function of a hypothetical decision-maker

10. Uses of a Neumann-Morgenstern Utility Function

Once a decision-maker's Neumann-Morgenstern utility function has been constructed, it can be used to indicate whether he or she should accept or reject particular gambles. To illustrate, consider the actual case of William Beard, one of the owners of the Beard Oil Company. Using the above procedures, C. Jackson Grayson constructed Mr. Beard's utility function, the result being shown in Figure 19.4.[9] Of course, Mr. Beard's actual utility function differs from that shown in Figure 19.3, since the latter was based on hypothetical data, not on Mr. Beard's responses.[10]

Suppose that Mr. Beard must decide whether or not to drill the well described in Section 5. If the assumptions in Section 8 hold, he should maximize expected utility. Thus he should drill the well if his expected utility if the well is drilled exceeds his expected utility if it is not drilled. As pointed out in the previous section, his expected utility if the well is drilled equals

$$0.60 \ U(-50) + 0.10 \ U(-20) + 0.15 \ U(30) + 0.10 \ U(430) + 0.05 \ U(930).$$

Now that Mr. Beard's utility function has been constructed, this expression can be evaluated. For Mr. Beard, $U(-50)$ equals -5, $U(-20)$ equals -2, $U(30)$ equals 2, $U(430)$ equals 25, and $U(930)$ equals 40, according to Figure 19.4. Thus, if the well is drilled, his expected utility is

$$0.60(-5) + 0.10(-2) + 0.15(2) + 0.10(25) + 0.05(40) = -0.2.$$

As pointed out in the previous section, if the well is not drilled, Mr. Beard's expected utility equals $U(0)$, which is zero, according to Figure 19.4. Thus he should not drill the well. Why? Because if he does not drill it, his expected utility is zero, whereas if he drills it, his expected utility is -0.2. Since he should maximize expected utility (if the assumptions in Section 8 hold), he should choose the action with the higher expected utility, which is not to drill. Note that this is not the decision that maximizes the expected monetary value. As we saw in Section 5, if Mr. Beard wants to maximize the expected monetary value, he should drill the well. But because of Mr. Beard's preferences with respect to risk, as shown by his utility function, this is not the best decision for him.

Besides being useful in indicating the sorts of decisions that individuals and firms should make, Neumann-Morgenstern utility functions can also be useful in predicting the decisions that they actually will make. To the extent that they conform to the assumptions in Section 8, decision-makers will choose the course of action that maximizes expected utility. Thus, if we have a decision-maker's Neumann-Morgenstern util-

---

9. C. Jackson Grayson, *Decisions under Uncertainty*. This utility function was read from Grayson's graph on page 304 and is only approximate, but it is sufficiently accurate for present purposes.

10. Note that, unlike the hypothetical case in the previous section, Grayson did not set $U(930)$ equal to 50 and $U(-50)$ equal to zero. See Figure 19.4.

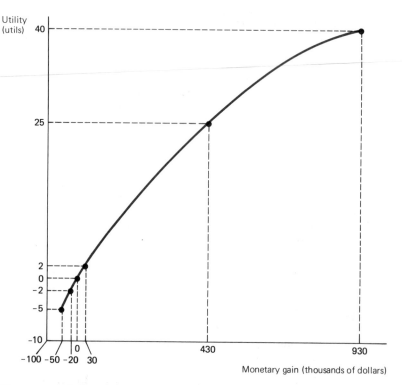

Figure 19.4   William Beard's Neumann-Morgenstern utility function

SOURCE: C. Jackson Grayson, *Decisions under Uncertainty: Drilling Decisions by Oil and Gas Operators* (Boston: Harvard University, 1960).

ity function, we can predict which course of action he or she will choose by comparing the expected utility of each one. For example, suppose that William Beard is confronted with a choice between (1) the certainty of a $430,000 gain and (2) a gamble where there is a 0.50 probability that he will gain $930,000 and a 0.50 probability that he will gain $30,000. Which will he choose?

Using Mr. Beard's utility function in Figure 19.4, we can readily determine the utility he attaches to $30,000, $430,000, and $930,000. These utilities are 2, 25, and 40, respectively. Thus the expected utility from the certainty of a $430,000 gain equals 25. And the expected utility from the gamble equals

$$0.50(2) + 0.50(40) = 21.$$

Since the expected utility from the certain gain of $430,000 exceeds that from the gamble, we would predict that Mr. Beard will choose the certainty of a $430,000 gain over the gamble.[11]

11. Of course, as pointed out in Section 8, decision-makers sometimes are inconsistent and, like all of us, they make mistakes. Thus it would be foolish to expect that predictions of this sort would always be correct, even if the theory were basically

11. Characteristics of Neumann-Morgenstern Utility Functions

Not all Neumann-Morgenstern utility functions look like the one in Figure 19.4. Although one can expect that utility increases with monetary gain, the shape of the utility function can vary greatly, depending on the preferences of the decision-maker. Figure 19.5 shows three general types of utility functions. The one in panel A is like that in Figure 19.4 in the sense that utility increases with monetary value, but *at a decreasing rate*. In other words, an increase in monetary gain of $1 is associated with

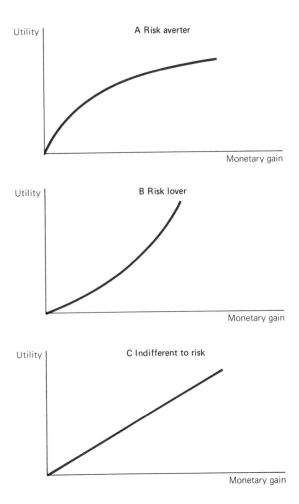

Figure 19.5 Three types of Neumann-Morgenstern utility functions

---

correct. For an early (and classic) study that attempted to determine the accuracy of such predictions, see F. Mosteller and P. Nogee, "An Experimental Measurement of Utility," *Journal of Political Economy* 59, (October 1951).

smaller and smaller increases in utility as the monetary gain increases in size. People with utility functions of this sort are *risk averters*. That is, when confronted with gambles with equal expected monetary values, they prefer a gamble with a more certain outcome to one with a less certain outcome.[12]

The utility function in panel B of Figure 19.5 is one where utility increases with monetary value, but *at an increasing rate*. In other words, an increase in monetary gain of $1 is associated with *larger and larger* increases in utility as the monetary gain increases in size. People with utility functions of this sort are *risk lovers*. That is, when confronted with gambles with equal expected monetary values, they prefer a gamble with a less certain outcome to one with a more certain outcome.[13]

Finally, the utility function in panel C is one where utility increases with monetary value and *at a constant rate*. In other words, an increase of $1 in monetary gain is associated with a *constant* increase in utility as the monetary gain grows larger and larger. Stated differently, utility in this case is a linear function of monetary gain:

$$U = a + bM \qquad \text{19.2}$$

where U is utility, M is monetary gain, and a and b are constants (of course, $b > 0$). People with utility functions of this sort are *indifferent to risk*.[14] That is, they maximize expected monetary value, regardless of risk. It is easy to show that this is true. If Equation 19.2 holds,

$$E(U) = a + bE(M) \qquad \text{19.3}$$

12. Consider a gamble where there is a probability of P that the gain is M_1 and a probability of $(1-P)$ that the loss is M_2. A person is a risk averter if the utility of the gamble's expected monetary value, $U[(P)M_1 + (1-P)M_2]$, is *greater than* the expected utility of the gamble, $PU(M_1) + (1-P) U(M_2)$.

　　Suppose that you are offered the opportunity to play a game in which a coin is tossed until it comes up heads. The game then ends and you receive a sum equal to $(\$2)^n$, where n is the number of times the coin was tossed. The expected value of this sum is $\frac{1}{2}(\$2) + \frac{1}{4}(\$4) + \frac{1}{8}(\$8) + \ldots = 1 + 1 + 1 + \ldots$ which is an infinitely large amount. (To see why this is the expected value of this sum, note that the probability of heads on the first toss is $\frac{1}{2}$, and of tails on the first and heads on the second toss is $\frac{1}{4}$. In general, the probability of $(n-1)$ tails followed by a heads on the nth toss equals $(\frac{1}{2})^n$.) You are unlikely to be willing to pay an infinite amount for the opportunity to play this game. Thus, with respect to this gamble, you are likely to be a risk averter. This is the so-called *St. Petersburg paradox*.

13. Consider a gamble where there is a probability of P that the gain is M_1 and a probability of $(1-P)$ that the loss is M_2. A person is a risk lover if the utility of the gamble's expected monetary value, $U[(P)M_1 + (1-P)M_2]$, is *less than* the expected utility of the gamble, $PU(M_1) + (1-P) U(M_2)$.

14. It is important to recognize that a person can be a risk averter under some circumstances, a risk lover under other circumstances, and indifferent to risk under still other circumstances. The utility functions in Figure 19.5 are "pure" cases where the person is always only one of these types, at least in the range covered by the graphs. For a "hybrid" case, see Example 19.2.

Example 19.2 The Utility Function for Income

In a famous article, Milton Friedman and L. J. Savage hypothesized that a person's Neumann-Morgenstern utility function for income typically has the shape indicated below.

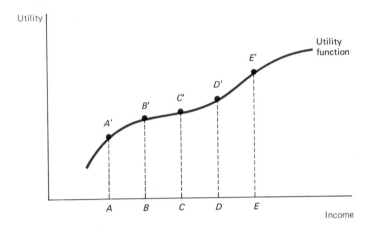

(a) If John Jones has this utility function, will he prefer the certainty of an income of B to a gamble in which there is a 0.5 probability that his income is A and a 0.5 probability that his income is C? (Note that B is the average of A and C.) (b) Will he prefer the certainty of an income of D to a gamble where there is a 0.5 probability that his income is C and a 0.5 probability that his income is E? (Note that D is the average of C and E.)

Solution

(a) Yes. The expected utility attached to the certainty of an income of B equals BB′ (the distance from B to B′). To determine the expected utility from the gamble, draw a straight line from A′ to C′. The vertical distance from B to this line equals the expected utility of the gamble because it equals 0.5 times AA′ plus 0.5 times CC′. (AA′ is the utility of an income of A, and CC′ is the utility of an income of C.) Since this vertical distance is less than BB′, the expected utility of the gamble is less than the expected utility of the certainty of an income of B. (b) No. The expected utility attached to the certainty of an income of D equals DD′. To determine the expected utility from the gamble, draw a straight line from C′ to E′. The vertical distance from D to this line equals the expected utility of the gamble because it equals 0.5 times CC′ plus 0.5 times EE′. Since this vertical distance is more than DD′, the expected utility of the gamble is more than the expected utility of the certainty of an income of D.*

---

* For further discussion, see Milton Friedman and L. J. Savage, "The Utility Analysis of Choices Involving Risk," *Journal of Political Economy* 56 (August 1948).

where $E(U)$ is expected utility and $E(M)$ is expected monetary value.[15] Thus, since expected utility is directly related to expected monetary value, it can only be a maximum when expected monetary value is a maximum.

12. Neoclassical Utility versus Neumann-Morgenstern Utility

In Chapter 3, we pointed out that some great nineteenth-century economists like William Stanley Jevons of England and Léon Walras of France believed that utility was measurable in a cardinal sense, which means that the difference between two measurements is itself numerically significant. To them, a person's utility was measurable in the same sense that his weight was measurable. It is important to recognize that a person's Neumann-Morgenstern utility function is quite different from the neoclassical concept of utility. As pointed out by William Baumol,

> It is *not* the purpose of the Neumann-Morgenstern utility index to set up any sort of measure of introspective pleasure intensity. Such a measure of "strength of feelings" is totally unnecessary . . . [for the purposes] for which the Neumann-Morgenstern theory was constructed. Rather, the utility measure was set up for purposes of . . . prediction . . . to permit the theorist to *determine in the absence of the player* which of several risky propositions the player will *prefer* . . . [T]his is not cardinal utility in the old-fashioned sense. Not a word has been said about successive increments of some item yielding diminishing (or increasing) marginal joy. Indeed, to a strict neoclassicist, the Neumann-Morgenstern index is a sheep in wolf's clothing—to him (but not to the mathematician) it is nothing but an ordinal measure! For while it can be used to predict, it can predict only the rankings of [alternatives].[16]

While it would be inappropriate in a book of this sort to go further into this topic, it is essential that the reader recognize that the Neumann-Morgenstern utility function is not the same as neoclassical utility.

13. The Optimal Amount of Insurance

One important way in which firms and individuals try to cope with risk is through a purchase of insurance. The analytical tools described in previous sections can help to solve the problem of how much insurance a person (or firm) should buy. To see how, let's consider a specific case.

15. To see that equation 19.3 is correct, suppose that M can assume two possible values, M_1 and M_2, and that the probability that M_1 occurs is P and the probability that M_2 occurs is $(1-P)$. Then, if $U = a + bM$,
$$E(U) = P(a + bM_1) + (1-P)(a + bM_2)$$
$$= a + b[(P)M_1 + (1-P)M_2]$$
$$= a + b\,E(M)$$
since $E(M)$ equals $(P)M_1 + (1-P)M_2$.

16. William Baumol, *Economic Analysis and Operations Analysis,* 3d ed. (Englewood Cliffs, N.J.: Prentice Hall, 1972), p. 547.

Suppose that Richard Abbot, a jeweler, owns a diamond worth $100,000, and that he wants to determine how much insurance he should purchase against the theft of the diamond. He can buy theft insurance at a cost of 20 percent of the face value of the insurance. That is, if he buys $100,000 worth of insurance, he must pay $20,000 for the insurance; and if he buys $50,000 worth of insurance, he must pay $10,000. If we measure Mr. Abbot's Neumann-Morgenstern utility function, we can determine how much insurance he should buy.

To see how the optimal amount of insurance can be determined, we must recognize that Mr. Abbot is in a situation where there are two possible outcomes: (1) the diamond is stolen and (2) it is not stolen. The more insurance he buys, the greater the value of his assets if the diamond is stolen, but the less the value of his assets if it is not stolen. For example, if he buys $50,000 worth of insurance, he will have $40,000 (that is, $50,000 less the insurance, cost of $10,000) if it is stolen, and $90,000 (the value of the diamond, which is $100,000, less the insurance cost of $10,000) if it is not stolen. But if he buys $100,000 worth of insurance, he will have $80,000 (that is, $100,000 less the insurance cost of $20,000) if it is stolen, and $80,000 (the value of the diamond, $100,000, less the insurance cost of $20,000) if it is not stolen.

Table 19.1 shows, for various possible amounts of insurance that he can buy, the value of his assets if the diamond is stolen, and their value if it is not stolen. Since the value of his assets if it is stolen is inversely related to their value if it is not stolen, we can plot the former value of his assets against the latter value in Figure 19.6. As you can see, the relationshp between these two values is a straight line. AB. To obtain the equation for this line, note that

$$Y_n = \$100,000 - 0.2I \qquad\qquad \textbf{19.4}$$

where Y_n is the value of his assets if the diamond is not stolen, and I is the amount of insurance he buys. The equation says that the value of his

Table 19.1 Outcomes for Mr. Abbot if the diamond is or is not stolen, given that he purchases various amounts of insurance

Amount of insurance (I) (dollars)	Cost of insurance (0.2I) (dollars)	Value of Mr. Abbot's assets if:	
		Diamond is stolen (Y_T) (dollars)	Diamond is not stolen (Y_n) (dollars)
0	0	0	100,000
10,000	2,000	8,000	98,000
20,000	4,000	16,000	96,000
30,000	6,000	24,000	94,000
40,000	8,000	32,000	92,000
50,000	10,000	40,000	90,000
60,000	12,000	48,000	88,000
70,000	14,000	56,000	86,000
80,000	16,000	64,000	84,000
90,000	18,000	72,000	82,000
100,000	20,000	80,000	80,000

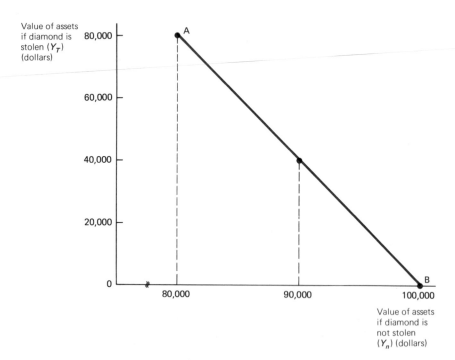

Value of assets
if diamond is   80,000
stolen (Y_T)
(dollars)

Value of assets
if diamond is
not stolen
(Y_n) (dollars)

Figure 19.6   Relationship between value of Mr. Abbot's assets if the diamond
is stolen and their value if it is not stolen

assets if the diamond is not stolen is $100,000 (the value of the diamond)
less the cost of the insurance (which is .2I). Also, note that

$$Y_T = I - 0.2I = 0.8I, \qquad\qquad 19.5$$

where Y_T is the value of his assets if the diamond is stolen. Under these
circumstances, he receives the insurance (I) less the cost of the insurance
(0.2I). From Equation 19.4, it follows that

$$I = \frac{1}{0.2}(\$100,000 - Y_n) = \$500,000 - 5Y_n \qquad\qquad 19.6$$

Substituting the right-hand side of Equation 19.6 for I in Equation 19.5,
we have

$$Y_T = 0.8\,(\$500,000 - 5Y_n) = \$400,000 - 4Y_n \qquad\qquad 19.7$$

which is the equation for the line in Figure 19.6.[17]

To determine the amount of insurance that Mr. Abbot should buy,
it is obvious that some account should be taken of his preferences regarding risk. If P is the probability that the diamond will be stolen, his

17. Since the amount of insurance, I, must be between zero and $100,000, the line in
Figure 19.6 only exists for the interval where $80,000 \leq Y_n \leq \$100,000$.

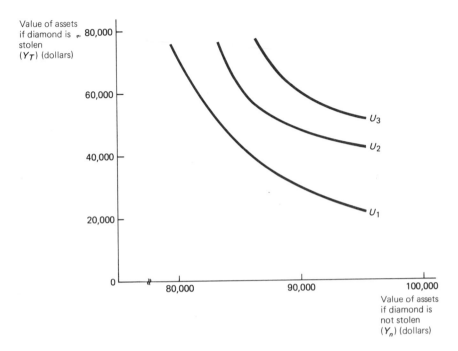

Figure 19.7   Combinations of Y_T and Y_n with same expected utility for Mr. Abbot

expected utility equals

$$P \cdot U(Y_T) + (1 - P) \cdot U(Y_n) \qquad\qquad 19.8$$

where $U(Y_T)$ is the utility he attaches to having assets equal in value to Y_T, and $U(Y_n)$ is the utility he attaches to having assets equal in value to Y_n. Mr. Abbott wants to choose values of Y_T and Y_n so that his expected utility is as large as possible.

Each curve in Figure 19.7 shows combinations of Y_T and Y_n that result in the same expected utility for Mr. Abbot. To derive each such curve, we set his expected utility equal to some constant, a. Thus

$$P \cdot U(Y_T) + (1 - P) \cdot U(Y_n) = a \qquad\qquad 19.9$$

Since increases in either Y_T or Y_n result in increases in his expected utility,[18] it follows that if his expected utility is held constant (at a), increases in Y_n must be accompanied by decreases in Y_T. (Why? Because if both Y_T and Y_n increased, or if one increased and the other remained constant, his expected utility would increase, not remain constant.)

---

18. Mr. Abbot's utility would be expected to increase with increases in the value of his assets. Thus, $U(Y_T)$ increases with increases in Y_T, and $U(Y_n)$ increases with increases in Y_n. And since both P and $(1-P)$ are positive, increases in either $U(Y_T)$ or $U(Y_n)$ result in increases in expected utility.

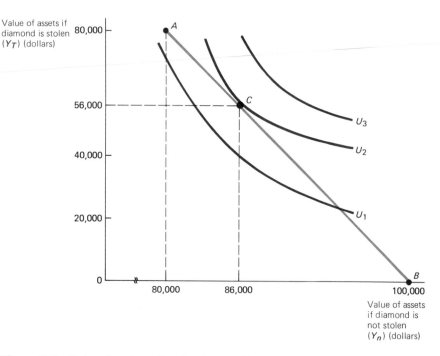

Figure 19.8   Determination of optimal expenditure on insurance

Thus each of the curves in Figure 19.7 is downward sloping to the right. Higher curves like U_3 represent higher levels of expected utility than lower ones like U_1. And since Mr. Abbot would like to maximize expected utility, points on higher curves like U_3 are preferred over points on lower curves like U_1.

To solve Mr. Abbot's problem, we must add line AB (in Figure 19.6) to Figure 19.7, the result being shown in Figure 19.8. As pointed out above, line AB contains all the possible combinations of the value of his assets if the diamond is stolen and their value if it is not stolen. In other words, line AB shows the combinations of Y_T and Y_n that he can achieve, given the existing insurance rates. Mr. Abbot must choose some point on line AB; but which point is best? Clearly, he should choose the point that is on the highest of the attainable curves shown in Figure 19.8, since each of these curves contains combinations of Y_T and Y_n that result in the same value of expected utility. Given that he must choose a point on line AB, the highest such curve that is attainable is U_2. He can reach this curve if he chooses point C, where $Y_T = \$56{,}000$ and $Y_n = \$86{,}000$.

To reach point C, he must buy \$70,000 of insurance. Why? Because, as shown in Table 19.1, if he buys this amount of insurance, the value of his assets if the diamond is stolen is \$56,000, and their value if it is not stolen is \$86,000. In other words, if he buys this amount of insurance, $Y_T = \$56{,}000$ and $Y_n = \$86{,}000$, which means that he attains point C. Thus, since point C is the optimal point, \$70,000 is the optimal amount of insurance for Mr. Abbot to purchase.

This sort of analysis can be used to determine the optimal amount of insurance of many types, not just insurance against theft. For example, suppose that a family owns a house that it wants to insure against fire. The techniques described in this section can be used to determine how much fire insurance this family should buy. (As an exercise, prove to yourself that this is true.) In addition, these techniques can be used to analyze certain aspects of investment behavior. Although this model is quite simple, it can shed considerable light on many kinds of decisions, if used with some imagination.

14. Uncertainty and the Minimax Rule

More than 60 years ago, Frank Knight called attention to the distinction between risk and uncertainty.[19] As pointed out at the beginning of this chapter, risk refers to a situation where the outcome is not certain, but where the probability of each possible outcome is known or can be estimated. *Uncertainty* refers to a situation where these probabilities are unknown. To illustrate the distinction, suppose that an insurance company is interested in predicting how many forty-five-year-old American males will die before their forth-sixth birthday. This is a case of risk, since (as we saw in Section 2) the probabilities that various numbers of males of this age will die can be estimated from mortality tables reflecting past experience. But if a biologist is interested in predicting the probability that life (in the sense that we know it) exists elsewhere in the universe, this is a case of uncertainty since he has no way of estimating what these probabilities are.

In previous sections, we have been concerned with risk. Now we turn to uncertainty. Unfortunately, although economists have devised a number of types of rules to help a decision maker choose among alternative courses of action under conditions of uncertainty, none of these rules is universally considered to be preferable. All of them have disadvantages and difficulties. To illustrate the sorts of rules that have been proposed, and their limitations, we take up the minimax rule. [20]

According to this rule, the decision-maker should determine the worst outcome that can occur if each possible course of action is chosen, and he or she should choose the course of action where this worst outcome is best. For example, consider a situation where the Miller Electronics Company, a hypothetical producer of electronic goods, must decide whether or not to build an assembly plant in a particular country in Southeast Asia. Miller Electronics Company is concerned that a revolution in this country might lead to the expropriation by the government of this plant, if it were built. As shown in Table 19.2, the Miller Electronics Company believes that, if it builds such a plant and expropriation of this sort occurs, it will lose $20 million. If it builds the plant and

19. Frank Knight, *Risk, Uncertainty, and Profit* (Boston: Houghton-Mifflin, 1921).

20. Frequently, this rule is referred to as the maximin rule, rather than the minimax rule. Both names are in common use.

Table 19.2 Miller Electronics Company's gains (or losses), with or without
expropriation, if it does or does not build plant

	OUTCOME	
COURSE OF ACTION	*Expropriation*	*No expropriation*
Firm builds plant	− $20 million	$100 million
Firm does not build plant	0	0

expropriation does not occur, it will gain $100 million. And if it does not
build the plant, it will gain (and lose) nothing.

The Miller Electronics Company, if it applies the minimax rule,
should determine the worst outcome under each course of action. There
are two possible courses of action: the firm can build this plant, or not
build it. Regardless of which course of action is chosen, there are two
possible outcomes: expropriation can occur or not occur. If this plant is
built, the worst outcome is a $20 million loss that will result if expro-
priation occurs. If this plant is not built, the worst (and only) outcome is
a zero gain. Thus, if the Miller Electronics Company applies the minimax
rule, it should not build this plant. Why? Because the worst outcome if
this plant is not built is preferable to the worst outcome if it is built.

At this point, it should be clear that the minimax rule has been
encountered before. In Chapter 12, the minimax rule was taken up as
part of our discussion of the theory of games. However, the present
situation is different from that which prevails in the theory of games.
Unlike the game situation, the decision maker here is not in a competitive situation where he or she faces an active opponent whose interests
are contrary to the decision maker's. Whether a revolution occurs in the
relevant Asian country will not be determined by a rival or competitor
who is out to inflict damages on the Miller Electronics Company. Instead, it will be determined by a host of political, social, and other factors
that have little to do with this particular firm. For this and other reasons,
the minimax rule has been criticized as being overly conservative. Critics
point out that there is no reason why the decision maker should assume
that whatever force (to borrow a term from *Star Wars*) determines the
outcome of the situation is out to hurt him or her. Thus, in choosing
among alternative courses of action, there is no reason why the decision
maker should pay attention only to the worst outcome that can occur if
each course of action is taken.

The minimax rule is by no means the only rule that has been proposed to help people make decisions under conditions of uncertainty.
Many others have been proposed both by economists and by statisticians.[21] However, each of these rules has its problems and limitations.
Which, if any, of these rules is appropriate depends on the attitudes
toward risk and the financial resources of the decision-maker, as well as

---

21. Other rules that are commonly encountered are the Bayes rule, the maximax rule,
    the Hurwicz α rule, and L. J. Savage's minimax regret rule. See Baumol, *Eco-
    nomic Analysis and Operations Analysis*.

on other aspects of the situation. There is no single rule that can be applied universally to decision making under uncertainty. Unless the probability of each outcome can be estimated, it is very difficult to formulate optimal general rules for decision-makers.[22]

15. Summary

The probability of a particular outcome is the proportion of times that this outcome occurs over the long run if this situation exists over and over again. The expected monetary value of a gamble is the sum of the amount of money gained (or lost) if each outcome occurs times the probability of occurrence of the outcome. The expected monetary value is important because it is the average amount that the decision-maker would gain (or lose) if he or she were to accept this gamble repeatedly. A decision tree represents a decision problem as a series of choices, each of which is depicted by a decision fork or a chance fork. A decision tree can be used to determine the course of action with the highest expected monetary value. As an example, we took up the decision of whether or not to drill an oil well.

The expected value of perfect information is the increase in expected monetary value if the decision-maker could obtain completely accurate information concerning the outcome of the relevant situation (but he or she does not yet know what this information will be). This is the maximum amount that the decision-maker should pay to obtain such information. Using methods described in this chapter, one can calculate the expected value of perfect information.

Whether a decision maker wants to maximize expected monetary value depends on his or her attitudes toward risk. If the assumptions in Section 8 hold, the decision-maker's attitudes toward risk can be measured by his or her Neumann-Morgenstern utility function. To construct such a utility function, we begin by setting the utility attached to two monetary values arbitrarily. Then we present the decision-maker with a choice between the certainty of one of the other monetary values and a gamble where the possible outcomes are the two monetary values whose utilities we set arbitrarily. Repeating this procedure over and over, we can construct the decision-maker's Neumann-Morgenstern utility function (which should not be confused with a cardinal utility function of the sort that nineteenth-century economists assumed to exist). This utility function is useful in indicating the courses of action that the decision-maker should choose, and in predicting those that he will choose. As an illustration, we described the utility function of William Beard, an actual owner of an oil firm.

22. Even when these probabilities can be estimated, there still are plenty of potential problems. If analyses of the sort described in this chapter are carried out with distorted, unreliable estimates of the probabilities, the results are likely to be incorrect and misleading. Unless these probabilities are meaningful, the results may be worse than useless, no matter how scientific the analysis may appear.

To cope with risk, firms and consumers often buy insurance. For example, a man must decide how much insurance (if any) to buy against the theft of an asset he owns. The more insurance he buys, the more money he will have if the asset is stolen, but the less money he will have if it is not stolen. Under the circumstances described above, the relationship between the amount of money he will have if it is stolen and the amount of money he will have if it is not stolen can be represented by a straight line. To find the optimal amount of insurance, we must find the point on this line where his expected utility is highest. The amount of insurance corresponding to this point is the optimal amount.

Risk refers to a situation where the outcome is not certain, but where the probability of each possible outcome is known or can be estimated. Uncertainty refers to a situation where these probabilities cannot be estimated. Many rules, including the minimax rule, have been proposed as aids to decision-making under conditions of uncertainty. According to the minimax rule, the decision-maker should choose the course of action where the worst possible outcome is least damaging. There are important problems in this rule, as well as others proposed to handle the situation of uncertainty. No universally acceptable rule exists to deal with cases where the relevant probabilities cannot be estimated.

QUESTIONS AND PROBLEMS

1. A true die is rolled twice. What is the probability of getting a total of 6? Is this a subjective probability?

2. According to R. A. Fisher, a famous British statistician, advocates of subjective probability "seem forced to regard mathematical probability not as an objective quantity measured by observed frequencies, but as measuring psychological tendencies, theorems respecting which are useless for scientific purposes." Do you agree? Do you think that subjective probabilities are useless in solving microeconomic problems?

3. The Tremont Corporation is considering the purchase of a firm that produces tools and dies. Tremont's management feels that there is a 50-50 chance, if Tremont buys the firm, that it can make the firm into an effective producer of auto parts. If the firm can be transformed in this way, Tremont believes that it will make $1 million if it buys the firm; if it cannot be transformed in this way, Tremont believes that it will lose $2 million. What is the expected monetary value to Tremont of buying the firm?

4. Construct a decision tree to represent Tremont's problem (described in the previous question). If Tremont maximizes expected monetary value, should it purchase the firm?

5. In fact, the Tremont corporation decides to purchase the firm described in Question 3. Does this mean that Tremont's management is (a) indifferent to risk, (b) a risk averter?

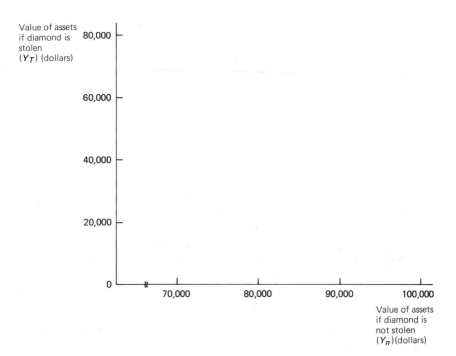

6. In Section 13, suppose that insurance rates go up. Theft insurance now costs 30 percent of the face value of the insurance. Will line AB in Figure 19.6 shift? If so, draw its new position in the graph above.

7. Mrs. Cherrytree's Neumann-Morgenstern utility function can be represented by the following equation:

$$U = 10 + 2M,$$

where U is utility and M is monetary gain (in thousands of dollars).[23] She has the opportunity to invest $25,000 in Archie Bunker's Bar and Grill. She believes that there is a 0.5 probability that she will lose her entire investment and a 0.5 probability that she will gain $32,000. (a) If she makes the investment, what is her expected utility? (b) Should she make the investment?

8. A firm must decide whether or not to go forward with an R and D project to develop a new process. If the project is successful, it will gain $5 million; if it is not successful, it will lose $1 million. It believes that the probability is 0.2 that it will be successful and 0.8 that it will not be successful. What is the expected value of perfect information concerning whether or not it will be successful?

23. As pointed out in note 8, this utility function is not unique. But that does not mean that this utility function cannot be used to solve this problem. Like any other such utility function, it is based on the arbitrary setting of the utilities attached to two monetary values.

9. In the previous question, suppose that the firm has no idea of what the probabilities of success or failure may be. If the minimax rule is applied, should the firm go forward with the R and D project? Why or why not?

10. In Question 3, what is the expected value of perfect information concerning whether or not the tool and die firm can be made into an effective producer of auto parts?

SELECTED REFERENCES

ALCHIAN, ARMEN. "The Meaning of Utility Measurement." Reprinted in Edwin Mansfield, *Microeconomics: Selected Readings,* 4th ed. New York: Norton, 1982.

EHRLICH, ISAAC, AND GARY BECKER. "Market Insurance, Self-Insurance and Self-Protection," *Journal of Political Economy* 80, July, 1972.

FRIEDMAN, MILTON, AND L. J. SAVAGE. "The Utility Analysis of Choices Involving Risk," *Journal of Political Economy* 56, August 1948.

KNIGHT, FRANK. *Risk, Uncertainty, and Profit.* Boston: Houghton-Mifflin, 1921.

LUCE, R. DUNCAN, AND HOWARD RAIFFA. *Games and Decisions.* New York: Wiley, 1957.

RAIFFA, HOWARD. *Decision Analysis.* Reading, Mass.: Addison-Wesley, 1968.

VARIAN, HAL. *Microeconomic Analysis.* New York: Norton, 1978.

VON NEUMANN, JOHN, AND OSCAR MORGENSTERN. *Theory of Games and Economic Behavior.* Princeton, N.J.: Princeton University Press, 1944.

Brief Answers to Odd-Numbered Questions and Problems

Chapter 1

1. No, because most of the disagreements stem from differences in ethical and political views.
3. No. This is the so-called fallacy of composition.
5. Yes, because the latter statements reflect the value judgments of the economist.
7. First, an economic system must allocate its resources among competing uses and combine these resources to produce the desired output efficiently.   Second, an economic system must determine the level and composition of output.   Third, an economic system must determine how the goods and services that are produced are distributed among the members of society.   Fourth, an economic system must determine the rate of growth of per capita income.
9. The most important test of a model is how well it predicts. Another is whether its assumptions are logically consistent. Another important consideration is the range of phenomena to which the model applies.

Chapter 2

1.

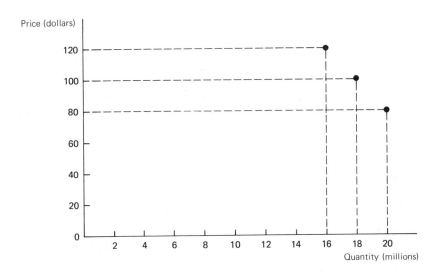

$$a.\ \eta = -\frac{(20-18)}{(20+18)/2} \div \frac{(80-100)}{(80+100)/2} = 0.47$$

$$b.\ \eta = -\frac{(18-16)}{(18+16)/2} \div \frac{(100-120)}{(100+120)/2} = 0.65$$

3. $100.   Excess demand.   Excess supply.

5. With the excise tax, the supply curve is

Price (dollars)	Quantity supplied
100	14
120	16
140	18
160	19

Thus the equilibrium price of a bicycle is $120, since at this price the quantity supplied equals the quantity demanded. If the government sets a price ceiling of $100, there will be a shortage of 4 million bicycles per year, since the quantity demanded will equal 18 million while the quantity supplied will equal 14 million.

7. Since the quantity supplied (Q_S) must equal the quantity demanded (Q_D), we have two equations to be solved simultaneously:

$$120 - 3Q_D = 5Q_S$$
$$Q_D = Q_S$$

Letting quantity equal Q, it follows that

$$120 - 3Q = 5Q$$
$$120 = 8Q$$
$$15 = Q$$

Since $P = 5Q$, it follows that $P = 75$. Thus the equilibrium price is 75 cents and the equilibrium quantity is 15 million pounds per year.

9. From question 7,

$$P = 120 - 3Q_D$$

or

$$3Q_D = 120 - P$$

$$Q_D = 40 - 1/3\,P$$

Also, $Q_S = 1/5P$. Thus, if $P = 80$, $Q_D = 40 - 80/3 = 13\frac{1}{3}$, and $Q_S = 80/5 = 16$. Consequently, $Q_S - Q_D = 16 - 13\frac{1}{3} = 2\frac{2}{3}$, which means that the resulting surplus equals $2\frac{2}{3}$ million pounds per year. To reduce this surplus, the government could attempt to reduce the amount of cantaloupes produced by farmers or expand the demand for cantaloupes.

Chapter 3

1. He should set the ratio of the marginal utility of good X to its price equal to the ratio of the marginal utility of good Y to its price. If he buys 5 units of good X and 1 unit of good Y, the total amount spent is $1,000, and this condition is met, since for each good this ratio equals 1 util $\div$ $10.

3. $1,000, since the budget line intersects the vertical axis at 20.
    $Q_A = 20 - 0.5 \, Q_B$, where Q_A is the quantity consumed of good A and
    Q_B is the quantity consumed of good B. $- 0.5$.   It must be
    $1,000 \div 40$, or $25.   0.5.

5. 1.   It does not vary at all, at least in this range.   No.

7. Utility is a number that indicates the level of enjoyment or preference
    attached to a market basket.   In the case of ordinal utility, no particu-
    lar meaning or significance attaches to the scale which is used to measure
    utility or to the size of the difference between the utilities attached to two
    market baskets. In the case of cardinal utility, it is assumed that utility is
    measurable in the same sense as a man's height or weight is measur-
    able.   Ordinal utility.

9. No.   Los Angeles, because the price of a pear divided by the price of an
    apple is higher in Los Angeles.

Chapter 4

1. *a.* Yes.   *b.* If all consumers are maximizing utility (and if the optimal
    point is a tangency point, not a corner solution), the marginal rate of
    substitution of telephone calls for newspapers must equal the price of a
    telephone call divided by the price of a newspaper.   *c.* Yes, it equals 15
    $\div$ 25, or 0.6.

3. Both part (*b*) and part (*c*) are true.

5. 3.   Price elastic.   Decrease.

7. The budget line is $Q_c + 0.5 \, Q_p = 100$. This line is tangent to an indifference
    curve when $Q_p = 100$.

9. The Laspeyres index equals:

$$L = \frac{100 \times \$0.50 + 120 \times \$40}{100 \times \$0.30 + 120 \times \$30} = 1.34$$

The Paasche index equals:

$$P = \frac{140 \times \$0.50 + 130 \times \$40}{140 \times \$0.30 + 130 \times \$30} = 1.34$$

Thus, in this case, the results are the same.

Chapter 5

1. Holding his income constant, the total amount he spends on Geritol is
    constant too; that is

$$PQ = I$$

where P is the price of Geritol, Q is the quantity demanded by the consumer, and I is his income. Thus

$$Q = \frac{I}{P}$$

Since I is held constant, this demand curve is a rectangular hyperbola, and the price elasticity of demand equals 1.   Since $Q = I/P$, it follows that a 1 percent increase in I will result in a 1 percent increase in Q, when P is held constant. Thus the income elasticity of demand equals 1.   Since Q does not depend on the price of any other good, the cross elasticity of demand equals zero.

3. Substitutes have a positive cross elasticity of demand. Thus cases (b) and (e) are likely to have a positive cross elasticity of demand.

5. It would indicate the extent to which fare increases would decrease subway travel. For example, if demand is price inelastic, fare increases would increase total revenue. Obviously this is an important fact.

7. Other factors — notably the general level of prices and incomes and the quality of the students — have not been held constant. Holding these factors — and the tuition rates at other universities — constant, it is almost surely untrue that large increases in tuition at this university would not cut down on the number of students demanding admission to the university.

9. The Engel curve shows the relationship between money income and the amount consumed of a particular commodity. If this relationship is a straight line through the origin, it follows that the amount consumed of this commodity is *proportional* to the consumer's money income. Thus, a 1 percent increase in the consumer's money income results in a 1 percent increase in the amount consumed of this commodity. Consequently, the income elasticity of demand for this commodity equals 1.

Chapter 6

1. The complete table is:

Number of units of variable input	Total output	Marginal product	Average product
3	90	Unknown	30
4	110	20	$27\frac{1}{2}$
5	130	20	26
6	135	5	$22\frac{1}{2}$
7	$136\frac{1}{2}$	$1\frac{1}{2}$	$19\frac{1}{2}$

3. Because of the law of diminishing marginal returns, the marginal product begins to decline at some point. If the marginal product exceeds the average product at that point, the marginal product can fall to some extent without reducing the average product. Only when it falls below the average product will the average product begin to decrease. The marginal product can continue to fall without reducing the total product. Only when it falls below zero will the total product begin to decrease.

5. 1.04 percent

7. Yes.

9. a. Yes, since it seems to reduce the amount of grain and protein that must be used to produce 150 pounds of pork. However, this assumes that it has no negative effect on the quality of the pork and that it does not increase the amount of other inputs that must be used.   b. At each quantity of protein, curve B is steeper than curve A. In other words, the absolute value

of its slope is greater. Thus, the marginal rate of technical substitution of protein for grain is greater when Aureomycin is added than when it is not (when the quantity of protein is held constant).

Chapter 7

1. The table is as follows:

Total fixed cost (dollars)	Total variable cost (dollars)	Average fixed cost (dollars)	Average variable cost (dollars)
50	0	—	—
50	20	50	20
50	50	25	25
50	70	$16\frac{2}{3}$	$23\frac{1}{3}$
50	85	$12\frac{1}{2}$	$21\frac{1}{4}$
50	100	10	20
50	110	$8\frac{1}{3}$	$18\frac{1}{3}$
50	115	$7\frac{1}{7}$	$16\frac{3}{7}$

3. The cost of each input combination (in the order they appear in the table in the question) is:

    8,654 P
    8,204 P
    7,892 P
    7,673 P
    7,529 P
    7,444 P

    The minimum-cost combination (of those considered here) is 7,500 pounds of hay and 3,694 pounds of grain.

5. The isocost curve is: Cost $= 1 \cdot L + 2 \cdot K$, or $L = $ cost $- 2K$. The relevant isoquant is $20 = 5L \cdot K$, or $L = 4 \div K$. The point on this isoquant that is on the lowest isocost curve is $K = \sqrt{2}$ and $L = 2\sqrt{2}$.

7. 1,000 copies sold.

9. It will probably shift the total cost function upward; that is, the total cost of producing a particular number of automobiles will increase.   To the extent that automobile manufacturers must increase their plant and equipment to produce and assemble such safety devices, fixed costs will rise.   Marginal cost will probably increase because the addition of the safety devices will probably increase the cost of producing an extra car.

Chapter 8

1. 3 or 4 units of output.

3. Yes. Food cost is the objective function, and the attainment of the proper amount of calories, fats, and proteins is a series of constraints. Also, there are nonnegativity constraints.

5. Yes, because each additional unit produced (up to and including 100) brings in $1 more than it costs.

7. The isorevenue lines are drawn on the next page.

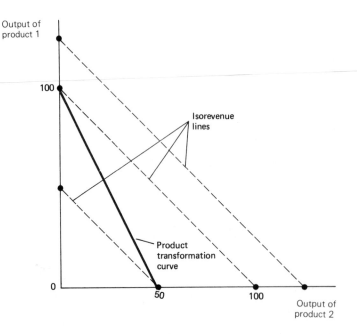

It should produce 100 units of product 1 and none of product 2, since this puts the firm on the highest isorevenue line that is attainable.   No. This is a corner solution. There is no point where the isorevenue line is tangent to the product transformation curve in this case.

9. The cost of making one unit of the good is $8 with process *A*, $7.50 with process *B*, and $7.70 with process *C*. Thus, all 100 units should be produced with process *B* since this is the cheapest procedure.

Chapter 9

1. The firm's marginal cost curve is

Output	Marginal cost (dollars)
0 to 1	10
1 to 2	12
2 to 3	13
3 to 4	14
4 to 5	15
5 to 6	16
6 to 7	17

a. If the price is $13, the firm will produce 2 or 3 units.   *b.* 3 or 4 units.   *c.* 4 or 5 units.   *d.* 5 or 6 units.   *e.* 6 or 7 units.

3. The industry supply curve is shown on the next page.

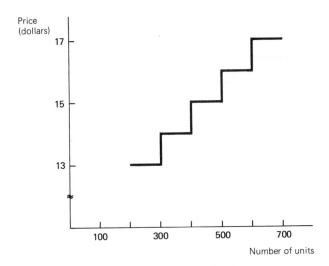

Price (dollars)

Number of units

5. $\eta_s = \dfrac{(8-7)}{(8+7)/2} \div \dfrac{(4-3)}{(4+3)/2} = 0.47.$

7. No, because the flat glass industry is dominated by a very few firms.

9. A difference of about 3.24 percent.

Chapter 10

1. The monopolist's total revenue, total cost, and total profit at each level of output are as follows:

Output	Total revenue (dollars)	Total cost (dollars)	Total profit (dollars)
5	40	20	20
6	42	21	21
7	42	22	20
8	40	23	17
9	36	24	12
10	30	30	0

Thus, the optimal output is 6, which means that price should be $7.

3. If the firm is producing 5 units in the first plant, the marginal cost in the first plant equals $20 + (2)(5)$, or 30. Thus, if the firm is minimizing costs, marginal cost in the second plant must also equal 30, which means that

$$10 + 5Q_2 = 30$$
$$5Q_2 = 20$$
$$Q_2 = 4$$

Consequently, the second plant must be producing 4 units of output.

5. Since the author's royalty is a fixed percentage of the price of the book, the total royalties per year earned by the author are proportional to the total revenue per year from the book. Consequently, the author would like to maximize total revenue, since this maximizes his or her royalties. To max-

imize total revenue, marginal revenue should be set equal to zero. On the other hand, the publisher would like to maximize profit, which means that marginal revenue should be set equal to marginal cost. Thus the author would like to set marginal revenue equal to a lower value than would the publisher. Holding constant the price elasticity of demand, marginal revenue decreases as price is lowered. Thus the author tends to prefer a lower price than does the publisher.

7. Marginal revenue $= 100 - 2Q$.
    Marginal cost $= 60 + 2Q$.
    Consequently, $100 - 2Q = 60 + 2Q$
    $$40 = 4Q$$
    $$10 = Q$$

    That is, you should choose an output of 10 units.

9. $MR_1 = 160 - 16Q_1$
    $MR_2 = 80 - 4Q_2$
    $MC = 5 + (Q_1 + Q_2)$
    Therefore $160 - 16Q_1 = 5 + Q_1 + Q_2$
    $80 - 4Q_2 = 5 + Q_1 + Q_2$
    Or $155 - 17Q_1 = Q_2$
    $75 - 5Q_2 = Q_1$
    Thus $155 - 17[75 - 5Q_2] = Q_2$
    $155 - 1275 + 85Q_2 = Q_2$
    $84Q_2 = 1120$
    $Q_2 = 13\frac{1}{3}$.

    It should sell $13\frac{1}{3}$ units in the second market, and the price in this market should be $53\frac{1}{3}$.

    $Q_1 = 75 - 5Q_2$
    $= 75 - 5(1120/84)$
    $= 75 - \dfrac{5600}{84}$
    $= 75 - 66\frac{2}{3}$
    $= 8\frac{1}{3}$

    It should sell $8\frac{1}{3}$ units in the first market, and the price in this market should be $93\frac{1}{3}$.

Chapter 11

1. No, because equilibrium can occur only at the point where the DD' demand curve intersects the dd' demand curve.

3. If the demand for the product is very price elastic, the demand curve will be tangent to the firm's long-run average cost curve at a point that is close to its minimum. Thus, the extent of the excess capacity will be relatively small. On the other hand, if the demand curve is not very price elastic, it will be tangent to the firm's long-run average cost curve at a point that is relatively far away from the minimum point, with the result that the extent of the excess capacity will be relatively great.

5. No.   Exit will occur, because at every output average cost exceeds price (based on the dd' demand curve).

7. Automobiles, furniture, cigarettes, tires, razor blades, and many others.

9. Yes. It is quite in keeping with the excess capacity theorem.

Chapter 12

1. The two producers will choose the monopoly output, where marginal revenue equals marginal cost. Since marginal cost equals zero, this means that

$$MR = 10 - 2Q = 0,$$

so

$$Q = \frac{10}{2} = 5$$

Thus, their combined output will be 5 gallons per hour.

3. They should set the marginal cost at one firm equal to the marginal cost at each other firm. If firm 1 produces 4 units, firm 2 produces 3 units, and firm 3 produces 4 units, the marginal cost at each firm equals $30. Thus, this seems to be the optimal distribution of output.

5. To earn 20 percent on its total investment of $250,000, its profit must equal $50,000 per year. Thus, if it operates at 80 percent of capacity (and sells 10,000 units), it must set a price of $15 per unit. (Since average cost equals $10, profit per unit will be $5, so total profit per year will be $50,000.) However, based on the information that is given, there is no assurance that it can sell 10,000 units per year if it charges a price of $15 per unit.

7. Firm I will choose strategy A.   Firm II will choose strategy 2.

9. Since $Q = 300 - P$, and the demand for the firm's output is $Q - Q_r$, it follows that the firm's demand curve is:

$$Q_b = Q - Q_r = (300 - P) - 49P$$
$$= 300 - 50P,$$

or

$$P = 6 - 0.02\,Q_b$$

Thus, the firm's marginal revenue curve is $MR = 6 - 0.04\,Q_b$. And since its marginal cost curve is $2.96Q_b$

$$6 - 0.04Q_b = 2.96\,Q_b$$
$$Q_b = 2$$

That is, your output level should be 2 million units.

Since $P = 6 - 0.02\,Q_b$, and $Q_b = 2$, it follows that

$$P = 6 - 0.02\,(2) = 5.96$$

That is, the price should be $5.96 per unit.

Since $Q = 300 - P$, and $P = 5.96$, it follows that

$$Q = 300 - 5.96 = 294.04.$$

That is, the industry output is 294.04 million units.

Chapter 13

1. No. It should set the marginal product of labor divided by $5 equal to the marginal product of capital divided by $6.

3. The value of the marginal product is shown below:

Number of days of labor	Output	Marginal product	Value of marginal product (dollars)
0	0		
1	8	8	40
2	15	7	35
3	21	6	30
4	26	5	25
5	30	4	20

Thus, if the daily wage of labor is $30, the firm should hire 2 or 3 days of labor.

5. 0.5   The ratio of capital's total income to labor's total income will decrease, since the elasticity of substitution is less than one.

7. Where discrimination exists, nonwhite labor is not allowed to compete with white labor. There are thus two quite different labor markets, one for whites, one for nonwhites. The demand curve for nonwhite labor reflects the fact that nonwhites are not allowed to enter many of the more productive jobs. Because of the differing positions of the demand (and supply) curves, the equilibrium wage for nonwhites is lower than for whites. Without discrimination, nonwhites and whites would compete in the same labor market, and it is likely that nonwhite wages would be higher at present, the white wage would be somewhat lower, and total output would rise.

9. The wage, P_L, will equal the price of the product, P, times the marginal product of labor, which equals

$$\frac{\delta Q}{\delta L} = 0.8L^{-2}K^2 = \frac{0.8Q}{L}$$

Thus $P_L = \dfrac{0.8Q}{L} \cdot P$, which means that

$$\frac{P_L L}{PQ} = 0.8$$

Since $P_L \cdot L$ equals the total wages paid by the firm and PQ equals its revenues, this completes the proof.

Chapter 14

1. 3 or 4 units of labor, because labor's marginal revenue product is $12 when between 3 and 4 units of labor are used. To see this, note that total revenue is $128 when 3 units of labor are used, and $140 when 4 units of labor are used.

3. Because union contracts tend to introduce rigidity in wage structures.

5.

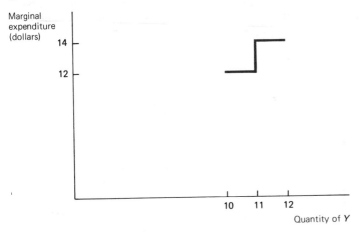

7. The supply curve for labor is shifted to the left, with the result that the price of labor will increase. There may be no effect on the demand curve for labor, unless employers are forced to hire more labor than they otherwise would have.

9. It would not necessarily reduce employment. The answer depends on the level at which the minimum wage is set. For a detailed explanation, see the case study in Chapter 14 of E. Mansfield, *Microeconomic Problems,* 4th ed. (New York: Norton, 1982).

Chapter 15

1. The quantity of lemon chicken might be measured along the horizontal axis; the quantity of sweet and sour pork might be measured along the vertical axis. The indifference curves of each person (A_1, A_2, A_3 for Joan; B_1, B_2, B_3 for John) might be inserted, as shown below:

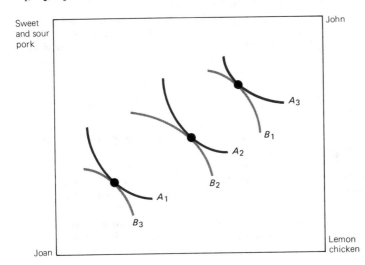

The optimal point would be on the contract curve connecting the dots.
   Probably not, since he probably gets satisfaction from her well-being (and in the interest of courtship, one hopes that she feels the same way).
3. Point Y represents your pretrade position.

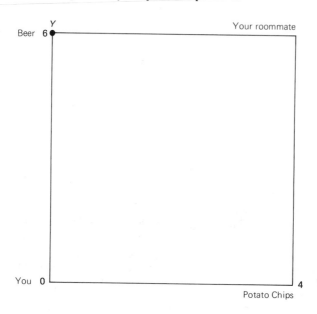

5. This trade would put her on her indifference curve 1, which is a higher indifference curve than that going through point Y. (To identify point Y, see the answer to Question 3.) Thus, she should agree to this.   This trade would put you on your indifference curve II, which is a higher indifference curve than that going through point Y. Thus, the trade will make you better off.

7. $E = 0.1E + 0.3X +$ final consumption of electric power, where E is output of electric power and X is output of coal.

9. Each point on the contract curve in such a box diagram corresponds to a certain level of production of each good. Plot these pairs of production levels, one against the other. The result is the product transformation curve.

Chapter 16

1. Government requirement of minimum schooling, probably accomplished through government subsidy.

3. No.   Because, if the two consumers arrive at any point off the contract curve, they can find a superior point on the contract curve, in the sense that one of them can be made better off without making the other worse off.

5. The plane's landing at that time may delay large commercial jets and impose substantial costs (in terms of delay and inconvenience) on the

passengers carried by these commercial aircraft. Increases in the landing fees paid by small private aircraft could help to eliminate such divergences.

7. No.

9. Social welfare depends only on the minimum of the two consumers' incomes. Holding Tom's income constant, social welfare is not affected by Dick's income, if Dick's income is at least equal to Tom's.

Chapter 17

1. A better criterion would be one that is based on a comparison of costs and benefits, assuming that these costs and benefits can be measured, at least roughly.

3. The Corps of Engineers included many kinds of benefits that the railroad consultants did not include, such as enhancement of waterfront land values. Also, the Corps of Engineers made a lower estimate of the costs. To some extent, as Prest and Turvey point out, the difference may be "due to the facts that the Corps likes to build canals and that the consultants were retained by the railroads."

5. 7 units of national defense.

7. It is not true that all public goods must be provided by the government. As pointed out in the text, some quantity of public goods may be provided privately, particularly if the number of people in the society is small. But the amount provided privately is likely to be less than the optimal amount.

9. No.   According to Parkinson, the bureaucracy tends to grow, regardless of whether there is a decline in the amount of work it must perform.

Chapter 18

1. $10 \div 1.08 = 9.26$. $10 \div 1.08 = 9.26$.

3. $200.

5. A profit-maximizing firm generally will not scrap existing equipment merely because somewhat better equipment is available. The new equipment must be sufficiently better to offset the fact that the old equipment is already paid for, whereas this is not the case for the new.   Yes.

7. Technological change shifts the production function, thus offsetting the tendency toward diminishing returns.

9. Yes.   Yes.

Chapter 19

1. $\frac{5}{36}$.   No.

3. $0.5 (\$1 \text{ million}) + 0.5 (-\$2 \text{ million}) = -\$0.5 \text{ million}$.

5. *a.* No, since it would have chosen not to purchase it if it were indifferent to risk.   *b.* No, since it would have chosen not to purchase it if it were risk averse.

7.   *a.* The utility of zero equals $10 + 2(0) = 10$. The utility of $-$ $25,000 equals $10 + 2(-25) = -40$. The utility of $+$ $32,000 equals $10 + 2(32) = 74$. Her expected utility equals $0.5(-40) + 0.5(74) = 17$.   *b.* Since the expected utility if she makes the investment (17) exceeds the expected utility if she does not make it (10), she should make it.

9.   No, because the maximum loss if it goes ahead with the project is $1 million, whereas the maximum loss if it does not go ahead with it is zero.

Index